Coming to Terms
with the Soviet Regime

Coming to Terms with the Soviet Regime

The "Changing Signposts" Movement

among Russian Émigrés

in the Early 1920s

Hilde Hardeman

Northern Illinois University Press   DeKalb   1994

Published by Northern Illinois University Press, DeKalb,
Illinois 60115   ✵   ∞

Manufactured in the United States using acid-free paper

Design by Julia Fauci

Uitgegeven met de steun van de Universitaire Stichting van België en van het Francqui-Fonds.

Library of Congress Cataloging-in-Publication Data

Hardeman, Hilde.

   Coming to terms with the Soviet regime : the "Changing
signposts" movement among Russian émigrés in the early
1920s / Hilde Hardeman.

          p.   cm.

   Includes bibliographical references and index.

   ISBN 0-87580-187-0

   1. Russians—Foreign countries—Politics and
government.   2. Russians—Foreign countries—Intellectual
life.   3. Soviet Union—History—Revolution, 1917-
1936.   I. Title.

DK35.5.H37   1994

947.084′1—dc20   94-7871

                              CIP

To Jan and Laura

Contents

Acknowledgments

I would like to take this opportunity to express my gratitude to the many people who have contributed to this project.

In the first place, I wish to thank Professor E. Waegemans, who introduced me to the world of Russia Abroad, for his enthusiasm and support. I am grateful also to Professor M. Raeff, whose suggestions and constant encouragement have been a great help to me.

This project was started during a one-year stay at the History Department of Stanford University, where I was fortunate to work with Professor T. Emmons. I wish to thank him, along with Professors L. Fleishman and M. Confino, for their counsel and inspiration. In the following years, I had the opportunity to study and do research in Paris, Amsterdam, and Moscow. There as well I was privileged to receive the support and advice of many people, including Professors A. Berelowitch, N. G. Dumova, M. Heller, Iu. V. Mukhachev, B. Naarden; Mme T. A. Ossorguine-Bakounine, V. A. Osipov, and Professors W. H. Roobol, J. Scherrer, and N. A. Struve. I am grateful to them all, especially to Professor Naarden, who took the time to go through a draft of this work. Warm thanks are extended also to I. B. Diushen for sharing memories of his father, B. V. Diushen, and to G. G. Derviz for sharing those of his uncle, Iu. N. Potekhin. My work has greatly benefited from the help of all these people; any mistakes and inadequacies, therefore, are my own.

While preparing the present book, I was fortunate to work in rich and accommodating archives and libraries, most importantly the collections of the Hoover Institution on War, Revolution, and Peace at Stanford University; the Bibliothèque de Documentation Internationale Contemporaine at Nanterre; the Bibliothèque Nationale, the Archives Nationales and the Bibliothèque Tourguénieff in Paris; the Internationaal Instituut voor Sociale Geschiedenis and the Oost-Europa Instituut in Amsterdam; the New York Public Library and the Bakhmeteff Archive at Columbia University in New York; the former Lenin Library, the former Central State Archive for Literature and the Arts (TsGALI), and the former Central State Archive of the October Revolution (TsGAOR) in Moscow. My gratitude goes to the staffs of these institutions, in particular to Hilja Kukk of the Hoover Institution and Tat'iana Gladkova of the B.D.I.C. and the Bibliothèque Tourguénieff. I am obliged also to Professor N. G. Dumova, without whose help in September 1989 I hardly would have seen more of TsGAOR than its cloakroom.

These numerous stays abroad were only possible thanks to the financial support of several institutions and the generous hospitality of many people. I gratefully acknowledge the support of the Belgian American Educational Foundation, which made possible my stay at Stanford, and of the Council of Europe, which funded my research in Paris. Special thanks go also to Mr. and Mrs. A. Waelkens. In addition, I enjoyed the warm hospitality of Sabine Breuillard, Mrs. Martine Cohen, Mr. and Mrs. L. Dewulf, N. G. Dumova, Hank Geerts, Marijke Hardeman, Jeff and Ingrid Keustermans, Mlle H. Morize, Ol'ga and Rafik Shakirov, and Galina Aleksandrovna.

I wish to thank also Professor A. K. Isaacs, Ania Krok-Paszkowska, and Amy Crawshaw, who reviewed the entire text and helped me with the English. In preparing this book for publication, I was privileged to work with the staff of Northern Illinois University Press, especially Mary Lincoln, Director. Publication of this book was supported by a grant from the "Universitaire Stichting van België."

My greatest debt, however, is owed to Jan Dings, my husband, who has borne the burdens of, and has guided me through, the most difficult stages of the process. With his sober advice and technical support, his loving assistance and encouragement, he has helped me in more ways than he knows.

Translation Note

Unless otherwise indicated, translations are mine, and the emphasis (italics) in quotations is from the original. Russian names, titles, and quotations have been transliterated according to the simplified Library of Congress System (i.e., without diacritical marks) for the modern Russian orthography. Dates before 1 February 1918 are given according to the Julian calendar, in so-called old style.

Coming to Terms with the Soviet Regime

We consider that the White tram, which has got stuck, has broken down completely, irreversibly, and will never start again. Others remain seated, imagining that this is only a temporary stop. When all will have become convinced of the contrary, all will get off, but for the time being they shout at those who are leaving that they are traitors. Yet we boarded the tram in order to ride. Now we are striving for the same goal by stepping off and going on foot toward this goal. This goal is Russia's well-being.

—A. V. Bobrishchev-Pushkin, *Patrioty bez otechestva*

The point is to use the only road along which Russia can sail as painlessly as possible between the Scylla and Charybdis of Communism and anarchy toward broad, worldwide expanses. This is the road of joint practical work by a physically and spiritually strong people, a firm regime, and an honest and principled intelligentsia.

—Iu. N. Potekhin in *Smena vekh: Sbornik statei*

The expulsion of scholars [in 1922] is the most graphic example of that notorious negative selection on which one is reflecting much these days, in an attempt to comprehend the sources and the mechanism of the present threat of social and human degradation. Having picked out not the criminals, not the enemies, but the thinkers of one's own people, the potentates put them on a ship, . . . and sent them to foreign shores. From those shores another ship arrived shortly thereafter. On 1 August 1923 those who had "changed signposts" disembarked from the steamer *Silesia*. . . . What could they [the authorities] achieve with all this? Only that what they in reality have achieved: the degradation of the moral and spiritual level of society. The cessation of the common work of national self-interpretation.

—S. Khoruzhii, *Literaturnaia gazeta,* 6 June 1990

INTRODUCTION

In the late summer of 1921, six young Russian émigré intellectuals, who all except one had taken an active part in the civil war on the side of the Whites, published in Prague a collection of articles, entitled *Smena vekh* (Change of Signposts). On its pages, they tried to answer two fundamental questions. What was the meaning of the revolution that had taken place in Russia in October 1917? And what should be the attitude of the Russian intelligentsia[1] toward this event?

By asking these questions, they involved themselves in a debate that had been going on for decades. Since the middle of the nineteenth century, Russian intellectuals had been discussing the issue of a revolution in their country with particular ardor. Gradually, within the Russian cultural and professional elite, a group had taken shape, united and defined by its moral commitment to the Russian people and by its belief that the Russian people would be liberated by revolutionary politics.[2]

The failed revolution of 1905 had presented these beliefs and commitments with their first important challenge. The unity with which workers, peasants, the intelligentsia, and commercial and industrial circles had first confronted the state proved ephemeral. By the end of 1905, the intelligentsia were deeply divided over whether they should accept or, on the contrary, completely reject partial concessions from above. Moreover, the workers and peasants turned out to be more radical than many intellectuals could accept. In 1906–1907 the Tsarist regime gradually restored its hold on the country. The intelligentsia remained deeply frustrated, especially the more moderate among them, who had seen their dreams of a liberal, parliamentary revolution both crushed by the government and rejected by the people.[3]

In 1909 a small group of leading intellectuals caused an uproar when they attempted to explain the outcome of 1905 as the deplorable result of the intelligentsia's maximalist revolutionary aspirations and their willingness to subject the absolute values of state, nation, law, truth, and religion to the relative values of politics and revolution. Economist P. B. Struve, philosophers N. A. Berdiaev, S. N. Bulgakov, and S. L. Frank, and three other colleagues set forth their views on the Russian intelligentsia (establishing the tradition in which the authors of *Smena vekh* explicitly wanted to place themselves) in a collection of articles entitled *Vekhi* (Signposts). The collection united in indignation Russian intellectuals from almost all tendencies except the right. Quite understandably, against the background of political reaction and because by that time many intellectuals no longer identified with revolutionary ideals, the *Vekhi* authors' appeal that the intelligentsia abandon their revolutionary ambitions and strive instead for self-perfection, in deference to the absolute values they had so long neglected, was generally misread as an appeal to yield to the Tsarist regime.[4] That the collection had raised a number of pertinent issues, such as the intelligentsia's disregard of the subjective dimension and their lack of respect for the law, was lost in the wave of resentment over *Vekhi*.

The successful revolution of February 1917, when the autocracy was overthrown without a struggle, seemed at first to confirm that the criticism of the *Vekhi* authors had been unwarranted, yet the developments of the following months made it clear that their analysis had been not that far off the mark. Against the background of growing anarchy in the country, the intelligentsia's initial euphoria over the downfall of Tsarism soon made way for increasing disillusionment with the revolution and for concern with Russia's future.

When the Bolsheviks seized power in late October, this did not particularly alarm their numerous opponents among the intelligentsia. Hardly anyone believed that Lenin and his colleagues would hold out.[5] This is not to say, however, that the intelligentsia's reaction to the Bolshevik coup was one of indifference. While a limited group of intellectuals, including the writer A. A. Blok (1880–1921),[6] the poet V. V. Maiakovskii (1893–1930),[7] the biologist K. A. Timiriazev (1843–1920)[8] and the neuropathologist V. M. Bekhterev (1857–1927),[9] were prepared to accept the Bolshevik revolution as "the Great Russian Revolution" they had been waiting for, many of their colleagues regarded the new regime with deep hostility. They resented both the Bolsheviks' autocratic methods and what was seen as their irresponsible incitement of the dark masses. Moreover, many feared that the new regime's political and economic program would lead to the destruction of the Russian economy and eventually of the Russian state.[10]

In the first weeks after the takeover, several professional groups including lawyers, physicians, and teachers, as well as the employees of various ministries and public services, declared a boycott against the new rulers. In some cases, for example that of the legal profession, this boycott continued well into 1918.[11] Hostility against the new regime was outspoken also in academic circles, among both professors and students.[12] The members of the Russian Academy of Sciences, for example, took a public stance against the Bolshevik "aggressors" in late November 1917, when they issued a joint statement strongly condemning the coup and declaring their full support for the Constituent Assembly, which was to convene in the near future.[13]

At about the same time, the Bolshevik authorities organized in Petrograd a meeting on "the Intelligentsia and the People," which was intended as a conciliatory signal to the intelligentsia. At the meeting, the People's Commissar of Enlightenment, A. V. Lunacharskii, appealed to the intelligentsia to accept the Bolshevik revolution, arguing that by opposing this expression of the popular will they were betraying their long tradition of service to the people. However, not only did the meeting fail to attract any sizeable attendance, the reaction of those present was predominantly hostile. The idea of "service to the people" had lost its appeal for many intellectuals, impressed as they were by the anarchic outbursts of the past months.[14] In the following weeks, the growing Bolshevik repression of political opponents, the forcible dissolution of the Constituent Assembly, and the conclusion of a separate peace with Germany on conditions that were most unfavorable for Russia only served to strengthen this hostility.

The first months of 1918 saw the creation of a number of organizations actively opposing the Bolsheviks, such as the Union for the Regeneration of Russia, the so-called Right Center, and B. V. Savinkov's Union for the Defense of Freedom and the Fatherland.[15] However, the number of people involved in those organizations of active resistance was small. In contrast, a growing group of intellectuals tried to find a modus vivendi with the new regime, often in the hope not only of protecting themselves and their families but of "softening" the regime as well. While they could not accept the Bolshevik government as such, they hoped that by remaining in, or returning to, their positions, they could contribute to preserving the country's economy, its institutions, and its culture. Thus, in late January 1918 the prominent Orientalist S. F. Ol'denburg—a former member of the Kadet Central Committee and minister of education in the Second Coalition Provisional Government—declared in his capacity as secretary of the Academy of Sciences that he and his colleagues were prepared to render their services to the People's Commissariat of Enlightenment and to the Supreme Council of the National Economy.[16] Many other intellectuals in Russia followed suit.[17]

The Soviet authorities, for their part, welcomed such moves. Starting in February 1918, they adopted a new policy vis-à-vis the intelligentsia, aimed at convincing non-Communist intellectuals that it was worth cooperating with the new regime as "bourgeois specialists."[18] In the words of A. V. Lunacharskii, intellectuals who let "the bearer of reason and social feelings" in their soul gain the upper hand over the petit bourgeois side of their character deserved protection and even encouragement.[19] This only applied, however, to those intellectuals who in some way or another could be useful to the Soviet state, be it by their skills, knowledge, or prestige. Among the "useful intellectuals," former officers of the Tsarist Army ranked high. When a number of them voluntarily joined the Red Army at the time of the German attack on Petrograd in February 1918 (including Lieutenant Generals D. P. Parskii and Iu. M. Sheideman; Major Generals A. A. Samoilo, P. P. Lebedev, P. P. Sytin, A. V. Stankevich, and V. F. Novitskii; and several colonels), they were given responsible positions. In the following weeks, especially after it had been decided in late April 1918 to abolish the principle of electing officers and to reintroduce the former discipline in the army, they were joined by several others, including Lieutenant General A. E. Snesarev and Colonels S. S. Kamenev and S. D. Kharlamov.[20]

While various motives may have prompted the former Tsarist officers to join the Red Army, feelings of patriotism and a sense of duty vis-à-vis the motherland certainly played an important role.[21] Former Tsarist Major General V. F. Novitskii, for example, wrote in April 1919 in the journal *Krasnyi ofitser* (Red Officer):

> Our red army [*sic*] distinctly presents itself to me in a historical perspective, as one of the links in the indissoluble chain of the Russian People's creative acts in the sphere of military ideas and military aspirations. . . . The old army will no longer revive. It has died. It has irrevocably perished; but Russia should not perish, and she will not perish, because the military power of our people is still great, its [the people's] energy is still sufficiently strong for armed struggle with its enemies.[22]

Not all former Tsarist officers who joined the Red Army did so voluntarily, however. In order to attract sufficient "military specialists"—something both Lenin and Trotskii, in his capacity as People's Commissar of War, considered a sine qua non for the formation of a regular army—the Bolshevik regime had to resort to coercive measures. In 1917 there were approximately 80,000 officers in the Red Army. On 29 July 1918 Trotskii declared that all Tsarist officers who refused to join the Red Army would be sent to concentration camps. On 30 September this threat was followed by a second order to the effect that the families of former officers who refused to serve would be detained as hostages.[23] How many of the 22,000 Tsarist officers who entered the Red Army during 1918 (by August 1920 this figure had risen to 48,000) did so voluntarily still remains unclear.[24]

The outbreak of civil war in the summer of 1918, which was also the immediate cause of Bolshevik coercion against the officer corps, thoroughly upset whatever beginnings of compromise there were between the intelligentsia and the regime. True, even after the launching of the Red Terror, considerable numbers of intellectuals remained at their posts, just as they had done in the previous months, trying to keep as far from politics as possible. Many others, however, became involved with the White movement, while still others sought refuge abroad.

In those times of terror and civil strife, cases of anti-Bolsheviks accepting the new regime were rare, but they did occur. Thus, on 12 November 1918, the day after an armistice between the Central and the Allied powers had been concluded, *Izvestiia* carried a letter to the editor by one of the leading journalists of the Moscow "Progressist" daily *Utro Rossii* (Russia's Morning), V. G. Tardov. In his letter Tardov stressed that Communism was utterly alien to him, yet added that the Soviet regime had been justified in his eyes as the only regime that would not turn the Russian people over to foreign rule. He therefore declared that as "a son of the working Russian people," he would devote himself to the young Russian socialist republic.[25]

The disappearance of the German threat and the increasing dimensions of foreign intervention against the Soviet regime had a serious impact on the intelligentsia's attitude vis-à-vis the Soviet regime, which now suddenly found itself in the role of Defender of the Motherland.[26] The writer M. A. Gor'kii, for example, who in the past months had sharply criticized the Bolsheviks for their violent and oppressive methods and for what he regarded as reckless playing on the barbaric instincts of the populace, appeared in late November 1918 at a meeting where he, along with A. V. Lunacharskii and G. E. Zinov'ev, made an appeal to the intelligentsia, urging them to join the Russian proletariat in resisting foreign intervention.[27]

In the course of 1919 the opposition to the new regime by those intellectuals who had remained in Russia further eroded.[28] The real turning point in this respect, however, came in the spring of 1920, when it became increasingly obvious that the Red Army had in effect won the civil war and that continuing the struggle could only cause more death and destruction, without affecting the war's outcome. In early March 1920 *Izvestiia* carried a declaration of the so-called Union of Working Intelligentsia, a group of intellectuals and businessmen including the academicians V. M. Bekhterev and S. F. Ol'denburg, the former director of the Siberian Bank V. V. Tarnovskii, the former shipowner N. S. Tsylev, and M. A. Gor'kii. In their declaration, which was printed in *Izvestiia* under the title "A sign of the times," the group stressed that, given the present situation in Russia, "it was imperative to immediately apply one's work and knowledge to the restoration of the country's productive forces and to the conservation of the culture that still remained intact after the World War and the revolutionary process." The "Working Intelligentsia" addressed themselves to the Russian émigré community and to European public opinion, asking them to leave the Soviet government and the Russian people in peace, to resume cultural and economic relations with Soviet Russia, and to help the country as much as possible restore its economic and cultural potential. They admitted that many things in the Soviet Republic were unacceptable, yet stressed that a change for the better would only be possible if normal life were restored. They argued that, in any case, continued armed intervention could only bring more suffering upon the people and would destroy even the last remnants of culture in the country.[29]

The Polish invasion of Soviet Russia in late April 1920 provided additional impetus for supporting the Soviet regime. On 30 April *Izvestiia* carried an official appeal "to all workers, peasants, and honest citizens of Russia" not to allow "the bayonet of the Polish *szlachta* to determine the will of the Russian people."[30] In the following days on the pages of the Soviet press the war against Poland was repeatedly presented as a Russian-national war.[31] On 4 May the Politburo received a letter from former Tsarist General and Supreme Commander under the Provisional Government A. A. Brusilov, in which he offered to establish a special convocation for coordinating the struggle against the Poles. The next day, a Special Convocation attached to the commander-in-chief was indeed created; it was chaired by Brusilov and included several other former Tsarist generals. On 30 May Brusilov and seven colleagues directed an appeal to "all former officers, wherever they found themselves," in which they stressed the Poles' annexationist intentions. As "senior comrades-in-arms," Brusilov and his colleagues appealed to the Russian officers' "feelings of love and devotion to the motherland," and urged them "to join the Red Army voluntarily, with full selflessness and willingness." If they failed to do so, Russia might be lost for good, and then their descendants would "rightfully accuse them that they, out of egoistic feelings of class war, had failed to apply their military learning and experience, had forgotten their own Russian people, and had ruined Mother Russia."[32]

At the time, it was suggested that Brusilov's letter to the Politburo was actually an evasive response to a proposal from the authorities that he assume a more important position; in any case, the general always tried to preserve as much as possible his independence from the Bolsheviks.[33] Be that as it may, Brusilov's appeal reportedly resulted in a true wave of patriotism. In the following days, thousands of officers and thousands more of volunteers, including many intellectuals, enlisted in the Red Army.[34]

Hardly a week later, on 5 June 1920, *Izvestiia* printed an article by law professor and former Kadet leader N. A. Gredeskul (1864–?), who not only endorsed Brusilov's call, but expressed his support for the cause of building socialism as well. As Gredeskul saw it, the Red victory in the civil war was a clear indication of the people's will, and therefore Russia should now move decisively in the direction of socialism. For "this right to start a great social revolution," a high historical price had been paid, and no time should be lost in starting to implement it. The destructive period of the revolution was over; a new constructive era could begin. However, the Polish invasion was preventing the Russian people from living as they wanted, and therefore all forces should be combined to repel the attack. Gredeskul urged the intelligentsia to fulfill their duty as "peaceful officers" and assure the army of a strong rear.[35] He repeated his appeal a few days later at a meeting of railway engineers,[36] and in July his first piece in *Izvestiia* was followed by a whole series of articles called "The intelligentsia at the turning point." In the series Gredeskul once again expressed his enthusiasm for the "great social revolution of the liberation of labor, . . . in the vanguard of which Russia had found herself," and through which Russia could lead mankind to a new world of universal justice and happiness.[37]

In this way, the course of events in 1919–1920, a time when the Soviet Republic was under continuous attack, induced a growing number of non-Communist intellectuals in Soviet Russia to make their peace with the new regime. Among the motives that prompted them to do so, the populist motive of "serving the people," which formerly had played such an important role in the intelligentsia's outlook, gave way to patriotic impulses of "serving the motherland."[38] Some intellectuals came to support the Bolsheviks for the sake of Russia, her culture, economy, and institutions, yet could not accept the October revolution or the Soviet regime as positive, per se. Others, in contrast, became impressed with the October revolution's message of a radically new and better world and took patriotic pride in that this grandiose event had taken place in their own country. General Brusilov no doubt belonged to the first group, while Professor Gredeskul should be rated among the second. More often than not, however, elements of both groups' attitudes were intertwined.

. . .

While the intelligentsia in Soviet Russia had no choice but to come to some kind of modus vivendi with the new regime, things were different for the hundreds of thousands of Russian émigrés who found themselves abroad because of their rejection of the Soviet regime. With the collapse of the White fronts in the course of 1920, their numbers rose steadily, reaching a total of almost one million by the end of 1921; exact numbers are unavailable.[39] The exodus spread over the Balkans, Central Europe, the Baltic countries, and Western Europe, with many Russians remaining in Poland, Germany, and France; and to the Far East, where Harbin, the Manchurian town on the Chinese Eastern Railroad, became a Russian émigré center of importance.[40] In this massive wave of emigration, members of almost all prerevolutionary social strata were involved, from noblemen and industrialists to peasants, mainly Cossacks who had been conscripts in the White armies. However, with the Bolshevik repression of all free thought, members of the professional and intellectual elites constituted a far greater share of this variegated group than they had of the population of prerevolutionary Russia as a whole.[41]

The émigrés had left Russia in the firm conviction that they would return home as soon as their country had been liberated from the Bolshevik usurpers. As a result, one of their main concerns in exile, at least initially, was to prepare themselves for that happy day. Cultural and political life continued abroad with this in mind. Given the presence among the émigrés of many prominent think-ers and artists, who, moreover, considered it their task to preserve and carry on Russian culture abroad in view of what they believed to be its total destruc-tion in Bolshevik Russia, cultural life in exile flourished.[42]

The idea of returning to a future non-Bolshevik Russia also determined political life in the émigré community. As the Bolsheviks did not tolerate any opposition, the whole gamut of political tendencies that had existed before the Bolshevik takeover was represented abroad, from Mensheviks to right-wing monarchists, the only exception being the Bolsheviks themselves. In exile, these various groups prepared themselves for assuming power in post-Bolshe-vik Russia.

Several attempts were made to create political bodies that would represent the Russian people abroad, and to work out concrete solutions for the coun-try's future political organization. In late 1918 a Russian Political Conference was convened in Paris, with the goal of assuring the representation of Russian interests abroad. The conference—which included representatives of Admiral Kolchak's Omsk Government, the Volunteer Army of the Don, the Northern Government, the Union of Regeneration, and the National Center—elected from among its ranks a council of four members, the so-called Russian Foreign Delegation. Chaired by the Kadet Prince G. E. L'vov, former prime minister in the first Provisional Government, the delegation adopted a program of de-mocracy, decentralization, and federalism and proposed to find a legal solution to the agrarian question. The delegation never received official international recognition or acceptance, however. Indeed, all attempts to enhance the in-fluence of this predominantly Kadet body by broadening the gamut of political tendencies represented in it failed, due to the irreconcilable antagonism be-tween socialist and right-wing parties in the emigration.[43]

This antagonism also wrecked all subsequent attempts to create a broadly representative organ of anti-Bolshevik forces. In late November 1920 a com-mittee of former members of the prerevolutionary State Council and the four State Dumas was set up; however, the SRs (Socialist Revolutionaries) among the former Duma delegates refused to join the committee, opposing the resto-ration of Tsarist institutions. Conversely, when in mid-December of that year the SRs launched an initiative of their own, calling for a conference of mem-bers of the Constituent Assembly that the Bolsheviks had disbanded in January 1918, they met with a wave of protest, as many political groups in the emigra-tion objected to the Constituent Assembly in the composition elected under the Bolsheviks.[44]

The Russian monarchists, for their part, who were particularly well repre-sented in Germany, France, and the Balkans, convened their first conference in May 1921 at the Bavarian resort of Bad Reichenhall. On that occasion they confirmed that only restoration of the monarchy could save Russia from ruin and that the old unity between tsar, church, and people should be restored.

However, the monarchists were also divided among themselves. Not only was there division between constitutionalists and extremist right-wing forces, but it also arose between supporters of each of the two Romanovs laying claim to the throne.[45]

In the meantime, the course of events in Russia made the émigrés' hopes for a rapid return ever more distant, and their discussions over Russia's future political organization ever more irrelevant. In November 1920 the White armies suffered their final defeat, and in the following months, the Soviet regime consolidated its support, both at home and abroad. Albeit often with a little "help" from the Red Army, several of the borderlands of the former Russian empire that had detached themselves from the center after the October revolution now rejoined it in the form of Soviet republics.[46] Outbursts of internal opposition such as the peasant revolts that flared up in the winter of 1920–21 and the Kronstadt uprising in March 1921 were forcibly suppressed.[47] The introduction of the New Economic Policy (NEP) at the Tenth Party Congress, which took place in early March 1921, seemed to promise further internal consolidation.

Internationally speaking, several border states entered into treaties with the Soviet government and recognized it de jure in the course of 1920 and 1921; moreover, in 1921 Soviet Russia concluded trade agreements with Great Britain, Germany, Italy, and Norway. The introduction of the NEP had an enormous impact in this respect. From late 1920, following a spectacular but brief economic upswing in 1919 and the first months of 1920, the countries of Western Europe found themselves in a deep economic crisis.[48] The partial return to private enterprise in Soviet Russia, which had thus far been totally isolated from the rest of Europe, raised hopes that this might help revive their own economies, so badly in need of new markets. Moreover, the move seemed to herald at least a partial return to "normality" in Russia.[49]

The final defeat of General Wrangel's Crimean forces, which signified the loss of the last acre of Russian soil under White control, sent a shock wave through the Russian émigré community and forced the émigrés to reexamine their course of action against the Soviet regime. The question of whether they should continue the armed struggle against the Bolsheviks was, in fact, not new. Starting in the last weeks of 1919, a number of SR emigrants had objected to carrying on the military action against the Bolsheviks because they opposed the White movement's undemocratic character. The emigrants also opposed maintaining the economic blockade of Soviet Russia because they felt that this was affecting not so much the Bolsheviks as the ordinary Russian people.[50] Objections to continued armed struggle surfaced also in Russian-nationalist circles, motivated by patriotic considerations of a special kind, namely, that Russians should never betray their motherland and always take Russia's side, whatever form of government prevailed there. If the choice was between foreign intervention and an unacceptable yet Russian regime, certain

Russian patriots considered it their duty to sacrifice their personal political convictions for Russia's sake and to stop the struggle against this regime. They felt that rather than hoping for its elimination with foreign help, they should try to achieve its gradual transformation from within. In the first months of 1920, appeals to this effect were launched by the editor of Prague's Russian-nationalist newspaper *Slavianskaia zaria* (Slavic Dawn), E. A. Efimovskii,[51] and, as will be seen, by the former director of Admiral Kolchak's press agency, the right-wing Kadet N. V. Ustrialov.

The Polish invasion of Soviet Russia in late April 1920 confirmed the opponents of continued armed struggle in their position;[52] however, only with the final defeat of the White armies did their stand gain more support. In contrast to the right-of-center political groups, who with an increasing lack of realism continued to advocate armed intervention,[53] the parties and factions on the other side of the political spectrum came to the conclusion that armed struggle should be abandoned. The Kadet party even split into two opposing groups over the issue, with the right-wing faction standing by the principle of military action and the left-wing faction, headed by the party's longtime leader P. N. Miliukov, proposing the adoption of a "new tactic," aimed at toppling the Soviet regime by encouraging popular revolt from within.[54]

In the meantime, the decree issued on 15 December 1921 by the All-Russian Central Executive Committee and the People's Commissariat of Foreign Affairs depriving all émigrés not prepared to solicit Soviet citizenship by 1 June 1922 of their Russian citizenship sent a shock wave through the Russian émigré community.[55] As hopes for a rapid return to a liberated Russia dwindled, the émigrés became increasingly concerned about what would happen to them if the Soviet regime did not fall, or fell only after a long period of time. Would it not then become impossible for them to reintegrate into Russian life? This "sore," "most smarting and vitally important question," as it was called on the pages of the émigré press,[56] could not but preoccupy the emigrants; however, none of the traditional émigré groups could come up with an answer.

Against this background, it is not surprising that some émigré intellectuals tried new means of finding a way out of the difficult and increasingly desperate situation in which they found themselves. Because the Soviet regime had so far withstood all attempts to undermine its authority, these émigrés found it increasingly difficult to dismiss the October revolution as merely a regrettable aberration from Russia's historical path. They became convinced that, on the contrary, the October revolution had a deeper historical meaning and that they should revise their position toward this event accordingly.

In 1921 four young émigré intellectuals, the linguist N. S. Trubetskoi, the theologian G. V. Florovskii, the economist P. N. Savitskii, and the music critic P. P. Suvchinskii, published in Sofia a collection of articles entitled *Iskhod k vostoku* (Exodus to the East). The "Eurasians," as the authors of *Iskhod k vostoku* called themselves, explained the October revolution as a healthy reaction against the Europeanization imposed on Russia since the time of Peter the Great, in addition to being the beginning of a new world culture in which Russia—the bridge between Europe and Asia, hence Eurasia—would play the leading role. They regarded the revolution both as the completion of Russia's Europeanization and as a way toward her cultural and spiritual rebirth. The Eurasians believed that this would be achieved by means of spiritually overcoming the European roots of Bolshevism, and they stressed in this respect the wholesome force of orthodoxy, which they considered the true essence of Russian nature.[57]

The Eurasians rejected the Bolshevik regime but believed at the same time that it served as a useful catalyst both in severing Russia's artificial links with Europe and in entering a new stage in Russia's history in which she would show her true face.[58] Conversely, by the early summer of 1920 the Kadet journalist P. I. Ryss, a close collaborator of P. N. Miliukov, came to the conclusion that the October revolution and the Soviet regime, reprehensible as they were in themselves, were helping Russia to become a full-fledged part of Europe.

Ryss argued that the revolution had been an enormous outburst of popular rebellion the Bolsheviks had tried to exploit for spreading their Communist ideas. However, they were clearly unable to retain the people's instincts on their side, and now that the great popular rebellion was coming to an end, Bolshevism was becoming obsolete *(izzhivaet sebia)* and would surely soon disappear from the scene.[59] In the meantime, however, Bolshevism had played a useful role in Russian history—"it had to the end unfolded the people's vengeance, and to the end destroyed the obsolete."[60] Brushing aside the Bolshevik refusal to recognize the principle of private property as a detail, Ryss regarded the fact that the people had obtained the land as the greatest achievement of the October revolution. He was convinced that this would radically alter the Russian people's psychology. As soon as peace returned to the country, the people would become engaged in developing and expanding their property, and in this process the last traces of their traditional rebelliousness and collectivism would give way to a new, individualistic psychology. Ryss believed that, as a result, the Russian people would finally accept Western ideas as their own, and Russia would join Europe on the path toward progress.[61]

While both the Eurasians and P. I. Ryss were prepared to accept the October revolution as ultimately a positive event, they rejected the Soviet regime. The Eurasians regarded it as the culmination of westernizing trends in the Russian intelligentsia and hence objectionable.[62] Ryss called every week the Bolsheviks remained in power a disaster, for he believed that this meant further destruction of the Russian state.[63]

In contrast, other groups and individuals in the émigré community were prepared to come to terms, not only with the October revolution but also with the Soviet regime. This was the case of the group *Mir i trud* (Peace and

Work), headed by the People's Socialist V. B. Stankevich, who in early 1920 launched an appeal to all Russian émigrés to cease the anti-Bolshevik struggle and return home, convinced as he was that peace would automatically lead to a normalization of the situation and a softening of the regime. It was true of the right-wing Kadet lawyer and ardent patriot N. V. Ustrialov, who believed that history unexpectedly had placed the Bolsheviks in the role of defenders of the Russian state and therefore felt that Russian patriots had no choice but to make their peace with the Soviet regime. It also applied to the group behind the Prague collection *Smena vekh,* who made an appeal to the Russian intelligentsia in emigration to "go to Canossa," accept the Soviet regime in the interests of the Russian nation and state, and return to Russia in order to cooperate with the Bolsheviks in reconstructing the devastated country.

This tendency to call for reconciliation with the Bolsheviks, generally in the belief that it would advance the Soviet regime's evolution toward more acceptable forms, became known under the name *smenovekhovstvo,* after the title of the programmatic collection *Smena vekh*. It influenced thinking in the émigré community until the mid-1920s.

. . .

Smenovekhovstvo has drawn scholarly attention ever since the late 1920s, both in the former Soviet Union[64] and elsewhere. Until the mid-1970s Soviet studies of the movement strongly emphasized that it should be seen in the framework of what was called the violent class struggle of the early 1920s, when the NEP created favorable conditions for the resurgence of bourgeois ideology. In these works, *smenovekhovstvo* was unequivocally presented as a movement aimed at undermining the Soviet regime and transforming it into a "bourgeois-capitalist" system.[65] To this effect, a whole range of phenomena and tendencies that had nothing to do with *smenovekhovstvo* were lumped together under one common denominator.[66] In this approach, more often than not, attention was focused on the Communist party's struggle against the movement. That the Soviet authorities had considered the movement useful and had even encouraged it was completely obscured; if this was mentioned, it was attributed solely to party leaders who in the meantime had fallen into disgrace, such as G. E. Zinov'ev.[67]

A first attempt to draw a more factual and balanced picture of the movement was made in 1977 by the historian S. A. Fediukin. While remaining within the official ideological framework, Fediukin distinguished between elements that did indeed pertain to the movement and phenomena that had been erroneously associated with it. He pointed out that *smenovekhovstvo* had not been aimed at undermining the Soviet regime but had, on the contrary, called for a conciliatory attitude vis-à-vis the Bolsheviks. In addition, he stressed that the movement had played a positive role in convincing bourgeois specialists to cooperate with the Soviet regime.[68]

Fediukin's work marked the beginning of a new trend in Soviet historiography on *smenovekhovstvo* that continued throughout the 1980s.[69] In contrast to their predecessors, who hardly used primary sources,[70] Fediukin and his followers have made use not only of the movement's original writings but also of archival materials. Of particular use were the collections held by the former Central Party Archive of the Institute of Marxism-Leninism (TsPA IML, now renamed the Russian Center for the Preservation and Study of Documents of Modern History) and the former Central State Archive of the October Revolution (TsGAOR, now renamed State Archive of the Russian Federation, or GARF). This included the collection of the former Russian Emigré Historical Archive in Prague, which was in large part transferred to TsGAOR after World War II.[71] Still, due to ideological restrictions and to the complete neglect of Western sources—a number of important archival materials on the movement seem to be available only in Western collections[72]—the overall value of these Soviet works remains limited. In view of the recent developments in Russian historiography, however, a change for the better is to be expected.[73]

In Western scholarship until the late 1960s, literature on *smenovekhovstvo* was limited to chapters or sections in works on a broader subject; some of these are, however, quite valuable.[74] The first studies focusing on the movement appeared in 1968, notably an article by E. Oberländer and one by R. C. Williams.[75] These essays were, however, limited in scope and only drew on a small number of sources. The first broader work appeared in 1980, when M. Agurskii published his book on "National-Bolshevism," in which he presented the *smenovekhovstvo* movement as one the main exponents thereof. A second revised and enlarged edition of this work appeared in 1987.[76] However, while M. Agurskii has used in his work a wealth of little-known sources, he deals with such a diversity of issues that his treatment of *smenovekhovstvo* remains rather summary. In addition, Agurskii's approach to his sources has not always been sufficiently critical.

No doubt, the great merit of Agurskii's work has been to draw attention to, and raise a number of questions about, the issue of *smenovekhovstvo*. Since 1980 several of the movement's aspects have been the subject of further research. M. Aucouturier, for example, has studied the movement's role in Russian literature; J. Burbank has devoted attention to N. V. Ustrialov's ideas in a panoramic study of non-Bolshevik Russian political thought in 1917–1922; M. Hagemeister has examined N. V. Ustrialov's contacts with followers of the philosopher N. F. Fedorov; and C. Read has dealt with the movement's place in Bolshevik cultural policies during the NEP.[77]

No detailed investigation of the movement as a whole has yet been made, however. My work is an attempt to fill this void. Making use of archival materials, both in Western collections and in the former USSR (insofar as Soviet repositories were accessible at the time this work was being prepared),[78] this book deals with the genesis, the ideas, and the principal exponents of *smenovekhovstvo*. In addition, it portrays the place the movement occupied, both in the émigré community and in Soviet Russia, as well as the way in which the Soviet authorities approached the movement.

Chapter One

MIR I TRUD

The Illusion of a Modus Vivendi between the
Soviet Regime and its Opponents

Among Russians abroad, one of the first appeals for peace with the Bolsheviks was heard in late January 1920. It came from the Berlin group *Mir i trud* (Peace and Work),[1] which had originated among Russian prisoners of war during 1919, that is, at a time when the civil war in Russia had not even reached its peak. These Russian captives had been shocked by the results of the World War, especially that both their own country and its main opponent, Germany, had come out of the war as losers and that the war had left even "victorious" countries in a state of utter devastation. A number of these prisoners came to reject the very idea of war as a means of solving major conflicts. They were convinced that technical progress had so expanded the power of mankind that war could only result in extreme destruction.

These antimilitaristic feelings were strengthened by reports of the disastrous civil war in Russia and by the unsatisfactory settlement of the World War at the Paris Peace Conference, which confirmed the pacifist Russians in their view that war could only create problems, not solve them. By the time the White armies of Bermondt, Iudenich, and Kolchak had been liquidated,[2] the pacifists' ideas had taken shape, and in early 1920 they decided to organize themselves in order to propagate their views. *Mir i trud,* as the circle was called, made its first public appearance at the end of January 1920.[3]

The moving spirit behind *Mir i trud* was Vladimir Benediktovich Stankevich (1884–1968),[4] a criminologist of Lithuanian origin, formerly a *privatdozent* at Petrograd University and a member of the Party of People's Socialists. From September 1917 to the October revolution he served as commissar of the Central Executive Committee, attached to the General Headquarters. In the turbulent days of the Bolshevik takeover he took part in the armed resistance against Lenin's party, subsequently had to go underground, and lived in a safe house in Kiev until, in August 1919, he escaped with his family to Berlin.[5]

Mir i trud had close links with the group behind the Berlin left-wing democratic daily *Golos Rossii* (Russia's Voice),[6] to which Stankevich regularly contributed. Several of the paper's collaborators participated in the circle, including A. S. Iashchenko, a lawyer and literary critic who in early 1919 had come to Berlin as a member of a Soviet delegation and had never returned;[7] M. O. Smil'g-Benario, a former consultant with the Soviet People's Commissariat of Justice and contributor to *Izvestiia* who had defected in February 1919;[8] and S. Ia. Shkliaver, the editor of *Golos Rossii*. Other active members of *Mir i trud* were V. V. Golubtsov; the lawyers N. N. Pereselenkov and G. L. Landau; the engineer I. G. Tsel'tner; the editor of the Berlin journal *Vremia* (Time),[9] G. N. Breitman; and a number of young literary men, including R. B. Gul' and Iu. V. Ofrosimov.[10]

Mir i trud set itself the goal "to further the peaceful solution of international, national, and class conflicts, and to promote the creation of opportunities for peaceful, productive, and creative work."[11] In the international sphere Stankevich and his colleagues placed high hopes in the League of Nations, which they expected to lay the foundation for a new world order, based on solidarity. They realized, however, that the League in its actual form—nullified as it was by the Treaty of Versailles—was merely a means for the victorious powers to consolidate their predominance. Therefore, *Mir i trud* advocated that all nations be admitted to the League on an equal basis, that the League's jurisdiction be extended, and that the Versailles Treaty be revised. Furthermore, they recommended abolishing conscription and applying the resolution on disarmament not only to Germany but also to the other nations.[12] Mankind had to break once and for all with its militaristic traditions, they felt, as these had led to absolutely unacceptable destruction.[13]

The members of *Mir i trud* were well aware that for the time being they carried far too little weight to have a voice in problems on a world scale.[14] Hence, to begin with, they concentrated their efforts on the Russian question. They defined their immediate goal as "to sum up the material and moral damages caused in Russia by the World War and the civil war and to further the establishment of peaceful life in the country."[15] To reach this goal, *Mir i trud* intended to rally public opinion by means of oral and written propaganda. Although the circle also addressed the German public,[16] it directed its propaganda primarily at the Russian émigré community, hoping through it to reach the people in Russia as well.

To begin with, *Mir i trud* issued a typewritten appeal to end the civil war in Russia, signed by V. B. Stankevich, V. V. Golubtsov, and I. G. Tsel'tner. Thanks to the financial contributions the circle received in response to this appeal, it was able to publish, in March 1920, a first collection of articles under the title *Mir i trud*.[17] In April *Mir i trud* started publishing a biweekly journal, entitled *Zhizn'* (Life), which appeared with the financial support of the publisher G. A. Gol'dberg and was edited by V. V. Golubtsov and V. B. Stankevich. The latter wrote nearly all the ideological articles for the journal,[18] assisted mainly by A. S. Iashchenko and G. L. Landau. *Zhizn'* also had a literary section, which carried work of Iu. V. Ofrosimov, R. B. Gul', F. V. Ivanov, and A. M. Drozdov.[19] In July *Mir i trud* launched a second appeal to restore peace in Russia; this appeared on the pages of *Zhizn'* and *Golos Rossii,* and also as a separate leaflet, both in Russian and German.[20] The appeal was directed at "all Russian citizens, public opinion in the whole world, and the governments of all countries." It called for the restoration not only of peace in and with Russia but of full international relations with that country. In November 1920, after the final defeat of the Whites, *Mir i trud* prepared yet another appeal; however, it is not clear whether this was ever made public.[21]

The basic idea behind all these appeals and publications was simple: peace in Russia should be restored immediately. To achieve this, *Mir i trud* considered it absolutely necessary that international relations with Russia be normalized. No government should continue to support any of the forces waging war in Russia or against Russia; at the same time, no efforts should be spared to mediate a peace agreement among them. Furthermore, the organization demanded that an international aid program for the starving Russian population be set up, that trade relations with Russia be renewed, and that the country be given the necessary credit. Finally, *Mir i trud* stressed that widespread introduction of foreign capital and organizational experience was indispensable to restore normal life in Russia; the Berlin group trusted that no foreigner would abuse Russia's temporary state of weakness and economic exhaustion to force excessive obligations upon her.[22]

Obviously, all international efforts were doomed to fail if the Russians themselves were not prepared to end the civil war. For *Mir i trud,* there was no doubt that the people *(narod)* in Russia yearned and thirsted for peace.[23] Rather, Stankevich stressed, the problem lay with the Russian intelligentsia: embittered as they were by the events of the past few years, reconciliation between Reds and Whites was unacceptable to their "sectarian" psychology.[24]

The contrast between the people on the one hand and the intelligentsia on the other hand played an important part in the thinking of Stankevich and his colleagues. They regarded the Russian people as unorganized, amorphous, and peace-loving by nature; it was the intelligentsia's task to organize and lead them.[25] Up to now, however, the Russian intelligentsia had seriously failed in this respect. They had not prepared the people to assume state power, setting an example of opposition for the sake of opposition instead. Nor had they imparted to the people a sense of practicality or economic creativity; on the contrary, it was no exaggeration to say that it was in spite of the intelligentsia that industrialization in Russia had reached a certain level. Finally, *Mir i trud* was convinced that by resorting to terror in the struggle against Tsarism, the intelligentsia had paved the way for the cruelty and ruthlessness the Russian people displayed during the civil war.[26]

As the members of the Berlin circle saw it, the course of events since the beginning of the revolution in February 1917 left no doubt that the intelligentsia in Russia did not understand the people at all. The revolution, Stankevich and his colleagues argued, had been not the creation of any political movement or party but a mighty, spontaneous process in which the people's soul and thoughts, their rejection of war and their thirst for peace and truth had sought an outlet. However, no one among the intelligentsia, neither the Bolsheviks nor their opponents, had been able to understand this in its fullness, let alone express it and give it shape.[27] In the circle's opinion, this was more than an accidental error. The intelligentsia were to blame for it, as a craftsman would be to blame if he did not know the workbench at which he was working.[28] The intelligentsia had to recognize their guilt and finally understand what the people wanted first and foremost: to work and live in peace.[29]

This call for peace, especially at a time when there seemed little hope left for the White cause, could easily be understood as outright capitulation to the Bolsheviks. However, *Mir i trud* decisively rejected such accusations. They repeatedly stressed that they were not blind to either the "undemocratic character of the Soviet regime or to its juridical and economic impracticability."[30] On the contrary, the organization stressed, it was hard to imagine a political system that, under the present conditions, would harm Russia more than the Bolshevik regime had.[31] Instead of peace, the Bolsheviks had brought the country civil war and, instead of bread and social equality, starvation and social hatred. The peasants had received the land, but because of wartime conditions they could not possibly work it.[32] In fact, Stankevich and his colleagues felt that the Bolsheviks had thrown Russia back into the times of serfdom, thus discrediting the great ideals of equality and fraternity to which the Bolsheviks so readily paid lip service.[33] They concluded that the Soviet state reminded them more of a torture chamber and of Arakcheev's military settlements than of the "state of the future" in the making.[34]

If the Bolshevik regime of that time was unacceptable to the members of *Mir i trud,* they were also convinced that many of the regime's defects stemmed at least in part from the general disruption and spiritual degeneration brought on by the incessant destruction and mutual extermination of war.[35] According to the Berlin group, this was especially true for Bolshevik terror, which had assumed serious proportions only in the summer of 1918 as a reaction to violent attacks against the regime.[36] The state of war had provided the Bolsheviks—and not only the Bolsheviks—with a justification for pitiless despotism. Under wartime conditions, even the most idealistic and democratic opponents of Bolshevism had fallen into military adventurism and dictatorial cruelty. The destructive force of war had perverted all the warring sides.[37]

Mir i trud did not dispute that armed struggle against the Bolsheviks would have made sense if the regime could have been swept away in one quick stroke. However, this had not been the case, and the protracted civil war was only making things worse. The Berlin group argued that while the Bolshevik economic policies of forced collectivization had seriously damaged the national economy, the civil war was making disruption complete and throwing the Russian people into total impoverishment. In the same way, the struggle for a "Great and United Russia" against those who "were leading Russia to national degradation and fragmentation" only accelerated Russia's disintegration. Consequently, *Mir i trud* thought it preferable to hope for an evolution of Bolshevism, rather than to continue an all-destructive war with the regime.[38]

After all, Stankevich and his colleagues argued, the Bolsheviks did have enormous creative potential, which in peacetime would have the opportunity to come to the surface. It would be worthwhile to see what these audacious innovators would then do in the educational and cultural spheres, or in the sphere of collective labor.[39] It was in the nature of things that the Bolsheviks would abandon their destructive methods in time of peace. *Mir i trud* stressed that the Bolsheviks had proven in the military sphere that they were flexible enough to do so. Although at first the Bolsheviks had not hesitated to liquidate the officers of the Russian Army, they had ended up reconstructing the army and protecting its officers and generals. The Berlin circle thought it therefore not utopian to believe that the Bolsheviks would finally stop annihilating the intelligentsia and destroying their professional opportunities and would proceed to restore Russia's productivity under the guidance of her former directors, technicians, and specialists.[40]

The members of *Mir i trud* considered that as soon as the war in Russia came to an end, an evolution of Bolshevism would not be long in coming. They believed that after a period of devastation, the revolutionary process was bound to reach a creative stage, whatever the regime's political mask.[41] Even if the Bolsheviks were overthrown, this would no longer significantly alter the course of events. Evolution toward democracy and the release of productive forces was sure to occur, if only peace were restored.[42] Indeed, the Berlin circle noted, in the months between the liquidation of most of the White armies (late 1919) and the beginning of the war with Poland (April 1920), the first signs of an evolution could already be discerned. The Bolsheviks transferred their efforts from the struggle against counterrevolution to the struggle against lice. The first indications of political freedom appeared: non-Communists were allowed to organize meetings, and Menshevik and Socialist Revolutionary (SR) newspapers were even permitted to reappear. The Poles and Wrangel had only to attack, however, for the terror to return with renewed force.[43]

Mir i trud brushed aside the objection that peace would merely serve to strengthen the Bolsheviks. It would strengthen everyone in Russia, they argued, especially those who would most efficiently utilize the regained peace to develop productivity and creativity, not only or even primarily the Bolsheviks. Material help from abroad, inevitable in the early stage of the peace process, would provide some breathing space for the whole population and give them the energy to stand up for their rights. Moreover, argued Stankevich and his colleagues, if Russia were opened up to influences from the outside world, the population would have the opportunity to take a sober view of the facts, and this would certainly not be to the Bolsheviks' advantage. Finally, *Mir i trud* stressed that to call for an end to armed struggle did not necessarily mean that all opposition to Bolshevism should cease. Under Tsarism it had been quite possible to oppose terror and revolts and, at the same time, be a staunch fighter for rights and freedom.[44]

In any case, the members of the Berlin circle trusted that evolution away from Bolshevism would be directed forward, not backward; a return to the old order was inconceivable for them. Eventually, they hoped to see Russia as a free and democratic federation of all nations that had formerly belonged to the Russian empire. On the economic level, they thought it indispensable that individual (capitalist) and cooperative forms of production have the right to exist alongside collective (socialist) forms. While they regarded a socialist economy as most suitable to both "the popular sense of justice" and economic theory, they stressed that from the point of view of productivity, free competition between all three forms of production was essential. It made no sense to force socialism upon the people, certainly not in conditions of complete economic disruption; this progressive form of production had to develop naturally and grow stronger in competition with other forms, not under the artificial circumstances of enforced monopoly.[45]

Politically speaking, the members of *Mir i trud* were convinced that a democracy after the "Allied" model was best suited both to the contemporary feeling for law and order *(pravosoznanie)* and to the way in which the modern economy was organized. They considered the shortcomings of contemporary democracy to be due to either growing pains or to the defects of man in general, and they regarded the deepening and universal dissemination of democratic principles as one of mankind's major tasks. These were the principles that Stankevich and his colleagues wanted to see as the basis for Russian government on all levels. The heart of Russian democracy was to be a new All-Russian Constituent Assembly, elected directly by universal, equal, and secret suffrage.[46]

The voluntary unification of all parts of the former Russian empire in a federation was an important issue to *Mir i trud*. In Stankevich's and his colleagues' all-too-optimistic view, peaceful cooperation would be to the advantage of all nations involved.[47] Furthermore, they felt that the border states, with their different political experience, would exert a beneficial influence on the development of the whole. More than that, they believed that one could already speak at the present stage of a certain mutual influence between the heartland and the border states. They argued, for instance, that at the border with the democratic Baltic states a noteworthy competition between two world views and two concepts of law was taking place. On the one hand, they believed, the menace of Bolshevism was forcing the newly formed governments of Lithuania, Latvia, and Estonia to take the need for radical internal reform seriously. On the other hand, by their realism and efficient organization these small states were causing envy among the Russian population, and this was not without effect on the Bolsheviks. This, at least, was the view of *Mir i trud*.[48]

The relationship between the Baltic border states and the Soviet Republic strengthened the circle's confidence in the future in two ways. First of all, they argued that the peace negotiations between Soviet Russia and the Baltic states showed that the Soviet government, for its part, was prepared to make peace. They admitted that the Bolsheviks often spoke of their intention to kindle world revolution, but stressed that in practice Moscow had invariably been the side that proposed peace and that defended itself, rather than attacked.[49] Second, their conviction that the democratic border states had a positive influence on the Soviet government confirmed the members of *Mir i trud* in their belief that peaceful opposition to Bolshevism was not utopian.[50]

. . .

As long as the civil war lasted, all calls to resume normal work and peacefully resist the Bolsheviks could not but sound extremely impracticable. The end to the war after the final defeat of the Whites in early November 1920 seemed to change this situation. In an appeal drafted immediately after the decisive events in the Crimea, *Mir i trud* made more concrete proposals for a course of action. The circle considered it the duty of every (Russian) intellectual to help Russia get back to work and establish relations with the outside world. In this respect especially, the Russians abroad had to assume responsibility, because help from without was a sine qua non for overcoming the material and technical ruin in Russia. Members of *Mir i trud* conceded that émigrés could lend such support only through the Soviet authorities, but they emphasized that help through official channels had to be combined with extensive, informal contacts with the Russian population. One had to make the most of all opportunities to send letters and parcels into Russia, to provide the people there not only with the bare necessities but also with literature, both scientific works and belles lettres. Through friends and relatives in Russia, the Russian émigré community had to establish a tangible link between Soviet Russia and the outside world, without any interference from the Soviet authorities.[51]

The circle admitted that material support from abroad was bound to help the Soviet regime survive, but stressed that such aid was nonetheless essential at this stage. This did not mean, however, that the political struggle against the regime's shortcomings would be abandoned. *Mir i trud* expected that all creative and productive forces in Russia would rally behind a number of concrete and, as the Berlin circle saw it, generally accepted demands. First of all, the Bolsheviks should stop squandering Russian property in trying to kindle revolution in the whole world. Second, they should abolish terror, eliminate the *Cheka,* and restore a minimum of personal liberty. Given the cessation of hostilities on all fronts, *Mir i trud* considered it only natural that this would happen. Third, the Soviet government should stop coercive collectivization and permit private enterprise. Furthermore, Russian citizens were to be given liberty of conscience and the freedom to fight for their political convictions through political organizations and propaganda. Finally, the Soviet constitution was to be put into practice, and the working population's rights in it were to be broadened, so as to give them real power in the country.[52]

Stankevich and his colleagues decided to concentrate their attention on backing these demands. The circle stressed the need for support from world public opinion and from Russia's democratic border states in this respect. Furthermore, they called for intensive agitation both among the Russians abroad and among the population in Soviet Russia, utilizing toward this goal all means and methods granted by the Soviet constitution.[53]

While the circle's proposals for action within the Soviet Republic were rather vague—they hoped somehow to organize branches of *Mir i trud* in Soviet Russia, but these plans never materialized[54]—Stankevich and his colleagues did put forward a more concrete course of action for the émigré community. It was time that the émigrés started negotiations with the Bolsheviks over how to settle the situation in Russia, they argued. The émigrés were to stop quarrelling among themselves and agree on a platform that could serve as a starting point for such negotiations.[55] In this respect it would be useful to set up a coordinating "political center" on a broad ideological basis, to represent the émigré community as a whole.[56]

So far, *Mir i trud* members had explicitly avoided becoming involved in the political divisions in the emigration and had invited people from all parties to join them.[57] At this point, however, they seemed to rule out the right wing's participation in formulating such a platform. They considered this the task of the community's left wing, of "Russian democracy" as they called it. In particular, they expected a lot from the Conference of Members of the Constituent Assembly, which was due to open in Paris on 8 January 1920, bringing together SRs and left-wing Kadets.[58]

Stankevich and his colleagues did not doubt that, given the situation, the émigrés would have no choice but to make concessions to the Bolsheviks. Of course, they admitted, if the opposition to the Bolsheviks had had enough strength, no one in the emigration would ever have abandoned the categorical demand for these usurpers to step down. But the actual balance of power was such that the émigrés would have to content themselves with minimal concessions from the Bolsheviks. At this point, *Mir i trud* considered it not unrealistic to insist on the abolition of terror, the expansion of opportunities for private enterprise, and the establishment of liberty of conscience and the freedom to work peacefully for one's convictions. By contrast, it seemed preferable temporarily to abandon the demand for immediate and complete popular sovereignty, as this would expose the people in Russia to far too much danger.

Mir i trud trusted that on this basis it would be possible to come to an acceptable agreement between the Soviet power and "Russian democracy." In any case, the Berlin circle argued, there was no reason to regard negotiations as being hopeless as such. First, the Bolsheviks had lately shown themselves to be *Realpolitiker* and would not refuse to talk. Second, although the émigré community was weak, they did hold a trump card. If the Bolsheviks wanted to get financial and technical aid from the outside world, *Mir i trud* argued, the shortest way to reach this goal would be through an agreement with Russian democracy. If the Soviet power aspired to recognition by the outside world, recognition by their democratic compatriots would be a decisive factor. Therefore, Stankevich and his colleagues stressed, all democratic groups in the émigré community should unite and agree on a platform as soon as possible; this would be an enormous contribution to improving conditions in Russia. And, if an agreement between "Russian democracy" and the Soviet power could be reached, this would be a truly historic event on a worldwide scale.[59]

That there was hardly a chance of such negotiations coming about in the immediate future, let alone of an agreement being reached, did not discourage *Mir i trud*'s supporters. They continued to close their eyes to reality. On 12 December 1920 Stankevich created a sensation in the émigré community by calling on the Russians abroad to return home. In the appeal, which appeared on the pages of *Golos Rossii,* Stankevich declared that irrespective of the present regime, the émigrés would in the future have to live and work in Russia. While in the past they had suffered many deprivations in that country, it was there that the best opportunities for the future lay. There, the émigrés had not only duties but also inalienable rights, which no decree could take away.[60] Moreover, Stankevich added, the majority of the émigrés were neither revolutionaries nor counterrevolutionaries, and for them life in emigration was miserable. Their only salvation was to return home. Consequently, he argued, the émigré community's only real, practical, and useful task was to prepare for return in a reasonable and intelligent way.[61] In this connection, Stankevich again stressed the importance of both informal, personal contacts with the population in Soviet Russia and support from public opinion in Russia's border states and in the West.[62]

So far, the émigré community had shown little interest in *Mir i trud*. If anything, they had regarded the circle as a bunch of exhausted people who had lost heart and desired rest and peace at any cost.[63] The circle did manage to attract a certain following, especially among émigrés in the Baltic states and Scandinavia, but this following was limited and inactive. Hardly any of these sympathizers took part in the circle's concrete activities. Moreover, General Wrangel's successes in the summer of 1920 considerably eroded the membership of *Mir i trud*.[64] In November 1920 the circle also had to give up the journal *Zhizn';* its publisher and financier G. A. Gol'dberg was no longer prepared to bear the losses the journal incurred.[65]

Stankevich's appeal to return home, however, attracted general attention among the émigré community and provoked many, chiefly negative reactions. The journal *Sovremennye zapiski* (Contemporary Annals), for example, representative of the moderate liberal left wing of the emigration, warned that returning home was nothing short of suicide,[66] and the Riga Socialist Revolutionary organ, *Narodnoe delo* (The People's Cause), even suspected *Mir i trud* of having counterrevolutionary intentions.[67] For its part, the Berlin daily *Rul'* (The Rudder)—organ of the right-wing Kadets, who remained confirmed advocates of armed intervention against the Soviet regime—called Stankevich's position a striking example of what it meant to give up the struggle against the Bolsheviks. If Russian émigrés lost their militancy, they would break with the motherland, compromise Russia's name abroad, and have no choice but to return to the hated Soviet Republic and surrender at the Bolsheviks' discretion. Stankevich's call could not possibly have a practical meaning, the paper stressed; it could not even serve as "elevating deception," for the truth was far too gloomy and suffocating.[68] Now that the Bolsheviks were clearly losing ground and were even calling on foreign capitalists to help revive the national economy, the staff of *Rul'* felt Stankevich's appeal was like a stab in the back for the Russian population. They did not doubt that Stankevich was acting with the best of intentions, but warned that his position amounted to betrayal of the Russian people.[69]

Yet, although almost all emigrants considered Stankevich's proposal to be unfeasible and naive, the idea of returning home did not leave them unmoved. At a lecture in Berlin in early January 1921, both Stankevich and the lawyer M. A. Taube[70] set forth their views on this subject. The latter proposed that the Russian émigré community should give up the idea of returning to Russia and form an independent nation, temporarily without a territory. This idea, however, found no favor in the eyes of the émigré community; if it came to that, their sympathies lay with Stankevich, rather than with Taube.[71] If need be, the émigrés were prepared to shelve the question of their return to Russia, but not to discard it. They did not want to sever all links with the motherland and kept hoping that one day they could go back to Russia—to a Russia they could accept and that would accept them. At the time of Stankevich's appeal, however, there really was no way the émigrés could go home, either practically or psychologically. So far, Soviet Russia remained unacceptable to almost all of them; nor, for its part, was the Soviet regime prepared to accept the émigrés.

In early 1921, even the rank and file of the White armies had not yet been granted amnesty by the Soviet government.[72] Moreover, the situation within the country was not yet consolidated; the civil war had hardly come to an end. In several parts of the country, especially in the Ukraine and the Volga region, the regime was still involved in a real war with peasant armies, and there were signs of growing unrest among the workers, especially in Petrograd. All this nourished hopes that sooner or later the regime would fall.

Under these circumstances, *Mir i trud* could not but peter out. Stankevich's hope that the defeat of the Whites would attract more people to the circle[73] proved ill-founded, and barely a few weeks after his sensational appeal, *Mir i trud* completely disappeared from the scene. This was also the end of Stankevich's participation in the political life of the émigré community. He became a collaborator of the Berlin publishing house *Znanie,* until in 1923 he received a chair at Kaunas University and returned to his native country, Lithuania.[74]

In the cultural sphere, however, the spirit of *Mir i trud* did not die down for a few more years. One of the circle's main concepts, that of "cultural appeasement *(kul'turnoe primirenchestvo),"* became the basic idea behind the critical-bibliographical journal *Russkaia kniga* (The Russian Book),[75] edited by A. S. Iashchenko, and behind the Berlin *Dom iskusstv* (House of the Arts),[76] in which Iashchenko also played a part.

In fact, while an almost unbridgeable gap separated the émigré community from Soviet Russia on the political and ideological level, in the early 1920s there was not yet such a sharp dividing line in the cultural sphere. Russian cultural life in Berlin embodied this relative unity. In 1921–1923, various factors such as the establishment of relations between the Soviet Republic and Germany, the easing of Soviet travel restrictions, the relatively low cost of living in Berlin, the resulting enormous number of Russian publishing houses, and finally even the city's geographic location made the German capital into a center where Russian literary figures of all political tendencies came together: émigrés, people who had chosen to remain in Soviet Russia, and others who had not made up their mind yet and "fell between two stools," as Gleb Struve termed it.[77] *Russkaia kniga* and *Dom iskusstv* reflected this peculiar situation.

The first issue of *Russkaia kniga* appeared in January 1921; in September of that year the monthly temporarily ceased publication, but reappeared in January 1922 under the title *Novaia russkaia kniga* (The New Russian Book). The contributors to the journal formed a most heterogeneous company, including G. V. Alekseev, A. V. Bakhrakh, V. S. Lur'e, B. K. Zaitsev, I. G. Erenburg, A. Belyi, A. M. Remizov, V. V. Maiakovskii, and B. A. Pil'niak. Several former members of *Mir i trud* actively took part in the journal: besides Iashchenko also A. M. Drozdov, R. B. Gul', Iu. V. Ofrosimov and F. V. Ivanov.[78] The ideas that had guided them at the time of *Mir i trud* also determined to a great extent the position of *Russkaia kniga.* On the journal's pages Iashchenko and his colleagues repeated their conviction that whatever regime would finally become consolidated in Russia, it would sooner or later have to work for the country's reconstruction and revival. They believed that at the present stage one of the few fields in which one could do something to promote this revival was the field of culture, in particular literature. Consequently, the editors of *Russkaia kniga* set themselves the goal of helping to preserve the cultural unity between Soviet Russia and the emigration, and declared that they would keep aloof from all politics, in order not to complicate their task.[79]

The journal carried book reviews, bibliographical information, and articles on individual authors, making no distinction between émigré and Soviet literature. Every issue also had an extensive bio-bibliographical section under the title "The fate and work of Russian writers, scholars and journalists during the period 1918–1922." To contemporaries, this section must have been tangible proof of the persistence of culture, of its continuity notwithstanding the incredibly difficult circumstances of the past few years.[80]

Dom iskusstv, for its part, was founded on 21 November 1921, as "an apolitical organization pursuing only cultural aims, the defense of legal and material interests of literary and artistic figures abroad, as well as inside Russia, and contact with writers living in Russia." Its founders included the authors A. Belyi, A. M. Remizov, and A. N. Tolstoi; the poet N. M. Minskii; the artists N. D. Miliuti and I. A. Puni; and A. S. Iashchenko.[81] *Dom iskusstv* organized regular meetings, where members from across the whole Russian cultural community met with one another, notwithstanding their ideological differences.

This situation of peaceful coexistence did not last long, however. It came to an end as a result of the community's increasing politicization. From the autumn of 1922 on, the meetings of *Dom iskusstv* were disturbed more and more often by political incidents.[82] *Novaia russkaia kniga* did not escape the general crisis either. In the course of 1923 it became more and more difficult for the editors to hold to their principle of political neutrality or, if they managed to do so, they did so only by ignoring what was really going on in the world of Russian literature. The journal finally ceased publication in the autumn of 1923.[83] *Dom iskusstv,* for its part, disappeared from the scene in early November 1923.[84] By the time the German economic crisis, which had become catastrophic by the end of 1923, dealt the deathblow to Russian cultural life in Berlin, the community there had already disintegrated.

Chapter Two

N. V. USTRIALOV

Joining the Bolsheviks for the Sake of "Great Russia"

At approximately the same time as the Berlin group *Mir i trud* launched its first call for peace in Russia, a similar appeal was heard among the Russians in Manchuria. It came from Nikolai Vasil'evich Ustrialov (1890–1938), a young *privatdozent* in constitutional law and a former director of Admiral Kolchak's press agency.

Ustrialov was educated at the Law Department of Moscow University, where his teachers included S. A. Kotliarevskii, Prince E. N. Trubetskoi, and I. A. Il'in. In 1916 he started teaching himself, both at his alma mater and at the Moscow Commerce Institute.[1] He was also active as a publicist and contributed regularly to the Moscow daily *Utro Rossii* (Russia's Morning), which was published by the group of liberal-minded Moscow industrialists who gathered around P. P. Riabushinskii.[2] Ustrialov joined the Kadets while still a student, and by 1918 was serving as chairman of the Kadet Party Committee of Kaluga province. In this capacity he barely escaped arrest at the beginning of the Red Terror in September 1918 by fleeing to Siberia. He found refuge in Perm, where he received the chair of public law at the local university.[3]

After the town was taken over by Kolchak's troops in late December 1918, Ustrialov traveled to Omsk and took up service in the White admiral's government. He initially served as a legal adviser to the Supreme Commander's Administration and the Council of Ministers, but he soon left this rather dull occupation for a more challenging position as director of the governmental press agency.[4] In this post he became one of the White dictatorship's most ardent advocates, opposing to the very end all proposals for democratization.[5] After the fall of Kolchak's government in early January 1920, Ustrialov again managed to escape and ended up in Harbin, the prosperous Manchurian town on the Chinese Eastern Railroad, predominantly inhabited by Russians.

Hardly a week after his arrival in Harbin, the local daily *Vestnik Man'chzhurii* (Manchuria Herald) published an interview with Ustrialov under the title *"Perelom"* (Turning Point), in which he called on the Whites to face the truth, and accept their final defeat. Although the anti-Bolshevik struggle in the South and the North of the country still continued, there could no longer be the slightest doubt about the White movement's complete bankruptcy. Ustrialov argued that although confirmed patriots had fought for Russia's national revival and unification on the side of the Whites, their nationalism had waned in practice, even though it had remained steadfast in principle. As opposed to this, the Soviet regime with its ideology of the International "had unexpectedly been advanced by the odd dialectic of history into the role of the national factor of contemporary Russian life."[6]

Ustrialov did not believe that the catastrophic defeat of the White movement had been caused by the reactionary character of its policies. As he saw it, the Bolshevik methods of administration were indisputably more reactionary than those of the Whites; indeed, the Kolchak government had fallen just as it was being democratized. Rather, the cause of the White defeat lay deeper. Ustrialov argued that it was clear from the course of events that Russia had not yet overcome Bolshevism. In his view, there was an element of fate in the Soviet regime's victories, as if such an outcome were the will of history. Moreover, by associating too closely with foreigners, the anti-Bolshevik movement had unwittingly lent Bolshevism a certain national aura, essentially alien to it. Ustrialov believed that, paradoxically, the Soviet regime had become an imperialist and centralist regime, and that the unification of Russia was now coming about under the aegis of Bolshevism. Therefore, though it was hard to face the White defeat, he felt there was also some consolation. The White movement's sacred goal was being realized, Russia was being unified and resurrected, and her power in the international arena was being restored.[7]

In Ustrialov's view, the only conclusion a *Realpolitiker* and patriot could draw from these "unbending arguments of life" was that armed struggle against Bolshevism should be abandoned. This did not mean, however, that one had to accept Bolshevism as such. He stressed that the ultimate goal remained unaltered: Bolshevism was to be overcome. However, he believed that while it had proven impossible to defeat Bolshevism by force of arms, it would gradually eliminate itself in an atmosphere of civil peace. He was even convinced that this process of "internal, organic transformation *(pererozhdenie)*" had already started. Therefore, he called upon "all opponents of Bolshevism, all advocates of a great and united Russia" to lay down their arms.[8]

Such an appeal from a man who just a few weeks before had advocated the continuation of armed struggle, stating that "there could be no peace with Bolshevism and its agents,"[9] was unexpected to say the least. Yet, while Ustrialov did actively support the White movement until the very last days of the Kolchak government, his about-face was not as sudden and surprising as it might first have seemed. It did not come about in the course of a few sleepless nights, as has been suggested,[10] but was rather the result of a long process, which had started even before the beginning of Bolshevik rule, and was largely determined by Ustrialov's world view.

In the first days after the February revolution, the general atmosphere of democratic enthusiasm that the downfall of Tsarism brought about among the Russian intelligentsia had affected also Ustrialov. He took an active part in the liberal propaganda campaign that the Kadet party set up in the spring of 1917.[11] As one of the main contributors to the Moscow daily *Utro Rossii,* Ustrialov also had close links with the liberal-minded Moscow business milieu. These circles eagerly welcomed the February revolution, seeing it as the beginning of an era in which the Russian bourgeoisie would finally play a leading role in the country.[12] In the spring and summer of 1917 the All-Russian Commercial-Industrial Union, in which the Moscow progressive industrialists played a prominent role, organized an extensive propaganda campaign, aimed at gaining broad support for the new "bourgeois" regime. Ustrialov was also involved. In this connection he went on a lecture tour to the Caucasus in May and June 1917.[13]

However, as anarchy in the country grew and the Provisional Government's successive coalitions proved incapable of dealing with the situation, the general euphoria gave way to despair. In the course of 1917 many who had formerly placed their hopes on the convening of a constituent assembly lost their faith in the people's capacity for democratic self-determination. True, in the first weeks after the Bolshevik takeover, the Constituent Assembly provided a platform upon which opponents of the new regime could rally against the common enemy. However, when, on 6 January 1918, the Bolsheviks disbanded the newly elected assembly, there was increasing skepticism about the practicability of democratic principles in Russia. In liberal circles, a decisive ideological revision took place. The traditional principles of democratic self-determination and full civic freedom were temporarily abandoned. The only way out of the crisis now seemed to be a dictatorship.[14]

Ustrialov entirely subscribed to this position. Indeed, as a man with Slavophile sympathies and an admirer of the conservative thinker K. N. Leont'ev,[15] Ustrialov's enthusiasm for the idea of implanting "arithmetic democracy" in Russia had never been very great. Within a few days of the fall of the monarchy, his sympathy for the Russian people's new power gave way to alarm and aversion.[16] However, it was not until later in that year that he openly expressed his feelings in this respect. By early 1918 he no longer hesitated to argue that the Constituent Assembly, given its composition, was a force no less destructive and disruptive than the Bolsheviks.[17] He was now thoroughly convinced that the Russian people were not ripe for democracy, and believed that for the present, the "yoke of freedom" was too heavy for them.[18]

In this light, the Bolsheviks' trampling of Russian democracy did not particularly shock Ustrialov; he later even indicated that their prorogation of the Constituent Assembly had been one of the decisive moments in his process of accepting the new regime.[19] The antinationalism of the new rulers, however, worried him. Ustrialov was an ardent patriot, who wholeheartedly believed in the idea of a "Great Russia." This concept, based on the thesis that Russia's internal development depended upon her external power, had been put forward in 1908 by P. B. Struve,[20] the man Ustrialov considered his mentor.[21] In the years preceding the First World War the concept had played an important ideological role in the circles of right-wing Kadets and progressive businessmen,[22] and the outbreak of the war had only enhanced its importance. In 1916 a special bimonthly journal entitled *Problemy velikoi Rossii* (Problems of Great Russia)[23] had been founded, dedicated entirely to the concept in all its aspects. Contributors included the rector of Petrograd University E. D. Grimm; the prominent Kadet F. I. Rodichev; the economists I. Kh. Ozerov and I. M. Gol'dshtein; the lawyers S. A. Kotliarevskii, E. A. Korovin, A. S. Iashchenko, and Iu. V. Kliuchnikov; the jurist and philosopher Prince E. N. Trubetskoi; and the jurist and historian Baron B. E. Nol'de.

Ustrialov contributed to the journal two articles, in which he set forth his opinions on the essence of nationalism and on Russian imperialism.[24] For Ustrialov, to believe in a "Great Russia" was first of all to believe in the Russian state. As a Hegelian, he considered the state as the unifying principle that alone could shape and strengthen the national "idea" of a people, and unite initially different groups of people into one nation. Moreover, inspired by the thought of the historical philosopher N. Ia. Danilevskii, Ustrialov regarded states as living organisms with both a body and a soul, and believed the development of these two aspects to be closely interrelated.[25] As he saw it, only a state with a powerful and great body could have a great culture. As a result, in his eyes, imperialism was a vital and deeply fruitful idea. If a state wanted to be great in every sense of the word, it had to strive for expansion.[26] As all healthy state organisms displayed this tendency, confrontations were inevitable. According to Ustrialov, the outcome of such conflicts was never accidental: in these confrontations the "true specific gravity of all participants was established before the Supreme court of historical Providence."[27] In Ustrialov's world view, History was a force, judging and directing the world toward progress according to certain laws. The protagonists in this process were the historical nations; as living organisms they were born, grew older, and died, incessantly succeeding each other and struggling against each other for predominance. History judged the "national idea" of each nation, and let the "better" force prevail, the "worse" disappear.[28] If Russia had been able to develop into a powerful state, this could only mean that History needed her. Therefore, it was her duty to continue the struggle for expansion.[29]

Ustrialov stressed that in this light, the ongoing world war should not be represented as a war for "European freedom" or for "the trampled rights of small nations," nor as a war against "imperialism" or against "German militarism." Rather, all participants in the war—Britain, France, and Russia, as well as Germany and Austria—were struggling to maintain their own territory and strengthen it with new acquisitions. In this struggle, the "Spirit of History" (*"Dukh istorii"*) would decide which of the warring parties was truly "great."[30]

In their declaration of intent, the editors of *Problemy velikoi Rossii* stated rather vaguely that they believed Russia's future lay in "the cultural development of her spiritual and material forces and in the peaceful conquest of the position she needed to give all the numerous peoples in the Empire the possibility to prosper."[31] While allowing Ustrialov to express his views on the journal's pages, the editors distanced themselves from his plea for imperialism,[32] as did some of his fellow contributors. The law professor A. M. Ladyzhenskii, for instance, published an answer to Ustrialov under the title "The Idea of Great Russia and Aggressive Imperialism," in which he called Ustrialov's article "an example of how one should not understand the idea of 'Great Russia.'" Ladyzhenskii argued that Ustrialov's position was an apology for the state standing above the law. In the name of Russian statehood and Russian culture, Ustrialov negated the value of a stable international legal order.[33] Here, Ladyzhenskii hit the nail on the head.[34] It was precisely Ustrialov's readiness to unconditionally subordinate the value of law to that of the state which distinguished his position from that of most of his fellow contributors to *Problemy velikoi Rossii,* and from that of P. B. Struve.

The February revolution had at first strengthened Ustrialov's hopes for a Russian victory in the world war. Against the background of the Tsarist regime's inability to defend Russia's international dignity, the idea of revolution had become "a symbol of patriotism, a national duty," Ustrialov wrote in April 1917. In his view, the revolution had been in the first place "an act of the country's will to reach victory."[35] Now that the old order had been overthrown, Ustrialov hoped that the Russian people would understand that the war was being waged, not for narrow class interests, but for the sake of the Russian nation as a whole, for its freedom and that of the whole world. He trusted that as citizens of a free country, his compatriots would exert all their efforts to bring the war to a victorious end.[36] However, from the spring of 1917, he could not suppress certain misgivings. He complained that not all Russians seemed to grasp the enormous importance of a victory for the country's freedom. In his view, this was especially true for the representatives of Bolshevism, "this peculiar, most misshapen phenomenon of Russian life." Their disruptive slogans were a crime against the motherland.[37]

The Bolshevik takeover confirmed Ustrialov's worst apprehensions. Not only did the Bolsheviks undermine the Russian empire by proclaiming the principle of national self-determination;[38] their open break with the Allies and their declaration of an immediate "just and democratic" peace made their betrayal of Russian national interests complete. Ustrialov admitted that the international situation was not ripe for peace, and that in the face of the continuing war the Bolsheviks merely looked ridiculous with their endless paper declarations. However, this did not make the results of their position any less regrettable. Russia had been ruled out as an international factor; the international life of the near future would develop without her, and in spite of her. Ustrialov feared that henceforth, she would become the mere object of international contention.[39]

The peace negotiations with Germany in Brest-Litovsk filled Ustrialov with anger and despair. He was deeply convinced that in international conflicts "a nation deserved life and victory only if it was *better* than its opponents, if its national 'idea' was superior."[40] Consequently, in Ustrialov's eyes to abandon the war was to recognize "Germany as being worthy of enslaving mankind," and to exclude Russia for a long time or even forever from the circle of the world's great powers.[41] Nonetheless, he could muster some respect for Trotskii's principled position of "neither war nor peace."[42] When the Bolsheviks finally capitulated after the Germans renewed their offensive on 18 February 1918, his contempt was all the more profound.[43]

Ustrialov did not share the opinion of many other anti-Bolsheviks who charged Lenin and his colleagues with being German agents. On the contrary, he regarded the Bolshevik revolution as a truly Russian phenomenon, as the victory of the "rebellious side" of the Russian soul over that side which had created "Great Russia." In Ustrialov's opinion the Bolsheviks were a peculiar mixture of Pugachev and Bakunin—of the unbridled Russian *muzhik* and the Russian intelligentsia as they had been characterized in the 1909 collection of articles *Vekhi* (Signposts).[44]

Meditating on the meaning of the October revolution, Ustrialov returned to the ideas contained in *Vekhi*. The authors of this collection had questioned the attitudes of the Russian intelligentsia in the years leading up to the revolution of 1905, and had blamed the fateful outcome of that revolution upon the intelligentsia's extremism and their alienation from the values of nation, state, truth, law, and religion.[45] In early 1918 the group behind *Vekhi* responded to the events of 1917 with a new collection of articles, *Iz glubiny* (From the Depths).[46] They regarded the October revolution as the total destruction of the Russian state, and identified the general alienation from the state as the deleterious force that had caused this downfall. In their view, this alienation now affected not only the intelligentsia, but the people as a whole.[47]

Ustrialov entirely subscribed to this analysis. He argued that although Bolshevism was the spiritual creation of the Russian intelligentsia, it had unconsciously been taken up by the Russian people, who had done away with its ideological cover of "internationalism," yet had preserved its destructive passion. In the Bolshevik revolution, the gap between the intelligentsia and the people had for a moment been overcome, and both sides had met in the primordial Russian passion for destruction.[48] Ustrialov concluded that therefore, perhaps even more than with the autocracy, the direct responsibility for the ongoing revolution lay with the Russian people as a whole.[49] It was precisely because he was convinced the origins of Bolshevism lay in the Russian soul itself that Ustrialov never completely lost his faith in Russia's future. The "illness" that had appeared in October 1917 was undoubtedly serious, he wrote on Christmas Eve of 1917, but it was the illness of a great organism. In spite of all its horror, destructiveness, and outrage, the Russian revolution's scale and grandiosity made it the greatest phenomenon in recent world history.[50]

Ustrialov believed that the revolution was realizing a complex of ideas that were erroneous and absurd, but nonetheless characteristic of the Russian national consciousness. In the Bolsheviks' declarations on Russia's mission to kindle the fire of world revolution, Herzen was meeting Khomiakov, and populism was meeting Marxism. As Ustrialov saw it, in this truly popular revolution old ideas were being put to the test, and new ideas were emerging from the national consciousness. The Russian nation was going through a period of fruitful self-examination, and at the end of this process only strong, viable, and healthy ideas would remain. Ustrialov argued that, therefore, it was *necessary* to live Bolshevism through to the very end.[51] He believed that in this way one of the main national vices, Russian destructiveness, would eliminate itself once and for all by force of its own negativity, and that then the future of Great Russia would be assured.[52]

Ustrialov was deeply convinced that in history periods of destruction were always followed by constructive eras.[53] While the Russian revolution indicated that the Russian nation was ill, this illness would eventually lead either to a "healthy reaction" from the organism or to death. Ustrialov did not believe in this second possibility; his faith in Russia's vitality was too great.[54] Rather, he trusted that, just as delirium sometimes gives a patient valuable insights, the crisis of the Russian revolution would entail a salutary reaction. It would lead to a new, deepened, and creative national self-consciousness, and to a great flourishing of the national culture, in which "Russia's secret would open itself before the reason of world history."[55]

Ustrialov believed that a spiritual revival in this sense would entail a political revival, in which the revolution's "equalizing democratism" would make way for "an aristocratic recognition of the indisputable values of culture."[56] Although the concrete form this political revival would take remained unclear to him, he was convinced that it would certainly not be based on one specific class. As he saw it, not only was the proletariat's inability to lead the state beyond doubt, but the Russian bourgeoisie had shown itself to lack the necessary creativity and statesmanship as well. He admitted that the present economic situation would inevitably give the bourgeoisie an organizing and creative role in society, but stressed that future political predominance by it, or by any class, was out of the question. He maintained that "the Russian republic would not be a republic of workers and peasants, or a republic of landowners and industrialists. It would be a republic of all Russians, or there would be no republic."[57]

Ustrialov was not alone in his belief that Russia's revival could only be a national revival.[58] When in April 1918 he started a new journal that was to propound this view, he managed to gather around it a number of prominent Kadets, including almost the complete group of contributors to *Iz glubiny,* several senior members of the staff of *Utro Rossii,*[59] the publicist A. S. Belevskii, and the editor of the Moscow liberal daily *Russkie vedomosti* (Russian Gazette), historian A. A. Kizevetter. Besides Ustrialov, the other initiators of *Nakanune* (On the Eve) were the young Kadets Iu. V. Kliuchnikov and Iu. N. Potekhin, both, as will be seen, future *smenovekhovtsy,* as the members of the *Smena vekh* circle would be called.[60]

In their declaration of intent, entitled "At the Crossing," the editors of *Nakanune* advocated political realism and a decisive break with revolutionary romanticism of any kind. They stated that, from the very beginning, the Russian revolution had been poisoned by the intelligentsia's pernicious illusions. In their opinion, the idea that it was necessary to immediately convoke a Constituent Assembly had deprived the Provisional Government of real power and meaning. "Democratic control" over governmental institutions had completely undermined the principle of legitimate state power. As they saw it, in October the Bolsheviks had only completed a process started long before. Clearly, Russia was not ripe for unrestricted democracy. Yet, as the Russian intelligentsia had failed to acknowledge this immaturity, the Russian state had fallen apart under the all-too-heavy yoke of democracy. Therefore, Ustrialov and his colleagues urged the intelligentsia to go through a catharsis and to take as the highest values the values of the state, the nation, the motherland, and the culture.[61]

In fact, the editors of *Nakanune* seemed to hope that Russia was "on the eve" of a prosperous period in its history, and that the revolution was only a temporary crisis that would be followed by a national revival.[62] In the editorial of the June issue they declared that Bolshevism had outlived itself *(izzhil sebia).* Apparently, they believed that the people's national consciousness was finally awakening, and that the legacy of Bolshevism was being liquidated.[63] However, *Nakanune*'s assessment of the situation proved to be mistaken. Before long, the Bolsheviks liquidated the entire non-Communist press, and the opposition lost its opportunities to speak out.[64] Moreover, when in early September the Bolsheviks launched the Red Terror, Ustrialov and many of his colleagues were forced to flee, or face liquidation themselves.

Judging from Ustrialov's writings between 1917 and 1918, it is clear that the basic assumptions that led him in early 1920 to accept the Bolshevik regime had already taken shape by the time he left Moscow.[65] At that time his disillusionment with formal democracy and with the poor statesmanship of the Russian bourgeoisie and the country's socialist and liberal politicians was already complete. In addition, his view of the October revolution as a deeply Russian phenomenon, as a grandiose, purifying, and invigorating crisis that would be of universal significance, was clearly delineated. Finally, his belief that Russia was to be a "great" state, and that all means were justified to reach this goal, had taken shape even before 1917. Nonetheless, in late 1918 Ustrialov still considered the Bolshevik regime as the major obstacle to Russia's rebirth as a great state. Consequently, when he was asked in early January 1919 to join the White movement in its struggle for "a great and united Russia," he did not hesitate. He left Perm, the city where he had found refuge after his flight from Moscow, and traveled to Omsk, the capital of White Admiral Kolchak.

For Ustrialov, his time in Omsk was a period of gnawing doubts and disillusionment. Although he had greeted the arrival of Kolchak's troops in Perm with high hopes,[66] from his very first days in Omsk he could not suppress his misgivings about the Kolchak government, with all its intrigues and all its relics of the old order. Was this the national dictatorship he had been waiting for, the strong power that would be able to restore Russia as a great state?[67] He kept his misgivings to himself, however, sharing them only with his old friend and colleague Iu. V. Kliuchnikov, who served as Kolchak's minister of foreign affairs until he resigned his post in early 1919.[68] At the time of Ustrialov's arrival in Omsk, Kliuchnikov was about to leave for the Paris Peace Conference.[69] When Ustrialov confessed to Kliuchnikov his doubts about the viability of the Kolchak government, which was so colorless compared to the Bolshevik regime, Kliuchnikov immediately and fully agreed with him, but argued that even though the center of history lay in Moscow, rather than in Omsk, people like Ustrialov and himself had the duty to join the White movement. As Kliuchnikov saw it, the Whites' task was to keep the revolution within certain limits, to consolidate it with prudence and common sense. He was convinced that if their movement was successful, it would be of great benefit to the country.

Ustrialov concurred with Kliuchnikov on this point; after all, the French revolution had needed a Napoleon to consolidate it. But what if the Whites were not victorious? Kliuchnikov saw but one possible answer to this tormenting question: victory by the Bolsheviks could only mean that Russia needed them, that the course of history had to pass through Lenin and his colleagues. Kliuchnikov added that, no matter what happened, one had to take Russia's side. Ustrialov agreed that if this were so, there would be no choice but to meet the Bolsheviks.[70]

Therefore, from his very first days in Omsk, Ustrialov did not exclude the possibility, however tormenting,[71] that at some point he could be forced to accept the Bolshevik regime if this were necessary for the good of Russia. This did not mean, however, one had to give up the anti-Bolshevik struggle. On the contrary, he felt that the struggle should be continued to the very end. Ustrialov realized that Kolchak was not the best possible incarnation of the national dictatorship that, Ustrialov believed, alone could help Russia out of her crisis, but was only too aware that there was no better Russian Napoleon available and that, in any event, "one should not change horses in midstream." There was nothing left but to strengthen Kolchak's authority as much as possible, close ranks around him, and give him complete and unconditional support. For all his doubts, Ustrialov considered opposition to Kolchak completely out of place. He felt that Russian society had been punished hard enough for its "itch for opposition."[72]

As director of the governmental press agency, Ustrialov consciously became the "bard" of the White dictatorship, limiting himself to what he called "positive criticism."[73] He did not hesitate to criticize the Omsk government when, in the late summer of 1919, it attempted to win over more popular support by putting forward a number of proposals for democratization.[74] Ustrialov opposed any mitigation of the dictatorship, convinced that this could only lead to a repetition of the scenario of 1917, and would undermine Kolchak's position completely.[75] While he continued to regard the Kolchak regime as a "dictatorship in the name of democracy,"[76] his experiences in the Kolchak administration and as chairman of the Eastern Section of the Kadet Central Committee[77] only enhanced his mistrust of party politics and deepened his doubts about the people's capacity to participate in government.[78]

Ustrialov's experiences in Omsk were also decisive for his attitude toward Russia's former allies. In fact, he had never been a proponent of unconditional support for the Allies, and in the weeks after the signing of the Brest-Litovsk Treaty, he had regarded such a position as untenable. At a meeting of the Kadet Central Committee in May 1918, he had urged that Russia adopt a policy of "open hands," in which the only criterion for taking a specific orientation would be its benefits for Russia's national interests. Still, when this position failed to win the support of his fellow party members, Ustrialov accepted the party's line of unconditional faithfulness to the Allies.[79] However, by the spring of 1919 the international situation had so changed that such an orientation seemed preferable even to Ustrialov. He set forth his views on the issue in a lecture to the Kadet Central Committee's Eastern Section in May 1919. As he saw it, Russia should make sure, first, that the powers with which she associated herself had enough weight on the international scene; second, that these powers took a positive attitude toward the Omsk government; and finally, that they could help Russia regain the status of a great European state. Taking all these factors into consideration, he felt that, under the circumstances, Russia should side with France, Britain, and, to a lesser degree, the United States.[80]

This did not mean that Ustrialov trusted the Allies completely. That Britain and the United States had recognized Finland as an independent state, for instance, had deeply disappointed him. He admitted that in light of President Wilson's Fourteen Points nothing else could have been expected, but this did not make the recognition any less damaging for Russia.[81] In the following months, Ustrialov's disappointment with the Allies grew considerably. He had always stressed that Russia's revival had to be brought about by the Russians themselves, but he also believed that, in compensation for her war efforts, Russia was entitled to effective help from the Allies in her struggle against the Bolsheviks.[82] By the late summer of 1919, Ustrialov found the Allies seriously wanting in this respect.[83] As time went by, he gradually became convinced that the Allies' only goal in their policy toward Russia was to prevent her from becoming a great and powerful state again. His disappointment became complete, following the Allies' refusal, in late December 1919, to support Kolchak against the so-called Political Center in Irkutsk, a coalition predominantly of SRs and Mensheviks, who after two weeks of fighting succeeded in overthrowing the Kolchak government on 5 January 1920.[84]

As Ustrialov's disillusionment with party politics and with the Allies grew stronger, so did his admiration for the Bolsheviks' strength. He could not help taking a patriotic pride in Lenin's strong character,[85] and at the conference of the Kadet Central Committee's Eastern Section in May 1919 he stressed that the scope and astonishing energy of Bolshevism made it strong enough to threaten the whole world.[86] In August 1919, when Kolchak's troops were retreating, while Denikin's men in the South were advancing, Ustrialov began to realize that this situation could lead to Russia's partition; in that case, he certainly preferred a complete Bolshevik victory.[87] In Ustrialov's eyes, the Bolsheviks were gradually attaining a national aura as the defenders of a united Russia.[88] By January 1920 he no longer doubted. On the eve of the Political Center's victory, he noted in his diary: "Bolshevism will be victorious. . . . It will unite Russia; honor and praise to it!"[89]

It was during these last days before the fall of the Kolchak government that Ustrialov formulated the ideas he would express a few weeks later in the sensational interview with the Harbin daily *Vestnik Man'chzhurii*.[90] In public, however, he continued to support Kolchak to the very end. He felt that launching an appeal to accept the Bolshevik victory at that time would have amounted to betraying the admiral and his government, and would have provided grist for the Political Center's mill. Moreover, he feared that friend and foe alike would consider him a coward and a renegade.[91]

After the fall of the Kolchak government, such considerations were no longer relevant, but Ustrialov realized that, given the threat of execution or imprisonment he was facing from the new authorities in Irkutsk, no one would believe his about-face to be sincere.[92] Consequently, he went into hiding and waited for an opportunity to escape. He was determined to make his views public once he had reached a safer place, where, he trusted, his appeal would not so easily be dismissed as mere "adaptation to the victors."[93] On 12 January

1920 Ustrialov finally left Irkutsk on board a Japanese railroad car. By that time, the Bolsheviks had started negotiations with the Political Center, which soon thereafter would lead to the installation of Bolshevik power in Irkutsk. Ustrialov's expectations were confirmed. Before leaving the city, he had written in his diary: "Everything is becoming all right, the country is being unified before one's eyes."[94]

Ustrialov had first intended to travel to Vladivostok; however, he got stranded in Harbin, where he would remain until his return to Moscow in 1935. Once in Harbin, Ustrialov decided to openly call for peace with the Bolsheviks. Rejecting the old White tactics, he proposed a new plan of action, based on using Bolshevism for national goals, and furthering its "evolutionary elimination from within."[95]

Ustrialov termed his position "National-Bolshevism," referring explicitly to the German movement of the same name.[96] Since its origin in the spring of 1919, he had been fascinated by the tendency in German nationalist circles to use Bolshevism as a weapon in the struggle against Germany's "enslavers," the Allies. To force the Allies to mitigate their demands upon the defeated country, the German "National-Bolsheviks" blackmailed them with the threat of a Bolshevist victory in Germany as well.[97] Ustrialov now believed that Bolshevism could be helpful to Russian patriots as well; with its international influence and its all-penetrating connections, Bolshevism was an excellent weapon of Russian foreign policy.[98] Moreover, he did not doubt that Bolshevism could be used also to bring about the reunification of the Russian empire. The border states that since 1917 had severed themselves from the center, Ustrialov argued, were able to hold out only because the Allies wanted to surround Russia with a *cordon sanitaire*. However, he was convinced that Moscow would not grant peace to these "pygmy states": in the name of world revolution, the Soviet government would strive to reunite them with the revolutionary heartland, and thus a great and united Russia would be restored.[99]

Ustrialov was also convinced that the Soviet government's aim to expand the revolution to the whole world would force it to adopt a more realistic economic policy and compromise with capitalism. He predicted that if the regime wanted to hold out, an economic "Brest" would be inevitable, and as a result, the "unbearable yoke of forcible communism" would gradually become less heavy for the population, and eventually become obsolete.[100] Finally, Ustrialov felt that the Soviet regime had proven to be the only force in Russia capable of curbing the anarchic forces of the masses, of " 'freezing' the corrupting waters of the revolutionary flood."[101] He warned that to destroy the regime now would be to throw Russia back into total anarchy.[102]

In short, by early 1920 Ustrialov was convinced that the evolution toward "Bonapartism" he expected—the process of resurrecting Russia as a great and powerful state, restoring order in Russian society, and normalizing the country's economy—was to take place through the revolution, not in spite of it.[103]

Although he had earlier believed that the White movement would lead Russia in this direction,[104] he now no longer doubted that it was the Red regime that would bring this about. "Bolshevism is evolving from Jacobinism to Napoleonism," he wrote in March 1920, "not as far as the concrete form of government is concerned, but with regard to the *style* of the state's aspirations."[105]

As Ustrialov saw it, to continue the armed struggle against the Soviet regime could only hamper this evolution, while peace with Moscow would, on the contrary, further it.[106] Therefore, he argued that, rather than giving one's life in the anti-Bolshevik struggle, the best sacrifice a Russian patriot now could make for Russia's national renaissance was to cooperate with the regime, notwithstanding its numerous and repellent shortcomings. He was convinced that the sooner opposition against the new regime died down, the sooner the process of Russia's national resurrection would begin. In this sense, "the way to Canossa would prove to be the way to Damascus."[107]

Ustrialov saw this position embodied in the person of Tsarist General Brusilov, who at the moment of the Polish invasion of Russia in the spring of 1920 had appealed to all Tsarist officers to join the Red Army in defense of Mother Russia.[108] As to his own role in this process, Ustrialov felt that his task lay rather on the ideological level. He considered it his patriotic duty to reveal the intrinsic meaning of National-Bolshevism,[109] help the outside world understand and interpret the Russian revolution, and "reconcile the 'civilized world' with the new Russia."[110]

Ustrialov realized that in order to perform this task, it was important both to assure his independence from the Soviet authorities and to maintain perspective by remaining outside Russia. In spite of his homesickness, he felt that he could not return to Russia until his mission had been fulfilled.[111] He twice declined an opportunity to return, first in 1923, when he was offered the chair of Public Law at the University of Irkutsk, and a second time in 1928, when he received a proposal to join the staff at Moscow University.[112] At the same time, Ustrialov did enter into contact with the Soviet representatives in Harbin, and adopted Soviet citizenship soon after his arrival there.[113] Moreover, albeit not without hesitation,[114] in 1925 he took up service in the Chinese Eastern Railroad, which had come under joint Chinese-Soviet management in 1924. He initially headed the railroad's Educational Division (in this connection he was sent in the summer of 1925 on a mission to Moscow), and in 1928 he was appointed director of the railroad's Central Library.[115] This service assured Ustrialov of a link with the homeland, without committing him too much to the Soviet authorities.[116]

In spite of his controversial ideological position, Ustrialov quickly became integrated into the Harbin Russian community, and seems to have been respected there as a person, even by his political opponents.[117] The time of his arrival coincided with the foundation of the first institution for higher education in Harbin, the so-called Higher Economic-Juridical Courses (in 1922 renamed "Harbin Juridical Faculty"), which was inaugurated on 1 March 1920.

Ustrialov was appointed professor of Public Law and General Theory of Law at the new institution, and was even elected its first dean. He held the chair of Public Law at the Juridical Faculty until 1934.[118] In the fall of 1920 he participated in founding a Popular University in Harbin, where he became a frequent lecturer. His lectures on themes such as "The History of Social Development in Russia" appear to have been well attended.[119] From 1922 on he also directed a literary-artistic circle for the youth, organized by the Harbin Commercial Assembly,[120] and a philosophical circle at the Juridical Faculty, where he introduced subjects such as Eurasianism, the Crisis of Democracy, and the thought of P. I. Novgorodtsev, Oswald Spengler, N. F. Fedorov, and V. S. Solov'ev.[121] Moreover, he participated regularly in public debates on ideological questions.[122]

During his years in Harbin, Ustrialov was extremely active as a publicist. Closely following the events in the Soviet Union, he tried to develop the ideological basis of his National-Bolshevik position, and to propagate his views as widely as possible. From the very beginning of his stay in Harbin he became a regular contributor to *Novosti zhizni* (News of Life), the newspaper of the local Russian commercial community, which had taken a pro-Bolshevik line soon after the fall of Kolchak.[123] He was one of the founders of the short-lived literary-artistic journal *Okno* (The Window),[124] and was the moving spirit behind the almanac *Russkaia zhizn'* (Russian Life), four issues of which appeared in 1922–1923. Besides this, he contributed for a while to *Vestnik Man'-chzhurii* (Manchuria Herald), the organ of the Directorate of the Chinese Eastern Railroad,[125] and, as will be seen, to several publications outside Manchuria. Moreover, he wrote a number of philosophical essays, including work on German National Socialism, Italian Fascism, the political ideal of Plato, and the problem of progress.[126]

In late October 1920, Ustrialov published a collection of the most important articles he had written for *Novosti zhizni*. He gave the brochure the title *V bor'be za Rossiiu* (In the Struggle for Russia), and dedicated it to General Brusilov.[127] The collection was a detailed exposition of Ustrialov's basic National-Bolshevik position.

In his afterword to the collection, Ustrialov admitted that most of the reprinted articles had been written in the days of the Red Army's victories over the Polish and White forces. That the tide had turned in the meantime, however, that the Red Army had been defeated by the Poles and was struggling against renewed attacks by General Wrangel's forces, did not alter his basic thesis. Even if Wrangel in the end managed to defeat Bolshevism with the help of starvation, foreign aid, and peasant anarchy, the price of such a victory would be ruinous. Ustrialov stressed that, compared to this, his own proposals for overcoming the country's revolutionary collapse were "incomparably more fruitful, efficient, and nationally expedient."[128]

With the publication of *V Bor'be za Rossiiu,* Ustrialov's views became known beyond his limited audience in Manchuria, and reached the Russian émigré community in Europe as well. However, apart from a not unsympathetic review by V. Stankevich, who limited himself to setting forth Ustrialov's main theses,[129] reactions in the émigré press were unanimously negative. According to the Socialist Revolutionary M. Vishniak in *Sovremennye zapiski,* Ustrialov's stand was the result of his mistrust of the Russian people and his unshakable confidence in dictatorship, combined with a considerable amount of opportunism.[130] On the pages of the Paris Kadet organ *Poslednie novosti* (Latest News), the journalist—and future *smenovekhovets*—I. Vasilevskii (Ne-Bukva) dismissed Ustrialov's position as sheer opportunism.[131]

The Kadet D. Pasmanik, for his part, rejected all accusations of opportunism. In his opinion, Ustrialov was blinded by hatred for Russia's former allies as well as for Russian socialists, and as a result of this failed to see how pernicious Bolshevism really was for Russia. Pasmanik agreed with Ustrialov that both the Allies and the SRs had done Russia much harm, but stressed that Bolshevism was even more harmful for the country. He argued that the idea of "Great Russia" was completely alien to the Moscow regime, and that the Bolsheviks were ruining the country's economy. Instead of curbing anarchic forces, as Ustrialov believed, the Bolsheviks were fueling them.[132]

Similar thoughts were expressed also by P. B. Struve. Even before *V Bor'be za Rossiiu* came off the press, Ustrialov had sent Struve a number of chapters, with a letter asking for his opinion.[133] Although Struve never answered Ustrialov directly, in April 1921 he published his reaction in *Rul',* the daily of the Berlin Kadets.[134]

Just as Pasmanik, Struve was unwilling to accuse Ustrialov of opportunism; as he saw it, Ustrialov's position was rather a gross mistake, caused by a misinterpretation of the facts.[135] Ustrialov's thesis that Bolshevism was realizing a national mission in spite of its antinational ideology was being totally refuted by Moscow's ruinous economic policy. Struve argued that the Bolsheviks were destroying the economy in the territories under their control, and if this was evil in itself, it was also evil in the national sense because it was radically changing the balance of power between Bolshevik Russia and the outside world.[136] Struve did not doubt that Ustrialov and his like-minded colleagues were being deceived by the Bolsheviks' "state-like" façade, the main element of which was the Red Army. For the sake of this façade, Ustrialov and his colleagues were prepared to idealize Bolshevism as a whole, overlooking the fact that behind its façade the Bolshevik state structure had no economic foundation, and was therefore doomed to collapse.[137] Struve concluded his comments on *V bor'be za Rossiiu* with the observation that, while reading Ustrialov's writings, it was hard to avoid the impression that National-Bolshevism was simply the result of that short-lived political climate caused by the Bolshevik victory over the Poles. (Apparently, Ustrialov had failed to include his afterword to *V Bor'be za Rossiiu* in the parcel for Struve.) As Struve saw it, the further course of events, ending in the Peace Treaty of Riga, had shown how ephemeral and illusory this climate was; National-Bolshevism had been refuted by experience.[138]

Ustrialov let most of the criticism of *V bor'be za Rossiiu* pass unanswered, but Struve's comments clearly disappointed him, and he reacted to them with a lengthy reply. In his opinion, Struve made a grave mistake in identifying Bolshevism with Communism. While Ustrialov fully agreed with Struve on the economic harmfulness of Communism, he stressed that one could not simply apply this judgment to Bolshevism as well. As Ustrialov saw it, "the Soviet regime was more than the economic policy of 'immediate Communism,' it was not even organically or indissolubly connected with it."[139]

In his reaction, Struve had completely passed over the fact that the Soviet government had in the meantime introduced the New Economic Policy (NEP). Ustrialov kindly drew his attention to this. He reminded Struve that the new economic course in Soviet Russia confirmed what Ustrialov had been predicting more than a year before: the overall situation was forcing the Bolsheviks to change their economic policy, and to abandon their devastating social experiments. Ustrialov admitted that whether the Bolsheviks would also succeed in getting the country onto "new economic rails" was another question, but he stressed that, under the present difficult circumstances, a "transformation of Bolshevism" was the best possible way out for Russia. A "return to capitalism" through a new political revolution would in any case be more ephemeral, tortuous, and destructive.[140]

Ustrialov was greatly surprised by Struve's counterargument, for some reason couched in Marxist terminology, that the Bolshevik state structure was doomed to collapse because it lacked an economic basis. How could Struve, one of the contributors to the 1909 collection *Vekhi,* doubt the enormous creative value of the principle of state organization as such? Ustrialov argued that the "superstructure" was not secondary and derivative, determined by its economic basis; it could find a basis in itself. Moreover, there was no mathematically established relationship between a given superstructure and its basis. Consequently, Ustrialov wondered "how one could ignore the political structure forged by our revolution, simply because this structure had *so far* been linked to a utopian and harmful economic system."[141]

Finally, Ustrialov could not possibly accept Struve's assertion that "National-Bolshevism had been refuted by experience." He admitted that the Soviet-Polish war had added inspiration to his position but stressed that the essence of National-Bolshevism had not been changed by the war's unfortunate outcome. In fact, it had only been strengthened by the further course of events: the defeat of General Wrangel, the growing spiritual impoverishment of the White movement, and, most important, the beginning of a tactical evolution of Bolshevism. Ustrialov concluded that events very clearly were confirming National-Bolshevism, justifying all its basic prognoses.[142]

Ustrialov also sent a copy of *V bor'be za Rossiiu* to Iu. V. Kliuchnikov, his former Moscow colleague, with whom he had had such a fateful exchange of thoughts during his first days in Omsk. By the summer of 1920 Kliuchnikov, now living in Paris, had come to the conclusion that Bolshevism was not an entirely negative phenomenon, but he was reluctant to take the next step and call for reconciliation with the Soviet regime. However, the news of Ustrialov's appeal, which reached Kliuchnikov in the fall of 1920, and even more so Ustrialov's collection of articles, which he received in early 1921, prompted him to take a stand.[143]

A small circle of like-minded émigrés soon formed around Kliuchnikov, including Iu. N. Potekhin, the young Kadet who along with Kliuchnikov and Ustrialov had founded the Moscow journal *Nakanune* in 1918. In the summer of 1921 the circle issued a collection of articles entitled *Smena vekh* (Change of Signposts), which would make the ideas of National-Bolshevism known both in the émigré community as a whole and in Soviet Russia. The collection also contained an essay entitled "Patriotica," attributed to Ustrialov; without Ustrialov's knowledge, Kliuchnikov had composed it out of fragments from *V bor'be za Rossiiu* and from separate articles Ustrialov had sent him.[144]

At first, Ustrialov sincerely welcomed his Paris allies. That he was no longer alone with his views, that these were now shared by a number of his friends, greatly encouraged him.[145] When, in early January 1922, he finally received a copy of *Smena vekh*,[146] he reacted immediately with a positive review in *Novosti zhizni*. He called the collection a deeply authentic human document, the result of agonizing attempts to grasp the meaning of the revolutionary whirlwind, and to work out an appropriate line of conduct. The collection showed a profound faith in Russia and a deep consciousness that the revolution had invested the Russian intelligentsia with enormous historical responsibility. Ustrialov added that as such, it was characteristic of that "school" of Russian national-minded intellectuals educated on *Vekhi*.[147]

As Ustrialov saw it, *Smena vekh* was primarily an appeal to the Russian intelligentsia to reconcile themselves with the revolution, and a search for new ways to serve the motherland, now that the "White dream" had shown itself to be mistaken. But there was also a spiritual aspect to the collection. Ustrialov regarded *Smena vekh* as an attempt to deepen the spiritual self-consciousness of the Russian intelligentsia, to understand the revolution's main "idea," and to describe the "face of Russian national culture as it had been revealed in the revolutionary awakening of the people and the nation."[148] In this respect, however, Ustrialov considered *Smena vekh* to be a failure. In his opinion, the "new" *Vekhi* could not possibly replace the "old" *Vekhi* of 1909. Yet, he stressed that the merit of the new collection was precisely that it had raised spiritual questions. Ustrialov proposed that the Russian intelligentsia now take as their motto "*Vpered ot Vekh!*" (Forward from *Vekhi*) and set themselves the task of "deepening and developing the principles of *Vekhi* in the light of the new revelations of national life and national culture."[149]

Happy as Ustrialov was with his newfound allies, his joy soon became mixed with misgivings. In his opinion, the Paris *smenovekhovtsy* and Kliuchnikov in particular were definitely going too far in their acceptance of the October revolution and the new regime. While he fully endorsed *Smena vekh* in public, in private he wrote to Kliuchnikov that there were many things in the collection with which he could not possibly agree, even though he subscribed to its overall conception. He warned Kliuchnikov and his colleagues that, "reconciling themselves to the revolution, they should not abandon their own understanding of the national idea, nor become imbued with esteem for Marx's beard, rather than for Solov'ev and others."[150]

Ustrialov's misgivings became stronger as he received successive issues of the new weekly founded in the meantime in Paris by Kliuchnikov and his colleagues, also under the name of *Smena vekh*. In his opinion, the Paris *smenovekhovtsy* were sliding to the left and falling prey to a dangerous revolutionary romanticism.[151] By not preserving the necessary distance from Moscow, they had brought upon themselves the disdain of Lenin and his colleagues, and had needlessly alienated émigré circles.[152] Nonetheless, Ustrialov preferred not to reveal his misgivings to the outside world. He continued to contribute to the weekly *Smena vekh*,[153] and even provided a few articles for publication in the Berlin daily *Nakanune*,[154] which in March 1922 had taken the Paris journal's place, and which Ustrialov described as an attempt to "be more Bolshevik than the Bolsheviks themselves *(perebol'shevit' bol'shevikov)*."[155] While Kliuchnikov and his colleagues on a number of occasions deemed it necessary to distance themselves from the "right-wing" Ustrialov,[156] Ustrialov insisted that unity in the circle be preserved, at least outwardly. He argued that for the time being, they were too small a group and had too many opponents to allow themselves the luxury of open internal polemics.[157] To be sure, Ustrialov often wondered whether this position was tenable, but, as he had done in Omsk, he repressed his doubts; there had already been enough "old intelligentsia sectarianism *(staro-intelligentskoe sektantstvo)*."[158]

When, however, during his visit to Moscow in 1925 he learned to what extent the group around Kliuchnikov had compromised itself with the Soviet regime, he regretted having been involved, albeit indirectly, in the whole undertaking.[159] By that time the public interest in *smenovekhovstvo* as such had died down, and it no longer made sense for Ustrialov to dissociate himself in firm terms from Kliuchnikov and his colleagues. After his return to Harbin Ustrialov published a small collection of travel impressions, in which he expressed his disapproval of the line the *smenovekhovtsy* had taken in rather mild tones. He stressed that the Prague collection had been most promising, yet added that the group behind the collection had slid to the left so fast and so carelessly they had completely lost their independence, and, as a result, both their influence among Russian intellectuals and the attention of the Soviet government. Ustrialov concluded regretfully that the movement's leaders had not been equal to the opportunities of the moment.[160]

In late 1921, after the introduction of the NEP in Soviet Russia, Ustrialov also gained the support of a small group of like-minded intellectuals in Harbin, including G. N. Dikii, an economist who first directed the Commercial Agency of the Ussuri River Railroad in Harbin, then in 1924 was appointed head of the Chinese Eastern Railroad's economic office;[161] N. S. Zefirov, former minister of provisions in the Omsk government, who in late 1921 took up Soviet service;[162] and E. E. Iashnov, also an economist and employee of the Chinese Eastern Railroad's economic office.[163] In 1922 the group began publishing the almanac *Russkaia zhizn'* (Russian Life). In the foreword to the first issue, Ustrialov and his colleagues stressed that they wanted to remain faithful to the Russian nation and state, and that they "refused to consider love for one's motherland as something *conditional,* subordinate to individual sympathies or antipathies toward a governing group or party, a social or political structure."[164]

Besides patriotism, the main motive of the *Russkaia zhizn'* group for accepting the Soviet regime was the hope that the NEP was the beginning of a Russian Thermidor.[165] After the Chinese Eastern Railroad came under joint Chinese-Soviet management in October 1924, the group acquired a following among the numerous émigrés employed there as non-Communist specialists. However, in 1926, when the railroad's director, who had taken the initiative of recruiting nationalist émigrés, was removed from his post—and a number of non-Communist specialists with him—the movement began to disintegrate.[166] The introduction of the five-year plans and the beginning of collectivization, which was to throw Ustrialov himself into a deep ideological crisis, and finally the Japanese invasion of Manchuria in 1931–1932, which caused many Russians in Harbin to give up their pro-Soviet position, marked the end of the Harbin group.[167]

In early 1923, through G. N. Dikii, one of his closest collaborators in Harbin, Ustrialov also entered into contact with the group behind the Moscow journal *Novaia Rossiia* (New Russia).[168] This group of nonparty intellectuals had, in the fall of 1921, obtained permission from the Moscow Politburo to set up a nonparty journal.[169] The first issue of the new "social, literary, and scientific monthly" appeared in Petrograd in March 1922. The journal was brought out by a private publishing house[170] and edited by I. G. Lezhnev (Al'tshuler), a journalist of Jewish origin, who in his youth had taken part in the underground labor movement, but who later had abandoned revolutionary politics. In the spring of 1917 Lezhnev had started contributing to the Petrograd newspaper *Russkaia volia* (Russian Liberty), which by that time had become the organ of industrialist circles in the capital.[171] However, soon after the October revolution he had joined the Red Army, and from 1918 to 1920 had served in a number of military institutions throughout the country. After his demobilization in late 1920 Lezhnev was employed by the newspaper *Izvestiia,* where he headed a department. At the same time, he contributed to several other Soviet periodicals, including *Trud* (Labor) and *Uchitel'skaia gazeta* (Teachers' Newspaper), as well as to Soviet organs abroad such as *Novyi mir* (The New World), *Put'* (The Path), and *Novyi put'* (The New Path), published by the Soviet missions in Berlin, Helsinki, and Riga, respectively.[172]

Lezhnev's closest collaborators in *Novaia Rossiia* were the well-known ethnographer V. G. Tan-Bogoraz[173] and the journalist and literary historian S. A. Adrianov,[174] both former contributors to *Russkaia volia.* In the course of 1921 they, too, began contributing to several publications of the Soviet missions abroad, and later in that year Adrianov was elected a nonparty member of the Petrograd Soviet.[175] In addition to this trio, regular contributors to *Novaia Rossiia* included the novelists A. Belyi, M. Shaginian, and O. Forsh; the poet M. Kuzmin; and the literary critic N. Asheshov.[176]

In the editorial to the first issue the editors proudly presented *Novaia Rossiia* as the first "nonparty organ" in the Soviet Republic. They stressed their faith in the New Russia they believed was being constructed out of both revolutionary and prerevolutionary elements. They compared Russia to a house whose façade had been badly damaged by the revolutionary storm, but added that this storm had also provided the house with reinforced concrete foundations and had eliminated all its rotten rafters.[177] According to Lezhnev and his colleagues, the revolution had brought about a creative synthesis between "the most worthy and healthy forces" among the popular masses, and the most businesslike, talented elements of the old intelligentsia. They intended *Novaia Rossiia* to be the organ of these "vital forces" among the intelligentsia, and set themselves the goal of formulating a new ideology for this group, based on "a combination of historical insight and creative, strong-willed aspirations."[178]

Except for two periods during which publication was interrupted, *Novaia Rossiia*—or *Rossiia,* as the journal was called during the greater part of its existence—continued its search for a new ideology until the spring of 1926, when it was closed down completely.[179] Even though *Novaia Rossiia* was a privately financed undertaking,[180] it enjoyed the moral support of the Soviet authorities, who apparently considered the journal useful because it called on the nonparty intelligentsia to cooperate with the Soviet regime, addressing them in their own language.[181]

Indeed, on the pages of *Novaia Rossiia* much attention was devoted to the role of the intelligentsia in the new Russian state. As Lezhnev and his colleagues saw it, the intelligentsia should accept the Soviet regime unconditionally and work honestly for the sake of "Soviet Russia and simply Russia."[182] They were convinced that, under the circumstances prevailing in the country, political activity outside the framework of the Communist party was bound to end either in counterrevolution or in ideological prostitution. Consequently, they stressed that, for the time being, the nonparty intelligentsia in Russia had no choice but to withdraw voluntarily from politics, and to limit themselves to "constructive criticism."[183] According to the editors of *Novaia Rossiia,* this was the only way the intelligentsia could maintain their tradition of ideological independence, something that Lezhnev and his colleagues considered of paramount importance.[184]

Ustrialov, who maintained a regular correspondence with Lezhnev until Lezhnev was expelled from the Soviet Union in 1926,[185] highly valued *Novaia Rossiia*'s stand of ideological independence, and subscribed entirely to the journal's appeal for conscientious practical work combined with political "abstinence."[186] Nevertheless, there were many aspects of *Novaia Rossiia*'s position with which he could not possibly agree. Generally speaking, Ustrialov's objection to the group's stance was the same he earlier had raised against Kliuchnikov and his colleagues: *Novaia Rossiia,* too, was being carried away by "revolutionary romanticism."[187]

Ustrialov decidedly rejected Lezhnev's thesis that internationalism was a "new religion" that "in power and repercussions surpassed Christianity and Buddhism." He argued that internationalism and socialism as such could not possibly replace religion, as these were entities on a completely different level. One should not yield to the "inspiration of the Tower of Babel."[188] Neither could he accept Lezhnev's notion of the new Russia as a "nation class," symbolizing all the oppressed in the world, and leading the struggle against worldwide imperialism. According to Ustrialov, this notion was merely a wellsounding but empty phrase, irreconcilable with any sociological reality.[189]

Even more categorical was Ustrialov's rejection of the idea that the Russian revolution was merely a phase in a larger, worldwide, historical "cataclysm," another motif that repeatedly appeared on the pages of *Novaia Rossiia.*[190] He felt that this idea not only overestimated the revolution's potential, but also completely ignored the Soviet government's retreat from Communism and the transformation of Russian life "in an unambiguously 'bourgeois' way."[191] Convinced as he was that the Russian economy was steadily developing toward a "bourgeois" system, he also opposed *Novaia Rossiia*'s appeal for a mixed economy.[192]

However, once again Ustrialov preferred to play down any differences of opinion and stress those elements that united him with the group behind *Novaia Rossiia.*[193] He sent Lezhnev several articles for publication in the journal, three of which did indeed appear on its pages,[194] giving the Soviet public the opportunity to become directly acquainted with some of Ustrialov's writings.

. . .

The introduction of the NEP in March 1921 had enormously strengthened Ustrialov in his position, as he saw his prediction that the Bolsheviks would be forced to adopt a more realistic economic policy come true. Since March

1920, when he first expressed his belief that an "economic Brest" was imminent, and throughout the years of the NEP, he had been convinced that if only the Bolsheviks took the first step, further evolution would be inevitable.[195] It was this belief that made him reject so decidedly the "revolutionary romanticism" of both the European *smenovekhovtsy* and the group behind *Novaia Rossiia*. Ustrialov felt that "to preach *intoxication* when the country was experiencing a *hangover,* meant completely to lose contact with the actual situation." In early 1922 he reminded Kliuchnikov that none of the *smenovekhovtsy* had sided with the Reds when the revolution was at its height; now, in his view, there was even less reason to become inspired by the revolution when it was on the decline.[196]

Ustrialov was convinced that the NEP was bringing about a complete transformation *(pererozhdenie)* of the Soviet economy. It would become a proprietary system, based primarily on a strong individual agricultural sector. As he saw it, the revolutionary government was in fact realizing the design of Tsarist Prime Minister P. A. Stolypin to create a strong class of peasant proprietors, a goal that Stolypin's reforms, introduced in 1906–1911, had failed to accomplish.[197] Ustrialov placed his hopes for Russia's economic development on the "sturdy little peasant *(krepkii muzhichek)*" and on the new "Soviet bourgeoisie" that originated as a result of the NEP. He maintained that, just as the Bolsheviks had been forced to introduce the NEP by the pressure of "worldwide capitalism," so they were now being "taken by the throat" by the postrevolutionary bourgeoisie, who were forcing them to evolve even further.[198] He believed that these people of the "revolution's second day" would "smother the Communist dream in loyal embraces."[199] In this light, Ustrialov considered it his duty to provide not only nonparty specialists but also these new, "postrevolutionary" social strata with an appropriate ideology, which would explicate the meaning of the "Soviet Thermidor" and interpret its prospects.[200] When the Menshevik organ *Sotsialisticheskii vestnik* (Socialist Messenger) classified the group behind *Smena vekh* as "ideologues of the Soviet bourgeoisie *(sovburzhuaziia)*," Ustrialov readily accepted this label.[201]

The evolution of the Soviet economy toward a "bourgeois" system was of paramount importance to Ustrialov. He considered this the only way to ensure the country's economic revival, which, in its turn, was a sine qua non for Russia's resurrection as a great and powerful state. He did not, however, nurse any hopes that a far-reaching economic evolution would be accompanied by corresponding political reforms; in his opinion, this was not even desirable. True, he did expect a certain mitigation of the system, especially in the legal sphere,[202] but he was also convinced that under the circumstances, it was in Russia's interest that the Bolsheviks maintain their dictatorial power.[203]

Ustrialov repeatedly stressed that the last thing he wanted to see in Russia was a formal democracy.[204] His faith in parliamentarism, already feeble since the winter of 1917–1918, had been dealt a deathblow; he now no longer doubted that formal, "arithmetic" democracy had outlived its usefulness.[205] In his opinion, the principles of 1789 had waned in the course of the nineteenth century, and the Great War of 1914–1918, waged and won precisely in the name of these principles, had instead marked their end. "Having won, democracy had fainted."[206]

In light of his conception of historical nations as living organisms that were born, grew older, and died, Ustrialov interpreted the crisis of Western democracy as a clear sign that the end of Western civilization was approaching. He noted with some satisfaction that *der Untergang des Abendlandes,* which so many Russian thinkers ranging from K. Leont'ev to A. Herzen had predicted, was now becoming so evident that Western thinkers such as Oswald Spengler and Guglielmo Ferrero also drew attention to it.[207] It was in this context that Ustrialov saw a worldwide mission reserved for his motherland. He was convinced that postrevolutionary Russia would create a new cultural and political model that would become authoritative also in the West,[208] fulfilling her "great vocation," as the Slavophiles, Herzen, and Dostoevskii had predicted, and so justifying the enormous sacrifices of the past revolutionary years.[209]

As Ustrialov saw it, "formal democracy" would give way to an "authentic democracy," a "superdemocracy *(sverkh-demokratiia)*" organically grown from the people.[210] He was convinced that the people, exhausted as they were by wars and revolutions, preferred to cede all power to an active vanguard from their own midst, thus creating a truly popular *(narodnyi),* rather than a democratic *(demokraticheskii),* regime.[211] In Ustrialov's view, the authority of such an "active minority" had to be based not on law or force but on a creative idea.[212] The Bolsheviks were the perfect embodiment of such an "aristocracy of the will."[213]

That Lenin and his colleagues were motivated by a "living idea" was an argument that Ustrialov had used in their favor before. Even though, in the fall of 1920, he had called this idea "erroneous" and a "temptation,"[214] by mid-1921 he no longer rejected the ideals of socialism and internationalism as such. He accepted them as the ideals that would determine the coming stage in world history,[215] but stressed that the way to reach this stage would be long, tortuous, and gradual.[216] That the Bolsheviks now also seemed to accept this made them rise in Ustrialov's estimation.[217]

In general, the years of the NEP were a period of relative peace of mind for Ustrialov. In his opinion, both from an economic and a patriotic point of view, the Bolsheviks seemed to be leading the country in the right direction,[218] although less directly than he might have desired.[219] While the failure of the Thirteenth Party Congress in May 1924 to unambiguously confirm the party's commitment to the NEP had somewhat alarmed Ustrialov,[220] the outcome of the Fourteenth Party Congress, held in December 1925, completely reassured him. At this "Council of the Twentieth Century," as he enthusiastically termed the congress, the party had decided on its future policy in accordance with the "inexorable demands of economic logic and national-historical dialectics."[221]

The adoption of the principle of "socialism in one country" and the party's commitment to a "proletarian economic offensive, based on the New Economic Policy," deeply satisfied Ustrialov. In his view, the party had taken exactly those decisions which were needed under the circumstances. He was now more than ever convinced that, wittingly or unwittingly, the Soviet regime was providing grist for the "great historical All-Russian mill." That the party justified the options it had taken with the help of an emphatically socialist ideology and terminology did not in the least disturb him. It was not, he argued, how the congress justified its decisions that was important, but what it had decided.[222]

In the summer of 1925 Ustrialov published a voluminous collection of articles under the title *Pod znakom revoliutsii* (Under the Sign of Revolution), which contained his most important writings over the period of March 1921–June 1925. In the months leading up to the Fourteenth Party Congress, the collection—with its characterization of the Soviet regime as a new "caesarism" and of the NEP as a real Thermidor—had given rise to a heated discussion among Soviet leaders.[223] Zinov'ev, voicing the opinion of the party's left wing, which believed that the party was going too far in its concessions to the "new bourgeoisie" and to the individual peasant in particular, had seized upon *Pod znakom revoliutsii* to show the party that unless it changed its policy, Ustrialov's predictions of a Soviet Thermidor would materialize.[224] The center, for its part, had answered Zinov'ev's attack through the person of Bukharin, who dismissed Ustrialov's predictions of a Thermidor as being the result of a totally erroneous interpretation of the facts, and attacked Ustrialov instead for dreaming of a "new autocracy."[225] However, these attacks against *Pod znakom revoliutsii* did not impress Ustrialov. In his opinion, they merely proved that his analysis of the situation was correct.[226]

So much greater was the shock when the NEP came to an end. After the Fifteenth Party Congress of December 1927, in which the party had decided to introduce a first five-year plan of accelerated industrialization and to start with the collectivization of the countryside, Ustrialov initially placed his hopes on the group around Bukharin, the so-called right deviation, which advocated the continuation of the NEP.[227] When in November 1929 the "right" was declared the party's main enemy, he was thrown into a deep crisis.[228] Yet once again, his boundless belief in Russia helped him to come to terms with what was happening in the country.[229] It would take until 1934 for him to overcome all his doubts and to accept the new course of the Soviet government completely, but then he did so with even greater enthusiasm.

In principle, Ustrialov did not object either to planned, accelerated industrialization or to a sweeping reorganization of agriculture through collectivization.[230] Indeed, the immensity of what was being undertaken in his motherland filled him with "lofty pride" and delight.[231] However, he found it hard to believe that the party's policy had any chance of succeeding under the given circumstances.[232] As a result, he did not know whether to shout "Hurrah!" or to cry "Help!"[233] Ustrialov stressed that he would most sincerely applaud the realization of the goals of the ongoing "socialist offensive." Nonetheless, he expected that sooner or later the party would have to recognize that these goals were beyond the country's strength, and as a result would be forced to return to the principles of the NEP.[234] He continued to believe in the probability of a Russian Thermidor, and hoped that the new course would prove to be merely a "left-wing zigzag," leading from the NEP to a neo-NEP.[235] Therefore, he called upon the *spetsovskaia intelligentsiia*" (intellectuals working as "bourgeois specialists") in the Soviet Union to "maintain an irreproachable and active loyalty." They should "compel themselves actively and honestly to serve the state of the Revolution," however difficult this at times might be. If they were not capable of suppressing their doubts about the results of the socialist reorganization, Ustrialov urged them to do whatever they could for this process to succeed as fully as possible, so that the sacrifices that had already been made would not be in vain. In his view, even the most skeptical old specialist should now repeat the exclamation from the Gospel "Lord, I believe; help thou mine unbelief!"[236]

Ustrialov did not shut his eyes to the terror and horrors that accompanied collectivization,[237] yet he refused to speak out against them.[238] Rather, he compared the ongoing events in Russia to the era of Peter the Great, when the present had been "consciously sacrificed for the sake of the future."[239] In Ustrialov's view, "the revolution was sacrificing the popular well-being for the sake of national wealth."[240] He also decisively rejected any criticism to the effect that the "socialist offensive" in the Soviet Union would come down to the restoration of serfdom. He argued that "in the decisive hours of their existence, nations with a great style had never been afraid . . . to stand on the throat of their own 'freedom' and recognize themselves as 'slaves' of the great idea that had been assigned to them."[241]

At the time, Ustrialov qualified his comparison of the ongoing events to the time of Peter the Great by adding that the analogy was merely formal, because the outcome of the current crisis in Russia was not yet known.[242] His last doubts were dispelled by the Seventeenth Party Congress (26 January–10 February 1934), where it was declared that the basis of a socialist economy had been constructed, and collectivization had been completed.[243] The facts were convincing, he wrote in a jubilant article[244] devoted to the congress: Soviet socialism had won.[245]

> With proud joy because it was one's native land, because of its worldwide cause and its public exploit one could now say: yes, a great program is being implemented, the miraculous transformation of the country is becoming flesh and

blood. Doubts and fears have been dispelled: above the peoples of the Soviet land the day of a really new and glorious life is breaking.[246]

The revolutionary romanticism for which he had earlier reproached Kliuchnikov and Lezhnev now also captivated Ustrialov himself. Not only was he aware of this, he even considered it a step forward on his part. As he wrote in November 1934, only now had he come fully to appreciate the revolution's authentic energy and its immediate innovative power.[247]

At the Seventeenth Party Congress in early 1934, the final elimination of classes and the transformation of the country's whole working population into conscious and active builders of a classless socialist society had been announced as the major political objectives of the second five-year plan. Ustrialov admitted that these goals could hardly be realized in five years' time. However, he also felt that this belief in a "classless Soviet nation, a union of Soviet peoples, appearing in the arena of world history as the outpost of the idea of universal humanity," was a clear sign of the Russian revolution's universal meaning.[248]

He now regarded the product of this revolution, the Soviet Union, as the prototype of a new world order, of a new united mankind. He stressed that for such an order to be realized, a far-reaching socioeconomic transformation would be needed, and felt that the Soviet Union was paving the way in this respect. Moreover, it would be necessary to come to a "supranational whole on a national basis," in which the nations would cease to be the basis of mankind's political division, while at the same time preserving their internal cultural individuality.[249] Ustrialov did not doubt that here too, the Soviet Union was setting an example. In this Union, different nations were being incorporated into a strong state, which was cemented by two creative ideas: the concept of a united mankind based on social justice and general labor, and that of the transformation of nature by human genius.[250] Ustrialov believed that these ideas, along with the fact that so far the rest of the world had not followed the Soviet example nor was likely to do so in the foreseeable future, were the basis of a peculiar Soviet self-consciousness. This, in turn was leading to a feeling of love for one's own state as the pioneer of a new world.[251]

Ustrialov was well aware that the Soviet state was not perfect; this could not be expected from a prototype. He believed that, before it reached its ideal form, it would undergo many changes, especially in its spiritual outlook. He even expected Bolshevism to evolve toward some form of philosophical idealism.[252] In any case, he was convinced that Bolshevism would play a decisive role in formulating the leading ideology of the coming era. Its commitment to "real democracy," as well as the universal character of its objectives—which in Ustrialov's opinion favorably distinguished Bolshevism from Italian Fascism and German National Socialism[253]—were a guarantee of this.[254]

It had been psychologically and ideologically impossible for Ustrialov to return to Russia as long as "the circle of his National-Bolshevik ideas had not been concluded by the logic of the revolution, as long as the [party's] general line . . . had neither laid an actual economic basis for Soviet socialism, nor assumed a positive, statelike foreign policy." After the Seventeenth Party Congress he felt that these conditions had been fulfilled, so that an "independent" political stand no longer made sense.[255]

The congress almost coincided with negotiations between the Soviet Union and Japan over the future of the Chinese Eastern Railroad. Japan had been occupying Manchuria since 1932, and it was not impossible that the railroad would pass into Japanese hands. Ustrialov decided that if it came to that, he would return home.[256] The railroad had always assured him of a link with the motherland; without it, he saw but two alternatives: either a complete break, or reunion. In the light of his stance of the previous fifteen years, Ustrialov felt that he should choose for the latter. Indeed, he considered this as his debt of honor.[257] By the fall of 1934 there was no longer any doubt that the railroad would be sold to Japan. Even though at that time it was still unclear which position the Soviet government would take vis-à-vis the railroad's personnel in general, and Ustrialov in particular, Ustrialov started to prepare for his return. He began arranging his notes and papers in order to send them to the Russian Historical Archive in Prague before leaving.[258]

Ustrialov was fully aware that if he returned, he would have to practice the political restraint he had been recommending to the national-minded intelligentsia within the Soviet Union for more than a decade. He stressed that such restraint had now become a matter of conscious and free subordination to the state, rather than of doubt, disbelief, and obedience "with gritted teeth."[259] Nonetheless, he admitted that such an attitude would be extremely hard for him, especially in the "historiosophical" field. Deep in his heart he could not help hoping for a "modest political 'spring' " in the Soviet Union, a return to the relative freedom of the years of the NEP, without, naturally, a return to the NEP itself.[260]

In the fall of 1934 Ustrialov, using the last opportunity to speak out freely, published a collection of his most important articles over the period 1931–1934. In *Nashe vremia* (Our Era) he tried to give an independent, "Soviet-patriotic" interpretation of the recent events in the Soviet Union, paying special attention to themes such as a classless society and the Soviet mission in world history. The collection had for Ustrialov the value of a "new, more mature *Smena vekh*."[261] Because of its far-reaching endorsement of the Soviet Communist party's policies, *Nashe vremia* put Ustrialov into serious trouble with the local authorities, for the first time since his arrival in Harbin. At a certain point he even faced expulsion, but in the end no legal action was taken against him.[262] On the other hand, before *Nashe vremia* was printed, Ustrialov's old friend G. N. Dikii had warned him that the collection's criticism of the Soviet leadership[263] might harm him now that he was planning to return to Russia.[264] However, Ustrialov refused to make any changes in the collection's content. He argued that as long as this was not necessary for the sake of the Soviet state, he was incapable of "killing the 'Ustrialov' in himself completely."[265]

Ustrialov and his family departed for Moscow around 10 May 1935. Ustrialov stressed that his return to Moscow was a source of joy to him. However, he certainly had not left Harbin with full peace of mind. It was still absolutely unclear what was awaiting him in the Soviet Union.[266] Moreover, he could not have forgotten what he had been repeating in his writings of the last few years, namely that there was no place for the old Russian intelligentsia in the new Soviet state.[267] Ustrialov was convinced that in order not to perish, the whole prerevolutionary generation would have to "be thoroughly cooked in the Soviet cauldron, apprentice themselves to the *Komsomol* youth," and surrender themselves to the elemental force of revolutionary reality. He added that if "this was not easy for Miliukov or Struve, neither was it so for . . . Ustrialov."[268] He, like them, was not a "new man," and he was painfully aware of this.[269]

In August 1934, Ustrialov had written to his friend Dikii:

> If the state . . . says to me: 'keep silent . . . , or even better, write what I order you,' then I will obey and keep quiet; maybe I will even try, insofar as I have the force, to write what they order me (although I do not guarantee that I will do the latter).[270]

Whether the three articles by Ustrialov that appeared in *Izvestiia* between December 1936 and April 1937 had been "ordered," remains unknown. However, in reading these articles, written on the occasions of the introduction of the "Stalin constitution,"[271] the centenary of Pushkin's death,[272] and the 125th anniversary of the birth of Herzen, respectively,[273] it is hard to doubt Ustrialov's sincerity.

Apparently, the introduction of the "Constitution of Victorious Socialism" removed Ustrialov's last reservations about the Soviet regime. In his opinion, the new constitution definitively resolved the problem of democracy by "combining freedom and authority into a dialectical unity," and "removed the former conflict between patriotism and internationalism" by making the USSR into both "a free union of free nations" and the "common fatherland" of all its inhabitants. He argued that the new constitution thus put an end, not only to the exploitation of man by man, but also to the exploitation of one nation by another.[274] For Ustrialov, the Stalin constitution marked the beginning of a "new, unprecedented stage in world history." He believed that the crisis that Russia had gone through during the past two decades had now come to an end.[275] In his view, the purifying and invigorating effect of that crisis was beyond question. While the bourgeois world was decaying ever more, the country of Pushkin and Herzen was, after a long illness, as if reborn. Russia was now ready to show the world the way to a "morally healthy, pure, realistic culture," to "real humanism," and to "the universal emancipation of man."[276]

No doubt, in his position as professor of geographical economics at the Moscow Institute of Transport Engineering, to which he had been appointed shortly after his arrival in Moscow, Ustrialov served the Soviet state conscientiously. However, in these years of terror that did not matter, and Ustrialov was arrested in June 1937. He was sentenced for alleged anti-Soviet activities by the Military Collegium of the Supreme Court of the Soviet Union, and perished on an unknown day in 1938.[277]

Chapter Three

SMENA VEKH

The Mystique of the Revolution

Although the idea of patriotic reconciliation with the Soviet regime was developed most extensively by N. V. Ustrialov, it became widely known chiefly through the agency of his European friends, who in the late summer of 1921 published a collection of articles under the title *Smena vekh* (Change of Signposts).

The initiator and inspirer of *Smena vekh* was Iurii Veniaminovich Kliuchnikov (1886–1938), one of Ustrialov's close friends. Kliuchnikov, the son of a prominent publisher,[1] had studied law with Ustrialov at Moscow University, where in 1916 he held a position as *privatdozent* in international law.[2] In that same year his first articles on international affairs appeared in the Moscow journal *Problemy velikoi Rossii*[3] and in the newspaper *Utro Rossii*. In the fall of 1917 he was appointed head of the foreign affairs department of the Moscow daily *Russkoe slovo* (The Russian Word).[4] As opposed to Ustrialov, who always devoted much attention to internal political questions, Kliuchnikov's primary interest was in international affairs. His views in this respect, which the prominent Kadet jurist and historian Baron B. E. Nol'de called a peculiar mixture of pacifism and imperialism,[5] would play an important role in his gradual acceptance of the Soviet regime.

Kliuchnikov had been a member of the Kadet party and belonged to that faction which was closely linked to the so-called Progressists among Moscow businessmen. In the summer of 1917 he accompanied his friend Ustrialov on a liberal propaganda tour, organized by the political division of the All-Russian Commercial-Industrial Union, to a number of Southern cities such as Astrakhan and Pyatigorsk.[6] He also contributed to the Kadet campaign in favor of Russia's continued participation in the war on the side of the Allies, with a pamphlet entitled *Revoliutsiia i voina* (The Revolution and the War).[7]

In the booklet, Kliuchnikov stressed that the Russian people had over-thrown the tsar precisely because they had realized that a victory against Germany was otherwise impossible. He argued that therefore, now that the revolution had taken place, Russia should remain true to her allies. Not only had she concluded a number of treaties with them, she was also linked to them by a common regime of freedom and by common interests, mainly in the Balkans and the Straits (Dardanelles and Bosporus).[8] It was significant for his future position that Kliuchnikov, unlike Ustrialov, did not radically reject the slogans of immediate peace and complete brotherhood between all peoples as they had been formulated by the Petrograd Soviet on 27 March 1917. In his opinion, revolutionary Russia had a perfect right to propose new answers to international questions. Yet, because other states were not inclined "to dedicate themselves so wholeheartedly to wonderful dreams as had the Russians, overwhelmed as they were by revolutionary rapture," he thought it better that, for the time being, Russia adopt a conventional foreign policy and comply with the wishes of her allies, in the first place Britain and France.[9]

With the Bolshevik takeover, Kliuchnikov's goodwill toward pacifist slogans decreased sharply: he now regarded these as being partly responsible for Russia's downfall. Instead of dreaming of worldwide peace and brotherhood, the Russians could better pray to God that their country would not be reduced to the status of a colony. Kliuchnikov was of the opinion that if the country remained in the hands of people like Lenin and Trotskii, such an outcome would be inevitable.[10] However, like so many of his contemporaries, Kliuchnikov consoled himself with the thought that the Bolsheviks lacked popular support and, thus, could not hold out for long. In his opinion "the wonder of Russia's resurrection" was attainable, if only the Russian people closed ranks and renounced all beautiful but impracticable slogans.[11]

Kliuchnikov trusted that Russia's allies would realize that the Russian people as a whole could not be held responsible for the actions of a small group of "criminal usurpers" and "German agents," and that they would refuse to recognize the Bolsheviks as the country's lawful government.[12] He was well aware, however, that the Allies' patience with Russia could not be endless. Therefore, he urged that, in the forthcoming elections to the Constituent Assembly, the Russian people should make it crystal clear whom they really supported. If the Bolsheviks were then unequivocally rejected, the Allies would be sure to lend Russia a helping hand, and give her the opportunity to recover.[13]

Kliuchnikov's confidence in the Allies was short-lived, however, as were his hopes in the Constituent Assembly. From their first weeks in power the Bolsheviks had warned that they would dissolve the Assembly at the least sign of refractoriness, and Kliuchnikov took these threats seriously.[14] Still, convinced as he was that the Bolshevik era would not be long-lasting,[15] it was clear that he did not consider such a course of action to be irreparable. What preoccupied him more in the spring of 1918 were Allied plans to intervene in

Siberia,[16] following the conclusion of a separate peace between Soviet Russia and the Central Powers. While Kliuchnikov was opposed to the Treaty of Brest-Litovsk as such,[17] he at the same time decisively rejected all projects for direct intervention on Russian territory. Not only did he consider this as meddling with Russian affairs, he also feared that it would further upset the already disrupted international balance. Kliuchnikov's opinion was that the status quo should be maintained until the creation of a League of Nations according to the proposal of the American President Wilson.[18]

The idea of a League of Nations particularly appealed to Kliuchnikov.[19] As a specialist in international law, he was convinced that mankind was evolving toward an "indivisible political and judicial union" in which all peoples of the world would live together in justice and peace.[20] In his opinion, the ongoing world war could not be understood unless it was seen in the light of this evolution.[21] Kliuchnikov argued that the moving force behind the Germans' imperialism was their conviction that they were so superior to other peoples they had the right to subjugate them and unite the world by means of force and oppression.[22] The Allied and Associated Powers, on the other hand, aspired to worldwide unity through "law and justice in international relationships."[23] Kliuchnikov regarded the position of President Wilson as the best evidence of this.[24]

In Kliuchnikov's eyes, a League of Nations would be an important step toward what he considered as being "the ideal of international history": either a single worldwide federal state or a single worldwide federation of states.[25] As opposed to President Wilson, who conceived the League as a family of nations on the basis of equality, Kliuchnikov believed that "the unification of all parts [of the world] into a number of very large and well organized states, rich in all indispensable resources," was a prerequisite for the League's success.[26] It was clear to Kliuchnikov that only peace-loving states could play a positive role in this unification process. He warned that further expansion on the part of militarist states such as Japan or Germany would lead to the deepest cultural, moral, and judicial fall of mankind.[27] He did not doubt that a truly great Russia could play a "positive and progressive role" here. He was convinced that as the "bearer of lofty international ideals" Russia could be a shining force of progress; she "had passed through the crucible of the revolution and had lived, albeit clumsily, chaotically and tragically, through many things which not even the most advanced peoples had experienced."[28] Consequently, the resurrection of Russia as a great state was in the interest not only of Russia itself but of mankind as a whole.[29]

Kliuchnikov recommended, therefore, that Russia base her foreign policy on the old and well-tried principle of "great powers *(velikoderzhavie),*"[30] rather than on the principle of "self-determination of the nations." He found the latter principle unacceptable, unless it stood for nothing other than the greatest possible freedom of every nation within the framework of large multinational states.[31] Kliuchnikov openly urged that, given the extreme importance of Russia's resurrection as a great power, the country should try to reach this goal by all means, "setting aside all sympathies, feelings, inclinations and even highest ideals." Like Ustrialov, Kliuchnikov advocated a policy of "open hands," and believed that Russia should side with whoever could help her to regain her power in the international sphere.[32]

In three articles in the "young Kadet" journal *Nakanune,* which he co-founded with Ustrialov and Iu. N. Potekhin in April 1918, Kliuchnikov extensively set forth his views on this subject. While he stressed that Russia's sympathies continued to be on the side of "the world's advanced democracies, i.e. of the Allies," and that collaboration with the Allies was most desirable, he made it clear that collaboration could not mean "one-sided subordination."[33] Under the present difficult circumstances, he argued, Russia could not afford the luxury of letting herself be guided by ideals. She had to follow her instinct of self-preservation and fight cunningly to regain her force, wealth, and greatness.[34]

Throughout the articles, Kliuchnikov continued to speak about Russia and the Russian people as though they had nothing to do with the Bolsheviks. Yet, in the second article of the series, which appeared on 14 April 1918, he noted, not without satisfaction, that in spite of their proclaimed internationalist policy, the Bolsheviks had taken the "first energetic steps" to halt the further disintegration of Russia into independent republics. The Soviet regime had tried to regain Bessarabia, and after the secession of the Ukraine, Finland, and the Baltic states, it had persistently intervened in their affairs.[35] However, in the spring of 1918 this observation did not suffice to make Kliuchnikov accept the Soviet regime as such. In June 1918, he wrote that the Bolsheviks were incapable of harmoniously combining morality, law, and politics, and as a result made normal life in Russia impossible. He hoped that they would understand this themselves and withdraw from power voluntarily. Kliuchnikov could even see a positive role for the Bolsheviks if they decided to do so: in that case they could serve as a warning to society, he explained, and prevent it from neglecting the demands of social progress.[36]

Unlike Ustrialov, who remained in Moscow until the outburst of the Red Terror in the late summer of 1918, Kliuchnikov left the city in late June. He traveled to Yaroslavl, where he intended to work on his dissertation, but instead became involved in the anti-Bolshevik uprising that broke out there on 6 July.[37] Whether Kliuchnikov had had any preliminary contacts with the uprising's initiators, the so-called Union for the Defense of Freedom and the Fatherland headed by the former Socialist Revolutionary B. V. Savinkov, is unclear, and little is known about his exact role in the rebellion. In any case, when Soviet troops forcibly suppressed it on 21 July, Kliuchnikov managed to escape and fled via Kazan and Ufa to Omsk.[38]

There, he became vice-minister of foreign affairs in the "business cabinet" of the so-called All-Russian Directory, which had been elected at the Ufa State Conference in September 1918 and had moved on to Omsk in October of that year. Kliuchnikov had been personally invited to that post by N. D. Avksent'ev, the directory's Socialist Revolutionary chairman.[39] This circumstance did not prevent him from remaining in his position after the military coup of 18 November 1918, when the directory was removed and Admiral Kolchak was installed as "Supreme Ruler" of Russia.[40] Kliuchnikov not only accepted this turn of events but even welcomed it. While it is doubtful he was personally involved in the coup,[41] he certainly regarded its outcome as a positive development. Like almost all members of the Kadet party in Siberia and the vast majority of military and commercial circles there, Kliuchnikov had been troubled by what he called the directory's "organic incapacity for work."[42] What in his opinion especially weakened the directory's position was the fact that, under the provisions of the Ufa State Conference, the directory was to subject itself by 1 January (or at the latest by 1 February) 1919 to a Conference of Members of the existing Constituent Assembly. Yet it was extremely unlikely that the necessary quorum for such a conference could ever be reached.[43]

On 16 November 1918, hardly two days before the coup took place, Kliuchnikov presented the directory with a memorandum in which he advocated that it free itself from this obligation. In light of the recent armistice between Germany and the Allies, Kliuchnikov regarded such a step as even more urgent. He stressed that in its present form, the directory was incapable of ensuring that Russia regain her greatness; yet, he contended, the world now more than ever needed a great, strong, and united Russia. This was a sine qua non for both a new international equilibrium and the successful formation of a League of Nations.[44] Kliuchnikov argued that although the withdrawal of German troops would no doubt bring about the formation of new centers of Russian anti-Bolshevik authority, it was unlikely that these would submit themselves to the directory, as hardly any of them would be prepared to accept the Ufa provisions. In view of this the directory had little chance of being recognized by the Allies as the legitimate All-Russian government. Therefore, Kliuchnikov recommended that the directory adopt a new constitutional document in which it abandoned the Ufa provisions, pledging instead to lay down its plenary powers as soon as all major Russian governments would be united. In the meantime, Kliuchnikov added, the directory should grant itself the right to alter the character and limits of its powers in agreement with the Council of Ministers and, in accordance with the requirements of its most important task, that of All-Russian unification.[45]

As could have been expected, the socialist members of the directory decisively rejected Kliuchnikov's recommendations. Yet the Council of Ministers, whom Kliuchnikov had also informed about his memorandum, decided to discuss the document during a special meeting scheduled for 18 November.[46] A few hours before it was to start, however, a group of officers arrested the directory's socialist members, whereupon the Council of Ministers assumed the directory's power and transferred it to Admiral Kolchak. The crisis for which Kliuchnikov had sought to offer a solution with his recommendations had thus been solved in another way, which he regarded as no less satisfactory. On the day after the coup, he told the press that the events of 18 November clearly showed that the principle of "statelikeness *(gosudarstvennost')"* was becoming ever stronger in Eastern Russia.[47]

In his new capacity as Admiral Kolchak's minister of foreign affairs, Kliuchnikov immediately dispatched telegrams to the Russian representatives abroad, urging them to explain to the governments to which they were accredited that the coup was the "natural" result of growing discontent with the directory, both among the military and among a substantial part of the public anxious to see state power strengthened. He underlined that the coup was a victory of "healthy, by no means reactionary tendencies," and "a new step forward toward the resurrection of a Great Russia."[48]

From the first days in his new position, Kliuchnikov fostered hopes that he, as the Russian minister of foreign affairs, would be sent to Paris to represent the country at the forthcoming peace conference. At that time it was not yet clear whether the Allies would invite a Russian delegation to the conference, and the government in Omsk was still hoping that this would be the case. The question of who should be delegated was under discussion. As the discussion dragged on, Kliuchnikov, in early 1919, gave the Council of Ministers an ultimatum in which he threatened to resign if he were not sent to Paris as Kolchak's official delegate.[49] Apart from ambition and personal scholarly interest in the peace conference, one of the factors which prompted Kliuchnikov to resort to an ultimatum was that he, as minister of foreign affairs, was being pushed aside by a successful young diplomat, I. I. Sukin. Almost immediately after Admiral Kolchak's accession as Supreme Ruler, Sukin had been appointed head of the General Headquarters' diplomatic office, and since then he had been dictating to the Ministry of Foreign Affairs, a situation Kliuchnikov found very hard to accept.[50] A mandate to the Paris Peace Conference would have provided Kliuchnikov with an interesting and most flattering way out of this situation and was therefore all the more desirable to him.

Given the importance of such a mandate on the one hand and Kliuchnikov's lack of authority on the other, the ministers rejected the ultimatum almost unanimously. In consequence, Kliuchnikov resigned.[51] However, the Council of Ministers tried to let him leave in an honorable way, characterizing his departure to the outside world as motivated purely by Kliuchnikov's own wish to attend the forthcoming peace conference. Moreover, he was commissioned to participate in the Russian delegation to the conference as a specialist on international law and to represent the Temporary Main Directorate of the Russian Red Cross in France as well as in its relationship with the Red Cross Headquarters in Geneva. The government even allotted him a stipend for this purpose.[52] Kliuchnikov was clearly happy with this outcome and left for the French capital in mid-February 1919.

Immediately after his arrival in Paris, Kliuchnikov became thoroughly involved in the life of the Russian émigré community there. He became a collaborator for the Russian Political Conference,[53] which had been founded in late 1918 to represent Russian national interests abroad. As one of its first acts, the conference had elected in January 1919 a "Russian Foreign Delegation," which it regarded as the only competent Russian representation to the Paris Peace Conference. The Allies refused to accept the delegation as a full participant in the conference, but nonetheless allowed it to express its views on a number of issues. In the framework of the Russian Political Conference, Kliuchnikov worked along with B. V. Savinkov and the Czech Prime Minister K. Kramá on a project for a "Constitution of the Russian State." In June 1919 this project was discussed at General Denikin's headquarters in Rostov. On 2 June 1919 Kliuchnikov delivered to the political conference an official report on the general situation in Omsk, in particular on the circumstances in which the coup of 18 November 1918 had taken place.[54]

Kliuchnikov joined the Paris Group of the Kadet party and in May 1920 was elected a member of the party's Paris Committee.[55] Moreover, he took part in the activities of the so-called Russian Academic Group, founded that spring, and under its auspices he taught a course on Russian political thought in June and July.[56]

In early 1920 Kliuchnikov edited a collection of articles on the situation in Russia, entitled *La Russie d'aujourd'hui et de demain,* to which a number of luminaries of the Russian émigré community in Paris, mainly members of the Kadet party, contributed. Besides articles by the prominent lawyer and politician M. M. Vinaver, the Ukrainian Kadet N. M. Mogilianskii, and the Moscow industrialist and former Provisional Government Minister of Trade and Industry A. I. Konovalov, the collection included an essay by P. N. Miliukov on Russia's relationship with Poland, and one by P. B. Struve on Lenin and the nature of Bolshevism. In his own contribution, which opened the collection and gave it its title, Kliuchnikov tried to convince the French public that the Russian revolution was a "historic necessity" that was leading Russia, albeit painfully, to the "democratic ideals of the advanced peoples of the West."[57]

In Kliuchnikov's opinion, the Russian revolution, just as any other revolution, should be seen as an organic process, consisting of three stages. A revolution started off with moderate demands, but soon became ever more radical, carried along by the atmosphere the revolution itself had created, until it reached its peak. Then, the revolutionary barometer began to fall, and the revolution entered into its third stage, in which it again assumed more moderate forms.[58]

The Russian revolution, Kliuchnikov explained, had started with the moderate demand of continuing the war against Germany, which ran counter to the pro-German atmosphere at the Russian court.[59] Then the revolutionary wave had swollen, and the revolution had turned into a social revolution, in which the Russian masses entered onto the political scene. Given certain traits of the Russian national character, such as extremism and the propensity to use the worst means to realize the most elevated goals, Kliuchnikov argued that it had been inevitable that the revolution assume extremist, violent forms.[60] The Bolsheviks had not caused this radicalization, Kliuchnikov argued, but rather had become the instrument of it. He added, however, that they had not always followed the will of the masses: in Brest-Litovsk, for example, they had acted completely against them. Kliuchnikov assured his audience that the people were therefore turning against the Bolsheviks, and that in this anti-Bolshevik struggle the best, most noble forces of the Russian people were being awakened. Moreover, struggling against the Bolsheviks, the Russian people were developing a number of new and valuable qualities: tenacity, persistence, and realism.[61]

Kliuchnikov trusted that the end of the second revolutionary phase was now in sight, that the victory of the anti-Bolshevik front was imminent, and that then the third phase of the revolution, its "liquidation," would begin. A new Russian society would come into being where, for fear of returning to one or another form of Bolshevism, a new respect for law and authority would develop. Kliuchnikov stressed that a return to the past was excluded: after all the hardships the Russian people had undergone during the war and the revolution, they would move unwaveringly toward "the most beautiful ideal of humanity," a democracy of the Western type.[62] Whether or not Kliuchnikov's praise for Western democracy was sincere, we will never know. Unlike Ustrialov, Kliuchnikov had never displayed an outspoken mistrust of democracy, and his attitude in Omsk at the time of the November coup may have been inspired by the peculiar circumstances of the moment. Still, even though he may have been sincere in *La Russie d'aujourd'hui et de demain,* before long he would take a diametrically opposed position.

Kliuchnikov had contacts not only with political circles but also with the literary milieu in the Paris émigré community. In the course of 1920 he completed a play, *Edinyi kust* (A Single Bush), which he read before I. Bunin, A. Kuprin, A. Tolstoi, M. Aldanov, I. Ehrenburg, and Don Aminado. None of the writers present, Don Aminado recalls, were impressed with Kliuchnikov's literary talents; A. Tolstoi, however, was struck by the play's main idea, which Don Aminado formulated as follows: "The fatherland is a single bush, and all its branches, even those which are growing sideways, are nourished by the same sap."[63]

The leitmotif of *Edinyi kust* is symptomatic of the radical change in Kliuchnikov's views on the situation in Russia and his attitude toward the Bolsheviks in the months immediately following the publication of *La Russie d'aujourd'hui et de demain.* As we have seen, during his last conversation with Ustrialov in

Omsk in February 1919, Kliuchnikov had stressed that he considered it his duty to join the White movement, because he hoped the Whites would keep the revolution within the limits of prudence and common sense. He had added the proviso that, whatever happened, one should always take the side of Russia. If in the end the Reds rather than the Whites should be victorious, this could only mean that Russia needed the Bolsheviks, and then there would be nothing left but to accept Lenin and his colleagues. While Ustrialov had found this idea tormenting, Kliuchnikov seemed to take it in stride.[64] Yet it took him longer than Ustrialov to decide that the time had come to accept the Bolsheviks. Clearly, the Paris émigré milieu gave little support for such a step.

In the spring of 1920, however, General Denikin's defeat and the transfer of the command over the remaining White forces to General Wrangel led the Kadet party to reexamine the policies of the White movement.[65] It was in the framework of this debate that Kliuchnikov called for an end to the armed struggle against the Bolsheviks. Unlike almost all his colleagues in the party, who agreed that one should abandon the idea of a military dictatorship but certainly not the armed anti-Bolshevik struggle as such, Kliuchnikov believed that to continue military action against the Bolsheviks was not only pointless, given the limited number of White troops remaining, but even harmful. He argued that continued civil war would needlessly enhance the anarchy in the country. Moreover, if the Bolsheviks were overthrown, this could only worsen the situation. In Kliuchnikov's opinion, the Soviet regime was the only force in Russia that had managed to take root in the country; its fall would engender a dangerous power vacuum and lead to complete anarchy.[66]

An element that greatly influenced Kliuchnikov's position was the renewed Polish offensive against Soviet Russia in late April 1920 and the Allied attitude toward it. Kliuchnikov found it unacceptable that General Wrangel was backing Russia's enemies with his actions.[67] Moreover, he felt that the Allies supported the Poles mainly because they wanted to weaken Russia. Under these circumstances, he argued, it was clear that Russia's national interests were being defended by the Bolsheviks.[68]

Once Kliuchnikov had become convinced that the struggle against the Bolshevik regime should be ended, he began to discover ever more positive sides to that regime. In a lecture he read to the Russian Academic Group on 6 July 1920, he presented Bolshevism as a necessary stage in the development of mankind. The world was going through such fundamental economic, social, and political changes, that the existing structures were no longer suitable. Radical structural changes, either through evolution or through a series of revolutions such as the one that took place in Russia, had become inevitable. In this context, Kliuchnikov now regarded the excesses of the Russian revolution as characteristic of an experimental stage, which would lead to Russia's revival and contribute to universal progress.[69]

Strange as it may seem, Kliuchnikov's first positive remarks about the Bolshevik regime went by unnoticed in the Paris émigré community. His statements in the closed meetings of the Kadet party's Paris Committee did not become public. His fellow members dismissed his call for an end to the armed struggle as a sign of fatigue and demoralization,[70] and apparently preferred to keep his remarks within the group. At his lecture to the Russian Academic Group, Kliuchnikov reminded his audience of his role in the White movement, apparently anxious to prevent his argument from being understood as a call for reconciliation with the Soviet regime.[71]

In the meantime, however, his conviction that to call for reconciliation was precisely the best attitude one could possibly take became ever stronger. He felt strengthened by the letters he received from Ustrialov in Harbin. He was especially encouraged by an article from a Japanese newspaper he came across, in which Ustrialov's declaratory article "*Perelom*" had been reprinted. When he showed these to two of his acquaintances from the Russian Political Conference, N. V. Chaikovskii and Prince G. E. L'vov, their reaction was merely one of sadness; the letters and the article did not convince them.[72] For Kliuchnikov, however, there was no longer the slightest doubt that he and Ustrialov were in the right.

The unexpected final defeat of the remaining White forces under General Wrangel's command on 14 November 1920 also brought several leading Kadets to the conclusion that it no longer made sense to continue the armed struggle. Headed by P. N. Miliukov, the party's leader since 1907, they proposed a "new tactic" in which they abandoned the idea of military action against the Bolsheviks.[73] An essential element of this "new tactic" was the conviction that the people in the Soviet Republic were fed up with the Bolsheviks and would soon topple them. The White movement had always neglected the aspirations of the people; Miliukov and his allies now stressed that anti-Bolshevik action could not succeed without popular support. Therefore, they felt the Kadet party should take a radical stand concerning agrarian and national questions and enter into a tactical coalition with the SRs, the party that supposedly had the confidence of the majority of the Russian people. Miliukov and his colleagues hoped that this new policy would in the end lead to a large-scale popular insurrection against the Bolsheviks.

Miliukov's "new tactic" was unacceptable to most Kadets, because they felt that the armed struggle against the Bolsheviks should be continued and because they objected to an agreement with the SRs, the party they regarded most culpable for the Bolshevik coup.[74] It was also unacceptable to Kliuchnikov, but for other reasons. First of all, Kliuchnikov argued, one should abandon all expectations vis-à-vis the anti-Bolshevik movement. In his opinion, all that was left of what he a few months earlier had called "the most noble forces of the Russian people" was "human dust."[75] Second, negotiations with the SRs over cooperation would be nothing more than a waste of time and energy.

Miliukov and his supporters were prepared to accept the call of a number of moderate SRs to convene a Conference of Members of the Constituent Assembly. Kliuchnikov strenuously objected. Since his experiences in Omsk, the Constituent Assembly, as it had been elected in the fall of 1917, had lost all credit with him. Such a conference could only be a step back into the past; he felt that the Kadet party should look instead to the future and prepare to assume a new place in the new Russia.[76]

Kliuchnikov agreed with the proponents of the "new tactic" that the Kadet party needed to revise its position radically. In taking a new course, the party should be guided by the general world situation and not just by the problems of the day. He rebuked the party leadership for failing to see that Bolshevism had become a world force containing indisputable elements of "historical and political truth." At the same time, he argued that in dealing with the Bolsheviks one should start from the assumption that they were holding out chiefly because of the disastrous situation within Russia and should believe that their power would disintegrate as soon as the internal situation improved. As a result, he urged the Kadets to follow a course that radically differed from old and new tactics alike.[77]

Convinced as he was of being in the right, Kliuchnikov considered it his duty to persuade the party's leadership to take the course he regarded as the only right one.[78] In the weeks following General Wrangel's defeat he prepared a detailed lecture on "The New Tasks of Kadetism," and in late December asked the Paris Committee to summon a general meeting so that the entire Paris Group could become acquainted with his views.[79] The committee reacted to Kliuchnikov's main theses with extreme reservation, feeling that they could not possibly give him the floor for such a lecture. However, because they did not want to take a final decision on the issue without having more details on his views, they asked him first to deliver his speech to a private meeting of the Paris Committee.[80]

Kliuchnikov read his lecture to the committee on 17 February 1921. To begin with, he repeated his premise that the Kadet mistakes of the past four years were the results of the party's having consistently determined its policies in accordance with the problems of the day and having always taken the line of least resistance. Kliuchnikov argued that the Bolsheviks had based their course of action on the international situation and that precisely this approach had ensured them of the final victory.[81] Elaborating on his thesis, put forward in 1918, that the recent world war was to be seen as a clash between two conflicting projects to unite the world, German and Allied, he now suggested that Bolshevism was a new major program for worldwide unification and pacification. In their aim for world revolution, he explained, the Bolsheviks were in fact trying to unite mankind in an entirely new society, founded on completely new social, political, and economic principles. Kliuchnikov was now convinced that the German imperialist project had been bound to fail because peace could not possibly result from violence and oppression. He also believed that the Allied liberal-democratic project, as proposed by President Wilson, had been doomed to collapse because it presupposed a world in which all countries were equally rich and benevolent. Yet he believed that for the Bolsheviks' revolutionary program the situation in the world was very favorable indeed.[82]

Kliuchnikov argued that the Bolshevik social experiment, with its emphasis on solidarity and "real equality," that is, "to each according to his needs," presupposed a situation of general ferment and discontent, and that in the aftermath of the Great War this was exactly the case. From their own point of view the Bolsheviks had achieved considerable successes, he stressed, not only within Russia but also in the world. In his opinion, the outbreak of world revolution was becoming ever more likely.[83] Kliuchnikov hastened to say that neither Bolshevism nor world revolution as such was attractive to him; he even called the Bolshevik social experiment "dreadful." Yet, he added, however "offensive and vile" Bolshevism might be, it had to be accepted as a real force, which had gained in strength and popular support as the struggle against it had increased.[84]

In Kliuchnikov's view, the only reasonable course of action left was to try to take the edge off Bolshevism, and here he saw a role of great importance for the Kadet party. As the party of evolutionary progress, he argued, the Kadets should stop trying to undermine the Soviet regime and conclude an agreement *(vstupat' v dogovornye otnosheniia)* with the Bolsheviks. This did not mean, he was quick to point out, that they had to give up their liberalism, their allegiance to the principles of equality, understanding, and cooperation; rather, they should try to convince the Bolsheviks of the value of these principles and "turn the Leninist movement from Communism into Kadetism."[85]

How exactly this was to be achieved, and what he meant by "Kadetism," Kliuchnikov did not spell out. On one point, however, he was crystal clear. The Kadets could not fulfill their task if they remained abroad; they should return to Russia and engage in both practical and political work, trying to reinforce the positive elements of Bolshevism and to mitigate its flaws. While Kliuchnikov admitted that this would be a difficult task, he was convinced that if the Kadets closed ranks and stopped wasting energy on transient futilities, they would be able to influence the situation in a historic way.[86]

With such a message Kliuchnikov could hardly expect a sympathetic response from his audience. Yet the reactions of the Paris Committee were evasive rather than indignant. Apparently, the Kadet Committee was unsure as to what its attitude should be toward Kliuchnikov's often vague and confused words. For V. A. Obolenskii, Kliuchnikov's speech was primarily an expression of dissatisfaction with émigré conditions. It was also an attempt to understand the grandiose processes taking place in Russia, and while Obolenskii admitted that such understanding was necessary, he considered Kliuchnikov's approach to be flawed. He objected to considering only the psychology of Lenin and Trotskii, men to whom the real mood in Russia was completely foreign.[87] P. Ia. Ryss, for his part, rejected Kliuchnikov's call for an agreement with the Bolsheviks because this could not possibly be reconciled with the Kadet party's *"vneklassnost',"* its aloofness from class concerns on principle. The Kadet party had always striven to reconcile class interests, Ryss argued; therefore, it could not possibly come to terms with an ideology that based itself on the idea of class struggle.[88]

Miliukov found it hard to formulate a reaction to Kliuchnikov's exposition because it had been unclear in many respects. For one thing, Kliuchnikov had spoken about reinforcing the positive elements in Bolshevism, without saying what he thought these were. Furthermore, Miliukov rejected Kliuchnikov's allegations that the Kadets' attitude toward the Bolsheviks went against "the spirit of Kadetism." Rather the opposite was true, the party leader argued: the point of departure in designing the party's "new tactic" had been to underline the essence of Kadet ideology.[89] In spite of their objections, however, the committee apparently felt it might be useful to give Kliuchnikov the opportunity to read his lecture to the entire Paris Group, and they scheduled a general meeting for four weeks later, on 17 March.[90]

In support of his argument, Kliuchnikov had referred in his lecture to a number of other young Kadets who had come to the same conclusion as he had. These included N. V. Ustrialov, Iu. N. Potekhin, and his former colleague at Moscow University E. N. Korovin, who had also been a fellow contributor to *Utro Rossii, Problemy velikoi Rossii,* and the Moscow journal *Nakanune.* Moreover, Kliuchnikov had referred as well to a lecture delivered a few days earlier before the anti-Bolshevik Parliamentary Committee by S. S. Luk'ianov.[91]

Sergei Sergeevich Luk'ianov (ca. 1888–1938), the son of a prominent pathologist and former chief procurator of the Holy Synod,[92] had joined the ranks of the emigration only in late 1920. In the years before the revolution he had held a modest position as Latin teacher at a Petrograd gymnasium and had, apart from a short period in which he had been a member of the Kadet party, not actively taken part in political life.[93] Apparently, he had continued this rather inconspicuous existence until late September 1920, when he left for the South under the pretext of a study excursion. Whether he really intended to join the forces of General Wrangel, as he declared during his first months in emigration, is unclear.[94] In any case, Luk'ianov never reached Wrangel's headquarters; instead, he turned up in Paris, where he became a teacher at the local Russian lycée and began contributing to *La Cause commune,* the French-language edition of the militantly anti-Bolshevik daily *Obshchee delo* (The Common Cause).[95]

By early 1921, Luk'ianov came to the conclusion that his abusive attacks against the Bolsheviks amounted to "doing foul things," and he changed his position.[96] He did so openly in a lecture on "Public opinion in Russia under the Soviets *(podsovetskaia Rossiia),*" which he read on 14 February 1921 before a closed meeting of the Parliamentary Committee. This committee had been founded in late November 1920 to fill the anti-Bolshevik power vacuum resulting from General Wrangel's defeat. It united former members of the pre-revolutionary State Council and the four State Dumas.

In his lecture, Luk'ianov put forward the thesis that, contrary to what most of the émigrés believed, an evolution of the Soviet system was quite possible. Moreover, he suggested that three years of Bolshevik rule had changed many aspects of Russian society for the better, so that the outcome of such an evolution was likely to be most favorable.[97] First of all, he argued, harsh reality had cured the Russian people of their penchant for beautiful words *(krasnobaistvo)* and had made them a great deal more realistic. Second, the people had learned from bitter experience that their individual fate depended upon that of the state; the unity of that state was of extreme importance to everyone of them, even for the supply of food.

Foreign intervention and the secession of several parts of the empire had, in fact, strengthened the Bolsheviks' position by awakening a feeling of wounded patriotism in the Russian people.[98] Furthermore, Luk'ianov declared, the Bolshevik regime had stimulated the people's desire for self-government. He believed that in the end this would lead to some kind of representative system, but found it impossible, for the present, to say whether this would be a conventional parliamentary system.[99]

Luk'ianov noted that the past three years had also seen a noticeable rapprochement between the people and the intelligentsia; the people, he claimed, had at last come to appreciate the value of intellectuals for the functioning of the country's economy. Finally, despite what many abroad believed, Luk'ianov stressed that the Bolsheviks had not destroyed Russian culture. While he admitted that the cultural level in Russia was now lower than before the revolution, he pointed out that this was due mainly to the diffusion of culture throughout the masses. He added that even in the sphere of higher learning the damage should not be overestimated.[100]

Luk'ianov hoped that the evolution of the Soviet regime would be hastened by a clash within the Communist party itself—a possible confrontation between "Communists," such as Trotskii and Zinov'ev, and "pure Bolsheviks" or "revolutionary opportunists," such as Lenin and Krasin. Luk'ianov expected that if it came to that, the population would support the Bolsheviks, and it was clear that he believed such a development would be an enormous step forward.[101]

Luk'ianov had made sure that his views were carefully worded, and this apparently helped him to avoid indignant reactions from the public. Because his lecture had been rather long, the public debate over his views was postponed to the Parliamentary Committee's next meeting.[102] In the meantime,

Luk'ianov's speech became a much-talked-of subject among the émigrés. As soon as Kliuchnikov learned about it, he contacted Luk'ianov, who promptly asked him for help at the upcoming meeting of the Parliamentary Committee. Deciding that the time had come to be open about the ideas he had bottled up for months, expressed only in closed meetings of the Paris Kadet Committee, Kliuchnikov agreed to support Luk'ianov.[103]

On the evening of the public debate, Kliuchnikov caused a sensation, not only by taking Luk'ianov's side, but by going even further and publicly calling for reconciliation and cooperation with the Soviet regime. As he had done in his recent speech to the Kadet Committee, Kliuchnikov argued once again that Bolshevism could be understood only in the broader context of the general world situation. He stressed that the situation of heightened international and social tension and general impoverishment during and after the world war had proven to be an excellent breeding ground for the ideology of Lenin and his colleagues. Bolshevism drew its force from enmity, war, and poverty; in order to overcome it, one needed to alleviate these factors, certainly not to aggravate them. In view of this, Kliuchnikov concluded, the Russian intelligentsia should act in a spirit of sacrifice, return to Russia, and cooperate with the Bolsheviks.[104]

As expected, reactions to Kliuchnikov's words were unanimously negative.[105] P. B. Struve, for example, objected that because the Bolshevik dictatorship was based on both political and economic coercion, there could not be the slightest opportunity for useful action within Soviet Russia.[106] To B. S. Mirskii (Mirkin-Getsevich), one of Miliukov's closest collaborators on the staff of *Poslednie novosti* (Latest News), the position of Kliuchnikov and Luk'ianov was unacceptable because it confused historical and moral categories. Mirskii argued that, for lack of historical perspective, the only attitude one could take toward contemporary events was a moral attitude, and in his view, a modus vivendi with the Bolsheviks, even if such could rationally be justified, was morally impossible.[107] P. S. Poliakov-Litovtsev, Mirskii's colleague in *Poslednie novosti,* completely subscribed to the latter's objections and called an agreement with the Bolsheviks tantamount to "complete spiritual death."[108]

It particularly disturbed the audience that Kliuchnikov and especially Luk'-ianov made no secret of their dislike of formal democracy. In his first appearance at the Parliamentary Committee, Luk'ianov had indicated he expected Russia to embrace some kind of "representative system" that might differ from classical parliamentarism; now, however, he stressed that the Russian people had lost all confidence in formal democracy, and he made it clear that he welcomed this.[109] As a result, Mirskii called Luk'ianov's position "a new variant of the old 'Black Hundred' movement."[110]

After the discussion at the Parliamentary Committee, Kliuchnikov and Luk'-ianov became very much isolated in the Paris émigré community.[111] Kliuchnikov's lecture before the entire Paris Group of the Kadet party, planned for 17

March but postponed because of the events in Kronstadt, was now canceled altogether because the Paris Committee feared it would cause a scandal.[112] Still, by June 1921 a small circle of supporters gathered around them, consisting of Iu. N. Potekhin, P. A. Sadyker, and A. V. Bobrishchev-Pushkin.[113]

A close friend of Kliuchnikov and Ustrialov, Iurii Nikolaevich Potekhin (1890–1938) had been trained as an agriculturalist, been a *zemstvo* employee, and by 1917 served as a representative of the Chief Committee of the All-Russian *Zemstvo* Union.[114] Like Kliuchnikov and Ustrialov, he was a member of the Kadet party, although he had not joined the party until early 1917. After the October Revolution Potekhin became involved in the White movement; he was a member of the so-called National Center and served as vice-minister of industry and trade in the government of White General Denikin.[115] In this position he was close to former Tsarist Minister of Agriculture A. V. Krivoshein, who now headed Denikin's Administration of Provisions.[116] After Denikin's defeat, Potekhin emigrated and settled with his family in the Austrian health resort of Gmunden.

In the summer of 1921 Potekhin spent two months in Paris, where he regularly met with Kliuchnikov and his supporters.[117] A few months earlier, in late March, Kliuchnikov had written to Ustrialov that "Potekhin agreed with them on almost everything," yet took a "sharply negative attitude toward the Bolsheviks."[118] Indeed, while Potekhin had by then concluded that it no longer made sense to continue the anti-Bolshevik struggle and that the best thing the Russian intelligentsia could do was to return to Russia, he found it hard to discover any positive elements in the Soviet regime. His position seemed to be dominated by a sense of fatality.[119] His views quickly evolved, however, and by the late summer of 1921 he felt a "more or less complete mental accord" with Kliuchnikov and his circle.[120]

As opposed to P. A. Sadyker, about whom hardly anything is known, the lawyer and politician A. V. Bobrishchev-Pushkin (1875–1938) was a well-known figure. The son of an attorney, he had a busy legal practice in Petersburg until 1905, when he entered politics. He was one of the founders of the Party of Legal Order. After this party joined the so-called Union of 17 October in January 1906, he became a member of the Octobrist Central Committee and, later, even the union's vice-chairman. Under the pseudonym "Gromoboi," he was also one of the Octobrists' chief publicists.[121]

After the February Revolution Bobrishchev-Pushkin temporarily left politics and resumed his work as an attorney. Like almost all members of the Russian legal profession, he reacted to the Bolshevik takeover with hostility. When, however, in the late summer of 1918, the Soviet authorities began to take serious measures against the defiant bar associations, he headed a small group of Petrograd lawyers who, without much success, advocated cooperation with the authorities.[122] This did not prevent him from joining the Volunteer Army in early 1919. He was employed by General Denikin's propaganda agency, the so-called *Osvag,* and contributed to several of its publications. After Denikin's defeat in late March 1920 Bobrishchev-Pushkin was evacuated together with thousands of other refugees from the port of Novorossiisk. He traveled to France and finally settled in Monte Carlo.[123]

From his home on the Riviera Bobrishchev-Pushkin began, in the spring of 1921, to work for the Berlin daily *Novyi mir* (The New World), the organ of the Soviet mission in Germany.[124] As he later wrote in a confidential letter to Ustrialov, he regarded this step as a recourse to "the weapon of the weak: to mimicry." He and his class had been defeated, he felt, and all they could do now was to draw the necessary conclusions from that situation and adopt a "slave tactic *(rab'ia taktika),*" however humiliating that might be.[125] Bobrishchev-Pushkin argued that there were no possibilities left to eliminate the Soviet government in a "proud and vigorous" way and that, even if Lenin and his colleagues were ousted, there was no one to take their place. He felt deep contempt for the different émigré factions, with their hollow quarrels over which of them should eventually assume power in Russia. Like Ustrialov, he placed his hopes rather in a gradual transformation of the revolution from within.[126] He stressed that while his ideals remained unaltered, while he continued to love Russia and wished her greatness above all, the only way left to work for the realization of these ideals was to try to "give them [the Bolsheviks] one's own [ideas] under the guise of theirs *(davat' im svoe pod vidom ikhnego).*"[127]

Bobrishchev-Pushkin's acquiescent attitude toward the Soviet regime was not merely the result of "mimicry," however. True, he labeled socialist ideology as "naive and grossly primitive," but since he believed that the growing social tension in Europe made the spread of the revolutionary fire inevitable, he also regarded it as an advantage for Russia to take her place at the helm of a possible international revolution. Again like Ustrialov, Bobrishchev-Pushkin felt that, from a Russian patriotic point of view, Bolshevism, with its internationalist ideology, was in a certain sense even useful, if only for the sympathy it aroused among the popular masses all over the world.[128]

Bobrishchev-Pushkin's first article in *Novyi mir*—which appeared under the pseudonym "Ne-Kommunist" on 5 April 1921—was published "on the basis of free discussion," as the accompanying editorial explained.[129] In the article, he dealt with the delicate question of the émigrés' return to the motherland. It seemed clear to him that the only thing preventing most of them from returning was their fear of prosecution by the Soviet authorities. In view of this, he advocated a general amnesty for all Russian émigrés, whatever the circumstances of their departure from Russia. He agreed that there was a risk that some people might return with evil intentions, but added that this could never be excluded completely; real terrorists always found a way to outwit the authorities.[130] Ne-Kommunist's later articles were often sharp attacks on the émigré community. In one article Bobrishchev-Pushkin reproached them with having left Russia merely "to save their own skin and their diamond rings,"[131] and in another he called the Russian émigrés "parasites."[132] No wonder that his articles met with indignant reactions, which grew even more vehement once it became clear who Ne-Kommunist really was.[133]

In the meantime, Kliuchnikov had entered into contact with Soviet representatives abroad. He contributed a number of articles to the organ of the Soviet mission in Helsinki, the daily *Put'* (The Path), where, as he expressed it in a letter to Ustrialov, he had been "received with outstretched arms."[134] A first article appeared on 3 July 1921, entitled "The Logic of Reconciliation," signed "Iu. K.," and "written [the editors announced] by a professor and 'bourgeois' public figure who had played an important role in the Russian 'White' movement but had realized as early as 1919 that it was imperative to recognize Soviet power and become reconciled to it."[135]

The article, in which Kliuchnikov once again expounded his main theses on the subject, was followed by a second, unsigned piece entitled "The disintegration of the Kadet party." This was a report of one of the Paris Kadets' last meetings before the split of the party, where Miliukov had again defended his "new tactic" in an extensive lecture. The second article in *Put'* centered on Kliuchnikov's reaction to this exposition and reproduced verbatim Miliukov's renewed plea for a reconciliatory approach to the Bolsheviks.[136] Appearing as it did in an "organ of Bolshevik tendency," it deeply angered Kliuchnikov's fellow party members, who asked him to resign.[137] By then, however, the Kadet party had split into two separate factions. Kliuchnikov had not taken part in the meetings of either faction, so the request to resign somewhat surprised him. In his response, he stressed that as long as there had been room for different positions within the Kadet party, he had considered it his duty to remain a member, hoping to help the party "avoid irremediable mistakes." Now that the party had split, however, he found it impossible to identify with, and therefore to join, either of the two resulting factions. He had not informed the factions about his withdrawal, regarding this as redundant, because the group to which he had belonged no longer existed. He now formally announced his resignation, adding that he would join Miliukov's faction as soon as it recognized that he, Kliuchnikov, was in the right. He trusted that that moment would not be long in coming.[138]

In the meantime, Kliuchnikov did what he could to propagate his views. In April 1921 he had complained to A. S. Iashchenko, the editor-in-chief of the Berlin journal *Novaia russkaia kniga,* that he had many "themes of his own" on which he wished to write, but that he could not find an appropriate Russian-language organ in France. He therefore had asked Iashchenko to let him contribute to *Novaia russkaia kniga,* but nothing ever came of it, and Kliuchnikov remained without an opportunity to express his views.[139] His contacts with the Soviet authorities through the intermediary of the Helsinki daily *Put'* put an end to this situation. With the support of Soviet officials,[140] yet not on their initiative, Kliuchnikov and his Paris circle were by mid-July 1921 working on a collection of articles that would soon make their views widely known, both in the émigré community and in Russia. Moreover, approximately at the same time Kliuchnikov received an offer—as it seems, also from Soviet officials—to become the editor of a new weekly "of the *Nakanune* type," which would shortly begin to appear in Paris. After months of isolation, Kliuchnikov and his Paris friends felt that their day was drawing closer.[141]

. . .

The collection *Smena vekh* (Change of Signposts), issued in the late summer of 1921 by the Prague publishing house "Nasha rech'," was to a large extent Kliuchnikov's work. The conception was his and so was the idea for the title, a clear allusion to the 1909 collection of articles *Vekhi*. It was also Kliuchnikov who approached the authors, coordinated the whole undertaking, and, as mentioned in chapter 3, also composed "Ustrialov's" contribution to *Smena vekh*, "Patriotica."[142]

Smena vekh is dated "July 1921," although at that time Kliuchnikov was still recruiting contributors. According to the initial plan the booklet was to appear in mid-August 1921, but it did not actually come out until mid-September, and even so, Kliuchnikov and his associates had to race against time to finish it by then.[143] The result of their hard work was a 180-page appeal to the Russian intelligentsia, urging them to accept the October revolution in the interest of the Russian nation and state, and to reconcile themselves with the Soviet regime.

The collection opened with an article by Kliuchnikov under the title "*Smena vekh*," in which he explicitly referred to *Vekhi*. In the aftermath of the 1905 revolution, *Vekhi* had questioned the attitude of the Russian intelligentsia in the years leading up to this event. Kliuchnikov felt that now, in light of a new eruption of revolutionary force, the same questions should be asked once again. What was the meaning of this new revolution, and what attitude was the intelligentsia to take with regard to it?[144] In his article, Kliuchnikov sought to provide new answers to these questions "in the spirit of *Vekhi*." He stressed that *Vekhi* had pointed out the dangers of an abortive revolution and had, in his opinion rightly, put the blame for the failure of 1905 on the intelligentsia's nihilism and maximalism, together with their "apostasy *(otshchepenstvo)*" from the state, their lack of national consciousness, and their worship of revolution.[145]

The authors of *Vekhi* had underlined the contrast between the mystique of the state and the mystique of the revolution. According to Kliuchnikov, this antithesis had lost its significance now that the October revolution had taken place. He argued that the mystique of the state had revealed itself in the revolution, so that now the mystique of the state and the mystique of the revolution coincided for Russia. Thus, reducing the message of *Vekhi* to a call for "understanding the 'mystique of the state,' " Kliuchnikov urged Russian intellectuals to forget their anti-Bolshevik maximalism—to cease their hostilities against the Soviet regime, accept it, and cooperate with it in the interest of the state.[146]

Kliuchnikov's article was followed by the "Ustrialov" essay, a collage of fragments from Ustrialov's National-Bolshevik writings over the preceding year and a half, combined with a rendering of a more recent article, *"Put' Termidora"* (The Path of Thermidor). To Kliuchnikov's credit, "Patriotica" gave a faithful picture of Ustrialov's position.

The main idea of Luk'ianov's contribution, "The Revolution and the Regime," was that the Soviet regime was the first in Russian history, since the times of the young Romanov dynasty in the early seventeenth century, that could pride itself in having a broad social basis. This, according to Luk'ianov, was the result both of the Whites' antipatriotic attitude during the civil war and of the Bolsheviks' right response in 1917 to the new socioeconomic and political circumstances.[147] Luk'ianov was convinced that through the revolution and the civil war a strong regime had originated that enjoyed the support of the whole people. Moreover, he believed that the people had become imbued with a new national, political, economic, and social consciousness. While this was realized at the expense of numerous victims, that was no reason, he argued, to turn away from revolutionary Russia. On the contrary, for these sacrifices not to have been in vain, the motherland should be lent a helping hand.[148]

In his essay "A New Faith," Bobrishchev-Pushkin portrayed Lenin and his colleagues both as Russia's saviors, who alone had been capable of averting anarchy and disintegration,[149] and as the harbingers of a new era, who by introducing a new understanding of the right of ownership had given the world a precious addition to the values of 1789.[150] So far, Bobrishchev-Pushkin stressed, a great part of the Russian intelligentsia had failed to grasp the enormous meaning of the events that had taken place in their country during the previous four years. He urged them now to realize that despite its many shortcomings, the Soviet regime was the herald of a new life; the Russian intelligentsia should accept it and try to influence it in a positive way by means of constructive criticism.[151]

In his "Physics and Metaphysics of the Russian Revolution," Potekhin stressed that while there was a close alliance between the Soviet regime and the Russian people, the intelligentsia had so far shown themselves incapable of accepting the utopian and violent revolution. However understandable, their attitude had brought Russia much needless suffering, and now that the Soviet regime was passing through an evolution toward realism and moderation, this could be justified even less. Concrete opportunities for constructive work to further Russia's resurrection were opening up, Potekhin argued. Consequently, the Russian intelligentsia in emigration should return home and participate honestly in Russia's reconstruction. In his view, such a step would further the regime's evolution.[152]

This was also the main theme of the sixth article of the collection, "To Canossa," written by Sergei Stepanovich Chakhotin (1883–1974), a well-known biophysicist, who only at the very last moment had become involved in Kliuchnikov's undertaking. The son of the former Russian vice-consul in Constantinople, in 1902 Chakhotin had been expelled from Russia as one of the initiators of student unrest at Moscow University. He had continued his studies in Würzburg as a student of W. C. Röntgen, but in 1912, at the insistence of I. P. Pavlov, he had been allowed to return to Russia to become Pavlov's assistant.[153] At the time of the October revolution, Chakhotin found himself in the Crimea. He soon became involved with the developing Volunteer Army. In the early fall of 1918 he founded the army's Department of Information and Agitation *(Osvedomitel'no-Agitatsionnoe Otdelenie),* the so-called *Osvag.* An adherent of Taylorism, Chakhotin tried to organize the *Osvag* according to the principles of "scientific management." However, his approach was not very successful, and in March 1919 he was sacked and his system dismantled. Subsequently, Chakhotin worked for a while at the rival Information Department of the United Military Government of the Don, but before long decided to emigrate, and by the end of 1919, he began teaching at Zagreb University.[154]

How exactly Chakhotin became involved with the group behind *Smena vekh* remains unclear. He does not seem to have personally known any of the other contributors before the revolution, although he was presumably acquainted with Potekhin and Bobrishchev-Pushkin from the time they had served in General Denikin's administration.[155] It had taken quite some time and effort, Kliuchnikov later told Ustrialov, to persuade Chakhotin to participate in the collection; moreover, once he had agreed, he apparently had negotiated for every phrase.[156] Yet, to judge from his article in *Smena vekh,* there were two main motives that had prompted Chakhotin to subscribe to the appeal of Kliuchnikov and his friends for reconciliation with the Soviet regime. First, he had come to realize that there was no reasonable alternative to the Soviet regime; second, he felt that the turmoil of revolution and civil war had lasted more than long enough and that, with the advent of the New Economic Policy in Soviet Russia, the time had come to resume one's usual work.

Chakhotin's article is definitely the most sober of all the contributions to the Prague collection. He argued that in the preceding four years the Russian intelligentsia had made three major mistakes—first, by relying blindly on the Russian people; second, by taking the side of the Whites purely out of hatred for the Bolsheviks; and finally, by naively putting all their hopes in Russia's former allies.[157] Now, Chakhotin continued, the Russian intelligentsia should finally face the truth, recognize their mistakes, and return to their motherland to actively take part in the country's economic and cultural reconstruction. This would also help in making the regime's evolution toward normalization irreversible.[158]

Reading the articles of *Smena vekh* one after the other, it is obvious that the contributors wrote their essays independently. One gets the impression of reading six speeches on the same subject, written more or less within the same ideological framework, but not otherwise related. Still, in justifying their appeal to accept the October Revolution and reconcile oneself with the Soviet regime, the six put forward largely the same arguments.

First, they showed that, contrary to all expectations, the Bolsheviks had not destroyed Russia but were strengthening her and, in spite of their internationalist ideology, were gathering together the territory of the former Russian empire around the core of the Russian Soviet Republic. As opposed to the so-called patriots of the White armies, the Bolsheviks had not sold out Russia to foreigners, but had defended the country against foreign attacks.[159] Moreover, the Revolution had given Russia enormous prestige among the masses of the whole world.[160] Second, Kliuchnikov and his colleagues stressed that the Bolsheviks had not thrown Russia into anarchy as many feared. On the contrary, they had shown themselves to be a strong power, alone capable of curbing the "anarchic forces" of the Russian people.[161] Finally, the contributors of the Prague collection were convinced that the Soviet regime was passing through an evolution toward moderation, a conviction considerably strengthened by the introduction of the NEP in March 1921. On the one hand, the contributors feared that continued opposition to the regime might jeopardize the continuation of this evolution. On the other hand, they believed that the moderating tendency would persist and could be deepened if non-Communists played a greater part in Russian society.[162]

With the collection *Smena vekh,* Kliuchnikov and his colleagues spoke out on a number of issues that had occupied the minds of Russian intellectuals for decades: the questions of Russia's place in the world and her role in world history, of the relationship between the Russian people and the state, and of the intelligentsia's role in society. These questions, the *smenovekhovtsy* felt, had been put in a totally new perspective by the revolutions of 1917 and deserved a new answer in light of recent developments at home and abroad. What was the meaning of the October revolution for Russia and the world, and what attitude should the Russian intelligentsia adopt vis-à-vis this event?

The *smenovekhovtsy*'s predominant concern in their assessment of the October revolution and its results was their striving for a strong, "great" Russia that would occupy a prominent place on the international scene. As shown in chapter 2, for Ustrialov, an adherent of N. Ia. Danilevskii's ideas on the state as a living organism with both a body and a soul and on the importance of imperialism for historical progress, the question of Russia's "specific gravity" on the international scene was of almost existential importance.[163] The other *smenovekhovtsy*, for their part, approached the question in a more pragmatic way, yet considered it no less important. Assessing the October revolution and the Soviet regime from the point of view of Russia's international interests, the authors of *Smena vekh* were all convinced that for the moment, "the revolutionary regime . . . alone was capable of restoring Russia's great-power status *(russkoe velikoderzhavie)*."[164] Thanks to the revolution, Bobrishchev-Pushkin argued, Russia was able to realize her age-old political tasks in a peaceful way. He pointed to the example of Turkey, which had turned from Russia's enemy into a friendly nation; the Turks now regarded Russia as their liberator from the Entente, and as a result, a favorable solution to the apparently insoluble question of the Straits seemed in the offing.[165]

Another element that made the *smenovekhovtsy* conclude that the Soviet government was strengthening, not undermining, Russia's international position was their firm belief that Soviet Russia could count on the support of the working masses in the whole world.[166] The refusal of French dockers to load arms for the White Army in December 1919; their British colleagues' attempts to prevent the shipping of arms to General Wrangel in May 1920; and the British Labour party's threat in the summer of 1920 to call a gquarreleneral strike if the British government supported either the Poles or General Wrangel against the Red Army had clearly made a great impression on Kliuchnikov and his colleagues.[167] It had become impossible to attack Russia, they believed, for henceforth no people would allow itself to be mobilized against the country of the revolution. In this way, the *smenovekhovtsy* concluded, the Bolsheviks' internationalist ideology had, however paradoxically, become a powerful weapon for the defense of Russia's national interests.[168]

Convinced statists, the *smenovekhovtsy* were also very much concerned with the repercussions of the October revolution for the Russian state. While Tsarist government had discredited the idea of the state as such in the eyes of many Russian intellectuals, others considered the state to be the most important organizational principle in Russian society and therefore a positive force. In the second half of the nineteenth century this view had been put forward by the so-called etatist school of Russian historiography and its leading theorist, B. N. Chicherin;[169] in the years preceding the revolution, a comparable position was taken by the group of liberal thinkers behind the collections *Voprosy idealizma* (Questions of Idealism) and *Vekhi*.[170] Evaluating the impact of the October revolution from the perspective of this statist tradition, with which they explicitly identified, Kliuchnikov and his colleagues felt that the Bolsheviks had shown themselves to be a positive force. As opposed to the authors of *Vekhi*, who considered the October revolution to be the final destruction of the Russian state,[171] the *smenovekhovtsy* were convinced that the Bolsheviks had on the contrary averted an outburst of anarchy in Russia. If it had not been for Lenin and his colleagues, Luk'ianov argued, "the Russian revolutionary force would have called into being something far more terrible, terrible not through murder and robbery, but terrible in the first place because the revolution would have threatened to degenerate into anarchy and revolt *(bunt)*."[172] For all its defects, the Soviet regime was the strongest regime there could possibly be in a Russia living through a revolutionary crisis.[173] In any case, the *smenovekhovtsy* stressed, there was no one to take the Bolsheviks' place, certainly not among the quarreling émigrés. At present, a change of power in the Kremlin could only throw Russia out of the frying pan into the fire.[174]

In the views of Chicherin and, following him, the authors of *Vekhi,* one of the main problems hampering the organization of Russian society was what they considered to be its lack of social cohesion and sense of community.[175] The *smenovekhovtsy* believed that as a result of the October revolution this problem had finally been overcome, if not fully, then at least as far as the relationship between the people and the state was concerned. Traditionally, the Russian intelligentsia had presumed an opposition between people and government, in which the intelligentsia were to speak for the people. After the October revolution, it was hard for several groups in the intelligentsia to face the Bolsheviks' popularity.[176] The *smenovekhovtsy,* however, considered popular support for the revolutionary regime in a positive light. As they saw it, the revolution had awakened the Russian people's national feelings and had imbued them with the mystique of the state. Luk'ianov, for instance, regarded the "colossal growth of the civil *(gosudarstvennyi),* national, economic, and social consciousness of the popular masses in Russia" as one of the revolution's greatest accomplishments.[177] Potekhin pointed out that under the Soviet regime the Russian people had come to see the state as something of their own, something which closely concerned them. This had a double cause, he explained: first, many millions of workers and peasants had become involved in practical work in the Soviet institutions; second, over the past four years the masses had come to know the pernicious results of anarchy from firsthand experience.[178] The *smenovekhovtsy* believed that the Bolsheviks had been able to bring about real unity between the people and the state and regarded this unity as a pledge for progress. In their view, the people would henceforth be the leading figure of Russian history. One of Kliuchnikov's "favorite ideas" in this connection was that "the revolution had released *(vypustila) the whole Russian people* onto the historical scene."[179] Potekhin, for his part, stressed that through the experiences of the past few years, the Russian people had become ready for independent economic and political activity and had overcome *(izzhiv)* its rebelliousness. He believed that from now on it would be the decisive factor in Russian history, and this gave him hope for the future.[180]

Not all contributors to *Smena vekh* shared this hope, however. According to Chakhotin, the experience of the revolution had rather shown that it was wrong to cherish high expectations of the Russian masses,[181] and Ustrialov's article in the Prague collection even contained an explicit reference to the bitter words of the conservative thinker K. N. Leont'ev, who, inspired by a feeling of deep doubt in the Russian people, in 1880 had written: "One should freeze Russia, if only a little, lest she would not 'decay.' "[182] Leont'ev, unlike the nineteenth-century Slavophiles and the Russian populists, did not believe in the creative force of the popular masses, whatever their nationality. In his view, what made a people great was not its own elemental force *(stikhiia)* but the compulsory idea that organized it.[183] Leont'ev's low opinion of the Russian people resulted from his feelings that it had never developed an organizing idea of its own and that it was chiefly characterized by an enormous propensity for anarchy.[184] All positive elements in the Russian character were of foreign origin, he stressed: German, Tatar, or Byzantine. The latter element was especially valuable in his eyes, for he considered Byzantine orthodoxy and autocracy as Russia's main organizing principles.[185]

Like Leont'ev, Ustrialov regarded the Russian people as primarily anarchic. His only hope was that these destructive forces would once and for all exhaust themselves in the revolutionary wave, a hope he had expressed from the first months after the Bolshevik takeover.[186] In 1920 and early 1921, when he wrote the articles from which Kliuchnikov would pick fragments for "Patriotica," Ustrialov's expectations toward the Russian people did not seem to reach any further. Rather, he repeatedly spoke about the threat of anarchy.[187]

Ustrialov was well aware that his remarks in this respect were sure to provoke accusations that "he did not believe in the Russian people," accusations that he described as not only "demagogic" and "of a nasty tone" but also unfounded. His argument was the following:

> The creativity of a people is many-sided, and does not only express itself directly, in the elemental, anarchic outbursts of the masses, but also in the regime against which these outbursts are directed. More than that, a regime always represents a more weighty product of the national 'genius' than the rebellious arrows that are directed against it. For the regime is, so to speak, the popular spirit that has already 'crystallized,' that has become self-conscious, while the discontent with this regime, especially when expressed in such forms . . . , must be seen as deception or ignorant temptation *(obman ili temnyi soblazn)* of the suffering popular soul. Therefore, in evaluating the debate between the regime and a rebellion against it, one should free oneself from 'referring *(kivanie)*' to the 'popular will.' This icon is always featureless or many-sided.[188]

In sharp contrast to the skepticism of Chakhotin and Ustrialov, the other contributors to *Smena vekh* not only believed that the Russian people had finally begun to play an active and positive role in Russian history, they were also convinced that the revolution had charged the Russian people with a task of universal importance. In their view, the Russian people had been called upon to take over the lead of world history from the declining West and "bring eternal justice." Messianic elements, reminiscent of the ideas of the nineteenth-century Slavophiles, play an important role in *Smena vekh,* especially in the articles of Kliuchnikov and Bobrishchev-Pushkin and to a lesser extent in those of Luk'ianov[189] and Potekhin.[190]

Kliuchnikov argued that the only thing that had been able to awaken the Russian workers and peasants was the realization that they had been called upon "to suffer for the workers and peasants, for the oppressed and offended *(unizhennye i oskorblennye)* of the whole world." Neither the Provisional Government's promises for land reform nor the idea of a Constituent Assembly had appealed to the Russian people, while a call "to kill the evil in the world and bring mankind eternal justice" had attracted them all the more.[191] In his article "A New Faith," Bobrishchev-Pushkin described the Russian people as the new messiah in truly flamboyant terms: " 'In the guise of slaves,' in the pangs of innumerable sufferings, the Russian people is bringing its tormented brothers universal ideals, and for this it is loved, by this it is reborn and purified in the very abyss of its fall, because of this it is mighty in its humiliation."[192] Bobrishchev-Pushkin believed that as a result of the revolution, "the light was shining again from the east." He now regarded the new Russia as the future, "official Europe" as the past.[193]

The idea that Western Europe was decaying and Russia was called upon to take over Europe's leading role in world history was not new among the Russian intelligentsia. In the nineteenth century it had played an important role in the thought of the Slavophiles and in the work of such thinkers as N. Ia. Danilevskii and K. N. Leont'ev. In the early 1920s, concepts of this kind apparently helped Russian intellectuals to deal with the shocking experiences of the world war and the revolution. Oswald Spengler's *Untergang des Abendlandes,* for instance, met with an enormous response among the Russian intelligentsia, both in Soviet Russia and in the emigration.[194] A number of Russian intellectuals even came to regard the October revolution as a clear sign of Russia's vigor and of her mission to radically renew the world.

In the first months after the October takeover, a striking example of such an attitude was the position of the group *Skify,* the so-called Scythians, that became well known through A. A. Blok's famous poems *The Scythians* and *The Twelve.* This group, led by the literary critic R. V. Ivanov-Razumnik and counting the poets A. Belyi and S. Esenin among its adherents, regarded the Russian revolution as an event of universal significance, no less important than the birth of Christ. In the Scythians' view, this revolution was bringing the world, through blood and torment, a new unifying idea, a promise of peace and brotherhood for all nations and for all generations to come. That this was happening amid barbarities did not put off the Scythians; on the contrary, they regarded this as a guarantee of the revolution's significance and genuineness.[195]

Similar ideas played roles in the émigré movement of Eurasianism and, from

1919 on, in the thought of the philosopher N. A. Berdiaev. As has been indicated above, the Eurasians accepted the October revolution as a turning point in the history of Russia and the world, marking both the conclusion of Russia's forced Europeanization and the beginning of a new universal culture in which Russia—the "point of tangency" between Europe and Asia—would take the lead.[196] Berdiaev, for his part, initially regarded the Russian revolution as the direct result of what, in his view, made up the Russian national character: anarchism, extreme egalitarianism, and an instinctive hatred for culture; but by 1919 he began to see the revolution as part of an overall crisis of Western culture.[197] According to Berdiaev, this crisis had taken on extreme forms in Russia because Russia had remained isolated from Western culture when that culture was at its height and had adopted Western culture's decadent products when it was on the decline. Yet, however bitter a fate this might be, Berdiaev felt that it was not entirely negative. In his view, Russia's destiny was now to follow through the destructive, decadent phase to the very end; he believed that, as a result of this experience, Russia would be capable of leading humanity into a new historical phase of spiritual rebirth.[198]

As the American historian J. Burbank has demonstrated, Berdiaev was not alone in succumbing to "the seductive 'logic' of 'light from darkness' "; this was also the case with P. B. Struve and the Kadet leader P. N. Miliukov.[199] In fact, even in the first months after the October revolution, it was not uncommon to speak about the revolution in terms of an illness that would eventually lead either to a healthy reaction from the organism or to death.[200] This motif was also present in *Smena vekh;* especially in the pieces by Ustrialov and Chakhotin, who believed that as a reaction to the "illnesses" of the past few years, the organism of the Russian state would develop new, healthy forces. In "To Canossa" Chakhotin pictured Bolshevism as a disease, and Russia was a patient who needed rest and loving treatment in order to overcome her delirium and recover. While he admitted that Russia's illness was deplorable, he tried to comfort his readers by reminding them that "after every illness one can observe in the organism the appearance of new forces, an intensified metabolism, an increase in health and strength."[201] The same image was used by Bobrishchev-Pushkin[202] and by Ustrialov, who stressed that in the eyes of contemporaries, a revolution manifested itself primarily "like a tornado or a whirlwind, which 'sprang up, stirred up, and whirled away like the typhus.' " However, "the organism recovered, tempered by the illness that had flashed through it. 'It was no longer the same,' but the wholesome fruits of the poison revealed themselves only gradually, furthering the creative development of soul and body."[203]

In their analysis of the October revolution, the authors of *Smena vekh* were guided by a Hegelian world view, in which history was considered a force, judging and directing the world toward progress.[204] Ustrialov spoke about the "odd dialectic of history" that had "unexpectedly advanced Soviet power with its ideology of the International into the role of the national factor of contemporary Russian life."[205] This idea was repeated by Chakhotin, who wrote that "history had compelled the Russian 'Communist' republic, in spite of its official dogma, to take upon itself the national task of uniting Russia, which was on the point of falling apart."[206] Luk'ianov admitted that the price that had been paid for Russia's future happiness was high, but added that "history, unfortunately, did not know either too high or too low prices." He stressed that "in relation to history the question whether it could have been otherwise was meaningless."[207] Bobrishchev-Pushkin, for his part, believed that history forgave bloodshed, if only the goal for which it had been committed was "wise and useful."[208] Potekhin stressed that "there was nothing fortuitous in the inexorable development of the Russian revolution,"[209] and Kliuchnikov was convinced that "the revolution had chosen for her fights and victories those whom she regarded most suitable."[210] That there was no stopping the revolution under the Bolshevik flag was, for him and his colleagues, the best proof that the driving force behind this revolution was the force of history itself.

In conclusion, the authors of the collection all agreed that, forced by the "logic of life," the Bolshevik regime was evolving toward more moderate forms. Ustrialov even spoke of a "Russian Thermidor,"[211] and Bobrishchev-Pushkin went still further, writing that "Russia was approaching the Directory."[212] While the four others avoided allusions to the French revolution, they too saw a clear evolution. Both Luk'ianov and Chakhotin stressed that the Soviet regime was increasingly compelled to take into account the actual social and economic situation in the country,[213] and Potekhin pointed out that Lenin and his colleagues had finally started to "overcome their own fanatical utopianism."[214] In short, as Kliuchnikov put it, the long revolutionary period was coming to a close, and "a period of fast and powerful evolutionary progress was opening."[215]

As to the concrete direction they expected this evolution to take, the *smenovekhovtsy* were vague. Politically speaking, they excluded the possibility that the Soviet regime would evolve toward a parliamentary system of the Western European model,[216] which, as Potekhin stressed, was no better suited for Russia than orthodox Communism.[217] Chakhotin, who did see the possibility of some kind of parliamentarism in Russia,[218] was in this respect a complete outsider. The others all agreed that the ultimate political system in Russia would be "something distinctive *(svoe)*, gained through suffering and forged by the revolution."[219] Potekhin and Bobrishchev-Pushkin even felt that "Sovietism," if freed from its excesses, might turn out to be the form of government best adapted to the Russian situation.[220]

On the economic level, Kliuchnikov and his colleagues applauded the introduction of the New Economic Policy, which they regarded as the best proof that Lenin and his colleagues were not dangerous dogmatists, but had a keen feeling of reality.[221] Ustrialov believed that Lenin's "tactical retreat" would prove to be irreversible, and further evolution toward a "bourgeois" economy was inevitable.[222] With this view, he seemed to be alone among the *smenove-khovtsy*. None of the other articles in *Smena vekh* hinted at this, and in future publications Ustrialov's colleagues would rather express their hopes that the NEP would lead to a new equilibrium between private initiative and state regulation.

Be that as it may, all participants in the Prague collection agreed that the evolutionary process they believed was taking place in Russia should be safe-guarded and deepened. They felt that in this respect the Russian intelligentsia could play an important role and should adjust their attitude toward the Soviet regime accordingly. In any case, they felt, the intelligentsia should now take the side of the Russian people, making the unity in Russian society complete.

Apart from Luk'ianov, all contributors to *Smena vekh* had taken part in the civil war on the side of the Whites. While Kliuchnikov and especially Bobrish-chev-Pushkin now renounced this episode because they believed it had brought Russia nothing but suffering and destruction,[223] Luk'ianov, Potekhin, and Chakhotin did not consider it a complete mistake. At least they managed to see a number of positive aspects to it.[224] Potekhin argued that the hard years of the civil war had toughened the Russian people,[225] and Luk'ianov regarded one of the civil war's positive aspects to be that it had prompted the people consciously and actively to support the Soviet regime, so that for the first time in centuries the regime in Russia had acquired a solid social basis.[226] Cha-khotin, for his part, pointed out that in the war "all [that was] old and inexpe-dient had been burned down and room had been made for something new, fresh, rational." In addition, he stressed that "if the Soviet regime had become capable of evolving toward a more realistic national policy—this was also to a considerable extent the result of the struggle of the last years."[227]

Chakhotin felt that the Russian intelligentsia did not need to repent of their former (White) position, for he was convinced that at the time they could not have acted otherwise. Moreover, he believed that the intelligentsia's involve-ment in the civil war had radically changed them for the better: "it had taught [us] to love the motherland more actively, more sacrificially than before, it had cured us of mocking at manifestations of healthy nationalism, it had cured us of naive sentimentalism in politics."[228] These new qualities, Chakhotin believed, would help the intelligentsia fulfill the task required of them in the changing situation in Russia. The intelligentsia should "go to Canossa," and recognize that they had lost the game. Their calculations had, to a great extent, been mistaken. They should return to Russia and take part in the country's recon-struction by means of practical, concrete work, especially in the economic and cultural fields. In this way, Chakhotin stressed, they could finally come to the aid of those non-Bolshevik intellectuals who had always considered it their duty not to leave the country and who, notwithstanding hunger, cold, coer-cion, and mockeries, had remained at their posts and tried to preserve Russian culture. In fact, Chakhotin added, only they, among the Russian intelligentsia, had nothing to reproach themselves with.[229]

Potekhin repeated Chakhotin's appeal and called upon the Russian intelligentsia abroad to return home and take up practical work. He was convinced that "the zigzag on Russia's true historic path," which, in his view, was the result of the Soviet system's shortcomings, "would be straightened into a broad, original road of real progress if the intelligentsia took up practical activity along with the people," and if "the regime's evolving core became enveloped *(obvolakivanie)* by hardworking and honest businesslike organs."[230] Potekhin stressed that he did not have in mind a Trojan horse tactic aimed at undermining Soviet Russia from within. On the contrary, he stated, the intelligentsia should learn from their former mistakes and, out of a sense of responsibility for the state, "give up all prejudices, refrain from that 'maximalism of claims' which was so reminiscent of Bolshevism," and cooperate with the regime in the Russian public interest.[231]

Luk'ianov and Kliuchnikov, for their part, were less specific in formulating their expectations toward the Russian intelligentsia. Luk'ianov limited himself to urging Russian intellectuals to "honestly lend the Motherland a helping hand."[232] Kliuchnikov's vague, even confused wording of the intelligentsia's task should be interpreted in light of his belief in a "mystical link" between the Russian intelligentsia and the revolution.[233] In Kliuchnikov's opinion, the Russian intelligentsia, with all the shortcomings *Vekhi* had reproached them for, was made for the revolution and could heal these shortcomings only if the revolution was completed.[234] As a result, he urged the Russian intelligentsia to accept the revolution and help the evolutionary process develop to the very end. Once this was accomplished, he believed, the intelligentsia would "in all probability be just as the authors of *Vekhi* in part saw them, in part would have wished to see them. Yet, all the negative in them, which formerly sprang from their revolutionary purpose, would no longer make itself felt, would disappear, would become softened."[235]

Kliuchnikov's vision of how the intelligentsia then would be was a chaotic blend of Fedorov and Dostoevskii, Solov'ev, Struve, and Herzen. In the new Russia, he believed, the intelligentsia would become an integral part of the people, and "in them the Russian people's God-seeking tendency would be concentrated." They would "become penetrated with 'the mystique of the state,'" and "through them the state—the Russian state—would finally become what it ought to be: 'the path of God on earth.'"[236] As a group, he continued, the intelligentsia would fight against the "sins and calamities of social life." Thus, they would become a "force of powerful social progress," which Russia as well as all other peoples would need in their struggle against "spiritual philistinism" and in their striving for social justice.[237]

Bobrishchev-Pushkin had advocated cooperation with the Soviet regime as early as the fall of 1918. He now repeated this appeal, pointing to the example of the Tsarist officers who had joined the Red Army. In the military sphere such cooperation had produced brilliant results, he argued; the same should be possible in other fields as well.[238] Still, this did not mean that he felt that he and his colleagues should return home immediately. In Bobrishchev-Pushkin's view, the time was not ripe to take this step. He agreed with Ustrialov that the patriotic-minded intelligentsia abroad first had another task to fulfill, namely to break the influence of the anti-Bolshevik émigrés. With their propaganda, Bobrishchev-Pushkin argued, the anti-Bolsheviks aimed at undermining the Russian (i.e., Soviet) government's attempts to conclude treaties and commercial agreements with other states, at galvanizing the former regime's representations abroad, at encouraging whoever intended to attack Russia, and at rousing internal anarchy. This was extremely damaging for Russia, he stressed. As long as this pernicious activity had not been neutralized, it was irresponsible to return.[239]

Thus, *Smena vekh* was both an appeal to and a frontal attack against Russian intellectuals in emigration. Apart from Bobrishchev-Pushkin's article, the contributions of Potekhin[240] and especially of Kliuchnikov were also charged with reproaches toward the émigré intelligentsia. Kliuchnikov not only had sharp words for the SRs,[241] with whom he had been at odds since the November coup in Omsk, but also violently attacked Miliukov[242] and even Struve. Kliuchnikov addressed Struve in a lengthy, pedantic, written speech, in which he called Struve guilty of all the shortcomings *Vekhi* had in 1909 reproached the Russian intelligentsia with: maximalism, intolerance, "exaggerated 'principledness,' " and, most important in Kliuchnikov's view, a lack of understanding of the "mystique of the state" that, he believed, had revealed itself in the revolution.[243]

Chapter Four

INDIGNATION AND CONDESCENSION

Reactions to *Smena Vekh*

Potekhin was right when, in a letter to Ustrialov shortly before *Smena vekh* was to come out, he described the collection as "defiant."[1] The booklet could not but provoke a storm of indignation among the Russians abroad. In spite of the deep ideological differences that divided the émigré community into a whole range of factions, there was one thing that united them, their rejection of the Soviet regime. As Kliuchnikov and his colleagues brought precisely this rejection into question, it was not surprising to see the émigrés united in their condemnation of *Smena vekh*. However, even on this issue émigré unity was not complete, with the different reactions clearly reflecting each group's ideological standpoint.

In the weeks immediately following the collection's publication, the whole émigré press featured comments on *Smena vekh,* from the ultraright monarchist daily *Novoe vremia* in Belgrade to the Menshevik organ *Sotsialisticheskii vestnik* in Berlin. The first to react was the Paris daily *Obshchee delo,* which at the time of General Wrangel's Crimean operation had been the organ of the general's government and, even after Wrangel's defeat, remained an ardent advocate of continuing the armed struggle against the Soviet regime. On 17 September 1921 the paper carried a short, sarcastic article by the well-known columnist A. Iablonovskii, Kliuchnikov's former colleague at the Moscow daily *Russkoe slovo.*[2] The article was entitled "Seven Educated Men *(Sem' obrazovannykh muzhchin)*"—the seventh "man" being "Ne-Kommunist," after Bobrishchev-Pushkin's pseudonym in the Berlin newspaper *Novyi mir.*

This was a somewhat forced allusion to D. S. Merezhkovskii's caustic reaction to *Vekhi,* which had appeared in April 1909 under the heading "Seven

Meek Men."[3] On that occasion Merezhkovskii had likened the authors of *Vekhi* with their attacks on the intelligentsia to the drunken men of Raskolnikov's dream in *Crime and Punishment,* who in an outburst of gratuitous cruelty had beaten to death a little old mare.[4] Iablonovskii did not reproach Kliuchnikov and his colleagues for anything so pitiless, but scornfully called them "turncoats." His disdain was directed especially against Bobrishchev-Pushkin, who, during his stay in Novorossiisk, as Iablonovskii reminded his readers, had written and staged a number of ultrapatriotic plays, cursing the Bolsheviks and "portraying the Third International as a devil with an enormous hooked nose."[5]

Clearly, of all six participants in *Smena vekh* Bobrishchev-Pushkin was the one who could most easily be accused of being unprincipled. As a former leading Octobrist, he was not only the best known of the six *smenovekhovtsy;* he was also from the very start a compromised figure in the eyes of many émigré intellectuals. To most of the Russian intelligentsia the Octobrists with their far-reaching willingness to compromise with the regime had always been contemptible, especially after the dissolution of the Second Duma and the promulgation of a new, unconstitutional electoral law on 3 June 1907. If it seemed an exceedingly great step for a former Octobrist to become a Bolshevik sympathizer, several commentators chose to interpret this move as a sign that Bobrishchev-Pushkin had not changed at all but was merely prepared to bow to whatever regime was in power.

From this interpretation, it was but a small step for the critics of *Smena vekh* to represent the whole Prague collection as an expression of shameless opportunism and servility. In a second article on *Smena vekh* in *Obshchee delo* L. Bernshtein, for example, explicitly referred to the Octobrist position toward the events of 3 June 1907. "*Novo-vekhizm*" was a peculiar kind of "neo-Octobrism," he argued: the *smenovekhovtsy* had accepted the Soviet regime only because it had shown itself sufficiently "hard" and "chastising." In fact, even to call Bobrishchev-Pushkin and his colleagues "obsequious 'neo-Octobrists' " was too great an honor for them.[6]

In the right-wing Menshevik monthly *Zaria* (Dawn), M. Lazerson labeled the message of *Smena vekh* as "Octobrist-Bonapartist."[7] For its part, the Berlin daily *Golos Rossii,* which since 5 August 1921 had become a sounding board for P. N. Miliukov,[8] even made it clear that it did not intend to waste words on *Smena vekh,* for it was "somehow awkward to speak about the revolution with people such as Bobrishchev-Pushkin."[9]

On 27 September 1921 *Volia Rossii* (Russia's Freedom), the left-wing Socialist Revolutionary organ in Prague, featured a review of *Smena vekh* entitled "From Octobrism to Bolshevism." The article was written by M. Slonim, who argued that the authors of the Prague collection had chosen the side of the Reds merely because the Reds had won the civil war. In doing so, Slonim stressed, "the Bobrishchev-Pushkins" had not "parted from their true essence, from Octobrism and servile love for autocracy." In his view, the Soviet regime impressed the *smenovekhovtsy* because it possessed the same attributes that the autocracy previously had: "a majestic façade, bayonets and iron rods for the disobedient."[10] In an article entitled " 'Fathers' and 'sons,' " which appeared in *Volia Rossii* on 5 February 1922, SR leader V. M. Chernov recalled that in their day, the Octobrists had been nicknamed "the party of the latest governmental instruction." He observed that, if the comparison did not completely hold water because Kliuchnikov and his colleagues did not really form a party, they could in any case be called "deferential commentators and popularizers of 'the latest Kremlin instruction.' "[11]

Ideologically speaking, it was indeed true that all articles in *Smena vekh*—not merely Bobrishchev-Pushkin's—contained several elements reminiscent of Octobrist thought:[12] the importance Kliuchnikov and his colleagues attached to the state, their ardent patriotism, their longing for "organic unity" between the people and the state, and their rejection of Western-style "numerical" democracy and individual freedom. Indeed, their view of freedom reflected the Octobrist ideal of "productive freedom," which the historian of the Octobrists, E. Birth, defined as "releasing the individual forces in order to use them in a controlled way for furthering the common good."[13] To be sure, a few critics of *Smena vekh,* notably the SRs V. Chernov and M. Slonim, did point out these ideological parallels.[14] In their eyes, however, the most striking resemblance between those Octobrists who "based themselves on 17 October" and those who "traced their origins to 25 October" was shameless servilism.[15]

Besides the "Octobrist connection," there was another aspect to *Smena vekh* many of the collection's critics were keen to seize upon, namely the link with *Vekhi,* in the tradition of which Kliuchnikov and his colleagues explicitly wanted to place themselves. At its appearance in March 1909, *Vekhi* had caused a real scandal in Russian educated society. With its criticism of the radical intelligentsia's traditionally revolutionary aspirations and its plea for their moral and political reeducation toward deference to the absolute values of state, nation, truth, law, and religion, the collection had angered and incensed Russian intellectuals almost without exception.[16]

At a time of political reaction, *Vekhi*'s appeal to the Russian intelligentsia to strive for self-perfection and assume responsibility in the light of those long-disregarded values had been readily misinterpreted as an appeal to submit to the regime.[17] That a number of right-wing figures had welcomed the collection had only added fuel to the flames.[18] From the Kadets to the Bolsheviks, Russian intellectuals had gone on the defensive, branding the authors of *Vekhi* as apostate defamers of the intelligentsia's holiest creeds.

In the emotional debate that followed *Vekhi*'s publication, critics forgot that the collection had touched upon a number of real problems, such as the lack of respect for law among some of the Russian intellectuals. The impression *Vekhi* left in the memory of most of the intelligentsia was that of a scandalous and reactionary document, the essence of which could, as SR leader V. M. Chernov put it, be expressed in a single word: "Octobrism,"[19] or, according to Kadet chairman Miliukov, in a single phrase: "the ideological slogan of all reaction."[20] Such recollections of *Vekhi* were still vivid in the early 1920s, when, in a response to the appeal by well-known law professor and former Kadet N. A. Gredeskul for reconciliation with the Bolsheviks on the pages of *Izvestiia* in June 1920, *Poslednie novosti* published a scathing article under the title "New 'Vekhi.' "[21]

As a result, the *smenovekhovtsy's* explicit identification with *Vekhi* gave many of their critics a convenient starting point for rejecting *Smena vekh.* V. Chernov, for example, stressed that the essence of *Smena vekh* was the same as that of *Vekhi,* the only difference being that Struve and his colleagues had preached their "Octobrism" in the days of the autocracy, while Kliuchnikov and his men did so under a "commissarocracy."[22] M. Slonim, for his part, argued that both *Vekhi* and *Smena vekh* had been born out of the same "defeatist" psychology, out of the "spiritual impoverishment and despair of those who could not endure the Russian intelligentsia's heavy cross."[23]

The right-wing Socialist Revolutionary M. Vishniak, who wrote a review of *Smena vekh* for *Sovremennye zapiski,* also believed that the *smenovekhovtsy's* claim to ideological kinship with *Vekhi* was largely justified. Vishniak saw this kinship especially in what he called the hatred for "Pinks," as opposed to Reds and Whites, which he felt was common to the two collections. In his view, the authors of *Vekhi* and *Smena vekh* were united by a shared aversion to "people of the Avksent'ev and Kerenskii type," since they were convinced that the latter, in the words of Kliuchnikov, had as their only vocation to "maintain the Russian chaos and the disintegration of the Russian state."[24] Unlike Chernov and Slonim, Vishniak stressed that from a moral point of view, there was a world of difference between the two collections. In this respect, he felt, the *smenovekhovtsy* were in a far worse, viler category. In fact, Vishniak remarked, people of the "Kliuchnikov type" unwittingly reminded one of the figure of Faddei Bulgarin.[25] This was hardly a gratifying comparison. Bulgarin (1789–1859), the founder of the servile Petersburg daily *Severnaia pchela* (The Northern Bee) and an informer to the secret police, acquired in his day the reputation of, as the historian of Russian literature D. S. Mirsky called it, "a vile sycophant whom all honest men abhorred."[26]

The link with *Vekhi* was also underlined by P. Ryss, the commentator of the Kadet daily *Poslednie novosti.* Ryss regarded *Smena vekh*—that is to say the article by Kliuchnikov, for that was the only contribution he considered worth commenting on—as a clear consequence of *Vekhi.* At the same time, however, he felt that the *smenovekhovtsy* had not properly understood their teachers.[27]

Ryss argued that the *vekhovtsy,* as the authors of *Vekhi* were called, disillusioned with socialism as a philosophical doctrine and a sociopolitical idea, had preached individualism, yet had by their demand to submit oneself to the "mystique of the state" also renounced the individual's full development. In his view, their failure to find a solution to the opposition between the individual and the state resulted in a built-in contradiction.[28] As Ryss saw it, Kliuchnikov and his colleagues, thrown far away from their homeland by the revolutionary whirlwind, young and mentally unstable, had become absorbed by the "facts." Guided by a simplified understanding of *Vekhi*, they had thought to recognize the "mystique of the state" in the Soviet regime, and they had jumped to conclusions without quite grasping the essence of what was happening. They had deified the irrational Leviathan of Bulgakov and Gershenzon in the person of Lenin.[29] If Struve and his colleagues had failed to solve the conflict between state and individual, Ryss concluded, Kliuchnikov and his colleagues had not even taken this problem into consideration. While they were the product of *Vekhi*'s reticent idealism, they themselves were people without any ideology at all. Therefore, Ryss suggested, the authors of *Vekhi* would hardly be keen to acknowledge the *smenovekhovtsy* as their children.[30]

This suggestion was also made by the Kadet G. K. Gins, the former administrative director of Admiral Kolchak's Council of Ministers, who labeled *Smena vekh* as a perversion of *Vekhi*.[31] Ryss and Gins were proven correct: the two *vekhovtsy* who publicly reacted to *Smena vekh*, A. S. Izgoev and P. B. Struve, did indeed refuse to consider the Prague collection as a continuation of the *Vekhi* tradition.

A. S. Izgoev voiced his comments on *Smena vekh* during a discussion on the collection organized by the Petrograd *Dom literatorov* (House of Litterateurs), an independent literary organization that united a substantial part of the former capital's literary community.[32] While Izgoev conceded that the authors of *Smena vekh* had grasped part of the ideas of *Vekhi*—the importance of the mystique of the state and the value of patriotism—he argued that they had at the same time failed to understand *Vekhi*'s leitmotif, namely, its call for the intelligentsia's moral and spiritual reeducation. The *smenovekhovtsy* had succumbed to the notion of deifying the state, Izgoev continued, and for the sake of this "god" they had been prepared to jettison all moral and spiritual values; yet it was precisely these values that constituted the intelligentsia's strength. Therefore, he concluded, if one could not deny that there was a certain external similarity between the old and the new *Vekhi*, there was nonetheless a huge difference of principle between the two collections.[33]

P. B. Struve, for his part, reacted to *Smena vekh* with utter contempt. On the pages of the monthly *Russkaia mysl'* (Russian Thought), he branded the Prague collection, with its "opportunist acceptance of the revolution elevated into an idea and a philosophy," as "the most monstrous phenomenon in the history of Russia's spiritual development." If the ideology of *Smena vekh* was essentially the apotheosis of the October revolution, Struve argued, psychologically speaking, it was primarily an act of adaptation to the regime that revolution had created. In *Smena vekh* "the revolution was accepted as a datum, a fact, and the Russian people were invited to bow to that fact-idol in all its sickening and obscene reality."[34]

As to the relationship between *Vekhi* and *Smena vekh*, Struve argued that the Prague collection was the exact opposite of *Vekhi*, both in psychology and in content. *Vekhi* had been the revolutionary negation of a revolutionary ideology, a rising against that ideology in the name of higher religious, cultural, and social principles of a general nature. *Smena vekh*, however, negated revolution as a form of struggle and did so in the name of accepting an accomplished revolution. *Vekhi* had been the product of free thought and had therefore freely combined in itself the principles of conservatism and revolutionariness; the authors of *Smena vekh*, on the contrary, slavishly linked these principles together. Hence, Struve concluded, the "striking ideological poverty and moral stench of this work: *Smena vekh* was reeking of lust for external success and personal luck."[35]

If certain commentators were prepared to accept that at least some of the *smenovekhovtsy*, especially Ustrialov and Kliuchnikov,[36] were sincere, others, both left-wing and right-wing, claimed that the group behind the Prague collection had been bought by Moscow to a man.[37] According to the Belgrade monarchist daily *Novoe vremia* (New Times), the Bolsheviks had come to realize that the Russian émigré community—all those teachers, nurses, professors, physicians, engineers, and students who would rather suffer hardships abroad than return to Soviet Russia—was by its sheer existence the best possible anti-Bolshevik propaganda. Therefore, the Belgrade paper continued, the Moscow rulers had decided to try to buy "émigré souls," aiming initially at the "morally versatile." It was only natural that the first to jump at Moscow's advances would be "venal" people such as the "Ustrialovs, Kliushnikovs [sic], and Bo-brishchev-Pushkins." Such opportunists, the paper trusted, would hardly have any influence in the émigré community; they were merely "dead souls," speaking dead, not living, words.[38]

In spite of their disdain for Kliuchnikov and his friends, the commentators of *Novoe vremia* managed to discover also a positive aspect to *Smena vekh*. Just as their like-minded colleagues had in the days of *Vekhi*, they seized upon the Prague collection, with its criticism of the émigré intelligentsia, in order to attack the liberal and socialist intelligentsia in their turn. It was an old axiom, *Novoe vremia* argued, that a lie could seem convincing only if there was a grain of truth to it, and according to the Belgrade paper, there was indeed such a core of truth in *Smena vekh*. As *Novoe vremia* saw it, the authors of the Prague collection rightly claimed that the revolution was of a certain national significance and correctly attributed this to the fact that Bolshevism had overcome the pernicious illusions of the traditional Russian intelligentsia. With unconcealed satisfaction, the paper noted: "All the cardboard figures *(kartonazhi)* that the revolutionary intelligentsia had solicitously glued and built, starting from the tragicomical clown of the Constituent Assembly *(Uchredilka)*, had been overcome by a simple kick of a *muzhik* boot."[39] *Novoe vremia* hastened to add, however, that this "grain of truth" was of a purely negative kind. True, the authors of *Smena vekh* had been right in arguing that the Russian intelligentsia had failed and were still failing to understand the preconditions for their country's greatness, happiness, and glory; yet the *smenovekhovtsy*'s assumption that Russia's national mission could be achieved by the *Comintern* was entirely mistaken.[40]

In any case, whether or not they regarded Kliuchnikov and his colleagues as shameless mercenaries in Lenin's service, most commentators on *Smena vekh* agreed that the Prague collection played into Moscow's hands. Not only was there a possibility that the collection would cause confusion in the émigré ranks; it could, as G. K. Gins suggested, also help the Bolsheviks to raise spirits at home and discourage potential internal opponents.[41] Moreover, the Soviet government might try to take advantage of *Smena vekh* in its pursuit of international recognition. According to Gins, if a number of émigrés "recognized their mistakes," public opinion abroad could waver in their attitude vis-à-vis Moscow, and Vishniak feared that Moscow would use the *smenovekhovtsy* as a claque in those countries where overt Communist propaganda was forbidden.[42]

Indeed, of all the political groups in the emigration only the Mensheviks did not regard the Prague collection as being a witting or unwitting tool in the hands of Moscow. In the fall of 1921 the Menshevik central organ in Berlin, *Sotsialisticheskii vestnik,* featured two articles on the subject by S. Sumskii,[43] who described *Smena vekh* as "the most significant and, in any case, the most interesting of all that had appeared in Russian political and social journalism over the last few years."[44] Sumskii admitted that the collection's authors were far from intellectual heavyweights and that their style was somewhat primitive and naive, but stressed that *Smena vekh* nonetheless deserved serious attention. In his view, the virtual unanimity with which the Russian émigrés had rejected the new collection merely showed how little understanding they had of what was really going on in their motherland.[45]

As the Mensheviks saw it, Lenin and his colleagues had seriously violated the laws of historical progress by attempting to bypass the historical stage of a bourgeois revolution and install socialism in Russia immediately. From the first days after the October revolution, Iu. O. Martov and his party had warned that this violation was bound to lead to economic regression and bourgeois reaction. When, in March 1921, the Soviet government introduced its New Economic Policy, the Mensheviks greeted it as a clear sign that their prophecy had been fulfilled.[46] It was in this framework that Sumskii placed *Smena vekh*. Entirely in line with his party's official viewpoint, he argued that Russia was going through a Thermidor. Economically speaking, a new bourgeoisie had gained the upper hand in the country, and this new class was now striving for political power as well. In order to reach this goal, Sumskii continued, the new

Soviet bourgeoisie needed a suitable ideology, and this was precisely what *Smena vekh* was offering them.[47]

As Sumskii saw it, the Prague collection "indicated the ways and methods of the Russian revolution's new stage," and spelled out the "ideology of our [Russian] Thermidor."[48] With the help of Communist phraseology, Sumskii argued, *Smena vekh* justified the new bourgeoisie's right to property, while at the same time rejecting Communism and socialism as such. He quoted in this respect Bobrishchev-Pushkin, who on the one hand had claimed in *Smena vekh* that "the Russian people were enjoying not what had been stolen, but taken . . . by the right of age-old sufferings, age-old slavery, and labor," and who on the other hand had assured his readers that "everything would be all right—in Russia there would be property and private initiative, commerce and cooperatives."[49] Moreover, Sumskii continued, now that the new Russian bourgeoisie had benefited from the revolution, they were longing for peace and order, and this yearning, too, was rationalized in the Prague collection. The *smenovekhovtsy* justified it with patriotic slogans and, what was particularly attractive to the Soviet bourgeoisie, advocated that peace and order be restored, not through a return to the past, but through the revolution's complete transformation *(vyrozhdenie)*.[50]

Sumskii's conclusion from his analysis of *Smena vekh* was that, notwithstanding its authors' loyalty toward the Soviet regime and even—albeit only in part sincere—toward the Communist party, the collection was a deeply counterrevolutionary phenomenon. He was convinced that the Soviet government fully realized how dangerous the development *Smena vekh* reflected was and that they would do their utmost to paralyze and delay this process. Yet, he did not doubt that their efforts would remain in vain. True to his Menshevik convictions, Sumskii believed that the spontaneous force of history would take its course and that in Russia this force was now at the side of the new bourgeoisie. In his view, it was this which lent the collection *Smena vekh* its strength.[51]

. . .

As opposed to the scornful outrage with which *Smena vekh* had been greeted by most of the émigrés, in Soviet Russia the Prague collection met with a reaction of condescending benevolence, both on the part of the Soviet leadership and among the non-Communist intelligentsia. Reactions there did not come out immediately, however. Commentators in Soviet Russia seemed to be waiting for a signal.[52]

On 12 October 1921 Lenin was shown a telegram, sent by the Soviet mission in Germany to People's Commissar of Foreign Affairs G. V. Chicherin, that referred to "an offer from Professor Iu. V. Kliuchnikov of the group 'New Signposts *(Novye Vekhi)*' " to travel to the international disarmament conference that was to open in Washington on 12 November of that year.[53] Because the Soviet government had not been officially invited to send a delegation, Kliuchnikov proposed that he go there "in a private, semiofficial role *(v chastnoi poluofitsial'noi roli),*" in order to try to influence American political circles "in a desirable spirit for Soviet Russia." This idea apparently appealed to Lenin; he immediately sent a note to V. M. Molotov, secretary of the Bolshevik Central Committee, calling his attention to this "very important" proposal and urging that "one ought to support this."[54] Accidentally or not, the following day, on 13 October, *Izvestiia* appeared with a lengthy, positive editorial on *Smena vekh* signed by its editor, Iu. Steklov,[55] and on 14 October *Pravda* carried an approving reaction to the collection by its leading publicist, N. Meshcheriakov.[56] The silence surrounding the collection was broken, and in the following days and weeks *Smena vekh* was constantly on the pages of the Soviet press. At one point, historian and Deputy People's Commissar for Education M. Pokrovskii even wondered whether readers "were not beginning to be fed up" with it.[57]

On 15 October the trade union organ *Gudok* (Horn) welcomed *Smena vekh* with a triumphant "The proletarian will be victorious."[58] Three days later, the popular Petrograd daily *Krasnaia gazeta* (Red Newspaper) carried an article by former Deputy Commander of the Baltic Fleet's Political Division N. Kuz'min, under the title "The defeat of democracy,"[59] and on 20 October *Petrogradskaia pravda* (Petrograd Truth) appeared with an editorial calling the Prague collection a "new victory for the Soviet regime."[60] The first comments on *Smena vekh* had scarcely appeared in the Moscow papers when the Soviet organs abroad, silent until then, also published reviews of the collection. *Novyi mir,* the organ of the Soviet mission in Berlin, did so on 16 October; its counterparts in Riga and Helsinki on 21 and 25 October, respectively.[61]

From mid-October to the end of December 1921 *Pravda* returned to *Smena vekh* five times,[62] *Petrogradskaia pravda* six times,[63] and *Krasnaia gazeta* and *Izvestiia* once each.[64] In late November *Zhizn' natsional'nostei* (Life of the Nationalities), the organ of the People's Commissariat for Nationalities, devoted an editorial to the issue and a few weeks later harked back to it in a more elaborate article.[65] Finally, in the last weeks of 1921 the first essays on *Smena vekh* appeared in Soviet political and literary magazines: the September–October issue of the literary monthly *Krasnaia nov'* (Red Virgin Soil) had an article by N. Meshcheriakov, the September issue of *Kommunisticheskii internatsional* (Communist International) had one by Iu. Steklov;[66] and the December issue of *Spravochnik Petrogradskogo agitatora* (Handbook of the Petrograd Agitator) carried not only an extensive essay by the rector of Sverdlov Communist University, V. Nevskii, but also a literal, unabridged rendering of Bobrishchev-Pushkin's contribution to the Prague collection.[67] Early in 1922 articles by M. Pokrovskii in *Kommunisticheskii internatsional* and by People's Commissar for Education A. Lunacharskii in *Kul'tura i zhizn'* (Culture and Life) followed,[68] and both *Krasnaia nov'* and *Izvestiia* featured reprints of materials from the new Paris weekly *Smena vekh.*[69]

Besides the numerous reactions to the Prague collection in the press, a number of prominent Soviet leaders also commented on *Smena vekh* in public. Apparently, the first to do so was Trotskii, who at the Second All-Russian Conference of Political Education, held in late October 1921, stressed the collection's usefulness as a means to convince former Tsarist officers to join the Red Army.[70] In the course of November 1921 G. Zinov'ev, head of the Petrograd party organization and chairman of the *Comintern,* referred to the collection in several speeches, including his speech at the inauguration of the Seventh Petrograd Soviet.[71] Lunacharskii spoke out on the issue at length in early December, when he told a journalist of the Soviet press agency ROSTA that Soviet government circles were following with great interest the enormous changes that, judging from the collection *Smena vekh,* were taking place among the Russian émigré community's "best elements."[72] Lenin, for his part, did not publicly react to the collection until the Eleventh Party Congress in March 1922, but told Gor'kii privately that he considered the Prague collection "capable of bringing part of the émigrés to reason."[73]

Where émigré critics had scolded and bitterly reproached Kliuchnikov and his colleagues for being mercenary, most Soviet comments tended to stress the *smenovekhovtsy's* personal integrity,[74] and, what is more, to represent them as people of a greater stature than they in reality were, thus adding to the significance of their conversion. Meshcheriakov called them "great literary names," Steklov termed them "prominent Kadets," and Kliuchnikov's having served in Admiral Kolchak's government was mentioned time and again.[75]

Generally speaking, in their reactions to *Smena vekh* Soviet commentators gave Kliuchnikov and his colleagues benevolent pats on the back, treating them as likely pupils who had come to grasp the obvious truth their teachers had been trying to explain to them, namely, that the proletariat had won a historic victory in Russia and that the anti-Soviet movement had lost the game once and for all.[76] What in this respect particularly appealed to Soviet observers was the *smenovekhovtsy's* outspoken rejection of formal democracy. Their statements on the total bankruptcy of socialism and liberalism were eagerly quoted,[77] and in *Krasnaia gazeta* N. Kuz'min even indicated this as the collection's most important aspect.[78]

At the same time, however, the commentators stressed that the *smenovekhovtsy's* acceptance of the Soviet regime in Russia did not mean that they had become Communists themselves. True, in the very first Soviet article on the Prague collection, Steklov had kept silent about the predominantly Russian nationalist feelings that had prompted Kliuchnikov and his colleagues to reconcile themselves with the new regime in Moscow,[79] but most commentators did draw attention to this and other "survivals *(perezhitki)* of the past" in the *smenovekhovtsy's* thought.[80] What is more, several Soviet observers were convinced that precisely these *perezhitki* made *Smena vekh* such a useful instrument in the hands of the Soviet authorities. Trotskii, for example, believed that the strongly patriotic motifs in *Smena vekh* were "excellent material" for the "ideological conquest" of former Tsarist officers.[81] Lunacharskii, for his part, hoped that *Smena vekh* would offer a platform for cooperating with the Bolsheviks to any remaining representatives of a "real, original bourgeois patriotism" who were concerned with the salvation and consolidation of their motherland and who believed that industrial and cultural progress in Russia was only possible on the basis of what had been achieved in the October revolution.[82]

As Meshcheriakov saw it, under the circumstances, one could say that the *smenovekhovtsy* had "*les qualités de leurs défauts.*" He stressed that even though they had taken the side of the revolution, with their nationalism, mysticism, and their vision of the intelligentsia as "the salt of the earth," Kliuchnikov and his colleagues remained in many ways linked to the past. Meshcheriakov argued, however, that these bourgeois "*perezhitki*" were useful, for they could help other intellectuals with the same ideological shortcomings to take the decisive step and accept the October revolution and the regime that resulted from it. In fact, he saw *Smena vekh* as a bridge, a "Pink" intermediate stage that could help non-Communist intellectuals gradually to pass from "White" to "Red," and join the Communists. Therefore, he concluded, it could prove helpful for attracting specialists into Soviet service and was sure to have a disintegrating influence on the émigré community.[83]

Not all Soviet commentators, however, were prepared simply to accept the "*défauts*" in the thought of Kliuchnikov and his colleagues as "*qualités.*" This was especially true of both left-wing Bolsheviks, who were alarmed by *Smena vekh*'s statements about an evolution of the regime, and officials of the *Comintern* and the People's Commissariat of Nationalities, who opposed the collection's strong nationalist tendency.

Thus, V. Nevskii, who for some time had been one of the leaders of the so-called Workers' Opposition,[84] was clearly displeased with the hopes for a transformation of the Soviet regime that some of the *smenovekhovtsy* expressed. He warned Kliuchnikov and his colleagues that, while they were welcome to offer their services to the new regime, unless they were honestly prepared to transform themselves, "the old lady History would make fertilizer out of them."[85]

M. Pokrovskii, who at the time of the Soviet-German negotiations at Brest-Litovsk had signed a letter of "Left Communists" to the Bolshevik Central Committee, protesting against a possible peace settlement and advocating that "revolutionary war" be continued,[86] was likewise displeased. For him, transmutation of the Soviet regime, or, as he saw it, the substitution of the regime's social basis by a new such basis, was only possible if a more progressive class took the place of a less progressive one. While Pokrovskii admitted that this had been the case in the Germany of Bismarck, where the bourgeoisie had replaced the class of the Junkers, in Soviet Russia such a transmutation was clearly impossible because there could be no more progressive class than the revolutionary proletariat. Consequently, he also advised Kliuchnikov and his colleagues that they should rather transform themselves.[87]

The staff of *Zhizn' natsional'nostei,* for their part, were troubled by the strongly patriotic tones in *Smena vekh,* and understandably, they felt that all this talk of Russia's greatness was "grating upon the ears." Still, for the time being, they were prepared to let the authors of *Smena vekh* find satisfaction for their national pride in the Russian people's achievements. In the end, the people of the Commissariat of Nationalities trusted, the *smenovekhovtsy* and their like would have to come around anyway; they, too, would be forced to realize that the ideal to which the victorious proletariat would remain true was "the universal, not 'Russian,' ideal of Communism."[88]

Even the most understanding Soviet commentators expected that the *smenovekhovtsy* would eventually take the side of the Soviet regime completely and unconditionally. Meshcheriakov did not doubt that Kliuchnikov and his colleagues were "talented pupils," and trusted that in the future "the National-Bolsheviks would lose ever more the bourgeois characteristics of their *Weltanschauung,* and come ever closer to the Bolshevik-Communists *(bol'sheviki-kommunisty)*."[89] Lunacharskii, for his part, expressed the hope that those "deeply patriotic elements" who accepted cooperation with the Soviet regime on the platform of *Smena vekh* would "gradually become absorbed by our party,"[90] and stressed that, in any case, political independence was completely out of the question.[91] The historian and editor of *Petrogradskaia pravda* V. Bystrianskii regarded the appearance of *Smena vekh* as a clear sign that the prediction of the *Communist Manifesto* had come true: "that on the eve of the crash of the old order, part of the representatives of the ruling class would renounce their class, and join that class to which the future belonged."[92] He hoped that the example of Kliuchnikov and his colleagues would not pass by unnoticed among the non-Communist intelligentsia in Russia and would lead to the latter's "direct and unconditional transition under the Soviet banner."[93]

Thus, the prevailing tone of the first Soviet reactions to *Smena vekh* was one of triumphant approval. Some commentators even considered the booklet so useful that they recommended its distribution in Soviet Russia as well. Trotskii, for instance, demanded during his speech at the All-Russian Congress of Political Education that at least one copy of the Prague collection be available in every province.[94] Iu. Steklov, for his part, urged the Soviet authorities to reprint the collection in Russia and distribute it in a great number of copies, both "for the instruction of the bourgeois intelligentsia and for the gratification of the broad working masses, who from reading this collection would become convinced that their sacrificial exploit had forced even people from the opposite camp to bow to the social revolution's great truth."[95]

While Trotskii's wish was most likely complied with, Steklov's call for the collection's wide distribution among Soviet readers remained largely unanswered. True, in late 1921 one thousand copies of the first Prague edition were imported into Soviet Russia,[96] and in January 1922 the collection was indeed republished by the Soviet State Publishing House. However, the imported copies were both hard to come by and beyond the means of many,[97] and the Soviet version of *Smena vekh,* which, incidentally, did not differ in any respect from the Prague version, was not brought out by *Gosizdat* in Moscow, but by its Tver' and Smolensk branches.[98] Moreover, the number of copies of these reprints was small: the Tver' edition came out in 10,000 copies, and the Smolensk version was limited to a mere 7,500 copies.[99] Apparently, the voice of the collection's opponents, which would gain in strength in the course of 1922, did not go entirely unheeded.

As a result, direct access to *Smena vekh* remained limited. If the collection became widely known in Soviet Russia, it was largely due to the numerous comments in the press. It was also on these comments that most non-Communist intellectuals within Soviet Russia had to rely in order to form an opinion,[100] which may have had a considerable influence on their reactions to the collection. Thus, the Moscow historian Iu. V. Got'e, a man of profoundly anti-Bolshevik views close to those of P. B. Struve,[101] withdrew his erstwhile rejection of *Smena vekh* that had been based on Steklov's article in *Pravda* after he had had a chance to read the collection for himself.[102]

Got'e noted in his diary entry for 14 October 1921 that Steklov's article had filled him with indignation toward this "group of flabby Russian intelligentsia renegades," as he called Kliuchnikov and his colleagues. If what had been written about them was true, he felt, "then in the first place they were late, and in the second place, either these were unprincipled fools or they had simply been bought."[103] After having read the collection, however, Got'e felt obliged to admit that it was better and more interesting than he had imagined and that there were no signs of insincerity or corruptness in it. Rather, he now saw the collection as "the voice of those émigrés who were having a hard time of it or were disenchanted."[104]

Got'e appreciated that the *smenovekhovtsy* paid "respect to those who were carrying on cultural work here in spite of everything," and that they did not "hush up" the dark sides of Bolshevism. Still, this did not mean that he endorsed the Prague collection. As T. Emmons, the editor of Got'e's diary, has indicated, while the national and statist themes in *Smena vekh* were dear to Got'e's heart, Got'e could not possibly accept the idea that the Bolshevik regime might have taken up a Russian national mission, and even less could he share the *smenovekhovtsy*'s underlying belief in the genius and "statism" of the Russian common people.[105] In Got'e's view, Kliuchnikov and his colleagues were mistaken in two ways. First, as a result of failing to realize to what extent the Russia of 1921 was decaying and disintegrating, they overestimated the Bolsheviks. Second, they were blinded by feelings of Russian messianism and therefore "did not want to understand that there was no world future in Russia and that Russia had demonstrated with her anarchic rebelliousness *(Pugachev-shchina)* that she was the lowest race." As Got'e saw it, *Smena vekh* was "a mixture of truth, ignorance, and falsehood, both conscious and unconscious," and combined in itself "the touching naïveté of the Russian intelligentsia . . . with its incurable feebleness and flaccidity."[106]

Got'e confined these remarks on *Smena vekh* to his diary. The number of public reactions to the Prague collection by non-Communist intellectuals in Soviet Russia was rather small, certainly compared to the large body of official Soviet reactions.[107] In spite of the relative openness of the NEP, opportunities to speak out were limited. The first public non-Communist reactions to *Smena vekh* came, in fact, from a semiofficial quarter. On 11 November 1921 *Izvestiia* carried an article on the Prague collection by the former prominent Kadet N. Gredeskul, who had taken the side of the Soviet regime in the spring of 1920. Later that month *Put'*, the Soviet organ in Helsinki, published an article on the issue by the literary historian and journalist S. A. Adrianov, also a "nonparty" supporter of the regime.[108]

In his reaction, Gredeskul found that *Smena vekh* was the result of a process that had started among the intelligentsia within Soviet Russia in the course of 1920. In this process, he explained, at least part of the Russian intelligentsia had begun to recant their initial rejection of the revolution in which the Russian people as a whole had entered onto the scene of world history. Indeed, more and more intellectuals had come to regard this historic event as an exploit rather than as a crime, as a germination rather than as a degeneration *(zarodysh* as opposed to *vyrodok)*.[109] According to Gredeskul, one could only be happy that this process now had affected the Russian émigré community as well, and one should sincerely welcome Kliuchnikov and his colleagues. He concluded his article with the solemn declaration that people in Soviet Russia would

> wait for their [the *smenovekhovtsy*'s] return for common work toward the cre-ation of that future great and radiant Russia, that would be 'great,' not in the old sense, but in a new sense, that would not put out the light coming from the West, but, having hoisted [the light] at her own place, would reflect it back to the West, in order eventually to enlighten the whole world with it.[110]

Adrianov's reaction to the Prague collection was entitled "Welcome!," but he kept a far greater distance from Kliuchnikov and his colleagues than Gredeskul, who had shown no reservations toward the *smenovekhovtsy*. Adri-anov found it necessary to assume a haughty attitude and draw a sharp distinc-tion between the Prague group on the one hand and people such as himself on the other. In his view, the main difference between them was this—the *smenovekhovtsy* by their emigration had escaped the hardships their colleagues in Soviet Russia had had to endure in the past few years and, as a result, had not been physically and spiritually hardened in the same way. Adrianov argued that Kliuchnikov and his colleagues lacked that "instinct of tireless searching" so typical of the "tempered" intelligentsia in Soviet Russia, that "eternal unsatisfied inquiry into life that inspired both sustained daily creative labor and, if necessary, fearless destruction." If the *smenovekhovtsy* did accept the revolutionary atmosphere, he added, they did so clearly *à contrecoeur,* preferring a "gentle, not very hasty evolution" instead.[111]

Still, Adrianov believed that émigrés who showed they had not lost all spiritual links with their colleagues in the motherland should be given credit. This was certainly the case with *Smena vekh's* authors, he felt, and therefore they should be encouraged in their undertakings. He hoped that they would "break loose as many victims as possible from the tangled snares of political circles abroad *(zagranichnaia kruzhkovshchina),* and win over as many workers as possible to return to our field *(niva).*" Such returnees should be given a warm welcome, he stressed, as Russia needed honest, educated, and self-denying workers now more than ever; "active work would give them at last the guts that they had so far been lacking."[112]

The practical significance of *Smena vekh* was also stressed by a third "fellow traveler" of the Soviet regime, the publicist I. Lezhnev. He considered it primarily a phenomenon of tactical revision, linked to the immediate needs of the Russian émigrés, who were psychologically incapable of returning home. Like Lenin, he felt that *Smena vekh's* campaign in favor of the Soviet regime might "sober up" at least some of the émigrés. He doubted, however, that the Prague collection could be of any significance for those intellectuals who had not left their country. They had long since gone through the process of accepting the revolution and revising ideological positions; to them, *Smena vekh* was of no concern.[113]

The first article on *Smena vekh* by an opponent of the Soviet regime appeared in early December 1921 on the pages of the Petrograd monthly *Vestnik literatury* (Bulletin of Literature), the organ of the Society for Mutual Aid among Litterateurs and Scientists.[114] Its author, the sociologist P. A. Sorokin, described the Prague collection as an expression of the ideology of the so-called *spetsy* or "bourgeois specialists" and what he called "*gosklienty,*" people who were commercially dependent on the state for orders and concessions. Sorokin argued that these groups were primarily interested in a strong, stable government, and that the actual nature of a regime was of no real concern to them. Still, he continued, it was a universal human tendency to color one's real motives with noble words, and this was exactly what was happening in *Smena vekh:* in the Prague collection, the longing for a supportive government was being dressed up in patriotic terms.[115] Sorokin predicted that, as a result, the collection would be an enormous success in circles of "state clients," while it was sure to meet with hostility among both revolutionaries and counterrevolutionaries, as neither could be expected to reconcile Communism and imperialism, the international and the national cause, or the interests of revolution

and counterrevolution. If thus far a number of Soviet representatives had reacted favorably to the collection, Sorokin argued, this merely showed that they
were no "real" revolutionaries; otherwise, they would have surely seen the
collection as a "slap in the face."[116]

In Sorokin's view, the *smenovekhovtsy's* appeal to the intelligentsia to "regis-
ter as state employees *(zapisyvat'sia v kazennye rabotniki)"* was both strange and
untimely. In the past few years almost all intellectuals had been in state service,
he argued, and the results of this were deplorable. It was precisely this situation
that had made initiative, creativity, and a serious attitude toward work impossible; instead, it had led to apathy and creative impotence. The regime had
finally admitted this in the economic field, Sorokin continued, and it was to
be expected that the same would happen on the cultural level as well. Consequently, even though the *smenovekhovtsy's* appeal for active participation in the
country's reconstruction was more than justified, it made no sense to suggest
that this could only be done in the guise of agents and functionaries of the
regime. Under the New Economic Policy, such an appeal was an absurd
anachronism.[117]

Few non-Communist intellectuals, however, shared Sorokin's belief that
intellectuals in Soviet Russia would in the near future have opportunities for
independent creative work. This became clear during a series of discussions on
Smena vekh organized by the Petrograd *Dom literatorov* in the winter of 1921–
22.[118] On 20 November 1921 *Dom literatorov* called a special assembly of its
members to discuss the Prague collection. The debate drew a full house,[119] yet
few participants were prepared to openly express their views on the subject,
even though the meeting was closed to outsiders. It seems at first that only two
speakers agreed to take the floor, S. A. Adrianov and the ethnographer V. G.
Tan-Bogoraz, the former populist who had come to support the Soviet regime
out of ardent nationalism and a strong belief in the advent of a completely new
world.[120]

Because few of those present had had a chance to read *Smena vekh* themselves, Adrianov opened his lecture with a detailed and, judging from articles
in the contemporary press, rather accurate account of the collection's contents,
in which he emphasized its patriotic motives. Just as he had done in his article
in the daily *Put'*, Adrianov welcomed the *smenovekhovtsy's* change of position
as a basically positive phenomenon, but distanced himself from their hope for
an evolution of the regime.[121] V. G. Tan, for his part, reacted to the collection
with outspoken contempt, feeling that the people in Soviet Russia should
"look down upon the booklet *Smena vekh*." "We are here in the fire, and they
[the collection's authors] are there at a distance," Tan argued. In his view, the
smenovekhovtsy's main mistake was that they interpreted the Russian revolution
from a narrowly nationalist point of view. They failed to see this event as part
of a greater worldwide cataclysm and therefore did not sufficiently appreciate
its significance for world history.[122]

On 24 November, four days after the first meeting, *Dom literatorov* held a second meeting on *Smena vekh,* to which members of different literary organizations had been invited. This time a lengthy and lively debate developed between representatives of a whole gamut of opinions, including N. A. Gredeskul, the journalist S. B. Liubosh (pseudonym of S. B. Liuboshits), the Communist poet Ia. P. Gamza, and the publicist P. K. Guber, a former contributor to the Kadet organ *Rech'* (Speech).[123]

Gredeskul opened the debate by welcoming the *smenovekhovtsy,* but also voiced some criticism of their position. While the feelings of nationalism and patriotism that had prompted them to accept the Soviet regime were absolutely irreproachable, he felt, Kliuchnikov and his colleagues seemed hesitant to draw the logical conclusion from their stand. Somehow, Gredeskul remarked, they appeared not to understand that Russia could only be ensured of a great future if the revolution that had started there conquered the whole world; otherwise she was doomed to become the vassal of the world's imperialist powers.[124] Ia. P. Gamza, for his part, objected to the sharp division between "goals" and "means" that played such an important role in the *smenovekhovtsy's* views. As a member of the Moscow Group of Proletarian Poets, he called on the intelligentsia to side with the Bolsheviks completely and unconditionally and to accept both their tactics and their ideology.[125] S. B. Liubosh set himself up as the guardian of what he regarded as the intelligentsia's time-honored values. A former contributor to the Moscow "Progressist" daily *Utro Rossii* and the Petrograd business paper *Birzhevye vedomosti* (Exchange Gazette),[126] he reportedly caused bewilderment among the audience by calling upon the intelligentsia to go into left-wing opposition to the Bolshevik regime. Ustrialov's remarks about a "descent with the brakes on *(spusk na tormozakh)*" were more than justified, he felt. The intelligentsia should do what they could to "prevent a victory of future philistinism *(pomeshat' torzhestvu budushchego meshchanstva)."*[127]

According to an account of the debate in the contemporary press, the publicist and literary critic P. K. Guber seemed to speak for the majority of those present, who greeted his remarks with lengthy applause. Guber, a former fellow party member of Kliuchnikov, Ustrialov, and Potekhin, saw the collection *Smena vekh* as an expression of both shaken emotions and a sober, considered political idea. In his view, the *"neo-vekhisty* were flesh of the flesh of the old *vekhisty,"* who had always been suspicious of revolution and for whom a great Russia had always been one of the highest ideals. For people like them, Guber argued, it had been impossible not to notice the metamorphoses that were taking place in Soviet Russia: the development of a mighty Red Army, the de facto imperialist policy of the Bolsheviks, their defiant attitude vis-à-vis the Entente, and the introduction of the NEP. If the *smenovekhovtsy* were prepared to accept the Soviet regime, he stressed, it was only because they felt the Bolsheviks had "tamed" the revolution.[128]

Guber agreed with the authors of the Prague collection that the Soviet regime was going through a considerable evolution. He doubted, however, that the *smenovekhovtsy* were drawing the right conclusions from this. In his view, to decide that the recent events in Soviet Russia were the beginning of a "Russian Thermidor" was like trying to use a large scale for a map of a huge territory. What is more, Guber felt that the positive program that Kliuchnikov and his colleagues were proposing was extremely naive. Their hopes to influence the regime for the better by cooperating with the Bolsheviks were unfounded, he feared, for there was not the least indication that the Bolsheviks would give them a chance to do so. The social, political, and legal conditions were not ripe for cooperation with the Bolsheviks. Still, Guber believed, the *smenovekhovtsy* would find support in Soviet Russia. Like Sorokin, he predicted that their views would catch on in circles of *spetsy* and among the most educated members of the NEP bourgeoisie.[129]

Dom literatorov concluded the series of debates on the Prague collection with a third meeting in early January 1922, when the Petrograd literary community assembled in large numbers for a lecture by A. S. Izgoev, one of the contributors to the "old *Vekhi.*" Izgoev admitted that Kliuchnikov and his colleagues had taken up a number of the ideas of *Vekhi,* but argued that at the same time, they had failed to understand the collection's most important aspect—its call for the intelligentsia's moral and spiritual reeducation. He reproached the *smenovekhovtsy* for having proclaimed the state as the absolutely supreme value, to which all other values were subordinated; by doing this, he felt, they had definitively broken with the spirit of *Vekhi.*[130]

Izgoev's speech appeared in a special collection of articles under the title *O Smene vekh* (On Smena vekh), which was published in the first weeks of 1921 by the *Dom literatorov* publishing house "Logos." Other contributors to the collection were P. K. Guber, the journalist and former collaborator of *Rech'* J. Clemens (pseudonym of I. A. Kleinman), and the publicist and writer A. B. Petrishchev, who, as opposed to his Kadet coauthors, was from a Socialist Revolutionary background.[131]

The contributors to *O Smene vekh* characterized the Prague collection as primarily a political declaration, but stressed that as such, it was of little value. What sense could statements about a radical and decisive evolution of the Soviet system have, Izgoev and his colleagues wondered, if they came from six émigrés, rather than from the Bolsheviks themselves.[132] In their view, the *smenovekhovtsy*'s assertions sounded very much like wishful thinking. J. Clemens suggested that this blindness to reality sprang from a messianic *ad astra per aspera* that was not an uncommon reaction to a national catastrophe. He referred in this respect to the messianic movement among nineteenth-century Polish intellectuals.[133] A. B. Petrishchev, for his part, reproached the *smenovekhovtsy* for outwardly showing repentance while in fact accusing others. In his view, this made *Smena vekh* very much a repetition of the old *Vekhi.*[134] He did welcome the collection's basic motif "Back to Russia!," but stressed that this appeal should not be interpreted as a call upon Russian intellectuals to abandon their spiritual independence. The intelligentsia would never give up their main force, Petrishchev reminded his readers.[135]

While the non-Communist intelligentsia in Soviet Russia dismissed *Smena vekh* as of no concern to them, the Soviet authorities found the Prague collection useful under the circumstances. In the coming months they would try to make the most of this opportunity and "squeeze the *Smena vekh* lemon dry."[136]

Chapter Five

THE WEEKLY *SMENA VEKH*

A Second Step toward Reconciliation

Ustrialov found Moscow's triumphant reactions to the collection *Smena vekh* "nauseating" and immediately responded to them with an article in the Harbin daily *Novosti zhizni,* reminding the Bolsheviks that he and his colleagues were "with them, but not theirs."[1] Kliuchnikov and his Paris friends, on the other hand, were delighted with the Soviet reactions. They felt that the Soviet authorities, when confronted with the Prague collection, "had tried to reflect on the sense of the new phenomenon conscientiously and . . . had completely understood it." In their view, the Soviet leaders' attitude vis-à-vis the booklet confirmed once again that it was "not a narrow and intolerant party spirit that governed Russia, but a broad *raison d'état (gosudarstvennyi razum)* and a clear understanding of the international situation."[2]

The Paris *smenovekhovtsy* did not hesitate to accept support from the Soviet authorities for their further undertakings. Kliuchnikov agreed to become the editor-in-chief of a new weekly under Moscow's control, which first appeared in Paris in late October 1921, under the title *Smena vekh.* The journal received regular Soviet funding, apparently channeled through the Soviet trade mission in London.[3] In this way, Kliuchnikov and his friends gave up their independence vis-à-vis the Soviet regime, although, understandably, they did try to keep up appearances in the émigré community.

Strengthened as they were by Moscow's encouragement and support, the Paris *smenovekhovtsy* would not allow anything to put them off. Shortly after the appearance of the Prague collection, Kliuchnikov had sent the writer M. Gor'kii a copy of it, asking him for his opinion on the booklet and on " 'compromising *(soglashatel'skie)*' or 'conciliatory *(primirencheskie)*' or 'pro-Bolshevik' " publications in general and proposing that he contribute to the projected weekly. Kliuchnikov hoped that Gor'kii's backing would prompt other writers and scholars in Soviet Russia to participate as well. He believed that this would further the mutual understanding between the Russian intelligentsia at home and abroad. His hopes were soon disappointed, however, as Gor'kii rejected the proposal, pointing out that the basic idea behind *Smena vekh* was unsound. In Gor'kii's view, the *smenovekhovtsy*'s call for reconciliation could not appeal to anyone, as it was completely outdated in the eyes of the intelligentsia at home, and at the same time absolutely unacceptable to the émigrés.[4]

Gor'kii's response was no doubt a setback for Kliuchnikov and his colleagues, but it did not dishearten them, nor did the indignation and outrage of their émigré critics, who did not always limit themselves to verbal abuse. Soon after the Prague collection's publication, Kliuchnikov and Luk'ianov were asked to give up their teaching positions at various émigré institutions.[5] At the Russian Academic Conference convened in Prague in late October 1921, Kliuchnikov and Potekhin, although given an opportunity to speak out, were shunned by all participants.[6] Moreover, in the fall of 1921 an attempt was made on the life of a Boris Markovich, apparently because of his involvement with the *smenovekhovtsy*.[7]

And still, even in this hostile environment Kliuchnikov and his colleagues did have some support, and from no less a person than the "dean" of the Russian emigration in France, V. A. Maklakov. A well-known lawyer and prominent conservative Kadet, Maklakov had in the summer of 1917 been appointed the Provisional Government's ambassador to France, a post at which he was to remain until the French government recognized the Soviet regime de jure in October 1924.[8]

Maklakov was clearly impressed with the Prague collection. While he did not take a stand on the issue in public, he described the booklet in a private letter to B. A. Bakhmetev, his counterpart in Washington, as "the most interesting of all that had lately been written." In Maklakov's view, the collection was remarkable in two ways: first, because it dealt with the most acute, burning topics of the day; and second, because it approached these questions in a completely new way.[9] This did not mean that Maklakov was prepared to subscribe to the *smenovekhovtsy*'s positions, however. In his letter to Bakhmetev, he stressed that the collection contained both "truth and falsehood," both "indisputable and very disputable things." While he could endorse to a great extent the *smenovekhovtsy*'s criticism of the first Provisional Government and of the White movement and its methods of struggle, he felt at the same time that there was something "from the Evil One" in the collection. The claim of Kliuchnikov and his colleagues "that Bolshevism had brought some new words, which were bound to be victorious also in Europe" was absolutely unacceptable to him.[10]

In spite of these objections, Maklakov found *Smena vekh* so interesting, that he decided to invite Kliuchnikov to the Russian Embassy for a tête-à-tête. On Sunday, 23 October, a week before the first issue of the journal *Smena vekh* was to appear, the two men talked for four hours, and this conversation left Maklakov even more impressed. Kliuchnikov had just returned from London, where he had had several conversations with People's Commissar of Foreign Trade L. B. Krasin, who was then the Soviet plenipotentiary representative in London and, as it seems, Moscow's contact with the Paris *smenovekhovtsy*. What Kliuchnikov told Maklakov about these conversations, especially with respect to the Soviet stand on the issue of Russia's territorial unity, was something of a revelation for him.[11] As Maklakov later wrote in a letter to Bakhmetev, Kliuchnikov had drawn his attention to the Bolsheviks' determination to stand up for Russia's unity, arguing that, although the Soviet leaders were being reproached by their opponents for having given away parts of Russia on all sides, in reality their actions had gone in exactly the opposite direction. Whenever Moscow recognized the independence of some part of the Russian state, this recognition had always been accompanied by actions to assure the reincorporation of this region into the heartland. This had happened in Georgia, Azerbaijan, and Armenia, and Kliuchnikov told Maklakov, so it would be in the case of the Baltic states and the Far East.[12]

For Maklakov, a longtime defender of an indivisible Russia,[13] this representation of Soviet foreign policy was surprising and attractive indeed. Moreover, he felt that the Soviet political system as such contained also a number of most valuable elements, most importantly, the principle of election by several stages *(mnogostepennye vybory)*, as opposed to that of universal, equal, direct, and secret suffrage (the so-called *chetyrekhkhovstka)*, which, in Maklakov's view, reached far beyond the possibilities of Russia's "dark masses," and which he "had hated from the heart already at [the time of] the State Duma." He had to admit that in this light, he could even understand the readiness of Kliuchnikov and his friends to accept the Soviet regime. However, as he confided to Bakhmetev, while his reason could see the possible expediency of the *smenovekhovtsy*'s stand, his conscience excluded the possibility of reconciliation with those who bore the responsibility for such horrors as the Treaty of Brest-Litovsk and the Red Terror.[14] Notwithstanding this criticism, the mere fact that Maklakov took their position seriously could not have but given heart to Kliuchnikov and his colleagues. At the time of the tête-à-tête in the Russian Embassy, they were putting the final touches to the first issue of their new weekly, which would come out in a few days. The stand they took there, however, would completely antagonize Maklakov.

The first issue of the new journal *Smena vekh,* a modest brochure with a grey-blue cover, appeared on the Paris newsstands on Saturday, 29 October 1921. Besides articles by Kliuchnikov, Luk'ianov and Ustrialov, it contained the contributions of new collaborators from the émigré community such as former Tsarist General A. Noskov, as well as a section "from Russia" with pieces by the renowned journalist V. M. Doroshevich and the poet A. A. Blok.

The first issue opened with a declaration of platform, presumably written by Kliuchnikov, in which the editors stated their aims. The new weekly was to be "a second step in the process of reconciliation of the Russian intelligentsia in emigration with Russia and the Russian revolution . . . and a bridge between the Russian intelligentsia abroad and the Russian intelligentsia in Russia." As such, the journal was directed at "all members of the intelligentsia who sincerely and honestly accepted the fact of the great Russian revolution and considered it a mighty historical shift and a first stage in Russia's striving toward vigorous sociopolitical progress." Within this framework, the editors stressed, everyone should be free "to set out for themselves the final goal and possible limits of the Russian revolution's realizations," as no one was "the bearer of absolute truth."[15] On the basis of this platform, which was wide enough to accommodate even Communists, Kliuchnikov attracted a most varied group of contributors to the journal. Besides his former colleagues of the collection *Smena vekh* and a number of émigré sympathizers, including several people of socialist background, it embraced intellectuals in Soviet Russia as well.[16]

The authors of the Prague collection played a rather important part in the new journal, except for Chakhotin, who, as soon as the collection had come out, regretted he had been "inveigled into the undertaking."[17] Over the twenty issues that appeared in all, he limited himself to two contributions, one on the psychology of reconciliation and a second on the need for rationalization of Russian society. Bobrishchev-Pushkin, for his part, provided no less than ten articles on subjects such as Soviet theater, the Russian émigrés' judicial situation, and the values of the French revolution, while Luk'ianov wrote on émigré attitudes toward the famine in Southern Russia, on the Soviet regime's evolution, and on revolutionary culture. Potekhin's contribution included two articles on the consequences of the world economic crisis for Europe and Soviet Russia, an essay on Russo-Austrian relations, and five short satirical pieces on the White emigration under the pseudonym "Skif."[18] Kliuchnikov wrote a whole series of articles for the journal, both under his own name and under the pseudonym "S. L.,"[19] dealing mainly with the role of Soviet Russia in international politics. Just as with the collection *Smena vekh,* it was he who coordinated the whole undertaking.

Over the signature of Ustrialov, finally, the editors printed eight articles nearly all of which had previously appeared in the Harbin daily *Novosti zhizni;*[20] Ustrialov had been regularly sending his writings to Kliuchnikov even before he knew about the latter's endeavors. In early 1922 he sent Kliuchnikov an article he had written especially for the Paris journal, trying to develop the themes that united him with his Paris colleagues, while avoiding what divided them. Under the title "The People in the Revolution," the article represented the October revolution as the deepest expression of the Russian people's soul, in which "instincts of anarchic rebelliousness . . . from time immemorial had come together with a striving for a healthy state organism of great scale and caliber."[21] While Ustrialov did what he could to conceal his ideological differences with the Paris *smenovekhovtsy* from the public, he did, however, criticize the journal's line in private letters, but his pleas for less "revolutionary romanticism" and more independence vis-à-vis Moscow fell on deaf ears.[22]

Besides the authors of the Prague collection, the list of contributors to the journal included a whole series of new names. However, hardly any of these new collaborators published more than a few articles in the weekly; they all remained more or less occasional associates. Moreover, among the émigrés who contributed to the journal, there were almost no people of real standing, the only exceptions being G. K. Lukomskii, a well-known art historian, and V. N. L'vov, the former chief procurator in the Provisional Government.

V. N. L'vov (1872–?), a Samara landowner and right-wing Octobrist, had served as chairman of the Center Faction in the Fourth Duma and as the Provisional Government's chief procurator of the Holy Synod. In the summer of 1919 he found himself in Siberia, and by the fall of 1920 he had joined the Russian émigré community in Paris.[23] After a rather inconspicuous year there, he suddenly raised his voice in favor of reconciliation with the Soviet regime. In mid-August 1921 two French dailies, the popular, moderate Catholic paper *Le Petit Journal* and the left-of-center *L'Oeuvre,* published interviews with L'vov, in which he argued that the Soviet regime was going through a far-reaching evolution toward democracy and advocated the resumption of trade relations with the country as the only way to further this evolution and deepen it.[24]

After these interviews, which angered many émigrés, especially because they portrayed L'vov as a champion of democracy,[25] the former chief procurator lapsed into silence until mid-November, when once again he publicly took a controversial stand. On 12 November 1921 he gave a talk (in Russian) at the Salles des Sociétés savantes in Paris entitled "The Soviet Regime in the Struggle for Russian Statehood *(gosudarstvennost')*." L'vov portrayed the Soviet regime as a regime that had the complete support of the population and argued that it was organizing the Russian state according to the best Slavophile traditions and thus, as L'vov saw it, in accordance with the Russian people's psychology.[26] He now had become convinced that the Soviet regime was a positive force for Russian statehood: it had saved the country from anarchy and would "lead the Russian people onto the road of universal progress . . . and bring them economic and political prosperity."[27]

On that same day, the Paris daily *L'Ere nouvelle,* the organ of E. Herriot's Radical-Socialist party, carried an interview with V. N. L'vov on the situation in the Soviet Republic. Addressing himself to the French public, L'vov prudently avoided expressions such as "Slavophile traditions," and in his careful phrasing suggested that the Soviet regime, now that it had abandoned its radicalism, in fact hardly differed from a Western-style democracy.[28] In the interview, L'vov announced the foundation of a *"mouvement politique russe des*

Ralliés," headed by Kliuchnikov, Luk'ianov, Ustrialov, Potekhin, and himself. He introduced the *Ralliés* to the French public as "liberals, but of the extreme left of the liberal party, equivalent . . . to your radical party, not socialists," and stressed that they had "associated themselves to the government of the soviets *(ralliés au gouvernement des Soviets)"* and were certainly not "converts to Bolshevism." As far as their policy was concerned, L'vov explained that it consisted in recognizing, first, that "the facts were the facts"; second, that the Soviet system was strong and valuable; and third, that the Soviet regime was not necessarily synonymous with Communism. Moreover, L'vov added, he and his colleagues felt they could not ignore the fact that the Soviet regime was going through an evolution and was adapting itself to "the current equilibrium in the world."[29]

This interview, followed by yet another article in which L'vov presented himself again as a democrat of many years' standing who "had never belonged to the reactionary camp,"[30] provoked protests from a whole range of émigré organizations. To their apparent surprise, the staff of *L'Ere nouvelle* were flooded with angry letters to the editor, in which it was strongly denied that L'vov had anything to do with the Russian liberals, or that the so-called *Ralliés* had any support whatsoever in the émigré community. As a result, *L'Ere nouvelle* was forced to conclude that the *Ralliés* were apparently just a small minority among the Russian émigrés and carried very little, if any, weight.[31] It was the last time L'vov's name appeared on the daily's pages.

Whether L'vov's statements in the French press on a movement of *Ralliés* had the endorsement of the Paris *smenovekhovtsy* as a group is unclear, but it seems unlikely. Indeed, in the months after the Prague collection's publication, Kliuchnikov and Potekhin had hoped to gather their following into a real party—Kliuchnikov even intended to christen it the "Neo-Kadet party"[32]— but nothing ever came of this. Not only did their following fall short of expectations but the Paris *smenovekhovtsy* could not agree on which face to assume. Kliuchnikov rejected the *Ralliés* concept as far too vague,[33] while Bobrishchev-Pushkin and L'vov could not possibly accept the "Neo-Kadet" idea.[34] As a result, the Paris circle failed to present itself to the outside world as a close-knit group with a distinct face.

Be that as it may, L'vov's involvement with the Paris *smenovekhovtsy* was short-lived. The former chief procurator contributed two articles on religious freedom under the Soviet regime to the weekly *Smena vekh,* but just ten days after the interview in *L'Ere nouvelle* in which he had linked his own name with that of Kliuchnikov and his colleagues, L'vov publicly distanced himself from the Paris circle. The fifth issue of *Smena vekh* carried a letter to the editor, dated 22 November, in which L'vov asked that he no longer be considered a collaborator for the weekly, because his "political views were now significantly more left-wing."[35] He returned to Soviet Russia in the summer of 1922, where he first served as a member of the so-called Supreme Church Direction and later was employed by various central economic institutions.[36]

The contribution of the art historian G. K. Lukomskii (1884–1940) to the weekly consisted of two small articles that rebutted the often-heard reproach that the Bolsheviks were destroying Russian culture. Until the spring of 1920 Lukomskii had worked in Tsarskoe Selo, Kiev, and Yalta on the cataloguing and restoration of several imperial art collections and residences, in order to prepare them to be opened to the public. In April of that year he traveled to Italy to carry out historical research;[37] he arrived in Paris in August 1920 and apparently never returned to his motherland. Most likely, Lukomskii did not leave Soviet Russia for political reasons. As an émigré, he engaged exclusively in artistic undertakings; his collaboration with *Smena vekh* was therefore rather occasional.

Several names appeared only once on the pages of *Smena vekh*. This was the case with V. M. Belov, a journalist who in 1920 and early 1921 had contributed to such émigré organs as the Berlin Kadet daily *Rul'* and P. N. Miliukov's *Poslednie novosti*.[38] In the spring of 1921 in Tallinn Belov founded the "democratic-national" daily *Svobodnoe slovo* (Free Word),[39] of which he also became editor-in-chief. In the late summer of that year he "changed signposts," taking a stand close to that of Ustrialov.[40] As a result, the outlook of *Svobodnoe slovo* changed dramatically, to such an extent that the Paris daily *Obshchee delo* claimed it was being subsidized by the Soviet mission in Tallinn.[41] Belov contributed one article to the weekly *Smena vekh*—on the Russian émigré community in Estonia—which appeared in the issue of 14 January 1922. As early as the summer of that year he returned to Russia, where he published a caustic booklet on the emigration called *Beloe pokhmel'e* (White Hangover), in which he did not make a single allusion to his former status as a *smenovekhovets,* or even as an émigré.[42]

Other once-only contributors to the Paris weekly were the journalist A. L. Blek (under the pseudonym A. L'vovich), a physician named P. Iakovlev, P. Strelugin, N. Nasvetevich, and S. Steletskii. Nothing is known to me of the latter four. A. L. Blek (1861?–1925), for his part, had been active in the revolutionary movement before the October revolution; he did not remain in the emigration and died in Leningrad in 1925.[43]

Five other emigrants also contributed one article each to the Paris journal, but continued to collaborate with the *smenovekhovtsy*. These were the writer R. B. Gul', the engineer and journalist B. V. Diushen, the economist G. G. Shvittau, the journalist K. Treplev, and P. A. Sadyker. All were to play a part in the Berlin daily *Nakanune*.

R. B. Gul' (1896–1986), the future editor of the major émigré journal *Novyi zhurnal* (New Review), which he would head from 1959 until his death, made his debut as a *smenovekhovets* with a lyrical article in the Paris journal's ninth issue, in which he represented the October revolution as an expression of the Russian people's suppressed soul.[44] Before the revolution Gul' had been a student at the Moscow Law Faculty, where he had met both Kliuchnikov and Ustrialov, until he was drawn into the army in 1916.[45] After the October revolution he joined General Kornilov's Volunteer Army and took part in the so-called Ice March.[46] In 1918 he was mobilized by the Ukrainian Hetman Skoropadskii, taken prisoner by the forces of S. A. Petliura, and finally found himself in a German prisoner-of-war camp.[47] One of V. B. Stankevich's associates in early 1920 in the Berlin group *Mir i trud,* Gul' became in 1921 a collaborator in A. S. Iashchenko's monthly *(Novaia) Russkaia kniga* and in 1922 was appointed the journal's editorial secretary.[48]

Gul' first contributed to *Nakanune* in May 1922, when his novel *V rasseian'i sushchie* (Those Who Are Existing in Dispersion), in which he describes how a young Russian worker in Germany decides to break away from the suffocating émigré community and return home,[49] appeared in the paper's weekly literary supplement. He joined the staff of *Nakanune* in the fall of 1923, after the return to Soviet Russia of A. N. Tolstoi, whom he replaced as the editor of the daily's literary supplement.[50]

B. V. Diushen (1886–1949), an electrotechnical engineer by training, had in 1917 been appointed "Commissar of the Provisional Government" in Yaroslavl province. In the fall of that year he was elected a member of the Constituent Assembly for the SRs, and in the summer of 1918 he played a major role in the Yaroslavl anti-Bolshevik uprising, in which Kliuchnikov was also involved. Diushen was arrested but escaped prosecution, apparently thanks to the mediation of his wife Valentina, who had been a Bolshevik since 1905 and was a personal friend of A. M. Kollontai. Fleeing to Siberia and from there to the Baltic region, Diushen became involved with the White forces of General Iudenich.[51] In the fall of 1919 he joined the staff of the Tallinn daily *Svoboda Rossii* (Russia's Freedom), the organ of Iudenich's "Northwestern" government, and in late December of that year, after the departure of the paper's editor G. I. Kirdetsov, became de facto its editor-in-chief.[52] In mid-1920 he moved to Berlin, where he started teaching correspondence courses organized by the Berlin division of the YMCA for Russian émigrés.[53]

In February 1921 Diushen gave a public speech distancing himself from the SRs and from the "slogans of the March revolution," which a year before he so ardently had defended on the pages of *Svoboda Rossii.*[54] In his lecture, Diushen argued that one should distinguish between the Communist party, which in his view would be granted only a short life in Russia, and the Soviet system, which he believed to contain many "healthy elements." As examples of such "elements," Diushen mentioned, first, the Red Army, which he considered a truly national Russian army; second, the thirst for knowledge among the lowest popular classes, who in his view were waking up after a thousand years of serfdom; and third, the role he believed the intelligentsia could play in the Soviet institutions. He was convinced that those intellectuals who had taken up work there would manage to raise these institutions to a high level *(vysoko podniat')*. On the question of who eventually would rule Russia if, as he predicted, the Communist party made its exit, Diushen remained vague. In any case, he believed, it would not be the political parties. In Russia, their historical mission had been fulfilled; their place would be taken by "new forces."[55] In the course of 1921 Diushen joined the Soviet trade mission in Berlin.[56] Because Kliuchnikov also joined the trade mission in October of that year,[57] it was presumably there that the two men met and decided to cooperate. Diushen contributed an article on the Soviet trade unions and the NEP to the weekly *Smena vekh*, which appeared in the very last issue. He became one of the leading figures in the Berlin daily *Nakanune*.

G. G. Shvittau was a young economist from Popular Socialist background,[58] a former privatdozent in political economy and statistics at Petrograd University.[59] The October revolution surprised him on a scientific mission to Germany, so he became an émigré involuntarily.[60] Shvittau participated in the Paris journal's last issue with an article on the situation of Russian cooperative societies *(kooperatsii)*, a form of economic organization of which he was a confirmed advocate.[61] He was to edit *Nakanune*'s weekly economic supplement until the spring of 1923.[62]

The journalist K. Treplev (pseudonym of A. S. Sorokin [1884–?])[63] had covered the civil war in the South as correspondent for a number of South Russian newspapers.[64] From his contribution to *Smena vekh*, it appears that after the civil war he found himself in the Russian émigré community in Greece.[65] In 1922 he became a contributor to *Nakanune* as well.

Finally, P. A. Sadyker had been a member of Kliuchnikov's Paris circle from the very beginning, but he had hardly played an important role in the group. Apparently, he "was no publicist";[66] he did not take part in the collection *Smena vekh*, and his contribution to the Paris weekly consisted of one article dealing with the explosive international situation,[67] and a highly confused account of a lecture on the Prague collection by the émigré law professor A. M. Gorovtsev.[68] Sadyker would become a member of *Nakanune*'s editorial board, but his role there would be limited to that of an accountant.[69]

Only three émigré participants played a more important part in the weekly *Smena vekh*. This was the case with F. Kudriavtsev, who provided thirteen articles on international politics, and M. Grigor'ev, who published seven articles on the economic situation in Soviet Russia. Grigor'ev was a proponent of a middle course between a Communist planned economy and a market economy for Russia. Despite their substantial contribution to the weekly *Smena vekh*, and later also to *Nakanune*, no further information on either of them has been found.

There was less difficulty in the case of A. A. Noskov, *Smena vekh*'s specialist on military affairs. A Tsarist major general, Noskov had served at the Chief Administration of the Tsar's General Staff,[70] and under Kerenskii had headed the Third Army. By the spring of 1920 he found himself in Paris, where he was initially in favor of international recognition of General Wrangel's Crimean government,[71] only to change his view as soon as the fortunes of war turned. By mid-October, Noskov withdrew his support for the White general; on the pages of the Paris daily *L'Information* he began to stress the latter's weakness and lack of popular support, and to praise the Red Army instead.[72]

In an article in *L'Information* of 8 December 1920, Noskov advocated that Western Europe adopt a policy of appeasement versus Soviet Russia and resume trade relations with the country. This would gradually bring about Russia's resurrection, Noskov argued, and at the same time help to overcome the economic crisis that was afflicting the whole world. While he admitted that this would also enhance the Soviet government's prestige, he asked his readers whether it was not "more dangerous for the West to continue to fan the hate of the Russian masses than to work toward the resurrection of their normal life?"[73]

The creation on 18 July 1921 of the so-called All-Russian Committee for Aid to the Hungry, which united leading Soviet officials, two former Provisional Government ministers, and a number of prominent Kadets and nonparty intellectuals,[74] was for Noskov a clear sign that, faced with the horrors of famine, Russia had found "the only way capable of regenerating the people in all its greatness: that of the reconciliation of all classes of the population."[75] However, when the committee was disbanded on 31 August of that year and its "bourgeois" members arrested, Noskov prudently kept silent.

In the meantime, he began to put into practice his own recommendations for resuming trade relations with Soviet Russia. By November 1921 he had established a commercial firm in Paris, situated in rue de Clichy, that had commercial dealings with Soviet Russia through the intermediary of the Soviet Trade Delegation in London. According to the observations of the French secret services, Noskov's firm also played a role in the process of transferring Soviet subsidies for *Smena vekh*.[76] After the Paris journal ceased publication, Noskov became a contributor to *Nakanune*. He remained in Paris, regularly sending his articles to Berlin until 1923, when the French authorities expelled him from the country, and he joined his colleagues in the German capital.[77]

If there were hardly any people of standing among the émigré contributors to *Smena vekh,* the opposite was true for the collaborators from Russia. On the pages of the Paris weekly appeared poetry by A. A. Blok (1880–1921), M. A. Kuzmin (1875–1936), and S. M. Gorodetskii (1884–1967), as well as prose by established authors such as the well-known publicist and former editor-in-chief of the Moscow daily *Russkoe slovo* V. M. Doroshevich (1865–1922), the writer V. V. Muizhel' (1880–1924), and the ethnologist and writer V. N. Tan-Bogoraz (1865–1936). Moreover, three not insignificant art critics and literary historians published in the journal: P. S. Kogan (1872–1932), a professor at Moscow University who in 1921 became chairman of the State Academy of

Arts; the young literary critic E. F. Gollerbakh (1895–1942), and the art critic N. P. Asheshov (1866–1923).

This did not mean that Kliuchnikov's hopes for widespread participation by intellectuals from Soviet Russia came true, however. Not only was the number of contributors from Soviet Russia limited, most remained merely casual associates. In certain cases, the use of the term *collaborator* was not even justified. Thus, the poetry of Blok, Kuzmin, and Gorodetskii that appeared in *Smena vekh* had not been written especially for the Paris journal; Kliuchnikov and his colleagues simply reprinted it with a few words of comment.

Muizhel', Asheshov, Tan, and Gollerbakh, in the summer and early fall of 1921, all began contributing to *Put'* (the organ of the Soviet mission in Helsinki,[78] where Kliuchnikov had entered into contact with the Soviet authorities). Before long their names also appeared on the pages of *Novyi put'* and *Novyi mir*, the dailies of the Soviet missions in Riga and Berlin. Because the Soviet authorities were involved in *Smena vekh* from the very beginning, it seems likely that it was through their intervention that Muizhel' and his friends began collaborating there. Most of their articles appeared in the Paris weekly after the Finnish authorities had forced *Put'* to cease publication in early January 1922;[79] they all became contributors to *Nakanune*, as well as to I. G. Lezhnev's journal, *(Novaia) Rossiia*.

As indicated, the part played by the different contributors "from Russia" in *Smena vekh* was limited: none of them published more than a few articles in the journal. Still, besides these rather occasional collaborators, the journal did have its "own Moscow *smenovekhovets*"[80]—to use the expression of G. P. Struve in his study of Russian literature in exile. This was S. B. Chlenov (1890–1938?), a young Moscow lawyer and economist,[81] whom the editors of *Smena vekh* introduced to the readers as "a representative of the 'old' intelligentsia—Chlenov had always been a leftist but never a Communist—who was animated by the enthusiasm of creating a new Russia."[82]

In the spring and summer of 1917, Chlenov had been a member of the so-called Commission for the Protection of the New Order *(Komissia po obespecheniiu novogo stroia)*, founded by the Moscow Soviet and consisting of representatives of the latter organ, the socialist parties, and the city's College of Judicial Investigators.[83] In the summer of 1921 he became a regular contributor to *Pechat' i revoliutsiia* and *Krasnaia nov'*, where he published mainly book reviews and articles on the situation in Germany.[84] By the time Chlenov started contributing to *Smena vekh*, he was teaching at the so-called Institute of Red Professors in Moscow, where he held seminars at the Institute's economic department. He would retain this position throughout the 1920s.[85]

Besides his work as a teacher and scholar, Chlenov also remained active as a counsel; he was a member of the Moscow College of Counsels for the Defense.[86] In the summer of 1922 he took part in the defense at the mammoth SR trial in Moscow, where the remaining Socialist Revolutionary leaders in

Soviet Russia were accused of having caused millions of casualties during the civil war.[87] On that occasion Chlenov was one of the defenders, not of the actual accused, but of a second group of "pseudodefendants." This group consisted of former SRs who were supposed to incriminate the accused SR leaders and at the same time sing the praises of the Soviet regime. While the first group was being defended by a number of well-established Russian lawyers and representatives of the international socialist movement, such as the Belgian socialists E. Vandervelde and A. Wauters, the second group was assisted mainly by Soviet political figures, including N. I. Bukharin. Apart from V. Veger, Chlenov was in fact the only lawyer among the defenders of the second group.[88] Furthermore, in November 1923 Chlenov acted as de facto public prosecutor on behalf of the Soviet government in the case against M. Konradi, a Russian émigré who in May 1923 had killed V. V. Vorovskii, the head of the Soviet delegation to the Conference of Lausanne.[89]

Judging from his role in both the SR and the Konradi trial, it is clear that, while Chlenov was not a party member, he did associate himself with the Soviet regime very closely indeed. That the editors of the Paris journal took the side of this "leftist," opposing him to Ustrialov, whose views they called "right-wing for a *smenovekhovets*,"[90] was symptomatic of the Paris *smenovekhovtsy*'s ideological evolution in the months after the Prague collection's publication.

. . .

Looking back on *smenovekhovstvo*, Ustrialov wrote in January 1925: "The ideological meaning of the movement . . . was expressed best of all by our Prague booklet. The Paris journal that followed it, and after that, even more so, the Berlin daily, obscured its true appearance because of imaginary tactical considerations."[91] In the eyes of I. Lezhnev, on the other hand, it was the weekly's practical aspect that stood out:

> At this moment the *practical* tasks of the émigré community make up the decisive motive for the *smenovekhovtsy*. That is why for a proper evaluation of this new movement the collection that appeared *last year* is absolutely insufficient. The physiognomy of the group is to a far greater extent revealed in the weekly *Smena vekh* than in the collection. . . . In the emigration up to two million people have accumulated, who should be returned to Russia but who, however, in their actual psychological state are incapable of returning. The group *Smena vekh* conducts among them large-scale agitation in favor of the Soviet regime, and considers this one of its most important tasks.[92]

Both Ustrialov's observation, pointing out the ideological shift between the collection *Smena vekh* and the journal of the same name, and Lezhnev's, which drew attention to the Paris weekly's practical side, were entirely justified. The Paris journal addressed itself primarily to Russian émigré intellectuals,[93] trying

to convince them that reconciliation with the Bolshevik regime was reasonable, and that it was now possible to return to Russia to live and work there.
Several subjects that were of obvious interest to potential repatriates, such as
the development of industry and trade in Soviet Russia since the introduction
of the NEP, the situation of Russian culture, and the state of the Red Army,
had been treated in the Prague collection only in a very general way; numerous
articles in the journal *Smena vekh* now dealt with those topics in greater detail.
The editors of the journal wanted to show their readers that Russia was no
longer the scene of horrors and atrocities, that it was no longer merely an
object for the experiments of Communist doctrinaires. Instead, they emphasized, the signs of normalization and stabilization were unmistakable.

Apparently anticipating the practical questions of those readers who had
already made up their minds to go back, *Smena vekh* published a series of letters
from Russia, describing the conditions of life in Moscow and Petrograd. These
letters showed that while there were no longer such problems as shortages of
provisions or heating, it was still very difficult to find housing in these cities.
Even so, the tone of the letters was optimistic. The government was taking
energetic measures to settle the problem, it was argued, and a change for the
better was soon to be expected.[94]

Several articles, dealing with the situation of art and theater in Soviet Russia
and with the efforts of the Soviet government to introduce changes to schools
and universities, assured the émigrés that intellectual and cultural life in Russia
was not dead.[95] The contributors to *Smena vekh* admitted that the October
revolution had caused part of the old culture to collapse, but they were quick
to point out that the only elements to have disappeared were those which, in
any case, no longer served a purpose. Basically, the Paris *smenovekhovtsy* argued,
the revolution had done away with all that had been decadent and fossilized in
Russian culture and had changed its character from an elite culture to a popular
culture. Inevitably, this had entailed a loss of sophistication, but this had been
balanced by the freshness and spontaneous strength that had been gained. The
revolution had breathed new life into culture, they stressed.[96]

Kliuchnikov and his colleagues were aware, however, that it was not sufficient for an intellectual to know that the culture in his motherland had not
died. There was another, even more important question on his mind: what
about intellectual freedom in Russia, what about freedom of speech and the
press? The answer that the contributors to *Smena vekh* gave in this respect was
simple: for the time being, freedom of opinion was impossible in Russia. They
stressed, however, that it was not the Soviet government that was to blame.
They compared the Soviet Republic to a besieged town, to a ship in a storm:
in a situation of mortal danger, individual freedom was out of the question.[97]
The Paris *smenovekhovtsy* were absolutely convinced that as soon as all enemies
of Soviet Russia ceased their hostilities, freedom would be restored. They

welcomed the replacement of the Cheka by the GPU in February 1922 as a milestone:

> The inevitable is coming true. On this [basis] did we make our call for civil peace in Russia—for reconciliation and creative work. The horrible weapon of revolutionary terror, which made conditions for creative work in Russia endlessly difficult, and infected both rulers and ruled with the spirit of arbitrariness, is disappearing from the scene of life. . . . The violence of dictatorship, inevitable in a period of harsh struggle, will be ousted further by a dictatorship of law.[98]

All the articles in the Paris journal on the situation of the Soviet economy stressed the necessity of coming to an intermediate form between planned economy and free-market economy. The authors rejected the possibility of returning to a genuine free-market economy as "reactionary, both economically and socially,"[99] but stressed at the same time that not only state property but also private property should be considered "inviolable," if only because of its benefit for the state.[100] Kliuchnikov and his colleagues believed that the NEP would lead to the desired intermediate form, and they published several enthusiastic articles on the new policy. However, the authors rarely substantiated their optimistic appraisals of the NEP with factual information. Indeed, in the twenty issues of the journal, only two articles provided any facts at all. In the issue of 12 November 1921 an article entitled "The NEP According to Statements of the Soviet Press over the Period September–October 1921" cited without comment such questionable sources such as *Izvestiia, Pravda,* and *Ekonomicheskaia zhizn'*.[101] In the issue of 4 March 1922 Iu. N. Potekhin answered criticism from the Paris daily *Poslednie novosti* that *Smena vekh* had failed to document its "creative process" thesis by listing various figures—he did not mention his sources—indicating substantial improvement in the economic situation of Soviet Russia. While Potekhin admitted that the production of the Russian economy still remained far below the prewar level, he pointed out that, given the destruction caused by more than seven years of war, nothing else could be expected. It was easy for those in emigration to write indignant articles about the miserable state of the Russian economy, Potekhin argued; at least, the Russian people were trying to do something about it. "With failures and errors, slowly and laborously the creative work of the popular masses is building Russia brick by brick."[102]

As opposed to Lezhnev, who regarded the Paris weekly as even more characteristic of *smenovekhovstvo* than the Prague collection, Ustrialov felt that in the journal *Smena vekh* the movement's "true appearance" was being "obscured." In Ustrialov's view, Kliuchnikov and his colleagues were sliding to the left, falling prey to "revolutionary romanticism." Indeed, while the Prague collection had attempted to show that, all things considered, the Bolsheviks were not merely the destructive force they had first appeared to be, the weekly

Smena vekh exalted the glorious future that Kliuchnikov and his Paris friends expected the October revolution and the Soviet regime would bring Russia and the world. And while the collection had stressed the national value of the October revolution, the weekly—the "second step" toward reconciliation with that revolution—emphasized its international importance.

In the editorial to the journal's first issue, the Paris *smenovekhovtsy* stressed that the revolution had turned out to be "more grandiose" than anyone could have supposed. It was now clear, they argued, that the cause of Russian progress was also the cause of worldwide progress and that, thanks to the new Russia "born out of the hell of revolution," it would eventually be possible to realize stable international peace. Once this was reached, Kliuchnikov and his colleagues trusted, the "Great Russian revolution's merits" would be recognized, not only by the Russians themselves but by the whole of mankind as well.[103]

A common observation on the journal's pages was that the crisis of the Russian economy should be placed in a broader perspective: the whole of Europe, if not the whole world, was passing through an economic crisis. What is more, the Paris *smenovekhovtsy* argued, the character of this crisis was not exclusively economic: it was also a social and political crisis. The contributors to *Smena vekh* drew attention to the rising unemployment, galloping inflation, and growing labor unrest in many countries; and to the highly volatile international situation. Indeed, they believed that as a result of the war, the social and political situation in the world had become as explosive as it had been in Russia on the eve of the October revolution.[104]

In contrast to Ustrialov, who thought of worldwide socialism only as a remote, regulatory idea and who ruled out world revolution under the given circumstances,[105] Kliuchnikov and his Paris colleagues were convinced that a world revolution was in the offing. Yet, even though they regarded a radical change of Western society as both unavoidable and desirable, at the same time they feared the horror and destruction that, in their view, would inevitably accompany a global revolution. They believed that this could be averted only if the other countries would learn from what had happened in Russia.[106] During its revolution, they argued, Russia had been the object of social, political and economic experiments. Many of the changes the Russian revolutionaries had tried to bring about had been extremist and infeasible; however, as time went on, moderation and realism had gained the upper hand, and the creative forces of evolution had taken the place of the destructive forces of revolution. As a result, Kliuchnikov and his colleagues stressed, a new social, political, and economic order was taking shape that was both revolutionary and realistic.[107] This new order would most likely offer a way out of the crisis, not only for the Russian people, but for mankind as a whole.[108] If the other nations were to learn from the results of the Russian experiment and adopt the ideals of the

Russian revolution in their developed, moderate form, it would be possible to bypass the painful shocks of revolution.

The contributors to the collection *Smena vekh* stressed that the social truth of the October revolution had ensured Soviet Russia of the sympathy of the working classes throughout the world. In several articles of the journal, it was argued that if the ruling classes of the capitalist countries maintained their hostility toward revolutionary Russia, the working classes would follow the Russian example and take their future in their own hands.[109] On the other hand, if the capitalist countries were to make overtures to the Soviet Republic, revolution would become superfluous. Therefore, Kliuchnikov and his colleagues argued, it was to the other countries' advantage to seek rapprochement with Soviet Russia; she should be invited to participate as an equal partner in the process of consultation and collaboration at an international level, not in spite of her revolutionary character, but exactly because of it.[110] As Kliuchnikov stated in the issue of 27 November 1921: "A world revolution cannot be avoided by struggle against (an officially Communist) Soviet Russia, but only by reconciliation with her, exactly as she is."[111]

The collection *Smena vekh* had advocated collaboration of non–Bolshevik intellectuals with the Soviet regime, arguing that this would deepen the regime's evolution toward moderation. In the same way, the journal *Smena vekh* preached international reconciliation and cooperation with Soviet Russia, alleging that such contact would influence this evolution in a favorable sense. In an article entitled "The International Significance of Russia," Kliuchnikov wrote:

> When Russia enters the world community, she will not only influence other peoples; she will experience their influence herself. The more complete the community between Russia and the other peoples becomes, the quicker Russia will recover from her revolutionary pains, and the greater the ease with which she will become a factor of universal progress.[112]

The *smenovekhovtsy* assigned a prominent role to Soviet Russia in defusing the explosive international situation. As has been indicated, they believed that the ideals of the Russian revolution could provide the basis for a new world order that would make wars in the future impossible.[113] In their view, Russia could show the world the way of real solidarity and justice and teach it a "healthy internationalism" that would at the same time preserve the singularity of the different nations and put an end to chauvinist nationalism and imperialism.[114] In this way, they believed, all nations of the world would be united in a peaceful union, of which revolutionary Russia would take the helm. This motif, merely touched upon in the Prague collection, played a most important role in the Paris weekly.

The idea of an "indivisible political and judicial union" in which all peoples of the world would live together in peace and justice had obsessed Kliuchnikov ever since the days of the world war. He had at first vested his hopes in the Allies and the League of Nations, but by early 1921 he turned toward Bolshevism, which he now considered a new, revolutionary program for worldwide unity. In the course of 1921 Kliuchnikov's vision on how universal unification and pacification should be achieved had taken an ever more distinct shape. In the summer of that year he had expressed his views on the issue in lectures in Paris and Brussels.[115] Moreover, he had been working on a book, entitled *Na velikom istoricheskom pereput'i* (At the Great Historical Crossroads), which would appear in Berlin in the spring of 1922 as a "publication of the weekly *Smena vekh*."[116]

On the pages of *Na velikom istoricheskom pereput'i* Kliuchnikov now unequivocally portrayed Bolshevism as the radical force that alone would be capable of breaking the deadlock in which the world found itself after the failure of both the German and Allied peace program.[117] The principles of inequality and equality on which, in his opinion, these programs had been based had shown their impracticability, he argued, and the only principle that offered a way out and could serve as the basis for uniting mankind was complete solidarity.[118] Moreover, he believed that to achieve this, the world would have to go through a revolution; in certain cases, as he stressed in the preface to *Na velikom istoricheskom pereput'i*, "revolution became the most natural *(estestvennoe)* and beneficial *(blagotvornoe)* social condition."[119]

Kliuchnikov was convinced the Russian people could play a leading role in this process. Not only had they gone through a revolution themselves, but even more importantly, the Russian national character with its far-reaching spirit of sacrifice and its innate universality was also most fitted for such a role. In Kliuchnikov's view, that Lenin had fully understood this had been one of the main reasons for the Bolsheviks' success.[120] As a result, he concluded, Russia was now better suited than any other nation to show the world the way to a new society based on pioneering social, political, and economic principles, to the "unity of mankind *(edinstvo chelovechestva)*."[121]

Here, too, Kliuchnikov made it clear that, notwithstanding the need for revolutionary change, one should try at all costs to keep the suffering and destruction in this process to an absolute minimum. He saw but one way to achieve this, to "humbly bow one's head before the inevitable course of events," and "voluntarily give way to [world revolution] in all its fundamental demands." "In the case of such obedience to destiny," Kliuchnikov stressed, "the Great Social Revolution would take place, neither as a revolution in our Russian experience of the word nor accompanied with shocks in the Russian style," but "smoothly and systematically."[122]

Undoubtedly, Kliuchnikov's views played a decisive role in setting the tone of the Paris journal, although similar views were expressed by other contributors to the weekly. Shvittau, for instance, believed that by understanding and accepting the inevitable process of global revolution, complete destruction of the world's cultural heritage could be avoided, and the whole of mankind would eventually attain unity.[123] For his part, Luk'ianov looked at the question from a somewhat different perspective, one closer to the official Moscow position. He dreamed aloud of a "united worldwide state of workers *(edinoe mirovoe gosudarstvo trudiashchikhsia)*" and argued that the universal adoption of revolutionary economic and social principles after the Soviet model was "a question of time—if the bourgeoisie of the world knew how to grant further concessions; or of world revolution—if the bourgeoisie were to stubbornly cling to its former positions."[124] In any case, the idea of a worldwide, peaceful union of nations in which Soviet Russia would play a leading role was for the participants in the journal, nationalists as they were, a most alluring prospect. As A. V. Bobrishchev-Pushkin put it: "The new Russia united her national tasks with those in the international sphere. The antithesis between the nation and internationalism was only a seeming antithesis. What can be more dignifying for a nation than to take the lead in the great international unification?"[125] Consequently, Soviet Russia could be sure of playing a prominent role in the future: depending on the attitude of the capitalist governments, revolutionary Russia would either become the vanguard of the working classes in a world revolution, or play a leading role in securing unity and peace among the nations.[126]

In this light, Kliuchnikov and his Paris friends considered it crucial that the Soviet regime retain its essentially revolutionary character.[127] In the editorial of the weekly's second issue, which was devoted to the forthcoming fourth anniversary of the October revolution, they made it clear that while they welcomed the "lowering of the revolutionary wave," they certainly did not want all "the Red, the new, that which justified the sacrifices that had been made" to be lost.[128] A few weeks later, they openly distanced themselves from Ustrialov, reproaching him for "understanding the evolution of the Soviet regime as a far-reaching reconciliation with the past and a return to social-political forms from which all the radically new, the daring, the 'October' *(oktiabr'skoe)* had been excluded."[129]

In fact, Kliuchnikov and his friends now felt that for the time being the "tactical retreat" of the NEP as it stood, with its limited liberalization in the economic, political, and judicial fields, went far enough. They seemed to consider the corrections the New Economic Policy had made to the Soviet regime irreversible. If the Soviet leaders reneged on this point, Kliuchnikov and his colleagues believed, it would surely deprive them of all popular support; this was a risk the Bolsheviks would not take. Luk'ianov referred in this respect to the assurance of People's Commissar of Foreign Affairs G. V. Chicherin that "the NEP stood for a true proletarian Thermidor *(podlinnyi proletarskii termidor)*."[130] As a result, the Paris *smenovekhovtsy* felt that "it was no longer so necessary or desirable for the Soviet regime soon to abandon the Communist ideal, i.e., to change Russia and the whole world." Not only would this "deprive the Russian revolution of its emotional content *(pafos)* and reduce its leaders to ordinary political opportunists,"[131] they feared, it would also make it impossible to justify the Russian people's sacrifices of the past four years.[132]

. . .

With its emphasis on the need for international reconciliation with Soviet Russia, the weekly *Smena vekh* appeared at a time when full, juridical recognition of the Soviet government was very much under discussion. Over the past two centuries Russia had become an important element in the European balance of power and had assumed a central place in the continent's economy, both as a supplier of raw materials and as a market for manufactured goods. That it had ceased to play this role after the October revolution was seriously hampering the process of political stabilization and economic recovery in postwar Europe. Therefore, as soon as hope had evaporated that the Soviet regime would soon disappear, government circles in Western Europe began to realize the need for some kind of relationship with the Soviet Republic. They increasingly understood that economic and political links with Soviet Russia would in the end be inevitable and that an acceptable formula for such relations should be found.[133]

A pioneering role in this respect was played by the British government, headed by Prime Minister David Lloyd George. In February 1920, immediately after the British decision to withdraw support for the Whites in the Russian civil war, Lloyd George had publicly expressed his belief that while all efforts to "restore Russia to sanity by force" had failed, she could be "saved" by trade.[134] He was convinced that establishing "normal" commercial and diplomatic relations between Soviet Russia and the rest of the world would have a "civilizing" effect on Bolshevism. As Lloyd George saw it, this would at least mitigate the harshness of the Soviet regime and eventually perhaps even cause it to fully adapt itself to the outside world. At the same time, he hoped that a resumption of Anglo-Russian trade relations would serve purely British interests as well. He trusted, first, that this would boost the British economy and thus reduce unemployment; and second, that it would be possible to use trade negotiations with Soviet Russia to secure an end to Soviet propaganda, something that was posing a serious threat to British imperial interests, especially in Asia.[135]

British-Soviet trade negotiations began in the spring of 1920, after the Allied Supreme Council's decision to lift the economic blockade of Soviet Russia, continued for several months, and after an interruption in the summer of 1920 caused by the Soviet-Polish war, concluded with the signing of a trade agreement on 16 March 1921.[136] In the following months several other countries took Britain's lead, the most important being Germany and Italy. Thus, on 6 May 1921 a somewhat broader agreement providing also for the exchange

of diplomatic missions was concluded between the Soviet and German governments, and on 26 December of that year the Italian government signed a trade
agreement with Moscow after the model of the Anglo-Russian accord.[137]

While these agreements represented de facto recognition of the Soviet regime, they fell short of conferring to it full de jure recognition. It was understood, however, that such would follow in due course, provided that the Soviet
government was willing to make certain concessions. Thus, the accord between the Soviet Republic and Germany was qualified as "provisional" *(vorläu-
fig)*,[138] and the Anglo-Russian agreement was explicitly presented as a
preliminary accord, "pending the conclusion of a formal general Peace Treaty
[between the two countries] . . . by which their economic and political relations would be regulated in the future."[139]

There were in fact two main issues that stood in the way of full international
recognition of the Soviet government: first, the nationalization of foreign
property by the Soviet government and its repudiation of foreign debts incurred by the Tsarist or Provisional governments; and second, the question of
Soviet propaganda. While Soviet propaganda was a source of especial irritation
to the British government, which feared its effects both in the colonies and at
home, the question of nationalized property and debts was of great concern to
France. Not only had the French invested more than any other nation in the
Russian economy, they also held the largest share of Russia's foreign debts.
Moreover, as opposed to Russia's debts to Britain, nearly three quarters of
which were due to the government, most of her debts to France were owed
to individual citizens. The estimated 1.5 million private claimants were a force
the French government could not afford to ignore.[140]

As long as this problem remained unsettled, Paris was not in the least inclined to mitigate its hostile attitude vis-à-vis the Soviet regime. Although the
French had supported the Allied decision to lift the economic blockade of
Soviet Russia in January 1920, unlike Britain, they had declined to enter into
trade negotiations with Soviet representatives. They argued that negotiations
were impossible with a government that refused to recognize the obligations
of its predecessors and, as they saw it, was not in the least representative of the
population.[141] If, for the British and the Italians, it was more important to
restore trade relations with Soviet Russia in the here and now than to secure a
promise for the restitution of old debts at some time in the future, for France,
such an approach remained unacceptable.[142]

The trade agreements concluded between the Soviet government and a
number of Western governments in the course of 1921 all contained explicit
provisions that both parties should refrain from agitation and propaganda
against each other,[143] yet on the issue of debts, no definite agreements had been
made. Thus, in the Anglo-Russian agreement it was briefly touched upon in a
separate "Declaration of Recognition of Claims," which followed the agreement's actual text, and in which both parties declared that "all claims of either

party or of its nationals against the other party in respect to property or rights or in respect to obligations incurred by the existing or former Governments of either country will be equitably dealt with in the formal general Peace Treaty referred to in the Preamble."[144]

In their dealings with other governments, Soviet representatives had, from the summer of 1920 onward, repeatedly put forward the demand for an international peace conference at which the Soviet government would be accepted as a full member of the international community.[145] Chicherin and his colleagues at the People's Commissariat of Foreign Affairs regarded such a conference as absolutely indispensable, given that the Soviet Republic found itself, internationally speaking, in a position of one against all. They argued that if, for instance, the British government pledged to refrain from hostile activities vis-à-vis Moscow, Britain's allies would still be free to continue such activities. With the foreign intervention during the civil war still fresh in their minds, full-fledged international recognition was a high priority for the Soviets.[146]

In the course of 1921 Moscow's willingness to establish a new relationship with the outside world became ever stronger. The Soviet leadership, in particular the People's Commissariat of Foreign Affairs, became increasingly aware that Russia's economic recovery would be impossible without foreign assistance, and therefore concessions to the outside world were inevitable. While recommendations that Moscow recognize at least part of the Tsarist debts had gone unheeded at the time of the Anglo-Russian trade negotiations, by the fall of 1921 such a step was no longer entirely unacceptable.[147] When, in October 1921, Chicherin proposed that Lenin and Trotskii leave the *Comintern*'s Executive Committee and that all Tsarist debts be recognized, Lenin rejected Chicherin's suggestions in their original form as too compromising, but asked him at the same time to prepare a second, less far-reaching proposal on the issue.[148]

According to Chicherin's second proposal, the Soviet government would formally declare its willingness in principle to recognize all state loans contracted by the Tsarist government before 1914, provided that (1) it was granted the necessary conditions to make their restitution a real possibility; (2) it was recognized de jure; (3) a general peace treaty with the Western powers was concluded; and (4) the inviolability of Soviet borders was guaranteed. For this purpose, Chicherin suggested, an international peace conference should be convened in the near future. This time, the people's commissar's suggestions met with approval by the Soviet leadership, and on 28 October 1921 they were signed by Chicherin and dispatched abroad.[149]

While the British responded to Chicherin's note with a reserved but certainly not negative request for clarification on certain issues, the French reaction to Chicherin's proposal was, as could have been expected, most skeptical. Paris did not even deem it necessary to respond formally to the Soviet proposal; the official position of the French government was that, as long as Moscow was not prepared to unconditionally recognize all its obligations, negotiations with the Soviet government were completely out of the question.[150]

In reality, the French no longer completely rejected the idea of some sort of relationship with Soviet Russia. In particular, they began to fear that their uncompromising stand vis-à-vis the Soviet regime might eventually cause them to be left behind if it came to developing the Russian economy. That the idea of an international consortium to that effect was being discussed by the Soviet trade representative L. B. Krasin with both London and Berlin in the last weeks of 1921 seriously alarmed the French government.[151] These fears eventually prompted the French to accept Lloyd George's proposal for a "great economic conference," to which also representatives of Germany and Soviet Russia would be invited. As a result, on 21 December 1921 the British prime minister and his French counterpart, Aristide Briand, decided that the Allied Supreme Council should meet in Cannes in early January 1922 to "discuss the general economic situation in Europe."[152]

On 6 January 1922 representatives of France, Great Britain, Italy, Belgium, the United States, and Japan met in Cannes, and they decided to organize in the coming spring an international financial and economic conference as an "urgent and essential step toward the economic reconstruction of Central and Eastern Europe." The Cannes Conference formulated a number of principles that were considered necessary conditions for such cooperation. Most important for the relationship with the Soviet government was the premise that no nation was to dictate to any other state the principles according to which its economy and government should be organized. The conference also declared that all governments were to organize legal and financial order at home so that trade with foreign countries would be possible, to recognize the state debts of their respective countries, and to refrain from attacks and propaganda directed against other states. The conference decided to invite a Soviet delegation to Genoa, whether the Soviet government accepted the Cannes principles or not. It was the first time the Soviet government received an invitation for an international conference, and it was generally expected that in Genoa the question of its juridical recognition would come up for discussion.[153]

It was against this background of feverish international consultation and cautious but decisive overtures toward Soviet Russia that the weekly *Smena vekh* developed its campaign for the Soviet regime's international recognition. The journal's first issue appeared on 29 October, the day after Chicherin publicly announced the Soviet government's willingness in principle to recognize prewar Tsarist debts; the last issue appeared on 25 March, two weeks before the start of the Genoa Conference. Over that period Kliuchnikov and his colleagues closely followed developments on the international scene, discussing them on the pages of their weekly. In doing so, they took care to adopt a moderate tone, admitting that probably, "it would be nicer if one had to do with a non-Soviet Russia, but given the fact that there was no such [Russia] nor was it to be foreseen, there was nothing left but to try to get on with a Russia that was Soviet."[154]

In their comments the Paris *smenovekhovtsy* invariably stressed that, without Soviet Russia's participation, there could hardly be a way out of the difficult international situation. In a number of articles on the Conference on Disarmament and Pacific Questions, which had opened in Washington on 12 November 1921 and to which no Russian delegation had been invited, it was stressed that as long as Russia remained absent from the international scene, there was a real danger that the world would again polarize into two hostile blocks. If Russia resumed its international role, however, this would become impossible. As Kliuchnikov and his colleagues saw it, not only would Soviet Russia then refuse to be drawn into one of the rival camps; also neither side would allow the other to join forces with Russia, for fear that this would irreversibly tip the balance of power. Therefore, the Paris *smenovekhovtsy* concluded rather unconvincingly, Russia's reappearance as a full member of the international community would once and for all do away with international coalitions and bring the whole world peace, progress, and freedom.[155]

Commenting on the "preliminary" agreements that various countries had concluded with Soviet Russia, Kliuchnikov wrote that while these accords were certainly steps in the right direction, they were not far-reaching enough. He and his colleagues would wait with impatience for the day when for the first time a truly worldwide conference would take place, in which Russia would take part as a full-fledged participant. Only such a conference could assure the well-being of Russia, of the whole of Europe, and of the whole world, Kliuchnikov emphasized.[156]

The outcome of the inter-Allied consultations in Cannes in early January 1921, followed by Moscow's acceptance of an invitation to the forthcoming Conference of Genoa, was hailed enthusiastically on the pages of the Paris journal. "Victory at Cannes/Cannae *(pri Kannakh)*," exclaimed F. Kudriavtsev, eagerly making the obvious allusion to Hannibal's formidable victory over the Romans.[157] In the eyes of the Paris *smenovekhovtsy,* the basic principles that had been agreed upon in Cannes seemed to offer the juridical framework for the process of "mutual adaptation and mutual concessions between revolutionary Russia and the nonrevolutionary states of the West" that played such an important role in their vision of the future.[158]

The campaign by the weekly *Smena vekh* for international recognition of the Soviet government seemed to be aimed not so much at the Russian émigré community as at European public opinion and even government circles. Indeed, as early as July 1921 Kliuchnikov had indicated that he and his Paris colleagues intended to address "serious elements abroad."[159] If the Prague collection had contained hardly anything that pointed in this direction, the Paris weekly's propagandist character was so obvious it drew the attention not only of I. Lezhnev[160] but also of the French secret police. To be sure, the Sûreté

Générale kept a close eye on the Russian émigré community as a whole in those days, but the weekly *Smena vekh* and its editors were certainly the object of special attention.[161] As early as two weeks before the first issue was to come out, the Sûreté was advised by an anonymous correspondent of the forthcoming publication of a new journal in Russian. The correspondent informed his employers that the new weekly "will not have an extremist outlook: it will take on a rather moderate tone and will deal especially with the question of the need for, and the usefulness of, an entente between France and Soviet Russia."[162]

If it was an exaggeration to consider the French attitude *Smena vekh*'s principal target, the Paris journal did indeed pay particular attention to the French position vis-à-vis the Soviet Republic, a question that had been broached earlier by Noskov and V. N. L'vov on the pages of the French press. In its attempts to persuade the French to abandon their irreconcilability, *Smena vekh* emphasized the dangers of such a position, playing mainly upon the traditional French-German enmity. In the first issue of the journal, Kliuchnikov wrote:

> What would happen if France, counting on some unrealizable Russia, would adopt a position that is unacceptable to Russia as it is now and as it will be after all gradual transformations and self-perfections? In that case, France itself would draw Russia toward Germany . . . On the other hand, in close and sincere cooperation with Russia it would be easy for France to establish such relations with Germany, that the French-German question would once and for all lose its sharpness.[163]

At the same time, the contributors to *Smena vekh* tried to kindle French fears of being left behind if it came to establishing economic relations with Soviet Russia.[164] On several occasions they referred to Chicherin's note of 28 October as if this document was proposing a conclusive solution to the question of Russia's prewar debts and all the French government had to do for the matter to be settled was to accept the Soviet proposal.[165] In any case, the Paris *smenovekhovtsy* maintained, "the interests of France did not lie in attempting to extort consolidated debts, but in restoring a field *(poprishche)* in which the French energy could create ever new values."[166]

In this context, one might wonder how a Russian-language journal could possibly affect European public opinion. *Smena vekh* was aimed in the first place at the Russian intelligentsia in emigration. By the early 1920s this was a group that, even in France, retained hardly any influence in matters concerning Russia, and certainly not enough to directly affect government decisions.[167] Nonetheless, the *smenovekhovtsy* seemed to believe that if they managed to "bring to reason part of the émigrés," as apparently even Lenin hoped, and succeeded in softening the émigrés' attitude vis-à-vis the Soviet regime, this would also exert influence on public opinion in their host countries. More-over, both the *smenovekhovtsy* and their supporters in Moscow seemed to as-sume that positive notes about the Soviet government coming from non-Communist quarters and, what is more, from previous opponents of the Soviet regime might catch on more easily among the European public than might overt Communist propaganda. In this respect, the anonymous correspondent of the French Sûreté observed:

> The soviets consider, and not without reason, that a tendency in public opinion in favor of a rapprochement with Russia would not be neglected by the French government. On the other hand, they reckon that the public opinion, incapable of generalizing, bases itself, in its sympathies for certain political principles, not so much on the profound ideological content of these principles as on the political physiognomy of the men who represent this ideology: an idea represented by acceptable people, becomes easily acceptable itself. . . . Bolshevik propaganda incarnated by men whose past does not have anything to do with communism, ceases to be Bolshevik. Hence the selection of the contributors of *Smena vekh*.[168]

Presumably, considerations of this kind had prompted Moscow to start col-laborating with the Paris *smenovekhovtsy*. The Soviet authorities, as mentioned above, had been involved in the Paris journal from the very beginning; in all likelihood, the initiative for this cooperation had been taken by L. B. Krasin, the Soviet representative in London. Given that the French authorities would not allow official Soviet representatives on their territory—not even Krasin, whom Lloyd George had called a "reliable, sober businessman" and a "good Bolshevik"[169]—Krasin probably considered Kliuchnikov and his colleagues suitable allies in the hostile French environment. That they still enjoyed some support in Russian émigré circles there, notably from Maklakov, in the early fall of 1921 must have made them seem even more interesting associates in Soviet eyes.

Yet, if Moscow ever aspired to use the weekly *Smena vekh* as an effective mouthpiece in France by way of the Russian émigrés, this turned out to be a miscalculation. Initially Kliuchnikov and his colleagues had also hoped to maintain contacts with the émigré community there,[170] but their stands soon made this impossible. With their enthusiastic talk of Russia as the revolutionary vanguard of nations, their warnings against an unlimited "lowering of the rev-olutionary wave," and their failure to keep a sufficient distance from the Soviet regime, the Paris *smenovekhovtsy* lost whatever support they might have en-joyed among leading émigré circles. Thus, commenting on the first issue of *Smena vekh* in a letter to Kliuchnikov, Maklakov pointed out that Kliuchni-kov's group seemed to have abandoned their "struggle by new means" against the Soviet regime and to have let themselves be overpowered by Moscow.[171] Moreover, the *smenovekhovtsy*'s reputation in émigré circles was tainted because their journal had begun to attract lesser men, inspired not so much by ideological motives as by "considérations d'intérêt," in words of the anonymous French correspondent.[172]

On the whole, after the first wave of indignation vis-à-vis the collection *Smena vekh,* émigré circles now preferred to ignore Kliuchnikov and his colleagues; apart from a few isolated reactions, they preserved a disdainful silence.[173] Nor did the Paris weekly receive any noticeable attention from the French press. After the controversy over V. N. L'vov's statements in *L'Ere nouvelle,* which, as has been indicated, had provoked a storm of angry émigré reactions, French journalists apparently decided that Kliuchnikov's group was not worth going into.[174]

Nonetheless, the Paris *smenovekhovtsy* managed to establish at least one valuable contact in the French political world, namely, Edouard Herriot, the chairman of the so-called Radical-Socialist party, whose organ was *L'Ere nouvelle.* If the editors of *L'Ere nouvelle* did not consider it opportune in late 1921 and early 1922 to give the *Smena vekh* group more coverage, Herriot himself apparently regarded the contact with the *"Ralliés"* useful. As early as January 1921 the Radical-Socialist leader had advocated that the French government abandon its hostility vis-à-vis Soviet Russia and extend a helping hand. It would be under his premiership that France would finally, in late October 1924, recognize the Soviet government de jure.[175] In the summer of 1922 the staff of the Berlin daily *Nakanune* would play an important part in organizing Herriot's much-publicized tour of Soviet Russia, which would be instrumental in determining the Radical politician's views on the Soviet regime.[176] Of course, in early 1922 the Soviet sponsors of Kliuchnikov's circle could not have foreseen Herriot's role in French relations with Soviet Russia with all its implications, but that this connection must have pleased them is beyond doubt.

. . .

While it is true that Kliuchnikov and his closest colleagues kept little distance from Moscow, it should be made clear that, if they had accepted closer collaboration with the Soviet authorities, they had done so because they believed this could further their cause. Except for Luk'ianov, who soon "took the bait" of Bolshevik secret service abroad,"[177] they were motivated to cooperate with Moscow for reasons definitely of their own.

In the case of Bobrishchev-Pushkin and Potekhin, who along with Kliuchnikov and Luk'ianov made up the core group behind the Paris journal, these were vague hopes that the fire of revolution would spread to Western Europe, so that Russia could take advantage of having already gone through that stage and take the lead over the European countries. Neither man could work up much enthusiasm for the revolutionary ideals as such—Potekhin called them "nonsense" and "a tale written by adults for themselves," Bobrishchev-Pushkin considered them "naive and grossly primitive"—but if the revolution could bring Russia leadership over the rest of Europe, even the rest of the world, that was an opportunity which should not be spurned, they felt. "It was time to be egoists," as Potekhin put it.[178]

Potekhin certainly did not believe that a new international order under Russia's leadership might also enhance the well-being of mankind as a whole.[179] Whereas Bobrishchev-Pushkin cherished hopes that the revolutionary character of such an order would cause existing international antagonisms to fade away and thus lead the world to a better future. In expressing these hopes on the pages of the Paris journal,[180] Bobrishchev-Pushkin made sure, however, not to give vent to his loathing of Communist ideology or his criticism of certain aspects of Moscow's internal policy, such as the persecution of the Church or the Soviet government's manipulation of elections. As Ustrialov rightly remarked, tactical considerations prompted Bobrishchev-Pushkin to take the stand he did. In the former Octobrist leader's opinion, open protests against the "victorious class" were absolutely useless; all one could do was suggest one's ideas to the Bolsheviks as though they were their own and cooperate with them in an attempt "to bring the people albeit just a little benefit."[181]

At the same time, Bobrishchev-Pushkin was a proponent of the "revolutionary romanticism" that troubled Ustrialov so much. If it were not for that, Bobrishchev-Pushkin wondered, how could one possibly come to terms with all the destruction and suffering the Russian revolution had brought about?[182] His opinion in this respect was shared by Potekhin, who also took care not to betray on the pages of *Smena vekh* his cynical views on Russia's future role in the world. In a letter to Ustrialov, Potekhin stressed that, as for himself, the term *revolutionary fatalism* might be more appropriate, maintaining at the same time that "romanticism was indispensable for life also in other periods" and that "it was not always good to see too early that the emperor had no clothes."[183]

Therefore, although Ustrialov's remarks on "tactical considerations" were certainly justified with regard to Potekhin and Bobrishchev-Pushkin, with respect to Kliuchnikov, the man whose views unquestionably determined the tone of the Paris journal, they were unwarranted. An enthusiastic letter he sent to Ustrialov in late 1921 leaves no doubt that Kliuchnikov's intentions and zeal as editor-in-chief of *Smena vekh* were sincere, something also confirmed by a number of contemporaries, including Maklakov.[184] Kliuchnikov honestly believed that an evolved Soviet regime would ensure his motherland a prosperous future and that Soviet Russia had been called upon to unite all nations of the world in peace. Kliuchnikov was also convinced that he and his colleagues could play an active role in bringing this about. Therefore, an offer for cooperation from the businesslike Krasin, with his outspoken patriotism, his vision of a modern, industrialized Russia firmly integrated in the world economy, and his apparent striving for a peaceful evolution to a new international order rather than for world revolution, must have seemed most valuable and promising in his eyes.[185] Moreover, the international developments in late 1921 and early 1922 were such, that Kliuchnikov could not but feel confirmed in his view that by accepting Krasin's offer, he and his colleagues had made the right decision.

The outcome of the Conference of Cannes and the subsequent invitation of a Soviet delegation to the planned economic conference in Genoa filled the Paris *smenovekhovtsy*, especially Kliuchnikov, with the highest expectations. True, the response from émigré circles to their appeal for reconciliation with Soviet Russia was not as positive as they had hoped,[186] but this disappointment was soon overshadowed and amply made up for by developments on the international scene. If the émigrés refused to recognize Soviet Russia, it seemed the rest of the world would not; if Russia's interests in the international community had so far been trampled on by these same émigrés,[187] at the upcoming Conference of Genoa her interests would be defended firmly and authoritatively by the Soviet delegation.[188]

As the Paris *smenovekhovtsy* saw it, the Conference of Genoa would be a "great debate *(velikii spor)*" between Russia and the rest of the world. In their view, there were but three possible outcomes to this dispute. Either Russia and all other countries would "come to an agreement with each other to the benefit of all," or "Russia's partners would helter-skelter withdraw from Genoa to other conference tables." Or, if neither of these possibilities materialized, the only other possible outcome was world revolution. In any case, Kliuchnikov and his colleagues stressed, "that outcome which still was being counted upon abroad had become absolutely impossible, i.e., that Russia would find itself in the position of a defendant among judges, of vanquished among victors. No, this was no longer ever to happen!"[189]

Although Kliuchnikov and his colleagues did not doubt that the Soviet delegation would "defend Russia" in Genoa as best it could, their confidence that the conference would be to Russia's advantage was strengthened even more when it became clear that they would have their own representative in the "debate" on the Italian Riviera. In February 1922, upon the personal recommendation of Lenin, who had been favorably impressed by Kliuchnikov's article on the forthcoming conference in the 21 January issue of *Smena vekh*, Kliuchnikov was invited to join the Soviet delegation to Genoa as an expert on international law.[190]

At Krasin's instigation, the Soviet government had in fact started to prepare for a possible international conference even before the actual decision to organize such a forum with Soviet participation had been taken, let alone an invitation to Genoa had been received. Thus, a preparatory commission, chaired by G. V. Chicherin, had been created for that purpose on 5 January 1922. Upon receipt and acceptance of a formal invitation to Genoa, the Soviet delegation was officially established on 27 January; besides Chicherin it included Krasin,

Deputy Commissar for Foreign Affairs M. M. Litvinov, and the Soviet trade representative in Italy, V. V. Vorovskii.[191]

In drafting the Soviet strategy for Genoa, a most active role was played by Lenin, who urged that the delegation's tactics should assume a "bourgeois-pacifist" character. As Lenin saw it, the Soviet representatives in Genoa should try to undermine the united capitalist front by bolstering pacifist sentiments within the bourgeois states. He advised the delegation to refer to "bourgeois-pacifist" writings rather than to Communist ideas in support of their propositions and especially recommended in this respect *The Economic Consequences of the Peace* by the young Cambridge economist J. M. Keynes, who had served as an economic advisor to the British delegation at the Paris Peace Conference. Keynes argued in his book against imposing too heavy reparations upon Germany because of the negative effects he believed this would have on the European economy as a whole. He also advocated both the cancellation of much of the inter-Allied debt and the restoration of economic relations with Soviet Russia as necessary conditions for Europe's postwar recovery.[192] Lenin believed that Keynes's views could be a most suitable point of reference for the Soviet delegation and therefore insisted that every member of the delegation have a thorough knowledge of the work.[193]

In light of these strategic designs, Lenin's interest in Kliuchnikov's article on the Genoa Conference was understandable. The article was, for Kliuchnikov, an exceptionally sober analysis of the international situation, in which the conference was represented as the outcome of a long process. As decisive factors in this process, Kliuchnikov mentioned, first, the gradual consolidation of the Soviet regime; second, the deterioration of the international political and economic situation as a result of Russia's absence from the international scene—an element that also Keynes had stressed; and third, the resultant growing danger of serious social unrest in the countries of Western Europe. Furthermore, Kliuchnikov devoted attention to the differences between French and British policies vis-à-vis Soviet Russia, and he stressed that in the long run the British strategy of gradual rapprochement would certainly be the most reasonable and beneficial for the old world. Continued isolation of the Soviet Republic would only be grist for the Third International's mill, he maintained.[194]

Kliuchnikov concluded his article in a somewhat different tone, but here as well he happened to touch upon one of Lenin's concerns. Kliuchnikov warned the members of the Russian delegation that the other participants in the Genoa Conference would surely try to "bring Soviet Russia to its knees in front of an international tribunal," and urged them to guard against such attempts.[195] No doubt, Kliuchnikov's remarks in this respect met with Lenin's approval, given the Soviet leader's apprehensions that some of the delegation's members, especially Chicherin, Krasin, and Litvinov, might take a too submissive attitude in Genoa, convinced as they were that foreign aid was a sine qua non for Russia's economic recovery.[196]

No details are known about the discussion between the members of the Politburo and the sitting members of the Soviet delegation to Genoa with regard to Kliuchnikov's inclusion into that delegation; in any case, Lenin's recommendations were heeded, and in early April 1922 Kliuchnikov made his way to Genoa in the role of legal expert.[197] It was a great occasion for him. From Genoa, he wrote Ustrialov a jubilant postcard in which he called his assignment "the first practical application of *smenovekhovstvo*."[198] Kliuchnikov's colleagues back in Paris also expected a lot from him. "If the Soviet regime had committed a mistake in Genoa, . . . Iurii Veniaminovich, as an expert, would have been able to avert it," Bobrishchev-Pushkin remarked later.[199]

The Paris *smenovekhovtsy*'s feeling that their day had finally come was reinforced when Krasin gave them the opportunity to expand their weekly into a daily. The first issue of *Nakanune* (On the Eve), as the paper was called, resuming the title of the short-lived Moscow journal of 1918, would appear on 26 March 1922 in Berlin, the city which for both economic and political reasons became the *smenovekhovtsy*'s new home base. Not only was the cost of living far lower in Berlin than in the French capital, but as a result of the rapprochement between Germany and the Soviet Republic in the beginning of 1922, Berlin was also a more hospitable place for the pro-Soviet *smenovekhovtsy* than Paris, where the authorities approached them with increasing hostility.[200]

In the editorial of *Smena vekh*'s last issue, which appeared on 25 March 1922, Kliuchnikov and his colleagues looked back to the day the journal's first issue had come off the press:

> we ourselves represented but a small group of audacious individuals, who had dared to throw down a challenge to the "innumerable masses *(nesmetnye polchish-cha)*" of our opponents. We knew that it was necessary to throw down the challenge, and believed in our rightness. But it was only a challenge, and only a belief. At that time we had little force. And the responsibility was great.[201]

In those early days, there had been three elements that might have undercut their position, they recalled: first of all, the attitude the émigré community would take with respect to their "challenge"; second, the course of events in Russia and the way the Soviet authorities would react to *Smena vekh;* and finally, the position of the other countries vis-à-vis Soviet Russia. Yet now, merely twenty weeks later, the developments with respect to all three elements were confirming the rightness of their stand.

First of all, the editors of *Smena vekh* argued, the anti-Bolshevik émigré community had not managed to raise a single serious objection to their position and, what is more, was showing unmistakable signs of moral and political decline.[202] Furthermore, the events in Soviet Russia were also going in the right direction. With their customary naïveté in this respect, Kliuchnikov and his colleagues even prided themselves that the debates over the Prague collection had ushered in a new era of free and public discussion of political questions there. As for Moscow's reaction to *Smena vekh*, several Soviet representatives had declared that "they were going the same way *(im s nami po puti)*," the Paris *smenovekhovtsy* told their readers. Thus, they went on, Lenin and his party had shown that they were above revenge against former participants in the anti-Bolshevik struggle, and that they had understood that Russian intellectuals could indeed cooperate with the Communists without becoming Communists themselves. Finally, Kliuchnikov and his colleagues remarked, developments on the international scene, the events in Cannes and the invitation to Genoa, were proving to what extent Soviet Russia's position in the world had been strengthened.[203]

Against this background, the *smenovekhovtsy* felt it was futile to carry on academic discussions about the role of the intelligentsia or to engage in further squabbles with the émigrés. As they saw it, "the change *(smena)* had been brought about, the positions had been taken, and the time had come to open the struggle on a wider front." Kliuchnikov and his colleagues now believed that their tasks no longer lay primarily outside Russia. A decisive regrouping of the émigré community was in the offing, they trusted. Everyone whose "brains had not yet dried up, [whose] heart had not turned sour, and in whose soul the Russian element had not yet died" would finally choose for Soviet Russia. By contrast, inside Russia "mistakes of political perspective and erroneous loyalty to the past" seemed to persist longer than could be justified, they believed. However understandable this might be—it was easier to gain insight in relative prosperity abroad than amid suffering and terror, the *smenovekhovtsy* admitted—it was most regrettable. Kliuchnikov and his colleagues stressed that they would do whatever they could to convince everyone, not only abroad but also and primarily in Russia, that a return to the past was both impossible and undesirable.[204]

The weekly *Smena vekh* had been intended in part as a "bridge between the Russian intelligentsia abroad and the Russian intelligentsia in Russia," but little had come of that because the Soviet public had had no access to the journal.[205] With *Nakanune*, things would be different. The Berlin daily would not only be distributed in Soviet Russia, something quite exceptional in itself,[206] it would also have its own office in Moscow. Thus, it was with great pride in what had been achieved and with the highest expectations for the future that Kliuchnikov and his colleagues bade farewell to the readers of *Smena vekh* and took up their new mission in Berlin. As *Nakanune*'s brand-new editor-in-chief, Kliuchnikov told a correspondent of *Izvestiia*:

> We have held out our hand to the Bolsheviks, and they are holding their hand out to us. If the Bolsheviks can, so to speak, celebrate a victory over us, then the victory is mutual. . . . We have gone through a "change of signposts" *(prodelali "smenu vekh")* and feel ourselves now on the eve of a new day in Russian life and in our own.[207]

Chapter Six

NAKANUNE

Smenovekhovstvo as an Instrument in Moscow's Hands

The first issue of the *smenovekhovtsy*'s new organ appeared in Berlin on 26 March 1922. According to the paper's masthead, *Nakanune* was edited by Iu. V. Kliuchnikov and G. L. Kirdetsov, "with the personal participation *(s blizhaishim uchastiem)* of S. S. Luk'ianov, B. V. Diushen, and Iu. N. Potekhin." Besides Kliuchnikov, Luk'ianov, and Potekhin, the other *smenovekhovtsy* from the beginning were involved in the new daily as well. Bobrishchev-Pushkin and Chakhotin contributed some sixty and forty articles, respectively. Even Ustrialov, who could not agree with the daily's position, sent the editors copy more or less regularly, believing it imperative at the time to preserve at least the outward unity of the movement.[1] Finally, almost all the staff of the Paris weekly also played a role in *Nakanune,* both émigrés and contributors "from Russia," the most striking exception being S. B. Chlenov.[2]

In their farewell letter to the readers of the weekly *Smena vekh,* Kliuchnikov and his colleagues had announced that in Berlin, their group would be enriched with new members, who would "bring in new ideas and a new impetus."[3] While the promise of new ideas would remain largely unfulfilled, from the first issue of *Nakanune* the *smenovekhovtsy* could indeed boast a whole range of new collaborators, including not only the well-known journalists G. L. Kirdetsov and I. M. Vasilevskii but also a literary luminary in the person of Count A. N. Tolstoi. Furthermore, in the following weeks the group behind *Nakanune* attracted the former Tsarist diplomat Iu. Ia. Solov'ev (1872–1934),[4] the lawyer A. S. Gurovich, and the journalists A. Vol'skii and B. M. Shenfel'd-Rossov, both former members of *Mir i trud.*[5] Vol'skii and Shenfel'd-Rossov were, along with R. B. Gul', not the only *Mir i trud* men to join the staff of

Nakanune. After the closing of *Novaia russkaia kniga* in late 1923, A. S. Ia-shchenko, the journal's editor, also began collaborating with the Berlin daily, contributing mainly articles on the decline of Western parliamentary democracy.[6] By contrast, V. B. Stankevich, the founder of *Mir i trud,* kept aloof from the *Nakanune* group, feeling that if he contributed to *Nakanune,* he might as well join the staff of *Izvestiia,* and that was apparently a step too far for him.[7]

In all, over the two and a half years of *Nakanune*'s existence the total number of collaborators to the daily and its diverse supplements—the paper had weekly supplements on literature and economics and, for some time, regular extra sections on the cinema and foreign affairs[8]—came close to four hundred. Well over two-fifths of these contributors lived in Soviet Russia, yet their share in the paper was comparatively small.[9] *Nakanune* remained essentially an émigré organ, although, as will be shown, it served both as an outpost of the Soviet press abroad and as a "corridor" for repatriation to Soviet Russia.

Four men stood out among the new faces on *Nakanune*'s staff: G. L. Kirdetsov, the paper's actual editor-in-chief; I. M. Vasilevskii and A. S. Gurovich, who distinguished themselves mainly by the number of articles they contributed to *Nakanune,* adding up to sixty feuilletons and over thirty political articles, respectively; and A. N. Tolstoi, who, as editor of *Nakanune*'s literary supplement, attracted to the paper a choice of talented young Soviet writers.

Grigorii L'vovich Kirdetsov (anagram of Dvoretskii) (1880– ?), an economist by training and a longtime acquaintance of A. V. Lunacharskii, had before the revolution collaborated with several liberal and socialist newspapers, including *Birzhevye vedomosti* (Exchange Gazette), *Russkaia volia* (Russian Freedom), *Tovarishch* (Comrade), and *Pravda.* Besides that, he had been a regular contributor to the encyclopedic dictionary *Brockhaus-Efron,* as well as to *Evreiskaia entsiklopediia* (Jewish Encyclopedia).[10] In 1914, he was sent to Copenhagen as a war correspondent for *Birzhevye vedomosti;* thanks to the patriotic tone of his articles, he soon became one of the paper's most popular contributors.[11]

In 1919 Kirdetsov was assigned to the post of Baltic correspondent for the London *Times.* In the late summer of that year he took part in the formation of General Iudenich's "Northwestern" government, headed the government's press and propaganda department, became editor-in-chief of its organ *Svoboda Rossii,* and was sent on diplomatic missions to London and Paris on its behalf.[12] After Iudenich's final defeat in December 1919, Kirdetsov returned to Estonia where, along with his colleague on the staff of *Svoboda Rossii,* B. V. Diushen, he undertook a successful attempt to appropriate the daily's assets and continued to bring it out until June of that year.[13] Apparently, it was in the process of writing a book about General Iudenich's march on Petrograd that Kirdetsov came to question the anti-Bolshevik struggle and "changed signposts."[14] As opposed to Diushen, he did not contribute to the weekly *Smena vekh.* In *Nakanune,* however, he was to play a most important role. Kirdetsov became the new daily's editor-in-chief, a position he at first had to share with Kliuchnikov, but before long occupied unchallenged.[15]

A second newcomer to the staff of *Nakanune* was Il'ia Markovich Vasilevskii (1883–1938), who had been a well-known feuilletonist before the revolution.[16] In late 1918 he had left Soviet Russia and had traveled first to Kiev and then to Odessa, only to emigrate in the beginning of the following year. He landed in Constantinople, where he founded the weekly *Russkoe ekho* (Russian Echo), but soon moved on to Paris, where he began contributing to *Poslednie novosti*. In the winter of 1920–21 he also served as editor-in-chief of the weekly newspaper *Svobodnye mysli* (Free Thoughts), of which, however, no more than twelve issues appeared.[17] It was on the pages of *Svobodnye mysli* that Vasilevskii first gave evidence of a more conciliatory attitude toward the Soviet regime. In protesting V. Burtsev's strong condemnation of former Kadet Professor N. A. Gredeskul, whom Burtsev had called a "lackey,"[18] Vasilevskii argued that the émigrés, as deserters who had fled the hardships in their motherland, had no right to criticize their brothers who had remained there, and that had they stayed in Soviet Russia themselves, they would also have tried to find a modus vivendi with the new regime.[19]

During a discussion following the controversial lectures by Kliuchnikov and Luk'ianov at the Parliamentary Committee in February 1921, Vasilevskii openly admitted that the least one could say was that the speakers had broached an important question.[20] Just a few weeks later, in an article entitled "At the Turning Point," which appeared in the *Poslednie novosti* of 15 March 1921, he spoke of "a certain secret meaning, a certain majestic harmony" in what was going on in his motherland and of his belief in a new Russia, "free *(vol'naia)*, strong and joyful," where "the harsh principle of 'he who does not work, shall not eat' would remain in force also after the withdrawal of the Bolsheviks." He warned the émigrés that they should try to keep pace with events; otherwise, "they would not understand the impetuous course of history and, ill-tempered *(zlobnye)* and misunderstanding, would remain far behind."[21] After this article Vasilevskii's name disappeared from the pages of *Poslednie novosti*, and by the end of 1921 the French secret police regarded him as yet another proponent of Moscow's new strategy of masked, indirect propaganda.[22] Vasilevskii did not contribute to the Paris weekly *Smena vekh*, but in *Nakanune* he played an important role from the very beginning. With more than sixty articles in just over two years, he was one of the daily's most prolific contributors.[23]

Aleksandr Samuilovich Gurovich, for his part, was a former Kadet lawyer. At the time of the October revolution he had been in charge of a division of the Central Committee of the All-Russian Union of Towns. In the spring of 1918 he had accepted a job as legal advisor to the presidium of the Supreme Council of the National Economy, hoping in this way to do his bit in "rescuing values" and "softening the regime." By the end of that year, however, he had been forced to conclude that he was open to accusations of being a counterrevolutionary and had left his post.[24] In early 1919 he decided to emigrate, and in the fall of that year he arrived with his family in Prague,[25] where he began contributing to the newly founded Russian nationalist newspaper *Slavianskaia zaria* (Slavic Dawn).[26] Along with E. A. Efimovskii, the paper's editor, Gurovich openly declared that he was against foreign intervention in the civil war,[27] and in the spring of 1920 even called upon the émigrés to "bring their irreconcilability to the altar of [Russia's] rescue." The Russian émigré community in Prague rejected this appeal with unqualified hostility, however, and the staff of *Slavianskaia zaria* felt obliged to back down.[28]

In emigration Gurovich remained an active member of the Kadet party. In the spring of 1921, when the party was divided over P. N. Miliukov's "new tactics," Gurovich took Miliukov's side; from April 1921 his name appeared regularly on the pages of *Poslednie novosti*.[29] In January 1922, a branch of Miliukov's Democratic Group of the Party of People's Freedom was founded in Berlin, and Gurovich, who by that time was living in the German capital, became the group's secretary.[30] In this capacity, he sent regular reports on the situation in Berlin to the headquarters in Paris, in which he warned that, given the great number of "Bolsheviks and Bolshevizers *(bol'shevistvuiushchie)* ('*smenovekhovtsy*,' '*Mir i trud*' and the like)" among the Russian émigrés there, the Democratic Group should not limit itself to irreconcilable anti-Bolshevism. As Gurovich saw it, the only way the group could gain influence among these circles was by presenting them with a positive program which would outline the way toward Russia's rebirth.[31]

Before long, however, Gurovich himself became involved with the "Bolshevizers" in the Berlin émigré community; in late April 1922 he secretly began contributing to *Nakanune* under the pseudonym *Iskatel'* (Seeker), and from early June of that year he did so openly, under his own name.[32] It was apparently, as he saw it, the realistic position of the Soviet delegation to the Conference of Genoa that finally led him to accept the Soviet regime. As he wrote in his first avowed contribution to *Nakanune*, Gurovich now regarded this regime as the "paradoxical road" along which "the craftiness of the World Spirit *(lukavstvo mirovogo dukha)*" was leading the Russian people to freedom and to the "promised land of right and law."[33]

The *smenovekhovtsy*'s most spectacular "acquisition," however, was undoubtedly the writer Count Aleksei Nikolaevich Tolstoi (1882–1945).[34] In the years before the revolution, Tolstoi had made a name for himself with such novels as *Khromoi barin* (The Limping Lord) and *Chudaki* (Eccentrics); during the world war he had traveled all over the front, both as a war correspondent for the daily *Russkie vedomosti* and as a representative of several voluntary organizations.[35] While his reaction to the February revolution had been unequivocally positive, the October revolution had filled him with ambivalence. On the one hand, he regarded it a mere popular revolt, brought about by the extreme suffering of the war; on the other, he felt that there was a deeper meaning to the revolution and saw it as a fire that would purify and heal the Russian soul. Referring to the writings of Dostoevskii, Tolstoi spoke in November 1917 of an "infernal abyss through which the Russian people had to go and were already going, in order to burn on the bottom of it in throes and fear, and to come out of it meek, pure, and creative."[36]

By the fall of 1918 Moscow had become a most dangerous place for a count, and Tolstoi left with his family for a literary tour of Southern Russia. They settled in Odessa, which, under the Treaty of Brest-Litovsk, was at that time occupied by German forces. In December 1918, following the German defeat in the world war, French forces took command of the city, only to withdraw barely four months later, in early April 1919. Many Russian refugees were left behind to fend for themselves, but Tolstoi and his family managed to escape from the city. After several weeks in an Allied quarantine station on the Princes Islands they arrived in Paris, where they would remain until the fall of 1921.[37] It was there that Tolstoi started working on a trilogy about the revolution and the civil war and began to reflect on what had happened in his motherland. Although he first joined the émigrés in cursing the Bolsheviks, calling Lenin and his colleagues "blood-stained phantoms, all trembling in vileness and lust,"[38] he gradually came to accept the new regime.

In a letter to his longtime friend A. S. Iashchenko, commenting on the platform of *Mir i trud,* which the Berlin group had sent to him, Tolstoi wrote on 16 February 1920 that since the past fall he "had understood and reappraised very, very much." It was now clear to him that Russia was becoming "menacing and strong *(groznaia i sil'naia)"* again. Comparing 1917 and 1920, he wrote to Iashchenko, "the curve of state power was from zero sharply going upwards." Tolstoi did not doubt that life in Russia was "now very much unpleasant, even foul," but "when the slumbering charioteer of history suddenly began to whip the horses," there was nothing left to do but adapt oneself to the situation, however unusual or uncomfortable. He believed that, in any case, the period of pure destruction was now over, and a "destructive-creative era in history" was beginning. He trusted that his generation would live to see also the ensuing period of construction.[39]

The Polish attack against Soviet Russia in the spring of 1920 fanned Tolstoi's patriotic feelings, as did Western Europe's hesitation to help the Soviet republic when, in mid-1921, Southern Russia was struck by a terrible famine.[40] At the same time, Tolstoi's experiences in France, a country recovering from the war with great difficulty, further convinced him that the end of Western culture was near and that Russia, purified by revolutionary fire, could bring the world something new, fresh, and healthy.[41] To be sure, among the motives that prompted Tolstoi to "change signposts," feelings of homesickness also played a role, as did fears that if they remained longer in emigration his children would grow up "without nationality or language" or he himself might lose his place in the Russian literary world for good.[42] It would be simplistic, however, to reduce Tolstoi's conversion to sheer opportunism or nostalgia *(toska)*. Clearly, as was the case with most of the *smenovekhovtsy*, Tolstoi sincerely believed that the Soviet regime was having a positive influence on the "curve of Russia's state power,"[43] and that the revolutionary Russia could show the world the way to a new, valuable type of society.

In the fall of 1921 Tolstoi moved his family from Paris to Berlin. "Life has moved from a standstill," he had written to his wife in the summer of that year, "I am burning everything behind me. . . . Let's go to Berlin and, if you wish, also farther."[44] In the German capital Tolstoi began collaborating with A. S. Iashchenko's monthly literary journal, *Novaia russkaia kniga*, which had set itself the goal of preserving the unity between Russian culture in the Soviet republic and in the emigration and had, for that matter, tried to keep aloof from politics. In November of that year Tolstoi also became one of the founders of the Berlin *Dom iskusstv*, which was intended to serve similar aims.[45] From participating in these basically apolitical undertakings to joining the *smenovekhovtsy* with their increasing willingness to exalt the Bolsheviks was, however, still an enormous step; a catalyzing role in this respect was played by the arrival in Berlin of the young Soviet novelist B. Pil'niak, in February 1922. Apparently, Pil'niak convinced not only Tolstoi to make this move but also a number of other literary men.[46]

B. A. Pil'niak (pseudonym of Vogau) (1894–1937) had risen to sudden fame in 1921 with his novel *Golyi god* (The Naked Year), in which he had pictured the revolution as a grandiose peasant rebellion *(bunt)*, a snowstorm in which Russia was being cleansed of all that was superfluous and foreign and freed from the corrupting Western civilization that Peter the Great had tried to impose on her. In early 1922 the Soviet authorities sent Pil'niak for a few weeks to Berlin, where the Russian community received him with great interest.[47] Literary evenings with this Soviet writer, who repeatedly emphasized his ideological independence, brought in full houses. On that particular occasion Pil'niak conveyed a special message from the non-Communist intelligentsia in Russia for their colleagues in emigration. Before leaving for Berlin, he had carried out a small poll, asking some seventy nonparty intellectuals for their opinions on what this message should be like. As a result, Pil'niak had been charged with telling the émigrés that it was time to "stop playing the fool," and that instead of doing Russia harm abroad they should return home and take up vital work there.[48]

During his stay in Berlin, Pil'niak became good friends with A. Tolstoi, as well as with a few younger novelists, in particular A. M. Drozdov (1895–1963),[49] G. V. Alekseev (1892–1938),[50] and I. S. Sokolov-Mikitov (1892–1975),[51] all of whom would return to Soviet Russia before long. As it seems, it was Pil'niak who convinced them to do so, assuring them that great opportunities awaited them in the homeland.[52] In any case, upon his own return to

Soviet Russia in April 1922, Pil'niak advised Tolstoi and Sokolov-Mikitov that he had seen the authorities, who would welcome them back in Russia "with honor *(pochetno)*."[53] By that time, however, Tolstoi and Sokolov-Mikitov had already made the first move in that direction and had joined the group behind *Nakanune*.[54] Drozdov and Alekseev, for their part, would do so shortly thereafter, in December 1922 and the fall of 1923, respectively.[55] For Tolstoi, as well as for several of his colleagues, *Nakanune* would in fact be an intermediate stage between the emigration and the return home.[56]

As editor of *Nakanune*'s weekly literary supplement, Tolstoi's role in the undertaking lay chiefly in the cultural field, although on a few occasions he did feel the need to make political statements on the paper's pages.[57] It was Kirdetsov and Diushen who determined the daily's ideological face, while the original *smenovekhovtsy*—with the exception of Luk'ianov—were soon pushed into the background. While this altered little in the group's fundamental position as it had been formulated in the journal *Smena vekh*, *Nakanune* continued the shift toward a predominance of people from a socialist background that had started at the time of the Paris weekly. As Ustrialov wrote regretfully to Potekhin in April 1923, "at the helm of the movement now had appeared Messrs. Kirdetsov and Diushen, people not at all of our traditions."[58] The new helmsmen did not steer the ship of *smenovekhovstvo* on their own, however, but sailed under close supervision from Moscow.

The Soviet authorities had their say in *Nakanune* from the very beginning; N. N. Krestinskii, then the Soviet representative in Germany, was one of the new daily's initiators.[59] As had been the case with the weekly *Smena vekh*, *Nakanune* received financial support from Moscow through Krasin; it is unclear, however, how this happened exactly. At the time, various rumors were circulating in the émigré community in this connection. One version was that the Soviet government subsidized *Nakanune* by taking out ten thousand subscriptions to the paper;[60] others held that the money was being transferred through a straw man.[61] A third version, proposed by the Berlin correspondent of the Belgrade émigré paper *Russkoe delo,* claimed that the funds were coming from a rich Estonian businessman doing big business with the Soviet government. According to this version, as people's commissar of foreign trade, Krasin had convinced the businessman to become *Nakanune*'s Maecenas in exchange for an important contract.[62]

Although the true answer to this question remains unknown, the *Russkoe delo* version is not entirely implausible, at least with respect to the first months of *Nakanune*'s existence, and it would also justify, in part, A. Tolstoi's claim that the daily "was being published with the means of a private person, who did not have any links at all with the present government of Russia."[63] Be that as it may, *Nakanune* did not suffer from a lack of funds, and up to the last days of the paper's existence, its staff could afford to live in great style.[64]

Compared to the modest weekly *Smena vekh, Nakanune* was quite a large-scale undertaking. While the émigrés had tried to ignore the Paris journal as best they could, they could hardly ignore the new daily. On 26 March 1922, the day the first issue of *Nakanune* came off the press, the Paris daily *Poslednie novosti* carried an editorial stating that it would not be worthwhile devoting much attention to these "court jesters," were it not that "the acquisition of a daily newspaper in Berlin added a new political meaning to this oil stain."[65] Over the two and a half years of *Nakanune*'s existence, Miliukov and his staff engaged in a continuous polemic against this "daily that distinguished itself from *Pravda* only by . . . less seriousness and a less consistent position."[66] The editors of *Sovremennye zapiski*, for their part, did not judge *Nakanune* worthy of a special article, but seized upon every opportunity to lash out against this "despicable and venal daily," which had been "created for the deception and catching of souls."[67]

In an interview with *Novyi mir*, the organ of the Soviet mission in Berlin, shortly before the first issue of *Nakanune* was to appear, Kliuchnikov had said that one of the new daily's main tasks would be to "finish off the émigré community *(dokonat' emigratsiiu),*" an expression that had greatly irritated the Russian exiles.[68] That the *smenovekhovtsy* now also had a man of such standing as A. N. Tolstoi in their midst could only add fuel to the flames. In the weeks following the appearance of *Nakanune*, émigré organizations called special meetings to exclude from their ranks anyone who dared to collaborate with the maligned paper. This was done, for instance, by the Union of Writers and Journalists in Berlin and its counterpart in Paris, by the Democratic Group of the Party of People's Freedom, and by the Paris Committee for Help to Scientists and Writers in Emigration.[69] Far from impressing them, these disciplinary measures presented the new *smenovekhovtsy* with an opportunity to explicitly distance themselves from the émigré community and to express their loyalty to the new regime.[70]

Certainly the most-talked-of example in this connection was A. N. Tolstoi's open letter to former People's Socialist leader N. V. Chaikovskii. Immediately after the appearance of *Nakanune*'s first issue, in his capacity as chairman of the Paris Committee for Help to Scientists and Writers in Emigration, Chaikovskii had sent Tolstoi a letter, calling on him to explain his participation in the new organ. In particular, Chaikovskii had asked Tolstoi to confirm whether his association with a newspaper "known to be published with Bolshevik money" meant that he openly took the side of the "fraudulent regime" in Russia. Tolstoi chose to reply to Chaikovskii with an open letter in *Nakanune*, in which he, possibly even in good faith, denied all allegations that the Berlin daily was being subsidized by Moscow, and stressed that he had joined the daily on the basis of absolute independence. At the same time, Tolstoi seized the opportunity to elaborate on his motives for accepting the Soviet regime. While he admitted that he, too, would prefer to see a government of untainted people in Russia, he nonetheless felt compelled to accept Lenin's as the only Russian government that could safeguard the unity of the Russian state. He argued that at this point the Soviet regime alone was capable of defending Russia on the international scene not only against attacks on its territory but also against possible enslavement and pillage by other countries.[71]

Tolstoi's open letter, which soon thereafter was reproduced on the pages of *Izvestiia*,[72] met with disapproval and disdain, both from among the émigrés and from some of Tolstoi's friends in Soviet Russia.[73] As long as *Nakanune*'s links with the Soviet regime remained unproven, however, at least some people were prepared to give Tolstoi and his colleagues the benefit of the doubt. In his letter to Chaikovskii, Tolstoi had suggested that by joining *Nakanune* he had subordinated his own personal longing for moral purity and integrity to the interests of the Russian state and the Russian people as a whole.[74] Indeed, his longtime friend the novelist K. I. Chukovskii, who had remained in Russia, regarded Tolstoi's step as an expression of a certain heroism and tried to defend him.[75] Before long, however, the group behind *Nakanune* made a move that shattered any last illusions with respect to the paper's relationship with Moscow, causing even Chukovskii to change his attitude vis-à-vis the Berlin daily and its staff.

On 31 May 1922 Kliuchnikov and Potekhin, the first émigrés to be offered this opportunity, traveled to Moscow as "special correspondents" of *Nakanune,* and the following day, on 1 June, an editorial office of the paper opened its doors in Moscow.[76] The Moscow office operated in close contact with the People's Commissariat of Foreign Affairs, in particular with the commissariat's press division, headed at the time by the diplomat and historian I. M. Maiskii, and the office's successive directors, M. Krichevskii and M. Levidov, were both employees of the commissariat.[77]

Krichevskii, a journalist and former collaborator of *Birzhevye vedomosti,* had been a member of the Soviet mission in Berlin, where he had served as editor of the mission's organ, *Novyi mir,* until mid-March 1922, when it had been closed down, presumably to make room for *Nakanune*.[78] He soon resigned as head of *Nakanune*'s Moscow office, however, and was replaced by M. Iu. Levidov, a writer and journalist who shortly after the October revolution had taken the side of the Soviet regime—one of the first representatives of his profession to do so. Levidov had served as agent of the Russian Telegraph Agency (ROSTA) in London; by the time of his appointment to the staff of *Nakanune,* he was directing ROSTA's foreign department at the People's Commissariat of Foreign Affairs.[79]

Nakanune's Moscow office took care of subscriptions, the acceptance of advertisements, and the paper's distribution in Moscow, Petrograd, and in the provinces. Every day, fresh issues of *Nakanune* were flown from Berlin to the Soviet capital, where they were sold on newspaper stands or shipped to other cities.[80] As for the editorial part of the work, the Moscow staff provided *Nakanune* with predominantly literary copy, twice a week sending the main office in Berlin a parcel with stories, poems and feuilletons by Soviet authors. Regular contributors included M. Bulgakov, V. Kataev, K. Fedin, E. Petrov, Iu. Slezkin, and M. Kuzmin.[81] In addition, the Moscow staff occasionally also contributed articles on current affairs to *Nakanune*. E. L. Mindlin, the daily's young editorial secretary in Moscow, wrote some twenty articles for the paper, mainly on cultural life in Soviet Russia.[82] According to Mindlin's own testimony, he had regular consultations in this connection with I. M. Maiskii; from time to time the latter would draw his attention to some event in Soviet Russia or on the international scene, or, more often, to developments in the Russian community abroad. Mindlin was also responsible for dispatching the parcels with copy to Berlin. He was supposed to bring them personally to the People's Commissariat of Foreign Affairs, from where they were sent to the German capital by diplomatic courier.[83]

Clearly, with the opening of an office in Moscow under close supervision of People's Commissar Chicherin and his staff, *Nakanune*'s claim of ideological independence became untenable. What is more, during their stay of well over three months in Soviet Russia, Kliuchnikov and Potekhin gave a whole series of lectures on *smenovekhovstvo,* at least part of which had been organized by the political propaganda division *(Glavpolitprosvet)* of the People's Commissariat of Enlightenment. At these lectures, the two men placed themselves decisively behind the Soviet regime. While they continued to insist on their ideological independence and that they were neither Communists nor socialists, they repeatedly stressed how well they understood that, for now at least, political freedom in Soviet Russia was out of the question.[84] At a time when a number of large political trials were taking place in Soviet Russia, notably the SR trial in Moscow and the so-called trial of clergymen in Petrograd, where, for the sake of political propaganda, tens of innocent people were condemned to years in jail or even to death,[85] this sounded particularly grim.

The lectures by Kliuchnikov and Potekhin brought in full houses,[86] yet did not add to the *smenovekhovtsy*'s popularity in Soviet Russia. On the contrary, they confirmed the reservations of both Communists and non-Communists in Soviet Russia vis-à-vis *smenovekhovstvo.*[87] In their farewell letter to the readers of the journal *Smena vekh,* Kliuchnikov and his colleagues stated that among the intelligentsia in Soviet Russia "mistakes of political perspective and erroneous loyalty to the past" had not yet completely disappeared, and they had set themselves the task to remedy this ill. Shortly after his arrival in Moscow as *Nakanune*'s special correspondent, Kliuchnikov repeated this idea in an interview with *Izvestiia,* adding that if his and Potekhin's presence in Soviet Russia could serve as an additional stimulus for their former colleagues to look at things with different eyes, this alone would be a considerable achievement.[88]

Such a paternalistic attitude was hardly well received among the non-Communist intelligentsia in the motherland; if anything, they found it insulting to be lectured by a couple of émigrés who, as Tan-Bogoraz expressed it, felt the need to "fawn on the Soviet regime *(prisluzhivat'sia)*."[89] As a result, the reputation of the Berlin *smenovekhovtsy* plummeted; one after another, Soviet intellectuals, including Pil'niak and Chukovskii, distanced themselves from the group behind *Nakanune*, as did the last émigrés who had been prepared to give them the benefit of the doubt.[90]

At the same time, in the ranks of the Communist party the lectures and interviews given by Kliuchnikov and Potekhin fanned the caution and hostility with which many had approached *smenovekhovstvo* ever since its origin. The two men's explicit declarations that they were far from being Communists or socialists, their insistence that the intelligentsia as a whole and *smenovekhovstvo* in particular assume the leading role in society, and their plea that, in the end, the revolution lead to a synthesis between old and new raised many an eyebrow in Communist circles. In the weeks of the *smenovekhovtsy*'s visit to Soviet Russia, both *Izvestiia* and *Pravda* carried a number of critical articles, which reprimanded Kliuchnikov and Potekhin for failing to understand that the leading role in society belonged to the working masses and to the working classes alone and admonished them not to cherish hopes that the NEP would lead to anything but economic change.[91] If the *smenovekhovtsy* were prepared to work honestly for the sake of the motherland, they were welcome, but they should not meddle in politics, was the message. As the journalist G. Bergman expressed it on the pages of *Pravda,* what poverty-stricken Russia needed now was workers, not politicians; with politics, the Bolsheviks would cope themselves.[92]

In the meantime, at the *Nakanune* headquarters in Berlin the reports of Kliuchnikov's and Potekhin's adventures in Soviet Russia were followed with growing uneasiness. Especially the emphasis with which the two had declared themselves to be neither Communists nor socialists seemed to irritate Kirdetsov and his staff. In the *Nakanune* of 20 July 1922, Kirdetsov tried to draw a line between the "non-socialist" *smenovekhovtsy,* among whom he included the two Russia travelers as well as Ustrialov, and the movement's "left wing." He drew attention to Ustrialov's belief that the NEP would eventually lead to a complete transformation *(pererozhdenie)* of the Soviet economy into a proprietary system based on a strong class of peasant landholders and, without saying it in so many words, suggested that the views of Kliuchnikov and Potekhin were no different. Kirdetsov stressed that, in contrast, the representatives of *smenovekhovstvo*'s left wing not only did "not intend to push Russia into the bourgeois swamp so that the Revolution would suffocate from the stench of the practical consequences of Stolypinian agrarian individualism," but they were also convinced that the "labor state *(trudovoe gosudarstvo)*" should have a socialist foundation.[93]

Kirdetsov's efforts to distinguish between "right" and "wrong" in *smenovek-hovstvo* could not, however, prevent further Soviet attacks on the movement's organ. Just three days after the appearance of Kirdetsov's article, *Pravda* published a scathing outburst against *Nakanune,* warning the *smenovekhovtsy* that if they were not prepared to fully support the Bolshevik revolution, they would at best remain its "parasitic spongers," and at worst become its "overt enemies."[94] The outburst had been prompted by a critical note in *Nakanune's* coverage of the Moscow SR trial, which had appeared in the issue of 15 July 1922, although on the whole *Nakanune's* reporting had hardly differed from that in the Soviet press.[95] In one of the very few critical remarks about the Soviet authorities that the staff of *Nakanune* ever allowed themselves, they regretted that the Moscow court had been turned into an arena for political struggle to such an extent that it would seriously affect the significance of a future verdict.[96] The paper immediately followed the piece with a soothing article by Bobrishchev-Pushkin that hailed the openly biased Soviet court for being far more fair than its supposedly impartial counterparts in Western Europe.[97] Still, opponents of *smenovekhovstvo* in the party seemed to consider the article a convenient pretext for an offensive against the movement.

The "spongers" outburst was followed, on 27 July, by yet another attack in *Pravda,* a long article by A. S. Bubnov (1884–1940), a former "Left Communist" who now headed the Communist party's section for agitation and propaganda.[98] In his essay Bubnov warned that *smenovekhovstvo* might serve not only as a Pink bridge for former opponents of the Soviet regime to join the ranks of its supporters, as N. L. Meshcheriakov had argued, but also as a legal and "decent *(prilichnyi)*" cloak for counterrevolutionary tendencies.[99] When shortly thereafter, at the Twelfth All-Russian Conference of the Communist Party, *smenovekhovstvo's* longtime enemy G. E. Zinov'ev called the movement's representatives "quasi-friends" who were joining the Mensheviks and SRs in hoping for a revival of bourgeois democracy,[100] Kirdetsov and his colleagues in Berlin felt the time had come to make things completely clear.

In the editorial of 13 August 1922, the staff of *Nakanune* welcomed Zinov'ev's remark as recognition of the socialist tendency in their movement. Kirdetsov and his colleagues admitted that there were indeed those within *smenovekhovstvo* who placed their hopes in a return of bourgeois structures, and they conceded that as a many-sided movement based on accepting the October revolution and the sociopolitical situation in Russia that resulted from it, *smenovekhovstvo* did not have "one definitive *(kanonicheskaia)* ideology." At the same time, however, they stressed that in the group behind *Nakanune* there were no representatives of so-called bourgeois-restorationist tendencies to be found and that de facto the paper was being directed by a unanimous editorial board.[101]

This was too much for Kliuchnikov, who as *Nakanune's* coeditor-in-chief felt disavowed by his own staff and who, in an interview with *Izvestiia,* in turn distanced himself from his colleagues in Berlin. Yet he apparently found it hard to pinpoint a distinct ideological difference between his colleagues' position and his own and reduced the problem to a difference in style. Potekhin's and his departure for Russia, he told his interviewer, had entailed a far greater change in the paper's tone than could have been expected; since they had left Berlin, *Nakanune*'s support for Soviet Russia had gradually lost all sophistication. Accusations of "semiofficialness *(ofitsioznost')*" against the Berlin daily, although unwarranted in themselves, were becoming ever more understandable and even justified. Moreover, given that Kirdetsov had thought it opportune to openly criticize Potekhin's and his political standpoint, Kliuchnikov continued, there had been nothing left for them to do but send a declaration to their paper, stating that, since their departure from Berlin, neither he nor Potekhin had taken part in editing *Nakanune*.[102]

This apparently was the moment Kirdetsov and Diushen had been waiting for to get rid of their embarrassing colleagues and to become the unchallenged leaders of *Nakanune,* which was, after all, an enticing prospect. On 22 August 1922 the names of Kliuchnikov and Potekhin appeared on the daily's masthead for the last time. The following day the editors of *Nakanune* announced that, because Kliuchnikov's and Potekhin's views no longer corresponded with those of *Nakanune,* they were no longer part of the daily's editorial board.[103] From that day on, Kliuchnikov and Potekhin were replaced by P. A. Sadyker and S. S. Chakhotin—neither of whom carried much weight on the paper's editorial board[104]—while Kirdetsov retained the position of editor-in-chief.[105]

For the two Russia travelers, and for Kliuchnikov in particular, this announcement came as a shock. This was not what they had intended with their letter to "their own paper" declining responsibility for *Nakanune*'s contents during their stay in Soviet Russia. Potekhin, to be sure, did not seem to be overly concerned by the affair; in Moscow he had been offered a position as "economic specialist *(spets-ekonomist)*" at the Supreme Council of the National Economy and had decided to return to Soviet Russia for good.[106] For Kliuchnikov, however, who ever since the publication of the collection *Smena vekh* had imagined himself the principal leader of a movement with great prospects[107]—an idea greatly fostered by his invitation to join the Soviet delegation to Genoa—the exclusion from *Nakanune* came as a sore disappointment. True, in Moscow he, too, had received an attractive offer, the chair of international law at Moscow University,[108] but such a proposal was, if flattering, hardly tempting. Rather, he had been hoping to return to Berlin, resume his position at the head of *Nakanune,* and set things right there.[109]

That proved to be impossible. Upon his return to the German capital, Kliuchnikov tried in vain to regain his influence. He first threatened to bring the case before court, then demanded that the paper be closed down, but all to no avail. The forum of *Nakanune* remained closed to him. While Potekhin continued to contribute to *Nakanune* from Moscow, Kliuchnikov's name never again appeared on the daily's pages. Eventually, he was forced to accept the situation. There was nothing he could do, given that his "dethronement" had taken place with the knowledge of the daily's sponsors, and possibly even at their instigation.[110]

Moscow's exact role in the palace revolution at *Nakanune* remains unclear; from the available evidence, it is impossible to infer to what extent feelings of jealousy and lust for power on the part of Kirdetsov and Diushen[111] played a role and to what extent the coup was prompted by political and tactical motives on the part of the Soviet government. Presumably, the authorities in Moscow preferred to see faithful implementers and even "hacks" at the helm of *smenovekhovstvo*, rather than people inspired by their own ideological dreams. Moreover, during his stay in Soviet Russia Kliuchnikov had irritated so many people with his naively self-important attitude that the movement's supporters among the Soviet authorities could not but come to regard him as a hindrance.

In the end, Kliuchnikov could do nothing more than proudly claim that *Nakanune* was lagging behind the actual developments in Soviet Russia and at the same time reproach the daily's staff with excessive servility.[112] Still, he readily joined in at the one moment in *Nakanune*'s existence when the daily served most outspokenly as an instrument in Moscow's hands, notably during its campaign following the murder of the Soviet diplomat V. V. Vorovskii, killed by a Russian émigré at the Conference of Lausanne in May 1923.

When the Swiss Bundesrat had denied the Soviet government the right to act as a plaintiff in the lawsuit against Vorovskii's murderers, *Nakanune* had taken it upon itself to defend Moscow's interests in the case, becoming, in effect, a continuation of Soviet intelligence. Moscow had decided to seize upon the event to launch an intensive propaganda campaign against international capitalism in general and the anti-Bolshevik Russian émigrés in particular, and the staff of *Nakanune* spared no efforts to do their bit in this respect. The paper published sharp attacks against several émigré leaders, accusing them of complicity in the crime, and sent a number of collaborators to the trial in Lausanne as witnesses for the prosecution, notably Major General S. Dobrorol-'skii, who had been Governor-General of Novorossiisk under General Denikin, and Major General E. Dostovalov, the former chief of staff of White General Kutepov.[113] In the courtroom, the two military men were joined by Kliuchnikov, who by that time had returned to Russia for good, where he was directing the seminar on international politics at the so-called Socialist Academy in Moscow and teaching international law at the Military Academy of the Red Army.[114] When asked in Lausanne whether it was not problematic for a non-Communist—he continued to stress his ideological independence—to cooperate this closely with the Bolsheviks, Kliuchnikov reportedly was thrown off balance for a moment. Then he answered that this was merely a theoretical problem, with which it was not worth occupying oneself at a time when one's country needed urgent help.[115] Be that as it may, Kliuchnikov appeared before the Swiss court at Dobrorol'skii's and Dostovalov's side and testified along with them to the unprecedented atrocities committed by the Whites during the civil war, as well as to the great humanity of the Soviet regime, "the most popular regime in the world," as he worded it.[116]

. . .

For all the reciprocal annoyance and reproaches between Kliuchnikov and his successors at the top of *Nakanune,* the changes in the daily's leadership made little difference to its fundamental position. As Kliuchnikov had suggested himself, it was all rather a question of style and tone than of principle. The decisive ideological shift in mainstream *smenovekhovstvo* had taken place earlier, in the days of the Paris weekly, when Kliuchnikov and his colleagues had moved from accepting that the October revolution was not exclusively a destructive phenomenon, to hailing it as an event that heralded a better future for the whole of mankind. Despite his insistence on the need for ideological independence and for a synthesis of old and new,[117] Kliuchnikov's vague vision of a new world order based on pioneering social, political, and economic principles was not fundamentally different from the equally sketchy concept of a worldwide "reign of labor *(tsarstvo truda)"* advanced by Kirdetsov and his friends.[118]

In both cases, the assumption was that, thanks to the October revolution, Russia could show mankind the way to a new and better world based on social and international solidarity, and in both cases, this was a source of great patriotic pride. In the editorial of 25 March 1923, on the occasion of *Nakanune*'s first anniversary, Kirdetsov and his colleagues stressed that they felt heartened by the knowledge that "amid the twilight of Europe, amid the crisis of the old world culture, our motherland—Russia is giving mankind the example of the first ever attempt to build a labor state, which is opening new, boundless horizons for the creation of a new, really human, and great culture."[119]

Politically speaking, both the original group of *smenovekhovtsy* and the group behind *Nakanune* were convinced that revolutionary Russia could offer the world a valuable alternative to the system of parliamentary democracy, which, in their view, had reached a state of complete decay;[120] on the precise form of this alternative, however, they both remained vague. In *Nakanune,* this alternative was characterized primarily in terms of the relationship between the individual and the state. As Kirdetsov and his friends saw it, only a system in which the individual identified his own good with that of the community could offer a way out of the impasse into which formal democracy had brought the world; they believed that, since the introduction of the NEP, the developments in Soviet Russia were going precisely in that direction. In their opinion, the Soviet republic was gradually moving from a dictatorship of the proletariat to what they called a "labor democracy," a system in which all social groups could play a part, provided that they were prepared to subject their immediate individual interests to the interests of the community and to the "great goals of the future"—the happiness of all.[121]

Like Kliuchnikov, Kirdetsov and his colleagues applauded the adjustments being made to the Soviet economic system as a result of the NEP. These adjustments, they stressed, were indispensable for Russia's economic resurrection and a clear proof of the Soviet government's sense of realism.[122] They all shared the conviction, however, that "the lowering of the revolutionary wave should not go too far," and warned against the danger of the "bourgeois swamp." The NEP should be merely another way to reach the ideals of October, nothing more.[123]

The former Kadet Kliuchnikov had always stressed his preference for peaceful evolution as opposed to revolution, and with respect to the developments in Soviet Russia, the Marxist Kirdetsov entirely agreed with him. The group behind *Nakanune* preferred the "healthy reasonableness" of 1923 to the "madness" of 1917,[124] and considered as its task the furtherance of "the peaceful evolutionary development of the seeds that October had thrown onto Russia's soil."[125] On the international level, Kliuchnikov had initially feared that world revolution would be inevitable if the Western world did not learn from the Russian experiment, but Russia's position at the Conference of Genoa had reassured him that it would not come to that.[126] The same was true for Kirdetsov and his staff, who trusted that in the transition to a new world order, further victims would be avoided "by affirming the unshakeableness of the central core of revolutionary forces—by means of the consolidation of the USSR."[127]

Another point of convergence between the original group of *smenovekhovtsy* and the group behind *Nakanune* consisted in their common longing for a great and strong Russian state. Just as Kliuchnikov and Ustrialov had done before them, the contributors to *Nakanune* spoke approvingly of the Soviet regime's "collecting of the Russian land" and its "great-power status *(velikoderzhavnost')*."[128] Reporting on the Soviet republic's external relations, they repeatedly stressed that the Soviet government was defending Russia's national interests with great dignity and determination.[129]

Finally, Kirdetsov and his colleagues agreed with their predecessors at the helm of European *smenovekhovstvo* that not only the workers and the peasants but also the intelligentsia should play a role in the new Russian state. Their opinions differed, however, with respect to the character of this role. On the pages of the collection *Smena vekh,* it had been argued that by taking up practical work in Soviet Russia, the non-Communist intelligentsia could contribute to safeguarding and deepening the evolutionary process that was taking place there.[130] Kliuchnikov, for his part, had added to this that if only the intelligentsia accepted the October revolution, they would become a "force of powerful social progress," and take the lead in the struggle against "spiritual philistinism."[131] During his and Potekhin's visit to Soviet Russia he had repeated this, arguing that the intelligentsia should not only place their knowledge and practical know-how at their country's disposal but manifest themselves also as a leading cultural force, serving the eternal values of good and beauty, and struggling against narrow-mindedness *(meshchanstvo)*.[132]

As opposed to this, the editors of *Nakanune* regarded the intelligentsia primarily as a force of cultural, technical, and scientific progress; the intelligentsia, as a whole, was to evolve toward a "labor intelligentsia *(trudovaia intelligentsiia),*" toward a group of "intellectual citizens of the labor state" who regarded their intellect primarily as an instrument to work for the good of the collective.[133] They advised the intelligentsia to take henceforth as their motto the slogan "culturedness is a profession *(intelligentnost' est' professiia),*" but added that this was not to say that the intelligentsia should be reduced to a group of *spetsy* ("bourgeois specialists"). While the *spets* was driven primarily by self-interest, the true "intellectual *(intelligent)*" was motivated by his concern for the common good, yet realized that this goal could be achieved only on the basis of true professionalism.[134]

Kirdetsov and his colleagues were convinced that there could be no place in the new Russia for intellectuals who were either unable or unwilling to understand this. When in the late summer and fall of 1922 tens of prominent intellectuals were expelled from Soviet Russia, including the philosophers N. A. Berdiaev and S. L. Frank, the economists B. D. Brutskus and S. N. Prokopovich, the sociologist P. A. Sorokin, and the historians A. A. Kizevetter and V. A. Miakotin, this move met with approval on the pages of *Nakanune*. While it was regretted that the list of deportees included also people "to whom anti-Soviet tendencies were foreign," it was stressed that on the whole, the measure was entirely justified.[135]

Kliuchnikov's reaction to the evictions is unknown to me—after his exclusion from *Nakanune* he no longer had a forum to express his views.[136] However, in light of his repeated remarks on the untimeliness of political freedom in Soviet Russia, his willingness to endorse the course of events at the SR trial, and his appearance later in the Konradi case, it seems likely that he agreed with the Berlin daily's editors on this point.[137] In all probability, when it came to curbing "anti-Soviet tendencies," Kliuchnikov shared the views of the *Nakanune* group.[138]

In the meantime, there was also a remarkable continuity between the goals that the editors of the journal *Smena vekh* had set themselves and those of the group behind *Nakanune*. The staff of the Paris weekly had regarded it as their task to reconcile the intelligentsia in emigration with the revolutionary Russia and to influence Western public opinion in a positive way in their attitude vis-à-vis the Soviet republic. Furthermore, in the last issue of *Smena vekh* Kliuchnikov and his colleagues had indicated that they intended to address the intelligentsia in Soviet Russia as well, because many intellectuals there seemed incapable of understanding and accepting the October revolution and its re-sults. The goals to which Kirdetsov and his colleagues referred throughout *Nakanune*'s existence were similar. To be sure, there was a substantial difference between the activities of the Berlin group and those of the *smenovekhovtsy* in the Paris days, but this was mainly because the group behind *Nakanune* had a far greater scope, financially speaking, and had more intimate links with the Soviet authorities.[139] As the editorial of *Nakanune*'s very last issue stressed, com-pared to *Smena vekh, Nakanune* was "a forward movement, toward more active work."[140] Whatever their differences, however, their purpose remained basi-cally the same.

Like the staff of the weekly *Smena vekh* before them, the editors of *Nakanune* hoped to expedite the émigré community's disintegration, winning the "healthy" elements among them over to the Soviet republic. They tried to do so by bringing the Russian émigrés "news on the Russia of the workers, on what [Russia] had achieved as the result of a great struggle."[141] Every day the paper carried a whole range of articles on the situation in the homeland, which usually hardly differed in tone and style from the coverage in the Soviet press. While this irritated many émigrés, the sheer volume of news on Soviet Russia nonetheless aroused interest. Moreover, that *Nakanune,* thanks to its substantial means, could offer its readers attractive literary work not only in its literary supplement but also in its ordinary issues was a great asset in finding an audi-ence in the émigré community.[142]

Kirdetsov and his colleagues did not limit themselves to newspaper propa-ganda, but also engaged in a campaign of lectures directed especially at émigré youth. In the spring and summer of 1923 the leading contributors to *Nakanune* gave lectures on such subjects as dictatorship and democracy (Luk'ianov), the evolution of religion (Bobrishchev-Pushkin), politics or organization (Chak-hotin), the British attitude vis-à-vis Soviet Russia (Kirdetsov), the Russian people's new national consciousness (A. Tolstoi), and the tasks of the Russian youth abroad (Diushen).[143] What is more, in cooperation with the Soviet Red Cross and the Soviet mission in Berlin, the staff of *Nakanune* played an active role in helping potential repatriates to return to Soviet Russia.[144] In fact, only a small group of emigrants passed through this "corridor," primarily the collab-orators of *Nakanune* themselves, as well as a few people from the literary world. Still, the return of these émigrés proved valuable for Soviet propaganda abroad, especially in its campaign for international recognition.[145]

Speaking as editor-in-chief in an interview with *Izvestiia* on the occasion of *Nakanune*'s founding, Kliuchnikov had stressed that "the international situation required that people abroad learn about Soviet Russia not only from Russian organs that were hostile to her but also from organs that supported her."[146] Kirdetsov and his colleagues stuck to this task of diffusing "the voice of Rus-sia's friends abroad" and counteracting that of Russia's enemies.[147] On the pages of *Nakanune* much attention was devoted to the Soviet international position in general and to de jure recognition of the Soviet government in particular.[148] As has been seen, *Nakanune* was sponsored and supervised by the People's Commissariat of Foreign Affairs in Moscow. Throughout the daily's existence, much of its space was reserved for articles in support of Soviet foreign policy; from the end of 1923 to the daily's closing in June 1924, this became the prevailing subject on *Nakanune*'s pages.[149]

The staff of *Nakanune* attempted also to build up a network of contacts among Western European politicians and public figures. In the summer of 1922 they were involved in organizing the journey to Soviet Russia of the French Radical-Socialist politician E. Herriot; on his way to Moscow Herriot even made a stop at *Nakanune*'s headquarters in Berlin, where a tea party was held in his honor.[150] The contacts with Herriot continued also after his return from Russia. In 1923 Bobrishchev-Pushkin took part in preparing the French politician's campaign for the parliamentary elections that were due in May 1924.[151] Further, it seems that the daily's staff played a role in the formation of "organizations of friends of Soviet Russia" abroad.[152] Within the scope of the present study, it was not possible to investigate this involvement in detail. It is known, however, that the staff of *Nakanune* played a part in the creation of the German organization *Freunde des neuen Russlands,* which was founded on 27 June 1923 with the assistance of both the International Workers' Aid Society and the Soviet mission in Berlin.[153] The organization's initiators from the German side included left-wing intellectuals such as the physicist A. Einstein, the sculptress K. Kollwitz, and the novelists B. Kellermann and M. Barthel, as well as a number of prominent politicians, including the vice-president and future president of the Reichstag, the socialist P. Löbe,[154] and the chairman of the democratic faction in the Reichstag, L. Haas.[155] Another remarkable name among the organization's founding members was that of P. Eltzbacher, a right-wing law professor who in April 1919 had caused a stir by openly advocating that Germany adopt Bolshevism, calling this the only way to save the country from enslavement by the Entente.[156] Moreover, when in early 1924 a new supplement on foreign affairs was added to *Nakanune,* Kirdetsov and his staff attracted a whole group of German politicians, academics, and journalists as contributors to the new publication, including the political editor of *Berliner Tageblatt,* E. Dombrowski, political scientist A. Grabowsky, pacifist leader and editor of *Welt am Montag,* H. von Gerlach, and economists M. Bonn and C. Brinkmann.[157]

Besides its tasks abroad, *Nakanune* also had a purpose to serve within Russia's borders. First, by demonstrating that the Russians in emigration were playing a "shameful, antinational, and wretched role" vis-à-vis their motherland, the daily was supposed to strip the émigrés of the "aura of 'fighters for the truth' " that they allegedly still had among part of the intelligentsia in the motherland. Second, *Nakanune*'s editors hoped to convince those in Soviet Russia who still had doubts about the new regime's credibility to accept it and to cooperate with it. Along with their sponsors, Kirdetsov and his colleagues believed that an organ published abroad and perceived as independent was more likely to have influence in these circles. While they admitted that for people who had lived through the hardships of wartime Communism it was not easy to recognize the revolution's beneficialness, they trusted that, as a group of intellectuals who had grasped the revolution's meaning in a long and difficult process, yet free from all pressure from the Soviet regime, they had a fair chance to find an audience among the "hesitaters and doubters" in Soviet Russia.[158]

While the weekly *Smena vekh* had never had the opportunity to address directly the intelligentsia in Soviet Russia, from June 1922 on, the Berlin-based *Nakanune* had daily access to the Soviet public. It was the only émigré periodical to be granted this right.[159] Fresh issues of *Nakanune* were flown to Moscow every day and were openly on sale in the Soviet capital and in other cities. Apparently, this was the result of a special resolution of the Central Committee's Division for Agitation and Propaganda, which in February 1922 had decided that it was "indispensable in the near future not to stand in the way of the periodical publications of the '*smenovekhovtsy*,' given that they struggled against counterrevolutionary tendencies in the upper circles of the Russian intelligentsia."[160]

Whether *Nakanune* did indeed have the expected effect on the Soviet public is, however, another question. The Soviet historian S. A. Fediukin has argued that a comparison between the Soviet press and *Nakanune* would force even the most deep-rooted skeptic to conclude that the domestic press's coverage of international events and of life in the Russian émigré community was objective and that the loathsomeness of the bourgeois society was a fact, not an invention, of Communist agitation and propaganda.[161] Fediukin does not put forward the slightest evidence to support his thesis, however.[162] While this may have been believed by certain less educated groups of the population, it remains doubtful whether *Nakanune* ever had this effect on a sizeable scale among intellectuals critical of the Soviet regime. In any case, the daily's prestige in Soviet Russia was hardly higher than that in the émigré community.[163]

No doubt, *Nakanune*'s shady reputation was largely the result of the way in which Kirdetsov and his colleagues performed their fourth task, a task that went beyond those which the editors of the Paris weekly had set themselves. In their various statements of purpose, Kirdetsov and his friends repeatedly stressed that they should take advantage of their position as observers from without in order to closely follow the developments in Soviet Russia and react to them with constructive criticism.[164] Writing in the *Nakanune* of 5 May 1922, Kirdetsov explained that, as outsiders and at the same time supporters of the Soviet regime, they could play a useful role in the process of Russia's development by "drawing the border between the realistic and the ideal *(provesti gran' mezhdu real'nym i ideal'nym)*."[165]

In reality, however, *Nakanune's* "constructive criticism" invariably came down to endorsing whatever measure the government in Moscow took. Reacting to the open letter in which B. Pil'niak had distanced himself from *Nakanune* because of its servile coverage of the SR trial, B. Diushen retorted that "in the camp of the enemy, one had to speak of a close and dear cause with great caution."[166] The editors carried this "caution" so far that even Bobrishchev-Pushkin complained it was simply impossible to voice a critical note vis-à-vis Moscow on the pages of *Nakanune*.[167] Rather, Kirdetsov and his colleagues seemed to consider it their duty to "justify everything that was coming from Soviet Russia."[168] It was this attitude that earned *Nakanune* the epithets of "semiofficial organ of the contemporary Octobrists *(ofitsioz sovremennykh oktiabristov)*"[169] and "reptile (mercenary newspaper) *(reptiliia)*."[170] One contributor to *Poslednie novosti* even suggested that *Nakanune,* in effect, served as a powerful instrument of anti-Bolshevik propaganda, which opened the eyes of whoever still doubted the Soviet regime's perniciousness.[171] It was this extreme obsequiousness that distinguished *Nakanune* most from its predecessor, *Smena vekh,* and that also put off Kliuchnikov, although it would be hard to draw a line in Kliuchnikov's reaction between genuine indignation and a feeling of having been badly done by.

In the meantime, *Nakanune's* sponsors in Moscow were not blind to the Berlin daily's increasingly bad reputation; the question of continued support for the paper was a controversial issue among the Soviet authorities. It seems that Bukharin, who met the staff of *Nakanune* during a visit to Berlin in the spring of 1923, strongly opposed further subsidies to the daily, while Trotskii on the contrary advocated that they be continued, arguing that *Nakanune* was useful as "an outpost of the Soviet press abroad."[172] This was apparently also the view of officials at the Press Division of the Central Committee, who noted approvingly: "The daily is sufficiently consistent, in the vast majority of cases the information coincides entirely with the corresponding communications of our newspapers, and also the paper's ideological side is sufficiently firm and consistent in its benevolence toward the Soviet regime."[173] *Nakanune's* most convinced supporters were, however, to be found at the People's Commissariat of Foreign Affairs, which had, after all, been directly involved with *Nakanune* ever since its founding. Presumably, it was also from this quarter that in June 1924 the decision came to close *Nakanune* down, a decision that has to be seen primarily in the light of international developments at the time, although rumors about bad management and even abuses in the daily's financial affairs could not have left the daily's sponsors unaffected either.[174]

In the course of 1924 the major European powers finally granted full, international recognition to the Soviet government. On 1 February the new British Labour government officially recognized the USSR, a step followed in the next few weeks by Italy, Austria, Greece, Norway, and Sweden. In France, where the Poincaré government had strongly opposed the resumption of official relations with Soviet Russia, things changed when the general elections of 11 May 1924 were won by the so-called *Cartel des Gauches,* which had made de jure recognition of the Soviet government a key plank in its platform.[175] To a great extent these events deprived *Nakanune* of its purpose, especially because they also entailed a substantial change in the position of the Russian émigré community in the countries concerned. When the Soviet government was recognized as Russia's legitimate rulers, the émigrés were stripped of whatever status they still had as representatives of the "real" Russia and were conclusively eliminated as a potential threat to the Soviet regime.[176] In this light, *Nakanune*'s Moscow sponsors no longer saw the need for an "outpost" abroad of this kind and cut off the flow of money to the Berlin daily. On 15 June 1924 *Nakanune* closed its doors because of its "uselessness."[177]

The daily's last editorial stressed with baffling self-assurance that *Nakanune* was ceasing publication "as an organ that had fulfilled its main tasks." Both in the USSR and abroad, it argued, the signposts had been changed for good: the so-called internal emigration had disappeared completely, the external emigration had disintegrated, and the USSR had regained its rightful place in the world. *Nakanune*'s departing editors concluded that although, as a movement typical of a transitional stage, "*Nakanunchestvo*" had outlived its usefulness, this did not mean their group would now disappear from the scene. They would take another step forward toward more active work, exactly as they had done in the spring of 1922, when they had made the transition from *Smena vekh* to *Nakanune.* The group behind *Nakanune* indicated that they saw their immediate task now in furthering cultural, social, and commercial contacts between the USSR and the countries of Western Europe, and they would henceforth dedicate themselves to this task both at home and abroad. They ended their farewell message with an expression of gratitude to the German authorities, who had met their activities with benevolence and fairness. Finally, *Nakanune*'s subscribers were assured that they would receive full refunds.[178] The business was shut down with dignity, at least to outside appearances.

After *Nakanune*'s closing, several members of its staff did take the announced "step forward"; indeed, many of them already had made such a move earlier. Kirdetsov, who served as press attaché at the Soviet mission in Berlin from the summer of 1923 and later at the Soviet mission in Rome until 1926, returned to Moscow, where he continued to work for the People's Commissariat of Foreign Affairs and became a regular contributor to *Mezhdunarodnaia zhizn'* (International Life), the commissariat's organ.[179] Diushen, for his part, had worked for the Soviet trade mission in Berlin from 1921 until his return to Moscow, also in 1926, when he was appointed head of the Central Office for Correspondence Courses for Vocational Training and became editor of the journal *Izobretatel'* (Inventor).[180] Kliuchnikov, who had had contacts with the

People's Commissariat of Foreign Affairs ever since 1921, continued to collaborate with the commissariat after his return to Soviet Russia in August 1923.[181] Besides his activities at his various teaching positions,[182] he was a regular contributor to *Mezhdunarodnaia zhizn'*,[183] and compiled several collections of diplomatic documents from recent European history, published by the commissariat.[184]

Upon Krasin's request, Chakhotin joined the Soviet trade mission in Berlin as well, but he remained in this post only for a short time and soon returned to his scientific interests.[185] He compiled a bibliography of European literature on the principles of "scientific management" and wrote an introduction to the subject, both of which appeared in the Soviet Union, at the Soviet State Publishing House and at the People's Commissariat for Worker-Peasant Inspection, respectively.[186] In the 1930s he did research into the mechanisms of German and Italian Fascist propaganda, basing his analysis on the concept of the conditioned reflex. He was arrested by the Gestapo in 1941 and sent to a concentration camp, but survived. He returned to Russia in the late 1940s, where he continued his research as a physiologist at the Institute for Biophysics of the Academy of Sciences.[187]

Luk'ianov had moved to Paris in early 1924 in order to explore the possibilities of setting up Soviet organizations there. He joined the Russian Section of the French Communist party,[188] and edited *Parizhskii vestnik–Le Messager russe de Paris,* the organ of the umbrella association of Soviet organizations in France, including the Union for Return to the Motherland, the Union of Russian Workers, and the Union of Students–Soviet Citizens in France. He also served as editor of *Nash soiuz–Notre Union,* the weekly that in May 1926 took the place of *Parizhskii vestnik.*[189] He left the staff of *Nash Soiuz* in July 1927 to join the Soviet press agency TASS, first in Paris and from 1930 on in Moscow. He was the first editor of the French-language Soviet weekly *Journal de Moscou,* which was published by the People's Commissariat of Foreign Affairs, but which was supposed to pass for an independent publication. As E. A. Gnedin, the weekly's last editor later remarked, the choice of a former *smenovekhovets* for this post was not coincidental.[190]

Several other contributors to *Nakanune* did not join Soviet organizations abroad, but returned to Soviet Russia, where many of them resumed the activities they had had before their emigration. Tolstoi, Vasilevskii, and Bobrishchev-Pushkin returned in August 1923 aboard the same ship as Kliuchnikov. Vasilevskii and Bobrishchev-Pushkin resumed their respective occupations as feuilletonist[191] and lawyer,[192] while Tolstoi made his comeback in the literary world and soon became a member of the Soviet cultural establishment. He would eventually be elected a member of the Soviet Academy of Sciences and a deputy to the Supreme Soviet.[193] On the whole, only a few of *Nakanune*'s collaborators did not pass through the Berlin daily's "corridor." Among them were P. A. Sadyker;[194] A. S. Iashchenko, who, to be sure, continued to hesitate whether to return home throughout the 1920s, finally deciding in 1930 to stay abroad;[195] and R. B. Gul', who fully "returned in the bosom of the émigré community,"[196] where, as editor of the major émigré periodical *Novyi zhurnal* (New Review), he would play a fairly important role in the years after World War II.[197]

Chapter *Seven*

THE EFFECTS OF
SMENOVEKHOVSTVO

Both Ustrialov and the European *smenovekhovtsy* addressed themselves primarily to the Russian émigré intelligentsia, appealing to them to accept the October revolution and the regime it had brought forth in the interests of the Russian nation and state. What is more, in contrast to Ustrialov, who felt that the time was not ripe for the émigrés to return, Kliuchnikov and his European friends urged the émigrés to rejoin their former colleagues in Soviet Russia and take up practical work there.

As has been seen, this call for reconciliation and cooperation with the Soviet regime was met with almost unanimous indignation on the part of the émigré intellectuals. The appeal touched upon the one element that united them, namely, their rejection of the Soviet regime, and it was therefore not surprising that hardly anyone among them was prepared to make this move. While intellectuals in Soviet Russia had no choice but to find a modus vivendi of some kind with the new regime, for their colleagues in emigration it took a most peculiar cast of mind to take such a step. Even the so-called *vozvrashchentsy* (returnees), a small group of intellectuals centered around A. V. Peshekhonov, M. A. Osorgin, and E. D. Kuskova who in 1925–1926 called upon the émigrés to return home, maintained an attitude of hostility vis-à-vis the Soviet regime.[1]

Clearly, a most instrumental element in accepting the new regime was unconditional Russian patriotism, unqualified love for the great motherland. As Potekhin insisted in the collection *Smena vekh,* quoting a passage from Gogol's moralizing *Izbrannye mesta iz perepiski s druz'iami* (Selected Passages from a Correspondence with Friends), which at the time had shocked the whole of educated Russia: if one really loved Russia, one "loved whatever there was in Russia."[2] A second element conducive to "changing signposts" was a strongly Hegelian world view and a view of world history as "*das Weltgericht,*" which was most obvious in the case of Gurovich and especially of Ustrialov, who combined it with an almost biological evolutionism. A third element, connected to this, was the conviction that Western culture and Western political forms in particular had reached the stage of decay and that Russia could show the world a way out of this impasse. Finally, a fourth element was an economic determinism close to the views of the English philosopher Herbert Spencer (1820–1903), which was particularly strong in the case of Chakhotin.[3] Judging from the example of the *smenovekhovtsy*, for former convinced opponents of the Soviet regime to change their minds about it, it took a combination of these elements in varying proportions, mixed with either a considerable amount of wishful thinking and naïveté, a substantial amount of opportunism, or a blend of both. In any case, this peculiar combination of elements in the right proportions did not occur often.

Indeed, besides the literary milieu, where cultural enthusiasm for the East made a few individuals "change signposts," the only group of émigré intellectuals where the *smenovekhovtsy*'s appeals did find an audience, albeit a limited one, was that of the Russian students in exile. Generally speaking, in the first half of the 1920s Russian students in emigration considered it their duty to prepare themselves for a career so that they could serve their country, once Russia was free again and they had the opportunity to return.[4] Not all students had the patience to wait for that day, however, and it was in their midst that the ideas of the *smenovekhovtsy* caught on. Reportedly, Ustrialov's *V bor'be za Rossiiu* aroused considerable interest among Russian students in Prague,[5] and there is evidence that the efforts of the *Nakanune* group to gain support in student circles also had a certain effect.[6]

In June 1922 the Berlin Democratic Group of the Party of People's Freedom was shocked by the decision of one of its youngest members, a student named Gershun who was generally considered a "good young man," to leave the group and join the *smenovekhovtsy*. In justifying his action, Gershun declared that he thought it indispensable for Russia's interests to cooperate with the existing regime there, although he did not identify himself with its ideals.[7] The Gershun case was not an isolated one: in July 1922 Bobrishchev-Pushkin wrote to Ustrialov that a group of 370 students had joined their movement,[8] and in that same month a Union of Russian Students–Citizens of the RSFSR was founded in Czechoslovakia.[9] In September 1922 a similar organization was created in Berlin,[10] and in November of that year both the chairman and vice-chairman of the mainstream student organization ORESO (Union of Russian Emigré Student Organizations), which united on an apolitical platform some 8,500 of the fifteen thousand students in emigration, "changed signposts."[11]

Starting in September 1922, *Nakanune* appeared with a weekly section on "Student life," in which the new organizations of *smenovekhovtsy* students could express their views.[12] The first conference held by the organizations took

place in Berlin from 27 to 30 December 1922 and was attended by twenty-
one delegates from Berlin, Prague, Vienna, Leipzig, Geneva, and a number of
other centers, representing some four hundred students in all. Most likely,
these were largely the same people as the group that Bobrishchev-Pushkin had
mentioned in his letter to Ustrialov. Among the participants in the conference
was also a representative of the Central Office of Moscow Student Organizations, M. Glebov, who played a leading role in the event.[13]

At the Berlin conference it was decided to found a new union of pro-Soviet
student organizations, which was to counterbalance the influence of ORESO.
The members of the new union set themselves the task of "educating from
their midst workers *(rabotniki)* who, after their arrival in Russia, would collaborate hand in hand with the working people *(trudiashchiesia)* of the RSFSR
in building a New Russia," and who would do so "without pretensions to
commanding positions, without pretensions to leadership or influence in the
politics of the workers' and peasants' state." On this occasion, the delegates
also distanced themselves from the *smenovekhovtsy.* They argued that, unlike
those former opponents of the regime, they were not replacing old signposts
with new ones, but were positioning their signposts for the first time; therefore, their acceptance of the October revolution was more radical.[14]

Whether Moscow had been involved in the new student organizations from
the outset is not clear; in any case, by the time of the Berlin conference the
movement's Soviet backing was beyond doubt. In fact, the pro-Soviet students
received subsidies and technical assistance from the Central Committee's Division for Agitation and Propaganda.[15] Notwithstanding this support, however,
the movement was never a great success. At the conference it was announced
that, so far, a total of 720 émigré students had chosen the side of the Soviet
regime.[16] In the summer of 1923, on the first anniversary of its foundation, the
Prague organization proudly declared that twenty-four of its members had
returned to Russia, but further diplomatically limited itself to reporting that its
membership figure had risen from a "two-digit to a three-digit number."[17] If
anything, these figures were not underestimated, yet even so they added up to
just a small part of the total number of émigré students; thus, in a total of
15,000, the figure of 720 amounted to less than five percent. Moreover, after
the summer of 1923 the tendency to "change signposts" among the émigré
students petered out.[18] Presumably, by that time those students who were re-
ceptive to influences of this kind had been persuaded, while the remaining
majority continued to stand firm and would not hear of such ideas. This is not
to say that pro-Soviet student organizations abroad disappeared altogether. In
Germany, for example, the Union of Students from the USSR was active
throughout the 1920s and up to 1933, when it was banned by Hitler; in 1928
it had a membership of 450. However, the great majority of its members were
Soviet students sent to Germany to study at the universities of Berlin, Leipzig,

and other cities, while émigrés or children of émigrés were hardly represented in the organization.[19]

The group behind *Nakanune* helped organize the return to Soviet Russia of only a limited number of émigrés, primarily the daily's contributors themselves, as well as a small group of literary figures. *Smenovekhovstvo* has also been associated with the larger scale repatriation of Cossacks from Czechoslovakia and, especially, the so-called Union for Return to the Motherland, which coordinated repatriation from Bulgaria. Contemporaries labeled this phenomenon *smenovekhovstvo*,[20] as did several scholars of the movement later.[21] Still, while there were contacts between the groups involved, and while the repatriation movement did fit in with the same broad sociopolitical tendency as *smenovekhovstvo* in the narrow sense, it would be straining the truth to represent the repatriation movement as an achievement of the *smenovekhovtsy*.

Indeed, a spontaneous repatriation movement had begun to take shape among the émigré masses—primarily the rank and file of the White armies—by the beginning of 1921, that is, even before the *smenovekhovtsy* as a group had appeared on the scene. In the months following the final defeat of the White armies, nostalgia—"zoological nostalgia *(zoologicheskaia toska)* for one's own land and family," as one of the Cossack returnees called it[22]—and the hardships of refugee life had made smaller groups of émigrés decide to return home at their own risk.[23] This movement intensified as a result of the Central Committee's decree of 3 November 1921, which granted amnesty to the rank and file of the White armies on the occasion of the October revolution's fourth anniversary. According to Soviet figures, some 120,000 émigrés returned home in the course of 1921.[24] This number is no doubt exaggerated,[25] but there is evidence that at least several thousands of émigrés did return to Russia in the course of that year.

In the meantime, the presence of large numbers of Russian refugees was becoming an all too heavy burden for several of the host countries. In the summer of 1921 the Council of the League of Nations decided to deal with the problem and appointed the famous Norwegian explorer F. Nansen as "High Commissioner on Behalf of the League in Connection with the Problem of Russian Refugees in Europe." From his first days in office, Dr. Nansen's approach to the problem was one that decisively favored voluntary repatriation as the best possible solution to the problem.[26]

In the spring of 1922 the first organization aimed at furthering repatriation with the High Commissioner's help, the so-called Union for Return to the Motherland, was created in Bulgaria. That country harbored by that time well over 30,000 Russian refugees, mostly former soldiers of General Wrangel's army, including several thousand Cossacks.[27] The initiative for setting up the union came from the Bulgarian Communist party, but it seems that Moscow had a hand in the union from the very beginning.[28] Presumably, the Soviet authorities felt a movement of this kind would help to improve their international reputation and at the same time prevent a loss of face vis-à-vis the League of Nations, which, after all, they regarded as an instrument of imperialist governments. Supposedly, to cooperate with the League at the request of an "independent" refugee organization was easier for Moscow than to do so on their own initiative. In any case, one of the union's first actions was not only to send the People's Commissariat for Internal Affairs a declaration promising the Soviet regime "unconditional loyalty and utmost support" but also to request the Soviet representatives in Vienna and Constantinople to provide for the repatriation of Russian refugees with the help of the League of Nations.[29]

In response to these requests, the Soviet government started negotiations with Dr. Nansen, and in July 1922 a limited repatriation agreement was signed between the Soviet People's Commissariat for Foreign Affairs and the High Commissioner's office. The agreement provided for the repatriation of common soldiers from the Don, Kuban, and Terek regions and stipulated that, in organizing the undertaking, Dr. Nansen's organization should cooperate with the Soviet Red Cross and the People's Commissariat for Internal Affairs.[30] From that moment, the Soviet authorities openly took control of the Union for Return to the Motherland. In the course of October 1922 a number of Soviet representatives arrived in Sofia to set up a mission of the Soviet Red Cross. Supported by the Bulgarian government, headed by the Agrarian party leader A. Stamboliiskii, the mission went on to conduct an intensive propaganda campaign for repatriation. With this goal, they founded a new pro-Soviet newspaper, *Novaia Rossiia* (New Russia), which replaced both the union's former organ *Na rodinu* (To the Motherland) and the Cossack daily *Vestnik zemledel'tsa* (Farmer's Messenger). The new paper probably received subsidies, not only from the Soviet Red Cross but also from Dr. Nansen's office.[31]

Clearly, the setting up of the Bulgarian Union for Return to the Motherland was not connected with *smenovekhovstvo*. It must be seen in the context of, first, the spontaneous repatriation movement of rank-and-file refugees that had started in early 1921; second, the Soviet government's desire to capitalize on this movement to enhance its credibility at a time when its international recognition was under consideration; and third, the action taken by the League of Nations to further repatriation. This is not to say that, ideologically speaking, the Bulgarian movement had nothing in common with *smenovekhovstvo* in the narrow sense of the word. When, besides a few thousand common soldiers, a number of high-ranking White officers, including Lieutenant General A. Sekretev and Major Generals Iu. Gravitskii, I. Klochkov, and E. Zelenin, joined the Bulgarian Union, they justified their step in terms very much reminiscent of Ustrialov's *V bor'be za Rossiiu* and the nationalist themes in the collection *Smena vekh*. On 29 October the newly converted generals published an appeal "To the Forces of the White Armies," in which they promised to be "loyal

citizens of the Soviet Republic and honest soldiers of its revolutionary army."
They stressed that, whereas the White movement had turned out to be directed against the Russian state and people, the Soviet regime had assured itself
of the Russian people's utmost support and was serving as the only protector
of Russia's national interests and sovereignty. The generals appealed to the
White forces to return to the motherland, adding that to remain in emigration
would be a crime vis-à-vis the Russian people.[32] In the next months, this
declaration was followed by several other, similarly worded statements.[33]

In their decision to support the Soviet regime, these military men may well
have been inspired by the ideas of *smenovekhovstvo;* however, from the available
evidence it is impossible to substantiate this. The same, for that matter, is true
for the step taken almost a year earlier by the White Lieutenant General Ia. A.
Slashchev (1885–1929), who at the invitation of, and after extensive negotiations with, the Soviet government,[34] returned to Soviet Russia in late November 1921, along with a small group of supporters. Naturally, his move was
eagerly publicized by the Soviet government. Upon his arrival in Moscow,
Slashchev launched an appeal to the White forces, warning them that unless
they followed his example, they would be merely mercenaries of foreign capital, directed against their own country and their own people.[35] Slashchev's
resentment of the role of foreign powers in the White movement was apparently sincere. The appearance of the collection *Smena vekh* and the positive
reactions to it in the Soviet press may have served as an extra stimulus in his
decision to take the side of the Soviet government, but, again, there is no
evidence to confirm this. Besides, Slashchev had seriously collided with General Wrangel and subsequently been cashiered, so that feelings of personal ran-
cor may also have played a role in his move.[36]

Among the contributors to *Novaia Rossiia,* the organ of the Union for Return to the Motherland, there were also people with a background similar to
that of Ustrialov, Kliuchnikov, and their colleagues, most importantly, the
Kadet historian E. D. Grimm (1870–?). Before the revolution, Grimm had
been rector of Petrograd University and had contributed to a whole range of
publications, including the journal *Problemy velikoi Rossii*. During the civil war
he had served as vice-director of General Denikin's *Osvag;*[37] after the evacua-
tion of Novorossisk he had settled in Bulgaria, where he had held a chair at
the Faculty of History and Philology of Sofia University.[38]

As early as 1921, Grimm had spoken admiringly of the Bolsheviks' decisiveness and vigor, as compared to the weakness of both the Provisional Government and the White movement; however, he did not "change signposts" until
the end of the following year, when he joined the staff of *Novaia Rossiia*.[39] Yet,
even then, Grimm seemed to lack the courage to be honest about his position
and initially worked for *Novaia Rossiia* in secret. What is more, he did not
immediately break with the White camp, but continued to serve as a political
advisor to the staff of General Wrangel, maintaining a strongly anti-Bolshevik

stand in public. Understandably, when Grimm's double life was revealed in February 1923, the émigré community reacted with great indignation.[40]

It is unclear whether Grimm's enthusiasm for the "grandiose scale . . . and worldwide significance of the processes of Russian popular life"[41] had in any way been inspired by the ideas of Ustrialov and European *smenovekhovstvo*. In any case, judging from the correspondence between Ustrialov and his European friends, there were no actual contacts between them. This does not mean that the group behind *Novaia Rossiia* had no connections with the European *smenovekhovtsy* whatsoever. Bobrishchev-Pushkin served as the paper's correspondent in France and regularly contributed to *Novaia Rossiia* under the pseudonyms A. Kol'chugin and Gromoboi.[42] B. Mironov, also a collaborator of *Nakanune,* contributed an article on the situation in Germany to the Sofia newspaper. On that occasion he was referred to as *Novaia Rossiia*'s "Berlin correspondent."[43] That, however, was as far as the cooperation went.

Even more so than *Nakanune, Novaia Rossiia* was primarily a propaganda organ of the Soviet government. An article such as the one in which a certain Petrovskii reported from Novorossiisk that "delicatessens were bursting with produce"; that the local GPU officials were "correct, polite people"; that there was complete religious and cultural freedom; and that cultural life in the city was sparkling, would presumably have been too much even for the Berlin daily's staff.[44]

Be that as it may, *Novaia Rossiia* and the Union for the Return to the Motherland were cut short by developments in Bulgaria's internal political situation. On 9 June 1923 the Stamboliiskii government was overthrown in a military coup, and soon thereafter the union and its organ were outlawed.[45] In July 1923 the organization's leaders were expelled from the country and sent to Odessa. Among them was E. D. Grimm; before long, he was employed by the People's Commissariat for Foreign Affairs as an advisor.[46] According to figures of the League of Nations, by the time of the union's liquidation some six thousand people, mostly Cossacks, had been repatriated through its agency; according to Soviet calculations, this figure ranged between eleven thousand and fourteen thousand persons.[47]

Efforts to promote repatriation were made also among the Cossack refugees in Czechoslovakia; in the summer of 1922 rumors circulated that a number of *smenovekhovtsy* were conducting a propaganda campaign in their midst. As a matter of fact, in early June of that year, representatives of the three main Cossack groups in the country—the Don, Kuban, and Terek Cossacks— directed an appeal to their fellow countrymen, urging them never to shed Russian blood again and to return home. Very little is known about this segment of the repatriation movement. Apparently, the men who launched this appeal had connections with the Union for Return to the Motherland in Sofia, yet it remains unclear whether or not they were merely agents from Moscow.[48] The appeal to return home caused a great deal of commotion among the

Cossacks in Czechoslovakia and seems to have convinced at least some of them to repatriate. The Russian historian L. K. Shkarenkov maintains that four thousand Cossacks were repatriated from Czechoslovakia in the course of 1922;[49] however, judging from the available evidence, the number of Cossacks who left Czechoslovakia in that year to return to their native land was rather in the order of four hundred.[50]

After the summer of 1923, the repatriation movement lost momentum. With the liquidation of the Bulgarian Union for Return to the Motherland, the only project for large-scale repatriation of Russian refugees came to an end, and in the following years the Soviet government showed no interest in setting up other ventures of this kind. Apparently, after its failure to secure international recognition at the Conferences of Genoa and The Hague, Moscow no longer felt the need to continue action in this field; Dr. Nansen's efforts to conclude new repatriation agreements with the Soviet government were unsuccessful.[51] On the whole, it must be concluded that *smenovekhovstvo* played, at best, a marginal role in the repatriation movement of the early 1920s; among the actual target group—émigré intellectuals—the *smenovekhovtsy's* appeal for reconciliation and cooperation with the new regime had hardly any effect.

A peculiar case was that of the former SR leader and Kerenskii's vice-minister of war, B. V. Savinkov (1879–1925), who joined the ranks of reconcilers in the late summer of 1924. Throughout the civil war and even after General Wrangel's final defeat, Savinkov had been one of the most active proponents of armed struggle against the Bolsheviks.[52] The circumstances of Savinkov's "changing signposts" are, to say the least, questionable. On 16 August 1924 the Soviet authorities arrested him while he was illegally crossing the Soviet-Polish border. Within days he was put on trial and sentenced to death, yet the Presidium of the Central Executive Committee of the USSR commuted this sentence to ten years in jail, presumably in response to Savinkov's declaration of full, unconditional support for the Soviet regime.[53]

At the lawsuit, Savinkov stressed that he had always been motivated by an enormous love for Russia and the Russian people and had struggled against the Bolsheviks as long as he had been convinced that their regime was disastrous for his native land. In the course of 1923, however, he had come to realize that his assessment of the situation had been completely misguided. First, the Constituent Assembly, in which he had fostered such high hopes, had turned out to be a nonentity; second, the separate peace with Germany had not marked the end of the Russian state, as he had feared; third, the Bolshevik takeover had not entailed reaction, but had on the contrary ruled out reaction for good; and, last but not least, the Bolsheviks were not the usurpers he had thought them to be, but had the full support of the Russian people. Savinkov added that, once he had realized this, it had become impossible for him to remain in emigration. He had decided to return home, whatever the risks he was running by this step. He concluded his speech before the court with an appeal to "every Russian, every man who loved his motherland," to bow before the regime of workers and peasants and recognize it without reservation.[54]

Savinkov's words in the courtroom may have saved him from the firing squad, but they never convinced the Soviet authorities completely. On 13 September 1924, two weeks after his conviction, *Pravda* carried a new declaration of loyalty to the Soviet regime over Savinkov's signature, but under the title "A *Smenovekhovets* with an Unexploded Bomb."[55] Furthermore, in a comment on a number of letters that Savinkov had written from his Moscow cell to former émigré associates, urging them to follow his example, the former SR leader was labeled superficial and egocentric, and his conversion was dismissed as "merely a new way to extol his image both politically and artistically."[56] In May 1925 it was announced that Savinkov had committed suicide. The circumstances of his death remain unclear to this day. Doubts as to whether Savinkov had indeed killed himself increased when, shortly after Savinkov's death, his warder took his own life.[57]

Apparently, Savinkov had been lured into the Soviet Union through *Trest,* a sham monarchist organization the Soviet secret police had set up in 1921 and operated until the fall of 1927.[58] However, the question remains whether Savinkov was purely the victim of Soviet undercover operations, or whether he had reached some accommodation with the Soviet regime. It seems reasonable to suppose that, if the latter had been the case, the former SR leader would have attempted to negotiate some agreement with Moscow before returning home and, in any case, would not have tried to enter Soviet Russia in secret. Yet revelations suggesting that, in December 1921, Savinkov had had contacts with L. B. Krasin, Soviet plenipotentiary representative in London at the time, have cast renewed doubt on the official accounts of the matter.[59]

Pravda had labeled Savinkov a *smenovekhovets*. Indeed, in style and argumentation Savinkov's various declarations of loyalty to the Soviet regime were comparable to the appeals and publications of the *smenovekhovtsy;* in his booklet *Patrioty bez otechestva* (Patriots without a Fatherland), which appeared in Leningrad in 1925, Bobrishchev-Pushkin welcomed Savinkov's move, calling it the completion of the counterrevolution's collapse.[60] However, there is not the slightest indication that Savinkov had any links with the *smenovekhovstvo* movement. Rather, the Soviet authorities' use of the term *smenovekhovets* in the Savinkov affair must be seen in the general framework of their campaign against the movement, which was to reach its height in 1923, but to continue well into 1924.

With their appeals for reconciliation with the new regime, the *smenovekhovtsy* had intended eventually to eliminate the anti-Bolshevik émigrés as a social force; the Soviet authorities' support to the movement had been prompted in part by hopes that *smenovekhovstvo* would further the émigré community's disintegration.[61] Soviet scholars have often credited the movement with actually achieving this;[62] however, it seems closer to the truth to say that *smenovekhovstvo* had the opposite effect. To be sure, individual "defections" to the *smenovekhovtsy*'s camp disheartened the immediate environment of the persons in question,[63] but that was certainly not the impact of the movement as a whole; the personal prestige of its representatives was too low for that. Rather, *smenovekhovstvo* provided the émigrés with yet another common enemy against which to form a united front. The thesis of the Soviet historian A. V. Kvakin, that *smenovekhovstvo* not only was the result of a crisis in the émigré community but also reinforced this crisis,[64] must be rejected, at least the second part of it.

If the practical results of *smenovekhovstvo* were, therefore, most limited, the group did play a role in the development of the so-called postrevolutionary movements in the Russian émigré community of the interbellum period. Along with the Eurasians, the *smenovekhovtsy* had been the first émigré grouping to insist that the October revolution was more than just a deplorable and temporary aberration in Russia's history. In the second half of the 1920s and the 1930s, the idea that one should accept the revolution as a fact and integrate Bolshevism into one's vision of Russia's future—which did not automatically mean that one should also accept the Bolshevik regime as such—became the basis of a whole range of new émigré movements.[65]

These movements adopted the common label of "postrevolutionary," opposing themselves to the traditional émigré groups, which continued the prerevolutionary political traditions. In fact, a strong feeling of disillusionment with the way the traditional émigré organizations had handled and were still handling the anti-Bolshevik struggle was one of the elements that united the postrevolutionaries of all political tendencies.[66] The new movements considered it their task to develop a new, comprehensive world view that would take into account Russia's characteristics as they had been revealed in the October revolution. Eventually, this world view was to serve as the basis for political programs that would enter into competition with Bolshevism, with platforms on which it should be possible to overcome the Soviet regime spiritually.[67] Understandably, these new movements found an audience primarily among émigré youth, the "lost" generation of émigré "sons" who, unlike their "fathers," did not have a pre-October life to hark back to and who reportedly felt themselves "the most superfluous of all superfluous men" in history.[68]

While the *smenovekhovtsy*'s call to accept the October revolution as an event of epochal importance for Russia and for mankind as a whole played a role in the inception of these movements—some postrevolutionaries openly admitted their intellectual indebtedness in this respect[69]—the views of Kliuchnikov and his colleagues had hardly any impact on their further development. In light of the new movements' ambitions to replace Bolshevism by an "ideocracy,"[70] or even a "neo-monarchy,"[71] the *smenovekhovtsy*'s advice that the best one could do for Russia's good was to cooperate loyally with the Soviet regime held little attraction and was even contemptible in their eyes.[72]

Ustrialov, who in the early 1930s maintained regular contacts with the so-called Postrevolutionary Club in Paris[73] and followed their undertakings with keen interest, decisively rejected this "activism."[74] He very much appreciated the postrevolutionaries' acceptance of the October revolution, their understanding that it was absolutely necessary for Russia's good that the USSR be a strong state, and their willingness to follow developments in the motherland without prejudice. Yet he dismissed as ridiculous and even dangerous their hopes of playing a role in replacing the Soviet regime. He warned that aggressive gestures from abroad might disturb the internal transformation processes that were going on in Soviet society.[75] In his view, the only possible activity for Russian patriots abroad was to continue the Russian cultural-historical tradition and to try to protect the Soviet state from dangers from without by means of political action.[76]

The postrevolutionaries, however, wanted to find a "third way" between the traditional émigré groupings' complete rupture with Russian reality and the *smenovekhovtsy*'s submission to the Soviet regime, between the old world and the new world of Bolshevik Russia.[77] With the outbreak of World War II, most postrevolutionaries saw their hopes for a "third way" shattered. Others, however, took advantage of the situation to enter into contact with their Soviet compatriots and to modify their programs according to the indications they received. This was the case with the so-called *Natsional'no-Trudovoi Soiuz Novogo Pokoleniia* (National-Labor Alliance of the New Generation), which has continued its quest for a "third way" to the present day.[78]

From the very beginning, the *smenovekhovtsy* had set themselves the task of reconciling the outside world with the new Russia,[79] something their Moscow supporters had eagerly encouraged. Because they failed to find an audience in émigré circles, the *smenovekhovtsy*'s efforts to influence foreign public opinion through the intermediary of the Russian émigré community were in vain. Yet, in their attempts to approach Western politicians directly, they were not entirely unsuccessful, as their contacts with the French Radical-Socialist leader E. Herriot and with a number of German politicians have shown. It must be stressed, however, that this was by no means exclusively their personal achievement. If, to be sure, in the France of the early 1920s any attitude other than hostility toward Soviet Russia was still seen as daring,[80] in Germany a positive stand vis-à-vis the new Russia was not exceptional, even in certain right-wing circles.[81] In their contacts with Western politicians, the *smenovekhovtsy* did not win over new sympathizers to the Soviet Republic's cause, but merely channeled existing sympathies.

Kliuchnikov and his colleagues also aspired to leave their mark on the Soviet government's foreign policy.[82] However, even Kliuchnikov's participation in the Soviet delegation to the Conference of Genoa, which he triumphantly had called *smenovekhovstvo*'s first practical application,[83] was limited to "playing the violin in the Soviet delegation's palazzo on May Day," even if accompanied on the piano by Chicherin himself.[84] The *smenovekhovtsy*'s day in this respect came later, after their return to Soviet Russia, when a number of them were employed by the People's Commissariat of Foreign Affairs. However, given their small number compared to the whole of the commissariat's staff, which, as the American historian T. J. Uldricks has shown, was a Communist stronghold,[85] their importance there should not be exaggerated. Besides, by that time, Soviet foreign policy had already been "normalized,"[86] and it had lost those characteristics that the *smenovekhovtsy* might have wanted to correct.

In the last issue of *Nakanune*, the European *smenovekhovtsy* claimed that their movement had left its imprint on Soviet society and had managed to win over to the Soviet regime those groups who still doubted its credibility.[87] Yet, the non-Communist intellectuals who had not left Soviet Russia either decisively condemned *smenovekhovstvo* or reacted to it in a haughty way, indicating that they had long since gone through the process of accepting the revolution and revising their ideological positions. As a matter of fact, in Soviet Russia quite a few non-Communist intellectuals were prepared to accept Soviet power as the Russian national power, without going so far as to accept Communist ideology. Because they had come to these conclusions, not under the influence of the Prague collection, but as a result of their own assessment of the situation, *smenovekhovstvo* was of no concern to them. Moreover, the way in which the European *smenovekhovtsy* compromised with the Soviet authorities greatly irritated these circles, who made sure to distance themselves from Kliuchnikov and his colleagues. Only Ustrialov found more favor in their eyes.

No doubt, one can reasonably presume that, under the circumstances of the NEP, many professionals, military men, and businessmen in Soviet Russia found an ideological justification for serving the new state in ideas such as those set forth by the *smenovekhovtsy*.[88] Ustrialov, for instance, had regular contacts with business circles in Moscow, in any case until 1927, when, in view of the violent attacks against him in the Soviet press, keeping in touch with him became too dangerous.[89] Earlier, in the fall of 1922, the heyday of *smenovekhovstvo*, *Pravda* published the results of a survey of 230 non-Communist engineers employed by Soviet institutions in Moscow. When they were questioned about their attitude toward Soviet power and their expectations for the future development of the Soviet economy, sixty-eight left the second part of the question unanswered, sixty-eight foresaw the strengthening of state capitalism as a transitory stage to Communism, and the other ninety-four expected the collapse of state capitalism as a transitory stage to Communism and a return, in part, to the former capitalist relations. As for their attitude toward Soviet power, thirty-four of the engineers did not answer the question, twelve described their attitude as "hostile," forty-six as "indifferent," twenty-eight as "sympathetic," and the remaining 110 called themselves "*smenovekhovtsy*."[90]

Obviously, the actual impact of *smenovekhovstvo* in this respect cannot be measured. In any case, no reader of the Soviet press could possibly remain ignorant of the movement, given the numerous articles that appeared on the subject in the course of 1921–1922. What the survey in *Pravda* definitely shows is that *smenovekhovets* and *smenovekhovstvo* had entered the Russian vocabulary and were widely used to describe any readiness on the part of non-Communists to accept the new regime.[91] Before long, however, the terms would take on an undertone of distrust and suspicion, as the discussion of the Communist party's attitude toward the movement will show.

Chapter Eight

SMENOVEKHOVSTVO AND THE BOLSHEVIKS

However limited the overall significance of *smenovekhovstvo,* it is clear that the movement never would have reached the dimensions it did without the support of the Soviet authorities, Lenin in particular. The hostile émigré community and the Soviet Russia of the NEP years—a period when the Communist party built up and even increased its ideological pressure[1]—were environments where *smenovekhovstvo* could not have expanded by itself. With the exception of Ustrialov, who insisted on maintaining independence from Moscow, the *smenovekhovtsy* accepted material and moral support from the Soviet government because they believed this would further their cause. The authorities in Moscow, for their part, sustained the movement because they regarded it as useful, both at home and abroad.

Moscow hoped, first, that *smenovekhovstvo* would help to emasculate the émigré community as a pressure group. After the experiences of the civil war and foreign intervention, the émigrés were a force which the Soviet authorities mistrusted and even feared, in any case, until the Conference of Genoa, which signaled the end of Moscow's complete isolation in international politics.[2] Second, the Soviet government believed that *smenovekhovstvo* could serve as an unsuspected instrument in campaigning for international recognition of the Soviet regime, hence, the close involvement of the People's Commissariat of Foreign Affairs with Kliuchnikov and his colleagues. It was this department that, supported by Lenin and Trotskii, enabled the *smenovekhovtsy* to set up the weekly *Smena vekh* and to expand it subsequently into a daily newspaper, *Nakanune.* And third, the Soviet authorities considered *smenovekhovstvo*—in which they included also the group behind *(Novaia) Rossiia*—as being useful in convincing non-Communist intellectuals to cooperate with the new regime and in curbing "counterrevolutionary tendencies" among them.

Indeed, Moscow had closely followed the émigré movement for reconciliation with the Soviet regime ever since its origin. The appeals of V. B. Stankevich and *Mir i trud,* for example, had been noted with satisfaction on the pages of *Izvestiia,*[3] while N. V. Ustrialov's *V bor'be za Rossiiu* had received two positive, if patronizing, reviews from *Pravda,*[4] reportedly even drawing the special attention of Lenin.[5] Finally, the collection *Smena vekh* had been the subject of a whole series of articles, mostly favorable, in the Soviet press, although there were also a few negative reactions, mainly from left-wing Bolsheviks and from officials of the *Comintern* and the People's Commissariat of Nationalities. Be that as it may, these critical remarks had not prevented the party's Central Committee from deciding in November 1921 to devote special attention to *smenovekhovstvo;* in February 1922, the committee had even ruled that the movement should be given active support as well.[6]

In the following weeks, as has been shown, a whole range of concrete measures were taken to this effect. Thus, it was decided to have the Prague collection reprinted by the Smolensk and Tver divisions of the State Publishing House. I. G. Lezhnev and his group were granted permission to publish their journal *Novaia Rossiia,* and when they met with opposition from the Petrograd party leader and chairman of the *Comintern,* G. E. Zinov'ev, Lenin personally interceded on their behalf.[7] In late May 1922, the Berlin daily *Nakanune* was admitted for distribution in Soviet cities and towns, and in June of that year Kliuchnikov and Potekhin arrived in Soviet Russia for a lecture tour organized by *Glavpolitprosvet,* the political propaganda division of the People's Commissariat of Enlightenment. In addition, the Central Committee decided to support the pro-Soviet movement among Russian students in emigration.

Notwithstanding this wide range of supporting measures, however, Moscow's patronage of *smenovekhovstvo* was never unconditional. Even the movement's most convinced defenders among the Bolsheviks stressed that independent political action was absolutely out of the question and made it clear that, in the end, they expected the *smenovekhovtsy* to take the side of the Soviet regime unequivocally. This was also the position of Lenin, who on several occasions personally intervened to protect and recommend the *smenovekhovtsy.* Lenin's first public statement on the movement, which he made at the Eleventh Party Congress in March 1922, was a mixture of endorsement and denunciation. He acknowledged the *smenovekhovtsy*'s support and praised them for their sincerity, yet stressed at the same time that they were "class enemies," striving for the restoration of bourgeois capitalism.[8]

At the Eleventh Party Congress, only a few radical opponents of a tolerant attitude vis-à-vis *smenovekhovstvo* had raised their voices on the issue, notably the left-wing Bolshevik and future chief of the Red Army's political administration, V. A. Antonov-Ovseenko (1884–1939), who resented the *smenovekhovtsy*'s talk of a "transformation" of the Soviet regime;[9] N. A. Skrypnik

(1872–1933), a leading Ukrainian Communist, who was alarmed by the movement's Russian nationalist overtones;[10] and finally, G. E. Zinov'ev, who was
careful, however, not to offend Lenin.[11] In March 1922, the time was clearly
not ripe for an outburst against the movement, not in the least because it had
Lenin's personal support.

Various circumstances, however, were to strengthen the hand of *smenovekhovstvo*'s opponents in the months that followed. After a first stroke in late
May 1922 had incapacitated him, Lenin's immediate grip on Soviet policy
weakened.[12] Apart from that, there was growing apprehension in party circles
that the economic concessions of the NEP were also leading to a revival of
bourgeois ideology,[13] and in this light, the issue of *smenovekhovstvo* was becoming ever more sensitive. Furthermore, as has been seen, feelings of hostility
toward *smenovekhovstvo* were boosted by the self-important and none-too-tact-
ful attitude that Kliuchnikov and Potekhin took during their visit to Soviet
Russia in June–August 1922; from the summer of that year, the tone of Soviet
comments on the movement became increasingly antagonistic. A. S. Bubnov,
chairman of the Central Committee's *Agitprop* division, which in February
1922 had called *smenovekhovstvo* useful in combating counterrevolutionary
tendencies, published on 27 July 1922 a long, belligerent article in *Pravda*.
Bubnov warned that the circumstances had changed since late 1921 and early
1922 and that, under the present conditions, *smenovekhovstvo* was more likely
to be a legal cloak for counterrevolutionary activities and a passport clearing
the way for all sorts of ideological deviations than a bridge leading toward
Communism.[14]

Just a few days later, at the Twelfth All-Russian Party Conference (4–7
August 1922), which was the first major party meeting at which Lenin was
absent, Zinov'ev launched an open attack against *smenovekhovstvo*. He called its
representatives "quasi-friends," arguing that the *smenovekhovtsy* did not support
the Communist party at all and in reality wished for nothing less than the
restoration of bourgeois democracy. At the conclusion of his speech, however,
Zinov'ev backed down a little and added that *smenovekhovstvo* had "to some
extent played a positive role."[15] Apparently, forces in favor of a tolerant attitude
toward the movement were still too strong for a complete denunciation. The
Party Conference's final resolution on *smenovekhovstvo* was entirely in the dual-
istic style that had characterized also Lenin's remarks on the issue at the Eleventh Party Congress:

> The so-called *smenovekhovstvo* orientation has played and still can play an objec-
> tively progressive role. It has rallied and continues to rally those groups of the
> emigration and the Russian intelligentsia who "have made their peace" with the
> Soviet authorities and are prepared to collaborate with them for the sake of the
> country's regeneration. That is why *smenovekhovstvo* has deserved and continues

to deserve positive treatment. However, it should not be forgotten for one minute that the *smenovekhovstvo* orientation contains powerful bourgeois-restorationist tendencies, that the *smenovekhovtsy* share the hope with Mensheviks and SRs that economic concessions will be followed by political concessions toward bourgeois democracy, and so forth.''[16]

This resolution stressed the positive role of *smenovekhovstvo,* albeit not without qualifications. However, it was part of a larger resolution on "Anti-Soviet Parties and Tendencies," in which it was argued that under the circumstances of the NEP, these groups were changing their tactics: "they are trying to use Soviet legality in their counterrevolutionary interests and are heading for their 'growing into' the Soviet regime, which they hope gradually to transform in the sense of a bourgeois democracy."[17] The resolution called for decisive action against tendencies of this nature, not only through propaganda and education but, if need be, with the help of repressive measures as well. True, the resolution also contained a clause to the effect that support should be given to those "truly nonparty elements . . . who, albeit only in basic lines, had grasped the real sense of the great revolution that had taken place."[18] However, in the weeks following the Party Conference, the Central Committee's *Agitprop* division under Bubnov's direction conducted a campaign in which this distinction was readily obscured.

Immediately after the Twelfth Party Conference's closing session, on 8 August 1922, a special meeting was convened on the question of the struggle against bourgeois ideology and *smenovekhovstvo.* The meeting was chaired by Bubnov and was attended by the secretaries of the provincial Party Committees, representatives of the press, and officials of *Glavpolitprosvet* and the Central Committee's *Agitprop* division.[19] Apparently, it was decided there to start an offensive against *smenovekhovstvo;* in the following weeks the movement became the object of a whole series of hostile articles in the central and regional press.[20] In the *Izvestiia* of 26 August, for example, the journalist D. I. Erde called *smenovekhovstvo* the "bourgeois-intellectual and petit bourgeois–radical ideology of the NEP *(nepovskaia burzhuazno-intelligentskaia i meshchanski-radikal'- naia ideologiia),*"[21] and in the issue of 31 October Erde argued that the *smenovekhovtsy*'s acceptance of the Soviet regime was only a cover for their nationalist and bourgeois democratic strivings.[22] On the pages of *Pravda,* the Petrograd *Komsomol* leader G. Safarov, a close associate of Zinov'ev, stressed that the *smenovekhovtsy* were trying to use the legal opportunities created by the NEP for counterrevolutionary goals.[23] In the November–December issue of *Sibirskie ogni* (Siberian Fires), M. Furshchik reproached the staff of *Smena vekh* and *Nakanune* with being "Kadet reserves," and branded the group behind *(Novaia) Rossiia* as "marauders of the revolution."[24]

In early January 1923 the Central Committee's Organization Bureau decided to prepare a collection of articles on the struggle with bourgeois ideology for the forthcoming Twelfth Party Congress.[25] The collection, entitled *Na ideologicheskom fronte bor'by s kontrrevoliutsiei* (On the Ideological Front of the Struggle with Counterrevolution), contained also an article on *smenovekhovstvo* by N. L. Meshcheriakov, one of the movement's longtime supporters. The tone of the article, which dealt mainly with the views of Ustrialov and the staff of *Nakanune,* was symptomatic. Meshcheriakov argued that the whole world was living through an era of struggle between the proletariat and the bourgeoisie. In this struggle the world was breaking up into two hostile camps, and all attempts to take a position in between those two camps were doomed to fail. There was no third position possible.[26] Despite this, Meshcheriakov went on, judging from their plea for an independent intelligentsia, it was clear that the *smenovekhovtsy* continued to believe in the possibility of an intermediate stance. They failed to understand that the intelligentsia could only be an instrument in the hands of one or the other of the warring camps: the bourgeoisie or the proletariat. Returning to the image of the "little Pink bridge" that he had used in his first comments on *smenovekhovstvo,* Meshcheriakov now observed that apparently the *smenovekhovtsy* wanted to turn this little bridge into "a permanent address" for themselves. This, he warned, was impossible; indeed, it was not a true "change of signposts." The *smenovekhovtsy* should realize that their choice was between only two possibilities, he said, and that they should take the side of the proletariat. Meshcheriakov urged those who could not immediately accept the ideology of the proletariat to become completely honest and diligent Soviet specialists and give up all pretensions to leading the proletariat. The Soviet authorities, he stressed, were not prepared to make any further concessions.[27]

At the Twelfth Party Congress, which took place in April 1923, there was not a trace of the tolerance that had marked the Twelfth Party Conference's resolution on *smenovekhovstvo.* Now attention was focused on the movement's "Great Russian" chauvinism and on what was called its petit bourgeois hopes for the Soviet regime's transformation.[28] At the Thirteenth Party Conference in January 1924, the struggle for ideological purity against petit bourgeois and *smenovekhovstvo* attempts to hedge in the Soviet system was declared one of the party's main tasks,[29] and this was repeated at the Thirteenth Party Congress in May 1924.[30] Against the background of a marked backlash by the Soviet leadership against the NEP in the second half of 1923 and 1924, the term *smenovekhovstvo* came to denote the ideology of the new bourgeoisie that originated as a result of the NEP. It gradually took on an undertone of distrust, and many suspected that it was merely their hope for the regime's return to bourgeois capitalism that had prompted the *smenovekhovtsy* to embrace reconciliation. Moreover, the meaning of the term was sometimes twisted so that it could include any form of dissent.[31]

In spite of these condemnations, Soviet support for *Nakanune* continued until June 1924, when international recognition of the Soviet regime sharply diminished the need for a pro-Soviet organ abroad. On the occasion of the Berlin daily's last issue, *Izvestiia* carried an article praising *Nakanune*'s staff for their role in the struggle against the anti-Bolshevik émigrés.[32] The journal *(Novaia) Rossiia,* for its part, continued to appear until the spring of 1926 and was allowed to reprint, without any intervention from the censor, a number of Ustrialov's articles, including "Secularization *(Obmirshchenie),*" in which he predicted the "decisive and irrepressible secularization of the Communist church's extremist deeds of derring-do *(derzaniia).*"[33] (According to I. G. Lezhnev, the authorities gave their permission only to have an excuse to subsequently attack Ustrialov,[34] something they did not fail to do.[35]) Finally, the *smenovekhovtsy* who returned to Russia in August 1923—A. N. Tolstoi, A. V. Bobrishchev-Pushkin, Iu. V. Kliuchnikov, and I. M. Vasilevskii—were given the opportunity to give public lectures throughout the country, speaking in a whole series of cities and towns including Moscow, Minsk, Kiev, Krasnodar, Novorossiisk, Baku, and Tbilisi.[36]

Yet, by the end of 1923, interest in the movement in Soviet Russia had fallen sharply. True, at the first soirée of lectures by the *smenovekhovtsy* returnees in Moscow, the hall reportedly was crammed full, but the lecturers could not really hold the public's attention.[37] Looking back on the tour of lectures, Bobrishchev-Pushkin was forced to admit that the audience had never been completely their own.[38] In the summer of 1924, on the occasion of *Nakanune*'s closing, D. I. Erde spoke in *Izvestiia* of "the end of *smenovekhovstvo,*"[39] and when N. V. Ustrialov visited Moscow a year later, he found that *smenovekhovstvo* was "*plusquamperfectum.*" From what Ustrialov observed, people in the Soviet capital either were not interested in the movement, or regarded it with suspicion.[40]

Before long, however, *smenovekhovstvo* became the focus of renewed public attention. The issue in its distorted form, charged with mistrust and suspicion, came to play a role in the power struggle within the party following Lenin's death. As has been seen, in the weeks preceding the Fourteenth Party Congress, G. E. Zinov'ev seized upon Ustrialov's new collection of articles *Pod znakom revoliutsii* to indirectly voice his opposition against two elements in the official party line that Ustrialov had applauded in his book: the party's encouragement of the individual peasant and its orientation toward "socialism in one country."[41] The center answered Zinov'ev's attack in the same fashion, that is, by means of an indirect attack, formally directed against Ustrialov, yet in reality intended to rebut Zinov'ev's criticism. This reply was written by Bukharin, who attacked Ustrialov for his longing for a "bourgeois dictatorship," and tried at the same time to justify the party's course.[42] Stalin, for his part, kept himself in the background during the debate on *Pod znakom revoliutsii,*[43] yet returned to *smenovekhovstvo* at the Fourteenth Party Congress in December 1925, branding it as the ideology of a new bourgeoisie dreaming of the regime's transformation, but added that dreaming as such was not forbidden, as long as the *smenovekhovtsy* continued to provide grist for the Bolshevik mill. He made it clear that it was not they who were his main enemies.[44]

Thereupon, Stalin's opponents within the Central Committee accused him of yielding to petit bourgeois, *smenovekhovstvo* influences himself. Reportedly, in the spring of 1926, Zinov'ev came to a meeting of the Politburo, angrily brandishing an issue of *Novaia Rossiia*—the journal had appeared again under its original title since January 1926—and complaining that, while he and his comrades were being prosecuted, the gentlemen of *Novaia Rossiia* had full freedom of speech. Shortly thereafter, the journal was closed down by the authorities, and Lezhnev, its editor-in-chief, was arrested and subsequently exiled. Apparently, Stalin considered it opportune to eliminate anything that might confirm allegations that he was succumbing to *smenovekhovstvo* influences.[45]

This was not sufficient to silence his opponents, however. Even Trotskii, formerly one of *smenovekhovstvo*'s main supporters, now joined in these accusations. In October 1926, at the Politburo meeting where he was excluded from its membership, Trotskii warned that under Stalin's direction, the Central Committee was letting the party slide back exactly in the direction Ustrialov and the new bourgeois classes wanted.[46] In December of that year, at a unified plenary session of the *Comintern* Executive Committee, the deposed chairman of the Moscow Soviet L. B. Kamenev, who had been ousted from the Politburo along with Trotskii, accused the Central Committee of adhering to Ustrialov's advice.[47] In the course of 1927, Zinov'ev and his allies published a number of articles in which they used the term *ustrialovshchina* to condemn the party's policy in the countryside.[48] Finally, at the tenth anniversary of the October revolution, the so-called left-wing opposition appeared on the streets, carrying banners with the slogan "Down with *Ustrialovshchina!*"[49]

Hardly a month later, at the Fifteenth Party Congress in December 1927, Trotskii, Zinov'ev, and Kamenev, along with their adherents, were expelled from the party. In the Central Committee's political account to the congress, it was admitted that *smenovekhovstvo* influences persisted in the countryside, as well as among the new bourgeoisie and the intelligentsia. However, it was stressed that the party had reacted and was reacting to this phenomenon by strengthening the dictatorship of the proletariat.[50] This was not the last time the term *smenovekhovstvo* came up at a party meeting. At the Sixteenth Party Congress in April 1929, it was used once again as an incrimination, now by the center against Bukharin. In the meantime, Stalin had espoused the defeated opposition's program of rapid industrialization and collectivization, while Bukharin continued to oppose such a policy. In 1928 one of Bukharin's associates within the party, A. K. Zaitsev, had published a book arguing that, in the debate over *Pod znakom revoliutsii*, only Bukharin had formulated a convincing and crushing answer to Ustrialov.[51] Now Bukharin himself was being accused of falling under Ustrialov's influence. That Ustrialov had praised him for his rejection of collectivization, saying that "when Bukharin speaks from the heart, the nonparty fellow travelers on the right can keep silent,"[52] was readily seized upon to inculpate him.[53] Shortly thereafter, Bukharin was expelled from the Politburo.[54]

In this way, *smenovekhovstvo* successively served two purposes for the Bolsheviks. First, Lenin and his colleagues backed the movement as a useful ally abroad, where it could play a role in undermining the émigré community's influence and in securing the Soviet government's international recognition, and at home, where it could help to convince nonparty intellectuals to cooperate with the new regime. Later, when the movement as such was no longer of any use, the concept of *smenovekhovstvo* in its distorted form, standing for strivings to transform the Soviet society into a bourgeois capitalist system, was seized upon as a convenient element in the struggle for power within the party. By means of a "guilt by association" technique, the concept was played off, first by the so-called left-wing opposition against the central party line and subsequently by the center against Bukharin and what was called the right-wing deviation.

It has also been argued that the idea of the revolution's national meaning, as it had been put forward by the *smenovekhovtsy,* had its place in the party discussions leading up to the adoption of the "socialism in one country" principle at the Fourteenth Party Conference in April 1925. In 1958 the British historian E. H. Carr advanced the thesis that the *smenovekhovstvo* movement "had helped to prepare the way for the reconciliation of the revolutionary and the national tradition that was a condition and concomitant of 'socialism in one country.' "[55] Carr relativized his contention, however, by placing it in a wider framework, pointing to "the uncovenanted beginnings of a 'national' foreign policy and the equally unforeseen strength of the appeal to a tradition of 'Russian' patriotism" as factors that laid the psychological foundations for the turn toward "socialism in one country."[56]

One of the principal students of the *smenovekhovstvo* movement, M. Agurskii, went a step further and tried to demonstrate that the ideas of Ustrialov directly influenced and inspired Stalin in this matter.[57] On the basis of the available evidence, however, it is hard to substantiate such a contention. In fact, Agurskii refers in this respect mainly to the heated discussion over *smenovekhovstvo* and the ideas of Ustrialov in Bolshevik party circles and to the protection that the *smenovekhovtsy* and the group behind *Novaia Rossiia* enjoyed on behalf of a number of leading Bolsheviks, including Stalin.[58] The mere fact that *smenovekhovstvo* and Ustrialov's publications were repeatedly under discussion in the party debates of the early and mid-1920s could hardly serve as a conclusive confirmation of the movement's influence on some party leaders. The same is true for the *smenovekhovtsy*'s protection by Stalin and his allies; moreover, the examples that Agurskii puts forward in this connection are not always convincing. That, for instance, there were plans to reprint a number of articles from Ustrialov's controversial *Pod znakom revoliutsii* in the Soviet Union in the spring of 1926 is sufficient to make Agurskii conclude that Ustrialov was backed by Stalin.[59] However, Zinov'ev, who hardly could be suspected of supporting Ustrialov, made a similar proposal in his reaction to the book, arguing that "the prophesies of our enemies . . . serve as yet another reminder about certain real dangers . . . that lie in the current situation. Maybe we will even straight away reissue Ustrialov's booklet and make the study of it obligatory in our party schools and other educational institutions."[60]

It must be added, however, that in the last version of his work on National-Bolshevism, M. Agurskii considerably watered down the extreme position he had taken in earlier versions. With his recognition that the idea of "socialism in one country" was not new, but had emerged as early as the spring of 1918,[61] he implicitly withdrew his earlier assertion that "Stalin, advancing his slogan [of socialism in one country], saw in the Harbin philosopher a source of inspiration."[62] Clearly, *smenovekhovstvo* came into being in reaction to the Soviet regime's consolidation as a strong, de facto Russian-national regime, not the other way round. Although some *smenovekhovtsy* considered the introduction of "socialism in one country" a victory, they could not take credit for it.

In the meantime, the *smenovekhovtsy* who returned to Soviet Russia in the course of the 1920s integrated into Soviet society, some of them even remarkably well. As noted above, Iu. V. Kliuchnikov, G. L. Kirdetsov, and E. D. Grimm became employed by the People's Commissariat of Foreign Affairs, a position that reportedly was considered a sign of great confidence on behalf of the authorities.[63] Vasilevskii Ne-Bukva and Bobrishchev-Pushkin returned to their former occupations as a journalist and a lawyer, respectively. A. N. Tolstoi, for his part, became a prominent writer and, in the words of G. P. Struve, "made his way in the world and even in high society *(vyshel v liudi i dazhe v bare)*,"[64] joining the ranks of the Soviet elite. As a gifted electrotechnical engineer, B. V. Diushen was offered upon his return in 1926 a three-room apartment and an interesting job at the People's Commissariat of Enlightenment;[65] he became a real Soviet *spets*. V. N. L'vov, as has been seen, was employed by one of the Soviet economic institutions; S. S. Luk'ianov worked first for Soviet organizations in France and subsequently for the Soviet press agency TASS; and General A. A. Noskov was given a position at the Military Academy of the Red Army.[66] Iu. N. Potekhin first worked for the Supreme Council of the National Economy and during the second half of the 1920s acted as the plenipotentiary in Moscow of the Leningrad-based Union of Theatrical and Musical Writers *(Dramsoiuz)*.[67] Apparently, Potekhin had connections with the highest circles of the Communist party: he reportedly was an acquaintance of Stalin and in the late 1920s served as literary editor of *Sovetskoe stroitel'stvo* (Soviet Construction), the journal of the Central Executive Committee of the USSR.[68] In 1929 he contributed to a collection of articles published by this journal, entitled *Sovetskaia demokratiia* (Soviet Democracy).[69] Clearly, the Soviet authorities did not hesitate to offer the *smenovekhovtsy* jobs in which they could serve the Soviet state according to their abilities and qualifications. However, this certainly was not the privilege of the *smenovekhovtsy* alone. Generally speaking, until the late 1920s the Soviet authorities took a tolerant attitude toward the non-Communist intelligentsia, including even former opponents, provided they, for their part, did not take an openly hostile stand vis-à-vis the regime.[70]

In the late spring of 1928, however, the Soviet leadership abandoned their former tolerance and launched a "cultural revolution." The old intelligentsia as a group came under suspicion and were accused of being wreckers and conspirators. Thus, they served as scapegoats for all the economic problems that accompanied the accelerated industrialization drive.[71] The so-called Shakhty trial in the early summer of 1928, in which fifty-three mining engineers and technical specialists of the Shakhty area in the Don coal basin were tried on charges of alleged sabotage, served as a first warning.[72] It was followed by a wave of arrests and purges among the old intelligentsia,[73] and by a second show trial in November–December 1930, the so-called *Prompartiia* (Industrial party) trial, where eight alleged leaders of an alleged underground organization were accused of large-scale "wrecking" activities. The leaders had supposedly received their orders from the French politician R. Poincaré, who from July 1926 to July 1929 had served a third term as prime minister, and from the Russian industrialist P. P. Riabushinskii, who, incidentally, had died in exile in 1924.[74]

It was against this background of imputations and arrests that, in January 1931, the literary journal *Krasnaia nov'* published a scathing article against the *smenovekhovtsy*, in which they were called "precursors of sabotage," and were even accused of being the brains behind *Prompartiia* and other "wrecking" organizations. It was argued in the article that, once the *smenovekhovtsy* had understood that the NEP would not lead to the "Thermidor" they desired, they had consciously changed their tactics and engaged in sabotage.[75] With the help of a series of quotations from the 1921 collection *Smena vekh*, taken out of context, the author tried to show that Kliuchnikov and his friends had never wanted anything else but the liquidation of the Soviet regime and the suppression of the proletariat.[76]

Obviously, such an attack did not bode well for the *smenovekhovtsy*. S. S. Luk'ianov immediately wrote a letter to the editors of *Izvestiia*, distancing himself from his former colleagues, Ustrialov in particular, and arguing that, unlike them, he could hardly be reproached with taking a counterrevolutionary stand, as he had long since joined the ranks of the Soviet proletariat.[77] Luk'ianov's letter apparently was acceptable to the daily's editors, and they printed it. However, when Ustrialov in his turn wrote a letter to *Izvestiia*, protesting that Luk'ianov had falsely accused him of being a counterrevolutionary, a wrecker, and an interventionist, the letter was never published.[78] Not everyone was given the right to defend himself against fabricated accusations. Still, the *smenovekhovtsy* seem to have been spared prosecution at that time. Indeed, from the summer of 1931 the wave of repressions against the old intelligentsia began to ebb. The pressures for restoring order were becoming ever stronger, and Stalin withdrew his support for the "cultural revolution."[79] Along with many other intellectuals, the *smenovekhovtsy* were granted some respite. Kliuchnikov could continue his research in the field of international law, Luk'ianov was appointed the first editor-in-chief of the new French-language Soviet weekly *Journal de Moscou,* and Ustrialov was allowed to return to Moscow and given a teaching position.

The actual repression of the *smenovekhovtsy* began in the first months after the murder of the Leningrad party leader S. M. Kirov, which marked the beginning of the Great Terror. In 1935 Diushen, Luk'ianov, and Kirdetsov—all good friends—were arrested together on charges of belonging to a counterrevolutionary organization. Luk'ianov reportedly had compromised himself as editor of *Journal de Moscou* by consistently deleting Stalin's name from its pages;[80] however, there seems to have been no immediate cause for the arrest of his two friends. The same was true for Bobrishchev-Pushkin, who was detained in 1935 as well, and for Kliuchnikov, Potekhin, Vasilevskii, and Ustrialov, who were arrested in 1937 and early 1938. Bobrishchev-Pushkin was executed in 1937; the others perished in the course of 1938.[81] Kirdetsov and Luk'ianov, who upon their arrest in 1935 had been sent to a concentration camp, never returned. Diushen, on the other hand, was spared thanks to his technical skills and inventiveness. As opposed to his two friends, he had been sent to jail, where he had been forced to continue his work as an engineer. In 1940 he invented a new antitank weapon, and as a result, People's Commissar for Defense Marshal K. E. Voroshilov ordered that he be freed. Diushen was appointed chief engineer of the special laboratories at the Ministry of State Security (MGB), where he worked until his death in 1949.[82] Chakhotin, finally, escaped the purges by living abroad in those years. He returned to the Soviet Union only in the late 1940s and worked at the Moscow Institute for Biophysics of the Academy of Sciences until his death in 1974.[83] No details are available on the fate of other former *smenovekhovtsy.* Presumably, they, too, perished in the late 1930s. With their White, émigré, and bourgeois background, the *smenovekhovtsy* were all too easy victims for the devastating terror of those years.

CONCLUSION

When in the course of 1920–1921 a number of Russian émigré intellectuals launched an appeal to cease the struggle against the Soviet regime and to come to terms with it, they did so because they believed that, under the given circumstances, this was the best course of action one could take for Russia and the Russian people. None of them accepted the Soviet regime wholeheartedly, yet they felt that to continue the struggle against it could only aggravate the situation. Not only would this cause even further devastation and needlessly increase anarchy in the country, it would also deepen the regime's darker side, providing the Bolsheviks with a justification for intensifying the terror against their opponents.

No one among the émigrés who called for acceptance of the Soviet regime was, however, guided purely by the desire to prevent further destruction and human suffering. Over the past few years they had all come to regard the October revolution as an expression of the Russian people's will and, hence, as a phenomenon that should not be disavowed. In addition, while none of them could accept Bolshevik ideology, they all had a certain admiration for Lenin and his colleagues. V. B. Stankevich, for example, praised the Bolsheviks as audacious innovators with an enormous creative potential; N. V. Ustrialov appreciated their vigor and that they were consolidating the territory of the former Russian empire; and Iu. V. Kliuchnikov valued them because he believed that they alone had rightly understood the need for radically new economic, social, and political principles which could serve as the basis for a just and peaceful world.

Finally, these advocates of reconciliation with Moscow believed that the Soviet regime would evolve toward more acceptable forms, if only it were left in peace. Stankevich trusted that peace would bring new opportunities for free economic competition and lead to the creation of a parliamentary democracy in Russia. Ustrialov expected the Soviet regime to evolve toward "Bonapartism," which he understood as being Russia's resurrection as a powerful state, the restoration of order, and the return to a "bourgeois" economic system. Kliuchnikov and his friends, for their part, believed that such evolution would lead to an intermediate form between private initiative and state regulation and to a new type of political system in which all social groups would play roles, provided that they identified their own interests with those of the community.

In making their peace with the Soviet regime, Stankevich, Kliuchnikov, and Ustrialov felt inspired by the convictions and principles that had guided them in the years preceding the revolution and that subsequently had motivated them to take the side of the anti-Bolshevik movement in the civil war. The People's Socialist Stankevich was motivated by his belief in democratic principles; the right-wing Kadet N. V. Ustrialov, an admirer of Vladimir Solov'ev, by his longing for a powerful "Great Russia" that would lead the world toward the ideal of a "united mankind"; and the Kadet and specialist in international law Iu. V. Kliuchnikov by his vision of a worldwide community of nations in which all peoples of the world would live together in justice and peace. Stankevich's hopes that negotiations between Moscow and all democratic émigré groups would lead to the creation of a parliamentary system in which the Bolsheviks would peacefully coexist with their political opponents were, however, so obviously unrealistic, that he and his group never received serious attention in the émigré community. By contrast, the expectations with which Kliuchnikov and Ustrialov approached the developments in their motherland were not entirely out of tune with the course of events.

For Ustrialov, the decisive element which had prompted him to revise his position vis-à-vis the Soviet regime had been the observation that the borderlands of the former Russian empire, several of which had detached themselves from the center in the months following the October revolution, were gradually being united around the core of the Russian Soviet Republic. That the Soviet regime had not hesitated to defend Russia against the Polish invaders had strengthened him in his belief that, notwithstanding their internationalist ideology, the Bolsheviks were protecting Russia's national interests. Moscow's decisive action against outbursts of popular rebellion had reassured him that Lenin's government was capable of stemming anarchy. In addition, with the introduction of the NEP, Ustrialov had seen his prediction confirmed that, in order to survive, the Soviet regime would be forced to compromise with capitalism. Finally, in a later stage he became impressed with what he considered the Soviet state's universal mission as the prototype of a new union of mankind, a supranational whole on a national basis, united by the ideas of social justice, general labor, and the transformation of nature by human genius.

The Polish invasion and the introduction of the NEP had been decisive moments for Kliuchnikov as well; he, however, was in the first place fascinated by what he regarded as the international significance of Bolshevism. Disillusioned by the outcome of the Paris Peace Conference, which he initially had hoped would mark the beginning of a new and more just system of international relations, and influenced by the deep economic and political crisis that struck Europe as it was struggling to recover from the world war, Kliuchnikov came to the conclusion that only a radical break with the past could resolve the impasse. Convinced that the world was on the brink of overall revolution, he came to believe that Bolshevism might prove to be a necessary stage in the development of mankind and that an evolved Soviet regime might take the lead in the world's progress toward a just and peaceful international order. This was a prospect he regarded as most gratifying for the Russian people.

In the light of these observations, and faced with what they regarded as the émigrés' incapability of taking constructive action, Ustrialov and Kliuchnikov felt compelled to make their peace with Lenin's government. As they saw it, if they were really concerned with the future of their country and their people, they had no choice but to give up their own desire for complete ideological purity and accept the Soviet regime, whatever crimes it had committed in the past and however "repugnant" its materialistic ideology and its doctrine of class struggle might be. As Russian patriots, they felt that this was the best sacrifice they could make for their motherland.

Kliuchnikov and Ustrialov belonged to the small group of young Russian intellectuals who had been educated in the traditions of the collection *Vekhi* of 1909. In an attempt to understand the underlying causes that had led to the failure of the revolution of 1905, the authors of *Vekhi* had pointed to the Russian intelligentsia's readiness to subjugate the absolute values of nation, state, law, truth, and religion to the relative values of politics and revolution. Moreover, P. B. Struve and his colleagues had argued that, in their reverence for abstract revolutionary ideas, the Russian intelligentsia had lost all contact with reality and had become incapable of constructive work.[1]

Searching for a way out of the impasse in which the October revolution had placed the Russian non-Communist intelligentsia, Ustrialov and Kliuchnikov tried to heed their teachers' warnings. In the émigré factions' endless squabbles over how Russia should be organized in an ever more remote post-Bolshevik future, they saw repeated what the *Vekhi* authors had written on the intelligentsia's devotion to abstractions and their alienation from reality. By calling for acceptance of the Soviet regime and cooperation with the Bolsheviks in Russia's reconstruction, the *smenovekhovtsy* tried to avoid the same shortcomings. In addition, by insisting on the need to give up one's own ideological purity for the sake of one's country and one's people, they wanted to avert the mistake S. L. Frank had observed with respect to the radical intelligentsia, namely, that by devotion to some abstract form of humanism they would augment the sufferings of their fellow men.[2]

The *smenovekhovtsy* accepted the Soviet regime in an attempt to place the absolute values of nation and state above the relative values of politics, as P. B. Struve and his colleagues had recommended. In doing so, however,

Kliuchnikov, Ustrialov, and their friends took into consideration only part of *Vekhi*'s message, thus crippling its true meaning. The *Vekhi* authors' urgent appeal for the intelligentsia's moral and spiritual reeducation was left unheeded; the message of *Vekhi* was reduced to the need for understanding the mystique of the state and for overcoming the intelligentsia's "itch for opposition," as Ustrialov called it.[3] Ustrialov, to be sure, was aware of this deficiency, while at the same time incapable of remedying it. As his friend G. N. Dikii rightly remarked in 1930, there was in him "not a grain of that legal consciousness for the absence of which Kistiakovskii had reproached the Russian intelligentsia in *Vekhi*." Ustrialov "knew only the rights of a despotic regime, yet completely ignored the yearning for rights—both political and social—of the individual."[4] In contrast, Kliuchnikov and his European followers did not even take the problem into consideration.

In the meantime, if the *smenovekhovtsy*'s interpretation of *Vekhi*'s message was inadequate, so was their understanding of the situation. They were all too willing to ascribe the enormous devastation in their homeland solely to the years of war and civil strife and to present the Bolshevik terror as merely a regrettable, yet inescapable, response to the attacks of the Soviet regime's opponents. In addition, they overestimated the regime's capability for evolution, as well as its willingness to accept "constructive criticism" and cooperate with non-Communists who wanted to retain ideological independence. They turned a deaf ear to the Soviet authorities' repeated and unequivocal warnings against misunderstandings of this kind. This was the case not only during Kliuchnikov and Potekhin's visit to Moscow in the summer of 1922; Ustrialov continued to hope for a "modest political 'spring' " in his motherland even in 1934. While the *smenovekhovtsy* blamed the Russian émigrés for living either in the past or in a delusive future, they lived in a world of illusions themselves. They cherished the illusion that the Soviet system would evolve and thus provide the world with a "new democracy" and a balanced economic model of state regulation combined with private initiative and, further, that Moscow would take them into account. In the end, this was their downfall.

No doubt, the *smenovekhovtsy*'s willingness to abandon their opposition to the Soviet regime was greatly facilitated by their disillusionment with what they called "arithmetic democracy." Ustrialov and Kliuchnikov, as well as a great part of their followers, had belonged to right-wing Kadet or Octobrist circles, where enthusiasm for parliamentary democracy based on universal, equal, direct, and secret suffrage had never been very great, and where the state had always been considered a positive value. However, both the right-wing Kadets and the Octobrists had remained constitutionalists;[5] by "changing signposts," Ustrialov and his colleagues broke with this tradition for good. Disillusioned with the way the traditional parties had handled the situation in the Provisional Government, in the various White governments, and later in emigration, they were favorably struck by the Bolsheviks' decisiveness. They came to regard Lenin's party as an "aristocracy of the will," motivated by a creative idea, and the Soviet system as a prototype of "authentic" democracy, organically grown from the people. If there was one element in the Soviet system that the *smenovekhovtsy* accepted with full willingness, even with a certain enthusiasm, it was its antidemocratic character. In this respect, they were true children of their time.

While the *smenovekhovtsy* admitted that the Soviet prototype still needed perfecting, they believed that it could offer a way out of the crisis in which Western democracy found itself. In any case, the Soviet model, with its stress on social and international justice, seemed to be far more valuable in their eyes than the answers to the problem being formulated elsewhere, in particular, Italian Fascism and German National-Socialism. In this light, they assumed that the time had come in which Russia would take over Europe's leading role in world history. This filled them with great national pride and tremendous messianic expectations. Gradually, they came to believe that the Russian people's sufferings would be redeemed by the bright future of universal justice and peace that would result from Russia's revolutionary experience. With this in mind, the *smenovekhovtsy* recognized the October revolution as the "Great Russian Revolution" for which the Russian intelligentsia had been waiting so long and as a decisive step toward fulfilling the prophecies of Vladimir Solov'ev and Fedor Dostoevskii on Russia's universal, "all-human" mission.

Just as all the other political groups in the Russian intelligentsia, the *smenovekhovtsy* started from the assumption that they were speaking for the Russian people. Moreover, they believed they were the truthful interpreters of the people's opinions and aspirations. They felt they should accept the Soviet regime because it had arisen from the people's spontaneous entrance on the political scene and because it corresponded to the people's desires. Kliuchnikov, Ustrialov, and their colleagues referred in this respect to the Russian people's yearning for "eternal justice"; to their need for clear and simple social and political goals; and, strange as it might seem, to their longing for a strong state, an element that the *smenovekhovtsy* held to be the other side of the anarchic trait in the Russian national character. The *smenovekhovtsy* maintained that, by taking these popular aspirations into consideration and endorsing them, the Bolsheviks had been able to control the eruption of popular revolt and avoid anarchy. In addition, this had ensured the Soviet regime of a broad social basis. As a result, unity between the people and the regime had been restored, and the lack of social cohesion that had affected the country for centuries had finally been overcome. The *smenovekhovtsy* felt that this was a guarantee of Russia's progress, greatness, and well-being. In any case, that it had been achieved at the price of immense suffering was no reason to turn one's back on Soviet Russia. On the contrary, to ensure that such suffering would not be in vain, the intelligentsia should not lag behind, but unequivocally take the people's side.

The *smenovekhovtsy*'s call to accept the Soviet regime convinced hardly anyone among the Russian intelligentsia in emigration. Other groups in the émigré community had their own interpretations of the situation in Soviet Russia and of the Russian people's desires, and they, too, were convinced of having the truth on their side. Moreover, to be susceptible to the *smenovekhovtsy*'s argumentation a most peculiar cast of mind was needed, the basic component of which was unconditional and imperialistic patriotism, mixed with elements such as economic determinism or a view of world history as *"das Weltgericht,"* and a considerable amount of wishful thinking, opportunism, or an amalgam of both. Clearly, this particular combination of factors in the right proportions did not occur frequently.

While it is apparent that opportunism was rampant among the people who joined the *smenovekhovtsy* at a later stage, when Soviet support for the movement had become substantial, it should be emphasized that the original group of *smenovekhovtsy* were prompted primarily by earnest, albeit erroneous and one-sided, considerations. For Ustrialov, Kliuchnikov, and their friends, one of the main incentives to accept the Soviet regime was their aspiration for Russia's greatness and her worldwide leadership. During the past seven decades of Soviet rule, their wish to see Russia as a superpower seemed to have materialized; however, the events of the last few years have made it clear that the Soviet Union was a giant with clay feet, and its superpower status only a façade. It turned out that the drive for accelerated industrialization and collectivization that had provoked Ustrialov's enthusiasm in the early 1930s was absolutely devastating. Also, the social and interethnic cohesion that the *smenovekhovtsy* had assumed formed the basis of a strong multinational Soviet Union—a state they, moreover, regarded as the prototype of a united mankind—was nothing but an illusion. In addition, the ideas of "authentic democracy" and universal solidarity that they had expected to inspire the Russian people—and with them the whole world—in their progress toward peace and justice proved to be merely empty shells. Well over seventy years of Soviet regime have left devastation not only in Russia but in all territories under Soviet control, an outcome many Russian intellectuals have predicted ever since the Bolshevik takeover. Blinded by messianic expectations and obsessed as they were by what they regarded as the all-surpassing value of the state, the *smenovekhovtsy* failed to realize this.

Abbreviations and Conventions

Belyi Omsk N. V. Ustrialov, "Belyi Omsk (1919–1934)," N. V. Ustrialov collection, Hoover Institution Archives, Stanford, California.

BN MT B. Nicolaevsky collection, series 143, box 211, folder 9, Hoover Institution Archives, Stanford, California.

BSE1 *Bol'shaia sovetskaia entsiklopediia.* 1st ed. 66 vols. Moscow: Sovetskaia entsiklopediia, 1926–1948.

BSE2 *Bol'shaia sovetskaia entsiklopediia.* 2d ed. 51 vols. Moscow: Sovetskaia entsiklopediia, 1950–1957.

BSE3 *Bol'shaia sovetskaia entsiklopediia.* 3d ed. 30 vols. Moscow: Sovetskaia entsiklopediia, 1970–1981.

Dikii "Moia perepiska s G. N. Dikim," N. V. Ustrialov collection, Hoover Institution Archives, Stanford, California.

Dvenadtsatyi s''ezd *Dvenadtsatyi s''ezd RKP(b), 17–25 aprelia 1923 g.: Stenograficheskii otchet.* Moscow: Gospolitizdat, 1968.

EGV *Grazhdanskaia voina i voennaia interventsiia v SSSR: Entsiklopediia.* 2d rev. ed. Moscow: Sovetskaia entsiklopediia, 1987.

Kadet Conferences "Civil War: Kadet Conferences in Omsk, November 1918 and May 1919," S. V. Panina collection, box 13, Bakhmeteff Archive, Columbia University, New York.

KD Archive Constitutional Democratic Party archive, Hoover Institution Archives, Stanford, California.

KLE *Kratkaia literaturnaia entsiklopediia.* 9 vols. Moscow: Sovetskaia entsiklopediia, 1962–1978.

KPSS v rezoliutsiiakh *KPSS v rezoliutsiiakh i resheniiakh s''ezdov, konferentsii i plenumov TsK.* Vols. 2–4. Moscow: Gospolitizdat, 1970.

MSE1 *Malaia sovetskaia entsiklopediia.* 1st ed. 10 vols. Moscow: Sovetskaia entsiklopediia, 1928–1931.

Notes russes 1920 "Notes de correspondants anonymes dites 'Notes russes' 1920," Archives de la Direction des Renseignements généraux du ministère de l'Intérieur, fol. F₇ 13.489, Archives Nationales, Paris.

Notes russes 1921 "Notes de correspondants anonymes dites 'Notes russes' 1920," Archives de la Direction des Renseignements généraux du ministère de l'Intérieur, fol. F₇ 13.490, Archives Nationales, Paris.

Notes russes 1922 "Notes de correspondants anonymes dites 'Notes russes' 1920," Archives de la Direction des Renseignements généraux du ministère de l'Intérieur, fol. F₇ 13.491, Archives Nationales, Paris.

Odinnadtsatyi s"ezd *Odinnadtsatyi s"ezd RKP(b), Mart–aprel' 1922 g.: Stenograficheskii otchet.* Moscow: Gospolitizdat, 1961.

OSV *O Smene vekh.* Petersburg: Izd-vo 'Logos' pri Dome literatorov, 1922.

Piatnadtsatyi s"ezd *Piatnadtsatyi s"ezd VKP(b), Dekabr' 1917 g.: Stenograficheskii otchet.* 2 vols. Moscow: Gospolitizdat, 1961–1962.

Porevoliutsionery "Moia perepiska s 'Porevoliutsionerami,' " N. V. Ustrialov collection, Hoover Institution Archives, Stanford, California.

Raznye liudi "Moia perepiska s raznymi liud'mi," N. V. Ustrialov collection, Hoover Institution Archives, Stanford, California.

Shestnadtsatyi s"ezd *Shestnadtsatyi s"ezd VKP(b), Aprel' 1929 g.: Stenograficheskii otchet.* Moscow: Gospolitizdat, 1962.

SIE *Sovetskaia istoricheskaia entsiklopediia.* 16 vols. Moscow: Sovetskaia entsiklopediia, 1961–1976.

Smenovekhovtsy "Moia perepiska so smenovekhovtsami," N. V. Ustrialov collection, Hoover Institution Archives, Stanford, California.

SSV *Smena Vekh: Sbornik statei.* Prague: Nasha rech', 1921.

Suvchinskii "Moia perepiska s P. P. Suvchinskim," N. V. Ustrialov collection, Hoover Institution Archives, Stanford, California.

SV *Smena Vekh,* Paris, 1921–1922.

Trinadtsatyi s"ezd *Trinadtsatyi s"ezd RKP(b), Mai 1924 g.: Stenograficheskii otchet.* Moscow: Gospolitizdat, 1963.

TsGALI: the former Tsentral'nyi Gosudarstvennyi Arkhiv Literatury i Iskusstva (Moscow), now renamed Russkii Gosudarstvennyi Arkhiv Literatury i Iskusstva.

TsGAOR: the former Tsentral'nyi Gosudarstvennyi Arkhiv Oktiabr'skoi Revoliutsii (Moscow), now renamed Gosudarstvennyi Arkhiv Russkoi Federatsii.

Ves' Peterburg (1912): *Ves' Peterburg na 1912 god: Adresnaia i spravochnaia kniga g. S-Peterburga.* Petersburg, A. S. Suvorin, 1912.

Ves' Leningrad (1926): *Ves' Leningrad na 1926 god: Adresnaia i spravochnaia kniga g. Leningrada.* Leningrad: Organizatsionnyi otdel Leningradskogo Gubispolkoma, 1926.

Vsia Moskva (1917 [1923, 1926, 1929, 1936]): *Vsia Moskva na 1917 [1923, 1926, 1929, 1936] god: Adresno-spravochnaia kniga g. Moskvy.* Moscow: A. S. Suvorin [Moskovskii Rabochii], 1917 [1923, 1926, 1929, 1936].

Notes

INTRODUCTION

1. I prefer to use the term *intelligentsia* in a broad sense, meaning those intellectuals who rose above strict individualism or professionalism, displayed social commitment, questioned the structures of Russian state and society, and were concerned with the country's future. While the authors of *Smena vekh* cannot be numbered among the revolutionary intelligentsia, as active participants in Russian political life they certainly belonged to the intelligentsia in this broader sense.

2. There is a large body of literature on this subject. An excellent point of departure is M. Confino, "On Intellectuals and Intellectual Traditions in Eighteenth- and Nineteenth-Century Russia," *Daedalus* 101 (Spring 1972): 117–49.

3. On the 1905 revolution see A. Ascher, *The Revolution of 1905: Russia in Disarray* (Stanford, Calif.: Stanford University Press, 1988); F.-X. Coquin, *La révolution russe manquée* (Brussels: Complexe, 1985); H. Rogger, *Russia in the Age of Modernisation and Revolution, 1881–1917* (London: Longman, 1983), 208–28.

4. *Vekhi: Sbornik statei o russkoi intelligentsii* (Moscow: V. M. Sablin, 1909; Frankfurt am Main: Posev, 1967). On *Vekhi* and the debate surrounding it, see C. Read, *Religion, Revolution and the Russian Intelligentsia 1900–1912: The Vekhi Debate and its Intellectual Background* (London: Macmillan, 1979); O. W. Müller, *Intelligentsiia: Untersuchungen zur Geschichte eines politischen Schlagwortes* (Frankfurt am Main: Athenäum, 1971), 352–75; J. Brooks, "*Vekhi* and the *Vekhi* Dispute," *Survey* 19, no. 1 (Winter 1973): 21–50; N. P. Poltoratzky, "The *Vekhi* Dispute and the Significance of *Vekhi*," *Canadian Slavonic Papers* 9, no. 1 (1967): 86–106; L. Schapiro, "The Vekhi Group and the Mystique of Revolution," *Slavonic and East European Review* 34 (1955): 66–68; N. Zernov, *Russkoe religioznoe vozrozhdenie XX veka* (Paris: YMCA-Press, 1974), 141–45; J. E. Zimmerman, "The Political Views of the Vekhi Authors," *Canadian-American Slavic Studies* 10 (Fall 1976): 307–27. On the changes in the intelligentsia's self-conception in the years preceding 1917 see Confino, "Intellectuals," 141–43; J. Burbank, *Intelligentsia and Revolution: Russian Views of Bolshevism, 1917–1922* (New York: Oxford University Press, 1986), 8–11.

5. C. Read, *Culture and Power in Revolutionary Russia: The Intelligentsia and the Transition from Tsarism to Communism* (London: Macmillan, 1990), 60; W. G. Rosenberg, *Liberals in the Russian Revolution: The Constitutional Democratic Party 1917–1923* (Princeton: Princeton University Press, 1974), 263–64.

6. See, for example, Blok's poem "Dvenadtsat' " and his article "Intelligentsiia

i Revoliutsiia" (both written in January 1918) in A. Blok and A. Belyi, *Dialog poetov o Rossii i revoliutsii*, comp. M. F. P'ianykh (Moscow: Vysshaia shkola, 1990), 168–78, 415–25. On Blok's initial enthusiasm and his subsequent disillusionment with the revolution see also R. Poznanski, *Intelligentsia et révolution: Blok, Gorki et Maïakovski face à 1917* (Paris: Anthropos, 1981), 61–118.

7. See, for example, Maiakovskii's poems "Oda revoliutsii" (1918), "My idem" (1919) and "Vladimir Il'ich" (1920) in V. V. Maiakovskii, *Polnoe sobranie sochinenii v trinadtsati tomakh*, vol. 2 (Moscow: Khudozhestvennaia literatura, 1956), 12–13, 30–34. See also Poznanski, *Intelligentsia et révolution*, 189–226.

8. Read, *Culture and Power*, 77.

9. On his reaction to the revolution, see S. A. Fediukin, *Velikii Oktiabr' i intelligentsiia: Iz istorii vovlecheniia staroi intelligentsii v stroitel'stvo sotsializma* (Moscow: Nauka, 1972), 231–32.

10. Read, *Culture and Power,* 47, 56; Burbank, *Intelligentsia and Revolution,* 7, 242. See also N. A. Gredeskul, *Rossiia prezhde i teper'* (Moscow: Gosizdat, 1926), 174–82.

11. See E. Huskey, "The Russian Bar and the Consolidation of Soviet Power," *Russian Review* 43 (1984): 119–34; K. V. Gusev, ed., *Intelligentsiia i revoliutsiia: XX vek* (Moscow: Nauka, 1985), 10, 135–36, 214; D. L. Golinkov, *Krushenie antisovetskogo podpol'ia v SSSR,* 2d rev. ed., 2 vols. (Moscow: Izd-vo politicheskoi literatury, 1978), 1:73–87. For contemporary accounts of the various boycott actions see, for example, "Protiv bol'shevikov," *Utro Rossii,* 10 November 1917; "V ministerstve Trotskogo," *Utro Rossii,* 15 November 1917; "Zabastovka gorodskikh sluzhashchikh v Moskve," *Utro Rossii,* 3 December 1917; "Razgon glavnogo komiteta zemskogo soiuza," *Utro Rossii,* 30 December 1917.

12. See S. Fedorov, "I v chastnosti—o vysshei shkole," *Pamiat': Istoricheskii sbornik,* no. 5 (1982): 411–14; G. D. Alekseeva, *Oktiabr'skaia revoliutsiia i istoricheskaia nauka v Rossii (1917–1923 gg.)* (Moscow: Nauka, 1968), 202–3; Iu. V. Got'e, *Time of Troubles: The Diary of Iurii Vladimirovich Got'e, Moscow, July 8, 1917 to July 23, 1922,* trans. and ed. T. Emmons (London: Tauris, 1988), 19–20, 106.

13. "Materialy k istorii Akademii Nauk," *Pamiat': Istoricheskii sbornik,* no. 4 (1981): 463–66. The statement appeared in a number of newspapers (see, for example, "Golos russkoi nauki," *Utro Rossii,* 28 November 1917).

14. Read, *Culture and Power,* 46–47.

15. Read, *Culture and Power,* 57–61; Rosenberg, *Liberals,* 289–93; Golinkov, *Krushenie,* 1:285–98, 2:11–17.

16. Alekseeva, *Oktiabr'skaia revoliutsiia,* 264.

17. Huskey, "Russian Bar," 127, 132–33; A. Gurovich, "Vysshii Sovet Narodnogo Khoziaistva: Iz vpetchatlenii goda sluzhby," *Arkhiv russkoi revoliutsii,* no. 6 (1922): 306–9, 328–31; A. Meerovich, "V Narkomindele, 1922–1939: Interv'iu s E. A. Gnezdinym," *Pamiat': Istoricheskii sbornik,* no. 5 (1982): 359; A. V. Krasnikova, "Iz istorii razrabotki V. I. Leninym politiki privlecheniia burzhuaznoi intelligentsii na sluzhbu sovetskoi vlasti," *Vestnik LGU,* ser. 2, 1970, no. 8:36; Gusev, *Intelligentsiia i revoliutsiia,* 27–28. See also "Sokhranenie russkoi promyshlennosti," *Utro Rossii,* 29 [16] March 1917.

18. See on this policy Krasnikova, "Iz istorii razrabotki"; Read, *Culture and Power,* 52–53.

19. A. V. Lunacharskii, "Mesto i rol' intelligentsii v obshchestve," *Narodnoe pro-sveshchenie*, 1918, no. 3:26.

20. See W. H. Chamberlin, *The Russian Revolution, 1917–1921*, 2 vols. (New York: Macmillan, 1954; Princeton: Princeton University Press, 1987), 2:25–31; Gusev, *Intelligentsiia i revoliutsiia*, 155–56; *EGV*, 255–56, s.v. "Kamenev, Sergei Sergeevich"; *EGV*, 324, s.v. "Lebedev, Pavel Pavlovich"; *EGV*, 399, s.v. "Novitskii, Fedor Fedoro-vich"; *EGV*, 429, s.v. "Parskii, Dmitrii Pavlovich"; *EGV*, 528, s.v. "Samoilo, Alek-sandr Aleksandrovich"; *EGV*, 551, s.v. "Snesarev, Andrei Evgen'evich"; *EGV*, 574, s.v. "Stankevich, Anton Vladimirovich"; *EGV*, 582, s.v. "Sytin, Pavel Pavlovich"; *EGV*, 639, s.v. "Kharlamov, Sergei Dmitrievich"; *EGV*, 678, s.v. "Sheideman, Iurii Mikhailovich."

21. See in this connection the remarks of N. Andreyev, "The Reality of Na-tional Bolshevism," *Soviet Jewish Affairs* 12 (February 1982): 77; Chamberlin, *Russian Revolution*, 2:31–32; S. Alin, "Smena vekh komandnogo sostava," 27 April 1922, PSR Archief, 2046, Internationaal Instituut voor Sociale Geschiedenis, Amsterdam; A. Skachko, *Poputchiki (Iz khroniki 1919 goda)* (Moscow: Vserossiiskii Proletkul't, 1923).

22. Quoted in I. Lezhnev, "Velikii sintez," *Novaia Rossiia*, no. 1 (March 1922): 19–20.

23. Chamberlin, *Russian Revolution*, 2:30–32: Gredeskul, *Rossiia prezhde*, 168–69; *EGV*, 298, s.v. "Krasnaia Armiia."

24. Gusev, *Intelligentsiia i revoliutsiia*, 153; *EGV*, 298, s.v. "Krasnaia Armiia"; Chamberlin, *Russian Revolution*, 2:32.

25. V. G. Tardov, "Pis'mo v redaktsiiu," *Izvestiia*, 12 November 1918.

26. Alin, "Smena vekh komandnogo sostava"; Gusev, *Intelligentsiia i revoliutsiia*, 214–15.

27. "Mitingi trudiashcheisia intelligentsii," *Severnaia kommuna*, 30 November 1918, referred to in Read, *Culture and Power*, 84. See also A. V. Lunacharskii, "Smena vekh intelligentskoi obshchestvennosti," *Kul'tura i zhizn'*, no. 1 (1 February 1922), reprinted in A. V. Lunacharskii, *Ob intelligentsii* (Moscow: Krasnaia nov', 1923), 45–46. Gor'kii's reaction to the October revolution was initially hostile. He considered the revolution untimely, and feared that it would entail anarchy and cultural destruction. On the pages of *Novaia zhizn'*, the newspaper he edited until July 1918 when it was shut down, Gor'kii raised his voice repeatedly against the Bolshevik methods of vio-lence and oppression. However, by late 1918 he tempered his hostility, kept aloof from politics, and devoted himself to the salvation and development of Russian culture. From the late 1920s on, his endorsement of the Soviet regime became ever more unconditional (see Poznanski, *Intelligentsia et révolution*, 119–88).

28. V., "Novye knigi: Intelligentsiia i sovetskaia vlast'," *Vestnik literatury*, 1919, no. 11:11–12; Bespartiinyi, "Ob intelligentsii (Pis'mo so storony)," *Vestnik literatury*, 1919, no. 4:9–19; K. Radek, "Intelligentsiia i sovetskaia vlast' " in *Intelligentsiia i sovet-skaia vlast': Sbornik statei* (Moscow: Sovetskii mir, 1919), 51–55; V. Kerzhentsev, "Intel-ligentsiia na perelome" in *Intelligentsiia i sovetskaia vlast'*, 56–59. See also A. V. Kvakin, "Novovekhovstvo kak krizis beloi emigratsii" (Kandidatskaia dissertatsiia, Kalininskii gosudarstvennyi universitet, 1981), 70–73; Gusev, *Intelligentsiia i revoliutsiia*, 215–16.

29. "Znamenie vremeni," *Izvestiia*, 3 March 1920. See in this connection also S. A. Fediukin, *Sovetskaia vlast' i burzhuaznye spetsialisty* (Moscow: Mysl', 1965), 124–25.

30. "Ko vsem rabochim, krest'ianam i chestnym grazhdanam Rossii," *Izvestiia,* 30 April 1920.

31. See M. Agursky, *The Third Rome: National Bolshevism in the USSR* (Boulder, Colo.: Westview Press, 1987), 217–19; K. Radek, *Voina pol'skikh belogvardeitsev protiv Sovetskoi Rossii* (Moscow: Gosizdat, 1920).

32. *Grazhdanskaia voina v SSSR,* 2 vols. (Moscow: Voennoe izd-vo Ministerstva oborony SSSR, 1980–86), 2:263; Got'e, *Time of Troubles,* 357–58 (diary notes for 5 and 7 May 1920). The appeal appeared both in *Pravda* and *Izvestiia:* "Vozzvanie ko vsem byvshim ofitseram, gde by oni ni nakhodilis'," *Pravda,* 30 May 1920, and *Izvestiia,* 30 May 1920.

33. Got'e, *Time of Troubles,* 358 (diary note for 7 May 1920), 345–46 (note for 19 March 1920); Andreyev, "Reality," 77.

34. Agursky, *Third Rome,* 219; A. Men'shoi, *Rossiia no 2, emigrantskaia* (Moscow: Tipografiia M.G.S.N.Kh., 1922), 55–56.

35. N. Gredeskul, "Pol'skoe nastuplenie i intelligentsiia," *Izvestiia,* 5 June 1920. The editors accompanied the article with the remark that "it was being printed as a voice from among the intelligentsia." For a biographical note on Gredeskul see *BSE1,* 19:40, s.v. "Gredeskul, Nikolai Andreevich."

36. "V sovetskoi Rossii: Prof. Gredeskul v stane bol'shevikov," *Poslednie novosti,* 18 June 1920.

37. N. Gredeskul, "Intelligentsiia i Sovetskaia Rossiia," *Izvestiia,* 11 July 1920. The other articles of the series were "Soglashenie ili razryv," *Izvestiia,* 13 July 1920; "Zhertvy i rezul'taty," *Izvestiia,* 15 July 1920; "Da ili net," *Izvestiia,* 29 July 1920. In the following months, Gredeskul launched repeated appeals, both to the intelligentsia and the workers, urging them to cooperate in the great cause of building a socialist Russia and defending the country from capitalist attacks. See "Gredeskul zovet intelligentsiiu," *Obshchee delo,* 13 January 1921; "Obrashchenie byvshego chlena Ts.K. Kadetskoi partii," *Izvestiia,* 5 June 1921; "Professor Gredeskul za rabotoi," *Obshchee delo,* 21 June 1921.

38. This is not to say that populist motives had disappeared altogether. See, for example, V., "Novye knigi," 12; Read, *Culture and Power,* 75–76.

39. For a discussion of the various estimates available see M. Raeff, *Russia Abroad: A Cultural History of the Russian Emigration, 1919–1939* (New York: Oxford University Press, 1990), 23–24; M. R. Marrus, *The Unwanted: European Refugees in the Twentieth Century* (New York: Oxford University Press, 1985), 60–61.

40. Raeff, *Russia Abroad,* 19–23. For tables giving an overview of the geographical distribution of the Russian refugees in 1922, 1930, and 1937, see there 202–3.

41. Raeff, *Russia Abroad,* 5, 25–27.

42. On cultural life in Russia abroad see Th. R. Beyer, G. Kratz, and X. Werner, *Russische Autoren und Verlage in Berlin nach dem Ersten Weltkrieg* (Berlin: Arnold Spitz, 1987); M. Beyssac, *La vie culturelle de l'émigration russe en France: Chronique (1920–1930)* (Paris: P.U.F., 1971); L. Fleishman, R. Kh'iuz, and O. Raevskaia-Kh'iuz, eds., *Russkii Berlin 1921–1923: Po materialam arkhiva B. I. Nikolaevskogo v Guverovskom institute* (Paris: YMCA-Press, 1983); R. H. Johnston, *New Mecca, New Babylon: Paris and the Russian Exiles, 1920–1945* (Kingston: McGill–Queen's University Press, 1988); S. Karlinsky and A. Appel, Jr., eds., *The Bitter Air of Exile: Russian Writers in the West,*

1922–1972 (Berkeley: University of California Press, 1977); P. E. Kovalevskii, *Zarube-zhnaia Rossiia: Istoriia i kul'turno-prosvetitel'naia rabota russkogo zarubezh'ia za polveka 1920–1970*, 2 vols. (Paris: Librairie des cinq continents, 1971–73); F. Mierau, ed., *Russen in Berlin, 1918–1933: Eine kulturelle Begegnung* (Weinheim: Quadriga, 1988); T. Ossorguine-Bakounine, comp., *L'émigration russe en Europe: Catalogue collectif des périodiques en lange russe, 1855–1940* (Paris: Institut d'Etudes slaves, 1976); S. P. Postnikov, ed., *Russkie v Prage, 1918–1928 gg.* (Prague, 1928); Raeff, *Russia Abroad;* C. Scandura, "Das 'Russische Berlin' 1921–1924: Die Verlage," *Zeitschrift für Slawistik* 32 (1987): 754–62; G. P. Struve, *Russkaia literatura v izgnanii*, 2d rev. ed. (Paris: YMCA-Press, 1984); H. E. Volkmann, *Die russische Emigration in Deutschland, 1919–1929* (Würzburg: Holzner, 1966).

43. H. von Rimscha, *Der russische Bürgerkrieg und die russische Emigration, 1917–1921* (Jena: Verlag der Frommannschen Buchhandlung, 1924), 52–54.

44. Rimscha, *Bürgerkrieg,* 107–115; H. von Rimscha, *Russland jenseits der Grenzen 1921–1926: Ein Beitrag zur russischen Nachkriegsgeschichte* (Jena: Verlag der Frommannschen Buchhandlung, 1927), 83–87; P. N. Miliukov, *Antibol'shevistskoe dvizhenie,* vol. 2 of *Rossiia na perelome* (Paris: Imprimerie d'Art Voltaire, 1927), 241–42.

45. Rimscha, *Russland jenseits der Grenzen,* 59–82; Volkmann, *Russische Emigration,* 61–120; R. C. Williams, *Culture in Exile: Russian Emigrés in Germany 1881–1941* (Ithaca: Cornell University Press, 1972), 159–81, 202–22; Burbank, *Intelligentsia and Revolution,* 184–89.

46. R. Pipes, *The Formation of the Soviet Union: Communism and Nationalism, 1917–1923,* 2d rev. ed. (Cambridge: Harvard University Press, 1964), 114–241.

47. On the peasant uprisings see O. H. Radkey, *The Unknown Civil War in Soviet Russia: A Study of the Green Movement in the Tambov Region 1920–1921* (Stanford, Calif.: Hoover Institution Press, 1976). On the events in Kronstadt see P. Avrich, *Kronstadt 1921* (Princeton: Princeton University Press, 1970); I. Getzler, *Kronstadt 1917–1921: The Fate of a Soviet Democracy* (Cambridge: Cambridge University Press, 1983).

48. On the economic crisis in Europe in the early 1920s see D. H. Aldcroft, *From Versailles to Wall Street 1919–1929* (London: Lane, 1977; Harmondsworth: Penguin Books, 1987), 55–96.

49. E. M. Carroll, *Soviet Communism and Western Opinion, 1919–1921,* ed. F. B. M. Hollyday (Chapel Hill: University of North Carolina Press, 1965), 234–37.

50. Rimscha, *Bürgerkrieg,* 65–67.

51. See, for example, E. Efimovskii, "Vse dlia Rossii," *Slavianskaia zaria,* 8 March 1920; see also [A.] I. [sic] Gurovich, *Zapiski emigranta* (Petrograd: 'Petrograd,' 1923), 165–67; M. Geller and A. Nekrich, *Utopiia u vlasti: Istoriia Sovetskogo Soiuza s 1917 goda do nashikh dnei,* vol. 1 (London: Overseas Publications Interchange, 1982), 152.

52. Rimscha, *Russland jenseits der Grenzen,* 165.

53. Rimscha, *Bürgerkrieg,* 104–7; Rimscha, *Russland jenseits der Grenzen,* 87–92; Miliukov, *Antibol'shevistskoe dvizhenie,* 233–39.

54. Rosenberg, *Liberals,* 445–49; Burbank, *Intelligentsia and Revolution,* 158–61; Iu. V. Mukhachev, *Ideino-politicheskoe bankrotstvo planov burzhuaznogo restavratorstva v SSSR* (Moscow: Mysl', 1982), 74–87; Miliukov, *Antibol'shevistskoe dvizhenie,* 242–43.

55. "Postanovlenie VTsIK i Sovnarkoma o lishenii prav rossiiskogo grazhdanstva," *Vestnik Narodnogo Komissariata po inostrannym delam,* 1992, no. 4–5:249–50. The

decree had first been published in *Izvestiia,* 19 December 1921. See also C. Gousseff and N. Saddier, "L'émigration russe en France, 1920–1930" (Mémoire de Maîtrise d'Histoire, Université de Paris I, 1983), 188–89.

56. Editorial remark to S. F.-n, "Bol'noi vopros: 'My' i 'oni,' " *Rul',* 17 December 1920. V. D. Nabokov, "Bol'noi vopros," *Rul',* early December 1921, was unavailable to me, but is referred to in Militsyn, "Bol'noi vopros," *Rul',* 28 [15] December 1921. Militsyn's article was continued in *Rul',* 30 [17] December 1920. See also "Bol'noi vopros," *Put',* 15 April 1921; E. Kuskova, "Zhguchii vopros," *Zveno,* no. 6 (12 March 1923): 1; Rimscha, *Bürgerkrieg,* 121–22.

57. See O. Böss, *Die Lehre der Eurasier: Ein Beitrag zur russischen Ideeengeschichte des 20. Jahrhunderts* (Wiesbaden: Otto Harrasowitz, 1961), 14–24; M. Gorlin, "Die philosophisch-politischen Strömungen in der russischen Emigration," *Osteuropa* 8 (1932): 284–86; N. V. Riasanovsky, "The Emergence of Eurasianism," *California Slavic Studies,* no. 4 (1967): 39–46; Burbank, *Intelligentsia and Revolution,* 215–19; L. Luks, "Die Ideologie der Eurasier im zeitgeschichtlichen Zusammenhang," *Jahrbücher für Geschichte Osteuropas* 34 (1986): 375–86.

58. Riasanovsky, "Emergence," 53.

59. P. Ryss, *Russkii opyt: Istoriko-psikhologicheskii ocherk russkoi revoliutsii* (Paris: Sever, 1921), 263–66, 281–83.

60. Ryss, *Russkii opyt,* 283.

61. Ryss, *Russkii opyt,* 281–86.

62. Riasanovsky, "Emergence," 53.

63. Ryss, *Russkii opyt,* 283.

64. For a comprehensive and instructive overview of Soviet publications up to 1980 see A. V. Kvakin, "Sovetskaia istoriografiia novovekhovstva" in *Istoriografiia i istochniki po istorii Oktiabr'skoi revoliutsii i sotsialisticheskogo stroitel'stva v SSSR* (Kalinin: Kalininskii gosudarstvennyi universitet, 1980), 18–40.

65. See, for example, E. B. Genkina, "Iz istorii bor'by bol'shevistskoi partii za ukreplenie ideologicheskogo fronta," *Voprosy istorii,* 1949, no. 1:16–38; N. Mamai, *Kommunisticheskaia partiia v bor'be za ideino-politicheskoe vospitanie mass v pervye gody NEPa* (Moscow: Gospolitizdat, 1954); I. Ia. Trifonov, "Iz istorii bor'by kommunisticheskoi partii protiv smenovekhovstva," *Istoriia SSSR,* 1959, no. 3:64–82; I. Ia. Trifonov, *Ocherki istorii klassovoi bor'by v SSSR v gody NEPa, 1921–1937* (Moscow: Gospolitizdat, 1960); I. Ia. Trifonov, *Lenin i bor'ba s burzhuaznoi ideologiei v nachale NEPa* (Moscow: Znanie, 1969); L. N. Suvorov, "Bor'ba V. I. Lenina protiv restavratorskoi ideologii 'smenovekhovstva,' " *Vestnik MGU, Filosofiia,* 1960, no. 2:45–56; L. N. Suvorov, *Bor'ba marksistko-leninskoi filosofii v SSSR protiv burzhuaznoi ideologii i revizionizma v perekhodnyi period ot kapitalizma k sotsializmu* (Moscow: Izd-vo Moskovskogo universiteta, 1961); L. G. Obichkina, "Iz istorii bor'by RKP(b) protiv antisovetskikh partii i techenii (1921–1923 gg.)," *Voprosy istorii KPSS,* 1969, no. 2:100–10; L. G. Orekhova, "Klassovyi podkhod V.I. Lenina i sovetskikh istorikov k kritike filosofskikh i sotsiologicheskikh vzgliadov smenovekhovstva" in *Partiinost' istoriko-filosofskogo issledovaniia i kritika antikommunizma: Sbornik* (Moscow: Izd-vo Moskovskogo universiteta, 1972), 145–61; O. I. Khokhunova, "Partiinaia pechat' v bor'be s burzhuaznoi ideologiei smenovekhovstva v pervye gody novoi ekonomicheskoi politiki" in *Sbornik nauchnykh rabot kafedr marksizma-leninizma, politicheskoi ekonomii i ekonomiki i organizatsiia proizvodstva,* vol. 1 (Ivanovo: Ivanovskii energeticheskii institut imeni V. I. Lenina, 1958),

71–93; O. I. Khokhunova, "Iz istorii bor'by kommunistischeskoi partii na ideolog-icheskom fronte (1921–1925 gg.)" in *Deiatel'nost' partiinykh organizatsii i sotsial'nyi prog-ress* (Ivanovo: Dom Politicheskogo prosveshcheniia Ivanovskogo Obkoma KPSS, 1968), 26–42; O. I. Khokhunova, "Iz istorii bor'by partii so smenovekhovstvom," *Vestnik MGU, Istoriia*, 1976, no. 4:3–21.

66. In 1973, G. G. Sharoeva mentioned among the adherents of this movement even the Kadet publicist A. S. Izgoev, who in early 1922 had openly taken position against *smenovekhovstvo*, as one of the few non-communist intellectuals in Soviet Russia to do so (see chap. 4) (see G. G. Sharoeva, "V. I. Lenin i bor'ba s burzhuaznoi ideolo-giei v zhurnalistike pervoi poloviny 20-kh godov," *Vestnik MGU, Zhurnalistika*, 1973, no. 2:21). For other striking examples of this "lumping together" see Mamai, *Kommun-isticheskaia partiia*, 52–53; Trifonov, *Ocherki istorii*, 96; E. A. Kozlov, "Bor'ba kommun-isticheskoi partii protiv velikoderzhavnogo shovinizma smenovekhovtsev v pervye gody Nepa" in *Bor'ba kommunisticheskoi partii Sovetskogo Soiuza protiv opportunizma i natsionali-zma* (Leningrad: Izd-vo Leningradskogo universiteta, 1978), 129; Khokhunova, "Iz istorii bor'by partii," 6.

67. See, for example, Trifonov, "Iz istorii bor'by," 80.

68. S. A. Fediukin, *Bor'ba s burzhuaznoi ideologiei v usloviiakh perekhoda k Nepu* (Moscow: Nauka, 1977), 12–14.

69. See, for example, L. K. Shkarenkov, *Agoniia beloi emigratsii*, 2d rev. ed. (Mos-cow: Mysl', 1986); G. F. Barikhnovskii, *Ideino-politicheskii krakh beloemigratsii i razgrom vnutrennei kontr-revoliutsii (1921–1924)* (Leningrad: Izd-vo Leningradskogo universiteta, 1978); Iu. V. Mukhachev and L. K. Shkarenkov, *Krakh 'Novoi taktiki' kontrrevoliutsii posle grazhdanskoi voiny* (Moscow: Znanie, 1980); Iu. V. Mukhachev, *Ideino-politicheskoe bankrotstvo*; Kvakin, "Novovekhovstvo kak krizis"; A. V. Kvakin, "Vliianie pobedy sovetskogo naroda nad belogvardeitsami i interventami na vozniknovenie 'smenove-khovstva'" in *Iz istorii interventsii i grazhdanskoi voiny v Sibiri i na Dal'nem Vostoke, 1917–1922 gg.*, ed. Iu. I. Korablev and V. I. Shishkin (Novosibirsk: Nauka, Sibirskoe otdelenie, 1985), 199–203.

70. See also Kvakin, "Sovetskaia istoriografiia," 32.

71. See N. Andreev, "O sud'be Russkogo Istoricheskogo Arkhiva v Prage," *Grani*, no. 125 (1982), 307–11; G. Fischer, "The Russian Archive in Prague," *American Slavic and East European Review* 8 (1959), 189–95; N. Davydova, "Arkhiv, o kotorom dolgo molchali," *Moskovskie novosti*, 1990, no. 15:16; R. J. Kneeley and E. Kasinec, "Slovanská knihovna in Prague and its RZIA Collection," *Slavic Review* 51 (Spring 1992): 122–31.

72. In particular the archive of N. V. Ustrialov seems to be unavailable in Russia. While Ustrialov in 1935 did send a copy of his papers to the Russian Emigré Historical Archive in Prague, it seems that this part of the collection was not moved to the Soviet Union after World War II, but remained in Prague (see chap. 2, n. 258). Another, less complete copy of Ustrialov's archive is in the Hoover Institution Archives in Stanford, California.

73. A first example seems to be the work of V. A. Osipov, who is preparing a *kandidat* dissertation on the daily *Nakanune* at the Institute for Scientific Information for the Social Sciences of the Russian Academy of Sciences (INION RAN) in Moscow.

74. See, for example, Rimscha, *Bürgerkrieg*; Rimscha, *Russland jenseits der Gren-zen*; Gorlin, "Philosophisch-politischen Strömungen"; W. Kolarz, *Stalin und das ewige*

Russland: Die Wurzeln des Sowjetpatriotismus (London: Lincolns-Prager, 1942); Schapiro, "Vekhi Group"; Struve, *Russkaia literatura* (the first edition of which appeared in 1956); E. H. Carr, *The Interregnum 1923–1924* (London: Macmillan, 1954); S. V. Utechin, *Russian Political Thought: A Concise History* (London: J. M. Dent and Sons, 1964); J. R. Azrael, *Managerial Power and Soviet Politics* (Cambridge: Harvard University Press, 1966). Especially the work of Gorlin, Struve, Carr and Utechin is useful.

75. E. Oberländer, "Nationalbolschewistische Tendenzen in der russischen Intelligenz: Die 'Smena Vech'-Diskussion 1921–1922," *Jahrbücher für Geschichte Osteuropas* 16 (1968): 194–211; R. C. Williams, " 'Changing Landmarks' in Russian Berlin, 1923–1924," *Slavic Review* 27 (December 1968): 581–93. R. C. Williams's essay on *smenovekhovstvo* is resumed in Williams, *Culture in Exile.*

76. M. Agurskii, *Ideologiia natsional-bol'shevizma* (Paris: YMCA-Press, 1980); Agursky, *Third Rome.* For M. Agurskii's other publications on the subject see the bibliography.

77. M. Okutiur'e, " 'Smena vekh' i russkaia literatura 20-kh godov" in *Odna ili dve russkikh literatury,* ed. Zh. Niva (Lausanne: L'Age d'Homme, 1981), 103–11; Burbank, *Intelligentsia and Revolution,* 222–34: M. Hagemeister, *Nikolaj Fedorov: Studien zu Leben, Werk und Wirkung* (Munich: Otto Sagner, 1989), 363–66, pt. 2, chap. 4; Read, *Culture and Power,* 186–200. See also P. C. Wagemaakers, "N. V. Ustrjalov en het Russische Nationaal-Bolsjevisme" (Doctoraalscriptie, Universiteit van Amsterdam, 1985); H. Hardeman, "De bundel en het tijdschrift 'Smena vech,' 1921–1922" (Licentiaatsthesis, Katholieke Universiteit Leuven, 1985); H. Hardeman, "The Journal 'Change of Landmarks' ('Smena vekh'), Paris 1921–1922: A Second Step toward Reconciliation with the Bolsheviks," *Slavica Gandensia,* no. 14 (1987): 49–67.

78. See in this regard the bibliography. I had the opportunity to work in the former Central State Archive of the October Revolution (TsGAOR) and the former Central State Archive of Literature and the Arts (TsGALI) in the fall of 1989; however, at that time access to a number of collections, especially to those which had belonged to the former Russian Emigré Historical Archive in Prague, was still very limited.

CHAPTER 1: *MIR I TRUD*

1. For a detailed account of the origin of *Mir i trud* see [V. B. Stankevich], "Istoriia vozniknoveniia organizatsii 'Mir i trud,' " *BN MT.* Judging from the text (see, for example, pp. 1, 22), the account must have been written at the end of 1920 or at the very beginning of 1921.

2. [Stankevich], "Istoriia," 1. Major General P. R. Bermondt was defeated in October 1919, General N. N. Iudenich in December of that year, and Admiral A. V. Kolchak in early January 1920. At the same place in his manuscript Stankevich also mentions the liquidation of Lieutenant General A. I. Denikin's army; however, this happened later, in early April 1920.

3. "Organizatsiia 'Mir i trud,' " *Golos Rossii,* 5 February 1920.

4. On V. B. Stankevich see R. B. Gul's obituary in *Novyi zhurnal,* no. 94 (1969): 269–71; R. B. Gul', *Rossiia v Germanii,* vol. 1 of *Ia unes Rossiiu: Apologiia emigratsii* (New York: Most, 1984), 44–45; V. Stankevich, *Vospominaniia, 1914–1919 gg.* (Berlin: 1921).

5. V. I. Startsev, *Krakh Kerenshchiny* (Leningrad: Nauka, 1982), 252; Gul', *Rossiia*

v Germanii, 45. During the World War, Stankevich had written a manual on fortification. In February 1918, at the time of the German advance on Petrograd, Stankevich believed he could contribute to the defense of the city, and offered his advice to the then Supreme Commander N. V. Krylenko. However, Krylenko had him arrested on the spot. Strongly condemning Stankevich's move, the Central Committee of the People's Socialists excluded him from the Party. See Simplex, "Prostye mysli: O prizyve 'Nazad v Rossiiu,' " *Rul'*, 17 December 1920.

6. *Golos Rossii: Ezhednevnyi organ nezavisimoi russkoi politicheskoi demokraticheskoi mysli* (Berlin: February 1919–15 October 1922). On the paper, see S. S. Ol'denburg, "Russkaia zarubezhnaia pechat'," *Russkii ekonomist*, no. 11–12 (May–June 1923): 58; and especially H. von Rimscha, *Der russische Bürgerkrieg und die russische Emigration 1917–1921* (Jena: Verlag der Frommannschen Buchhandlung, 1924), 62–63. It was von Rimscha who, in my opinion, rightly qualified it as "left-wing democratic."

7. On Iashchenko see L. Fleishman, R. Kh'iuz, and O. Raevskaia-Kh'iuz, eds., *Russkii Berlin 1921–1923: Po materialam arkhiva B. I. Nikolaevskogo v Guverovskom institute* (Paris: YMCA-Press, 1983), 9–13.

8. See M. Smil'g-Benario, "Na sovetskoi sluzhbe," *Arkhiv russkoi revoliutsii*, no. 3 (1921): 147–89; "Sud'ba i raboty russkikh pisatelei, uchenykh i zhurnalistov za 1918–1922 g.," *Russkaia kniga*, 1920, no. 2:30.

9. *Vremia: Nezavisimyi organ sblizheniia narodov* (Berlin: 1919–1925). See also Ol'denburg, "Russkaia zarubezhnaia pechat'," 58.

10. See the list of signatures under the appeal *Mir i trud* launched in July 1920: "Ot organizatsii 'Mir i trud' " and "Kundgebung des Vereins 'Friede und Arbeit' (Mir i trud)," *BN MT;* "Ot organizatsii 'Mir i trud,' " *Zhizn'*, no. 7 (1 July 1920): 1–3; "Ot organizatsii 'Mir i trud,' " *Golos Rossii*, 4 July 1920. Among the émigrés who subsequently endorsed the appeal were the literary specialist E. A. Liatskii and the journalists V. Gorvits-Samoilov and K. M. Bal'nitskii, from the Warsaw paper *Varshavskoe slovo* and from the L'vov journal *Prikarpatskaia Rus'*, respectively. See Fleishman, Kh'iuz, and Raevskaia-Kh'iuz, *Russkii Berlin*, 15; Gul', *Rossiia v Germanii*, 44–52.

11. "Ustav organizatsii 'Mir i trud' (Germanskaia Gruppa)," *BN MT.*

12. "Osnovnye polozheniia organizatsii 'Mir i trud,' " *BN MT*, 2.

13. [Stankevich], "Istoriia," 12–13.

14. [Stankevich], "Istoriia," 16.

15. "Ustav" (see n. 11).

16. *Mir i trud* published a brochure in German on the senselessness of war in general, and of the Russian civil war in particular: W. Stankewitsch, *Fragen, die zu lösen sind* ([Berlin]: Verlag Friede und Arbeit, [1920]). Furthermore, the appeal which the circle launched in July 1920 was distributed also in German translation (see n. 10).

17. [Stankevich], "Istoriia," 1. It seems that no copy of this typewritten appeal has been preserved; however, most likely it is this appeal which appeared in *Mir i trud: Neperiodicheskii sbornik*, vol. 1 (Berlin: Ladyzhnikov, 1920), 1–4. On the collection see also V. D., "Bibliografiia: 'Mir i trud,' " *Golos Rossii*, 9 March 1920. There were plans to publish a second issue of the collection (a project for the second issue is in *BN MT*), but these never materialized.

18. According to R. B. Gul', the contributions to the journal of the other collaborators were merely garnish for the ideas of Stankevich. See Gul', *Rossiia v Germanii*, 50.

19. Fleishman, Kh'iuz, and Raevskaia-Kh'iuz, *Russkii Berlin,* 17–18, 53–54; Gul', *Rossiia v Germanii,* 44–52. R. B. Gul', for example, published extracts from his novel *Ledianoi pokhod* in *Zhizn'*.

20. "Ot organizatsii" (see n. 10).

21. Two versions of a draft for this appeal are in *BN MT*: "Ot organizatsii 'Mir i trud' (proekt)" and "Ot organizatsii 'Mir i trud' (II redaktsiia)." Hereafter I will quote the second version of the draft as "Krym 2."

22. "Osnovnye polozheniia" (see n. 12), 4; "Ot organizatsii" (see n. 10).

23. "Dva goda grazhdanskoi voiny" in *Mir i trud,* 1:21–22.

24. V. Stankevich, "Pod novym lozungom," *Zhizn',* no. 11 (15 September 1920): 3. Stankevich uses here the term *russkie liudi* (Russian people); from the context, however, it is clear that he has in mind Russian intellectuals and politicians, as opposed to the ordinary people. See also the report of one of Stankevich's lectures, where he makes the same distinction: S. Laskii, "Vozvrat k Rossii," pts. 1, 2, *Golos Rossii,* 5, 6 January 1921.

In any case, *Mir i trud* members understood the term *intelligentsiia* to mean the educated stratum of Russian society, including the Bolsheviks. See especially "Ot redaktsii," *Zhizn',* no. 1 (1 April 1920): 1.

25. "Dva goda" (see n. 23), 21.

26. V. Stankevich, "Intelligentsiia i narod," *Zhizn',* no. 1 (1 April 1920): 3–8.

27. "Ot redaktsii" (see n. 24); Stankevich, *Vospominaniia,* 356.

28. Stankevich, "Intelligentsiia," 3.

29. "Dva goda" (see n. 23), 21.

30. "Ot organizatsii" (see n. 10).

31. [Stankevich], "Istoriia," 6.

32. "Dva goda" (see n. 23), 10–12.

33. V. Stankevich, "Kak ispol'zuet Sovetskaia vlast' pobedu?" *Zhizn',* no. 2 (15 April 1920): 1–3.

34. [Stankevich], "Istoriia," 4. General A. A. Arakcheev (1769–1834) was minister of war and later supervisor of the Council of Ministers' handling of domestic affairs under Tsar Alexander I. He implemented a system of military-agricultural colonies, where in peacetime soldiers could combine military service with farming, and continue their normal family life. Between 1816 and 1821, almost one third of Russia's standing army was based in such settlements. While the colonies offered the soldiers several advantages such as schools and hospitals, the strict, even cruel discipline in the settlements made them extremely unpopular, and resulted eventually in revolts and mutinies. The system was abandoned by Nicholas I.

35. [Stankevich], "Istoriia," 6, 20.

36. "Dva goda" (see n. 23), 16–17. It is true that Bolshevik terror did not begin on a large scale before the summer of 1918, taking on particularly acute forms after the Left Socialist Revolutionary insurrection in early July, and especially after the assaults on Lenin and M. Uritskii, the Chief of the Petrograd *Cheka,* both on 30 August. Subsequently, on 5 September 1918 *Sovnarkom* issued the so-called Decree on the Red Terror, which gave the green light for widespread terror against "enemies of the people." This does not mean, however, that Bolshevik terror was nonexistent before that time. At the end of November 1917, for example, the Kadet Party as a whole had been

declared to be "enemies of the people," and in December Lenin had called on the masses to take the law into their own hands. Moreover, the All-Russian Extraordinary Commission for Combating Counterrevolution and Sabotage *(Cheka)*, established by *Sovnarkom* on 7 December 1917, had begun sentencing and executing by way of summary justice as early as February 1918.

37. "Krym 2" (see n. 21), 1; [Stankevich], "Istoriia," 4–5.

38. "Dva goda" (see n. 23), 13–17; "Ot organizatsii" (see n. 10).

39. Stankevich, "Pod novym lozungom," 2; "Chto budet (Mneniia trekh russkikh emigrantov)," *Mir i trud,* 1:41.

40. [Stankevich], "Istoriia," 7.

41. "Ot redaktsii" (see n. 24), 1.

42. [Stankevich], "Istoriia," 7–8.

43. [Stankevich], "Istoriia," 6. In reality, no significant mitigation of Bolshevik policy versus the SRs took place in the spring of 1920. The situation of the Mensheviks, for their part, was somewhat easier: throughout 1920 they had party offices in Moscow and held regular meetings, even after the beginning of General Wrangel's attacks. Contrary to what the people of *Mir i trud* believed, the opposition's freedom of action during the civil war varied in converse proportion to the Red Army's fortunes. What may have deceived Stankevich and his colleagues, however, were reports of the visit of a British Labour delegation to Moscow in May 1920. The delegation's members were allowed to meet with politicians from opposition parties, and also to attend a meeting organized by the Moscow Printers' Union, where not only Menshevik speakers but even the Socialist Revolutionary leader V. M. Chernov, albeit in disguise, delivered speeches. See E. H. Carr, *The Bolshevik Revolution 1917–1923,* 3 vols. (London: Macmillan, 1950–1953; Harmondsworth: Penguin Books, 1966), 1:182–83; J. Burbank, *Intelligentsia and Revolution: Russian Views of Bolshevism, 1917–1922* (New York: Oxford University Press, 1986), 78–79.

44. [Stankevich], "Istoriia," 21.

45. "Osnovnye polozheniia" (see n. 12), 3.

46. "Osnovnye polozheniia" (see n. 12), 2.

47. "Osnovnye polozheniia" (see n. 12), 2; [Stankevich], "Istoriia," 9–10, 16.

48. Stankevich, "Pod novym lozungom," 4–5. According to the relevant literature, however, no such influence seems to have existed. See, for example, G. von Rauch, *The Baltic States: The Years of Independence: Estonia, Latvia, Lithuania, 1917–1940* (Berkeley: University of California Press, 1974).

49. [Stankevich], "Istoriia," 20. The Soviet government had concluded a peace treaty with Estonia on 2 February 1920, with Lithuania on 12 July, and with Latvia on 11 August of that year.

50. Stankevich, "Pod novym lozungom," 4–5.

51. "Krym 2" (see n. 21).

52. "Krym 2" (see n. 21). On the RSFSR constitution of 1918 see A. L. Unger, *Constitutional Development in the USSR: A Guide to the Soviet Constitutions* (New York: Pica Press, 1981), 7–41.

53. "Krym 2" (see n. 21).

54. [Stankevich], "Istoriia," 15.

55. V. Stankevich, "Nuzhno reshit'sia (Posviashchaetsia chlenam Uchreditel'nogo Sobraniia)," *Golos Rossii,* 8 January 1921.

56. "Politicheskii tsentr: Anketa 'Poslednikh novostei,'" *Poslednie novosti,* 25 November 1920.

57. "Ot organizatsii 'Mir i trud,'" *Mir i trud,* 1:3–4.

58. Stankevich, "Nuzhno reshit'sia." On the Conference of Members of the Constituent Assembly see the introduction.

59. Stankevich, "Nuzhno reshit'sia."

60. It was only on 15 December 1921 that *VTsIK* and *Sovnarkom* issued a decree, depriving all émigrés not prepared to solicit Soviet citizenship by 1 June 1922 of their Russian citizenship (see Iu. Fel'shtinskii, *K istorii nashei zakrytosti: Zakonodatel'nye osnovy sovetskoi immigratsionnoi i emigratsionnoi politiki* [London: Overseas Publications Interchange, 1988], 178).

61. Quoted in Rimscha, *Bürgerkrieg,* 162. There was no copy of the *Golos Rossii* issue carrying Stankevich's appeal "Nazad v Rossiiu" available to me.

62. Stankevich elaborated on this at a lecture held in Berlin on 4 January 1921. See S. La-skii, "Vozvrat."

63. See, for example, Iv. Petrunkevich, "Rossiia na rasput'i," *Evreiskaia tribuna* (25 July 1920), quoted in M. Smolenskii, "Raskol v russkoi intelligentsii," *Golos Rossii,* 4 August 1920.

64. [Stankevich], "Istoriia," 2, 15.

65. Gul', *Rossiia v Germanii,* 52.

66. M. Vishniak, "Na Rodine," *Sovremennye zapiski,* no. 2 (1920): 205–31.

67. A. Damanskaia, "Vozvrat v Rossiiu (Pis'mo iz Berlina)," *Narodnoe delo,* 11 January 1921, mentioned in Fleishman, Kh'iuz, and Raevskaia-Kh'iuz, *Russkii Berlin,* 16.

68. "Novaia pozitsiia," *Rul',* 15 December 1920.

69. I. Gessen, "Isteriia," *Rul',* 11 January 1921.

70. Baron Mikhail Aleksandrovich (von) Taube was a specialist in international law and a former professor of the Petrograd Juridical Institute (see "Sud'ba i raboty," 30).

71. E. Raikh, "Novogodnie nastroeniia," *Poslednie novosti,* 13 January 1921.

72. A decree granting amnesty to the rank and file of the White armies was issued by *VTsIK* on 3 November 1921, at the occasion of the fourth anniversary of the October revolution (see *SIE,* 16:496, s.v. "Emigratsiia posle Oktiabr'skoi revoliutsii 1917").

73. [Stankevich], "Istoriia," 2.

74. Gul', *Rossiia v Germanii,* 52; Fleishman, Kh'iuz, and Raevskaia-Kh'iuz, *Russkii Berlin,* 17, 53 n. 43. Stankevich lived in Kaunas until the end of World War II, when he returned to Germany to head the so-called Baltic University; in 1949 he emigrated to the United States, where he lived until his death.

75. On *(Novaia) Russkaia kniga* see G. P. Struve, *Russkaia literatura v izgnanii,* 2d rev. ed. (Paris: YMCA-Press, 1984), 35–39, and especially Fleishman, Kh'iuz, and Raevskaia-Kh'iuz, *Russkii Berlin,* 7–67.

76. See T. R. Beyer, "The House of the Arts and the Writers' Club, Berlin 1921–1923" in T. R. Beyer, G. Kratz, and X. Werner, *Russische Autoren und Verlage in Berlin nach dem Ersten Weltkrieg* (Berlin: Arnold Spitz, 1987), 9–38.

77. Struve, *Russkaia literatura,* 36. On "Russian Berlin" in these years see Struve,

Russkaia literatura, 24–29; R. C. Williams, *Culture in Exile: Russian Emigrés in Germany 1881–1941* (Ithaca, N.Y.: Cornell University Press, 1972), 121–58; and especially Fleishman, Kh'iuz, and Raevskaia-Kh'iuz, *Russkii Berlin*, which is devoted entirely to the subject.

78. Struve, *Russkaia literatura*, 35–37.

79. See, for example, "Ot redaktsii," *Russkaia kniga*, 1921, no. 1:1; A. S. Iashchenko, "Kniga i vozrozhdenie Rossii," *Russkaia kniga*, 1921, no. 4:1; "Ot redaktsii," *Novaia russkaia kniga*, 1922, no. 1:1.

80. See on this section and its value for the history of Russian literature Fleishman, Kh'iuz, and Raevskaia-Kh'iuz, *Russkii Berlin*, 19–25.

81. Beyer, "House of the Arts," 12–13. T. R. Beyer is quoting the aims of the group as they were formulated in *Novaia russkaia kniga*, 1922, no. 1:34.

82. Beyer, "House of the Arts," 26–32.

83. Fleishman, Kh'iuz, and Raevskaia-Kh'iuz, *Russkii Berlin*, 48–49.

84. Beyer, "House of the Arts," 33–34.

CHAPTER 2: N. V. USTRIALOV

1. N. V. Ustrialov, *Pod znakom revoliutsii* (Harbin: Russkaia mysl', 1925), 203–5; R. B. Gul', *Rossiia v Germanii*, vol. 1 of *Ia unes Rossiiu: Apologiia emigratsii* (New York: Most, 1984), 20; *Vysshaia shkola v Kharbine: Izvestiia Iuridicheskogo fakul'teta*, no. 1 (1925): 239–40.

2. On *Utro Rossii* and its publishers see M. Agurskii, "U istokov natsional-bol'-shevizma," *Minuvshee: Istoricheskii al'manakh*, no. 4 (1987): 141–47, 154–57; H. Hardeman, "A 'bourgeois' newspaper in the Russian revolution: 'Utro Rossii,' Moscow 1917–1918," *Rossiia/Russia*, no. 6 (1988): 61–80. Both in M. Agurskii's and in my article it is assumed that Ustrialov contributed to *Utro Rossii*, not only under his own name but also under the pseudonym P. Surmin. Although I. F. Masanov *(Slovar' psevdonimov russkikh pisatelei, uchenykh i obshchestvennykh deiatelei*, 4 vols. [Moscow: Izd-vo Vsesoiuznoi knizhnoi palaty, 1956–1960], 3:145) identifies P. Surmin as the pseudonym of a journalist and pedagogue named Petr Ivanovich Maigur, the statement in *BSE3* (27:133, s.v. "Ustrialov, Nikolai Vasil'evich") that P. Surmin was the pseudonym of Ustrialov, together with the fact that the tone of the Surmin articles in *Utro Rossii* is in many cases similar to that of the articles by Ustrialov, misled me at that time. However, after a closer reading of other publications by P. Surmin, I had to conclude that this could not possibly be Ustrialov's work. Especially the anti-Kadet and prosocialist position in one of Surmin's brochures of early 1917 *(Izbiratel'noe pravo* [Moscow: D. Ia. Makovskii, 1917], especially 15–16), and even more so the explicit antimilitarism and anti-imperialism of one of his articles ("V chem bor'ba za tsivilizatsiiu (Imperializm i demokratiia)" in *Evropa i voina: Rossiia i ee soiuzniki v bor'be za tsivilizatsiiu* [Moscow: D. Ia. Makovskii, 1917], 3–1:5–15) could not possibly be reconciled with Ustrialov's position at that time. Moreover, I have not found a single other source which would confirm the information given by *BSE3*. Consequently, I retract the statement about this matter which I made in my 1988 article.

3. N. V. Ustrialov to N. A. Tsurikov, 20 January 1927, *Raznye liudi*, 124–25; N. V. Ustrialov to N. A. Tsurikov, 27 October 1926, *Raznye liudi*, 119–21; *Vysshaia shkola v Kharbine: Izvestiia Iuridicheskogo fakul'teta*, no. 1 (1925): 239–40.

4. *Belyi Omsk,* 3, 4–5; "Vypiski iz zhurnala Soveshchaniia po delam pechati i perepiska o sekretnom fonde na izdatel'stvo dlia informatsii naseleniia i ob assignovanii sredstv na eti tseli za 1919 god," TsGAOR, f. 176, op. 4, d. 219, l. 8.

5. See, for example, N. Ustrialov, "Na perevale," *Russkoe delo,* 12 December 1919; N. Ustrialov, "Prizraki," *Russkoe delo,* 17 December 1919.

6. The article in question was reprinted in N. V. Ustrialov, *V bor'be za Rossiiu* (Harbin: Okno, 1920), 3–5.

7. Ustrialov, *V bor'be,* 4–5.

8. Ustrialov, *V bor'be,* 5.

9. N. Ustrialov, "V Irkutske," *Russkoe delo,* 9 December 1919; N. Ustrialov, "V groznyi chas," *Russkoe delo,* 26 December 1919.

10. The version that Ustrialov's conversion took place in the course of three sleepless nights was until recently maintained by the historian M. Agurskii on the basis of the testimony of M. Shkliaver, who knew Ustrialov personally (see M. Agurskii, *Ideologiia natsional-bol'shevizma* [Paris: YMCA-Press, 1980], 67; M. Agursky, "Defeat as Victory and the Living Death: The Case of Ustrialov," *History of European Ideas* 5 [1984]: 170). However, judging from his latest work on the subject (Agurskii, "U istokov"), Agurskii now has completely abandoned this version. Much earlier, in reaction to an article in the Harbin daily *Russkoe slovo* of 1 July 1930, in which a certain Zhitenev had claimed the same, Ustrialov dismissed this version as a "naive myth" (see *Belyi Omsk,* 121–22).

11. N. V. Ustrialov, "Fevral'skaia revoliutsiia (K vos'miletnemu iubileiu)," *Vestnik Man'chzhurii,* 1925, no. 3–4:109–10. On this campaign see N. G. Dumova, "Iz istorii kadetskoi partii v 1917 g.," *Istoricheskie zapiski,* no. 90 (1972): 125–30; V. Ia. Laverychev, *Po tu storonu barrikad: Iz istorii bor'by moskovskoi burzhuazii s revoliutsiei* (Moscow: Mysl', 1967), 222–24; V. Ia. Laverychev, "Vserossiiskii Soiuz Torgovli i Promyshlennosti," *Istoricheskie zapiski,* no. 70 (1961): 51–56. Ustrialov contributed four popular brochures to the campaign: N. Ustrialov, *Otvetstvennost' ministrov* (Moscow: D. Ia. Makovskii, 1917); N. Ustrialov, *Chto takoe uchreditel'noe sobranie* (Moscow: D. Ia. Makovskii, 1917); N. Ustrialov, *Revoliutsiia i voina* (Moscow: Izd-vo "1917 god," 1917); N. Ustrialov, *Chetyre Gosudarstvennye Dumy* (Moscow: D. Ia. Makovskii, 1917). I have not been able to locate the last pamphlet.

12. On their position see J. E. Zimmerman, "Russian Liberal Theory, 1900–1917," *Canadian-American Slavic Studies* 14 (Spring 1980): 13–19; Hardeman, "Bourgeois newspaper," 61–63.

13. Laverychev, "Vserossiisskii Soiuz," 54.

14. W. G. Rosenberg, *Liberals in the Russian Revolution: The Constitutional Democratic Party 1917–1923* (Princeton: Princeton University Press, 1974), 285–86; Hardeman, "Bourgeois newspaper," 71–72.

15. M. Hagemeister, *Nikolaj Fedorov: Studien zu Leben, Werk und Wirkung* (Munich: Otto Sagner, 1989), 363 n. 1; N. N. Alekseev to N. V. Ustrialov, 26 August 1931, *Porevoliutsionery,* 12. On Leont'ev and his thought see N. Berdiaev, *Konstantin Leont'ev: Ocherk iz istorii russkoi religioznoi mysli* (Paris: YMCA-Press, 1926); E. C. Thaden, *Conservative Nationalism in Nineteenth-Century Russia* (Seattle: University of Washington Press, 1964), 165–82; A. Walicki, *A History of Russian Thought: From the Enlightenment to Marxism* (Oxford: Oxford University Press, 1979), 300–8; A. V. Korolev, "Kul'turno-istoricheskie vozzreniia K. N. Leont'eva" in *Pamiati Konstantina Nikolaevicha Leont'eva,* + *1891: Literaturnyi sbornik* (Petersburg: Sirius, 1911), 327–63.

16. Ustrialov, "Fevral'skaia revoliutsiia," 110.

17. N. Ustrialov, "Vo vlasti raspada," *Utro Rossii,* 21 January 1918.

18. N. Ustrialov, "Tragediia demokratizma," *Zaria Rossii,* 1 May 1918.

19. *Belyi Omsk,* 129. Also I. G. Lezhnev admitted later that he had been favorably struck by this action. See I. Lezhnev, "Ob Uchreditel'nom Sobranii i o Nepe," *Rossiia,* no. 4 (December 1922): 14; I. G. Lezhnev to V. G. Tan-Bogoraz, 6 July 1934, TsGALI, f. 2252, op. 1, d. 105, ll. 3–4. A second event which impressed Ustrialov in a positive way during the first months of Bolshevik rule was the crushing of the anarchists, beginning in April 1918 (see *Belyi Omsk,* 129).

20. R. Pipes, *Struve: Liberal on the Right, 1905–1944* (Cambridge: Harvard University Press, 1980), 88–93.

21. Ustrialov, *V bor'be,* 66. Ustrialov's respect for Struve always remained very high. See N. V. Ustrialov to K. A. Chkheidze, 29 January 1935, TsGAOR, f. 5911, op. 1, d. 78, l. 45.

22. Hardeman, "Bourgeois newspaper," 62–63.

23. *Problemy velikoi Rossii: Zhurnal vneshnei politiki i prava.* The journal appeared semimonthly from April to December 1916, when it abruptly ceased publication.

24. N. V. Ustrialov, "K voprosu o sushchnosti 'natsionalizma,' " *Problemy velikoi Rossii,* no. 18 (10 [23] December 1916): 9–12; N. V. Ustrialov, "K voprosu o russkom imperializme," *Problemy velikoi Rossii,* no. 15 (15 [28] October 1916): 1–5.

25. Ustrialov, "O russkom imperializme," 1–2. On the thought of Danilevskii see Walicki, *History,* 291–97; R. E. McMaster, *Danilevsky: A Russian Totalitarian Philosopher* (Cambridge: Harvard University Press, 1967).

26. Ustrialov, "O russkom imperializme," 3.

27. Ustrialov, "O russkom imperializme," 4.

28. N. V. Ustrialov, "Natsional'naia problema u pervykh slavianofilov," *Russkaia mysl',* 1916, no. 10:10, 15, 20; see also N. Ustrialov, "Russkaia kul'tura," *Nakanune,* no. 3 (April 1918): 1.

29. Ustrialov, "O russkom imperializme," 2.

30. Ustrialov, "O russkom imperializme," 5.

31. *Problemy velikoi Rossii,* no. 1 (7 April 1916): 1–2.

32. Ustrialov's article on Russian imperialism (Ustrialov, "O russkom imperializme") was followed by a note from the editors, stating that they did not subscribe to all of the article's theses but, given the great importance of the questions dealt with, had decided that this difference of opinion should not stand in the way of the article's publication.

33. A. Ladyzhenskii, "Ideia velikoi Rossii i aggressivnyi imperializm (Otvet N. V. Ustrialovu)," *Problemy velikoi Rossii,* no. 16 (1 [14] November 1916): 2–3. See also B. L., "Nuzhen li Rossii imperializm?" *Problemy velikoi Rossii,* no. 17 (15 [28] November 1916): 4–6.

34. Earlier, Ustrialov had written explicitly that "universal history hardly would have been able to make much progress if mankind had adopted long ago the principle of the inviolability and freedom of the peoples in its literal sense" (Ustrialov, "Natsional'naia problema," 10).

35. N. V. Ustrialov, *Revoliutsiia i voina* (Moscow: Izd-vo "1917 god," 1917), 5, 7. He repeated this idea in "Vneshniaia politika revoliutsionnoi Rossii," *Utro Rossii,* 31 December 1917. See also Ustrialov, "Fevral'skaia revoliutsiia," 109.

36. Ustrialov, *Revoliutsiia i voina,* 4, 24, 27.

37. Ustrialov, *Revoliutsiia i voina,* 22–23, 26.

38. N. Ustrialov, "Sever i Iug," *Utro Rossii,* 23 December 1917.

39. Ustrialov, "Vneshniaia politika."

40. Ustrialov, *Revoliutsiia i voina,* 3.

41. Ustrialov, *Revoliutsiia i voina,* 4; N. Ustrialov, "U vrat mira," *Utro Rossii,* 17 January 1918.

42. N. Ustrialov, "Itogi," *Utro Rossii,* 2 [15] February 1918.

43. N. Ustrialov, "Ideinaia smert'," *Utro Rossii,* 9 [22] February 1918.

44. N. Ustrialov, "Russkii bunt," *Utro Rossii,* 26 November 1917.

45. See n. 4 to the introduction.

46. *Iz glubiny: Sbornik statei o russkoi revoliutsii* (Moscow: Russkaia mysl', 1918; Paris: YMCA-Press, 1967). The initiative for the collection was taken by P. B. Struve; contributors included N. A. Berdiaev, S. N. Bulgakov, S. L. Frank, and A. S. Izgoev (all contributors to *Vekhi*) as well as P. I. Novgorodtsev, S. A. Kotliarevskii, and V. N. Murav'ev. The last two were Ustrialov's colleagues on the staff of *Utro Rossii* (see Hardeman, "Bourgeois newspaper," 66–68). On the peculiar circumstances under which the collection appeared see J. Burbank, *Intelligentsia and Revolution: Russian Views of Bolshevism, 1917–1922* (New York: Oxford University Press, 1986), 132; for an analysis of the collection's contents see there 191–99, 132–37.

47. P. B. Struve, "Istoricheskii smysl russkoi revoliutsii i natsional'nye zadachi" in *Iz glubiny,* 291–92.

48. Ustrialov, "Russkii bunt."

49. N. Ustrialov, "V Rozhdestvenskuiu noch'," *Utro Rossii,* 24 December 1917.

50. Ustrialov, "V Rozhdestvenskuiu noch'."

51. Ustrialov, "V Rozhdestvenskuiu noch'."

52. Ustrialov, "Russkii bunt"; Ustrialov, "Vo vlasti raspada."

53. He wrote on Christmas Eve 1917: "Eras of destruction are the threshold of constructive eras; Providence destroys only to create" (Ustrialov, "V Rozhdestvenskuiu noch' ").

54. Ustrialov "Sever i Iug."

55. N. Ustrialov, "Vozrozhdenie," *Zaria Rossii,* 18 [5] May 1918.

56. Ustrialov, "Vozrozhdenie."

57. N. Ustrialov, "Klassy i natsiia v revoliutsionnoi Rossii," *Utro Rossii* 3 March [18 February] 1918.

58. P. B. Struve, for example, affirmed in his contribution to *Iz glubiny* that only when the idea of the Nation became the supreme value for all, would Russia and the Russian nation be able to rise from the dead. Struve, "Istoricheskii smysl," 303–5.

59. On their position see Hardeman, "Bourgeois newspaper," 73–75.

60. *Nakanune* was published by the publishing house Makovskii, and printed in Riabushinskii's printing house. Seven issues seem to have appeared, the first on 7 April 1918, the last in June of that year. On the journal see Ustrialov, *Pod znakom,* 196–98. There is also an interesting piece of testimony on the journal in Iu. V. Got'e, *Time of Troubles: The Diary of Iurii Vladimirovich Got'e, Moscow, July 8, 1917 to July 23, 1922,* trans. and ed. T. Emmons (London: Tauris, 1988), 142–43.

61. "Na perevale," *Nakanune,* no. 1 (7 April 1918): 1–2.

62. "Na perevale" (see n. 61), 2.

63. "Likvidatsiia bol'shevikov," *Nakanune*, no. 7 (June 1918): 1.

64. On the final liquidation of the opposition press see A. Z. Okorokov, *Oktiabr' i krakh russkoi burzhuaznoi pressy* (Moscow: Mysl', 1970); Hardeman, "Bourgeois newspaper," 65–66. It seems that *Nakanune* had already disappeared from the scene by that time. See Ustrialov, *Pod znakom,* 198.

65. This has also been argued by D. P. Hammer (see D. P. Hammer, "N. V. Ustrialov and the Origins of National Bolshevism" [Paper presented at the Third World Congress of Soviet and East European Studies, Washington D.C., 31 October–4 November 1985], 7). Later, this position was also taken by M. Agurskii (see Agurskii, "U istokov"); however, in my opinion, Agurskii overestimates the degree to which Ustrialov was prepared to accept socialism at that stage. Apparently, this is mainly a result of the fact that Agurskii identifies Ustrialov with P. Surmin (see n. 2 above). See in this respect especially Agurskii, "U istokov," 149–50, 154.

66. *Belyi Omsk,* 39.

67. *Belyi Omsk,* 1, 46.

68. On Kliuchnikov see chap. 3.

69. "Omsk-Parizh: Beseda s byvshim Upravliaiushchim Ministerstvom Inostrannykh Del professorom Iu. V. Kliuchnikovym," *Pravitel'stvennyi vestnik* (Omsk), 11 February 1919.

70. *Belyi Omsk,* 47–48; Ustrialov, *Pod znakom,* 63–64.

71. Recalling his conversation with Kliuchnikov, Ustrialov wrote in October 1921: "Since that day I consciously and unconsciously returned to this problem, seeking a way out in case *they* should be victorious: how could one neutralize their poison while at the same time having accepted their force?" *(Belyi Omsk,* 48).

72. *Belyi Omsk,* 105–6.

73. *Belyi Omsk,* 67, 71, 105. See also I. I. Serebrennikov, *V revoliutsii (1917–1919),* vol. 1 of *Moi vospominaniia* (Tientsin: Nashe znanie, 1937), 271.

74. P. N. Miliukov, *Antibol'shevistskoe dvizhenie,* vol. 2 of *Rossiia na perelome* (Paris: Imprimerie d'Art Voltaire, 1927), 137–39, 144; G. K. Gins, *Sibir', soiuzniki i Kolchak: Povorotnyi moment russkoi istorii 1918–1920 gg.,* 2 vols. (Peking: Tipo-Litografiia Russkoi dukhovnoi missii, 1921), 2:213–31, 293–301, 446–70.

75. "Obshchestvennye deiateli o gosudarstvennom zemskom soveshchanii," *Svobodnyi krai* (Irkutsk), 9 October [26 September] 1919; Ustrialov, "Na perevale." The latter article was accompanied by a quotation from Herbert Spencer: "The great political superstition of the past was the divine right of the monarch. The great superstition of present politics is the divine right of parliament." On Ustrialov's position see also Gins, *Sibir',* 2:396–97.

76. N. Ustrialov, "Russkoe delo," *Russkoe delo,* 5 October 1919; Session of 21 May 1919, *Kadet Conferences,* 31.

77. *Belyi Omsk,* 39; P. B. Struve, "Istoriko-politicheskie zametki o sovremennosti," pt. 1, *Russkaia mysl',* 1921, no. 5–7:219.

78. *Belyi Omsk,* 17, 140–43.

79. Ustrialov, *Pod znakom,* 202–6; L. A. Krol', *Za tri goda: Vospominaniia, vpechatleniia i vstrechi* (Vladivostok: Svobodnaia Rossiia, 1921), 46; Hardeman, "Bourgeois newspaper," 73.

80. Session of 21 May 1919 (see n. 76), 18, 20–24. The text of Ustrialov's lecture can be found there on 7–9.

81. Session of 21 May 1919 (see n. 76), 29.

82. N. V. Ustrialov, "Mezhdunarodnaia peregruppirovka," *Pravitel'stvennyi vestnik* (Omsk), 16 March 1919; "Tezisy Konferentsii po inostrannoi politike," Session of 21 May 1919 (see n. 76), 35. The author of these theses was Ustrialov *(Belyi Omsk,* 57).

83. See, for example, N. V. Ustrialov to P. N. Miliukov, 11 August 1919, P. N. Miliukov Collection, Bakhmeteff Archive, Columbia University, New York.

84. *Belyi Omsk,* 34, 38; N. U.[strialov], "Novyi fazis," *Biulleten' gazety Russkoe delo* (Irkutsk), 31 December 1919. On the Political Center see Miliukov, *Antibol'shevistskoe dvizhenie,* 148–51; G. Z. Ioffe, *Kolchakovskaia avantiura i ee krakh* (Moscow: Mysl', 1983), 236–37, 253–55.

85. *Belyi Omsk,* 2, 6, 18.

86. Session of 21 May 1919 (see n. 76), 6, 35.

87. *Belyi Omsk,* 20.

88. Ustrialov to Miliukov, 11 August 1919 (see n. 83).

89. *Belyi Omsk,* 38–39.

90. *Belyi Omsk,* 125.

91. *Belyi Omsk,* 39, 129–30, 149. See also Serebrennikov, *V revoliutsii,* 272.

92. *Belyi Omsk,* 130.

93. *Belyi Omsk,* 125.

94. *Belyi Omsk,* 41, 135. The transfer of power took place on 22 January 1920.

95. *Belyi Omsk,* 43, 131–32.

96. N. V. Ustrialov to P. B. Struve, 15 October 1920, quoted in Struve, "Istoriko-politicheskie zametki," pt. 1, 216.

97. Session of 21 May 1919 (see n. 76), 6, 13, 17–18. On German National-Bolshevism see L. Dupeux, *'Nationalbolschewismus' in Deutschland, 1919–1933: Kommunistische Strategie und konservative Dynamik* (Munich: C. H. Beck, 1985), 18–205. Given the fact that Ustrialov referred to the German movement as early as May 1919, it is clear that he had in mind the tendency in German conservative circles to welcome Bolshevism as an ally, not the "National-Bolshevik" tendency among German Communists. The former tendency manifested itself for the first time in early April 1919, while the latter came to the surface only in the fall of that year. See in this connection Dupeux, *Nationalbolschewismus,* 53–62, 87, 95–99.

98. Ustrialov, *V bor'be,* 35.

99. Ustrialov, *V bor'be,* 10, 35.

100. Ustrialov, *V bor'be,* 12–13.

101. Ustrialov, *V bor'be,* 33–34.

102. Ustrialov, *V bor'be,* 64.

103. Ustrialov, *V bor'be,* 36.

104. *Belyi Omsk,* 105–6.

105. Ustrialov, *V bor'be,* 13.

106. N. V. Ustrialov to kn. L. V. Golitsyna, [fall 1920], *Raznye liudi,* 7v–7d.

107. Ustrialov, *V bor'be,* 63.

108. See the introduction.

109. *Belyi Omsk*, 40; N. V. Ustrialov, Diary, 1 July 1922, *Smenovekhovtsy*, 61a.

110. Ustrialov, *Pod znakom*, 40.

111. *Belyi Omsk*, 41, 43, 131; Ustrialov, *Pod znakom*, 43, 82; M. Agurskii, "Perepiska I. Lezhneva i N. Ustrialova," *Slavica Hierosolymitana*, no. 5–6 (1981): 552; N. V. Ustrialov to K. A. Chkheidze, 25 June 1934, TsGAOR, f. 5911, op. 1, d. 78, l. 21.

112. G. Iu. Manis to N. V. Ustrialov, 4 June 1923, *Raznye liudi*, 61. Ustrialov noted in his diary that an invitation to Moscow, rather than to Irkutsk, would very much tempt him; however, he added that even in that case, he would probably be deterred by the prospect of losing his independence, of "getting his lips sealed" (see N. V. Ustrialov, Diary, 21 February [*sic*, i.e., June—H. H.] 1923, *Raznye liudi*, 64; N. V. Ustrialov to A. A. Kotel'nikov, 13 February 1931, *Raznye liudi*, 194).

113. N. V. Ustrialov to S. S. Luk'ianov, 19 October 1922, *Smenovekhovtsy*, 70.

114. G. N. Dikii to N. V. Ustrialov, 19 March 1931, *Dikii*, 71.

115. Ustrialov, *Pod znakom*, pp. ii–iii; *Vysshaia shkola v Kharbine: Izvestiia Iuridicheskogo fakul'teta*, no. 3 (1926): 310; *BSE1*, 56:392, s.v. "Ustrialov, Nikolai Vasil'evich"; N. V. Ustrialov to P. P. Suvchinskii, 30 January 1928, *Suvchinskii*, 30. His impressions of this mission to Moscow appeared in 1926 under the title "Rossiia (u okna vagona)," both in the Harbin journal *Vestnik Man'chzhurii*, 1926, no. 1–2:82–97; and in the Moscow journal *Novaia Rossiia*, 1926, no. 2:31–48, and 3:25–38. Moreover, they appeared as a separate booklet under the same title: N. V. Ustrialov, *Rossiia (u okna vagona)* (Harbin: Tipografiia KVzhd, 1926). During his stay in Moscow, Ustrialov did not have any contacts with Soviet leaders. He was asked to give an interview to the staff of *Izvestiia*, but the interview was never printed (see N. V. Ustrialov, Diary, 24 August 1925, *Smenovekhovtsy*, 113).

116. N. V. Ustrialov to K. A. Chkheidze, 30 November 1934, TsGAOR, f. 5911, op. 1, d. 78, l. 40.

117. Ustrialov, *V bor'be*, 2, 14; L. A. Zander to N. V. Ustrialov, [December 1920?], *Raznye liudi*, 7e; Golitsyna to Ustrialov, [fall 1920] (see n. 106), 7–7b; I. I. Serebrennikov, *V emigratsii (1920–1924)*, vol. 2 of *Moi vospominaniia* (Tientsin: Nashe znanie, 1940), 31.

118. *BSE1*, 56:392, s.v. "Ustrialov, Nikolai Vasil'evich"; *Vysshaia shkola v Kharbine: Izvestiia Iuridicheskogo fakul'teta*, no. 1 (1925): 202, 240. On the history of the institution see there 201–13.

119. M. A. Krol', "Stranitsy iz moei zhizni," M. A. Krol' Archief, 239–41, Internationaal Instituut voor Sociale Geschiedenis, Amsterdam; *Vysshaia shkola v Kharbine: Izvestiia Iuridicheskogo fakul'teta*, no. 1 (1925): 216.

120. "Kratkii obzor deiatel'nosti Literaturno-Khudozhestvennogo Kruzhka pri Kharbinskom Kommercheskom Sobranii," *Sungariiskie vechera*, no. 1 (1923): 63.

121. *Vysshaia shkola v Kharbine: Izvestiia Iuridicheskogo fakul'teta*, no. 1 (1925): 212; *Vysshaia shkola v Kharbine: Izvestiia Iuridicheskogo fakul'teta*, no. 3 (1926): 335; *Vysshaia shkola v Kharbine: Izvestiia Iuridicheskogo fakul'teta*, no. 5 (1928): 369–70.

122. On 20 November 1920, for example, he was one of the speakers at a discussion on "The Intelligentsia and the Spirit of the Age" (see "Disput 'Okna': 'Intelligentsiia i dukh vremeni,'" *Okno*, no. 2 [December 1920]: 56); in early December of that year he presided over a debate on "The Religion of Revolution," organized by the Harbin Commercial Assembly (see "Religiia Revoliutsii," *Okno*, no. 2 [December

1920]: 57); and in April 1922 he participated in a well-attended discussion, organized by the Railroad Assembly, on "The Intelligentsia at the Crossroads" (see "Intelligentsiia na rasput'i (Disput v zh.-d. Sobranii)," *Russkii golos* [Harbin], 6 April 1922).

123. N. V. Ustrialov to Iu. N. Potekhin, 8 September 1923, *Smenovekhovtsy*, 99; Agurskii, "Perepiska," 555 n. 6.

124. See M. Agursky, *The Third Rome: National Bolshevism in the USSR* (Boulder, Colo.: Westview Press, 1987), 247. *Okno* was not, however, merely a collection of songs, as M. Agurskii alleges, but was intended as a "Literary-artistic Monthly." However, only two issues ever came out. Apart from poems by S. Alymov, Nik. Aseev, Vs. Ivanov, S. Tret'iakov, and others, *Okno* also contained articles on literary and philosophical subjects. Besides N. V. Ustrialov contributors included F. Kubka, a Czech friend of Ustrialov, who later became a well-known novelist and playwright; and L. Zander, a young philosopher and former student of Ustrialov, who after World War II made himself a name as the author of numerous works on Russian religious philosophy. As soon as Zander saw the first issue of *Okno,* he deeply deplored having become involved in this "impious" undertaking. Indeed, only Ustrialov's and Kubka's contributions to the publication were acceptable to him. See L. A. Zander to N. V. Ustrialov, [March 1921], *Raznye liudi,* 10. Ustrialov's reaction to Zander's complaints is unknown.

125. The journal had been founded in 1923 as a weekly called *Ekonomicheskii vestnik Man'chzhurii,* and was published by the Chinese Eastern Railroad's economic office; in January 1925 it became a monthly under the title *Vestnik Man'chzhurii.* Ustrialov began contributing to the journal in 1925, when three articles written by him appeared on its pages. In 1926 the journal carried his impressions from his journey to Moscow in the summer of 1925 (see n. 115 above), but soon thereafter Ustrialov put an end to the collaboration because of some difference of opinion with the editors. See M. Ia. Pergament to N. V. Ustrialov, 28 April 1926, *Raznye liudi,* 104.

126. See the bibliography.

127. Ustrialov dedicated the collection to "General A. A. Brusilov, the steadfast and loyal servant of Great Russia in times of glory and in the hard days of sufferings and misfortune" (Ustrialov, *V bor'be,* 2).

128. Ustrialov, *V bor'be,* 2, 79–80.

129. V. Stankevich, "Prof. N. Ustrialov, V bor'be za Rossiiu," *Russkaia kniga,* 1921, no. 3:6–7.

130. M. Vishniak, "N. Ustrialov, V bor'be za Rossiiu (Kritika i bibliografiia)," *Sovremennye zapiski,* no. 3 (1921): 271.

131. I. Vasilevskii (Ne-Bukva), "Ivan Ivanovich," *Poslednie novosti,* 30 January 1921.

132. D. Pasmanik, "Prisposoblenie ili protest? (Po povodu knigi prof. Ustrialova)," *Obshchee delo,* 3 March 1921; D. Pasmanik, "Primirenchestvo prof. N. Ustrialova," *Obshchee delo,* 6 July 1921.

133. Struve, "Istoriko-politicheskie zametki," pt. 1, 216.

134. It appeared originally as a series of seven articles under the title "Po sushchevstu" in *Rul'* of 21, 30 April, 1 May, and 6, 9, 16, 27 July 1921; it was republished under the title "Istoriko-politicheskie zametki o sovremennosti," pts. 1, 2, *Russkaia mysl',* 1921, no. 5–7:208–24, 10–12:317–24.

135. P. B. Struve, "Proshloe, nastoiashchee, budushchee: Mysli o natsional'nom vozrozhdenii Rossii," *Russkaia mysl'*, 1922, no. 1–2:228.

136. Struve, "Istoriko-politicheskie zametki," pt. 1, 217–18.

137. Struve, "Istoriko-politicheskie zametki," pt. 1, 218–19.

138. Struve, "Istoriko-politicheskie zametki," pt. 1, 219.

139. Ustrialov's reply to Struve appeared under the title "Natsional-Bol'shevizm (Otvet P. B. Struve)" in *Novosti zhizni*, 18 September 1921, and in *SV*, no. 3 (12 November 1921). It was reprinted in Ustrialov, *Pod znakom*, 25–30.

140. Ustrialov, *Pod znakom*, 26–27.

141. Ustrialov, *Pod znakom*, 27.

142. Ustrialov, *Pod znakom*, 28–29.

143. See chap. 3.

144. Iu. V. Kliuchnikov to N. V. Ustrialov, 13 July 1921, *Smenovekhovtsy*, 9–11. In the collection itself, Kliuchnikov claimed that Ustrialov did know about the undertaking *(SSV*, 65). It has to be added, however, that Kliuchnikov did not distort the sense of Ustrialov's argument. The title "Patriotica" was also the title of one of the articles in *V bor'be za Rossiiu* (Ustrialov, *V bor'be*, 30–36), and is a reference to a collection of articles by P. B. Struve, *Patriotica: Politika, kul'tura, religiia, sotsializm. Sbornik statei za piat' let (1905–1910)* (Petersburg, 1911).

145. N. V. Ustrialov, Diary, 1 January 1921, *Smenovekhovtsy*, 4; Iu. V. Kliuchnikov to N. V. Ustrialov, late March 1921, *Smenovekhovtsy*, 6.

146. Ustrialov received in early January 1922 both a copy of the collection and the first three issues of the Paris journal. See N. V. Ustrialov to Iu. V. Kliuchnikov, 3 January 1922, *Smenovekhovtsy*, 25; N. V. Ustrialov to Iu. V. Kliuchnikov, 11 January 1922, *Smenovekhovtsy*, 28.

147. N. V. Ustrialov, "Vpered ot Vekh! ('Smena Vekh.' Sbornik statei. Praga, 1921 god)," *Novosti zhizni*, 7 January 1922, reprinted in Ustrialov, *Pod znakom*, 62–67.

148. Ustrialov, "Vpered ot Vekh!," 65–66.

149. Ustrialov, "Vpered ot Vekh!," 66–67. Ustrialov had earlier formulated the slogan *Vpered ot Vekh* in a letter to Potekhin. See N. V. Ustrialov, Diary, 24 October 1921, *Smenovekhovtsy*, 15.

150. Ustrialov to Kliuchnikov, 11 January 1922 (see n. 146), 28.

151. N. V. Ustrialov to Iu. V. Kliuchnikov, 30 January 1922, *Smenovekhovtsy*, 30–31; N. V. Ustrialov, Diary, 4 March 1922, *Smenovekhovtsy*, 37; Ustrialov to Kliuchnikov, 3 January 1922 (see n. 146), 26.

152. Ustrialov to Kliuchnikov, 30 January 1922 (see n. 151), 30–31; N. V. Ustrialov to A. V. Bobrishchev-Pushkin, 25 April 1922, *Smenovekhovtsy*, 42; N. V. Ustrialov, Diary, 1 January 1923, *Smenovekhovtsy*, 77. Ustrialov's misgivings were confirmed by the news he received from his old friend F. Kubka on Kliuchnikov's reputation among the émigrés. See F. F. Kubka to N. V. Ustrialov, 13 November 1921, *Raznye liudi*, 24; N. N. [F. Kubka] to N. V. Ustrialov, 16 January 1922, *Smenovekhovtsy*, 29.

153. In all, the Paris journal carried eight articles by Ustrialov, most of which had appeared in September–November 1921 in the Harbin daily *Novosti zhizni*. They were all reprinted in Ustrialov, *Pod znakom:* "Natsional-bol'shevizm" (25–30); "Dve reaktsii" (31–37); "Problema vozvrashcheniia" (38–43); "Dukhovnye predposylki revoliutsii" (233–39, under the title "Intelligentsiia i revoliutsiia"); "Evoliutsiia i taktika"

(50–54); "Tri bor'by" (55–61); "Prorocheskii bred" (309–17); "Fragmenty: O razume prava i prave istorii" (265–72, under the title "O razume prava i prave istorii").

154. Ustrialov contributed eight articles to *Nakanune:* "Narod v revoliutsii," 26 March 1922, reprinted in Ustrialov, *Pod znakom,* 240–47; "Smysl vstrechi," 7 May 1922, reprinted in Ustrialov, *Pod znakom,* 68–74; "Perspektivy primireniia," 17 May 1922; "Starorezhimnym radikalam," 14 November 1922, reprinted in Ustrialov, *Pod znakom,* 248–52; "1917–1922," 31 December 1922; "Dal'nii vostok," 10 March 1923; "Rossiia i Kitai," 17 March 1923; and "Fragmenty (K modnoi teme o 'krizise demokratii')," 21 February 1924, reprinted in Ustrialov, *Pod znakom,* 257–60.

155. Agurskii, "Perepiska," 558.

156. See, for example, *SV,* no. 12 (14 January 1922): 20; S. Luk'ianov, "Ravnodeistvuiushchaia," *Nakanune,* 16 August 1922.

157. Ustrialov to Kliuchnikov, 3 January 1922 (see n. 146), 27; Ustrialov to Kliuchnikov, 30 January 1922 (see n. 151), 30; N. V. Ustrialov to S. S. Luk'ianov, early October 1922, *Smenovekhovtsy,* 68.

158. N. V. Ustrialov, Diary, 28 July 1922, *Smenovekhovtsy,* 63; N. V. Ustrialov to Iu. N. Potekhin, 3 April 1923, *Smenovekhovtsy,* 81; N. V. Ustrialov to Iu. N. Potekhin, 8 September 1923, *Smenovekhovtsy,* 99.

159. N. V. Ustrialov, Diary, 24 August 1925, *Smenovekhovtsy,* 110–13.

160. Ustrialov, *Rossiia (u okna vagona),* 32–33; N. V. Ustrialov to N. A. Tsurikov, 27 October 1926, *Raznye liudi,* 120.

161. On Dikii see Ustrialov's introduction to *Dikii,* pp. i–ii.

162. N. V. Ustrialov, Diary, 15–16 November 1921, *Smenovekhovtsy,* 21–22; "Intelligentsiia na rasput'i" (see n. 122).

163. On Iashnov see Ustrialov's "Primechaniia" to *Raznye liudi,* p. vi.

164. The almanac's first issue was not available to me. However, the editorial of the first issue was reprinted in *Al'manakh russkaia zhizn',* no. 4 (October 1923): 1.

165. See, for example, E. Iashnov, "Poputnye mysli," *Al'manakh russkaia zhizn',* no. 3 (October 1922): 12; E. Iashnov, "Posle poezdki v Rossiiu (Vyvody i razmyshleniia)," *Al'manakh russkaia zhizn',* no. 4 (October 1923): 25–29; N. Zefirov, "Neizbezhnaia evoliutsiia," *Vestnik Man'chzhurii,* 1923, no. 11:5–7; "Intelligentsiia na rasput'i" (see n. 122).

166. Ustrialov, Introduction (see n. 161), p. i; Remark by Ustrialov, *Dikii,* 60; Dikii to Ustrialov, 19 March 1931 (see n. 114), 67–70.

167. N. V. Ustrialov to G. N. Dikii, 23 June 1933, *Dikii,* 155–56.

168. See on *Novaia Rossiia* Agurskii, "Perepiska"; M. Chudakova, ed., "Neokonchennoe sochinenie Mikhaila Bulgakova," *Novyi mir,* 1987, no. 8:180–84; O. P. Fedorova, "Zhurnal 'Novaia Rossiia' ('Rossiia') i otnoshenie burzhuaznoi intelligentsii k revoliutsionnoi deistvitel'nosti," *Problemy istorii SSSR,* 1973, no. 2:90–104: O. P. Fedorova, *Zhurnal'naia publitsistika 20-kh godov kak istochnik po istorii sovetskoi intelligentsii* (Moscow: Izd-vo Moskovskogo universiteta, 1985), 26–37, 40–50; S. A. Fediukin, *Bor'ba s burzhuaznoi ideologiei v usloviiakh perekhoda k Nepu* (Moscow: Nauka, 1977), 271–80; I. Lezhnev, *Istoki,* vol. 1 of *Zapiski sovremennika* (Moscow: Khudozhestvennaia literatura, 1934), 208–27.

169. *Novaia russkaia kniga,* 1922, no. 3:32.

170. Private publishing houses had been made possible by a special decree of the

Council of People's Commissars, issued on 12 December 1921. See Fediukin, *Bor'ba s burzhuaznoi ideologiei,* 71; L. Meshcheriakov, "O chastnykh izdatel'stvakh," *Pechat' i revoliutsiia,* 1922, no. 3:128–34.

171. On *Russkaia volia* see Iu. Oksman, " 'Russkaia volia,' banki i burzhuaznaia literatura," *Literaturnoe nasledstvo,* no. 2 (1930): 165–86.

172. I. Lezhnev, Autobiographical note, TsGALI, f. 2252, op. 1, d. 268, ll. 1–2; Fediukin, *Bor'ba s burzhuaznoi ideologiei,* 272; H. E. Schulz, P. K. Urban, and A. I. Lebed, eds., *Who was who in the USSR: A Biographic Directory* (Metuchen, N.J.: Scarecrow Press, 1972), 350; Agurskii, "Perepiska," 545–46; M. Koriakov, "Listki iz bloknota: K 'Vospominaniiam' N. Ia. Mandel'shtam," pts. 1–10, *Novoe russkoe slovo,* 2, 6, 9, 13, 16, 20, 23, 27, 30 May, 3 June 1984; G. Struve, "Koe-chto ob Isae Lezhneve i ego zhurnale: Po povodu statei M. Koriakova," *Novoe russkoe slovo,* 20 June 1984.

173. On Tan-Bogoraz see *Pamiati V. G. Bogoraza (1865–1936)* (Moscow-Leningrad: AN SSSR, 1937), pp. xvi–xviii; Agursky, *Third Rome,* 286–87.

174. Before the revolution, Adrianov had been a regular contributor to several periodicals, including *Vestnik Evropy* and *Birzhevye vedomosti.* By 1912, he had a position as privatdozent in the Department of History and Philology at the University of Petersburg, and was a member of the Imperial Archeological Commission. After the revolution he continued to teach at Petrograd (Leningrad) University; his courses included Russian, Ukrainian, and Byelorussian literature.

175. "Est' eshche porokh," *Put',* 5 November 1921; "Pechat'," *Poslednie novosti,* 16 October 1921; "Pechat' i zhizn'," *Volia Rossiia,* 24 September 1921.

176. On the regular contributors to *Novaia Rossiia* see Fedorova, *Zhurnal'naia publitsistika,* 19–20.

177. *Novaia Rossiia,* no. 1 (March 1922): 1–2.

178. *Novaia Rossiia,* no. 1 (March 1922): 3.

179. Upon order of G. E. Zinov'ev, then chairman of the Petrograd Executive Committee and of the Comintern, the second issue of *Novaia Rossiia* was confiscated in May 1922 because of an article entitled "The Emancipation of the Soviets." In this article Lezhnev had advocated a greater separation of party and state, and had called upon nonparty intellectuals to increase their influence within the soviets as much as possible (a copy of the confiscated article is in TsGALI, f. 2252, op. 1, d. 2, ll. 20–22). However, upon Lenin's personal intervention the journal resumed publication in August of that year, in Moscow, and under the title *Rossiia* (see Agurskii, "Perepiska," 547; Fediukin, *Bor'ba s burzhuaznoi ideologiei,* 301–2). As a result of organizational problems, the journal once again disappeared from the scene in mid-1925, to reappear in January 1926 under its initial title *Novaia Rossiia* (see Agurskii, "Perepiska," 585–86). Yet, after no more than three issues, the Soviet authorities closed the journal down, and this time for good (see Agurskii, "Perepiska," 550, 588–89; Agursky, *Third Rome,* 314–15).

180. Agurskii, "Perepiska," 564.

181. Fediukin, *Bor'ba s burzhuaznoi ideologiei,* 280.

182. I. Lezhnev, "Razmen vekh (Otvet Iu. N. Potekhinu. Mozhet byt', dazhe bol'she togo)," *Rossiia,* no. 5 (January 1923): 19.

183. I. Lezhnev, "Pis'mo prof. N. Ustrialovu," *Al'manakh russkaia zhizn',* no. 4 (October 1923): 45. This letter had appeared earlier in *Rossiia,* no. 9 (May–June 1923):

5–11; however, as opposed to the version in *Russkaia zhizn'*, the *Rossiia* version had been cut by the censor. See Agurskii, "Perepiska," 560.

184. Lezhnev, "Razmen vekh," 18.

185. See Agurskii, "Perepiska." Lezhnev was arrested and expelled from the Soviet Union after the final liquidation of *Novaia Rossiia* in the spring of 1926. The break with the Soviet Union, however, was never complete, as in the fall of 1926 Lezhnev was employed by the Soviet Trade Delegation in Berlin. In 1929 he wrote a letter to the Central Committee of the Communist party, asking for permission to return to the Soviet Union. In 1930 he was allowed to return to Moscow; in December 1933 he was even accepted as a member of the party, and from 1935 to 1939 he headed the literary section of *Pravda*. See Lezhnev, Autobiographical note; Agurskii, "Perepiska," 545–46.

186. Agurskii, "Perepiska," 585 n. 1; Ustrialov, *Pod znakom*, 139–40. See also N. V. Ustrialov, "Obmirshchenie," *Rossiia*, no. 9 (May–June 1923): 14–17, reprinted in Ustrialov, *Pod znakom*, 114–20.

187. Ustrialov, *Pod znakom*, 82; Agurskii, "Perepiska," 574.

188. Ustrialov, *Pod znakom*, 145–47; Agurskii, "Perepiska," 554, 557.

189. I. Lezhnev, "Pis'mo prof. N. Ustrialovu," *Al'manakh russkaia zhizn'*, no. 4 (October 1923): 37–39; Ustrialov, *Pod znakom*, 142.

190. See, for example, I. Lezhnev, "Na 'stydnuiu' temu," *Rossiia*, no. 13 (1925): 225; S. A. Adrianov, "Tret'ia Rossiia (Ne ozhivet ashche ne umret)," *Novaia Rossiia*, no. 1 (March 1922): 11–12.

191. Ustrialov, *Pod znakom*, 82–83.

192. Agurskii, "Perepiska," 575. See also I. Lezhnev, "NEP—Natsional'naia ekonomicheskaia politika," *Novaia Rossiia*, no. 2 (February 1926): 15–24.

193. Agurskii, "Perepiska," 569.

194. The articles in question were "Obmirshchenie" (see n. 186); "Sud'ba Evropy: Razmyshleniia k desiatiletiiu mirovoi voiny," *Rossiia*, no. 3 (1924): 121–32, reprinted in Ustrialov, *Pod znakom*, 331–40; and "U okna vagona (Moskva-Kharbin)," pts. 1, 2, *Novaia Rossiia*, 1926, no. 2:31–48, 3:25–38.

195. Ustrialov, *V bor'be*, 12–13.

196. Ustrialov to Kliuchnikov, 3 January 1922 (see n. 146), 25. See also N. V. Ustrialov to Iu. N. Potekhin, 27 March 1922, *Smenovekhovtsy*, 38; Ustrialov to Bobrishchev-Pushkin, 25 April 1922 (see n. 152), 40; Ustrialov, *Pod znakom*, 44.

197. N. V. Ustrialov to Iu. V. Kliuchnikov, 16 May 1922, *Smenovekhovtsy*, 47; Ustrialov, *Pod znakom*, 112–13.

198. Ustrialov to Bobrishchev-Pushkin, 25 April 1922 (see n. 152), 42–43; Ustrialov, *Pod znakom*, 98.

199. Ustrialov to Bobrishchev-Pushkin, 25 April 1922 (see n. 152), 43; see also Ustrialov to Potekhin, 8 September 1923 (see n. 158), 102; Ustrialov, Diary, 1 January 1923 (see n. 152), 76.

200. Ustrialov to Potekhin, 8 September 1923 (see n. 158), 101–2; N. V. Ustrialov tot Iu. V. Kliuchnikov, 2 January 1926, *Smenovekhovtsy*, 122.

201. Ustrialov to Bobrishchev-Pushkin, 25 April 1922 (see n. 152), 42; S. Sumskii, "Ideologiia sovburzhuazii," *Sotsialisticheskii vestnik*, 1921, no. 19:3–6.

202. Ustrialov, *Pod znakom*, 54, 69, 73.

203. Ustrialov, *Pod znakom,* 11, 36, 73.

204. Ustrialov, *Pod znakom,* 73, 108.

205. Ustrialov, *Pod znakom,* 250, 349.

206. Ustrialov, *Pod znakom,* 333.

207. Ustrialov, *Pod znakom,* 249–50, 332, 335–36. The Italian historian Guglielmo Ferrero (1871–1942) attracted Ustrialov's attention with his essay "La ruine de la civilisation antique" (see Ustrialov, *Pod znakom,* 332), which appeared first in the French journal *La revue des deux mondes* (1920), and was subsequently published as a separate volume (1921). Ferrero concluded his study of the Roman Empire in the third century A.D. with a reflection on twentieth-century Europe, in which he warned against the danger of all-embracing anarchy in Europe. He argued that, just as in the third century, the existing principles of authority—monarchy and democracy—had been destroyed in Europe, the only exceptions being France and Switzerland, where the democratic principle had survived. However, Ferrero stressed that, in the centuries following the downfall of the Roman Empire, complete anarchy had been avoided thanks to the influence of two religious creeds, Christianity and paganism. He believed that, in contrast, twentieth-century Europe found itself in a situation of complete intellectual and moral anarchy. He feared therefore that the disintegration of political authority might easily bring about the complete decomposition of European civilization. See Guglielmo Ferrero, *La ruine de la civilisation antique* (Paris: Plon, 1921), 245–52.

208. Ustrialov, *Pod znakom,* 108.

209. Ustrialov, *Pod znakom,* 300–3.

210. Ustrialov, *Pod znakom,* 263.

211. Ustrialov, *Pod znakom,* 253–54.

212. Ustrialov, *Pod znakom,* 339.

213. Ustrialov, *Pod znakom,* 349–50.

214. Ustrialov to Golitsyna, [fall 1920] (see n. 106), 7v.

215. Ustrialov, *Pod znakom,* 15; Ustrialov to Kliuchnikov, 3 January 1922 (see n. 146), 26; N. V. Ustrialov to Iu. N. Potekhin, 14 February 1922, *Smenovekhovtsy,* 31–32; N. V. Ustrialov, "Obstrel sprava," *Novosti zhizni,* 20 June 1922.

216. Ustrialov, *Pod znakom,* 48; Ustrialov to Bobrishchev-Pushkin, 25 April 1922 (see n. 152), 41.

217. Ustrialov, *Pod znakom,* 16–17.

218. See, for example, Ustrialov, *Pod znakom,* p. i; N. V. Ustrialov, *Pod znakom revoliutsii,* 2d enl. ed. (Harbin: Politgraf, 1927), pp. v, 212–18.

219. Ustrialov, *Pod znakom,* 2d enl. ed., pp. vi–vii.

220. "13-i s"ezd" in Ustrialov, *Pod znakom,* 155–59.

221. "14-i s"ezd" in Ustrialov, *Pod znakom,* 2d enl. ed., 222–32.

222. Ustrialov, *Pod znakom,* 2d enl. ed., 228–31.

223. See on this discussion Agursky, *Third Rome,* 310–13; Ustrialov, *Pod znakom,* 2d enl. ed., p. v; N. V. Ustrialov, Diary, 13 December 1925, *Smenovekhovtsy,* 113–14; Iu. V. Kliuchnikov to N. V. Ustrialov, 2 December 1925, *Smenovekhovtsy,* 115–19.

224. G. Zinov'ev, *Filosofiia epokhi* (Leningrad: Priboi, 1925), 23. The article had originally appeared in *Pravda* on 19 and 20 September 1925. See also G. Zinov'ev, *Leninizm,* 2d ed. (Leningrad: Gosizdat, 1926), 196–99.

225. N. I. Bukharin, *Tsezarizm pod maskoi revoliutsii: Po povodu knigi N. Ustrialova 'Pod znakom revoliutsii'* (Moscow: Pravda, 1925), 44. Before being issued as a separate brochure, the article had appeared in *Pravda* on 13 and 15 November 1925.

226. Ustrialov to Kliuchnikov, 2 January 1926 (see n. 200), 120–21; N. V. Ustrialov to P. P. Suvchinskii, 5 October 1927, *Suvchinskii,* 23.

227. N. V. Ustrialov to E. E. Iashnov, 12 November 1929, *Raznye liudi,* 157; N. V. Ustrialov to P. P. Suvchinskii, 11 June 1929, *Suvchinskii,* 52; N. V. Ustrialov, *Hic Rohdus [sic], hic salta!* (Harbin, 1929), 11–13. Ustrialov had written "Hic Rohdus" especially for *Novosti zhizni;* however, because of "some difficulties" the article did not appear in the Harbin newspaper, so that Ustrialov had to publish it himself as a separate brochure (see Ustrialov, *Hic Rohdus,* 1). The editors of *Novosti zhizni* had refused to print the article, preferring not to act against the party's official policy (see N. V. Ustrialov to P. P. Suvchinskii, 8 May 1929, *Suvchinskii,* 48). Soon thereafter, the article appeared also on the pages of the Paris journal *Evraziia,* no. 25 (11 May 1929): 3–4, and no. 26 (18 May 1929): 3–4.

228. Ustrialov, "Primechaniia" (see n. 163), p. vi n. 87.

229. N. V. Ustrialov to G. N. Dikii, 19 March 1930, *Dikii,* 16.

230. N. V. Ustrialov to G. N. Dikii, 3 May 1930, *Dikii,* 28; N. V. Ustrialov, *Na novom etape* (Shanghai: Tsenturion, 1930), 18.

231. Ustrialov, *Na novom etape,* 13, 17; N. V. Ustrialov to G. N. Dikii, 1 February 1931, *Dikii,* 57–58.

232. Ustrialov to Dikii, 3 May 1930 (see n. 230), 28; Ustrialov, *Na novom etape,* 18.

233. N. V. Ustrialov to G. N. Dikii, 6 April 1931, *Dikii,* 73: Ustrialov, *Na novom etape,* 13; N. V. Ustrialov, *Nashe vremia* (Shanghai, 1934), 50.

234. Ustrialov, *Na novom etape,* 22.

235. Ustrialov, *Na novom etape,* 22; N. V. Ustrialov to A. Ia. Avdoshchenkov and E. I. Titov, 22 December 1929, *Raznye liudi,* 179; Ustrialov to Dikii, 3 May 1930 (see n. 230), 28.

236. Ustrialov, *Na novom etape,* 27–29.

237. Ustrialov, *Nashe vremia,* 2–3; N. V. Ustrialov to Iu. A. Shirinskii-Shikhmatov, 16 February 1935, *Porevoliutsionery,* 45.

238. N. V. Ustrialov to G. N. Dikii, 3 December 1930, *Dikii,* 46; N. V. Ustrialov to G. N. Dikii, 9 March 1934, *Dikii,* 187.

239. Ustrialov, *Na novom etape,* 14.

240. Ustrialov, *Nashe vremia,* 51.

241. Ustrialov, *Nashe vremia,* 50, 56.

242. Ustrialov, *Na novom etape,* 14.

243. See Ustrialov's introduction to *Smenovekhovtsy,* p. ii; Ustrialov to Dikii, 9 March 1934 (see n. 238), 187.

244. Ustrialov, *Nashe vremia,* 6, 8.

245. Ustrialov, *Nashe vremia,* p. vii.

246. Ustrialov, *Nashe vremia,* 10–11.

247. Ustrialov, introduction (see n. 243), p. ii. See also the analysis of Ustrialov's position by G. P. Fedotov, "V plenu stikhii," *Novyi grad,* no. 4 (1932): 8–20.

248. Ustrialov, *Nashe vremia,* 21, 26–27.

249. Ustrialov, *Nashe vremia*, 107.

250. Ustrialov, *Nashe vremia*, 34–36.

251. Ustrialov, *Nashe vremia*, 30, 34, 40.

252. Ustrialov, *Nashe vremia*, 97–98, 107; N. V. Ustrialov to G. N. Dikii, 10 August 1934, *Dikii*, 197.

253. Ustrialov, *Nashe vremia*, 75–76, 92–95, 100–1. Ustrialov's attitude toward Italian Fascism was not unsympathetic, but rather condescending. He considered it a phenomenon of far lesser significance than Bolshevism. In the first place, he argued that Italy's "specific gravity" was incomparably lower than that of Russia; secondly and mainly, he regarded Italian Fascism with its "old-fashioned imperialism" merely as a "new moment in the development of the old world," as opposed to the radically progressive, universal force of Bolshevik internationalism (see Ustrialov, *Pod znakom*, 2d enl. ed., 409–10; N. V. Ustrialov, "Ital'ianskii fashizm," *Vysshaia shkola v Kharbine: Izvestiia Iuridicheskogo fakul'teta*, no. 5 [1928]: 192–200; Ustrialov, *Nashe vremia*, 94). German National Socialism, for its part, could not arouse Ustrialov's sympathy at all. In his view it had, like Italian Fascism, not a single new idea to offer. Moreover, as he regarded nations as sociohistorical formations, Ustrialov rejected the National Socialist notion of race as the basis of the nation as both anthropologically and sociologically mistaken. Its "zoological biologism" was morally completely unacceptable to him (see N. V. Ustrialov, *Germanskii natsional-sotsializm* [Harbin: Chinarev, 1933], 10–11, 83; Ustrialov, *Nashe vremia*, 77–78).

254. Ustrialov, *Nashe vremia*, 68, 74, 87, 107–9.

255. N. V. Ustrialov to K. A. Chkheidze, 27 April 1935, TsGAOR, f. 5911, op. 1, d. 78, l. 56.

256. N. V. Ustrialov to G. N. Dikii, 27 February 1934, *Dikii*, 185–86; N. V. Ustrialov to K. A. Chkheidze, 27 February 1934, TsGAOR, f. 5911, op. 1, d. 78, l. 4.

257. N. V. Ustrialov to K. A. Chkheidze, 30 November 1934, TsGAOR, f. 5911, op. 1, d. 78, l. 40; Ustrialov to Chkheidze, 27 April 1935 (see n. 255), l. 56.

258. N. V. Ustrialov to K. A. Chkheidze, 8 October 1934, TsGAOR, f. 5911, op. 1, d. 78, ll. 36–37; N. V. Ustrialov to Iu. A. Shirinskii-Shikhmatov, 22 December 1934, *Porevoliutsionery*, 39; N. V. Ustrialov to K. A. Chkheidze, 16 November 1934, TsGAOR, f. 5911, op. 1, d. 78, l. 34; Ustrialov to Chkheidze, 30 November 1934 (see n. 257), l. 41. Ustrialov did indeed send the archive to Prague, with the request not to open it until 1 January 1950 (see Ustrialov to Chkheidze, 27 April 1935 [see n. 255], l. 58). It has been preserved there to this day, as part of the so-called Fedoroviana Pragensia collection in the Literární archiv Národního muzea in Prague (see Hagemeister, *Nikolaj Fedorov*, 363 n. 1). I hereby wish to thank Dr. Hagemeister for informing me about the exact contents of the Ustrialov papers in the "Fedoroviana Pragensia collection" (see the bibliography).

259. Ustrialov to Chkheidze, 27 April 1935 (see n. 255), 56–57.

260. N. V. Ustrialov to G. N. Dikii, 1 April 1934, *Dikii*, 190.

261. N. V. Ustrialov to G. N. Dikii, 12 May 1934, *Dikii*, 194–95; N. V. Ustrialov to K. A. Cheidze, 15 May 1934, TsGAOR, f. 5911, op. 1, d. 78, l. 15.

262. Ustrialov to Chkheidze, 16 November 1934 (see n. 258), 33–34; N. V. Ustrialov to N. A. Perfil'ev, 22 November 1934, *Porevoliutsionery*, 39; Ustrialov to Chkheidze, 30 November 1934 (see n. 257), 40–41; Ustrialov to Shirinskii-Shikhmatov, 22 December 1934 (see n. 258), 40.

263. See, for example, Ustrialov, *Nashe vremia,* 10, 46, 131–32. Earlier, Ustrialov had called the Soviet leadership even a "kakistocracy" (Ustrialov, *Na novom etape,* 41), and "a goverment of [people who are] a little (or even rather) insane" (see Ustrialov to Potekhin, 8 September 1923 [see n. 158], 99).

264. G. N. Dikii to N. V. Ustrialov, 15 July 1934, *Dikii,* 196.

265. Ustrialov to Dikii, 10 August 1934 (see n. 252).

266. Ustrialov to Chkheidze, 27 April 1935 (see n. 255), 56, 58.

267. Ustrialov, *Nashe vremia,* 45, 54–55, 131–32.

268. Ustrialov, *Na novom etape,* 43; Ustrialov, *Nashe vremia,* 132.

269. See Ustrialov's introduction to *Raznye liudi,* p. i; Ustrialov, introduction (see n. 243), p. i.

270. Ustrialov to Dikii, 10 August 1934 (see n. 252), 198.

271. N. V. Ustrialov, "Samopoznanie sotsializma," *Izvestiia,* 18 December 1936.

272. N. V. Ustrialov, "Genii vekov," *Izvestiia,* 10 February 1937.

273. N. V. Ustrialov, "Revoliutsioner-demokrat," *Izvestiia,* 6 April 1937.

274. Ustrialov, "Samopoznanie sotsializma."

275. Ustrialov, "Samopoznanie sotsializma."

276. Ustrialov, "Genii vekov"; Ustrialov, "Revoliutsioner-demokrat."

277. *BSE1,* 56:392, s.v. "Ustrialov, Nikolai Vasil'evich"; *BSE3,* 27:386, s.v. "Ustrialov, Nikolai Vasil'evich"; Schulz, Urban, and Lebed, *Who was who,* 564; V. I. Lenin, *Polnoe sobranie sochinenii,* 5th ed., 55 vols. (Moscow: Gospolitizdat, 1958–1965), 45:657.

Chapter 3: *Smena Vekh*

1. V. A. Osipov, "Vozniknovenie smenovekhovstva i sozdanie gazety 'Naka-nune' " (Avtoreferat, I.N.I.O.N., Moscow, 1989), 5.

2. R. B. Gul', *Rossiia v Germanii,* vol. 1 of *Ia unes Rossiiu: Apologiia emigratsii* (New York: Most, 1984), 20; H. E. Schulz, P. K. Urban, and A. I. Lebed, eds., *Who was who in the USSR: A Biographic Directory* (Metuchen, N.J.: Scarecrow Press, 1972), 282; *Vsia Moskva* (1917), div. 1, 258.

3. Kliuchnikov's contribution to the journal consisted of two articles: "Mezhdu-narodnoe obozrenie: Russko-Iaponskii soiuz," no. 9 (15 [28] July 1916): 12–16; and "Franko-Russkii soiuz," no. 10 (1 [14] August 1916): 2–4.

4. "Omsk-Parizh: Beseda s byvshim Upravliaiushchim Ministerstvom Inostran-nykh Del professorom Iu. V. Kliuchnikovym," *Pravitel'stvennyi vestnik* (Omsk), 11 February 1919. *Russkoe slovo* continued to appear for several months after the Bolshevik takeover, albeit with several interruptions. In the first months of 1918 it was repeatedly closed down by the authorities, only to reappear a few days later under a new title: successively, *Novoe slovo, Nashe slovo, Narodnoe slovo, Svobodnoe slovo,* and finally *Chest-noe slovo.* In early August 1918 it was shut down completely (see A. Z. Okorokov, *Oktiabr' i krakh russkoi burzhuaznoi pressy* [Moscow: Mysl', 1970], 344). The last article over Kliuchnikov's signature appeared in the paper on 30 June 1918.

5. Bar. B. E. Nol'de, "Novye knigi: Iu. V. Kliuchnikov, Internatsionalizm (Os-novnye voprosy mezhdunarodnykh otnoshenii)," *Nash vek,* 28 [15] April 1918.

6. V. Ia. Laverychev, "Vserossiiskii Soiuz Torgovli i Promyshlennosti," *Istor-icheskie zapiski,* no. 70 (1961): 54.

7. Iu. V. Kliuchnikov, *Revoliutsiia i voina* (Moscow: Universal'naia biblioteka, 1917). This pamphlet was issued by the Moscow Committee of the Kadet party (see W. G. Rosenberg, *Liberals in the Russian Revolution: The Constitutional Democratic Party 1917–1923* [Princeton: Princeton University Press, 1974], 480).

8. Kliuchnikov, *Revoliutsiia i voina*, 18–24.

9. Kliuchnikov, *Revoliutsiia i voina*, 29–32.

10. Iu. Kliuchnikov, "Smert' i voskresenie," *Russkoe slovo*, 9 November 1917; Iu. K.[liuchnikov], "So stupen'ki na stupen'ku," *Russkoe slovo*, 26 November 1917.

11. Kliuchnikov, "Smert'."

12. Iu. Kliuchnikov, "Velikoe reshenie i velikii obman," *Russkoe slovo*, 19 November 1917.

13. Iu. Kliuchnikov, "Rossiia i ee soiuzniki," *Russkoe slovo*, 16 November 1917; Kliuchnikov, "Smert'."

14. Kliuchnikov, "Velikoe reshenie." On 8 November 1917, for example, Petrograd Commissar for Affairs of the Press, Propaganda and Agitation M. Volodarskii had declared at a party meeting that the Bolsheviks "might have to dissolve the Constituent Assembly with bayonets" (see W. H. Chamberlin, *The Russian Revolution, 1917–1921*, 2 vols. [New York: Macmillan, 1954; Princeton: Princeton University Press, 1987], 1:365).

15. See, for example, Iu. Kliuchnikov, "Pered neizbezhnym," *Nashe slovo*, 30 June 1918.

16. After the Soviet government had started negotiations with Germany over a separate peace, Britain and France began to consider intervention in Russia as an absolute necessity to prevent the Germans from seizing Allied supplies in Northern Russia, and especially to maintain an anti-German Eastern front. In the Allies' opinion, a victory on the Western front would otherwise be impossible. It did not occur to them, however, that the few troops they could spare from the Western front could not possibly suffice to achieve this goal, and that Japan, on which they counted for help, could hardly be expected to cooperate. While the Japanese were eager to intervene in Manchuria, an area where they wanted to establish themselves, they were not in the least interested in expanding their operations further to the West, as Britain and France hoped. President Wilson, for his part, opposed intervention because he feared that this, especially if it were carried out chiefly by Japanese troops, would merely give rise to resentment among the Russian population, and drive them to seek German support. He believed that the possible military advantages of such a step could by no means outweigh its disadvantages. It was only when he became convinced that the Northern ports were indeed threatened by the Germans that he agreed, on 1 June 1918, to send troops to safeguard these ports, still opposing any intervention in Siberia. The factor that in early July finally made Wilson accept intervention as well was the fate of the 60,000-strong Czech force in Siberia, which was under protection of the Allied and Associated Powers, and which he felt obliged to help. See R. Ullman, *Intervention and the War*, vol. 1 of *Anglo-Soviet Relations, 1917–1921* (Princeton: Princeton University Press, 1961), 92–93, 101–7, 129, 192–98, 207, 212–29.

17. In the set of *Russkoe slovo* which I had at my disposal, issues immediately following the signing of the peace treaty are missing. However, Kliuchnikov's negative attitude is obvious also in later articles. See, for example, Iu. Kliuchnikov, "Argumenty Lenina," *Novoe slovo*, 16 [3] March 1918.

18. Iu. Kliuchnikov, "Iaponskaia pomoshch' Rossii," *Novoe slovo,* 10 March [25 February] 1918; Iu. Kliuchnikov, "Rech' Bal'fura," *Novoe slovo,* 21 [8] March 1918; Iu. Kliuchnikov, "Soiuzniki i Rossiia," *Nashe slovo,* 13 June 1918.

19. Iu. Kliuchnikov, "Liga Narodov," *Russkoe slovo,* 6 October 1917; Kliuchnikov, "Iaponskaia pomoshch'."

20. "Omsk-Parizh" (see n. 4); Iu. Kliuchnikov, "Nasha vneshniaia politika," pt. 2, *Nakanune,* no. 2 (14 [1] April 1918): 4; Iu. V. Kliuchnikov, *Na velikom istoricheskom pereput'i: Piat' glav po sotsiologii mezhdunarodnykh otnoshenii* (Berlin: Smena vekh, 1922), 31; V. M. Zenzinov, *Gosudarstvennyi perevorot admirala Kolchaka v Omske, 18 noiabria 1918 goda: Sbornik dokumentov* (Paris: Rirakhovskii, 1919), 27–28.

21. Kliuchnikov put forward his ideas in this respect in a lecture on "German Imperialism and American Federalism" that he read before the "Moscow Legal Society" on 19 February 1918, and in a book, *Internatsionalizm: Osnovnye voprosy mezhdunarodnykh otnoshenii* (Moscow: Gran', 1918). In 1922 he used the contents of this book as chapter 2 and 3 of his work *Na velikom istoricheskom pereput'i.* See Kliuchnikov, *Na velikom istoricheskom pereput'i,* 5; Iu. V. Kliuchnikov to N. V. Ustrialov, late March 1921, *Smenovekhovtsy,* 8.

22. Kliuchnikov, *Na velikom istoricheskom pereput'i,* 70–71.

23. Iu. V. Kliuchnikov, "Iaponiia i derzhavy Soglasiia" in *Evropa i voina: Rossiia i ee soiuzniki v bor'be za tsivilizatsiiu* (Moscow: D. Ia. Makovskii, 1917), 2–1:24. See also Iu. V. Kliuchnikov, "Na velikom istoricheskom pereput'i," *Golos Rossii,* 24 May 1921.

24. Kliuchnikov, *Na velikom istoricheskom pereput'i,* 85, 97.

25. Iu. Kliuchnikov, "Nasha vneshniaia politika," pt. 1, *Nakanune,* no. 1 (7 April [25 March] 1918): 4; Kliuchnikov, "Liga."

26. Kliuchnikov, "Nasha vneshniaia politika," pt. 2, 4; Kliuchnikov, "Liga."

27. Kliuchnikov, "Liga"; Kliuchnikov, "Nasha vneshniaia politika," pt. 1, 4.

28. Kliuchnikov, "Nasha vneshniaia politika," pt. 2, 5.

29. Kliuchnikov, "Nasha vneshniaia politika," pt. 1, 5.

30. Kliuchnikov, "Nasha vneshniaia politika," pt. 1, 4; Iu. Kliuchnikov, "Vneshniaia politika Ukrainy," *Nashe slovo,* 19 May 1918.

31. Kliuchnikov, "Nasha vneshniaia politika," pt. 2, 4.

32. Kliuchnikov, "Nasha vneshniaia politika," pt. 2, 4–5. In the spring of 1918 Kliuchnikov, along with Ustrialov and the young lawyer E. A. Korovin, their colleague at Moscow University and fellow contributor to *Problemy velikoi Rossii* and *Utro Rossii,* were invited to a session of the Kadet Central Committee's "Commission for Foreign Affairs," in order to present their point of view in this respect. However, they were unable to convince the Central Committee (see N. V. Ustrialov, *Pod znakom revoliutsii* [Harbin: Russkaia mysl', 1925], 203–4). On Korovin see n. 91 below.

33. Iu. Kliuchnikov, "Nasha vneshniaia politika," pt. 3, *Nakanune,* no. 6 (May 1918): 6. See also Kliuchnikov, "Nasha vneshniaia politika," pt. 2, 4.

34. Kliuchnikov, "Nasha vneshniaia politika," pt. 2, 4–5.

35. Kliuchnikov, "Nasha vneshniaia politika," pt. 2, 4.

36. Kliuchnikov, "Pered neizbezhnym."

37. A. Iablonovskii, " 'Podkidyshi,' " *Obshchee delo,* 4 November 1921; Schulz, Urban, and Lebed, *Who was who,* 282. On the uprising see Ullman, *Intervention,* 230–31; D. L. Golinkov, *Krushenie antisovetskogo podpol'ia v SSSR,* 2d rev. ed., 2 vols.

(Moscow: Izd-vo politicheskoi literatury, 1978), 1:175–83; D. L. Golinkov, "Kak byl likvidirovan kontrrevoliutsionnyi miatezh v Iaroslavle, Rybinske i Murome v 1918 godu," *Voprosy istorii*, 1965, no. 4:212–13.

38. Gul', *Rossiia v Germanii*, 176; Ustrialov, *Pod znakom*, 63; *Belyi Omsk*, 47.

39. G. Gins, "Chlen direktorii ob Omskom pravitel'stve," *Russkii golos* (Harbin), 3 June 1921; Iu. V. Kliuchnikov, "S-R i kolchakovskii perevorot (Po lichnym vospominaniiam)," *Nakanune* (Berlin), 2 April 1922; Kliuchnikov, "Omsk-Parizh" (see n. 4); Schulz, Urban, and Lebed, *Who was who*, 282.

40. On the coup see Rosenberg, *Liberals*, 393–95; N. G. Dumova, *Kadetskaia kontrrevoliutsiia i ee razgrom (oktiabr' 1917–1920 gg.)* (Moscow: Nauka, 1982), 192–207; G. K. Gins, *Sibir', soiuzniki i Kolchak: Povorotnyi moment russkoi istorii 1918–1920 gg.* 2 vols. (Peking: Tipo-Litografiia Russkoi dukhovnoi missii, 1921), 1:306–16; Zenzinov, *Gosudarstvennyi perevorot;* S. P. Mel'gunov, *Tragediia admirala Kolchaka*, 3 vols. (Belgrade: Russkaia tipografiia, 1930–1931), 2:95–158; G. Z. Ioffe, *Kolchakovskaia avantiura i ee krakh* (Moscow: Mysl', 1983), 120–46.

41. This is, for example, alleged by the Socialist Revolutionary N. V. Sviatitskii in his book *K istorii Vserossiiskogo Uchreditel'nogo Sobraniia: S"ezd chlenov Uchreditel'nogo Sobraniia (sentiabr'–dekabr' 1918)* (Moscow, 1921), 95, quoted in Mel'gunov, *Tragediia,* 2:134. It has, however, not been proven. Kliuchnikov himself first maintained that he did not know anything about the coup (see [Iu. V. Kliuchnikov,] "Reziume doklada v Russkom Politicheskom Soveshchanii v Parizhe b. Upravliaiushchego Ministerstvom Inostrannykh Del Omskogo Pravitel'stva Iu. V. Kliuchnikova, 2 iiunia 1919 g.," 4, S. P. Melgunov collection, box 13, Hoover Institution Archives, Stanford, California); later, however, he merely said that the coup had taken place against his will (see Kliuchnikov, "S-R i kolchakovskii perevorot"). While it is extremely unlikely that his first claim is true, given the fact that several members of the Kadet party in Omsk and of the All-Russian Directory's government were informed about the coup (see Dumova, *Kadetskaia kontrrevoliutsiia*, 195–204; Rosenberg, *Liberals*, 395; Mel'gunov, *Tragediia,* 2:135), it is on the other hand quite possible that Kliuchnikov did indeed oppose the idea of a coup. As has been suggested by S. P. Mel'gunov (see Mel'gunov, *Tragediia,* 2:134), the fact that Kliuchnikov—only two days before the coup—openly presented the directory with a proposal for its restructuring, a proposal that he afterwards said might have avoided the coup (see Zenzinov, *Gosudarstvennyi perevorot*, 30), seems to point in this direction.

42. [Kliuchnikov,] "Reziume doklada" (see n. 41), 3. See also Rosenberg, *Liberals,* 392–95.

43. [Kliuchnikov,] "Reziume doklada" (see n. 41), 1; Zenzinov, *Gosudarstvennyi perevorot,* 28–29. The quorum had been established at 250 for 1 January, and at 170 for 1 February 1919.

44. [Kliuchnikov,] "Reziume doklada" (see n. 41), 4. A copy of the memorandum is in the collection of the former TsGAOR in Moscow (see Dumova, *Kadetskaia kontrrevoliutsiia*, 389 n. 24), but has so far been unavailable to me. An account of its contents can be found in Zenzinov, *Gosudarstvennyi perevorot*, 29–30, and Gins, *Sibir',* 1:303–4.

45. Zenzinov, *Gosudarstvennyi perevorot,* 29–30; Gins, *Sibir',* 1:303.

46. Mel'gunov, *Tragediia,* 2:134; Zenzinov, *Gosudarstvennyi perevorot,* 30.

47. Zenzinov, *Gosudarstvennyi perevorot*, 30–32.

48. The text of the telegram can be found in Zenzinov, *Gosudarstvennyi perevorot*, 25–26. See also Dumova, *Kadetskaia kontrrevoliutsiia*, 204.

49. Gins, *Sibir'*, 2:71. On the Allied attitude toward possible Russian representation at the conference see R. Ullman, *Britain and the Russian Civil War*, vol. 2 of *Anglo-Soviet Relations, 1917–1921* (Princeton: Princeton University Press, 1968), 86–87.

50. Gins, *Sibir'*, 2:19, 36, 42, 71; *Belyi Omsk*, 44.

51. Gins, *Sibir'*, 2:2, 71–72.

52. Kliuchnikov, "Omsk-Parizh" (see n. 4); *Belyi Omsk*, 44–45; Iu. V. Kliuchnikov to N. V. Ustrialov, 25 February 1919, *Smenovekhovtsy*, 1–2; *Notes russes 1920*, 1 June 1920, doc. P.4392.U.

53. Members included former Prime Minister of the First Provisional Government Prince L'vov, the Provisional Government's ambassador to France, V. A. Maklakov, former President of the so-called Supreme Administration of the Northern Region N. V. Chaikovskii, and former Tsarist Minister of Foreign Affairs S. D. Sazonov, who represented in Paris the governments of both Admiral Kolchak and General Denikin. See *EGV*, 525, s.v. "Russkoe Politicheskoe Soveshchanie"; H. von Rimscha, *Der russische Bürgerkrieg und die russische Emigration 1917–1921* (Jena: Verlag der Frommannschen Buchhandlung, 1924), 52–54.

54. *EGV*, 525, s.v. "Russkoe Politicheskoe Soveshchanie"; for the contents of Kliuchnikov's report see [Kliuchnikov,] "Reziume doklada" (see n. 41).

55. L. Fleishman, R. Kh'iuz, and O. Raevskaia-Kh'iuz, eds., *Russkii Berlin 1921–1923: Po materialam arkhiva B. I. Nikolaevskogo v Guverovskom institute* (Paris: YMCA-Press, 1983), 106; "Protokol obshchego sobraniia Parizhskoi gruppy," 6–7 May 1920, *KD Archive*, box 2, 1.

56. "Lektsii po russkoi istorii i literature," *Poslednie novosti*, 12 May 1920; *Notes russes 1920*, 1 June 1920, doc. P.4392.U. The Russian Academic Group had been founded in the spring of 1920 by a number of Russian émigré academics in Paris, including the lawyer and former professor at Petrograd University Gronskii and the lawyer and historian Baron B. E. Nol'de. The Group worked under the auspices of the Paris Institut d'Etudes slaves, and had the tacit support of the Faculty of Law at Paris University. See M. Raeff, "Institutions of a society in exile: Russia abroad, 1919–1939," *Rossiia/Russia*, no. 6 (1988): 106.

57. G. Klutchnikoff, ed., *La Russie d'aujourd'hui et de demain* (Paris: Attinger, 1920), 17, 24.

58. Klutchnikoff, *Russie*, 12–13.

59. Klutchnikoff, *Russie*, 5–6.

60. Klutchnikoff, *Russie*, 8–11, 16.

61. Klutchnikoff, *Russie*, 15, 17–19.

62. Klutchnikoff, *Russie*, 21–24.

63. Don Aminado, *Poezd na tret'em puti* (New York: Izd-vo imeni Chekhova, 1954), 282–83. The play itself did not appear until 1923; it was published by the "Izdatel'stvo pisatelei v Berline" and appeared with the subtitle *Dramaticheskie kartiny iz russkoi zhizni 1918 goda*.

64. Ustrialov, *Pod znakom*, 63–64.

65. On this debate see Rosenberg, *Liberals*, 439–43.

66. "Protokol zasedaniia Komiteta Parizhskoi gruppy Partii Narodnoi Svobody," 17 May 1920, *KD Archive*, box. 2, 534–35. See also Fleishman, Kh'iuz, and Raevskaia-Kh'iuz, *Russkii Berlin*, 107.

67. It never came to an actual agreement between Wrangel and the Poles, however. See *EGV*, 121, s.v. "Vrangelevshchina."

68. "Protokol," 17 May 1920 (see n. 66), 534–35.

69. *Notes russes 1920*, 9 July 1920, doc. P.4479.U.

70. "Protokol," 17 May 1920 (see n. 66), 534

71. *Notes russes 1920*, 9 July 1920, doc. P.4479.U.

72. Iu. V. Kliuchnikov to N. V. Ustrialov, 20 November 1920, *Smenovekhovtsy*, 3.

73. On the "new tactics" see Rosenberg, *Liberals*, 445–49; Iu. V. Mukhachev, " 'Novaia taktika' rossiiskoi kontrrevoliutsii i ee proval, 1920–1922 gg.," *Istoricheskie zapiski*, no. 99 (1977): 55–87; Iu. V. Mukhachev, *Ideino-politicheskoe bankrotstvo planov burzhuaznogo restavratorstva v SSSR* (Moscow: Mysl', 1982), 74–87; J. P. Nielsen, *Miliukov i Stalin: O politicheskoi evoliutsii P. N. Miliukova v emigratsii (1918–1943)* (Oslo: Universitetet i Oslo, 1983), 5–10.

74. Rosenberg, *Liberals*, 449–50; Nielsen, *Miliukov i Stalin*, 10.

75. "Protokol zasedaniia chlenov Parizhskoi gruppy Partii Narodnoi Svobody," 25 November 1920, *KD Archive*, box 2, 26.

76. "Protokol zasedaniia Parizhskogo Komiteta Partii Narodnoi Svobody," 2 December 1920, *KD Archive*, box 2, 933; "Protokol sobraniia chlenov Parizhskoi gruppy Partii Narodnoi Svobody," 25 January 1921, *KD Archive*, box 2, 28–29. On the Conference of Members of the Constituent Assembly see the introduction.

77. "Protokol zasedaniia Parizhskogo Komiteta Partii Narodnoi Svobody," 3 December 1920, *KD Archive*, box 2, 942.

78. See, for example, "Protokol zasedaniia Parizhskogo Komiteta Partii Narodnoi Svobody," 17 February 1921, *KD Archive*, box 2, 1150.

79. "Protokol zasedaniia Parizhskogo Komiteta Partii Narodnoi Svobody," 30 December 1920, *KD Archive*, box 2, 1050.

80. "Protokol," 30 December 1920 (see n. 79), 1050. A list of Kliuchnikov's theses is included in the protocol of this meeting, 1051–52.

81. "Protokol," 17 February 1921 (see n. 78), 1147.

82. "Protokol," 17 February 1921 (see n. 78), 1147–48.

83. "Protokol," 17 February 1921 (see n. 78), 1147–48.

84. "Protokol," 17 February 1921 (see n. 78), 1147–48, 1150.

85. "Protokol," 17 February 1921 (see n. 78), 1150.

86. "Protokol," 17 February 1921 (see n. 78), 1147–48, 1150.

87. "Protokol," 17 February 1921 (see n. 78), 1150.

88. "Protokol," 17 February 1921 (see n. 78), 1149.

89. "Protokol," 17 February 1921 (see n. 78), 1149.

90. "Protokol Parizhskogo Komiteta gruppy Partii Narodnoi Svobody," 10 March 1921, *KD Archive*, box 2, 1173.

91. "Protokol," 17 February 1921 (see n. 78), 1148. It seems that Kliuchnikov was bluffing when he mentioned Korovin. In a letter to Ustrialov, several weeks after his lecture before the Paris Committee, Kliuchnikov wrote: "Now it is E. A. Korovin's

turn. How good would it be if he, too, in spite of everything, started thinking just as we. And yet, if he were true to the old points of view, I would forgive him more easily than anyone of us" (Kliuchnikov to Ustrialov, late March 1921 [see n. 21], 7). In reality, Korovin was already cooperating with the Soviet regime in 1919, and at that time was serving as director of the foreign section of the Soviet Red Cross (see Iu. V. Got'e, *Time of Troubles: The Diary of Iurii Vladimirovich Got'e. Moscow, July 8, 1917 to July 23, 1922,* trans. and ed. T. Emmons [London: Tauris, 1988], 262). He was appointed professor at Moscow State University and at the Moscow Institute of Oriental Studies in 1923. He rose to prominence as a specialist in international law, was included in the Soviet delegation to several international conferences, and in 1946 became a correspondent member of the Academy of Sciences (see Schulz, Urban, and Lebed, *Who was who,* 300). Judging from Ustrialov's correspondence, the contact between Korovin and his old friends Kliuchnikov and Ustrialov was never reestablished.

92. Gul', *Rossiia v Germanii,* 176. On Luk'ianov senior see N. O. Lossky, *History of Russian Philosophy* (New York: International University, 1951), 81, 178.

93. *Ves' Petrograd* (1915), div. 1, 437; *Novaia Rossiia,* no. 1 (March 1922), 61.

94. Osipov, "Vozniknovenie smenovekhovstva," 35; Al. P-o, "Novye veianiia (Doklad prof. Luk'ianova)," *Poslednie novosti,* 15 February 1921.

95. "Russkaia literatura za rubezhom," *Obshchee delo,* 26 September 1921; "Udostoilis'," *Obshchee delo,* 28 October 1921; Iablonovskii, " 'Podkidyshi.' "

96. Kliuchnikov to Ustrialov, late March 1921 (see n. 21), 6.

97. Al. P-o, "Novye veianiia."

98. Al. P-o, "Novye veianiia."

99. Al. P-o, "Novye veianiia."

100. Al. P-o, "Novye veianiia."

101. Al. P-o, "Novye veianiia."

102. Kliuchnikov to Ustrialov, late March 1921 (see n. 21), 6–7; Al. P-o, "Novye veianiia."

103. Kliuchnikov to Ustrialov, late March 1921 (see n. 21), 7.

104. A. V., "Mirit'sia li s bol'shevikami?" *Poslednie novosti,* 22 February 1921.

105. Iak. B., "Vozvrashchat'sia li v Sovetskuiu Rossiiu?" *Poslednie novosti,* 26 February 1921; A. R., " 'Razdavite gadinu!' (Na doklade prof. Luk'ianova)," *Obshchee delo,* 1 March 1921.

106. A. V., "Mirit'sia li."

107. Iak. B., "Vozvrashchat'sia li."

108. S. Poliakov(-Litovtsev), "O soglashatel'stve," *Poslednie novosti,* 1 March 1921.

109. Iak. B., "Vozvrashchat'sia li"; A. R., " 'Razdavite.' "

110. B. Mirskii, "O primirenii i primiriaiushchikhsia," *Poslednie novosti,* 26 February 1921.

111. Kliuchnikov to Ustrialov, late March 1921 (see n. 21), 7.

112. "Protokol," 10 March 1921 (see n. 90), 1172–74; N. Obolenskii to Iu. V. Kliuchnikov, 15 August 1921, *KD Archive,* box 2, 1352.

113. Iu. V. Kliuchnikov to N. V. Ustrialov, 13 July 1921, *Smenovekhovtsy,* 9; A. V. Bobrishchev-Pushkin, *Patrioty bez otechestva* (Leningrad: Kubuch, 1925), 116–17.

114. Iu. N. Potekhin to Mobshtab Narkomzema SSSR, 6 March 1930, TsGALI, f. 675, op. 2, d. 499, l. 36; Iu. N. Potekhin, "Anketa v Dramsoiuz," 17 April

1929, TsGALI, f. 675, op. 2, d. 499, l. 37. On Potekhin see also V. A. Osipov, "Kto takoi F. Iks: Iz pisatel'skikh biografii," *Literaturnaia Rossiia,* 25 August 1989.

115. Iu. N. Potekhin to N. V. Ustrialov, 1 September 1921, *Smenovekhovtsy,* 14; "Protokol," 17 February 1921 (see n. 78), 1149. On the National Center see Rosenberg, *Liberals,* 297–300; Dumova, *Kadetskaia kontrrevoliutsiia,* 118–27.

116. "Protokol," 17 February 1921 (see n. 78), 1149. On the position of A. V. Krivoshein in General Denikin's administration see K. A. Krivoshein, *A. V. Krivoshein (1857–1921 gg.): Ego znachenie v istorii Rossii nachala XX veka* (Paris: I. U. F., 1973), 307–8.

117. Potekhin to Ustrialov, 1 September 1921 (see n. 115), 12–14.

118. Kliuchnikov to Ustrialov, late March 1921 (see n. 21), 7.

119. Iu. N. Potekhin to N. V. Ustrialov, 3 March 1921, *Smenovekhovtsy,* 5–6.

120. Potekhin to Ustrialov, 1 September 1921 (see n. 115), 13.

121. *BSE1,* 6:553–54, s.v. "Bobrishchev-Pushkin, Aleksandr Vladimirovich"; Schulz, Urban, and Lebed, *Who was who,* 73; E. Birth, *Die Oktobristen (1905–1913), Zielvorstellungen und Struktur: Ein Beitrag zur russischen Parteiengeschichte* (Stuttgart: Ernst Klett, 1974), 27.

122. *BSE1,* 6:554, s.v. "Bobrishchev-Pushkin, Aleksandr Vladimirovich"; E. Huskey, "The Russian Bar and the Consolidation of Soviet Power," *Russian Review* 43 (1984): 134.

123. *BSE1,* 6:554, s.v. "Bobrishchev-Pushkin, Aleksandr Vladimirovich"; I. Ia. Trifonov, "Iz istorii bor'by kommunisticheskoi partii protiv smenovekhovstva," *Istoriia SSSR,* 1959, no. 3:66; *SSV,* 119; Iablonovskii, " 'Podkidyshi' "; A. V. Bobrishchev-Pushkin to N. V. Ustrialov, 10 June 1922, *Smenovekhovtsy,* 49, 59; Bobrishchev-Pushkin, *Patrioty,* 117–18.

124. Kliuchnikov to Ustrialov, 13 July 1921 (see n. 113), 10.

125. A. V. Bobrishchev-Pushkin to N. V. Ustrialov, 15 February 1922, *Smenovekhovtsy,* 33–35.

126. Bobrishchev-Pushkin to Ustrialov, 15 February 1922 (see n. 125), 34–35.

127. Bobrishchev-Pushkin to Ustrialov, 15 February 1922 (see n. 125), 33–35.

128. Bobrishchev-Pushkin to Ustrialov, 15 February 1922 (see n. 125), 33–34.

129. Editorial, *Novyi mir,* 5 April 1921.

130. Ne-Kommunist, "K vozvrashchenii v Rossiiu: Vopros ob amnistii," *Novyi mir,* 5 April 1921.

131. Quoted in B. Mirskii, "Oblichitel' ushedshikh," *Poslednie novosti,* 19 May 1921.

132. Ne-Kommunist, "Malen'kii terevsat," *Novyi mir,* 2 April 1922.

133. See, for example, Mirskii, "Oblichitel' "; "Evoliutsiia bol'shevizma," *Rul',* 1 September 1921; "Pechat'," *Poslednie novosti,* 23 September 1921; Iablonovskii, " 'Podkidyshi.' "

134. Kliuchnikov to Ustrialov, 13 July 1921 (see n. 113), 10.

135. Iu. K., "Logika primireniia," *Put',* 3 July 1921.

136. "Razval K.D. partii," *Put',* 9 August 1921. On the last, decisive meetings of the united Kadet party see Rosenberg, *Liberals,* 456–61.

137. "Protokol zasedaniia Parizhskogo Komiteta Partii Narodnoi Svobody," 15 August 1921, *KD Archive,* box 2, 1345–46; Obolenskii to Kliuchnikov, 15 August 1921 (see n. 112).

138. Iu. V. Kliuchnikov to the Committee of the Paris Group of the Party of People's Freedom, 18 August 1921, *KD Archive*, box 2, 1353.

139. Fleishman, Kh'iuz, and Raevskaia-Kh'iuz, *Russkii Berlin*, 108. Iashchenko's answer to Kliuchnikov is unknown.

140. This is suggested in Kliuchnikov to Ustrialov, 13 July 1921 (see n. 113), 9–10.

141. Kliuchnikov to Ustrialov, 13 July 1921 (see n. 113), 10–11.

142. Iu. V. Kliuchnikov to N. V. Ustrialov, 8 November 1921, *Smenovekhovtsy*, 17; Iu. V. Kliuchnikov to M. Gor'kii, 17 September 1921, quoted in Osipov, "Vozniknovenie smenovekhovstva," 18; N. V. Ustrialov, Diary, 24 August 1925, *Smenovekhovtsy*, 110.

143. Kliuchnikov to Ustrialov, 13 July 1921 (see n. 113), 9; Potekhin to Ustrialov, 1 September 1921 (see n. 115), 13. This is also clear from the collection's contents. Potekhin, for example, mentioned a lecture by I. Novgorodtsev *(SSV,* 182), which took place on 18 August 1921. On the lecture in question see B. Mirskii, "Krushenie zapadnichestva," *Poslednie novosti,* 19 August 1921.

144. *SSV,* 6.

145. *SSV,* 11, 35.

146. *SSV,* 17–18, 35–36.

147. *SSV,* 76–77, 85–87.

148. *SSV,* 85–90.

149. *SSV,* 97–100.

150. *SSV,* 123–28.

151. *SSV,* 117–18, 144–48.

152. *SSV,* 170–72, 179–80.

153. A. Khar'kovskii, "Chakhotinskaia odisseia," *Ogonek,* 1974, no. 8:6–7.

154. K. N. Sokolov, *Pravlenie gen. Denikina (Iz vospominanii)* (Sofia: Rossiisko-Bolgarskoe knigo-izdatel'stvo, 1921), 95–99; Osipov, "Vozniknovenie smenovekhovstva," 36; "Russkaia literatura za rubezhom" (see n. 95).

155. Kliuchnikov to Ustrialov, 13 July 1921 (see n. 113), 10: Potekhin to Ustrialov, 1 September 1921 (see n. 115), 13.

156. Ustrialov, Diary, 24 August 1925 (see n. 142), 110.

157. *SSV,* 150–53.

158. *SSV,* 158–59, 162–63.

159. *SSV,* 57–59 (Ustrialov); 136–37 (Bobrishchev-Pushkin); 156–57 (Chakhotin); 176 (Potekhin).

160. *SSV,* 40 (Kliuchnikov); 59 (Ustrialov); 133 (Bobrishchev-Pushkin); 176–77 (Potekhin).

161. *SSV,* 46 (Kliuchnikov); 60 (Ustrialov); 90 (Luk'ianov); 97, 100 (Bobrishchev-Pushkin); 179–80 (Potekhin).

162. *SSV,* 49 (Kliuchnikov); 62–65, 71 (Ustrialov); 87–88 (Luk'ianov); 129–30 (Bobrishchev-Pushkin); 161–66 (Chakhotin); 172, 177 (Potekhin).

163. See chap. 2.

164. *SSV,* 57.

165. *SSV,* 136. The Turkish nationalist government in Ankara, headed by Mustafa Kemal, concluded a treaty of friendship with the Soviet government on 16 March

1921. The nationalists could count on Soviet support in their conflict with the Entente and more particularly with the British government, which refused to recognize the Ankara government. The Straits question, however, was not to be solved so soon and so exclusively to Russia's advantage as Bobrishchev-Pushkin expected. At the Conference of Lausanne, which was convened in late 1922–early 1923, it was decided that free passage through the Straits should be guaranteed to all merchant ships without distinction.

166. *SSV,* 40.

167. *SSV,* 93. See in this connection S. R. Graubard, *British Labour and the Russian Revolution 1917–1924* (Cambridge: Harvard University Press, 1956), 64–114; R. Ullman, *The Anglo-Soviet Accord,* vol. 3 of *Anglo-Soviet Relations, 1917–1921* (Princeton: Princeton University Press, 1972), 51–52, 220–24.

168. *SSV,* 133, 176, 59.

169. On the Russian "etatist" school see K.-D. Grothusen, *Die historische Rechtsschule Russlands: Ein Beitrag zur russischen Geistesgeschichte in der zweiten Hälfte des 19. Jahrhunderts* (Giessen: Schmitz, 1962).

170. J. E. Zimmerman, "Russian Liberal Theory, 1900–17," *Canadian-American Slavic Studies* 14, no. 1 (Spring 1980): 17–18; J. E. Zimmerman, "The Political Views of the *Vekhi* Authors," *Canadian-American Slavic Studies* 10, no. 3 (Fall 1976): 314–16.

171. *Iz glubiny: Sbornik statei o russkoi revoliutsii* (Moscow: Russkaia mysl', 1918; Paris: YMCA-Press, 1967), 291–92. On this collection see chap. 2, n. 46.

172. *SSV,* 90.

173. *SSV,* 100.

174. *SSV,* 47–48, 60.

175. Zimmerman, "Russian Liberal Theory," 4–5, 8, 14–17.

176. J. Burbank, *Intelligentsia and Revolution: Russian Views of Bolshevism, 1917–1922* (New York: Oxford University Press, 1986), 246.

177. *SSV,* 89.

178. *SSV,* 176.

179. Kliuchnikov to Ustrialov, 8 November 1921 (see n. 142), 17.

180. *SSV,* 176.

181. *SSV,* 151–52.

182. K. N. Leont'ev, *Vostok, Rossiia i Slavianstvo: Sbornik statei,* vol. 2. (Moscow: I. N. Kushnerev, 1886), 86, referred to by Ustrialov in *SSV,* 56. See in this connection also N. Berdiaev, *Konstantin Leont'ev: Ocherk iz istorii russkoi religioznoi mysli* (Paris: YMCA-Press, 1926), 203.

183. Berdiaev, *Leont'ev,* 182–83, 186.

184. Berdiaev, *Leont'ev,* 196, 199–201.

185. Berdiaev, *Leont'ev,* 186, 193.

186. N. Ustrialov, "Russkii bunt," *Utro Rossii,* 26 November 1917; N. Ustrialov, "Vo vlasti raspada," *Utro Rossii,* 21 January 1918.

187. See especially "Zelenyi shum" (see N. V. Ustrialov, *V bor'be za Rossiiu* [Harbin: Okno, 1920], 64–70), which was written in late September 1920 in reaction to the wave of peasant wars which struck the country at that time; and "Nad bezdnoi" (see Ustrialov, *Pod znakom,* 1–5), which was a direct reaction to the Kronstadt uprising in March 1921.

188. Ustrialov, *V bor'be,* 68; *SSV,* 60.
189. *SSV,* 89.
190. *SSV,* 173.
191. *SSV,* 40–41.
192. *SSV,* 148.
193. *SSV,* 148.
194. See S. A. Fediukin, *Bor'ba s burzhuaznoi ideologiei v usloviiakh perekhoda k Nepu* (Moscow: Nauka, 1977), 45–49; F. Stepun, *Byvshee i nesbyvsheesia,* 2 vols. (New York: Izd-vo imeni Chekhova, 1956), 2:275–79; R. C. Williams, *Culture in Exile: Russian Emigrés in Germany 1881–1941* (Ithaca, N.Y.: Cornell University Press, 1972), 248–49, 313–18; B. Shletser, " 'Zakat Evropy,' " *Sovremennye zapiski,* no. 12 (1922): 339–48; V. Vaganian, "Nashi rossiiskie shpengleristy," *Pod znamenem marksizma,* 1922, no. 1–2:28–33; K. Grasis, " 'Zakat Evropy': Vekhisty o Shpenglere," *Krasnaia nov',* 1922, no. 2:196–211.
195. On this movement see G. Nivat, "Du 'Panmongolisme' au 'mouvement eurasien': Histoire d'un thème littéraire," *Cahiers du monde russe et soviétique* 7 (July–September 1966): 470–78; Williams, *Culture in Exile,* 252–58; M. Agursky, *The Third Rome: National Bolshevism in the USSR* (Boulder, Colo.: Westview Press, 1987), 170–79. The Scythians issued a first collection in 1917: A. I. Ivanchin-Pisarev, R. V. Ivanov-Razumnik, and S. D. Mstislavskii, eds., *Skify: Sbornik 1-i* (Petrograd, 1917), and a second in 1923: *Puti revoliutsii* (Berlin: Skify, 1923). See also A. Blok and A. Belyi, *Dialog poetov o Rossii i revoliutsii,* comp. M. F. P'ianykh (Moscow: Vysshaia shkola, 1990).
196. See n. 57 to the introduction.
197. Burbank, *Intelligentsia and Revolution,* 193–205.
198. Burbank, *Intelligentsia and Revolution,* 205–8; Williams, *Culture in Exile,* 248–49, 251–52.
199. Burbank, *Intelligentsia and Revolution,* 251–52.
200. See, for example, T. Ardov, "Pered kontsom," *Utro Rossii,* 24 November 1917; Iu. V. Got'e, *Smutnoe vremia: Ocherk istorii revoliutsionnykh dvizhenii nachala XVII stoletiia* ([Moscow]: Gosizdat, 1921), 5–6.
201. *SSV,* 159–60.
202. *SSV,* 115–16.
203. *SSV,* 61.
204. On the Hegelian tradition in Russian thought see A. Walicki, *A History of Russian Thought: From the Enlightenment to Marxism* (Oxford: Oxford University Press, 1979), 114–34, 397–405; D. I. Chizhevskii, *Gegel' v Rossii* (Paris: Dom knigi i Sovremennye zapiski, 1939).
205. *SSV,* 59.
206. *SSV,* 160.
207. *SSV,* 89–90.
208. *SSV,* 122.
209. *SSV,* 168.
210. *SSV,* 31.
211. *SSV,* 69–71.
212. *SSV,* 115.

213. *SSV*, 87 (Luk'ianov); 161 (Chakhotin).

214. *SSV*, 180.

215. *SSV*, 49.

216. *SSV*, 48.

217. *SSV*, 172.

218. *SSV*, 165–66.

219. *SSV*, 48.

220. *SSV*, 116 (Bobrishchev-Pushkin); 173 (Potekhin).

221. *SSV*, 129, 161, 180.

222. *SSV*, 62–65.

223. *SSV*, 48, 118–21.

224. Ustrialov did not consider the civil war a complete mistake either (Ustrialov, *V bor'be*, 1); he only condemned what he considered to be its pointless continuation after the fall of Kolchak.

225. *SSV*, 176.

226. *SSV*, 87.

227. *SSV*, 161–62.

228. *SSV*, 161.

229. *SSV*, 162–63.

230. *SSV*, 173, 180.

231. *SSV*, 180–81.

232. *SSV*, 90.

233. *SSV*, 33.

234. *SSV*, 31–33.

235. *SSV*, 49.

236. *SSV*, 49–50.

237. *SSV*, 50.

238. *SSV*, 142. On this issue see the introduction.

239. *SSV*, 145.

240. *SSV*, 169–70.

241. *SSV*, 24–26, 43–44.

242. *SSV*, 22–23, 41–43.

243. *SSV*, 34–39.

CHAPTER 4: INDIGNATION AND CONDESCENSION

1. Iu. N. Potekhin to N. V. Ustrialov, 1 September 1921, *Smenovekhovtsy*, 13.

2. A. Iablonovskii, "Sem' obrazovannykh muzhchin," *Obshchee delo*, 17 September 1921.

3. J. Brooks, "*Vekhi* and the *Vekhi* Dispute," *Survey* 19 (Winter 1973): 45, 46. Merezhkovskii's article had been entitled "Sem' smirennykh" and had appeared in *Rech'* of 9 May 1909.

4. F. M. Dostoevskii, *Sobranie sochinenii v piatnadtsati tomakh*, vol. 5 (Leningrad: Nauka, Leningradskoe otdelenie, 1989), 55–59.

5. Iablonovskii, "Sem'."

6. L. Bernshtein, " 'Novo-vekhovtsy,' " *Obshchee delo*, 15 January 1922.

7. M. Lazerson, "Natsional-bol'shevizm," *Zaria* (Berlin), no. 2 (18 May 1922): 42–43.

8. *Golos Rossii,* 31 July 1921.

9. A. Kulisher, "Ne-Kommunist," *Golos Rossii,* 11 October 1921; St. Ivanovich, "O 'priiatii,' " *Golos Rossii,* 31 December 1921.

10. M. Slonim, "Ot oktiabrizma k bol'shevizmu ('Smena vekh,' sbornik statei. Praga, 1921)," *Volia Rossii,* 27 September 1921.

11. V. Chernov, " 'Ottsy' i 'deti,' " *Volia Rossii,* 1922, no. 5:9.

12. On Octobrist ideology see E. Birth, *Die Oktobristen (1905–1913), Zielvorstellungen und Struktur: Ein Beitrag zur russischen Parteiengeschichte* (Stuttgart: Ernst Klett, 1974), especially 106–60.

13. See Birth, *Oktobristen,* 121–23, 130.

14. Slonim, "Ot oktiabrizma"; M. Slonim, "Metamorfozy natsional-liberalizma," *Volia Rossii,* 1922, no. 2:14–16; Chernov, " 'Ottsy.' "

15. Slonim, "Ot oktiabrizma."

16. See n. 4 to the introduction.

17. Brooks, "*Vekhi,*" 40–41.

18. Brooks, "*Vekhi,*" 42–44.

19. *Vekhi kak znamenie vremeni: Sbornik statei* (Moscow: Zveno, 1910), 34.

20. *Intelligentsiia v Rossii: Sbornik statei* (Petersburg: Zemlia, 1910), 105, quoted in Brooks, "*Vekhi,*" 45.

21. B. Mirskii, "Novye 'vekhi,' " *Poslednie novosti,* 3 July 1920.

22. Chernov, " 'Ottsy,' " 8–9.

23. Slonim, "Ot oktiabrizma."

24. M. Vishniak, " 'Smena vekh' (Kritika i bibliografiia)," *Sovremennye zapiski,* no. 8 (1921): 383–84. The quotation from Kliuchnikov is in *SSV,* 24, 26.

25. Vishniak, " 'Smena vekh,' " 384.

26. On Bulgarin see D. S. Mirsky, *A History of Russian Literature From its Beginnings to 1900* (New York: Vintage Books, 1958), 124–25.

27. P. Ryss, "Bez vekh," *Poslednie novosti,* 21 September 1921.

28. Ryss, "Bez vekh."

29. Ryss, "Bez vekh."

30. Ryss, "Bez vekh."

31. Gins reacted to *Smena vekh* with a series of articles in the Harbin daily *Russkii golos:* G. K. Gins, "Smena vekh," pts. 1–3, *Russkii golos,* 12, 23, 26 April 1922.

32. For an account of Izgoev's appearance in *Dom literatorov* see Ia. Livshits, " 'Vekhi' i 'Smena vekh' (Disput v Dome literatorov)," *Letopis' Doma literatorov,* 1922, no. 1–2:10–11; A. S. Izgoev, " 'Vekhi' i 'Smena vekh,' " *Russkaia mysl',* 1922, no. 3:176–78; "A. S. Izgoev o 'Smene vekh,' " *Volia Rossii,* no. 9 (4 March 1922): 22–23.

33. A. S. Izgoev, " 'Vekhi' i 'Smena vekh' " in *OSV,* 7–24.

34. P. B. Struve, "Proshloe, nastoiashchee, budushchee: Mysli o natsional'nom vozrozhdenii Rossii," *Russkaia mysl',* 1922, no. 1–2:227–228.

35. Struve, "Proshloe," 228.

36. See for instance D. Pasmanik, "Blagotvornye plody iada (Po povodu sbornika statei 'Smena vekh')," *Obshchee delo,* 12 October 1921; Struve, "Proshloe," 228; "Intelligentskoe primirenchestvo i bol'shevizm," *Revoliutsionnaia Rossiia,* no. 14–15

(November–December 1921): 1; S. Poliakov-Litovtsev, "Zhivoi trup," *Zveno,* no. 1 (5 February 1923): 1; A. M. Gorovtsev, " 'Smene vekh': Skhema lektsii, chitannoi avtorom v Parizhe" in *'Skrepa vekh': Vtoroi vypusk politicheskogo zhurnala-al'manakha 'Tribuny'* (Paris, [1922]), 13; P. Danilov, "Sharlatany," *Obshchee delo,* 14 November 1921.

37. See "Skupshchiki 'Mertvykh dush,' " *Novoe vremia,* 9 December 1921; Iuvenal, "Natsional-bol'shevizm," *Novoe vremia,* 14 December 1921; Vishniak, " 'Smena vekh,' " 385.

38. "Skupshchiki 'Mertvykh dush' " (see n. 37).

39. Iuvenal, "Natsional-bol'shevizm."

40. Iuvenal, "Natsional-bol'shevizm."

41. Gins, "Smena vekh," *Russkii golos* (Harbin), 23 April 1922. See also S. S. Ol'denburg, "Politicheskii obzor: Dela russkie, Smena vekh," *Russkaia mysl',* 1922, no. 1–2:307

42. Gins, "Smena vekh" (see n. 280); Vishniak, " 'Smena vekh,' " 385.

43. S. Sumskii, "Ideologiia sovburzhuazii," *Sotsialisticheskii vestnik,* 1921, no. 19:3–6; S. Sumskii, "O natsional-bol'shevizme," *Sotsialisticheskii vestnik,* 1921, no. 21:3–6.

44. Sumskii, "Ideologiia," 4.

45. Sumskii, "Ideologiia," 4.

46. See J. Burbank, *Intelligentsia and Revolution: Russian Views of Bolshevism, 1917–1922* (New York: Oxford University Press, 1986), 18–34, 59–62; L. H. Haimson, ed., *The Mensheviks from the Revolution of 1917 to the Second World War* (Chicago: University of Chicago Press, 1974), 247–49.

47. Sumskii, "Ideologiia," 6.

48. Sumskii, "Ideologiia," 6.

49. Sumskii, "Ideologiia," 6–7. For the quotations from Bobrishchev-Pushkin see *SSV,* 128, 130.

50. Sumskii, "Ideologiia," 6–7; Sumskii, "O natsional-bol'shevizme," 3.

51. Sumskii, "Ideologiia," 6.

52. The article by Iu. Steklov in *Izvestiia* of 14 August 1921 that M. Agurskii calls "the first badly hidden reaction to *Smena vekh*" (see M. Agursky, *The Third Rome: National Bolshevism in the USSR* [Boulder, Colo.: Westview Press, 1987], 259) cannot possibly refer to the Prague collection, for at that time it had not yet appeared. Most likely, Steklov was referring to the articles by Kliuchnikov in *Put'* of 3 July and 9 August 1921 ("Logika primireniia," *Put',* 3 July 1921; "Razval K.D. partii," *Put',* 9 August 1921), which dealt with the plea for reconciliation with the Bolsheviks Kliuchnikov had made in the Paris Kadet Committee in February of that year. See in this respect also Iu. Steklov, "Ne nachalo li otrezvleniia? (K voprosu 'o tretei taktike')," *Izvestiia,* 17 August 1921.

53. The Washington conference lasted from 12 November 1921 to 6 February 1922. Its main achievements were the so-called Four-Power Pacific Treaty, concluded between the United States, Britain, Japan, and France on 13 December 1921; and the Naval Armament Limitation Treaty, signed on 6 February 1922 by the four abovementioned states and by Italy.

54. *Vladimir Il'ich Lenin: Biograficheskaia khronika,* vol. 11 (Moscow: Izd-vo politicheskoi literatury, 1980), 471; *Leninskii sbornik,* vol. 39 (Moscow: Izd-vo politicheskoi literatury, 1980), 321. Nothing ever came of this plan, however.

55. Iu. Steklov, "Psikhologicheskii perelom," *Izvestiia*, 13 October 1921.

56. N. Meshcheriakov, "Znamenie vremeni," *Pravda*, 14 October 1921.

57. M. Pokrovskii, "Razlozhenie prodolzhaetsia," *Pravda*, 27 December 1921. For an (incomplete) overview of the reactions in the Soviet press see N. S. Zelikina, "Iz istorii bor'by sovetskoi publitsistike s burzhuazno-restavratorskimi ideiami smenovekhovstva," *Vestnik LGU*, ser. 2, 1983, no. 8:86–88.

58. "Pobedit Proletarii," *Gudok*, 15 October 1921.

59. N. Kuz'min, "Gibel' 'demokratii,' " *Krasnaia gazeta*, 18 October 1921.

60. "Novaia pobeda Sovetskoi vlasti," *Petrogradskaia pravda*, 20 October 1921.

61. S. Borisov, "Na novom puti," *Novyi mir*, 16 October 1921; D. Varvarin, "Smena 'vekh,' " *Novyi put'*, 21 October 1921; "Ideologiia 'vtorogo dnia,' " *Put'*, 25 October 1921.

62. N. Meshcheriakov, "Gor'koe priznanie," *Pravda*, 16 October 1921; N. Meshcheriakov, "Myl'nyi puzyr'," *Pravda*, 2 November 1921; N. Meshcheriakov, "Eshche o 'Smene vekh,' " *Pravda*, 19 November 1921; Pokrovskii, "Razlozhenie"; N. Meshcheriakov, "Iz belogvardeiskoi pechati," *Pravda*, 28 December 1921.

63. V. Bystrianskii, "Kontr-revoliutsiia i mrakobesie," *Petrogradskaia pravda*, 25 October 1921; V. Bystrianskii, " 'Smena vekh' o mirovoi revoliutsii," *Petrogradskaia pravda*, 20 November 1921; V. Bystrianskii, "Intelligentsiia i Sovetskaia vlast'," *Petrogradskaia pravda*, 22 November 1921; "Vokrug 'Smeny vekh,' " *Petrogradskaia pravda*, 22 November 1921; Vl. Vasilevskii, "Intelligentsiia i revoliutsiia (ezhenedel'nik 'Smena vekh')," *Petrogradskaia pravda*, 10 December 1921; V. Bystrianskii, "Na novykh pozitsiiakh," *Petrogradskaia pravda*, 11 December 1921.

64. N. Kuz'min, " 'Vekhi' i 'Smena vekh,' " *Krasnaia gazeta*, 6 December 1921; N. A. Gredeskul, " 'Smena vekh,' " *Izvestiia*, 11 November 1921.

65. "Ne k smenivshimsia vekham, a pod znamia internatsionalizma (Po povodu gruppy 'Smena vekh')," *Zhizn' natsional'nostei*, 1921, no. 27:1; Iu. Borisov, " 'Smena vekh,' " *Zhizn' natsional'nostei*, 1921, no. 30:2–3.

66. N. Meshcheriakov, "Novye vekhi," *Krasnaia nov'*, 1921, no. 3:256–71, reprinted in N. Meshcheriakov, *Na perelome: Iz nastroenii belogvardeiskoi emigratsii* (Moscow: Gospolitizdat, 1922), 38–61 (further references are to the latter version); Iu. Steklov, "Burzhuaznaia intelligentsiia v russkoi proletarskoi revoliutsii," *Kommunisticheskii internatsional*, no. 19 (1 September 1921): 4977–94.

67. V. I. Nevskii, "Metod revoliutsionnogo obucheniia (O 'Smene vekh')," *Spravochnik Petrogradskogo agitatora*, no. 12–13 (1 December 1921): 60–68; A. V. Bobrishchev-Pushkin, "Novaia vera," *Spravochnik Petrogradskogo agitatora*, no. 12–13 (1 December 1921): 20–59.

68. M. N. Pokrovskii, "Kaiushchaiasia intelligentsiia" in *Intelligentsiia i revoliutsiia* (Moscow: Dom pechati, 1922), 72–89; A. V. Lunacharskii, "Smena vekh intelligentskoi obshchestvennosti," *Kul'tura i zhizn'*, no. 1 (1 February 1922): 5–10, reprinted in A. V. Lunacharskii, *Ob intelligentsii* (Moscow: Krasnaia nov'), 42–51 (further references are to the latter edition).

69. P. A. Sadyker, "Voiny budushchego," first printed in *SV*, no. 12 (14 January 1922): 11–14, reprinted in *Krasnaia nov'*, 1922, no. 1:299–303; A. V. Bobrishchev-Pushkin, "Koshmar Ivana Ivanovicha," first printed in *SV*, no. 11 (7 January 1922): 14–17, reprinted in *Izvestiia*, 27 January 1922; Skif [Iu. N. Potekhin], "Pliuskvamperfektum," first printed in *SV*, no. 11 (7 January 1922): 17–18, reprinted in *Izvestiia*, 28

January 1922. All these articles were reprinted in unabridged form and without any comment.

70. "Rech' tov. Trotskogo na II. Vserossiiskom s"ezde politprosvetov (prodolzhenie)," *Pravda*, 27 October 1921.

71. S. A. Adrianov, "Dobro pozhalovat'," *Put'*, 2 December 1921.

72. Quoted in "Les Soviets et l'émigration russe (Rosta)," *L'Humanité*, 4 December 1921.

73. M. Gor'kii to Iu. V. Kliuchnikov, [November 1921], Arkhiv M. Gor'kogo, KG-P, 35-14-1, quoted in V. A. Osipov, "Vozniknovenie smenovekhovstva i sozdanie gazety 'Nakanune' " (Avtoreferat, I.N.I.O.N., Moscow, 1989), 19.

74. See, for example, Steklov, "Psikhologicheskii perelom"; Steklov, "Burzhuaznaia intelligentsiia," 4992; "Rech' tov. Trotskogo" (see n. 70); Lunacharskii, "Smena vekh," 46–47; Pokrovskii, "Kaiushchaiasia," 74.

75. Meshcheriakov, "Znamenie vremeni"; Steklov, "Psikhologicheskii perelom." See also Varvarin, "Smena 'vekh' "; Lunacharskii, "Smena vekh," 46. In many cases, there were mistakes in the biographical data mentioned: Trotskii, for instance, claimed that Potekhin had directed Kolchak's Information Agency ("Rech' tov. Trotskogo" [see n. 70]); Lenin had it that Ustrialov had been one of Admiral Kolchak's ministers (V. I. Lenin, *Polnoe sobranie sochinenii*, 5th ed., 55 vols. [Moscow: Gospolitizdat, 1958–1965], 45:93), and Lunacharskii believed that Bobrishchev-Pushkin had been "one of the brains behind the Wrangel adventure [*Vrangelevshchina*]" (Lunacharskii, "Smena vekh," 46); finally, Meshcheriakov mistakenly called Chakhotin and Potekhin former collaborators of Admiral Kolchak (Meshcheriakov, "Novye vekhi," 44).

76. Steklov, "Psikhologicheskii perelom"; Steklov, "Burzhuaznaia intelligentsiia," 4984; Meshcheriakov, "Znamenie vremeni"; Meshcheriakov, "Novye vekhi," 42, 55; "Pobedit Proletarii" (see n. 58); "Ideologiia 'vtorogo dnia' " (see n. 61); Kuz'min, "Gibel' "; "Novaia pobeda" (see n. 60); Bystrianskii, "Intelligentsiia."

77. Steklov, "Psikhologicheskii perelom"; Meshcheriakov, "Myl'nyi puzyr' "; Meshcheriakov, "Novye vekhi," 53; Lunacharskii, "Smena vekh," 46; "Novaia pobeda" (see n. 60).

78. Kuz'min, "Gibel'."

79. Steklov, "Psikhologicheskii perelom."

80. Meshcheriakov, "Znamenie vremeni"; Meshcheriakov, "Novye vekhi," 45; "Rech' tov. Trotskogo" (see n. 70); Borisov, "Na novom puti"; Varvarin, "Smena 'vekh' "; Lunacharskii, "Smena vekh," 46, 48; "Novaia pobeda" (see n. 60); Bystrianskii, "Smena vekh.' " Iu. Steklov did mention this in his "Burzhuaznaia intelligentsiia v russkoi proletarskoi revoliutsii," 4990.

81. "Rech' tov. Trotskogo" (see n. 70).

82. Lunacharskii, "Smena vekh," 50.

83. Meshcheriakov, "Novye vekhi," 54–59. See also Steklov, "Psikhologicheskii perelom" and Bystrianskii, "Intelligentsiia."

84. *EGV*, 396, s.v. "Nevskii, Vladimir Ivanovich." On the "Workers' opposition" see R. V. Daniels, *The Conscience of the Revolution: Communist Opposition in Soviet Russia* (Cambridge: Harvard University Press, 1960), 138–65.

85. Nevskii, "Metod," 68.

86. H. Shukman, ed., *The Blackwell Encyclopedia of the Russian Revolution* (Oxford: Blackwell, 1988), 365. On the "Left Communists" see Daniels, *Conscience*, 70–94.

87. Pokrovskii, "Kaiushchaiasia," 84–89.
88. "Ne k smenivshimsia" (see n. 65).
89. Meshcheriakov, "Znamenie vremeni"; Meshcheriakov, "Novye vekhi," 58.
90. Lunacharskii, "Smena vekh," 50–51.
91. "Les Soviets et l'émigration" (see n. 72).
92. Bystrianskii, " 'Smena vekh.' "
93. Bystrianskii, "Intelligentsiia."
94. "Rech' tov. Trotskogo" (see n. 70).
95. Steklov, "Psikhologicheskii perelom."
96. "Vstretilis': Pis'mo iz Moskvy," *Sotsialisticheskii vestnik,* 1921, no. 21:11.
97. In late December 1921, imported copies of the first edition went on sale in Petrograd for 200,000 rubles apiece. See "Literaturnaia khronika: V Peterburge," *Letopis' Doma literatorov,* 1921, no. 4:10; I. L., "Disput o 'Smene vekh,' " *Put',* 8 December 1921; Ia. Livshits, " 'Vekhi,' " 11. In the fall of 1921 and the winter of 1921–22 the value of the ruble was plummeting. Nonetheless, in December 1921, 200,000 rubles was still a considerable amount of money, as is clear from remarks in Iu. V. Got'e's diary: on 7 November 1921 a pound of bread cost 3,500 rubles, a pound of meat an average of 10,000 rubles; on 23 November a pound of bread was 4,800 rubles, and on 20 December 10,000 rubles (see Iu. V. Got'e, *Time of Troubles: The Diary of Iurii Vladimirovich Got'e, Moscow, July 8, 1917 to July 23, 1922,* trans. and ed. T. Emmons [London: Tauris, 1988], 434, 435, 439).
98. S. A. Fediukin, *Bor'ba s burzhuaznoi ideologiei v usloviiakh perekhoda k Nepu* (Moscow: Nauka, 1977), 286–87; "Literaturnaia khronika: V provintsii," *Letopis' Doma literatorov,* 1922, no. 1–2:9. The Smolensk edition was in fact published by the management of the Smolensk Printing Industry. The claim in the Berlin journal *Novaia russkaia kniga* of April 1922 that "the collection *Smena vekh* was being republished by the State Publishing House in Moscow and in Tver" (see *Novaia russkaia kniga,* 1922, no. 4:33) seems to be wrong: I have never seen any trace of, or reference to, a possible Moscow edition.
99. The number of copies that appeared in Tver was told to me by V. A. Osipov, conversation with author, Moscow, September 1989. See also A. V. Kvakin, "Osnovnye cherty novovekhovskoi ideologii" (Avtoreferat, Kalininskii gosudarstvennyi universitet, 1980), 8.
100. See N. A. Gredeskul, "Proryv molchaniia," *Put',* 23 December 1921; I. L., "Disput" (see n. 97).
101. On Got'e's views see T. Emmons's introduction to Got'e, *Time of Troubles,* 13–17.
102. Most likely, Got'e had the opportunity to read the collection in his quality as associate director and chief librarian of the Rumiantsev Museum (later the V. I. Lenin Public Library of the USSR, currently the Russian State Library), where émigré publications were regularly received starting from the spring of 1921. See Got'e, *Time of Troubles,* 17–18, 409.
103. Got'e, *Time of Troubles,* 429–30 (14 October 1921).
104. Got'e, *Time of Troubles,* 433 (2 November 1921).
105. Got'e, *Time of Troubles,* 15, 433–34 n. 105.
106. Got'e, *Time of Troubles,* 433.

107. See N. M. Somov, *Bibliografiia russkoi obshchestvennosti*, pt. 1 (Moscow: N. M. Somov, 1927), 44–62; N. M. Somov, *Bibliografiia russkoi obshchestvennosti (K voprosu ob intelligentsii)*, pt. 2 (Moscow: Russkoe bibliograficheskoe obshchestvo pri 1-i MGU, 1931), 30–37.

108. Gredeskul, " 'Smena vekh' "; Adrianov, "Dobro pozhalovat'." On Adrianov see chap. 2, n. 174.

109. Gredeskul, " 'Smena vekh.' "

110. Gredeskul, " 'Smena vekh.' "

111. Adrianov, "Dobro pozhalovat'."

112. Adrianov, "Dobro pozhalovat'."

113. I. Lezhnev, " 'Smena vekh,' " *Novaia Rossiia*, no. 1 (March 1922): 61–65.

114. The editors of *Vestnik literatury* had announced the article by Sorokin as the first in a series on *Smena vekh*, in which both opponents and supporters of the Prague collection would be given the opportunity to speak out. See A. K., "O 'Smene vekh,' " *Vestnik literatury*, 1921, no. 12:1. Following Sorokin's contribution, however, the monthly published only one more article related to the subject, signed by K. Bozhenko, in which the author vented his disapproval, not so much of the *smenovekhovtsy*'s position, as of V. G. Tan's statement that the intelligentsia had finally been liberated of their guilt vis-à-vis the people (see K. Bozhenko, "Rubka vekh," *Vestnik literatury*, 1922, no. 1:3–4; V. Polonskii, *Ocherki literaturnogo dvizheniia revoliutsionnoi epokhi (1917–1927)* [Moscow: Gosizdat, 1928], 7).

115. P. Sorokin, "O 'Smene vekh': 'Smena vekh' kak sotsial'nyi simptom," *Vestnik literatury*, 1921, no. 12:1–2.

116. Sorokin, "O 'Smene vekh,' " 2–3.

117. Sorokin, "O 'Smene vekh,' " 3.

118. Apparently, a similar debate took place at the Petrograd Free Philosophical Association [*Vol'naia filosofskaia assotsiatsiia*] (see A. K., "O 'Smene vekh' "). There were no records of this debate available to me.

119. I. L., "Disput" (see n. 97); Ia. Livshits, "Novye i starye vekhi (Dva sobesedovaniia v Dome literatorov o sbornike 'Smena vekh')," *Letopis' Doma literatorov*, 1921, no. 3:4; I. L., "Iz Rossii: Disput," *SV*, no. 10 (31 December 1921): 16.

120. Gredeskul, "Proryv molchaniia." On V. G. Tan-Bogoraz see chap. 2 n. 173.

121. I. L., "Disput" (see n. 97); Livshits, "Novye i starye."

122. I. L., "Disput o 'Smene vekh': Doklad V. G. Tana," *Put'*, 10 December 1921; I. L., "Disput o 'Smene vekh,' " *Put'*, 12 December 1921; Livshits, "Novye i starye."

123. Livshits, "Novye i starye"; I. L., "Iz Rossii" (see n. 119), 16.

124. I. L., "Disput o 'Smene vekh': Preniia," *Put'*, 14 December 1921; I. L., "Disput o 'Smene vekh,' " *Put'*, 15 December 1921; Livshits, "Novye i starye."

125. I. L., "Disput o 'Smene vekh,' " *Put'*, 17 December 1921; Livshits, "Novye i starye."

126. I. F. Masanov, *Slovar' psevdonimov russkikh pisatelei, uchenykh i obshchestvennykh deiatelei*, 4 vols. (Moscow: Izd-vo Vsesoiuznoi knizhnoi palaty, 1956–1960), 1:169.

127. I. L., "Disput," 14 December 1921 (see n. 124).

128. I. L., "Disput," 15 December 1921 (see n. 124); I. L., "Disput o 'Smene vekh,' " *Put'*, 16 December 1921; Livshits, "Novye i starye."

129. I. L., "Disput," 16 December 1921 (see n. 128).

130. Livshits, " 'Vekhi' "; Vl. Lavretskii, "Petrogradskie pis'ma: Novye i starye vekhi," *SV*, no. 16 (11 February 1922): 21–24. See also E. Oberländer, "Nationalbol-schewistische Tendenzen in der russischen Intelligenz: die 'Smena Vech'-Diskussion 1921–1922," *Jahrbücher für Geschichte Osteuropas* 16 (1968): 208–10. According to the account by Ia. Livshits, Izgoev concluded the debate by saying that "among all absolute values Russia should be one of the greatest values" (Livshits, " 'Vekhi,' " 11). Izgoev immediately reacted to this, saying that he "knew only one absolute value," and that "this was in all its diversity that, which people call God" (see "Dopolnenie k zametke 'Vekhi' i 'Smena vekh,' " *Russkaia mysl'*, 1922, no. 4:224).

131. See "Iz khroniki," *SV*, no. 12 (14 January 1922): 24. According to an announcement of the collection in *Put'*, 29 December 1921, besides Izgoev, Guber, and Clemens, the philosophers L. Karsavin and N. O. Losskii had also agreed to con-tribute to the collection. For some reason, however, they withdrew, and the article by A. B. Petrishchev was included instead.

132. *OSV*, 9–10, 24, 68–69.

133. *OSV*, 45–53.

134. *OSV*, 80.

135. *OSV*, 73–76.

136. After his conversations with Kliuchnikov during his visit to Moscow in the summer of 1925, Ustrialov wrote in his diary that "the *Smena vekh* lemon had been squeezed dry at a rather high speed" (see N. V. Ustrialov, Diary, 24 August 1925, *Smenovekhovtsy*, 111).

CHAPTER 5: THE WEEKLY *SMENA VEKH*

1. N. Ustrialov, " 'Vekhi' i revoliutsiia," *Novosti zhizni* (November 1921), re-printed in N. V. Ustrialov, *Pod znakom revoliutsii* (Harbin: Russkaia mysl', 1925), 47. This article was written in response to Meshcheriakov's reaction to the Prague collec-tion in *Pravda* (N. Meshcheriakov, "Znamenie vremeni," *Pravda*, 14 October 1921). At that time, Ustrialov had not even had a chance to read the collection himself (see chap. 2). With respect to Steklov's reaction in *Izvestiia* (Iu. Steklov, "Psikhologicheskii perelom," *Izvestiia*, 13 October 1921), Ustrialov wrote in a letter to Kliuchnikov: ". . . does Steklov's vulgar, as always, article really not sicken you, and do you really not feel the depressing poverty of thought of all articles to the last?" (N. V. Ustrialov to Iu. V. Kliuchnikov, 30 January 1922, *Smenovekhovtsy*, 31).

2. "S drugogo berega (Sovetskaia i pro-sovetskaia pechat' o 'Smene Vekh')," *SV*, no. 6 (3 December 1921), 12.

3. *Notes russes 1921*, 12 October 1921, doc. P.5436.U; *Notes russes 1921*, No-vember 1921, doc. P.5565.U; *Notes russes 1922*, 28 January 1922, doc. P.5789.U. See also A. Vetlugin, *Tret'ia Rossiia* (Paris: Franko-Russkaia pechat', 1922), 307–8; L. M., "Zametki," *Sotsialisticheskii vestnik*, 1922, no. 11:11. Unfortunately, Krasin's papers in the L. B. Krasin Archief, Internationaal Instituut voor Sociale Geschiedenis, Amster-dam, do not contain anything that could confirm this.

4. V. A. Osipov, "Vozniknovenie smenovekhovstva i sozdanie gazety 'Naka- nune' " (Avtoreferat, I.N.I.O.N., Moscow, 1989), 18–19. V. A. Osipov suggests that Gor'kii may have been acquainted with Kliuchnikov before 1917, given the fact that Gor'kii's *Moi universitety* contains a passage, referring to the printing house of Kliuchni- kov's father, V. M. Kliuchnikov. See in this connection Osipov, "Vozniknovenie smen- ovekhovstva," 19 n. 1; M. Gor'kii, *Detstvo, V liudiakh, Moi universitety* (Kiev: Dnipro, 1982), 502. See further also *Letopis' zhizni i tvorchestva A. M. Gor'kogo,* vol. 3 (Moscow: AN SSSR, 1959), 252, whose editors wrongly suggest that "the journal that is being organized by Kliuchnikov" is *Novaia Rossiia,* rather than *Smena vekh.*

5. Iu. V. Kliuchnikov to N. V. Ustrialov, 8 November 1921, *Smenovekhovtsy,* 18; A. V. Bobrishchev-Pushkin to N. V. Ustrialov, 10 June 1922, *Smenovekhovtsy,* 60.

6. NN to N. V. Ustrialov, 16 January 1922, *Smenovekhovtsy,* 29; Z. G. Ashkinazi, "Kaiushchiesia intelligenty: Pis'mo iz Pragy," *Poslednie novosti,* 8 November 1921; Iu. Kliuchnikov, "Nash otvet," *SV,* no. 4 (19 November 1921): 6.

7. M. Gor'kii to E. P. Peshkova, November 1921, Arkhiv M. Gor'kogo, PG- RL, 30–19, quoted in Osipov, "Vozniknovenie smenovekhovstva," 20. I was unable to identify this Boris Markovich.

8. R. H. Johnston, *New Mecca, New Babylon: Paris and the Russian Exiles, 1920– 1945* (Kingston, Ont.: McGill-Queen's University Press, 1988), 32. On Maklakov see G. Adamovich, *Vasilii Alekseevich Maklakov: Politik, iurist, chelovek* (Paris: V. V. Vyrobov, 1959). On his political views see W. G. Rosenberg, *Liberals in the Russian Revolution: The Constitutional Democratic Party 1917–1923* (Princeton: Princeton University Press, 1974), chaps. 1, 6, 7 *passim;* on his position in emigration see Johnston, *New Mecca,* 32–34, 65–67; Rosenberg, *Liberals,* 436–38.

9. V. A. Maklakov to B. A. Bakhmetev, 24 October 1921, 30, V. A. Maklakov collection, box 13, Hoover Institution Archives, Stanford, California.

10. Maklakov to Bakhmetev, 24 October 1921 (see n. 9), 30.

11. Maklakov to Bakhmetev, 24 October 1921 (see n. 9), 30–31.

12. Maklakov to Bakhmetev, 24 October 1921 (see n. 9), 31–32.

13. Rosenberg, *Liberals,* 171–72, 436.

14. Maklakov to Bakhmetev, 24 October 1921 (see n. 9), 33–34; V. A. Makla- kov to B. A. Bakhmetev, 3 January 1922, 12, V. A. Maklakov collection, box 14, Hoover Institution Archives, Stanford, California. See also Rosenberg, *Liberals,* 219.

15. Editorial, *SV,* no. 1 (29 October 1921), 2–3.

16. For a complete index see *SV,* no. 20 (25 March 1922), 22–24.

17. Ustrialov, Diary, 24 August 1925, *Smenovekhovtsy,* 110.

18. A collection of his satirical articles, including those published in *Smena vekh,* appeared in Moscow in 1924, under the title *Pavliny bez per'ev: Iz arkhiva kontr-revoliutsii* (Moscow: Novye vekhi, 1924). The dedication of the booklet ran: "The author dedi- cated this without love to the brothers Benzinov, Liberdan, Miliukent'ev, and other Kadets who have turned into SRs." V. M. Zenzinov and N. D. Avksent'ev were prominent SRs; in early 1921 they joined forces with the Kadet leader P. N. Miliukov in the framework of the so-called Conference of Members of the Constituent Assem- bly. M. I. Liber and F. I. Dan, for their part, were Menshevik leaders; in the months between the February and October revolutions they had advocated that their party cooperate with the SRs and the Kadets.

19. Luk'ianov had given him permission to use these initials. See Iu. V. Kliuchnikov to N. V. Ustrialov, 13 July 1921, *Smenovekhovtsy*, 10.

20. See chap. 2, n. 153. Apparently, of the articles Ustrialov sent to Kliuchnikov, Kliuchnikov published only those which were acceptable to him. Thus, the articles "Sumerki revoliutsii" (Ustrialov, *Pod znakom*, 44–46) and "Vpered ot Vekh!" (Ustrialov, *Pod znakom*, 62–67), which Ustrialov himself supposed "might somewhat embarrass" Kliuchnikov (Ustrialov to Kliuchnikov, 30 January 1922 [see n. 1], 30), never appeared on the pages of the Paris journal.

21. Ustrialov to Kliuchnikov, 30 January 1922 (see n. 1), 29–30. Apparently, the article arrived too late to appear in the weekly *Smena vekh;* it was included instead in the first issue of the Berlin daily *Nakanune*, which in late March 1922 took the Paris journal's place. See N. Ustrialov, "Narod v revoliutsii," *Nakanune*, 26 March 1922, reprinted in Ustrialov, *Pod znakom*, 240–47. For the quoted passage see there, 244.

22. See, for example, N. V. Ustrialov to Iu. V. Kliuchnikov, 3 January 1922, *Smenovekhovtsy*, 25–27; N. V. Ustrialov to A. V. Bobrishchev-Pushkin, 25 April 1922, *Smenovekhovtsy*, 44.

23. See Vl. L'vov, "Rokovaia oshibka," *Sibirskaia rech'* (Omsk), 10 August [28 July] 1919; V. N. L'vov, "Memuary russkogo ministra," *Poslednie novosti*, 27 November–9 December 1920.

24. "Une démocratie succédera au Bolchevisme? L'ancien ministre L'vov nous explique comment, selon lui," *Le Petit Journal*, 15 August 1921; V. Lvoff, "La France fera-t-elle de la Russie une démocratie alliée ou une autocratie ennemie?" *L'Oeuvre*, 19 August 1921.

25. See, for example, A. Iablonovskii, "Sumbur-pasha," *Obshchee delo*, 17 August 1921; "Pechat'," *Poslednie novosti*, 25 August 1921.

26. Vl. L'vov, *Sovetskaia vlast' v bor'be za russkuiu gosudarstvennost' (Doklad chitannyi v 'Salles des Sociétés savantes' v Parizhe 12 noiabria 1921 g.* (Berlin: Vl. L'vov, 1922), especially 5–6, 10, 18–19.

27. L'vov, *Sovetskaia vlast'*, 24.

28. P. Bonhomme, "Vers un Bloc des gauches russe: Les émigrés russes qui se rallient à la République des Soviets," *L'Ere nouvelle*, 12 November 1921.

29. Bonhomme, "Vers un Bloc."

30. V. L'vov, "Une enquête: L'émigration russe et les Soviets," *L'Ere nouvelle*, 24 November 1921.

31. P. B., "Vers un 'Bloc des Gauches' russe? Les émigrés ne semblent pas d'accord," *L'Ere nouvelle*, 21 November 1921; P. B., "Chez les émigrés russes: Où en est le ralliement aux Soviets 'seconde manière'?" *L'Ere nouvelle*, 5 December 1921; "Nedorazumenie," *Poslednie novosti*, 15 November 1921.

32. Iu. N. Potekhin to N. V. Ustrialov, 22 December 1921, *Smenovekhovtsy*, 24; Bobrishchev-Pushkin to Ustrialov, 6 June 1922 (see n. 5), 59.

33. Kliuchnikov, "Nash otvet," 5.

34. Bobrishchev-Pushkin to Ustrialov, 6 June 1922 (see n. 5), 59.

35. Vl. L'vov, "Pis'mo v redaktsiiu," *SV*, no. 5 (26 November 1921): 20.

36. See A. Volkov, "Obnovliaemaia tserkov' (Beseda s chlenom vysshego tserkovnogo upravleniia V. N. L'vovym)," *Izvestiia*, 2 August 1922; *MSE1*, 4:759, s.v. "L'vov, Vladimir Nikolaevich"; H. E. Schulz, P. K. Urban, and A. I. Lebed, eds., *Who*

was who in the USSR: A Biographic Directory (Metuchen, N.J.: Scarecrow Press, 1972), 359.

37. An extensive note on Lukomskii can be found in "Sud'ba i raboty russkikh pisatelei, uchenykh i zhurnalistov za 1918–1921 g.," *Russkaia kniga*, 1921, no. 4:18–21.

38. See, for example, V. Belov, "V Sovetskoi Rossii: Chelovek iz zastenka," *Rul'*, 2 March [17 February] 1921; V. Belov, "Oblomki krusheniia (K pokhodu na Petrograd)," *Poslednie novosti*, 18 November 1920.

39. *Svobodnoe slovo: Ezhednevnaia demokraticheskaia natsional'naia gazeta*. Red. Vadim Belov. See T. Ossorguine-Bakounine, comp., *L'émigration russe en Europe: Catalogue collectif des périodiques en lange russe, 1855–1940* (Paris: Institut d'Etudes slaves, 1976), 279. See also V. Belov, *Belaia pechat': ee ideologiia, rol', znachenie i deiatel'nost' (Materialy dlia budushchego istorika)* (Petrograd: Gosizdat, 1922), 23.

40. See V. Belov, *Po novym vekham* (Revel': Novaia zemlia, 1922), and, to a lesser extent, Belov, *Belaia pechat'*, especially 30–31, 118–25.

41. Del'ta, "Vadim Belov," *Obshchee delo*, 1 August 1921. On *Svobodnoe slovo* and its change in position see also V. A. Dutsman, comp., *Obzor inostrannoi i russkoi zarubezhnoi pressy* (Moscow: Razvedyvatel'noe upravlenie shtaba RKKA, 1922), 100, 102.

42. V. Belov, *Beloe pokhmel'e: Russkaia emigratsiia na rasput'e (Opyt issledovaniia psikhologii, nastroenii i bytovykh uslovii russkoi emigratsii v nashe vremia)* (Moscow: Gosizdat, 1923). The booklet was dated "Petrograd, August 1922" (p. 149). The tone of Belov's remarks on the phenomenon of *Smena vekh* (pp. 135–49) was approving, but detached.

43. I. F. Masanov, *Slovar' psevdonimov russkikh pisatelei, uchenykh i obshchestvennykh deiatelei*, 4 vols. (Moscow: Izd-vo Vsesoiuznoi knizhnoi palaty, 1956–1960), 4:69.

44. R. Gul', "Dom v vechnosti," *SV*, no. 9 (24 December 1921): 13–14.

45. R. B. Gul', *Rossiia v Germanii*, vol. 1 of *Ia unes Rossiiu: Apologiia emigratsii* (New York: Most, 1984), 20. On Gul' see also L. Rzhevsky, "Roman Borisovich Gul' " in *The Modern Encyclopaedia of Russian and Soviet Literatures*, vol. 9 (Gulf Breeze, Fla.: Academic International Press, 1989): 143–47.

46. Gul's literary debut was an account of this undertaking called *Ledianoi pokhod*. Extracts of it appeared in 1920 in the *Mir i trud* journal *Zhizn'*, and in 1921 the novel was published as a separate volume by the Berlin publishing house Efron. In Soviet Russia, *Ledianoi pokhod* was initially given a rather positive reception (see, for example, N. Meshcheriakov's review of the book in *Pechat' i revoliutsii*, 1921, no. 3:176–78), but subsequently it was banned there, as it became clear that Gul' condemned in it not only the Whites' part in the civil war, but the civil war as such. See P. Gorelov, "Sleduia krestnomu puti" in R. Gul', A. I. Denikin, and A. Budberg, *Ledianoi pokhod: Pokhod i smert' generala Kornilova (Dnevnik)* (Moscow: Molodaia gvardiia, 1990), 10.

47. Gul', *Rossiia v Germanii*, 21–36; R. Gul', "Kievskaia epopeia," *Arkhiv russkoi revoliutsii*, no. 2 (1921): 59–86. See also N. Andreev, "Romanu Borisovichu Guliu—85 let: O ego memuarakh 'Ia unes Rossiiu,' " *Russkaia mysl'*, no. 3382 (15 October 1981): 11.

48. Gul', *Rossiia v Germanii*, 70.

49. The novel appeared as a separate volume in 1923: R. Gul', *V rasseian'i sushchie: Povest' iz zhizni emigratsii 1920–1921* (Berlin: Manfred, 1923).

50. Gul', *Rossiia v Germanii,* 197–200.

51. Osipov, "Vozniknovenie smenovekhovstva," 34; I. B. Diushen, interview with author, Moscow, 25 September 1989; Gul', *Rossiia v Germanii,* 202–4.

52. Gul', *Rossiia v Germanii,* 202–4; Sekretar' gruppy S-R Severno-zapadnoi Oblasti Rossii to Redaktsiia gazety "Volia Rossii," 9 January 1921, PSR Archief, 2192, Internationaal Instituut voor Sociale Geschiedenis, Amsterdam. See also Ossorguine-Bakounine, *Catalogue collectif,* 166, 277, 279.

53. L. Fleishman, R. Kh'iuz, and O. Raevskaia-Kh'iuz, eds., *Russkii Berlin 1921–1923: Po materialam arkhiva B. I. Nikolaevskogo v Guverovskom institute* (Paris: YMCA-Press, 1983), 131.

54. See, for example, B. Diushen, "Nravstvennaia podderzhka," *Svoboda Rossii,* 15 November 1919; B. Diushen, "Znamia," *Svoboda Rossii,* 18 January 1920.

55. For an account of Diushen's lecture see S. Labrovskii, "Kto budet pravit' Rossiei," *Golos Rossii,* 11 February 1921.

56. Osipov, "Vozniknovenie smenovekhovstva," 34.

57. *Vladimir Il'ich Lenin: Biograficheskaia khronika,* vol. 11 (Moscow: Izd-vo politicheskoi literatury, 1980), 471.

58. V. Chernov, "Staraia i novaia burzhuaziia," *Volia Rossii,* 1922, no. 13:6. See also Prof. G. G. Shvittau, *Osnovy kapitalisticheskogo stroia* (Odessa: Agitatsionnaia sektsiia Ts. K. Ob"edinennogo studenchestva g. Odessy, 1917), especially 19.

59. *Ves' Petrograd* (1915), div. 3.

60. G. G. Shvittau, *Revoliutsiia i narodnoe khoziaistvo v Rossii (1917–1921)* (Leipzig: Tsentral'noe t-vo kooperativnogo izdatel'stva, 1922), 9.

61. See G. G. Shvittau, *Russkaia kooperatsiia na mezhdunarodnom rynke* (Berlin: Ladyzhnikov, 1920); Shvittau, *Revoliutsiia i narodnoe khoziaistvo,* especially 371–72.

62. Ossorguine-Bakounine, *Catalogue collectif,* 207.

63. Masanov, *Slovar' psevdonimov,* 3:174, 4:449.

64. K. Treplev, "Iz nedavnego proshlogo: Belyie 'patrioty' i angliiskaia kopeika," *Nakanune* 17 July 1923.

65. K. Treplev, " 'Deviatyi Val,' " *SV,* no. 17 (18 February 1922): 15–18.

66. Iu. N. Potekhin to N. V. Ustrialov, [May 1923], *Smenovekhovtsy,* 90.

67. P. Sadyker, "Voiny budushchego," *SV,* no. 12 (14 January 1922): 11–14.

68. P. Sadyker, " 'Vekhi smen' (Lektsiia prof. Gorovtseva)," *SV,* no. 11 (7 January 1922): 18–20. Gorovtsev even wrote a letter to the editor, protesting the misrepresentation of his views by Sadyker. See *SV* 12 (14 February 1922): 24. For Gorovtsev's own account of his lecture see A. M. Gorovtsev, " 'Smene vekh': Skhema lektsii, chitannoi avtorom v Parizhe" in *'Skrepa vekh': Vtoroi vypusk politicheskogo zhurnala-al'manakha 'Tribuny'* (Paris, [1922]), 13–17.

69. For a characteristic of Sadyker see E. L. Mindlin, *Neobyknovennye sobesedniki: Kniga vospominanii* (Moscow: Sovetskii pisatel', 1968), 136–37; N. A. Ukhtomskii to N. V. Ustrialov, 8 March 1923, *Raznye liudi,* 55; Potekhin to Ustrialov, [May 1923] (see n. 66), 90–91; A. V. Bobrishchev-Pushkin, *Patrioty bez otechestva* (Leningrad: Kubuch, 1925), 125.

70. *Ves' Peterburg* (1912), div. 3, col. 647.

71. Général Noskoff, "La nouvelle lutte dans le sud de la Russie: La situation de l'armée Wrangel," *L'Information,* 16 August 1920.

72. Général Noskoff, "La situation dans la Russie méridionale," *L'Information,* 13 October 1920; Général Noskoff, "La situation de Wrangel devient périlleuse," *L'Information,* 6 November 1920. See also Gen. Noskov, "Pis'mo v redaktsiiu," *Poslednie novosti,* 21 November 1920.

73. Général Noskoff, "La résurrection de la Russie est-elle possible?" *L'Information,* 8 December 1920.

74. On the committee see M. Geller, " 'Pervoe predosterezhenie'—udar khlystom," *Vestnik R. Kh. D.,* no. 127 (1978): 194–211; E. H. Carr, *The Bolshevik Revolution 1917–1923,* 3 vols. (London: Macmillan, 1950–1953; Harmondsworth: Penguin Books, 1966), 1:185–87.

75. Général Noskoff, "L'heure qui vient en Russie," *L'Information,* 5 August 1921.

76. *Notes russes 1921,* 12 November 1921, doc. P.5534.U.

77. V. A. Osipov, conversation with author, Moscow, September 1989.

78. The name of V. Muizhel' appeared for the first time on the pages of *Put'* in the issue of 10 July 1921, Tan's name on 2 October of that year, and that of Gollerbakh and Asheshov on 9 October and 30 September, respectively. *Smena vekh* would also print a "Letter from Petrograd" by Ia. B. Livshits, a Petrograd journalist who, under the initials I. L. and the pseudonym Vl. Lavretskii, regularly contributed to *Put'* starting from 6 July 1921 (see chap. 4, n. 97, 119–30).

79. "Priostanovka gazety 'Put'," " *Put',* 8 January 1922.

80. G. P. Struve, *Russkaia literatura v izgnanii,* 2d rev. ed. (Paris: YMCA-Press, 1984), 34.

81. *Vsia Moskva* (1917), div. 3, 536.

82. *SV,* no. 4 (19 November 1921): 21–22.

83. S. B. Chlenov, *Moskovskaia okhranka i ee sekretnye sotrudniki: Po dannym Komissii po obespecheniiu novogo stroia (s prilozheniem spiskov sotrudnikov, opublikovannykh komissiei)* (Moscow: Otdel pechati Moskovskogo Soveta R. i K. D., 1919), 3–6.

84. See, for example, S. Chlenov, "Otzyvy o knigakh: K. M. Takhtarev, Nauka ob obshchestvennoi zhizni," *Pechat' i revoliutsiia,* 1921, no. 1:125; S. Chlenov, "Germanskaia revoliutsiia i sotsial-demokratiia," *Krasnaia nov',* 1922, no. 2:161–70.

85. See S. Chlenov, "Novaia intelligentsiia," *SV,* no. 4 (19 November 1921): 22–24; T., "Institut krasnoi professury," *Pravda,* 8 August 1922; *Nauchnye rabotniki Moskvy* (Leningrad: AN SSSR, 1930), 312. The Institute of Red Professors had been founded by a special decree, issued by the Council of People's Commissars in February 1921, as a school where party members, on recommendation of the Central or Provincial Party Committees, were trained as "Red professors" in history and the social sciences. Initially, there were several non-Communists among the Institute's staff.

86. *Vsia Moskva* (1923), div. 4, 395; *Vsia Moskva* (1929), div. 9, 623.

87. On this trial see M. Jansen, *Een showproces onder Lenin: Het voorspel van de Grote Terreur* (Haarlem: De Haan, 1980).

88. Jansen, *Showproces,* 68–76. The text of Chlenov's intervention during the trial can be found in *Rechi zashchitnikov i obviniaemykh,* vol. 2 of *Protsess eserov* (Moscow: Krasnaia nov', 1922). For extracts from his speech see Jansen, *Showproces,* 106, 143.

89. "K delu Konradi," *Rul',* 30 October 1923; S. B. Chlenov, *Rech' po delu ob ubiistve V. V. Vorovskogo* (Moscow, 1923); S. B. Chlenov, *Ubiistvo V. V. Vorovskogo i*

burzhuaznoe pravosudie (Kharkov, 1924). On this case see E. H. Carr, *The Interregnum 1923–1924* (London: Macmillan, 1954), 169–74; A. E. Senn, *Assassination in Switzerland: The Murder of Vatslav Vorovsky* (Madison: University of Wisconsin Press, 1981). On Chlenov's exact role in the process see there, 121–22. Incidentally, both at the SR trial in Moscow and at the Konradi case, Kliuchnikov was present as a witness for the prosecution. While he was not interrogated in Moscow (see Jansen, *Showproces,* 184), Kliuchnikov did testify in Lausanne, stressing the White movement's barbarity and praising at the same time the Soviet regime's humanitarianism. See Senn, *Assassination,* 154–56; "Delo ubiitsy t. Vorovskogo," *Izvestiia,* 10 November 1923; "Dépositions d'un ancien ministre russe," *La Tribune de Genève,* 9 November 1923. See also chap. 6.

90. Introduction to S. Chlenov, "Revoliutsionnaia zakonnost'," *SV,* no. 12 (14 January 1922): 20.

91. Ustrialov, *Pod znakom,* 168.

92. I. Lezhnev, " 'Smena vekh,' " *Novaia Rossiia,* no. 1 (March 1922): 61–62.

93. Editorial, *SV,* no. 1 (29 October 1921): 2.

94. T. "Iz Moskvy," *SV,* no. 9 (24 December 1921): 22–23; S-a M., "Pis'ma iz Moskvy," *SV,* no. 17 (18 February 1922): 21–22.

95. See especially E. G., "V Ermitazhe," *SV,* no. 8 (17 December 1921): 23–24: E. Gollerbakh, "Okhrana predmetov iskusstva v Detskom Sele," *SV,* no. 13 (21 January 1922): 20–21; A. Bobrishchev-Pushkin, "Dramaticheskii teatr v Rossii," *SV* 2 (5 November 1921), 17–21; Chlenov, "Novaia intelligentsiia," 22–23; T., "Iz Moskvy."

96. See, for example, Vl. L'vov, "Russkaia revoliutsiia i religioznaia svoboda," *SV,* no. 2 (5 November 1921): 9–11; P. S. Kogan, "Poeziia epokhi oktiabr'skoi revoliutsii," *SV,* no. 7 (10 December 1921): 21–24; S. Chakhotin, "Psikhologiia primireniia," *SV,* no. 15 (4 February 1922): 9–11. See in this connection also M. Okutiur'e, " 'Smena vekh' i russkaia literatura 20-kh godov" in *Odna ili dve russkikh literatury,* ed. Zh. Niva (Lausanne: L'Age d'Homme, 1981), 108–9.

97. S. Chlenov, "Revoliutsionnaia zakonnost'," *SV,* no. 12 (14 January 1922): 21–22; S. Chakhotin, "Psikhologiia primireniia," *SV,* no. 15 (4 February 1922): 11.

98. Editorial comment to "Uprazdnenie V.Ch.K.," *SV,* no. 18 (25 February 1922): 9.

99. M. Grigor'ev, "Denatsionalizatsiia promyshlennosti," *SV,* no. 3 (12 November 1921): 6.

100. S. Luk'ianov, "Evoliutsiia," *SV,* no. 5 (26 November 1921): 12.

101. "NEP (Po soobshcheniiam sovetskikh gazet za sent.–okt. mes. 1921 g.): Obzor," *SV,* no. 3 (12 November 1921): 16–19.

102. Iu. Potekhin, "Mirovoi krizis (2: Rossiia)," *SV,* no. 19 (4 March 1922): 10.

103. Editorial, *SV,* no. 1 (29 October 1921): 2–3.

104. Iu. Kliuchnikov, "Iz perepiski," *SV,* no. 5 (26 November 1921): 8–9; Iu. Kliuchnikov, "Priznanie Sovetskogo Pravitel'stva," *SV,* no. 9 (24 December 1921): 1; S. S. Luk'ianov, "Mysli o revoliutsii," *Novaia Rossiia,* no. 1 (March 1922): 57–60; A. V. Bobrishchev-Pushkin to N. V. Ustrialov, 15 February 1922, *Smenovekhovtsy,* 34; Bobrishchev-Pushkin to Ustrialov, 10 June 1922 (see n. 5), 49–52; Iu. Potekhin, "Pered katastrofoi: Pis'mo iz Veny," *SV,* no. 5 (26 November 1921): 15–17; Iu. N. Potekhin to N. V. Ustrialov, 2 May 1922, *Smenovekhovtsy,* 45–46; S. Chlenov, "Berlinskie vpechatleniia," *Pravda,* 21 February 1922; S. Chlenov, "Germanskaia revoliutsiia i

sotsial-demokratiia," *Krasnaia nov'*, 1922, no. 2:170; S. Chlenov, "Sumerki bozhkov," *Krasnaia nov'*, 1922, no. 3:163; S. Chlenov, "Plachushchie tsifry," *Krasnaia nov'*, 1923, no. 4:128–48; Shvittau, *Revoliutsiia i narodnoe khoziaistvo*, 14–15. On the alarming socioeconomic situation in Europe in the early 1920s see D. H. Aldcroft, *From Versailles to Wall Street 1919–1920* (London: Lane, 1977; Harmondsworth: Penguin Books, 1987), 55–77.

105. N. V. Ustrialov, "Obstrel sprava," *Novosti zhizni*, 20 June 1922.

106. Kliuchnikov, "Iz perepiski," 8–9; Potekhin, "Pered katastrofoi," 16.

107. Luk'ianov, "Evoliutsiia," 11–13.

108. Iu. Kliuchnikov, "Mezhdunarodnoe znachenie Rossii," *SV*, no. 1 (29 October 1921): 10; Kliuchnikov, "Priznanie Sovetskogo Pravitel'stva," 3.

109. Luk'ianov, "Evoliutsiia," 14; Iu. Kliuchnikov, "Genuezskaia konferentsiia," *SV*, no. 13 (21 January 1921): 3.

110. Kliuchnikov, "Mezhdunarodnoe znachenie," 8; Kliuchnikov, "Priznanie Sovetskogo Pravitel'stva," 1–3.

111. Kliuchnikov, "Iz perepiski," 8–9.

112. Kliuchnikov, "Mezhdunarodnoe znachenie," 11.

113. Iu. Kliuchnikov, "Vashington i Moskva," *SV*, no. 2 (5 November 1921): 5–6; P. Sadyker, "Voiny budushchego," *SV*, no. 12 (14 January 1922): 14.

114. S. Luk'ianov, "Vchera i segodnia," *SV*, no. 20 (25 March 1922): 18.

115. Iu. V. Kliuchnikov, *Na velikom istoricheskom pereput'i: Piat' glav po sotsiologii mezhdunarodnykh otnoshenii* (Berlin: Smena vekh, 1922), 5. In Paris Kliuchnikov delivered a lecture at the Salles des Sociétés savantes on 18 and 23 May 1921; in Brussels, he spoke at the Université Internationale on 30 and 31 August of that year (Kliuchnikov, *Na velikom istoricheskom pereput'i*, 5).

116. Kliuchnikov had dedicated the book to his "dear friend Nikolai Vasil'evich Ustrialov" (Kliuchnikov, *Na velikom istoricheskom pereput'i*, 3). This was much to Ustrialov's displeasure and embarrassment, however, as Ustrialov felt the book's whole concept was "deeply foreign to him." Not only did he, rightly, find that Kliuchnikov's argumentation was at times forced, contradictory, and superficial; what bothered him even more was the fact that the book was "an unconditional panegyric and absolute apologia of Bolshevism." See N. V. Ustrialov, Diary, 28 July 1922, *Smenovekhovtsy*, 62–63. See on the book also A. I., "Prof. Iu. V. Kliuchnikov, Na velikom istoricheskom pereput'i," *Literaturnye zapiski*, no. 3 (1 August 1922): 18–19; M. Pavlovich, "Professor-idealist na velikom pereput'i," *Pechat' i revoliutsiia*, 1923, no. 2:13–26; B. Gimel'farb, "Kritika i bibliografiia: Prof. Iu. V. Kliuchnikov, Na velikom istoricheskom pereput'i," *Izvestiia*, 10 June 1922.

117. Kliuchnikov, *Na velikom istoricheskom pereput'i*, 41, 115.

118. Kliuchnikov, *Na velikom istoricheskom pereput'i*, 39, 132–33.

119. Kliuchnikov, *Na velikom istoricheskom pereput'i*, 6, 179–80.

120. Kliuchnikov, *Na velikom istoricheskom pereput'i*, 133, 177–79.

121. Kliuchnikov, *Na velikom istoricheskom pereput'i*, 133, 179.

122. Kliuchnikov, *Na velikom istoricheskom pereput'i*, 7, 184.

123. Shvittau, *Revoliutsiia i narodnoe khoziaistvo*, 14–16.

124. Luk'ianov, "Mysli," 60.

125. A. Bobrishchev-Pushkin, "Mistika na sluzhbe," *SV*, no. 3 (12 November 1921): 8.

126. Luk'ianov, "Evoliutsiia," 14; Kliuchnikov, "Priznanie Sovetskogo Pravitel'stva," 3–4; Iu. Kliuchnikov, "Istoricheskaia nedelia," *SV,* no. 12 (14 January 1922): 9.

127. Kliuchnikov, "Iz perepiski," 10.

128. Editorial, *SV,* no. 2 (5 November 1921): 1.

129. Introduction to S. Chlenov, "Revoliutsionnaia zakonnost'," 20.

130. Luk'ianov, "Evoliutsiia," 14.

131. Luk'ianov, "Evoliutsiia," 13.

132. Kliuchnikov, "Mezhdunarodnoe znachenie," 10; Editorial (see n. 128), 1; Kliuchnikov, "Nash otvet," 2. See also Kliuchnikov to Ustrialov, 8 November 1921 (see n. 5), 17; Kliuchnikov, *Na velikom istoricheskom pereput'i,* 177.

133. See in this connection S. White, *The Origins of Detente: The Genoa Conference and Soviet-Western Relations, 1921–1922* (Cambridge: Cambridge University Press, 1985), 1–29.

134. R. Ullman, *The Anglo-Soviet Accord,* vol. 3 of *Anglo-Soviet Relations, 1917–1921* (Princeton: Princeton University Press, 1972), 37.

135. Ullman, *Anglo-Soviet Accord,* 99–102, 113, 415–18, 438, 463–68.

136. These negotiations are the subject of Ullman, *Anglo-Soviet Accord.* See also M. Glenny, "The Anglo-Soviet Trade Agreement, March 1921," *Journal of Contemporary History* 5, no. 2 (1970): 63–82.

137. White, *Origins,* 20–21. On the coming about of the German-Soviet agreement see G. Rosenfeld, *Sowjetrussland und Deutschland, 1917–1922* (Cologne: Pahl-Rugenstein, 1984), 323–35.

138. Rosenfeld, *Sowjetrussland und Deutschland, 1917–1922,* 334.

139. For the text of the agreement see Ullman, *Anglo-Soviet Accord,* 474–78. Lloyd George had from the very beginning regarded the trade negotiations with Moscow as a step toward complete normalization of Anglo-Russian relations. To begin with, however, he had deliberately limited their scope, as he understood that a gradual approach was essential in order not to shock public opinion and to avoid a split of his cabinet over the issue (see Ullman, *Anglo-Soviet Accord,* 40–41, 131).

140. See in this connection White, *Origins,* 23–28; Ullman, *Anglo-Soviet Accord,* 103–8; A. Hogenhuis-Seliverstoff, *Les Relations franco-soviétiques 1917–1924* (Paris: Publications de la Sorbonne, 1981), 69–86. On the issue of Russian debts see A. M. Michelson, P. N. Apostol, and M. W. Bernatzky, *Russian Public Finance During the War* (New Haven: Yale University Press, 1928), 320–22, 450.

141. Hogenhuis-Seliverstoff, *Relations franco-soviétiques,* 165–176; White, *Origins,* 20–22, 37. The hope, however feeble, for a solution to the problem of Russia's foreign debts was apparently also one of the motives that had prompted the French in August 1920 to recognize General Wrangel's government in the Crimea. They were the only Western power to do so. See Ullman, *Anglo-Soviet Accord,* 240–41; Hogenhuis-Seliverstoff, *Relations franco-soviétiques,* 181–84.

142. White, *Origins,* 27–28, 68–69; Ullman, *Anglo-Soviet Accord,* 102.

143. White, *Origins,* 24–25. For the clause in the Anglo-Russian trade agreement see Ullman, *Anglo-Soviet Accord,* 474.

144. Ullman, *Anglo-Soviet Accord,* 421–22. For the text of the "Declaration" see there, 478.

145. Ullman, *Anglo-Soviet Accord*, 126–28, 427; White, *Origins*, 34–36.

146. Ullman, *Anglo-Soviet Accord*, 126. See also W. Eichwede, *Revolution und internationale Politik: Zur kommunistischen Interpretation der kapitalistischen Welt 1921–1925* (Cologne: Böhlau Verlag, 1971), 133.

147. White, *Origins*, 39, 106–7, 112–13; Ullman, *Anglo-Soviet Accord*, 120–21.

148. White, *Origins*, p. 39.

149. White, *Origins*, 34–36, 38–39.

150. White, *Origins*, 36–37.

151. See in this connection White, *Origins*, 38–44; Hogenhuis-Seliverstoff, *Relations franco-soviétiques*, 193–98; Johnston, *New Mecca*, 60.

152. White, *Origins*, 47.

153. See White, *Origins*, 52–57, 83–85; Hogenhuis-Seliverstoff, *Relations franco-soviétiques*, 198–201; I. Maiskii, *Vneshniaia politika RSFSR 1917–1922* (Moscow: Krasnaia nov', 1923), 117–18. For the so-called Cannes principles see White, *Origins*, 55–56; Hogenhuis-Seliverstoff, *Relations franco-soviétiques*, 200.

154. Kliuchnikov, "Priznanie Sovetskogo Pravitel'stva," 1.

155. See Kliuchnikov, "Mezhdunarodnoe znachenie," 8–11; Kliuchnikov, "Vashington i Moskva," 5–6; Editorial, *SV*, no. 3 (12 November 1921): 1–3.

156. Iu. Kliuchnikov, "Priznanie Sovetskogo Pravitel'stva," 2–3.

157. [F. Kudriavtsev], "Istoricheskaia nedelia," *SV*, no. 12 (14 January 1922): 5.

158. Kliuchnikov, "Genuezskaia konferentsiia," 4.

159. Kliuchnikov to Ustrialov, 13 July 1921 (see n. 19), 9.

160. Lezhnev, " 'Smena vekh,' " 62.

161. The archives of the Direction des Renseignements généraux du Ministère de l'Intérieur in Paris contain a whole series of notes on the weekly and its editors. In the so-called *Notes russes* for late 1921 and early 1922, the *smenovekhovtsy* occupy a prominent place.

162. *Notes russes 1921*, 12 October 1921, doc. P.5436.U.

163. Kliuchnikov, "Mezhdunarodnoe znachenie," 10–11.

164. [F. Kudriavtsev], "Ot okruzheniia k soglasheniiu," *SV*, no. 10 (31 December 1921): 5–8; S. L., "Beseda s prof. Ipat'evym," *SV*, no. 17 (18 February 1922): 19; [F. Kudriavtsev], "Rossiia i Frantsiia," *SV*, no. 7 (10 December 1921): 6.

165. See in this respect especially [Kudriavtsev], "Rossiia i Frantsiia," 5; Kliuchnikov, "Priznanie Sovetskogo," 3; [Kudriavtsev], "Ot okruzheniia," 6. Russia's wartime debts were owed mainly to Britain (see Ullman, *Anglo-Soviet Accord*, 107).

166. [Kudriavtsev], "Rossiia i Frantsiia," 6.

167. See Johnston, *New Mecca*, 60–64.

168. *Notes russes 1921*, November 1921, doc. P.5541.U.

169. Ullman, *Anglo-Soviet Accord*, 43–44, 131.

170. See Iu. N. Potekhin to N. V. Ustrialov, 1 September 1921, *Smenovekhovtsy*, 13; Bobrishchev-Pushkin to Ustrialov, 10 June 1922 (see n. 5), 59; Maklakov to Bakhmetev, 3 January 1922 (see n. 14), 12.

171. This letter is reprinted, without naming the author, in Kliuchnikov, "Iz perepiski," 1. Maklakov confirmed in a letter to Bakhmetev that he had written the letter in question. Apparently, Kliuchnikov had printed it on the pages of *Smena vekh*

against Maklakov's will, and this had angered Maklakov. See Maklakov to Bakhmetev, 3 January 1922 (see n. 14), 12–13.

172. *Notes russes 1921,* November 1921, doc. P.5541.U. See also Ustrialov, Diary, 24 August 1925 (see n. 17), 110; Bobrishchev-Pushkin, *Patrioty,* 120–24; V. A. Maklakov to B. A. Bakhmetev, 8 November 1921, 2, V. A. Maklakov collection, box 14, Hoover Institution Archives, Stanford, California.

173. The Soviet observer V. A. Dutsman spoke in this respect of "absolute boycott and slight." See Dutsman, *Obzor pressy,* 119. Reactions to the weekly *Smena vekh* appeared in P. N. Miliukov's mouthpiece *Poslednie novosti,* in V. N. Burtsev's daily *Obshchee delo,* and in the Menshevik journal *Sotsialisticheskii vestnik.* The editors of *Poslednie novosti* disdainfully wondered why one would publish a weekly if one did not even have one's own opinion and limited oneself to echoing Moscow (see "Pechat'," *Poslednie novosti,* 30 October 1921). In *Obshchee delo,* A. Iablonovskii reproached the *smenovekhovtsy,* mistakenly as it seems, for being paid by Steklov (A. Iablonovskii, "Perelety," *Obshchee delo,* 28 November 1921). The editors of *Sotsialisticheskii vestnik,* for their part, could no longer restrain themselves after a remark by Bobrishchev-Pushkin in the fourth issue of *Smena vekh,* that "no state structure had ever been based on freedom" (Editorial, *Sotsialisticheskii vestnik,* 1921, no. 21:1–3). Bobrishchev-Pushkin's article in question was "Svoboda-ravenstvo-bratstvo," *SV,* no. 4 (19 November 1921): 18–20.

174. I have been unable to detect any further reactions to *Smena vekh* in the French press.

175. See Johnston, *New Mecca,* 61–63; Hogenhuis-Seliverstoff, *Relations franco-soviétiques,* 262–69.

176. See E. Herriot, *La Russie nouvelle* (Paris: Ferenczi, 1922), 5–6. See also N. A. Ukhtomskii to N. V. Ustrialov, 30 June 1924, *Raznye liudi,* 83, where with respect to this tour the relationship between Herriot and the *Nakanune* group was even called "intimate." On Herriot's trip see further Johnston, *New Mecca,* 62–64; Hogenhuis-Seliverstoff, *Relations franco-soviétiques,* 234–35; F. Kupferman, *Au pays des Soviets: Le voyage français en Union soviétique 1917–1939* (Paris: Gallimard-Julliard, 1979), 51–53.

177. Ustrialov, Diary, 24 August 1925 (see n. 17), 110.

178. Potekhin to Ustrialov, 2 May 1922 (see n. 104), 45–46; Bobrishchev-Pushkin to Ustrialov, 15 February 1922 (see n. 104), 33–36; Bobrishchev-Pushkin to Ustrialov, 10 June 1922 (see n. 5), 49–54.

179. Potekhin to Ustrialov, 2 May 1922 (see n. 104), 45.

180. Bobrishchev-Pushkin, "Mistika na sluzhbe" (see n. 125), 8.

181. Bobrishchev-Pushkin to Ustrialov, 15 February 1922 (see n. 104), 33–36; Bobrishchev-Pushkin to Ustrialov, 10 June 1922 (see n. 5), 55–59.

182. Bobrishchev-Pushkin to Ustrialov, 15 February 1922 (see n. 104), 34; Bobrishchev-Pushkin to Ustrialov, 10 June 1922 (see n. 5), 55.

183. Potekhin to Ustrialov, 2 May 1922 (see n. 104), 45–46.

184. Kliuchnikov to Ustrialov, 8 November 1921 (see n. 5), especially 17–18. This is confirmed by Gul', *Rossiia v Germanii,* 178; Maklakov to Bakhmetev, 24 October 1921 (see n. 9), 32; Ustrialov, Diary, 24 August 1925 (see n. 17), 110, 112.

185. On Krasin see Ullman, *Anglo-Soviet Accord,* 89–93: L. Krassine, *Krassine: Sa vie et son oeuvre* (Paris: Gallimard, 1932), especially 142, 245; White, *Origins,* 112–113;

A. Gurovich, "Vysshii Sovet Narodnogo Khoziaistva: Iz vpetchatlenii goda sluzhby," *Arkhiv russkoi revoliutsii,* no. 6 (1922): 324–26. See also N. V. Ustrialov to A. V. Bobrishchev-Pushkin, 20 October 1922, *Smenovekhovtsy,* 70–72, where Ustrialov included Krasin as well as Chicherin and Lunacharskii among those Bolsheviks whom he regarded as supporters of a Soviet Thermidor (71).

186. Potekhin, for example, wrote in a letter of 1 September 1921 to Ustrialov that he and his colleagues "undoubtedly had tens of thousands of sympathizers" (see Potekhin to Ustrialov, 1 September 1921 [see n. 170], 13).

187. [Kudriavtsev], "Istoricheskaia nedelia," 6; [F. Kudriavtsev], "Za nedeliu: Rossiia na Vashingtonskoi konferentsii," *SV,* no. 17 (18 February 1922): 1–2; S. Luk'ianov, "Vchera i segodnia," *SV,* no. 20 (25 March 1922): 17.

188. [Kudriavtsev], "Istoricheskaia nedelia," 6.

189. Editorial, *SV,* no. 20 (25 March 1922): 2–3. In the preface to his *Na velikom istoricheskom pereput'i,* Kliuchnikov even put it this way: "There, in Genoa, the question will be solved: either worldwide evolution or worldwide revolution. One hasn't long to wait at all. But if the wrong answer will be given, if the necessary concessions to the spirit of the time and to progress will not be made there, how long will it then take for mankind to correct its new error and in what difficult forms will its correction then inevitably take place!" (see Kliuchnikov, *Na velikom istoricheskom pereput'i,* 7).

190. V. I. Lenin, *Polnoe sobranie sochinenii,* 5th ed., 55 vols. (Moscow: Gospolitizdat, 1958–1965), 44:380.

191. On the Soviet preparations for the Genoa Conference see White, *Origins,* 102–13.

192. J. M. Keynes, *The Economic Consequences of the Peace* (London: Macmillan, 1919), especially 105–13, 162–88. See also White, *Origins,* 8–9.

193. White, *Origins,* 105–9. Keynes's work had appeared in Russian translation in 1921: *Ekonomicheskie posledstviia mira* (Stockholm: Severnye ogni, 1921). The translation was the work of the young Russian émigrés G. P. Struve and T. S. Lur'e.

194. Kliuchnikov, "Genuezskaia konferentsiia," 1–7.

195. Kliuchnikov, "Genuezskaia konferentsiia," 8.

196. White, *Origins,* 112–13.

197. Lenin, *Polnoe sobranie sochinenii,* 44:628.

198. Iu. V. Kliuchnikov to N. V. Ustrialov, 17 April 1922, *Smenovekhovtsy,* 39.

199. Bobrishchev-Pushkin to Ustrialov, 10 June 1922 (see n. 5), 57.

200. *Notes russes 1922,* 29 March 1922, doc. P.6019.U; Bobrishchev-Pushkin, *Patrioty,* 117–18; Osipov, "Vozniknovenie smenovekhovstva," 20. See also R. C. Williams, *Culture in Exile: Russian Emigrés in Germany 1881–1941* (Ithaca: Cornell University Press, 1972), 132; Struve, *Russkaia literatura,* 24: Rosenfeld, *Soujetrussland und Deutschland, 1917–1922,* 371–73.

201. Editorial (see n. 189), 1.

202. In this respect, Kliuchnikov and his colleagues referred to the split in the Kadet Party, the very limited success of the Conference of Members of the Constituent Assembly, and the great financial difficulties of several émigré periodicals, most importantly *Obshchee delo,* which appeared but with lengthy interruptions from February 1922 on (on the problems of *Obshchee delo* see Dutsman, *Obzor pressy,* 116). See Editorial (see n. 189), 1.

203. Editorial (see n. 189), 1–2.

204. Editorial (see n. 189), 3.

205. One of the historians of *smenovekhovstvo,* M. Agurskii, maintains that the weekly *Smena vekh* was "freely on sale in Soviet Russia and had a good circulation" (see M. Agursky, *The Third Rome: National Bolshevism in the USSR* [Boulder, Colo.: Westview Press, 1987], 258). This must, however, be strongly denied. True, Lenin received the journal, albeit with great difficulty and not always regularly (see O. I. Khokhunova, "Iz istorii bor'by partii so smenovekhovstvom," *Vestnik MGU, Istoriia,* 1976, no. 4:10; Lenin, *Polnoe sobranie sochinenii,* 45:137), and also I. Lezhnev had the chance to read it; presumably, Kliuchnikov or Potekhin, who were acquainted with him, sent him the issues privately. These were exceptional cases, however; the Paris weekly was never imported into Soviet Russia on a regular basis or on a large scale. This is also confirmed by S. A. Fediukin, *Bor'ba s burzhuaznoi ideologiei v usloviiakh perekhoda k Nepu* (Moscow: Nauka, 1977), 288–89; Osipov, "Vozniknovenie smenovekhovstva," 23.

206. See in this connection Osipov, "Vozniknovenie smenovekhovstva," 23–24.

207. "O gazete 'smenovekhovtsev' v Berline (Beseda s prof. Iu. V. Kliuchnikovym)," *Izvestiia,* 28 March 1922.

CHAPTER 6: *NAKANUNE*

1. Ustrialov wrote three private letters to Luk'ianov, urging him to correct the course that *Nakanune* was taking, but Luk'ianov did not even respond to them (see N. V. Ustrialov to S. S. Luk'ianov, early October 1922, *Smenovekhovtsy,* 67–69; N. V. Ustrialov to S. S. Luk'ianov, 19 October 1922, *Smenovekhovtsy,* 69–70; N. V. Ustrialov to S. S. Luk'ianov, 14 December 1922, *Smenovekhovtsy,* 75–76).

2. For a list of the most important contributors to *Nakanune* and the number of articles they contributed see V. A. Osipov, "Vozniknovenie smenovekhovstva i sozdanie gazety 'Nakanune' " (Avtoreferat, I.N.I.O.N., Moscow, 1989), 28–29. A detailed list of collaborators appeared also in *Nakanune,* 5 September 1922.

3. Editorial, *SV,* no. 20 (25 March 1922): 3.

4. At the time of the October revolution, Solov'ev was serving as counsellor at the Russian embassy in Madrid. As the only Russian diplomat to take such a stand at that time, he offered his services to the new Russian government immediately after the Bolshevik takeover. In Berlin, where he found himself by late 1920, Solov'ev did what he could to further the process of rapprochement between Germany and the Soviet Republic, and to reconcile hesitant Russian émigrés with the new regime. With this goal in mind, he founded a small weekly under the title *Voskresen'e* in late 1921 (see T. Ossorguine-Bakounine, comp., *L'émigration russe en Europe: Catalogue collectif des périodiques en lange russe, 1855–1940* [Paris: Institut d'Etudes slaves, 1976], 140; Iu. Ia. Solov'ev, *Vospominaniia diplomata, 1893–1922* [Moscow: Izd-vo sotsial'no-ekonomicheskoi literatury, 1959], 385–86). Apparently, the weekly ceased publication after the appearance of *Nakanune,* to which Solov'ev began contributing shortly after its founding. His first article in the paper appeared on the occasion of the Conference of Genoa (see Iu. Solov'ev, "Uchastniki konferentsii," *Nakanune,* 21 May 1922; Solov'ev, *Vospominaniia,* 394–95). In August 1922 he returned to Moscow, where he served at the People's

Commissariat of Foreign Affairs, and later at the Soviet Red Cross. Solov'ev's memoirs were published in Moscow in 1959, on the twenty-fifth anniversary of his death.

5. R. B. Gul', *Rossiia v Germanii*, vol. 1 of *Ia unes Rossiiu: Apologiia emigratsii* (New York: Most, 1984), 196; Osipov, "Vozniknovenie smenovekhovstva," 16.

6. Iashchenko's first contribution to *Nakanune* was a series of articles "Iz politicheskikh razmyshlenii na sovremennye temy," with titles such as "Krakh formal'noi demokratii," *Nakanune*, 1 December 1923; "Vseobshchee izbiratel'noe pravo i partii," *Nakanune*, 15 December 1923; and "Sovremennaia Evropa," *Nakanune*, 22 December 1923.

7. Gul', *Rossiia v Germanii*, 196; L. Fleishman, R. Kh'iuz, and O. Raevskaia-Kh'iuz, eds., *Russkii Berlin 1921–1923: Po materialam arkhiva B. I. Nikolaevskogo v Guverovskom institute* (Paris: YMCA-Press, 1983), 16.

8. The various supplements to *Nakanune* were *Literaturnoe prilozhenie* (30 April 1922–22 July 1923), which, after the departure of its editor, A. N. Tolstoi, was renamed *Literaturnaia nedelia* (29 July 1923–15 June 1924); *Ekonomicheskoe obozrenie* (8 June 1922–2 September 1923); *Kino-obozrenie* (February–April 1923); and *Inostrannaia zhizn'* (25 January–13 June 1924) (see Ossorguine-Bakounine, *Catalogue collectif*, 177, 189, 207).

9. Osipov, "Vozniknovenie smenovekhovstva," 28–29.

10. Osipov, "Vozniknovenie smenovekhovstva," 34–35; M. Agurskii, ed., "Perepiska I. Lezhneva i N. Ustrialova," *Slavica Hierosolymitana*, no. 5–6 (1981): 558 n. 4; "Sud'ba i raboty russkikh pisatelei, uchenykh i zhurnalistov za 1918–1921 g.," *Russkaia kniga*, 1921, no. 7–8:24–25.

11. I. Trotskii, "Bol'shoi chelovek (posviashchaetsia byvshemu kollege)," *Dni*, 7 October 1923.

12. L. M. Khlebnikov, "Iz istorii gor'kovskikh izdatel'stv: 'Vsemirnaia literatura' i 'Izdatel'stvo Z. I. Grzhebina,' " *Literaturnoe nasledstvo*, no. 80 (1971): 689; I. Trotskii, "Bol'shoi chelovek."

13. Sekretar' gruppy S-R Severno-zapadnoi Oblasti Rossii to Redaktsiia gazety "Volia Rossiia," 9 January 1921, PSR Archief, 2192, Internationaal Instituut voor Sociale Geschiedenis, Amsterdam; Ossorguine-Bakounine, *Catalogue collectif*, 277.

14. See G. Kirdetsov, "O Lenine i smenovekhovtsakh," *Nakanune*, 5 May 1922. The book appeared in 1921 in Berlin under the title *U vorot Petrograda, 1919–1920 gg.* (Berlin: Gutnov, 1921). On the book see also A. Voronskii, "Pokhmel'e," *Krasnaia nov'*, 1921, no. 3:352–55.

15. N. A. Ukhtomskii to N. V. Ustrialov, 8 March 1923, *Raznye liudi*, 55; see also A. V. Bobrishchev-Pushkin, *Patrioty bez otechestva* (Leningrad: Kubuch, 1925), 126–27.

16. See *KLE*, 9:177, s.v. "Vasilevskii (Ne-Bukva), Il'ia Markovich."

17. "Sud'ba i raboty russkikh pisatelei, uchenykh i zhurnalistov za 1918–1920 gg.," *Russkaia kniga*, 1921, no. 1:19; Ossorguine-Bakounine, *Catalogue collectif*, 279.

18. V. Burtsev, "Raby! Ne bud'te po krainei mere lakeiami!" *Obshchee delo*, 3 July 1920.

19. Quoted in S., "O rabakh i lakeiakh," *Obshchee delo*, 2 November 1920.

20. Iak. B., "Vozvrashchat'sia li v Sovetskuiu Rossiiu?" *Poslednie novosti*, 26 February 1921.

21. I. Vasilevskii (Ne-Bukva), "Na perelome," *Poslednie novosti,* 15 March 1921.

22. *Notes russes 1921,* 3 December 1921, doc. P.5610.U.

23. Osipov, "Vozniknovenie smenovekhovstva," 29.

24. See in this connection A. Gurovich, "Vysshii Sovet Narodnogo Khoziaistva: Iz vpetchatlenii goda sluzhby," *Arkhiv russkoi revoliutsii,* no. 6 (1922): especially 306–9, 328–31. Gurovich wrote this article on his experiences as an employee of the Supreme Council in early 1919. See A. Gurovich, "Pis'mo v redaktsiiu," *Nakanune,* 22 August 1922.

25. Gurovich's memoirs of his emigration appeared in 1923 in Petrograd under the title *Zapiski emigranta;* by mistake, however, on the cover of that publication the author's name was printed as I. Gurovich, instead of A. S. Gurovich. See in this connection Gurovich's "Pis'mo v redaktsiiu," *Nakanune,* 4 August 1923.

26. Ossorguine-Bakounine, *Catalogue collectif,* 283. See on the paper also [A.] I. [*sic*] Gurovich, *Zapiski emigranta* (Petrograd: 'Petrograd,' 1923), 128–33.

27. See, for example, A. Gurovich, "Eshche zhiva," *Slavianskaia zaria,* 28 November 1919; A. Gurovich, "Vokrug dobychi," *Slavianskaia zaria,* 10 December 1919; E. Efimovskii, "My Vas preduprezhdaem," *Slavianskaia zaria,* 17 April 1920.

28. See E. Efimovskii's declaratory article "Vse dlia Rossii," *Slavianskaia zaria,* 8 March 1920. See also Gurovich, *Zapiski,* 165–67.

29. See, for example, A. Gurovich, "Soderzhanie revoliutsii," *Poslednie novosti,* 2 April 1921; A. Gurovich, "Budushchaia vlast'," *Poslednie novosti,* 6 May 1921; A. Gurovich, "Sushchnost' raznoglasii," *Poslednie novosti,* 9 August 1921; A. Gurovich, "Istochniki separatizma," *Poslednie novosti,* 22 December 1921.

30. P. Miliukov, "Logika renegata," *Poslednie novosti,* 20 July 1922; "Protokol zasedaniia Parizhskoi Respublikansko-Demokraticheskoi gruppy Partii Narodnoi Svobody," 19 January 1922, TsGAOR, f. 7506, op. 1, d. 71, l. 18.

31. A. S. Gurovich to Parizhskaia Respublikansko-Demokraticheskaia gruppa Partii Narodnoi Svobody, 11 January 1922, TsGAOR, f. 7506, op. 1, d. 71, l. 18; A. S. Gurovich to Parizhskaia Respublikansko-Demokraticheskaia gruppa Partii Narodnoi Svobody, 27 January 1922, TsGAOR, f. 7506, op. 1, d. 71, ll. 50–51.

32. A. Gurovich to P. N. Miliukov, 5 August 1922, TsGAOR, f. 579, op. 5, d. 204, l. 7; A. Gurovich, "Puti i tseli," *Nakanune,* 9 June 1922.

33. Gurovich to Miliukov, 5 August 1922 (see n. 32); Gurovich, "Puti i tseli." The motive of History as a leading force was present in several of Gurovich's articles in *Nakanune,* especially in "Dve oshibki," *Nakanune,* 22 July 1922; and "Tragediia i sovremennost'," *Nakanune,* 16 December 1922. In this connection, it is interesting to note that in 1919, according to Gurovich, L. B. Krasin, who would be one of the main participants of the Soviet delegation to Genoa, hoped it would be possible "to lead Russia under Bolshevik flag from Bolshevik fiction to a normal social order." See Gurovich, "Vysshii Sovet," 326.

34. On Tolstoi see A. M. Kriukova, ed., *A. N. Tolstoi: Materialy i issledovaniia* (Moscow: Nauka, 1985); V. Baranov, *Revoliutsiia i sud'ba khudozhnika: A. Tolstoi i ego put' k sotsialisticheskomu realizmu,* 2d rev. ed. (Moscow: Sovetskii pisatel', 1983); M. Gurenkov, *Bez Rossii zhit' nel'zia: Put' A. Tolstogo k revoliutsii* (Leningrad: Lenizdat, 1983); V. Shcherbina, *A. N. Tolstoi: Kritiko-biograficheskii ocherk* (Moscow: Khudozhestvennaia literatura, 1951); M. Charnyi, *Put' Alekseia Tolstogo: Ocherk tvorchestva,* 2d ed.

(Moscow: Khudozhestvennaia literatura, 1981); Z. A. Nikitina and L. I. Tolstaia, comps., *Vospominaniia ob A. N. Tolstom* (Moscow: Sovetskii pisatel', 1973). On Tolstoi in the years immediately after the October revolution see Fleishman, Kh'iuz, and Raevskaia-Kh'iuz, *Russkii Berlin,* especially 31–44, 108–31.

35. Fleishman, Kh'iuz, and Raevskaia-Kh'iuz, *Russkii Berlin,* 123.

36. A. N. Tolstoi, "Na kostre," *Luch pravdy,* no. 1 (November 1917), quoted in Kriukova, *Tolstoi,* 148–49.

37. "Sud'ba i raboty" (see n. 17), 32; Fleishman, Kh'iuz, and Raevskaia-Kh'iuz, *Russkii Berlin,* 124.

38. A. N. Tolstoi, "Torzhestvuiushchee iskusstvo" in *Skorb' zemli rodnoi: Sbornik statei 1920 goda* (New York: Initsiativnaia gruppa "Narodnoi gazety," 1920), 52. This article first appeared in the *Obshchee delo* of 9 October 1919.

39. A. N. Tolstoi to A. S. Iashchenko, 16 February 1920, in Fleishman, Kh'iuz, and Raevskaia-Kh'iuz, *Russkii Berlin,* 115.

40. See A. N. Tolstoi, "Otkrytoe pis'mo N. V. Chaikovskomu" in *Pochemu my vernulis' na Rodinu: Svidetel'stva reemigrantov* (Moscow: Progress, 1983), 17. The letter first appeared in the *Nakanune* of 14 April 1922 (this issue was unavailable to me), and was reprinted in the *Izvestiia* of 25 April of that year. See Fleishman, Kh'iuz, and Raevskaia-Kh'iuz, *Russkii Berlin,* 60, 62.

41. A. N. Tolstoi to K. I. Chukovskii, 20 April 1922, in Kriukova, *Tolstoi,* 492–94.

42. Kriukova, *Tolstoi,* 492; Nikitina and Tolstaia, *Vospominaniia,* 124.

43. See in this connection M. Agursky, *The Third Rome: National Bolshevism in the USSR* (Boulder, Colo.: Westview Press, 1987), 254.

44. Nikitina and Tolstaia, *Vospominaniia,* 124–25.

45. Fleishman, Kh'iuz, and Raevskaia-Kh'iuz, *Russkii Berlin,* 110.

46. Fleishman, Kh'iuz, and Raevskaia-Kh'iuz, *Russkii Berlin,* 31.

47. Fleishman, Kh'iuz, and Raevskaia-Kh'iuz, *Russkii Berlin,* 187. On Pil'niak see V. T. Reck, *Boris Pil'niak: A Soviet Writer in Conflict with the State* (Montreal: McGill-Queen's University Press, 1975). On Pil'niak's reception in Berlin see Gul', *Rossiia v Germanii,* 153–55.

48. A. Voronskii, "Sovetskaia Rossiia v osveshchenii belogo obozrevatelia," *Krasnaia nov',* 1922, no. 1:221.

49. On Drozdov and his "change of signposts" see Fleishman, Kh'iuz, and Raevskaia-Kh'iuz, *Russkii Berlin,* 80–87.

50. On Alekseev see Fleishman, Kh'iuz, and Raevskaia-Kh'iuz, *Russkii Berlin,* 95.

51. On Sokolov-Mikitov see Fleishman, Kh'iuz, and Raevskaia-Kh'iuz, *Russkii Berlin,* 204–6.

52. Fleishman, Kh'iuz, and Raevskaia-Kh'iuz, *Russkii Berlin,* 188–89.

53. Fleishman, Kh'iuz, and Raevskaia-Kh'iuz, *Russkii Berlin,* 192.

54. Sokolov-Mikitov contributed to *Nakanune*'s literary supplement, but, unlike Tolstoi, did not really feel himself a member of the group, and even distanced himself from Kliuchnikov and his colleagues. He returned to Soviet Russia as early as August 1922 (see Fleishman, Kh'iuz, and Raevskaia-Kh'iuz, *Russkii Berlin,* 204–7).

55. Fleishman, Kh'iuz, and Raevskaia-Kh'iuz, *Russkii Berlin,* 86–87. Drozdov

returned to Moscow in December 1923 (see Fleishman, Kh'iuz, and Raevskaia-Kh'iuz, *Russkii Berlin*, 95). Alekseev returned quite unexpectedly in November 1923. See also Gul', *Rossiia v Germanii*, 205–6.

56. G. P. Struve, *Russkaia literatura v izgnanii*, 2d rev. ed. (Paris: YMCA-Press, 1984), 35.

57. See Tolstoi's "Otkrytoe pis'mo N. V. Chaikovskomu," 18–19, and especially his "Neskol'ko slov pered ot"ezdom," *Nakanune*, 27 July 1923 (reprinted in *Pochemu my vernulis'*, 20–24), where he stressed that in Russia, "the individual was going toward its liberation through the affirmation and creation of a powerful state."

58. N. V. Ustrialov to Iu. N. Potekhin, 3 April 1923, *Smenovekhovtsy*, 82.

59. I. B. Diushen, interview with author, Moscow, 25 September 1989.

60. "Protokol zasedaniia Parizhskoi gruppy Partii Narodnoi Svobody," 18 December 1922, *KD Archive*, box 2, 354. The total number of copies of *Nakanune* is unknown. As a point of reference, *Poslednie novosti*, by far the most widely read émigré newspaper, had a circulation of 23,000 copies in the early thirties, and of 39,000 copies in 1938. See M. Raeff, *Russia Abroad: A Cultural History of the Russian Emigration 1919–1939* (New York: Oxford University Press, 1990), 82–83; R. H. Johnston, *New Mecca, New Babylon: Paris and the Russian Exiles, 1920–1945* (Kingston, Ont.: McGill-Queen's University Press, 1988), 41. The Berlin daily *Golos Rossii*, for its part, appeared in 1921 in a mere 1,000 copies (see V. A. Dutsman, comp., *Obzor inostrannoi i russkoi zarubezhnoi pressy* [Moscow: Razvedyvatel'noe upravlenie shtaba RKKA, 1922], 108).

61. Gul', *Rossiia v Germanii*, 196; "Protokol zasedaniia Parizhskoi Respublikan-sko-Demokraticheskoi gruppy Partii Narodnoi Svobody," 23 March 1922, TsGAOR, f. 7506, op. 1, d. 71, l. 203.

62. This version was mentioned in "Pechat'," *Poslednie novosti*, 13 April 1922. Krasin occupied the post of people's commissar of foreign trade from June 1920 to January 1924 (see H. Shukman, ed., *The Blackwell Encyclopedia of the Russian Revolution* [Oxford: Blackwell, 1988], 171).

63. Tolstoi, "Otkrytoe pis'mo," 16.

64. N. A. Ukhtomskii to N. V. Ustrialov, 30 June 1924, *Raznye liudi*, 83; E. L. Mindlin, *Neobyknovennye sobesedniki: Kniga vospominanii* (Moscow: Sovetskii pisatel', 1968), 121–22.

65. "'Smenovekhovtsy,' emigratsiia i Rossiia," *Poslednie novosti*, 26 March 1922.

66. "Pechat'," *Poslednie novosti*, 28 March 1922. Space prevents my mentioning any more than a small number of the polemical articles against *Nakanune* that appeared in the Paris daily. A few examples are P. Miliukov, "Neproshennye soiuzniki," *Poslednie novosti*, 6 April 1922; P. Miliukov, "Evoliutsiia—moia ili Rossii?" *Poslednie novosti*, 21 July 1922; B. Mirskii, "Advokaty zastenka," *Poslednie novosti*, 24 August 1922; "Pechat'," *Poslednie novosti*, 23 January 1923; B. Mirskii, "Rodina i vlast'," *Poslednie novosti*, 21 March 1923; "Kritika 'Nakanune,'" *Poslednie novosti*, 31 August 1923; "Pechat'," *Poslednie novosti*, 19 December 1923.

67. See, for example, M. Tsetlin, "Plemia mladoe (o 'Serapionovykh Brat'iakh')," *Sovremennye zapiski*, no. 12 (1922): 332; V. R., "'Edinyi sotsialisticheskii front' s bol'shevikami," *Sovremennye zapiski*, no. 12 (1922): 363–64.

68. The issue of *Novyi mir* in question was unavailable to me. Kliuchnikov's

statement to this effect is mentioned in two independent sources, however (see A. V. Bobrishchev-Pushkin to N. V. Ustrialov, 10 June 1922, *Smenovekhovtsy,* 60; " 'Smeno-vekhovtsy', emigratsiia" [see n. 65]). See further also "Pechat'," *Rul'*, 25 [12] March 1922; "Pechat'," *Rul'*, 28 [15] March 1922. In the latter article, the contributors to *Nakanune* were called "executioners' servants [*prisluzhniki palachei*]."

69. See Gul', *Rossiia v Germanii,* 198–99; M. Beyssac, *La vie culturelle de l'émigra-tion russe en France: Chronique (1920–1930)* (Paris: P.U.F., 1971), 27–28; Th. R. Beyer, G. Kratz, and X. Werner, *Russische Autoren und Verlage in Berlin nach dem Ersten Weltkrieg* (Berlin: Arnold Spitz, 1987), 24; "Protokol zasedaniia Parizhskoi Respublikansko-De-mokraticheskoi gruppy Partii Narodnoi Svobody," 8 June 1922, TsGAOR, f. 7506, op. 1, d. 71, l. 338; "Iskliuchenie smenovekhovtsev," *Poslednie novosti,* 3 June 1922.

70. See, for example, I. Vasilevskii (Ne-Bukva), "Parizhskaia kontr-razvedka," *Nakanune* 27 April 1922; A. Gurovich, "Pis'mo v redaktsiiu," *Nakanune,* 15 June 1922.

71. On Tolstoi's open letter see Fleishman, Kh'iuz, and Raevskaia-Kh'iuz, *Russkii Berlin,* 31–32; Baranov, *Revoliutsiia i sud'ba,* 102–3; Charnyi, *Put' Tolstogo,* 73–76; Tolstoi, "Otkrytoe pis'mo," 16.

72. The letter was reprinted in *Izvestiia* of 25 April 1922, along with an article by P. S. Kogan, entitled "Raskol emigratsii." See also Fleishman, Kh'iuz, and Raev-skaia-Kh'iuz, *Russkii Berlin,* 62.

73. Fleishman, Kh'iuz, and Raevskaia-Kh'iuz, *Russkii Berlin,* 32, 268–69; P. Miliukov, " 'Sluchai' gr. A. Tolstogo," *Poslednie novosti,* 16 April 1922.

74. Tolstoi, "Otkrytoe pis'mo," especially 19–20.

75. With this goal, Chukovskii published, in the organ of the Petrograd *Dom literatorov,* part of a private letter Tolstoi had written to him on 20 April 1922. In the letter, Tolstoi spoke of his enormous longing to join the literary community in Russia; he avoided every allusion to politics, and presented his position exclusively as the result of homesickness and disillusionment with the declining culture of the West. See "Iz pis'ma Alekseia N. Tolstogo," *Literaturnye zapiski,* no. 1 (25 May 1922), 4; the full text of the letter is in Kriukova, *Tolstoi,* 492–94. See also Fleishman, Kh'iuz, and Raevskaia-Kh'iuz, *Russkii Berlin,* 32–33.

76. "Khronika," *Nakanune,* 1 June 1922.

77. Mindlin, *Neobyknovennye sobesedniki,* 119–20, 128–29; S. A. Fediukin, *Bor'ba s burzhuaznoi ideologiei v usloviiakh perekhoda k Nepu* (Moscow: Nauka, 1977), 130–31. Krichevskii contributed also to the bulletin of the People's Commissariat of Foreign Affairs: see, for example, M. Krichevskii, "Rossiia no 2 i Genua," *Vestnik Narodnogo Komissariata po inostrannym delam,* 1922, no. 4–5:60–67.

78. See Mindlin, *Neobyknovennye sobesedniki,* 119; Dutsman, *Obzor pressy,* 109–10; "Smenovekhovtsy v Moskve," *Poslednie novosti,* 18 July 1922.

79. Mindlin, *Neobyknovennye sobesedniki,* 119, 128–29.

80. Mindlin, *Neobyknovennye sobesedniki,* 120, 122. This was indicated also in *Nakanune*'s masthead.

81. Mindlin, *Neobyknovennye sobesedniki,* 122–23.

82. See, for example, E. Mindlin, "Iubilei Iuzhina (Pis'mo iz Moskvy)," *Naka-nune,* 26 September 1922; E. Mindlin, "Literaturno-izdatel'skaia zhizn' Moskvy (Pis'mo iz Moskvy)," *Nakanune,* 4 January 1923; E. Mindlin, "Neosushchestvlennyi Sankt-Peterburg," *Nakanune,* 4 September 1923. According to the calculations of the

Russian historian V. A. Osipov, Mindlin was the only collaborator from Soviet Russia who made more than five contributions to *Nakanune,* apart from M. Bulgakov, who contributed some thirty feuilletons and stories (see Osipov, "Vozniknovenie smenove-khovstva," 28–29).

83. Mindlin, *Neobyknovennye sobesedniki,* 129.

84. Kliuchnikov and Potekhin gave lectures in Moscow, Petrograd, Kharkov, Poltava, and Rostov; in Kiev, however, where a lecture had also been planned, the local authorities refused to give the necessary permission (see A. Volkov, "Beseda s prof. Iu. V. Kliuchnikovym," *Izvestiia,* 17 August 1922). On the lectures see further Mindlin, *Neobyknovennye sobesedniki,* 123–25; "Perelety," *Poslednie novosti,* 24 September 1921; F., " 'Smenovekhovtsy' v Petrograde (Pis'mo iz Petrograda)," *Rul',* 20 [7] September 1922; Leri, "Chto videli smenovekhovtsy," *Rul',* 21 [8] September 1922; M. Kantor, "O 'Smene vekh' (Vnimaniiu Sverdlovtsev)," *Pravda,* 28 June 1922; G. Bergman, "Diktatura proletariata, Nep, intelligentsiia (Po povodu nekotorykh vys-tuplenii prof. Kliuchnikova)," *Pravda,* 8 July 1922; Erde, "Russkaia intelligentsiia, emi-gratsiia i 'Smena vekh,' " *Izvestiia,* 29 June 1922; "Disput o 'Smene vekh,' " *Izvestiia,* 11 July 1922); V. G. Tan-Bogoraz, " 'Smenovekhi' v Petrograde," *Rossiia,* no. 1 (August 1922): 12–14. On *Glavpolitprosvet* see P. Kenez, *The Birth of the Propaganda State: Soviet Methods of Mass Mobilization, 1917–1929* (Cambridge: Cambridge University Press, 1985), 123–25.

85. On the SR trial see M. Jansen, *Een showproces onder Lenin: Het voorspel van de Grote Terreur* (Haarlem: De Haan, 1980). At the so-called Petrograd clergymen trial ten people were sentenced to death, including the Metropolitan Veniamin, whom the de-fense had proven to be innocent (see Johannes Chrysostomus, *Patriarch Tichon, 1917–1925,* vol. 1 of *Kirchengeschichte Russlands der neuesten Zeit* [Munich: Anton Pustet, 1965], 184–85; Shukman, *Blackwell Encyclopedia,* 385).

86. A. V. Kvakin, "Novovekhovstvo kak krizis beloi emigratsii" (Kandidatskaia dissertatsiia, Kalininskii gosudarstvennyi universitet, 1981), 50.

87. See in this connection also Ustrialov to Potekhin, 3 April 1923 (see n. 58), 81.

88. "Intelligentsiia i sovetskaia vlast' (Beseda s redaktorom gazety 'Nakanune' prof. Iu. V. Kliuchnikovym)," *Izvestiia,* 9 June 1922.

89. See, for example, I. Lezhnev, "Razmen vekh (Otvet Iu. N. Potekhinu. Mozhet byt', dazhe bol'she togo)," *Rossiia,* no. 5 (January 1923): 17–18; Tan-Bogoraz, " 'Smenovekhi,' " 13; "Disput" (see n. 84), according to which it was E. Korovin, a former friend and collaborator of Kliuchnikov, Potekhin, and Ustrialov (see chap. 3, n. 91), who expressed irritation vis-à-vis the *smenovekhovtsy* for their servility to the Soviet regime.

90. See in this connection "Pechat'," *Poslednie novosti,* 21 July 1922; Fleishman, Kh'iuz, and Raevskaia-Kh'iuz, *Russkii Berlin,* 43–46, 83–84, 200–1; Reck, *Pil'niak,* 98–99; L. Fleishman, *Boris Pasternak v dvadtsatye gody* (Munich: Wilhelm Fink, 1981), 22–24.

91. Erde, "Russkaia intelligentsiia"; Kantor, "O 'Smene vekh' "; Bergman, "Diktatura"; G. Bergman, "Priskorbnye zabluzhdeniia prof. Kliuchnikova," *Izvestiia,* 18 August 1922; A. Bubnov, "Vozrozhdenie burzhuaznoi ideologii i zadachi agitprop-raboty," *Pravda,* 27 July 1922.

92. Bergman, "Diktatura."

93. G. Kirdetsov, "Paralleli," *Nakanune*, 20 July 1922. He referred to Ustrialov's article "Poteriannaia i vozvrashchennaia Rossiia," which appeared first in *Al'manakh russkaia zhizn'* of 20 May 1922, and was reprinted in N. V. Ustrialov, *Pod znakom revoliutsii* (Harbin: Russkaia mysl', 1925), 92.

94. "Prizhival'shchiki revoliutsii ili storonniki ee? (O smenovekhovtsakh)," *Pravda*, 23 July 1922.

95. Jansen, *Showproces*, 184–85.

96. The article in question was the editorial of *Nakanune*, 15 July 1922; this issue was not available to me.

97. A. Bobrishchev-Pushkin, "Itogi protestov Es-erovskoi zashchity," *Nakanune*, 16 July 1922.

98. *EGV*, 77, s.v. "Bubnov, Andrei Sergeevich"; Agursky, *Third Rome*, 293.

99. Bubnov, "Vozrozhdenie," reprinted in A. Bubnov, *Burzhuaznoe restavratorstvo na vtorom godu NEPa* (Petrograd: Priboi, 1923), 16–18.

100. Agursky, *Third Rome*, 293–94. The conference was convened from 4 to 7 August 1922.

101. Editorial, *Nakanune*, 13 August 1922.

102. Volkov, "Beseda."

103. "Ot redaktsii," *Nakanune*, 23 August 1922.

104. Ukhtomskii to Ustrialov, 8 March 1923 (see n. 15), 55. The same was true for Bobrishchev-Pushkin, who contributed to the daily from Monte Carlo, but hardly had a say in its editorial affairs (see A. V. Bobrishchev-Pushkin to N. V. Ustrialov, 9 October 1922, *Smenovekhovtsy*, 67; Bobrishchev-Pushkin, *Patrioty*, 126–27).

105. Kirdetsov left this post officially in October 1923, when he was appointed press attaché at the Soviet Embassy in Berlin; in reality, he began working at the Soviet mission in August of that year. He continued to play a role in the paper's management, however, in any case until March 1924, when he assumed the function of press attaché at the Soviet Embassy in Rome (see N. A. Ukhtomskii to N. V. Ustrialov, 29 August 1923, *Raznye liudi*, 72; "Ot redaktsii," *Nakanune*, 3 October 1923; "Khronika," *Nakanune*, 11 March 1924; Bobrishchev-Pushkin, *Patrioty*, 126–27).

106. Volkov, "Beseda"; Bobrishchev-Pushkin to Ustrialov, 9 October 1922 (see n. 104), 67. Potekhin returned to Moscow on 10 October 1922 (see Iu. N. Potekhin to N. V. Ustrialov, 23 February 1923, *Smenovekhovtsy*, 78).

107. Iu. V. Kliuchnikov to N. V. Ustrialov, 8 November 1921, *Smenovekhovtsy*, 16; Bobrishchev-Pushkin to Ustrialov, 10 June 1922 (see n. 68), 59; Iu. N. Potekhin to N. V. Ustrialov, 7 May 1923, *Smenovekhovtsy*, 87; N. V. Ustrialov, Diary, 24 August 1925, *Smenovekhovtsy*, 110.

108. Volkov, "Beseda"; Fleishman, Kh'iuz, and Raevskaia-Kh'iuz, *Russkii Berlin*, 106; A. V. Bobrishchev-Pushkin to N. V. Ustrialov, 2 November 1922, *Smenovekhovtsy*, 73.

109. Ukhtomskii to Ustrialov, 8 March 1923 (see n. 15), 56.

110. Bobrishchev-Pushkin to Ustrialov, 9 October 1922 (see n. 104), 67; Ustrialov, Diary, 24 August 1925 (see n. 107), 111.

111. Bobrishchev-Pushkin to Ustrialov, 10 June 1922 (see n. 68), 59; Ukhtomskii to Ustrialov, 8 March 1923 (see n. 15), 55.

112. Leri, "Chto videli"; Ukhtomskii to Ustrialov, 8 March 1923 (see n. 15), 55–56.

113. See in this connection A. E. Senn, *Assassination in Switzerland: The Murder of Vatslav Vorovsky* (Madison: University of Wisconsin Press, 1981), 121–23; A. V. Bobrishchev-Pushkin, *Voina bez perchatok* (Leningrad: Kubuch, 1925), 80–109; Osipov, "Vozniknovenie smenovekhovstva," 23; "Posobnichestvo belomu terroru? Zhdem otveta," *Nakanune,* 21 October 1923; S. B. Chlenov, "Zhdem otveta! Pis'mo v redaktsiiu," *Nakanune,* 25 October 1923; "Dva ubiistva, dve meri," *Nakanune,* 1 November 1923. See also chap. 5, n. 89. Dobrorol'skii had been responsible for the mobilization of the Russian Army in 1914 (see General Sergei Dobrorolski, *Die Mobilmachung der russischen Armee 1914* [Berlin: Deutsche Verlaggesellschaft für Politik und Geschichte, 1922], 6).

114. Fleishman, Kh'iuz, and Raevskaia-Kh'iuz, *Russkii Berlin,* 106; [Kliuchnikov, Iu. V.], "Stenogramma lektsii professora Kliuchnikova po mezhdunarodnomu pravu" (Voennaia Akademiia RKKA, Moscow, 1924).

115. "Dépositions d'un ancien ministre russe," *La Tribune de Genève,* 9 November 1923.

116. Senn, *Assassination,* 152–56; "Les 'beautés du bolchevisme,' vantées par les témoins à charge," *La Tribune de Genève,* 8 November 1923; "Dépositions d'un ancien ministre"; "Der Prozess Conradi-Polounine," pts. 1, 2, *Basler Vorwärts,* 7, 8 November 1923.

117. Thus, in the editorial of *Nakanune's* first issue, which undeniably bore Kliuchnikov's hallmark, it had been argued that the state of uninterrupted tension in which the world found itself since the world war could only be broken by a new "bold and broad ideal," to which one should "devote oneself sacrificially." Yet, Kliuchnikov added, this was not to say that the past was dead, or that to become impregnated with a great ideal would suffice for it to be realized. He stressed that "everything valuable that the world had accumulated over centuries with incessant creativity was to be carefully preserved, and to be handed over to the coming generations with love." At the same time, he argued that new ideals, however great, could become influential only if "someone reconciled them with life and incorporated them into it"; in his view, it was there that *Nakanune's* main task lay (see "Nakanune," *Nakanune,* 26 March 1922).

118. This was also Ustrialov's view, who in December 1922 wrote in a letter to Luk'ianov: "By the way, where does your disagreement with Kliuchnikov lie? From here that is absolutely incomprehensible to me!" (Ustrialov to Luk'ianov, 14 December 1922 [see n. 1]), 76).

119. "God: 25 marta 1922–25 marta 1923," *Nakanune,* 25 March 1923. See also "O sebe," *Nakanune,* 16 December 1923.

120. See, for example, S. Luk'ianov, "Ravnodeistvuiushchaia," *Nakanune,* 16 August 1922; A. Bobrishchev-Pushkin, "Dva retsepta," *Nakanune,* 7 October 1922; " 'Prizhival'shchiki revoliutsii ili storonniki ee,' " *Nakanune,* 2 August 1922; G. Kirdetsov, "Chto takoe sovetizm," *Nakanune,* 4 February 1923.

121. A. Gurovich, "Logika upriamstva (Otvet P. N. Miliukovu)," *Nakanune,* 6 August 1922; S. Luk'ianov, "Lichnost' i gosudarstvo," *Nakanune,* 10 January 1923; S. Luk'ianov, "Eshche o diktature," *Nakanune,* 15 January 1923; S. Luk'ianov, "Demokratiia i diktatura," *Nakanune,* 27 April 1923; "Pobedy revoliutsii," *Nakanune,* 12 March 1924.

122. See, for example, Editorial, *Nakanune*, 28 October 1922; Editorial, *Nakanune*, 25 November 1922; S. S. Luk'ianov, "Sovetskii chervonets," *Nakanune*, 21 August 1923.

123. Editorial, *Nakanune*, 13 October 1922; "Po gazetnym stolbtsam," *Nakanune*, 27 October 1922.

124. S. S. Luk'ianov, "Puti novogo," *Nakanune*, 7 November 1923; Kirdetsov, "Paralleli."

125. "O sebe" (see n. 119).

126. Iu. Kliuchnikov, "Iz itogov," *Nakanune*, 21 May 1921; Volkov, "Beseda."

127. "7 noiabria 1917–7 noiabria 1922," *Nakanune*, 7 November 1922; "Na novykh putiakh," *Nakanune*, 13 February 1924.

128. G. Kirdetsov, "Piat' let," *Nakanune*, 7 November 1922.

129. See, for example, "Rossiiu oboiti nel'zia," *Nakanune*, 27 September 1922; G. Kirdetsov, "Vesenniaia kampaniia," *Nakanune*, 29 May 1923; " 'Anglo-russkii spor' (Publichnoe sobranie)," *Nakanune*, 5 June 1923.

130. *SSV*, 90, 162–63, 173, 180–81.

131. *SSV*, 49–50.

132. "Intelligentsiia i sovetskaia vlast' " (see n. 88); "Disput" (see n. 84); Volkov, "Beseda."

133. Editorial in *Nakanune*, 23 September 1922; Prof. S. Chakhotin, "Intelligentsiia, smenovekhovstvo, kommunizm," *Nakanune*, 16 September 1922; S. Chakhotin, "Litso trudovoi intelligentsii," *Nakanune*, 19 September 1922.

134. B. Diushen, "Na novom puti," *Nakanune*, 17 February 1923.

135. B. Diushen, "Izgnanie intelligentov," *Nakanune*, 26 November 1922. On the expulsion see M. Geller, " 'Pervoe predosterezhenie'—udar khlystom," *Vestnik R. Kh. D.*, no. 127 (1978): 218–24; S. Khoruzhii, "Filosofskii parokhod: Kak eto bylo," pts. 1, 2, *Literaturnaia gazeta*, 9 May, 6 June 1990; T. Krasovitskaia, "Chto imeem, ne khranim," *Moskovskie novosti*, 20 May 1990.

136. Ukhtomskii wrote with respect to Kliuchnikov: "Knocked out of *Nakanune* by Kirdetsov, he is deprived of a pulpit. . . . He asked even me to help him to find means for the publication of a journal or an almanac" (Ukhtomskii to Ustrialov, 8 March 1923 [see n. 15], 56).

137. Another indicative episode in this respect, albeit much later, in 1925, was Kliuchnikov's appearance at a dispute on the "fate of the contemporary intelligentsia," in which he took part along with A. V. Lunacharskii, N. I. Bukharin, and the literary critic and academician P. N. Sakulin. On that occasion, Kliuchnikov advocated once again that the intelligentsia be given "freedom of creation," yet added that "it would be dangerous to give at this moment full political freedom to us, the nonparty intellectuals, even to those who in a steadfast way kept step with the Soviet regime—we would get out of hand" (see *Sud'by sovremennoi intelligentsii: Doklad A. V. Lunacharskogo i rechi P. I. Sakulina, N. I. Bukharina i Iu. V. Kliuchnikova* [Moscow: Moskovskii rabochii, 1925], 34).

138. Ustrialov also responded to the expulsions with qualified assent. In his view, the eviction showed that Russia's complete recovery was still a long way off, yet, compared to the cruel repression to which the regime had resorted little more than a year before, the sanction was "relatively humanitarian." Ustrialov explained that Russia

was going through a healing process of a "purely animal" nature, which should not be hindered by the "country's brain." He stressed that if some people of pure thought apparently could not accept this, there was unfortunately nothing left but to drive this home to them by force (see Ustrialov, *Pod znakom*, 117–18).

139. See in this respect Bobrishchev-Pushkin, *Patrioty*, 124.

140. "Vsegda vpered," *Nakanune*, 15 June 1924.

141. "God: 25 marta 1922" (see n. 119).

142. Fediukin, *Bor'ba s burzhuaznoi ideologiei*, 131; Osipov, "Vozniknovenie smenovekhovstva," 25–26, 29–30; Mindlin, *Neobyknovennye sobesedniki*, 133, 144–45; Dutsman, *Obzor pressy*, 109.

143. " 'Diktatura i demokratiia' (Doklad prof. S. S. Luk'ianova)," *Nakanune*, 10 April 1923; "Evoliutsiia religii (Doklad A. V. Bobrishcheva-Pushkina)," *Nakanune*, 25 April 1923; "Vpechatleniia o sovremennoi Moskve (Doklad prof. S. Chlenova)," *Nakanune*, 17 May 1923; "Lektsii v 'O.,' " *Nakanune*, 27 May 1923; B. Sh-d., "Doklad S. S. Chakhotina," *Nakanune*, 29 May 1923; " 'Anglo-russkii spor' (Publichnoe sobranie)," *Nakanune*, 5 June 1923; "Lektsiia A. N. Tolstogo i S. S. Luk'ianova v Iene," *Nakanune*, 3 July 1923; A. Drozdov, "Zametka na begu," *Nakanune*, 20 July 1923.

144. Bobrishchev-Pushkin to Ustrialov, 9 October 1922 (see n. 104), 67; Bobrishchev-Pushkin, *Patrioty*, 125.

145. See in this connection R. S., "Za chuzhoi spinoi," *Poslednie novosti*, 27 July 1923; H. von Rimscha, *Russland jenseits der Grenzen 1921–1926: Ein Beitrag zur russischen Nachkriegsgeschichte* (Jena: Verlag der Frommannschen Buchhandlung, 1927), 173–74.

146. "O gazete 'smenovekhovtsev' v Berline (Beseda s prof. Iu. V. Kliuchnikovym)," *Izvestiia*, 28 March 1922, 1.

147. "God: 25 marta 1922" (see n. 119); "O sebe" (see n. 119); "Vsegda vpered" (see n. 140).

148. According to the Russian historian V. A. Osipov, who is working on a detailed analysis of *Nakanune*'s contents, international politics was the subject given most attention on the daily's pages (see Osipov, "Vozniknovenie smenovekhovstva," 30–31).

149. R. C. Williams, *Culture in Exile: Russian Emigrés in Germany 1881–1941* (Ithaca: Cornell University Press, 1972), 272.

150. "Po puti v Moskvu: Beseda s Errio," *Nakanune*, 16 September 1922; F. Kudriavtsev, "Vozvrashchenie Errio," *Nakanune*, 22 October 1922. In his travel account Herriot gratefully mentioned the help which the "*Ralliés*" had offered him in organizing his visit to Soviet Russia (see E. Herriot, *La Russie nouvelle* [Paris: Ferenczi, 1922], 5).

151. A. V. Bobrishchev-Pushkin to N. V. Ustrialov, 3 March 1923, *Smenovekhovtsy*, 80.

152. "Vsegda vpered" (see n. 140).

153. "Nemetskaia intelligentsiia i Novaia Rossiia," *Nakanune*, 2 September 1923; "Freunde des Neuen Russlands," *Neue Kulturkorrespondenz*, no. 3 (15 June 1923), 10. Apparently, also the group behind the Moscow journal *Rossiia* had contacts with this organization (see Agurskii, "Perepiska," 562). On the organization see G. Rosenfeld, *Sowjetrussland und Deutschland, 1923–1939* (Cologne: Pahl-Rugenstein, 1984),

191–95. The International Workers' Aid Society was founded in September 1921 in Berlin, initiated by W. Münzenberg, the leader of the Communist Youth International. At first, the society concentrated on aid to the famished regions in Southern Russia; from 1922 on, it served also as a channel for Soviet propaganda. The society was supervised by the Communist International, albeit not officially. See E. H. Carr, *The Bolshevik Revolution 1917–1923,* 3 vols. (London: Macmillan, 1950–1953; Harmondsworth: Penguin Books, 1966), 3:401–2.

154. On Löbe see W. Benz and H. Graml, eds., *Biographisches Lexikon zur Weimarer Republik* (Munich: C. H. Beck, 1988), 211–12.

155. See M. Schwarz, *Biographisches Handbuch der Reichstage* (Hannover: Verlag für Literatur und Zeitgeschehen, 1965), 661.

156. See in this respect L. Dupeux, *'Nationalbolschewismus' in Deutschland, 1919–1933: Kommunistische Strategie und konservative Dynamik* (Munich: C. H. Beck, 1985), 53–69. It was presumably to Eltzbacher's call that Ustrialov had referred in his speech at the Kadet Conference in Omsk in May 1919 (see chap. 2, n. 97).

157. "Inostrannaia zhizn'," *Nakanune,* 13 January 1924. The supplement was edited by A. S. Iashchenko.

158. "God: 25 marta 1922" (see n. 119); "Vsegda vpered" (see n. 140).

159. This was most exceptional—all other requests to publish a Russian language journal abroad and import it into Soviet Russia had met with a staunch refusal from Moscow, whatever the publication's character. This was the case with the journal *Beseda,* founded in Berlin in 1923 by the writer M. Gor'kii with the goal of breaking the cultural and scientific isolation of Soviet Russia at that time. See Struve, *Russkaia literatura,* 38–39; Fleishman, Kh'iuz, and Raevskaia-Kh'iuz, *Russkii Berlin,* 339; Williams, *Culture in Exile,* 278–80; Osipov, "Vozniknovenie smenovekhovstva," 23–24. There was, to be sure, besides *Nakanune* one other journal that had access to the Soviet public, *Voina i mir: Vestnik voennoi nauki i tekhniki,* a publication with close links to the Berlin daily and, as the title indicates, a military journal of a purely technical character. Contributors included B. V. Diushen and General A. Noskov, as well as the Major Generals S. Dobrorol'skii and E. Dostovalov, all collaborators of *Nakanune.* The journal appeared under the motto "Si vis pacem, para bellum"; in the editorial of the first issue, the journal's staff argued: "Military science is . . . impassive, impartial. It is only a means, only a weapon, that serves him who has mastered it and who skillfully directs it to reach his goals. Therefore not a single state, not a single people should neglect the indications of the military science, of military experience, of the evolution of military affairs" (see "Ot redaktsii," *Voina i mir,* no. 1 [April] 1922]: 3). The journal appeared until 1924. See Dutsman, *Obzor pressy,* 112; Osipov, "Vozniknovenie smenovekhovstva," 23; B. Prianishnikov, *Nezrimaia pautina* (N.p.: B. Prianishnikov, 1979), 125.

160. Quoted in Kvakin, "Novovekhovstvo kak krizis," 83.

161. Fediukin, *Bor'ba s burzhuaznoi ideologiei,* 132.

162. Fediukin does not mention it, but this was one of the achievements with which *Nakanune*'s editors credited themselves in the daily's very last editorial. See "Vsegda vpered" (see n. 140).

163. Ukhtomskii to Ustrialov, 8 March 1923 (see n. 15), 55. Revealing in this respect is also a remark in the diary of M. Bulgakov, who was a regular contributor to *Nakanune* until the daily's closure: "A company of exceptional dregs is gathering

around *Nakanune*. I can congratulate myself, that I am in their midst. . . . Yet there is one thing which I can say with a clear conscience to myself. It was sheer necessity that forced me to publish in it. Had it not been for *Nakanune*, *Zapiski na manzhetakh* would never have seen the light, nor would have many other things, in which I can truthfully express the literary word. One had to be an exceptional hero to keep silent for four years, keep silent without hope that one might be able to open one's mouth in the future. I, unfortunately, am not a hero." Note for 26 October 1923 in K. N. Kirilenko and G. S. Faiman, eds., "Mikhail Bulgakov: 'Ia mogu byt' odnim—pisatelem . . .': Dnevniki M. A. Bulgakova," *Teatr*, 1990, no. 2:149.

164. "God: 25 marta 1922" (see n. 119); G. Kirdetsov, "Kto my," *Nakanune*, 7 March 1923; "O sebe" (see n. 119); "Vsegda vpered" (see n. 140).

165. Kirdetsov, "O Lenine i smenovekhovtsakh."

166. B. Diushen, "Smeshchenie iazykov," *Nakanune*, 13 July 1922. On Pil'niak's open letter see Reck, *Pil'niak*, 98–99; Fleishman, Kh'iuz, and Raevskaia-Kh'iuz, *Russkii Berlin*, 200–1.

167. Bobrishchev-Pushkin to Ustrialov, 10 June 1922 (see n. 68), 56–57.

168. Mindlin, *Neobyknovennye sobesedniki*, 126. See in this connection also Ukhtomskii to Ustrialov, 8 March 1923 (see n. 15), 54. Ukhtomskii wrote that one had the impression that *Nakanune*'s editors were continuously guessing what Moscow wanted to hear on a certain subject.

169. "Leidenskaia banka," *Dni*, 17 May 1923.

170. "Pechat'," *Rul'*, 25 [12] March 1922.

171. Mirskii, "Advokaty zastenka."

172. Ukhtomskii to Ustrialov, 30 June 1924 (see n. 64), 82–83. See also "Bol'sheviki i smenovekhovtsy," *Poslednie novosti*, 6 April 1923.

173. Report in the collection of the former TsPA IML (now the Russian Center for the Preservation and Study of the Documents of Modern History), Moscow, quoted in Fediukin, *Bor'ba s burzhuaznoi ideologiei*, 131. Unfortunately, Fediukin does not mention the exact date of the report.

174. Ukhtomskii to Ustrialov, 30 June 1924 (see n. 64), 82–83.

175. See in this connection E. H. Carr, *The Interregnum 1923–1924* (London: Macmillan, 1954), 243–53; A. Hogenhuis-Seliverstoff, *Les Relations franco-soviétiques 1917–1924* (Paris: Publications de la Sorbonne, 1981), 262–69. The Soviet regime's official recognition was welcomed triumphantly on the pages of *Nakanune*, which greeted the news that the British government had finally taken the long-awaited step with the words "The Worldwide Role of Russia: England Recognized the Soviet Government de Jure" printed in capitals over the daily's front page *(Nakanune,* 3 February 1924). See also "Vozvrashchenie Rossii," *Nakanune*, 12 February 1924.

176. See in this connection "Emigratsiia posle priznaniia," *Nakanune*, 28 May 1924; Raeff, *Russia Abroad*, 35–36; Johnston, *New Mecca*, 64–68. R. H. Johnston describes how, following the Soviet regime's legal recognition by the French government in late October 1924, V. A. Maklakov had to hurriedly vacate the Russian Embassy, which he had been occupying as the Provisional Government's ambassador to France, to make room for the incoming Soviet representation to France, headed by L. B. Krasin (65–66).

177. Gul', *Rossiia v Germanii*, 200; Ukhtomskii to Ustrialov, 30 June 1924 (see

n. 64), 82–83. It seems that for the operation of actually closing down *Nakanune,* the GPU official M. A. Trilisser (1883–1940) was sent to Berlin (see Agursky, *Third Rome,* 291).

178. "Vsegda vpered" (see n. 140).

179. Osipov, "Vozniknovenie smenovekhovstva," 35. The 1926 through 1929 volumes of *Mezhdunarodnaia zhizn'* contain several articles by Kirdetsov, mainly on Italian foreign policy. He also served as editor of several popular publications, including a popular dictionary on foreign policy, which first appeared in 1929 and was reprinted eight times in the course of 1930, and a collection of satirical portraits of politicians from the capitalist world (see G. L. Kirdetsov, ed., *Ves' mir: Politicheskii slovar'-spravochnik* [Moscow: Krest'ianskaia gazeta, 1929]; G. L. Kirdetsov, ed., *Kto oni takie: Kapitalisticheskii mir v 100 politicheskikh portretakh* [Moscow: Krest'ianskaia gazeta, 1931]).

180. Osipov, "Vozniknovenie smenovekhovstva," 34.

181. Agurskii, "Perepiska," 566; "Khronika," *Nakanune,* 29 July 1923; "Russkaia zhizn': Novosti dnia," *Nakanune,* 29 August 1923.

182. See n. 114 above. Moreover, in 1925–1926 Kliuchnikov was a member of the Section of Public and Administrative Law at the Institute for Soviet Law of the so-called Russian Association of Scientific Institutes for the Social Sciences (RANION) (see "Otchet Instituta Sovetskogo prava Raniona za 1925/1926 g.," *Sovetskoe pravo,* 1927, no. 2:163).

183. Several articles by Kliuchnikov appeared in the 1925 through 1928 volumes of the journal. His favorite subjects were international disarmament and the League of Nations.

184. In 1925–1927, along with the law professor and former Tsarist diplomat A. V. Sabanin, Kliuchnikov published six volumes with annotated translations of the diverse peace treaties which had been signed in Paris after the world war. In 1925–1929 he worked with A. V. Sabanin on four volumes of diplomatic documents, covering the period from the French revolution up to 1927, the tenth anniversary of the October revolution. See Iu. V. Kliuchnikov and A. Sabanin, eds., *Itogi imperialisticheskoi voiny,* 6 vols. (Moscow: Litizdat N.K.I.D., 1925–1927); Iu. V. Kliuchnikov and A. Sabanin, eds., *Mezhdunarodnaia politika noveishego vremeni v dogovorakh, notakh i deklaratsiiakh,* 4 vols. (Moscow: Litizdat N.K.I.D., 1925–1929). Kliuchnikov's introduction to the former work got a most favorable review on the pages of *Izvestiia* (see A. E., "Kritika i bibliografiia: Itogi imperialisticheskoi voiny," *Izvestiia,* 29 June 1926).

185. A. Khar'kovskii, "Chakhotinskaia odisseia," *Ogonek,* 1974, no. 8:7; S. A. Fediukin, *Velikii Oktiabr' i intelligentsiia: Iz istorii vovlecheniia staroi intelligentsii v stroitel'stvo sotsializma* (Moscow: Nauka, 1972), 267–68.

186. S. S. Chakhotin, *Organizatsiia: printsipy i metody v proizvodstve, torgovle, administratsii i politike* (Berlin: Opyt, 1923); S. S. Chakhotin, *Evropeiskaia literatura po N.O.T.* (Moscow: NKRKI SSSR, 1924); S. S. Chakhotin, *Organizatsiia: printsipy i metody v proizvodstve, torgovle, administratsii i politike,* 2d ed. (Leningrad: Gosizdat, 1925). A positive review of the bibliography is in *Organizatsiia truda: Ezhemesiachnyi organ Tsentral'nogo Instituta Truda,* 1924, no. 5:89. He published another work on this issue in 1938: S. S. Tchakhotine, *Organisation rationelle de la recherche scientifique* (Paris: Hermann, 1938).

187. Fediukin, *Velikii Oktiabr',* 267–68; Khar'kovskii, "Odisseia," 7. The results

of his work on Fascist propaganda appeared in Paris in 1939; the French edition was reprinted seven times, and was also translated into English.

188. Ukhtomskii to Ustrialov, 30 June 1924 (see n. 64), 84; "Pis'mo S. S. Luk'ianova v redaktsiiu Moskovskikh 'Izvestii,' " 24 March 1931, *Smenovekhovtsy,* 124.

189. Ossorguine-Bakounine, *Catalogue collectif,* 212, 234; P. N. Miliukov, *Emigratsiia na pereput'i* (Paris: Resp.–Dem. Ob"edinenie, 1926), 115; Osipov, "Vozniknovenie smenovekhovstva," 35–36. On the Union for Return to the Motherland see Johnston, *New Mecca,* 150; on the Union of Russian Workers in France and the Union of Students–Soviet Citizens in France see *Nash soiuz,* no. 24 (7 November 1926): 20–22.

190. "Pis'mo S. S. Luk'ianova" (see n. 188), 124; Osipov, "Vozniknovenie smenovekhovstva," 36; A. Meerovich, "V Narkomindele, 1922–1939: Interv'iu s E. A. Gnezdinym," *Pamiat': Istoricheskii sbornik,* no. 5 (1982): 383. The weekly *Journal de Moscou; Hebdomadaire politique, économique, social et littéraire* appeared from 1934 to April 1939.

191. Vasilevskii became a regular contributor to several publications including *Vecherniaia Moskva* and *Ogonek* (see Osipov, "Vozniknovenie smenovekhovstva," 34).

192. Bobrishchev-Pushkin returned to Soviet Russia earlier than he had intended, in order to help his ailing father, also a lawyer, with whom he had shared a practice in Petrograd before the revolution. Bobrishchev-Pushkin joined the Leningrad College of Counsels for the Defense, and continued his father's practice. See Bobrishchev-Pushkin to Ustrialov, 3 March 1923 (see n. 151), 80; Osipov, "Vozniknovenie smenovekhovstva," 34; H. E. Schulz, P. K. Urban, and A. I. Lebed, eds., *Who was who in the USSR: A Biographic Directory* (Metuchen, N.J.: Scarecrow Press, 1972), 73–74; *Ves' Leningrad* (1926), div. 10, 38.

193. Kriukova, *Tolstoi,* 231–49.

194. Osipov, "Vozniknovenie smenovekhovstva," 28. What happened to Sadyker is unknown to me.

195. Fleishman, Kh'iuz, and Raevskaia-Kh'iuz, *Russkii Berlin,* 12–14. In 1924 Iashchenko had received the chair of international law at Kaunas University. He died in Berlin in 1934.

196. Struve, *Russkaia literatura,* 29.

197. See L. Rzhevsky, "Roman Borisovich Gul' " in *The Modern Encyclopaedia of Russian and Soviet Literatures,* vol. 9 (Gulf Breeze, Fla.: Academic International Press, 1989), 143–47. Gul' became editor-in-chief of *Novyi zhurnal* in 1959, and had served in the years before as its editorial secretary.

CHAPTER 7: THE EFFECTS OF *SMENOVEKHOVSTVO*

1. The statistician and former Minister of Food Supply in the Provisional Government A. V. Peshekhonov, the novelist M. A. Osorgin, and the publicist E. D. Kuskova had been expelled from Soviet Russia in 1922, along with a whole group of other intellectuals; they were, therefore, not émigrés in the full sense of the word. In 1923 Peshekhonov published a pamphlet under the title *Pochemu ia ne emigriroval,* in which he argued that to return home—even without guarantees of tolerable living conditions or personal security—was the only way the émigrés could do something for their motherland. In his view, all they could do abroad was slouch along the streets (see

A. V. Peshekhonov, *Pochemu ia ne emigriroval* [Berlin: Obelisk, 1923], 28–30; P. N. Miliukov, *Emigratsiia na pereput'i* [Paris: Resp.- Dem. Ob"edinenie, 1926], 76–77). In 1925 Peshekhonov received the support of E. D. Kuskova and M. A. Osorgin, who took a position very much reminiscent of that of the Berlin group *Mir i trud*. Osorgin admitted that Russia was a prison, but added that it was impossible to saw through its bars and kick down its doors from abroad. In Russia, however, the people would one day succeed in bringing down even that Bastille. He stressed that, by saying this, he was not hinting at revolutionary activities of any kind, but was speaking "simply of life, of real cultural work, great and small, of strengthening the people's power and their capacity to resist, of working for the country's good" (quoted in Miliukov, *Emigratsiia*, 78). The *vozvrashchentsy* hoped to see Russia eventually as a parliamentary democracy and to reach this goal through peaceful action, yet declared themselves also prepared to engage, if need be, in active political struggle. Clearly, their position was absolutely impracticable. None of the *vozvrashchentsy* returned to the motherland; the Soviet authorities refused to admit them. Peshekhonov, to be sure, returned to Russia posthumously; he died in 1933 in Riga, where he had been working as a consultant for the local Soviet trade mission since 1927, yet was buried in Leningrad (see H. E. Schulz, P. K. Urban, and A. I. Lebed, eds., *Who was who in the USSR: A Biographic Directory* [Metuchen, N.J.: Scarecrow Press, 1972], 442). For a (polemical) account of their views see Miliukov, *Emigratsiia*, 73–122; see further T. B. Koons, "Histoire des doctrines politiques de l'émigration russe, 1919–1939" (Thèse pour le Doctorat d'Université, Université de Paris, Faculté des Lettres, 1952), 171–78.

2. *SSV*, p. 182. The quotation is from N. V. Gogol', "Nuzhno liubit' Rossiiu—Iz pis'ma k gr. A. P. Tolstomu" in N. V. Gogol', *Polnoe sobranie sochinenii*, vol. 8 (Moscow, 1952), 301.

3. J. R. Azrael, *Managerial Power and Soviet Politics* (Cambridge: Harvard University Press, 1966), 38–40, 213.

4. "Ideologicheskie osnovy ORESO," *Student*, no. 3 (October 1922): 38–39. On the émigré community's academic life see M. Raeff, *Russia Abroad: A Cultural History of the Russian Emigration 1919–1939* (New York: Oxford University Press, 1990), 59–71. On the situation in Prague, the community's "academic center," see S. P. Postnikov, ed., *Russkie v Prage, 1918–1928 gg.* (Prague, 1928), 69–99, 166–77; and J. H. Simpson, *Refugees: Preliminary Report of a Survey* (London: Royal Institute of International Affairs, 1938), 128–29.

5. F. F. Kubka to N. V. Ustrialov, 16 January 1922, *Raznye liudi*, 30.

6. R. C. Williams, *Culture in Exile: Russian Emigrés in Germany 1881–1941* (Ithaca: Cornell University Press, 1972), 273; "Protokol zasedaniia Parizhskoi Respublikansko-Demokraticheskoi gruppy Partii Narodnoi Svobody," 29 June 1922, TsGAOR, f. 7506, op. 1, d. 71, l. 421.

7. "Protokol zasedaniia Parizhskoi Respublikansko-Demokraticheskoi gruppy Partii Narodnoi Svobody," 8 June 1922, TsGAOR, f. 7506, op. 1, d. 71, ll. 339–40.

8. A. V. Bobrishchev-Pushkin to N. V. Ustrialov, 30 July 1922, *Smenovekhovtsy*, 65.

9. "Studentam, vekhi smenivshim," *Poslednie novosti*, 23 July 1922. On the organization see also "Protokol zasedaniia Parizhskoi Respublikansko-Demokraticheskoi gruppy Partii Narodnoi Svobody," 13 July 1922, TsGAOR, f. 7506, op. 1, d. 71, ll. 468–73.

10. "Studencheskaia zhizn,' " *Nakanune,* 17 November 1922; M. Glebov, " 'Pervye vekhi,' " *Proletarskoe studenchestvo,* no. 1 (April 1923): 127.

11. "Studencheskii s"ezd," *Poslednie novosti,* 11 November 1922; "Organizatsiia russkogo emigrantskogo studenchestva (za proshedshee vremia)," *Student,* no. 3 (October 1922): 24; "Polozhenie russkogo studenchestva v emigratsii," *Student,* no. 3 (October 1922): 59; L. K. Shkarenkov, *Agoniia beloi emigratsii,* 2d rev. ed. (Moscow: Mysl', 1986), 81; A. V. Bobrishchev-Pushkin, *Patrioty bez otechestva* (Leningrad: Kubuch, 1925), 136–38.

12. "Studencheskaia zhizn'," *Nakanune,* 20 September 1922.

13. On the conference see Iv. Savich, "Ocherednaia komediia," *Poslednie novosti,* 11 January 1923; "S"ezd smenovekhovskogo studenchestva," *Dni,* 29 December 1922; "Konferentsiia smenovekhovskogo studenchestva," *Dni,* 30 December 1922; "S"ezd smenovekhovskogo studenchestva," pts. 1, 2, *Dni,* 31 December 1922, 3 January 1923; Glebov, " 'Pervye vekhi.' "

14. Glebov, " 'Pervye vekhi,' " 127–29; "S"ezd smenovekhovskogo studenchestva," pts. 1, 2, *Dni,* 29 December 1922, 3 January 1923; Savich, "Ocherednaia komediia."

15. G. F. Barikhnovskii, *Ideino-politicheskii krakh beloemigratsii i razgrom vnutrennei kontr-revoliutsii (1921–1924)* (Leningrad: Izd-vo Leningradskogo universiteta, 1978), 130.

16. Savich, "Ocherednaia komediia"; Glebov, " 'Pervye vekhi,' " 127; "S"ezd smenovekhovskogo studenchestva," *Dni,* 3 January 1923.

17. "Obrazovanie Sovetskoi studencheskoi kolonii v Prage," *Nakanune,* 8 August 1923.

18. In any case, after that time the number of reports on such a tendency dropped sharply, and before long they disappeared altogether.

19. G. Rosenfeld, *Soujetrussland und Deutschland, 1917–1922* (Cologne: Pahl-Rugenstein, 1984), 197.

20. The most striking example is the account of the journalist V. V. Slavich, who under the pseudonym V. Patek wrote a pamphlet entitled *Ispoved' smenovekhovtsa,* in which he recalled his adventures as a member of the Bulgarian Union for Return to the Motherland (V. Patek, *Ispoved' smenovekhovtsa* [Sofia: Obzor, 1924]). See further Grigorii R., "Rabota smenovekhovtsev sredi kazachestva," *Dni,* 19 January 1923.

21. See, for example, H. von Rimscha, *Russland jenseits der Grenzen 1921–1926: Ein Beitrag zur russischen Nachkriegsgeschichte* (Jena: Verlag der Frommannschen Buchhandlung, 1927), 172–78; H. von Rimscha, "Probleme der russischen Emigration," *Wille und Weg* 4 (1 February 1929): 525–26; M. Agursky, *The Third Rome: National Bolshevism in the USSR* (Boulder, Colo.: Westview Press, 1987), 255–57; A. V. Kvakin, "Novovekhovstvo kak krizis beloi emigratsii" (Kandidatskaia dissertatsiia, Kalininskii gosudarstvennyi universitet, 1981), 125–33.

22. I. Lunchenkov, *Za chuzhie grekhi (kazaki i emigratsiia)* (Moscow: Zemlia i fabrika, 1925), 169.

23. Simpson, *Refugees,* p. 43; Shkarenkov, *Agoniia,* 85–86; V. V. Komin, *Krakh rossiiskoi kontr-revoliutsii za rubezhom* (Kalinin: Kalininskii gosudarstvennyi universitet, 1977), 31, 33–34; *Russkie v Gallipoli 1920–1921* (Berlin: Gutman, 1923), 494. How these groups of spontaneous repatriates were received in Russia remains unclear. At the

time, the émigré press reported arrests and executions, yet Soviet sources denied this. See, for example, "Vozvrashchenie na rodinu," *Poslednie novosti*, 25 March 1921; "Vozvrashchenie 'Reshid Pashi,'" *Poslednie novosti*, 20 April 1921; Shkarenkov, *Agoniia*, 86.

24. *BSE1*, 64:162, s.v. "Emigratsiia, belaia"; Komin, *Krakh rossiiskoi kontr-revoliutsii*, 35–36.

25. Simpson, *Refugees*, 172–73.

26. M. R. Marrus, *The Unwanted: European Refugees in the Twentieth Century* (New York: Oxford University Press, 1985), 88–91; Simpson, *Refugees*, 41, 45, 74–78.

27. Simpson, *Refugees*, 40–41.

28. G. I. Cherniavskii and D. Daskalov, "Sud'by russkoi beloemigratsii v Bolgarii," *Istoriia SSSR*, 1961, no. 1:112; Lunchenkov, *Za chuzhie grekhi*, 169–74; Patek, *Ispoved'*, 46–54; R. S., "Uezhaiushchie i ostaiushchiesia," *Poslednie novosti*, 8 November 1922.

29. Quoted in A. Bulatsel', *Na rodinu iz stana belykh* (Moscow: Gosizdat, 1924), 14.

30. See Bulatsel', *Na rodinu*, 14–16; Simpson, *Refugees*, 78; Patek, *Ispoved'*, 22–24; "Repatriatsiia," *Poslednie novosti*, 1 November 1922.

31. Bulatsel', *Na rodinu*, 16–17, 25–26; Shkarenkov, *Agoniia*, 86–88; Cherniavskii and Daskalov, "Sud'by," 111–15; N. Kazmin, "Emigrantskie gazety (Opyt obzora)," *Pechat' i revoliutsiia*, 1923, no. 4:71; I. Lezhnev, "Pis'mo prof. N. Ustrialovu," *Rossiia*, no. 9 (May–June 1923): 9–10.

32. V. Patek, *Ispoved'*, 85–86; Bulatsel', *Na rodinu*, 37–39. Patek insisted that all these men had been bought (83–84).

33. Bulatsel', *Na rodinu*, 39–42; Shkarenkov, *Agoniia*, 88–89; *Pochemu my vernulis' na Rodinu: Svidetel'stva reemigrantov* (Moscow: Progress, 1983), 35–38.

34. I. A. Slashchev, *Krym v 1920 g.: Otryvki iz vospominanii* (Moscow: Gosizdat, [1924]), 143; J. M. Meijer, ed., *The Trotsky Papers 1917–1922*, 2 vols. (The Hague: Mouton, 1971), 2:616–19. M. Agurskii asserts that these negotiations had started as early as the summer of 1920 (see Agursky, *Third Rome*, 198); it is, however, doubtful that this was so. In any case, it is impossible to reach such a conclusion on the basis of the document in *The Trotsky Papers* (p. 280) to which Agurskii refers. Agurskii may have more evidence to this effect, but, if he has, he does not mention it.

35. "Pribytie gen. Slashcheva i drugikh byvshikh Vrangelevskikh ofitserov v Sovetskoi Rossii: Pravitel'stvennoe soobshchenie," *Petrogradskaia pravda*, 25 November 1921; "Un ancien lieutenant de Wrangel invite les émigrés russes à se rallier aux soviets," *L'Humanité*, 25 November 1921; "K vozzvaniiu Slashcheva," *Novyi put'*, 24 November 1921.

36. Meijer, *Trotsky Papers*, 2:618; *EGV*, 550, s.v. "Slashchev, Iakov Aleksandrovich"; I. A. Slashchev, *Trebuiu suda obshchestva i glasnosti (Oborona i sdacha Kryma): Memuary i dokumenty* (Constantinople: Shul'man, 1921).

37. K. N. Sokolov, *Pravlenie gen. Denikina (Iz vospominanii)* (Sofia: Rossiisko-Bolgarskoe knigo-izdatel'stvo, 1921), 100–111; N. G. Dumova, *Kadetskaia kontrrevoliutsiia i ee razgrom (oktiabr' 1917–1920 gg.)* (Moscow: Nauka, 1982), 295; S., " 'Oba luchshe' (pis'mo iz Sofii)," *Poslednie novosti*, 7 August 1923.

38. K. Parchevskii, "Russkie bezhentsy v Bolgarii," *Russkie sborniki*, no. 2 (1921): 108.

39. E. D. Grimm, "Tri tsveta," *Russkie sborniki,* no. 2 (1921): 31–38. See also E. D. Grimm, *Kak bol'sheviki zakhvatili vlast' na Rusi* (Rostov na Donu: Narodnaia pol'za, 1919), 36.

40. Grimm's name first appeared on the masthead of *Novaia Rossiia* on 14 February 1923. See also S., " 'Oba luchshe' "; Patek, *Ispoved',* 100–105; E. Grimm, "Pro Domo," *Novaia Rossiia,* 4 March 1923.

41. E. D. Grimm, "O russofil'stve i russofobste v Bolgarii," in *Russkie v Bolgarii* (Sofia: Ob-vo Russko-Bolgarskaia druzhba, 1923), 20; Grimm, "Pro Domo".

42. See, for example, A. Kol'chugin, "Bez prava," *Novaia Rosiia,* 2 February 1923; A. Kol'chugin, "Boitsy i mirotvortsy," *Novaia Rossiia,* 4 March 1923; Gromoboi, "Iz emigrantskoi khrestomatii," *Novaia Rossiia,* 18 February 1923; Gromoboi, "O pravykh studentakh," *Novaia Rossiia,* 25 April 1923. In a letter to Ustrialov, Bobrishchev-Pushkin confirmed that he used the pseudonym A. Kol'chugin (see A. V. Bobrishchev-Pushkin to N. V. Ustrialov, 3 March 1923, *Smenovekhovtsy,* 80).

43. B. Mironov, "Germaniia na perevale," *Novaia Rossiia,* 27 April 1923.

44. A. Petrovskii, "V Rossii, na Rodine: Dve Rossii (ot nashego spetskora)," *Novaia Rossiia,* 28 March 1923.

45. Bulatsel', *Na rodinu,* 101–137; Lunchenkov, *Za chuzhie grekhi,* 189–90.

46. S. " 'Oba luchshe' "; Agursky, *Third Rome,* 255.

47. Simpson, *Refugees,* 78; Shkarenkov, *Agoniia,* 89; Komin, *Krakh rossiiskoi kontr-revoliutsii,* 36.

48. Grigorii R., "Rabota smenovekhovtsev"; "Protokol zasedaniia Parizhskoi gruppy Partii Narodnoi Svobody," 22 June 1922, TsGAOR, f. 7506, op. 1., d. 71, ll. 405–6.

49. Shkarenkov, *Agoniia,* 91. Shkarenkov indicates no source for his figure, which seems highly exaggerated and would have amounted to half the total number of Russian refugees in Czechoslovakia. If accurate, it would be inexplicable that no other source mentions it. In Simpson, *Refugees,* repatriation from Czechoslovakia is not even mentioned.

50. "Protokol," 29 June 1922 (see n. 6), ll. 429–33; "Protokol," 13 July 1922 (see n. 9), ll. 459–66.

51. Simpson, *Refugees,* 78. See in this connection also R. S., "Za chuzhoi spinoi," *Poslednie novosti,* 7 July 1923.

52. Savinkov was one of the founders of the Volunteer Army. During the Soviet-Polish War in the summer of 1920, he coordinated the Russian units that fought with the Poles against the Red Army. With the help of Western intelligence services, in the spring of 1921 he revived the so-called National Union for the Defense of Freedom and the Fatherland, the organization which in the summer of 1918 had staged a number of armed uprisings against the Bolsheviks. Apparently, Savinkov hoped to develop a network of mainly SR allies in Soviet Russia. However, due to the SRs' final suppression in Soviet Russia in the course of 1922, his efforts were in vain. On Savinkov see H. Shukman, ed., *The Blackwell Encyclopedia of the Russian Revolution* (Oxford: Blackwell, 1988), 373–74; *EGV,* 527, s.v. "Savinkov, Boris Viktorovich."

53. Shukman, *Blackwell Encyclopedia,* 374; *EGV,* 527, s.v. "Savinkov, Boris Viktorovich"; *Protsess Borisa Savinkova* (Berlin: Russkoe ekho, 1924), 117–24. On the Savinkov affair see also P. A. Arskii, ed., *Zagadka Savinkova: Sbornik statei* (Leningrad: Izdvo Gubkompoma, 1925).

54. *Protsess Borisa Savinkova,* 28–33, 107–16.

55. "Smenovekhovets s nevzorvavsheisia bomboi," *Pravda,* 13 September 1924. The text was issued as a separate pamphlet by the Kharkov Society for Assistance to the Young Leninist: B. V. Savinkov, *Pochemu ia priznal sovetskuiu vlast'* (Kharkov: Ob-vo sodeistviia iunomu lenintsu, 1924), and was included also in *Delo Borisa Savinkova,* 146–52.

56. "Ot redaktsii," in B. V. Savinkov, *Posmertnye stat'i i pis'ma* (Moscow: Ogonek, 1926), 3–5.

57. Rimscha, *Russland jenseits der Grenzen,* 181.

58. See in this connection B. Prianishnikov, *Nezrimaia pautina* (N.p.: B. Prianishnikov, 1979), 40–50; J. J. Dziak, *Chekisty: A History of the KGB* (Lexington, Mass.: Lexington Books, 1988), 45–47; on *Trest* see there 47–50. See further also G. Bailey, *The Conspirators* (New York: Harper, 1960); S. L. Voitsekhovskii, *Trest: Vospominaniia i dokumenty* (London, Ontario: Zaria, 1974); B. L. Dvinov, *Politics of the Russian Emigration* (Santa Monica, Calif.: B. L. Dvinov, 1955), 360–76; R. Gaucher, *L'opposition en U.R.S.S., 1917–1967* (Paris: Albin Michel, 1967), 99–121.

59. See M. Heller, "Krasin-Savinkov: Une rencontre secrète," *Cahiers du monde russe et soviétique* 26 (January–March 1985): 63–67.

60. Bobrishchev-Pushkin, *Patrioty,* 11–13.

61. N. V. Ustrialov to P. P. Suvchinskii, 25 December 1928, *Suvchinskii,* 45.

62. See, for example, Kvakin, "Novovekhovstvo kak krizis," 129; Iu. V. Mukhachev, *Ideino-politicheskoe bankrotstvo planov burzhuaznogo restavratorstva v SSSR* (Moscow: Mysl', 1982), 189; S. A. Fediukin, *Bor'ba kommunisticheskoi partii s burzhuaznoi ideologiei v pervye gody Nepa* (Moscow: Znanie, 1977), 121–33.

63. See, for example, the reaction to the departure of Gurovich and the student Gershun from the Berlin Democratic Group of the Party of People's Freedom: "Protokol," 22 June 1922 (see n. 48), l. 403. For a report on the reaction of ORESO members to the "changing signposts" of their chairman see "Studencheskii s"ezd" (see n. 11).

64. Kvakin, "Novovekhovstvo kak krizis," 134.

65. On these movements see R. H. Johnston, *New Mecca, New Babylon: Paris and the Russian Exiles, 1920–1945* (Kingston, Ont.: McGill-Queen's University Press, 1988), 90–97; G. P. Struve, *Russkaia literatura v izgnanii,* 2d rev. ed. (Paris: YMCA-Press, 1984), 222–31; Koons, "Histoire des doctrines," 183–92; B. Waignein, "Het tijdschrift 'Novyj Grad' 1931–1939" (Licentiaatsthesis, Katholieke Universiteit Leuven, 1988), 14–16, 134–40; V. S. Varshavskii, *Nezamechennoe pokolenie* (New York: Izd-vo imeni Chekhova, 1956); M. Hagemeister, *Nikolaj Fedorov: Studien zu Leben, Werk und Wirkung* (Munich: Otto Sagner, 1989), 417–18, 443–57; M. Gorlin, "Die philosophisch-politischen Strömungen in der russischen Emigration," *Osteuropa* 8 (1932): 287–94; C. Andreyev, *Vlasov and the Russian Liberation Movement: Soviet Reality and Emigré Theories* (Cambridge: Cambridge University Press, 1987), 170–71, 180–93.

66. Struve, *Russkaia literatura,* 223.

67. Hagemeister, *Nikolaj Fedorov,* 417–18; Andreyev, *Vlasov,* 185–86.

68. Editorial introduction to Varshavskii, *Nezamechennoe pokolenie,* 9; Johnston, *New Mecca,* 92–93.

69. Hagemeister, *Nikolaj Fedorov,* 418; Johnston, *New Mecca,* 93–94; N. N. Bylov to N. V. Ustrialov, 20 March 1928, *Porevoliutsionery,* 3.

70. Hagemeister, *Nikolaj Fedorov,* 418–19; Struve, *Russkaia literatura,* 225. This was also the goal the *evraziitsy* set themselves. See O. Böss, *Die Lehre der Eurasier: Ein Beitrag zur russischen Ideeengeschichte des 20. Jahrhunderts* (Wiesbaden: Otto Harrasowitz, 1961), 82–83; N. V. Riasanovsky, "The Emergence of Eurasianism," *California Slavic Studies,* no. 4 (1967): 51; L. Luks, "Die Ideologie der Eurasier im zeitgeschichtlichen Zusammenhang," *Jahrbücher für Geschichte Osteuropas* 34 (1986): 387–88; Gorlin, "Philosophisch-politischen Strömungen," 285.

71. This was the case with the so-called *Mladorossy,* or Young Russians, an openly fascist group. In 1928 the *Mladorossy* launched the slogan "Tsar and Soviets," advocating both the return of the Romanov monarchy and the preservation of what they regarded the most valuable element of the new Russian regime, notably the soviets. They were convinced that such a "neo-monarchist" synthesis would bring about the final unification of Russian society into a close-knit and harmonic whole. On the *Mladorossy* see N. Hayes, "Kazem-Bek and the Young Russians' Revolution," *Slavic Review* 39 (June 1980): 255–68; Koons, "Histoire des doctrines," 187–92; Gorlin, "Philosophisch-politischen Strömungen," 287–89; Johnston, *New Mecca,* 93–94; R. Petrovich, *Mladorossy: Materialy k istorii smenovekhovskogo dvizheniia* (London, Ontario: Zaria, 1973); Andreyev, *Vlasov,* 181–82.

72. See, for example, L. B., *Natsional-maksimalizm i natsional-bol'shevizm* ([Nice]: Nitstskii kruzhok politicheskogo samoobrazovaniia, 1927), 14–15; *Zavtra,* no. 5 (1 January 1935), 2–3; N. B., "Tret'e reshenie," *Zavtra,* no. 7 (15 April 1935), 41; "V poriadke obsuzhdeniia (Ot redkollegii)," *Utverzhdeniia,* no. 3 (October 1932), 106.

73. The "Postrevolutionary Club" was founded in late 1932 by the group behind the journal *Utverzhdeniia* (Affirmations) (1931–1932), which counted among its members not only "sons" but also a number of "fathers," including N. A. Berdiaev and F. A. Stepun. They advocated an "irreconcilably revolutionary attitude" vis-à-vis the Soviet regime, yet were at the same time prepared to consider the regime as an important step forward toward more social justice. They were convinced that the Russian revolution was an event of worldwide importance, which had clearly shown that Russia had a universal mission in the spiritual, cultural, and social fields. In the *utverzhdentsy's* view, the October revolution had put forward a materialistic antithesis to the equally materialistic thesis of bourgeois capitalism; they regarded it the task of the postrevolutionary movements to further the process of coming to a fruitful synthesis between both, in which the spiritual principle would prevail (see Struve, *Russkaia literatura,* 223–26; Johnston, *New Mecca,* 95; Varshavskii, *Nezamechennoe pokolenie,* 44–51; "Ot redaktsii," *Utverzhdeniia,* no. 1 [February 1931], 3–8). On the Club's foundation and activities see "Otkrytie porevoliutsionnogo kluba," *Zavtra,* no. 1 (7 January 1933), 25–30; Iu. A. Shirinskii-Shikhmatov to N. V. Ustrialov, 12 January 1934, *Porevoliutsionery,* 17–20; "Porevoliutsionnyi klub," *Ezhemesiachnik porevoliutsionnogo kluba,* no. 1 (15 December 1935), 1–4. The club published three periodicals: *Zavtra,* which was primarily the organ of the younger members (seven issues between January 1933 and April 1935); *Ezhenedel'nik porevoliutsionnogo kluba,* which appeared from late October 1934 to May 1935; and the short-lived *Ezhemesiachnik porevoliutsionnogo kluba,* the only issue of which appeared on 15 December 1935 (see T. Ossorguine-Bakounine, comp., *L'émigration russe en Europe: Catalogue collectif des périodiques en lange russe, 1855–1940* [Paris: Institut d'Etudes slaves, 1976], 160–61, 166; Varshavskii, *Nezamechennoe pokolenie,* 46–47). The initiative for starting a correspondence with Ustrialov came from the side of the postrevolutionaries, yet Ustrialov was more than happy

with this contact (see Porevoliutsionnyi Klub to N. V. Ustrialov, 20 September 1933, *Porevoliutsionery*, 13; N. V. Ustrialov to Iu. A. Shirinskii-Shikhmatov, 14 October 1933, *Porevoliutsionery*, 14).

74. This had always been also Ustrialov's main objection against *evraziistvo*, which he regarded as ideologically more valuable than *smenovekhovstvo* (see N. V. Ustrialov, *Pod znakom revoliutsii* [Harbin: Russkaia mysl', 1925], 246; N. V. Ustrialov to P. P. Suvchinskii, 18 December 1928, *Suvchinskii*, 41–43; N. V. Ustrialov to A. V. Bobrishchev-Pushkin, 25 April 1922, *Smenovekhovtsy*, 44). In his correspondence with the Eurasian leader P. P. Suvchinskii, Ustrialov tried to convince Suvchinskii of the dangers of activism (see, for example, N. V. Ustrialov to P. P. Suvchinskii, 9 October 1928, *Suvchinskii*, 36–39). See also N. Ustrialov, "Moia perepiska s P. P. Suvchinskim," *Suvchinskii*, pp. i–iii.

75. N. V. Ustrialov, "Zarubezhnaia smena," *Utverzhdeniia*, no. 3 (October 1932): 112–13; N. V. Ustrialov to Iu. A. Shirinskii-Shikhmatov, 23 July 1934, *Porevoliutsionery*, 7.

76. Ustrialov, "Zarubezhnaia smena," 114.

77. N. B. "Tret'e reshenie," 42; G. P. Fedotov, "V plenu stikhii," *Novyi grad*, no. 4 (1932): 9.

78. See Andreyev, *Vlasov*, 189–93; B. Prianishnikoff, *Novopokolentsy* (Silver Spring, Maryland: n. p., 1986).

79. Iu. V. Kliuchnikov to N. V. Ustrialov, 13 July 1921, *Smenovekhovtsy*, 9; Ustrialov, *Pod znakom*, 40–42.

80. F. Kupferman, *Au pays des Soviets: Le voyage français en Union soviétique 1917–1939* (Paris: Gallimard-Julliard, 1979), 17–18.

81. See Williams, *Culture in Exile*, 364–69; L. Dupeux, *'Nationalbolschewismus' in Deutschland, 1919–1933: Kommunistische Strategie und konservative Dynamik* (Munich: C. H. Beck, 1985), 41–205.

82. A. V. Bobrishchev-Pushkin to N. V. Ustrialov, 10 June 1922, *Smenovekhovtsy*, 57.

83. Iu. V. Kliuchnikov to N. V. Ustrialov, 17 April 1922, *Smenovekhovtsy*, 39.

84. Ustrialov, Diary, 24 August 1925, *Smenovekhovtsy*, 112. Reportedly, Chicherin was an excellent pianist (see S. White, *The Origins of Detente: The Genoa Conference and Soviet-Western Relations, 1921–1922* [Cambridge: Cambridge University Press, 1985], 25). Afterwards, Kliuchnikov himself was forced to admit that his role in Genoa had been absolutely insignificant (see "Intelligentsiia i Sovetskaia vlast' [Beseda s redaktorom gazety 'Nakanune' Iu. V. Kliuchnikovym]," *Izvestiia*, 9 June 1922).

85. T. J. Uldricks, *Diplomacy and Ideology: the Origins of Soviet Foreign Relations 1917–1930* (London: Sage, 1979), 98–99, 106–7.

86. Uldricks, *Diplomacy*, 143–68, 189, 192–93.

87. "Vsegda vpered," *Nakanune*, 15 June 1924.

88. See K. Bozhenko, "Ob obshchestvennykh nastroeniiakh," *Nakanune*, 5 September 1922; K. E. Bailes, *Technology and Society under Lenin and Stalin: Origins of the Soviet Technical Intelligentsia, 1917–1941* (Princeton: Princeton University Press, 1978), 72.

89. N. V. Ustrialov to P. P. Suvchinskii, 30 January 1928, *Suvchinskii*, 30.

90. F. Kin, " 'Spetsy' (Opyt statisticheskogo obsledovaniia)," *Pravda*, 3 September 1922.

91. See, for example, Ia. M. Okunev, *'Smena vekh' v tserkvi* (Kharkov: Proletarii, 1923), 17; I. Stepanov, "O 'Smene vekh' v tserkvi i o nashikh zadachakh," *Kommunisticheskaia revoliutsiia,* no. 9–10 (1 September 1922): 10; O. L. Vainshtein, *Ocherki po istorii frantsuzskoi emigratsii v epokhu velikoi revoliutsii (1789–1796)* (Kharkov: Gosizdat Ukrainy, 1924), 6–7.

CHAPTER 8: *SMENOVEKHOVSTVO* AND THE BOLSHEVIKS

1. See in this connection C. Read, *Culture and Power in Revolutionary Russia: The Intelligentsia and the Transition from Tsarism to Communism* (London: Macmillan, 1990), 188–89, 201–3, 231–32.

2. M. Agursky, *The Third Rome: National Bolshevism in the USSR* (Boulder, Colo.: Westview Press, 1987), 259; M. Krichevskii, "Rossiia no 2 i Genuia," *Vestnik Narodnogo Komissariata inostrannykh del,* 1922, no. 4–5:62–65.

3. Iu. Steklov, "Ne nachalo li otrezvleniia? (K voprosu 'o tretei taktike')," *Izvestiia,* 17 August 1921.

4. Em. Iaroslavskii, " 'Patriotika,' " *Pravda,* 15 March 1921; A. Voronskii, "Vynuzhdennye priznaniia," *Pravda,* 6 April 1921.

5. P. D. Iakovlev-Dunin to N. V. Ustrialov, 26 May 1921, *Smenovekhovtsy,* 19.

6. S. A. Fediukin, *Bor'ba s burzhuaznoi ideologiei v usloviiakh perekhoda k Nepu* (Moscow: Nauka, 1977), 283.

7. Agursky, *Third Rome,* 292–93; Fediukin, *Bor'ba s burzhuaznoi ideologiei,* 301–3.

8. V. I. Lenin, *Polnoe sobranie sochinenii,* 5th ed., 55 vols. (Moscow: Gospolitizdat, 1958–1965), 45:93–94. On the discussion of the movement at the Eleventh Party Congress see also Agursky, *Third Rome,* 264–65.

9. *Odinnadtsatyi s"ezd,* 78. On Antonov-Ovseenko see *EGV,* 39, s.v. Antonov-Ovseenko, Vladimir Aleksandrovich; H. Shukman, ed., *The Blackwell Encyclopedia of the Russian Revolution* (Oxford: Blackwell, 1988), 299–300.

10. *Odinnadtsatyi s"ezd,* 73–75. On Skrypnik see there, 849.

11. *Odinnadtsatyi s"ezd,* 407–9; Agursky, *Third Rome,* 265.

12. E. H. Carr, *The Bolshevik Revolution 1917–1923,* 3 vols. (London: Macmillan, 1950–1953; Harmondsworth: Penguin Books, 1966), 3:422.

13. Fediukin, *Bor'ba s burzhuaznoi ideologiei,* 137–38.

14. A. Bubnov, "Vozrozhdenie burzhuaznoi ideologii i zadachi agitproraboty," *Pravda,* 27 July 1922. In 1923 the article was included in a collection by Bubnov entitled *Burzhuaznoe restavratorstvo na vtorom godu NEPa* (Petrograd: Priboi, 1923), 5–33.

15. Agursky, *Third Rome,* 293–94.

16. *KPSS v rezoliutsiiakh,* 2:393.

17. *KPSS v rezoliutsiiakh,* 2:390–91.

18. *KPSS v rezoliutsiiakh,* 2:394–95.

19. See L. G. Obichkina, "Iz istorii bor'by RKP(b) protiv antisovetskikh partii i techenii (1921–1923 gg.)," *Voprosy istorii KPSS,* 1969, no. 2:106–7.

20. See chap. 6, nn. 91–92.

21. Erde, " 'Rossiiskie' i 'zagranichnye,' " *Izvestiia,* 26 August 1922.

22. Erde, "Politicheskii obzor," *Izvestiia,* 31 October 1922.

23. G. Safarov, "Rossiia no 2 1/2," *Pravda,* 27 August 1922.

24. M. Furshchik, "K voprosu o vozrozhdenii burzhuaznoi ideologii," *Sibirskie ogni,* no. 5 (November–December 1922): 90, 95.

25. Obichkina, "Iz istorii bor'by," 107.

26. N. Meshcheriakov, "Mechty smenovekhovstva i ikh sud'ba," in *Na ideologicheskom fronte bor'by s kontr-revoliutsiei* (Moscow: Krasnaia nov', 1923), 97.

27. Meshcheriakov, "Mechty," 99–103.

28. *KPSS v rezoliutsiiakh,* 2:437; *Dvenadtsatyi s"ezd,* 45, 228, 595–96, 607, 614, 693; Agursky, *Third Rome,* 295–97.

29. *KPSS v rezoliutsiiakh,* 2:501.

30. *KPSS v rezoliutsiiakh,* 3:112.

31. In 1925, for example, this term was used on the pages of *Bol'shevik* with respect to the agronomist A. V. Chaianov (see Agursky, *Third Rome,* 293). On the change in Soviet policy vis-à-vis the private sector in 1923–1924 see A. M. Ball, *Russia's Last Capitalists: The Nepmen, 1921–1929* (Berkeley: University of California Press, 1990), 39–44.

32. Erde, "Konets smenovekhizma," *Izvestiia,* 25 June 1924.

33. The article appeared first in the *Novosti zhizni* of 10 December 1922. It was reprinted in *Rossiia,* no. 9 (May–June 1923): 14–17, and in N. V. Ustrialov, *Pod znakom revoliutsii* (Harbin: Russkaia mysl', 1925), 114–20. The quoted passage is there on p. 115.

34. M. Agurskii, ed., "Perepiska I. Lezhneva i N. Ustrialova," *Slavica Hierosolymitana,* no. 5–6 (1981): 560.

35. Agurskii, "Perepiska," 562; A. Bubnov, "Tri lozunga," *Pravda,* 15 July 1923; A. Bryntsev, "Tozhe askety," *Dni,* 28 July 1923.

36. E. L. Mindlin, *Neobyknovennye sobesedniki: Kniga vospominanii* (Moscow: Sovetskii pisatel', 1968), 141–142; "Russkaia zhizn': Novosti dnia," *Nakanune,* 29 August 1923; A. Bobrishchev-Pushkin, "Vpechatleniia (pis'mo iz Rossii)," *Nakanune,* 28 February 1924; A. Bobrishchev-Pushkin, "Zapiski," *Nakanune,* 1 May 1924.

37. Mindlin, *Neobyknovennye sobesedniki,* 142.

38. Bobrishchev-Pushkin, "Zapiski."

39. Erde, "Konets smenovekhizma."

40. N. V. Ustrialov, Diary, 24 August 1925, *Smenovekhovtsy,* 113. See also Fediukin, *Bor'ba s burzhuaznoi ideologiei,* 309. Ustrialov's visit to Moscow provoked a very hostile article on *smenovekhovstvo* in *Planovoe khoziaistvo,* which called for a "protracted mass campaign of unmasking and explanation" (see Arslan, "Dvoinaia bukhgalteriia kommunoidov," *Planovoe khoziaistvo,* 1926, no. 6:223).

41. See G. Zinov'ev, *Filosofiia epokhi* (Leningrad: Priboi, 1925); G. Zinov'ev, *Leninizm,* 2d ed. (Leningrad: Gosizdat, 1926), 196–99. I am referring to the second edition of Zinov'ev's *Leninizm;* the first edition, which appeared in late 1925, was unavailable to me. On Zinov'ev's attack see also E. H. Carr, *Socialism in One Country 1924–1926,* vol. 1 (London: Macmillan, 1958): 300–5.

42. N. I. Bukharin, *Tsezarizm pod maskoi revoliutsii: Po povodu knigi N. Ustrialova 'Pod znakom revoliutsii'* (Moscow: Pravda, 1925), especially 14–19, 34–35, 39–45. See also Carr, *Socialism,* 309–10.

43. Behind the scenes, however, Stalin was involved in organizing the response to Zinov'ev's attacks (see Carr, *Socialism,* 302).

44. I. V. Stalin, *Sochineniia,* 13 vols. (Moscow: Gosudarstvennoe izd-vo politicheskoi literatury, 1946–1955), 7:341–42.

45. Agurskii, "Perepiska," 553; Agursky, *Third Rome,* 314–15. On Lezhnev's arrest and expulsion see chap. 2, n. 185.

46. Agursky, *Third Rome,* 332.

47. Agursky, *Third Rome,* 333. Stalin's answer to Kamenev's accusation is in Stalin, *Sochineniia,* 9:69–74. Stalin reminded Kamenev, who had reproached him for being supported by Ustrialov, that Ustrialov had even more words of praise for Lenin (p. 71).

48. See G. Zinov'ev, "Manifest kulatskoi partii," *Bol'shevik,* no. 13 (1927): 33–47; G. Safarov, "Nastuplenie kapitala v sibirskoi derevne," *Bol'shevik,* no. 15–16 (1927): 90–99. See also J. Hughes, *Stalin, Siberia and the Crisis of the New Economic Policy* (Cambridge: Cambridge University Press, 1991), 87.

49. *Piatnadtsatyi s"ezd,* 2:287.

50. *KPSS v rezoliutsiiakh,* 4:19; *Piatnadtsatyi s"ezd,* 2:1433, 1:70–71.

51. A. Zaitsev, *Ob Ustrialove, 'neo NEPe' i zhertvakh ustrialovshchiny* (Moscow: Gosizdat, 1928), 11, 65–99.

52. N. V. Ustrialov, *Hic Rohdus [sic], hic salta!* (Harbin, 1929), 6.

53. *Shestnadtsatyi s"ezd,* 319. At the congress Ustrialov was misquoted, as though he had written: "Indeed, as long as Bukharin speaks, the *smenovekhovtsy* can keep silent."

54. Shukman, *Blackwell Encyclopedia,* 313.

55. Carr, *Socialism,* 59.

56. Carr, *Socialism,* 7.

57. Agursky, *Third Rome,* 211, 247, 299, 311–12.

58. Agursky, *Third Rome,* 299, 312, 314–15.

59. Agurskii, "Perepiska," 587, 549–50.

60. Zinov'ev, *Filosofiia epokhi,* 23. In 1959 the Soviet historian I. Ia. Trifonov even seized upon this passage to demonstrate Zinov'ev's absolute corruptness as a supporter of *smenovekhovstvo* (I. Ia. Trifonov, "Iz istorii bor'by kommunisticheskoi partii protiv smenovekhovstva," *Istoriia SSSR,* 1959, no. 3:80).

61. Agursky, *Third Rome,* 305.

62. M. Agurskii, *Ideologiia natsional-bol'shevizma* (Paris: YMCA-Press, 1980), 204.

63. A. Meerovich, "V Narkomindele, 1922–1939: Interv'iu s E. A. Gnezdinym," *Pamiat': Istoricheskii sbornik,* no. 5 (1982): 358.

64. G. P. Struve, *Russkaia literatura v izgnanii,* 2d rev. ed. (Paris: YMCA-Press, 1984), 39.

65. I. B. Diushen, interview with author, Moscow, 25 September 1989.

66. V. A. Osipov, conversation with author, Moscow, September 1989.

67. TsGALI, f. 675, op. 2, d. 499, ll. 5, 28.

68. V. A. Osipov, "Vozniknovenie smenovekhovstva i sozdanie gazety 'Nakanune'" (Avtoreferat, I.N.I.O.N., Moscow), 36.

69. Iu. M. Steklov, ed., *Sovetskaia demokratiia: Sbornik statei* (Moscow: izdanie zhurnala 'Sovetskoe stroitel'stvo,' 1929). Potekhin's contribution was entitled "Zhenshchina na sovetskoi rabote" (pp. 60–72).

70. S. Fitzpatrick, ed., *Cultural Revolution in Russia, 1928–1931* (Bloomington: Indiana University Press, 1984), 8–9, 68; Read, *Culture and Power,* 186–87.

71. See in this regard Fitzpatrick, *Cultural Revolution.*

72. On the "Shakhty" trial see M. Geller and A. Nekrich, *Utopiia u vlasti: Istoriia Sovetskogo Soiuza s 1917 goda do nashikh dnei* (London: Overseas Publications Interchange, 1982), 1:219–21.

73. Fitzpatrick, *Cultural Revolution,* 21–23.

74. On the *"Prompartiia"* trial see Geller and Nekrich, *Utopiia,* 241–42.

75. R. Katanian, "Predshestvenniki vreditel'stva. 1: Smena vekh," *Krasnaia nov',* 1930, no. 1:121, 115.

76. Katanian, "Predshestvenniki," 118–19.

77. "Pis'mo S. S. Luk'ianova v redaktsiiu Moskovskikh 'Izvestii,' " 24 March 1931, *Smenovekhovtsy,* 123–25; printed in *Izvestiia* 91 (1931).

78. N. V. Ustrialov to editor of *Izvestiia,* 21 April 1931, *Smenovekhovtsy,* 125–26.

79. Fitzpatrick, *Cultural Revolution,* 34–36.

80. Osipov, "Vozniknovenie smenovekhovstva," 36.

81. Osipov, Vozniknovenie smenovekhovstva," 34–36; M. Chudakova, *Zhizneopisanie Mikhaila Bulgakova,* 2d enl. ed. (Moscow: Kniga, 1988), 609.

82. Osipov, "Vozniknovenie smenovekhovstva," 34; I. B. Diushen, interview with author, Moscow, 25 September 1989.

83. A. Khar'kovskii, "Chakhotinskaia odisseia," *Ogonek,* 1974, no. 8:7.

Conclusion

1. *Vekhi: Sbornik statei o russkoi intelligentsii* (Moscow: V. M. Sablin, 1909; Frankfurt am Main: Posev, 1967), 79–80.

2. *Vekhi,* 193.

3. *Belyi Omsk,* 105–6. See also N. V. Ustrialov, *Pod znakom revoliutsii* (Harbin: Russkaia mysl', 1925), 69; N. V. Ustrialov to P. P. Suvchinskii, 19 October 1928, *Suvchinskii,* 36–37; N. V. Ustrialov to A. A. Kotel'nikov, 13 February 1931, *Raznye liudi,* 194–95; N. V. Ustrialov to S. V. Dmitrievskii, 5 October 1932, *Raznye liudi,* 200–1.

4. G. N. Dikii to N. V. Ustrialov, 10 May 1930, *Dikii,* 31. The reference is to B. V. Kistiakovskii, "V zashchitu prava," *Vekhi,* 125–56.

5. See in this connection J. E. Zimmerman, "Russian Liberal Theory, 1900–1917," *Canadian-American Slavic Studies* 14 (Spring 1980): 10–13; T. Emmons, *The Formation of Political Parties and the First National Elections in Russia* (Cambridge: Harvard University Pres, 1983), 90.

Bibliography

PRIMARY SOURCES

Archives

Amsterdam. Internationaal Instituut voor Sociale Geschiedenis:
    L. B. Krasin Archief
    M. A. Krol' Archief
    PSR Archief
Moscow. Russkii Gosudarstvennyi Arkhiv Literatury i Iskusstva (formerly Tsentral'nyi Gosudarstvennyi Arkhiv Literatury i Iskusstva [TsGALI]):
    f. 108. I. M. Vasilevskii
    f. 484. Skitalets [St. G. Petrov]
    f. 629. Izdatel'stvo "Academia"
    f. 675. Soiuz dramaticheskikh i muzykal'nykh pisatelei
    f. 878. A. I. Iuzhin
    f. 2252. I. G. Lezhnev
    f. 2567. Iu. G. Oksman.
Moscow. Gosudarstvennyi Arkhiv Russkoi Federatsii (formerly Tsentral'nyi Gosudarstvennyi Arkhiv Oktiabr'skoi Revoliutsii [TsGAOR]):
    f. 176. Sovet Ministrov Rossiiskogo pravitel'stva (Kolchaka)
    f. 579. P. N. Miliukov
    f. 5783. P. N. Savitskii
    f. 5818. M. M. Vinaver
    f. 5911. K. A. Chkheidze
    f. 7506. Tsentral'nyi komitet partii "Narodnoi Svobody"
New York. Bakhmeteff Archive, Columbia University:
    S. V. Panina collection. Box 13. "Civil War. Kadet Conferences in Omsk, November 1918 and May 1919"
    P. N. Miliukov collection
Paris. Archives Nationales: Archives de la Direction des Renseignements généraux du ministère de l'Intérieur:
    fol. F$_7$ 13.489. "Notes de correspondants anonymes dites 'Notes russes' 1920"
    fol. F$_7$ 13.490. "Notes de correspondants anonymes dites 'Notes russes' 1921"
    fol. F$_7$ 13.491. "Notes de correspondants anonymes dites 'Notes russes' 1922"

Prague. Literární archiv Národního muzea:*
  Fedoroviana Pragensia. IV: N. V. Ustrialov:
    "Moia perepiska s G. N. Dikim"
    "Moia perepiska s I. G. Lezhnevym"
    "Moia perepiska s 'Porevoliutsionerami' "
    "Moia perepiska s raznymi liud'mi"
    "Moia perepiska so smenovekhovtsami"
    "Chlam Dum: Iunost' (1910–1912), Na rubezhe (1913–1916), Revoliut-
      siia (1917–1918), Belyi Omsk (1919)"
    "Byloe"
Stanford, California. Hoover Institution Archives:
  S. Botkine collection
  Constitutional Democratic Party archive
  G. K. Guins. "Collection of clippings from the Russian newspapers in the Far
    East, covering politicial events of 1920–1923; articles by G. K. Guins and
    others"
  V. A. Maklakov collection
  A. Markov collection. "Entsiklopediia belogo dvizheniia: vozhdi, partizany,
    fronty, pokhody i narodnye vosstaniia protiv sovetov v Rossii"
  S. P. Mel'gunov collection
  B. Nicolaevsky collection. Series 143. Box 211. "Dokumenty organizatsii 'Mir i
    trud' Berlin, 1920–1921 gg."
  P. B. Struve collection
  N. V. Ustrialov collection:
    "Moia perepiska s G. N. Dikim"
    "Moia perepiska s I. G. Lezhnevym"
    "Moia perepiska s 'Porevoliutsionerami' "
    "Moia perepiska s raznymi liud'mi"
    "Moia perepiska so smenovekhovtsami"
    "Belyi Omsk (1919–1934)"

Newspapers and Journals

Al'manakh russkaia zhizn', Harbin, 1922–1923
Arkhiv russkoi revoliutsii, Berlin, 1921–1937
Belyi arkhiv, Paris, 1926–1928
Beseda, Berlin, 1923–1925
Dal'nevostochnoe obozrenie, Vladivostok, 1919–1920
Dni, Berlin, 1922–1923
Ekonomist, Petrograd, 1921–1922
L'Ere nouvelle, Paris, 1920–1922
Evraziia, Clamart, 1928–1929
Evraziiskaia khronika, Paris, 1925–1928
Ezhenedel'nik porevoliutsionnogo kluba, Issy-les-Moulineaux, 1934–1935

---

*These holdings were not available to me but are mentioned here for the sake of completeness.

Golos Rossii, Berlin, 1920–1921
L'Humanité, Paris, 1921–1922
L'Information, Paris, 1920–1922
Izvestiia, Moscow, 1920–1924
Krasnaia gazeta, Petrograd, 1920–1922
Krasnaia nov', Moscow, 1921–1925
Kul'tura i zhizn', Moscow, 1922
Letopis' Doma literatorov, Petrograd, 1921–1922
Literaturnye zapiski, Petrograd, 1922
Mezhdunarodnaia zhizn', Moscow, 1920–1930
Na chuzhoi storone, Berlin, Prague, 1923–1925
Nakanune, Berlin, 1922–1924
Nakanune, Moscow, 1918
Nash soiuz, Paris, 1926–1928
Neue Kulturkorrespondenz, Berlin, 1923
The New Russia, London, 1920
Novaia Rossiia, Petrograd, 1922, Moscow, 1926
Novaia Rossiia, Sofia, 1922–1923
Novaia russkaia kniga, Berlin, 1922–1923
Novoe vremia, Belgrade, 1921
Novye zaprosy, Prague, 1921
Novyi mir, Berlin, 1921–1922
Novyi put', Riga, 1921–1922
Obshchee delo, Paris, 1920–1922
L'Oeuvre, Paris, 1921–1922
Okno, Harbin, 1920
Parizhskii vestnik, Paris, 1925–1926
Pechat' i revoliutsiia, Moscow, 1921–1925
Le Petit Journal, Paris, 1921–1922
Petrogradskaia pravda, Petrograd, 1920–1922
Poslednie novosti, Paris, 1920–1925
Pravda, Moscow, 1920–1924
Pravitel'stvennyi vestnik, Omsk, 1919
Problemy velikoi Rossii, Moscow, 1916
Proletarskoe studenchestvo, Moscow, 1923
Put', Helsinki, 1921–1922
Revoliutsionnaia Rossiia, Berlin, 1920–1922
Rossiia, Moscow, 1922–1925
Rul', Berlin, 1920–1922
Russkaia kniga, Berlin, 1921
Russkaia mysl', Moscow, Sofia, Prague, Berlin, 1917–1918, 1921–1923
Russkie sborniki, Sofia, 1920–1921
Russkii ekonomist, Berlin, 1922–1923
Russkii kolokol, Berlin, 1927–1930
Russkoe delo, Omsk-Irkutsk, 1919
Russkoe slovo, Moscow, 1917–1918

Sibirskaia rech', Omsk, 1919
Sibirskie ogni, Novonikolaevsk, 1922–1925
Slavianskaia zaria, Prague, 1919–1920
Smena vekh, Paris, 1921–1922
Sotsialisticheskii vestnik, Berlin, 1920–1925
Sovetskoe stroitel'stvo, Moscow, 1926–1930
Sovremennye zapiski, Paris, 1920–1940
Spravochnik Petrogradskogo agitatora, Petrograd, 1921
Student, Prague, 1921–1922
Sungariiskie vechera, Harbin, 1923
Svoboda Rossii, Riga, 1919–1920
Svobodnaia Rosiia, Riga, 1919
Svobodnyi krai, Irkutsk, 1919
Svobodnaia Sibir', Krasnoiarsk, 1919
Utro Rossii, Moscow, 1917–1918
Utverzhdeniia, Paris, 1931–1932
Vestnik literatury, Petrograd, 1919–1922
Vestnik Man'chzhurii, Harbin, 1919, 1925–1927
Vestnik Narodnogo Komissariata po inostrannym delam, Moscow, 1922
Voina i mir, Berlin, 1922–1924
Volia Rossii, Prague, 1920–1925
Vysshaia shkola v Kharbine: Izvestiia Iuridicheskogo fakul'teta, Harbin, 1925–1929
Zaria, Berlin, 1922–1925
Zaria Rossii, Moscow, 1918
Zavtra, Paris, 1933–1935
Zhizn', Berlin, 1920
Zhizn' natsional'nostei, Moscow, 1921–1922
Zveno, Paris, 1923

Books and Essays

A. K. "O 'Smene vekh.' " *Vestnik literatury*, 1921, no. 12:1.
A. R. " 'Razdavite gadinu!' (na doklade prof. Luk'ianova)." *Obshchee delo*, 1 March 1921.
A. V. "Mirit'sia li s bol'shevikami?" *Poslednie novosti*, 22 February 1921.
Adrianov, S. A. "Dobro pozhalovat'." *Put'*, 2 December 1921.
———. "Tret'ia Rossiia (Ne ozhivet ashche ne umret)." *Novaia Rossiia*, no. 1 (March 1922): 4–13.
Agurskii, M., ed. "Perepiska I. Lezhneva i N. Ustrialova." *Slavica Hierosolymitana*, no. 5–6 (1981): 543–89.
Al. P-o. "Novye veianiia (Doklad prof. Luk'ianova)." *Poslednie novosti*, 15 February 1921.
Aleksandrov, Iv. G. "Russkaia intelligentsiia i ee sovremennye zadachi." *Rossiia*, no. 9 (May–June 1923): 17–19.
Alekseev, N. N. "Otpravnye tochki nashei politiki." *Evraziia*, no. 1 (24 November 1928): 3–4.

"Un ancient lieutenant de Wrangel invite les émigrés russes à se rallier aux Soviets." *L'Humanité*, 25 November 1921.

Arsen'ev, D. "Otryvki iz dnevnika 'Smenovekhovtsa.'" *Proletarskoe studenchestvo*, no. 1 (April 1923): 35–38.

Arskii, P. A., ed. *Zagadka Savinkova: Sbornik statei*. Leningrad: Izd-vo Gubkompoma, 1925.

Arslan. "Dvoinaia bukhgalteriia kommunoidov." *Planovoe khoziaistvo*, 1926, no. 6:215–23.

Avksent'ev, N. D. "Patriotica." *Sovremennye zapiski*, no. 1 (1920): 125–35.

B-oi, Sergei. "Formy razvitiia burzhuaznoi ideologii v usloviiakh Nepa." In *Na ideologicheskom fronte bor'by s kontrrevoliutsiei*, 63–84. Moscow: Krasnaia nov', 1923.

Belov, V. *Belaia pechat': ee ideologiia, rol', znachenie i deiatel'nost' (Materialy dlia budushchego istorika)*. Petrograd: Gosizdat, 1922.

———. *Po novym vekham*. Revel': Novaia zemlia, 1922.

———. *Beloe pokhmel'e: Russkaia emigratsiia na rasput'e (Opyt issledovaniia psikhologii, nastroenii i bytovykh uslovii russkoi emigratsii v nashe vremia)*. Moscow: Gosizdat, 1923.

Bergman, G. "Diktatura proletariata, Nep, intelligentsiia (Po povodu nekotorykh vystuplenii prof. Kliuchnikova)." *Pravda*, 8 July 1922.

———. "Priskorbnye zabluzhdeniia prof. Kliuchnikova." *Izvestiia*, 18 August 1922.

Bernshtein, L. " 'Novo-vekhovtsy.' " *Obshchee delo*, 15 January 1922.

Blok, A. A. *Rossiia i intelligentsiia: Sbornik statei (1907–1918)*. Moscow: Revoliutsionnyi sotsializm, 1918.

———. "[Mozhet li intelligentsiia rabotat' s bol'shevikami?]." In A. A. Blok, *Sobranie sochinenii v 6 tomakh*. Vol. 4, *Ocherki, Stat'i, Rechi, 1905–1921*, 228. Leningrad: Khudozhestvennaia literatura, 1982.

Bobrishchev-Pushkin, A. V. "Novaia vera." *Spravochnik Petrogradskogo agitatora*, no. 12–13 (1 December 1921): 20–59.

——— [Nekommunist, pseud.]. "Demokraticheskie retsepty." *Al'manakh russkaia zhizn'*, no. 3 (October 1922): 37–39.

———. "Petrogradskie kritiki 'Smeny vekh.'" *Al'manakh russkaia zhizn'*, no. 3 (October 1922): 13–15.

———. *Patrioty bez otechestva*. Leningrad: Kubuch, 1925.

———. *Voina bez perchatok*. Leningrad: Kubuch, 1925.

Borisov, Iu. " 'Smena vekh.' " *Zhizn' natsional'nostei*, 1921, no. 30:2–3.

Borisov, S. "Na novom puti." *Novyi mir*, 16 October 1921, 1.

Bozhenko, K. "Rubka vekh." *Vestnik literatury*, 1922, no. 1:3–4.

Brusilov, A. A. *Moi vospominaniia*. Moscow: Voenizdat, 1963.

Bryntsev, S. "Perekrashivaiutsia." *Dni*, 30 June 1923.

Bubnov, A. "Vozrozhdenie burzhuaznoi ideologii i zadachi agitpraproty." *Pravda*, 27 July 1922.

———. *Burzhuaznoe restavratorstvo na vtorom godu NEPa*. Petrograd: Priboi, 1923.

Bukharin, N. I. *Proletarskaia revoliutsiia i kul'tura*. Moscow: Priboi, 1923.

———. *Tsezarizm pod maskoi revoliutsii: Po povodu knigi N. Ustrialova 'Pod znakom revoliutsii'*. Moscow: Pravda, 1925.

Bulatsel', A. *Na rodinu iz stana belykh*. Moscow: Gosizdat, 1924.

Bystrianskii, V. *Kontr-revoliutsiia i ee vozhdi.* Moscow: Gosizdat, 1921.

————. " 'Smena vekh' o mirovoi revoliutsii." *Petrogradskaia pravda,* 20 November 1921.

————. "Intelligentsiia i Sovetskaia vlast'." *Petrogradskaia pravda,* 22 November 1921.

————. "Na novykh pozitsiiakh." *Petrogradskaia pravda,* 11 December 1921.

————. "O liubvi k otechestvu v Sovetskoi Rossii." *Petrogradskaia pravda,* 25 January 1922.

Chakhotin, S. S. *Organizatsiia: printsipy i metody v proizvodstve, torgovle, administratsii i politike.* Berlin: Opyt, 1923.

————. *Evropeiskaia literatura po N.O.T..* Moscow: NKRKI SSSR, 1924.

————. *Organizatsiia: printsipy i metody v proizvodstve, torgovle, administratsii i politike.* 2d ed. Leningrad: Gosizdat, 1925.

[————] Tchakhotine, S. S. *Organisation rationelle de la recherche scientifique.* Paris: Hermann, 1938.

[————] Tchakhotine, S. S. *Le viol des foules par la propagande politique.* Paris: Gallimard, 1939.

Chernov, V. "Paralleli i kontrasty (mysli o russkom termidore)." *Volia Rossii,* 1922, no. 1:9–12.

————. " 'Ottsy' i 'deti.' " *Volia Rossii,* 1922, no. 5:5–9.

————. "Staraia i novaia burzhuaziia." *Volia Rossii,* 1922, no. 13:3–9.

Chetyrnadtsatyi s"ezd VKP(b), 18–31 dekabria 1925 g.: Stenograficheskii otchet. Moscow: Gosizdat, 1926.

Danilov, P. "Sharlatany." *Obshchee delo,* 14 November 1921.

Delo Borisa Savinkova. Moscow: Gosizdat, [1924].

Desiatyi s"ezd RKP(b), mart 1921 goda: Stenograficheskii otchet. Moscow: Gospolitizdat, 1963.

D'iakonov, L. P., comp. *Vyezd za granitsu i v"ezd v SSSR: Prakticheskoe rukovodstvo dlia grazhdan SSSR, emigrantov i reemigrantov i inostrantsev.* Moscow: Glavnoe upravlenie kommunal'nogo khoziaistva NKVD, 1925.

"Disput o 'Smene vekh.' " *Izvestiia,* 11 July 1922.

Diushen, B. V. *Osnovy sovremennoi aviatsii.* Moscow: Ogonek, 1931.

————. *Sotsialisticheskii zakaz izobretateliam na transporte.* Moscow: Ogiz-Gostransizdat, 1931.

————. *Sputnik izobretatelia.* Moscow: Zhurnal'no-gazetnoe ob"edinenie, 1931.

"Dopolnenie k zametke 'Vekhi' i 'Smena vekh.' " *Russkaia mysl',* 1922, no. 4:224.

Dutsman, V. A., comp. *Obzor inostrannoi i russkoi zarubezhnoi pressy.* Moscow: Razvedyvatel'noe upravlenie shtaba RKKA, 1922.

Dvenadtsatyi s"ezd RKP(b), 17–25 aprelia 1923 goda: Stenograficheskii otchet. Moscow: Gospolitizdat, 1968.

Efimov, R. " 'Vneklassovyi' professor I. G. Aleksandrov." *Planovoe khoziaistvo,* 1925, no. 1:263–65.

Eikalovich, igum. G., ed. "N. V. Ustrialov: Iz pis'ma." *Novyi zhurnal,* no. 164 (1986): 161–66.

"Emigranty u Bogomolova." *Novyi zhurnal,* no. 100 (1970): 269–79.

Erde. "Russkaia emigratsiia o genuezskoi konferentsii." *Izvestiia,* 14 April 1922.

————. "Russkaia intelligentsiia, emigratsiia i 'Smena vekh.' " *Izvestiia,* 29 June 1922.

————. " 'Rossiiskie' i 'zagranichnye.' " *Izvestiia*, 26 August 1922.

————. "Konets smenovekhizma." *Izvestiia*, 25 June 1924.

Fedotov, G. P. "V plenu stikhii." *Novyi grad*, no. 4 (1932): 8–20.

Fleishman, L.; Kh'iuz, R; and Raevskaia-Kh'iuz, O., eds. *Russkii Berlin 1921–1923: Po materialam arkhiva B. I. Nikolaevskogo v Guverovskom institute.* Paris: YMCA-Press, 1983.

Furshchik, M. "K voprosu o vozrozhdenii burzhuaznoi ideologii." *Sibirskie ogni*, no. 5 (November–December 1922): 84–101.

Gershenzon, M. O., and Ivanov, V. I. *Perepiska iz dvukh uglov.* Moscow: Ogon'ki, 1922.

Gessen, I. V. *Gody izgnaniia: Zhiznennyi otchet.* Paris: YMCA-Press, 1979.

Gimel'farb, B. "Kritika i bibliografiia: Prof. Iu. V. Kliuchnikov, Na velikom istoricheskom pereput'i." *Izvestiia*, 10 June 1922.

Gins, G. K. *Sibir', soiuzniki i Kolchak: Povorotnyi moment russkoi istorii 1918–1920 gg.* 2 vols. Peking: Tipo-Litografiia Russkoi dukhovnoi missii, 1921.

————. " 'Smena vekh.' " Parts 1–3. *Russkii golos*, 12, 23, 26 April 1922.

Glebov, M. " 'Pervye vekhi.' " *Proletarskoe studenchestvo*, no. 1 (April 1923): 123–29.

Gol'man, M. "Smenovekhovskie illiuzii (Po povodu 'Osnov khoziaistvennogo raionirovaniia SSSR' prof. I. G. Aleksandrova)." *Bol'shevik*, no. 5–6 (1925): 115–25.

"Gor'kii o bol'shevikakh i intelligentsii." *Poslednie novosti*, 23 September 1922.

Gorovtsev, A. M. " 'Smene vekh': Skhema lektsii, chitannoi avtorom v Parizhe." In *'Skrepa vekh': Vtoroi vypusk politicheskogo zhurnala-al'manakha 'Tribuny,'* 13–17. Paris, [1922].

Got'e, Iu. V. *Time of Troubles: The Diary of Iurii Vladimirovich Got'e, Moscow, July 8, 1917 to July 23, 1922.* Translated and edited by T. Emmons. London: Tauris, 1988.

Gredeskul, N. A. *Rossiia i ee narody: 'Velikaia' Rossiia, kak programma razresheniia natsional'nogo voprosa v Rossii.* Petrograd: Samoobrazovanie, 1916.

————. "Die Krise in der Intelligenz." *Russische Korrespondenz*, no. 14–16 (October 1920): 929–32.

————. " 'Smena vekh.' " *Izvestiia*, 11 November 1921.

————. *Rossiia prezhde i teper'.* Moscow: Gosizdat, 1926.

"Gredeskul zovet intelligentsiiu." *Obshchee delo*, 13 January 1921.

Grigorii R. "Rabota smenovekhovtsev sredi kazachestva." *Dni*, 19 January 1923.

Grimm, E. D. *Kak bol'sheviki zakhvatili vlast' na Rusi.* Rostov na Donu: Narodnaia pol'za, 1919.

————. "Tri tsveta." *Russkie sborniki*, no. 2 (1921): 19–39.

————. "O russofil'stve i russofobste v Bolgarii." In *Russkie v Bolgarii*, 13–20. Sofia: Ob-vo Russko-Bolgarskaia druzhba, 1923.

Guber, P. "Nakazannaia oprometchivost'." *Literaturnye zapiski*, no. 2 (23 June 1922): 6–7.

Gul', R. B. *V rasseian'i sushchie: Povest' iz zhizni emigratsii 1920–1921.* Berlin: Manfred, 1923.

————. *Ia unes Rossiiu: Apologiia emigratsii.* Vol. 1, *Rossiia v Germanii.* New York: Most, 1984.

Gurovich, A. "Vysshii Sovet Narodnogo Khoziaistva: Iz vpetchatlenii goda sluzhby." *Arkhiv russkoi revoliutsii*, no. 6 (1922): 304–31.

Gurovich, [A.] I. [sic]. Zapiski emigranta. Petrograd: 'Petrograd', 1923.

Herriot, E. La Russie nouvelle. Paris: Ferenczi, 1922.

I. L. "Disput o 'Smene vekh.' " Parts 1–7. Put', 8, 10, 12, 14–17 December 1921.

Ia. L. "Besedy s intelligentsiei Rossii vnutrennei." Belyi arkhiv, no. 3–4 (1928): 261–68.

Iablonovskii, A. "Sem' obrazovannykh muzhchin." Obshchee delo, 17 September 1921.

———. " 'Podkidyshi.' " Obshchee delo, 4 November 1921.

Iaroslavskii, Em. " 'Patriotika.' " Pravda, 15 March 1921.

———. "Smena vekh." Sovetskaia Sibir', 19 October 1921.

Iashnov, E. E. "Nishcheta ratsionalizma (Iz neosoznannykh urokov revoliutsii)." Al'-
    manakh russkaia zhizn', no. 2 (July 1922): 16–30.

Iat'. "Intelligentsiia i sovetskaia vlast' (Pis'mo iz Petrograda)." Dni, 9 December 1922.

"Ideologiia vtorogo dnia." Put', 25 October 1921.

Il'in, I. S. "Omsk, direktoriia, Kolchak." Parts 1, 2. Novyi zhurnal, no. 72, 73 (1963):
    198–217, 216–43.

Intelligentsiia i revoliutsiia: Sbornik statei. Moscow: Dom pechati, 1922.

Intelligentsiia i sovetskaia vlast': Sbornik statei. Moscow: Sovetskii mir, 1919.

"Intelligentsiia i sovetskaia vlast' (Beseda s redaktorom gazety 'Nakanune' prof. Iu. V.
    Kliuchnikovym)." Izvestiia, 9 June 1922.

"Intelligentskie nastroeniia i chaianiia ot oktiabr'skikh dnei do porazheniia belogvar-
    deishchiny." Sputnik kommunista, no. 15 (1922): 48–59.

"Intelligentskoe primirenchestvo i bol'shevizm." Revoliutsionnaia Rossiia, no. 14–15
    (November–December 1921): 1–4.

Isbakh. "Uells, Kliuchnikov i Vandervel'de." Rabochaia Moskva, 8 July 1922.

Iuvenal. "Natsional-bol'shevizm." Novoe vremia, 14 December 1921.

Ivanovich, St. "O 'priiatii.' " Golos Rossii, 31 December 1921, 2.

Iz glubiny: Sbornik statei o russkoi revoliutsii. Moscow: Russkaia mysl', 1918; Paris:
    YMCA-Press, 1967.

"Iz pis'ma Alekseia N. Tolstogo (Berlin, 20 aprelia 1922)." Literaturnye zapiski, no. 1
    (25 May 1922): 4.

Izgoev, A. S. "O zadachakh intelligentsii." Parfenon, no. 1 (1922): 32–39.

———. " 'Vekhi' i 'Smena vekh.' " Russkaia mysl', 1922, no. 3:176–78.

———. "Piat' let v Sovetskoi Rossii (otryvki vospominanii i zametki)." Arkhiv russkoi
    revoliutsii, no. 10 (1923): 5–55.

"Kak pishut smenovekhovtsy." Russkii ekonomist, no. 11–12 (May–June 1923): 56.

Kamenetskii, V. "Karfagen ili Kanossa?" Rul', 15 February 1923.

Kantor, M. "O 'Smene vekh' (Vnimaniiu Sverdlovtsev)." Pravda, 28 June 1922.

Karzhinskii, N. "Zarubezhnaia Rossiia." Novyi mir, 1926, no. 8–9:282–93.

Katanian, R. "Predshestvenniki vreditel'stva. 1: Smena vekh." Krasnaia nov', 1930, no.
    1:113–24.

Kazmin, N. "Emigrantskie gazety (Opyt obzora)." Pechat' i revoliutsiia, 1923, no.
    4:61–72.

Kedr-Livanskii. "Ob ekonomistakh iz 'Ekonomista' i intelligentsiia za granitsei." Kniga
    i revoliutsiia, no. 7 (1922): 13–15.

Kin, F. " 'Spetsy' (Opyt statisticheskogo obsledovaniia)." Pravda, 3 September 1922.

Kirdetsov, G. L. U vorot Petrograda, 1919–1920 gg. Berlin: Gutnov, 1921.

———. Kto oni takie: Kapitalisticheskii mir v 100 politicheskikh portretakh. Moscow: Kres-
    t'ianskaia gazeta, 1931.

————, ed. *Ves' mir: Politicheskii slovar'-spravochnik.* Moscow: Krest'ianskaia gazeta, 1929.

Kliuchnikov, Iu. V. *Revoliutsiia i voina.* Moscow: Universal'naia biblioteka, 1917.

————. "Iaponiia i derzhavy Soglasiia." In *Evropa i voina: Rossiia i ee soiuzniki v bor'be za tsivilizatsiiu,* 2–1:7–25. Moscow: D. Ia. Makovskii, 1917.

————. *Internatsionalizm (Osnovnye voprosy mezhdunarodnykh otnoshenii).* Moscow: Gran', 1918.

————. "Na velikom istoricheskom pereput'i." *Golos Rossii,* 24 May 1921.

[————] Iu. K. "Logika primireniia." *Put',* 3 July 1921.

[————]. "Razval K.D. partii." *Put',* 9 August 1921.

————. *Na velikom istoricheskom pereput'i: Piat' glav po sotsiologii mezhdunarodnykh otnoshenii.* Berlin: Smena vekh, 1922.

————. *Edinyi kust: Dramaticheskie kartiny iz russkoi zhizni 1918 goda.* Berlin: Izd-vo pisatelei v Berline, 1923.

————. *Mirnye dogovory imperialisticheskoi voiny v konspektivnom izlozhenii.* Moscow: Izd-vo Kommunisticheskoi akademii, 1925.

[————] Klutchnikoff, G., ed. *La Russie d'aujourd'hui et de demain.* Paris: Attinger, 1920.

[————], ed. *Konstitutsii burzhuaznykh stran.* Moscow: Gosudarstvennoe sotsial'no-ekonomicheskoe izd-vo, 1935.

Kliuchnikov, Iu. V., and Sabanin, A., eds. *Itogi imperialisticheskoi voiny.* 6 vols. Moscow: Litizdat N.K.I.D., 1925-27.

————. *Mezhdunarodnaia politika noveishego vremeni v dogovorakh, notakh i deklaratsiiakh.* 4 vols. Moscow: Litizdat N.K.I.D., 1925–1929.

"Kommunist o 'novovekhovtsakh.' " *Vestnik literatury,* 1922, no. 1:4.

KPSS v rezoliutsiiakh i resheniiakh s"ezdov, konferentsii i plenumov TsK. Vols. 2–4. Moscow: Gospolitizdat, 1970.

Krainskii, N. V. *Bez budushchego: Ocherki po psikhologii revoliutsii i emigratsii.* Belgrade: Sviatoslav, 1931.

Krichevskii, M. "Rossiia no 2 i Genuia." *Vestnik Narodnogo Komissariata inostrannykh del,* 1922, no. 4–5:60–67.

Krol', L. A. *Za tri goda: Vospominaniia, vpechatleniia i vstrechi.* Vladivostok: Svobodnaia Rossiia, 1921.

Kuskova, E. "Zhguchii vopros." *Zveno,* no. 6 (12 March 1923): 1.

Kuz'min, N. "Na novom fronte." *Krasnaia gazeta,* 30 November 1920.

————. "Gibel' 'demokratii.' " *Krasnaia gazeta,* 18 October 1921.

————. " 'Vekhi' i 'Smena vekh.' " *Krasnaia gazeta,* 6 December 1921.

L. B. *Natsional-maksimalizm i natsional-bol'shevizm.* [Nice]: Nitstskii kruzhok politicheskogo samoobrazovaniia, 1927.

Ladyzhenskii, A. "Ideia velikoi Rossii i aggressivnyi imperializm (Otvet N. V. Ustrialovu)." *Problemy velikoi Rossii,* no. 16 (1 [14] November 1916): 2–3.

Lakhtin, S. "Problema vozvrashcheniia na rodinu." *Rossiianin-porevoliutsioner,* no. 1 (January 1936): 3.

Larin, Iu. *Intelligentsiia i sovety: Khoziaistvo, revoliutsiia, gosapparat.* Moscow: Gosizdat, 1924.

Lazerson, M. "Natsional-bol'shevizm." *Zaria* (Berlin), no. 2 (18 May 1922): 40–43.

Lebedev, V. I. "Vozvrashchenie v Rossiiu." *Volia Rossii,* 1922, no. 3:3–5.

———. "Mysli o russkoi emigratsii." Parts 1, 2. *Volia Rossii,* 1922, no. 25:5–9, 26–27:8–10.

Lenin, V. I. *Polnoe sobranie sochinenii.* 5th ed. 55 vols. Moscow: Gospolitizdat, 1958–1965.

Letopis' zhizni i tvorchestva M. Gor'kogo. 4 vols. Moscow: AN SSSR, 1958–1960.

Lezhnev, I. " 'Smena vekh.' " *Novaia Rossiia,* no. 1 (March 1922): 60–65.

———. "Velikii sintez." *Novaia Rossiia,* no. 1 (March 1922): 14–28.

———. "Razmen vekh (Otvet Iu. N. Potekhinu. Mozhet byt', dazhe bol'she togo)." *Rossiia,* no. 5 (January 1923): 17–19.

———. "Pis'mo prof. N. Ustrialovu." *Rossiia,* no. 9 (May–June 1923): 5–11.

———. "Pis'mo prof. N. Ustrialovu." *Al'manakh russkaia zhizn',* no. 4 (October 1923): 35–47.

———. *Zapiski sovremennika.* Vol. 1, *Istoki.* Moscow: Khudozhestvennaia literatura, 1934.

Liubimov, L. D. *Na chuzhbine.* Moscow: Sovetskii pisatel', 1963.

Livshits, Ia. "Novye i starye vekhi (Dva sobesedovaniia v Dome literatorov o sbornike 'Smena vekh')." *Letopis' Doma literatorov,* 1921, no. 3:4.

———. " 'Vekhi' i 'Smena vekh' (Disput v Dome literatorov)." *Letopis' Doma literatorov,* 1922, no. 1–2:10–11.

Luk'ianov, S. S. *Kak skoree konchit' voinu.* Petrograd: Lur'e, 1917.

———. "Mysli o revoliutsii." *Novaia Rossiia,* no. 1 (March 1922): 57–60.

Lunacharskii, A. V. "Mesto i rol' intelligentsii v obshchestve." *Narodnoe prosveshchenie,* 1918, no. 3:24–26.

———. "Smena vekh intelligentskoi obshchestvennosti." *Kul'tura i zhizn',* no. 1 (1 February 1922): 5–10.

———. *Ob intelligentsii.* Moscow: Krasnaia nov', 1923.

———. *Intelligentsiia v ee proshlom, nastoiashchem i budushchem.* Moscow: Novaia Moskva, 1924.

Lunchenkov, I. *Za chuzhie grekhi (kazaki i emigratsiia).* Moscow: Zemlia i fabrika, 1925.

Luppol, I. K. "Ob otnoshenii sovetskikh uchenykh k uchenym emigratsii." *Nauchnyi rabotnik,* 1928, no. 12:13–22.

L'vov, Vl. *Sovetskaia vlast' v bor'be za russkuiu gosudarstvennost' (Doklad chitannyi v 'Salles des Sociétés savantes' v Parizhe 12 noiabria 1921 g.).* Berlin: By Vl. L'vov, 1922.

M. S. "A. S. Izgoev o 'Smene vekh.' " *Volia Rossii,* 1922, no. 9:22–23.

Maiskii, I. *Vneshniaia politika RSFSR 1917–1922.* Moscow: Krasnaia nov', 1923.

Mandel'shtam, N. *Vospominaniia.* New York: Izd-vo imeni Chekhova, 1970.

———. *Vtoraia kniga.* Paris: YMCA-Press, 1972.

Manuilov, V., ed. "Iurii Kliuchnikov, 'Chtoby ne bylo vmeste tesno ...' " *Novoe vremia,* 1992, no. 1:42–43.

Meerovich, A. "V Narkomindele, 1922–1939: Interv'iu s E. A. Gnezdinym." *Pamiat': Istoricheskii sbornik,* no. 5 (1982): 357–93.

Meisner, D. *Ispoved' starogo emigranta.* Moscow: Sovetskii Komitet po kul'turnym sviaziam s sootechestvennikami, 1963.

———. *Mirazhi i deistvitel'nost'.* Moscow: Novosti, 1966.

Mel'gunov, S. P. "Iz smenovekhovskoi literatury." *Na chuzhoi storone,* no. 3 (1923): 235–38.

Men'shoi, A. *Rossiia no 2, emigrantskaia.* Moscow: Tipografiia M.G.S.N.Kh., 1922.

Meshcheriakov, N. "Russkaia pechat' za granitsei (obzor)." *Pechat' i revoliutsiia,* 1921, no. 1:63–66.

———. "Bez dorogi." *Pechat' i revoliutsiia,* 1921, no. 2:7–15.

———. "O novykh nastroeniiakh russkoi intelligentsii." *Pechat' i revoliutsia,* 1921, no. 3:33–43.

———. "Novye Vekhi." *Krasnaia nov',* 1921, no. 3:256–71.

———. "Znamenie vremeni." *Pravda,* 14 October 1921.

———. "Gor'koe priznanie." *Pravda,* 16 October 1921.

———. "Myl'nyi puzyr.' " *Pravda,* 2 November 1921.

———. "Eshche o 'Smene vekh.' " *Pravda,* 19 November 1921.

———. *Na perelome: Iz nastroenii belogvardeiskoi emigratsii.* Moscow: Gospolitizdat, 1922.

———. "Russkie smenovekhovtsy." *Krasnaia nov',* 1922, no. 2:337–42.

———. "Volna mistiki (Iz nastroenii sovremennoi emigratsii)." *Pechat' i revoliutsiia,* 1922, no. 2:32–43.

———. "Mechty smenovekhovstva i ikh sud'ba." In *Na ideologicheskom fronte bor'by s kontr-revoliutsiei,* 85–103. Moscow: Krasnaia nov', 1923.

Miliukov, P. N. *Emigratsiia na pereput'i.* Paris: Resp.-Dem. Ob"edinenie, 1926.

[———]. "Evraziiskaia teoriia i praktika." *Poslednie novosti,* 3 December 1927.

Mindlin, E. L. *Neobyknovennye sobesedniki: Kniga vospominanii.* Moscow: Sovetskii pisatel', 1968.

Mir i trud: Neperiodicheskii sbornik. vol. 1. Berlin: Ladyzhnikov, 1920.

[Mirkin-Getsevich, B. S.] Mirkine-Guetzévich, B. *Les Scythes: Quelques théories russes sur la crise européenne.* Paris: Povolozky, 1924.

———— [B. Mirskii, pseud.]. *V izgnanii: Publitsisticheskie ocherki.* Paris: Franko-Russkaia pechat', 1922.

Na ideologicheskom fronte bor'by s kontr-revoliutsiei: Sbornik statei. Moscow: Krasnaia nov', 1923.

Nauchnye rabotniki Moskvy. Leningrad: AN SSSR, 1930.

Nauchnye uchrezhdeniia Leningrada. Leningrad: AN SSSR, 1926.

"Ne k smenivshimsia vekham, a pod znamia internatsionalizma (Po povodu gruppy 'Smena vekh')." *Zhizn' natsional'nostei,* 1921, no. 27:1.

Nevskii, V. I. "Intelligentsiia i sovety." *Petrogradskaia pravda,* 29 October 1921.

———. "Metod revoliutsionnogo obucheniia (O 'Smene vekh')." *Spravochnik Petrogradskogo agitatora,* no. 12–13 (1 December 1921): 60–68.

———. "Restavratsiia idealizma i bor'ba s 'novoi burzhuaziei.' " *Pod znamenem marksizma,* no. 7–8 (1922): 117–31.

Nol'de, Bar. B. E. "Novye knigi: Iu. V. Kliuchnikov, Internatsionalizm (Osnovnye voprosy mezhdunarodnykh otnoshenii)." *Nash vek,* 28 [15] April 1918.

"Novaia pobeda Sovetskoi vlasti." *Petrogradskaia pravda,* 20 October 1921.

"O gazete 'smenovekhovtsev' v Berline (Beseda s prof. Iu. V. Kliuchnikovym)." *Izvestiia,* 28 March 1922.

"O russkikh bezhentsakh." *Novoe vremia,* 15 December 1921.

O Smene vekh. Petersburg: Izd-vo 'Logos' pri Dome literatorov, 1922.

Odinnadtsatyi s"ezd RKP(b), mart–aprel' 1922 g.: Stenograficheskii otchet. Moscow: Gospolitizdat, 1961.

Okunev, Ia. M. *'Smena vekh' v tserkvi.* Kharkov: Proletarii, 1923.

Ol'denburg, S. S. "Politicheskii obzor: Dela russkie, Smena vekh." *Russkaia mysl',* 1922, no. 1–2:307.

———. "Russkaia zarubezhnaia pechat'." *Russkii ekonomist,* no. 11–12 (May–June 1923): 57–59.

"Omsk-Parizh: Beseda s byvshim Upravliaiushchim Ministerstvom inostrannykh del professorom Iu. V. Kliuchnikovym." *Pravitel'stvennyi vestnik* (Omsk), 11 February 1919.

Osorgin, M. "Priiatie Rossii." *Dni,* 4 February 1923.

Ozeretskovskii, G. *Rossiia malaia.* Vol. 1, *Russkii blistatel'nyi Parizh do voiny.* Paris, 1973.

P. Sh. " 'Smena vekh.' " *Rul',* 1921, no. 313.

Parnakh, V. "Emigratsiia v Parizhe i Berline." *Izvestiia,* 29 December 1922.

Pasmanik, D. "Prisposoblenie ili protest? (Po povodu knigi prof. Ustrialova)." *Obshchee delo,* 3 March 1921.

———. "Primirenchestvo prof. N. Ustrialova." *Obshchee delo,* 6 July 1921.

———. "Blagotvornye plody iada (Po povodu sbornika statei 'Smena vekh')." *Obshchee delo,* 12 October 1921.

Patek, V. *Ispoved' smenovekhovtsa.* Sofia: Obzor, 1924.

Pavlovich, M. "Professor-idealist na velikom pereput'i." *Pechat' i revoliutsiia,* 1923, no. 2:13–26.

Pchelintsev, I. "Smena vekh: Rasskaz." *Molodaia gvardiia,* 1923, no. 6:37–45.

Peshekhonov, A. V. *Pochemu ia ne emigriroval.* Berlin: Obelisk, 1923.

Petrishchev, A. "Smenovekhovskie retsepty." *Dni,* 31 January 1923.

———. "Smenovekhovstvo ili bezvekhovstvo?" *Dni,* 28 February 1923.

Piatnadtsatyi s"ezd VKP(b), dekabr' 1927 goda: Stenograficheskii otchet. 2 vols. Moscow: Gospolitizdat, 1961–1962.

"Pobedit Proletarii." *Gudok,* 15 October 1921.

Pochemu my vernulis' na Rodinu: Svidetel'stva reemigrantov. Moscow: Progress, 1983.

Pokrovskii, M. N. "Kaiushchaiasia intelligentsiia." In *Intelligentsiia i revoliutsiia,* 72–89. Moscow: Dom pechati, 1922.

Polonskii, V. "Iskateli 'ob"ektivnoi' istiny." *Pechat' i revoliutsiia,* 1921, no. 2:15–27.

———. "Na rasput'i." *Pechat' i revoliutsiia,* 1921, no. 3:15–23.

———. "Ob intelligentsii i revoliutsii." *Kul'tura i zhizn',* no. 2–3 (1–15 March 1922): 34–39.

———, ed. *Russkaia istoricheskaia literatura v klassovom osveshchenii.* Moscow: Izd-vo Kommunisticheskoi akademii, 1927.

———. *Ocherki literaturnogo dvizheniia revoliutsionnoi epokhi (1917–1927).* Moscow: Gosizdat, 1928.

Postnikov, S. P., ed. *Russkaia zarubezhnaia kniga: Trudy komiteta russkoi knigi.* Prague: Komitet russkoi knigi, 1924.

———. *Russkie v Prage, 1918–1928 gg.* Prague, 1928.

Potekhin, Iu. N. "Russkii internatsional." *Al'manakh russkaia zhizn',* no. 4 (October 1923): 32–35.

——— [Skif, pseud.]. *Pavliny bez per'ev: Iz arkhiva kontr-revoliutsii.* Moscow: Novye vekhi, 1924.

———. *Liudi zakata: Roman.* Leningrad: Zhizn' iskusstva, 1925.

————. *Operatsiia professora Foksa.* Moscow: Zemlia i fabrika, 1926.

————. *Rasskazy.* Moscow: Gosudarstvennoe voennoe izd-vo, 1926.

————. *Oshibka Oskara Bush.* Moscow: Izd-vo Puchina, 1927.

————. *Million nalichnymi: Liricheskii fars v 4-kh deistviiakh i 6-i kartinakh.* Moscow: Tea-kinopechat', 1928.

————. *Za udamoe silosovanie.* Moscow: Ogiz. Gos. izd. s.-kh. i kolkh. koop. lit., 1931.

————. *Za udamyi senokos.* Moscow: Ogiz. Gos. izd. s.-kh. i kolkh. koop. lit., 1931.

Preobrazhenskii, E. "Oblomki staroi Rossii." *Pod znamenem marksizma,* no. 1–2 (1922): 33–35.

"Prizhival'shchiki revoliutsii ili storonniki ee? (O smenovekhovtsakh)." *Pravda,* 23 July 1922.

"Prof. Gredeskul za raboti." *Obshchee delo,* 21 June 1921.

Protsess Borisa Savinkova. Berlin: Russkoe ekho, 1924.

Radek, K. *Voina pol'skikh belogvardeitsev protiv Sovetskoi Rossii.* Moscow: Gosizdat, 1920.

Rakovskii, G. N. *V stane belykh (Ot Orla do Novorossiiska).* Constantinople: Pressa, 1920.

————. *Konets belykh (Ot Dnepra do Bosfora): Vyrozhdenie, agoniia i likvidatsiia.* Prague: Volia Rossii, 1921.

————. "O russkoi emigratsii." *Volia Rossii,* 1922, no. 20:13–15.

Razumovskii, I. "Ustrialovshchina v prave." *Revoliutsiia prava,* 1927, no. 1:48–73.

Riutin, M. *Smenovekhovtsy i proletarskaia revoliutsiia.* Rostov na Donu: Priboi, 1924.

"Rossiia: Arrest reemigrantov." *Dni,* 14 July 1923.

Rostovtsev, M. "Bol'sheviki i intelligentsiia." *Rodnaia zemlia,* no. 1 (1920): 30–37.

————. "Should scientists return to Russia? A reply to prof. Bekhterev." *The New Russia,* no. 25 (22 July 1920): 370–72.

Rozenberg, V. A. "Russkaia zarubezhnaia periodicheskaia pechat'." In *Russkaia zarubezhnaia kniga: Trudy komiteta russkoi knigi,* edited by S. P. Postnikov, 131–42. Prague: Komitet russkoi knigi, 1924.

Rubinshtein, N. "Intelligentnye meshochniki ('Novaia Rossiia', 1–2)." *Bol'shevik,* no. 7–8 (1926): 119–23.

Rusov, N. N. "Zhivaia smert': Posviashchaetsia N. V. Ustrialovu." *Vestnik Man'-chzhurii,* 1925, no. 3–4:111–14.

Russkie v Bolgarii. Sofia: Ob-vo Russko-Bolgarskaia druzhba, 1923.

"Russkie v Chekhoslovakii: 'Smenovekhovtsy.'" *Volia Rossii,* 1922, no. 9:24.

Russkie v Gallipoli 1920–1921. Berlin: Gutman, 1923.

Ryss, P. *Russkii opyt: Istoriko-psikhologicheskii ocherk russkoi revoliutsii.* Paris: Sever, 1921.

————. "Bez Vekh." *Poslednie novosti,* 21 September 1921.

S. "Otnoshenie k revoliutsii russkoi intelligentsii v sovetskoi Rossii i za rubezhom." *Russkaia mysl',* 1923, no. 1–2:161–81.

S. Ia. "Ob emigratsii i sovetskoi Rossii (Doklad A. V. Peshekhonova i preniia)." *Dni,* 25 May 1923.

Safarov, G. "Nepman na sluzhbe u nepmana." *Pravda,* 28 May 1922.

————. "Rossiia no 2 1/2." *Pravda,* 27 August 1922.

Savinkov, B. V. *Pochemu ia priznal Sovetskuiu vlast'.* Kharkov: Ob-vo sodeistviia iunomu lenintsu, 1924.

————. *Posmertnye stat'i i pis'ma.* Moscow: Ogonek, 1926.

Semenoff, M., ed. *Les Relations de la France avec les Soviets russes.* Les Ecrits Pour et Contre, no. 3. Paris: Delpeuch, 1923.

Serebrennikov, I. I. *Moi vospominaniia.* Vol. 1, *V revoliutsii (1917–1919).* Tientsin: Nashe znanie, 1937.

———. *Moi vospominaniia.* Vol. 2, *V emigratsii (1920–1924).* Tientsin: Nashe znanie, 1940.

Sergeev, V. *Tri goda v Sovetskoi Rossii: Ocherki.* Paris: Povolozky, 1921.

Shafir, Ia. "Smenovekhovskaia tabakerka." *Knigonosha,* no. 13 (1926): 7–9.

Shestnadtsatyi s''ezd VKP(b), aprel' 1929 goda: Stenograficheskii otchet. Moscow: Gospolitizdat, 1962.

Shletser, B. "Russkii spor o kul'ture: Viacheslav Ivanov i M. O. Gershenzon—'Perepiska iz dvukh uglov.' " *Sovremennye zapiski,* no. 11 (1922): 195–211.

———. " 'Zakat Evropy.' " *Sovremennye zapiski,* no. 12 (1922): 339–48.

Shostakovskii, P. P., 1960. *Put' k pravde.* Minsk: Gosizdat BSSR, 1960.

Shreider, Dm. "Mozhno-li s nimi rabotat'?" *Volia Rossii,* 20 February 1921.

Shul'gin, V. V. *1920 god: Ocherki.* Sofia: Rossiisko-Bolgarskoe knigo-izdatel'stvo, 1921.

———. *Dni.* Belgrade: Suvorin i 'Novoe vremia', 1925.

———. *Tri stolitsy: Puteshestvie v Krasnuiu Rossiiu.* Berlin: Mednyi vsadnik, 1927.

Shvittau, G. G. *Revoliutsiia i narodnoe khoziaistvo v Rossii (1917–1921).* Leipzig: Tsentral'noe t-vo kooperativnogo izdatel'stva, 1922.

Skachko, A. *Poputchiki (Iz khroniki 1919 goda).* Moscow: Vserossiiskii Proletkul't, 1923.

"Skupshchiki 'Mertvykh dush.' " *Novoe vremia,* 9 December 1921.

Slashchev, Ia. A. *Trebuiu suda obshchestva i glasnosti (Oborona i sdacha Kryma): Memuary i dokumenty.* Constantinople: Shul'man, 1921.

———. *Krym v 1920 g.: Otryvki iz vospominanii.* Moscow: Gosizdat, [1924].

Slavin, I. "Vesti iz-za rubezha: 'Smena vekh,' ezhenedel'nyi zhurnal, no 12, Parizh, 14 Ianv. 1922 g." *Ezhenedel'nik sovetskoi iustitsii,* 1922, no. 8:11–13.

Slobodskoi, A. *Sredi emigratsii: Moi vospominaniia, Kiev-Konstantinopol', 1918–1920.* Kharkov: Proletarii, 1925.

Slonim, M. "Ot oktiabrizma k bol'shevizmu ('Smena vekh,' sbornik statei. Praga 1921)." *Volia Rossii,* 27 September 1921.

———. "Metamorfozy natsional-liberalizma." *Volia Rossii,* 1922, no. 2:14–16.

———. "Krizis emigratsii." *Volia Rossii,* 1922, no. 6:3–6.

Smena vekh: Sbornik statei. Prague: Nasha rech', 1921.

Smena vekh: Sbornik statei. 2d ed. Smolensk: Zavodoupravlenie Poligraficheskoi Promyshlennosti g. Smolenska, 1922.

Smena vekh: Sbornik statei, pereizdannyi Tverskim izdatel'stvom. Tver: Tverskoe izd-vo, 1922.

"Smenovekhovets s nevzorvavsheisia bomboi." *Pravda,* 13 September 1924.

" 'Smenovekhovtsy,' emigratsiia, Rossiia." *Poslednie novosti,* 26 March 1922.

Smil'g-Benario, M. "Na sovetskoi sluzhbe." *Arkhiv russkoi revoliutsii,* no. 3 (1921): 147–89.

Sokolov, K. N. *Pravlenie gen. Denikina (Iz vospominanii).* Sofia: Rossiisko-Bolgarskoe knigo-izdatel'stvo, 1921.

Solov'ev, Iu. Ia. *Vospominaniia diplomata, 1893–1922.* Moscow: Izd-vo sotsial'no-ekonomicheskoi literatury, 1959.

Sorokin, P. "O 'Smene vekh': 'Smena vekh' kak sotsial'nyi simptom." *Vestnik literatury,* 1921, no. 12:1–3.

"Les Soviets et l'émigration russe (Rosta)." *L'Humanité,* 4 December 1921.

Stalin, I. V. *Sochineniia.* 13 vols. Moscow: Gosudarstvennoe izd-vo politicheskoi literatury, 1946–1955.

[Stankevich, V.] Stankewitsch, W. *Fragen, die zu lösen sind.* [Berlin]: Friede und Arbeit, [1920].

———. "Prof. N. Ustrialov, V bor'be za Rossiiu." *Russkaia kniga,* 1921, no. 3:6–7.

Steklov, Iu. "Ne nachalo li otrezvleniia? (K voprosu 'o tretei taktike')." *Izvestiia,* 17 August 1921.

———. "Burzhuaznaia intelligentsiia v russkoi proletarskoi revoliutsii." *Kommunisticheskii internatsional* 19 (1 September 1921): 4977–94.

———. "Psikhologicheskii perelom." *Izvestiia,* 13 October 1921.

Stepanov, I. "O 'Smene vekh' v tserkvi i o nashikh zadachakh." *Kommunisticheskaia revoliutsiia,* no. 9–10 (1 September 1922): 3–12.

Stepun, F. *Byvshee i nesbyvsheesia.* 2 vols. New York: Izd-vo imeni Chekhova, 1956.

Struve, P. B. "Razmyshleniia o russkoi revoliutsii." *Russkaia mysl',* 1921, no. 1–2:6–37.

———. "Po sushchestvu." Parts 1–7. *Rul',* 19 April–27 July 1921.

———. "Istoriko-politicheskie zametki o sovremennosti." Parts 1, 2. *Russkaia mysl',* 1921, no. 5–7:208–24, 10–12:317–24.

———. "Proshloe, nastoiashchee, budushchee: Mysli o natsional'nom vozrozhdenii Rossii." *Russkaia mysl',* 1922, no. 1–2:222–31.

———. "Rossiia." *Russkaia mysl',* 1922, no. 3:101–15.

Sud'by sovremennoi intelligentsii: Doklad A. V. Lunacharskogo i rechi P. I. Sakulina, N. I. Bukharina i Iu. V. Kliuchnikova. Moscow: Moskovskii rabochii, 1925.

Sukhomlin, V. "Emigranty i 'ostavshiesia' (po povodu broshiury Peshekhonova)." *Volia Rossii,* 1923, no. 13:37–43.

Sumskii, S. "Ideologiia sovburzhuazii." *Sotsialisticheskii vestnik,* 1921, no. 19:3–6.

———. "O natsional-bol'shevizme." *Sotsialisticheskii vestnik,* 1921, no. 21:3–6.

Tan-Bogoraz, V. G. " 'Smenovekhi' v Petrograde." *Rossiia,* no. 1 (August 1922): 12–14.

Trainin, I. "Chelovecheskii dokument (po povodu broshiura V. L'vova 'Sovetskaia vlast' v bor'be za russkuiu gosudarstvennost')." *Zhizn' natsional'nostei,* 1922, no. 4:2–4.

Trinadtsatyi s"ezd RKP(b), Mai 1924 goda: Stenograficheskii otchet. Moscow: Gospolitizdat, 1963.

Trotskii, L. *Literatura i revoliutsiia.* Moscow: Krasnaia nov', 1924.

———. *Moia zhizn'.* Berlin: Granit, 1930.

Trubetskoi, kn. E. N. *Velikaia revoliutsiia i krizis patriotizma.* N.p.: Biblioteka Dobrovol'tsa, 1919.

———. *Vospominaniia.* Sofia: Rossiisko-Bolgarskoe knigo-izdatel'stvo, 1921.

Ustinov, G. "Printsipy i deistvitel'nost' (Ob 'intelligentskoi ideologii')." *Izvestiia,* 29 May 1918.

Ustrialov, N. V. "Natsional'naia problema u pervykh slavianofilov." *Russkaia mysl',* 1916, no. 10:1–22.

————. "K voprosu o russkom imperializme." *Problemy velikoi Rossii,* no. 15 (15 [28] October 1916): 1–5.

————. "K voprosu o sushchnosti 'natsionalizma.' " *Problemy velikoi Rossii,* no. 18 (10 [23] December 1916): 9–12.

————. *Chetyre Gosudarstvennye Dumy.* Moscow: D. Ia. Makovskii, 1917.

————. *Chto takoe Uchreditel'noe Sobranie.* Moscow: D. Ia. Makovskii, 1917.

————. *Otvetstvennost' ministrov.* Moscow: D. Ia. Makovskii, 1917.

————. *Revoliutsiia i voina.* Moscow: Izd-vo "1917 god", 1917.

————. "Mezhdunarodnaia peregruppirovka." *Pravitel'stvennyi vestnik* (Omsk), 16 March 1919.

[————] N. U. "Voskresenie." *Russkoe delo* (Omsk), 17 October 1919.

————. " 'Petushki.' " *Svobodnaia Sibir'* (Krasnoiarsk), 2 November [19 October] 1919.

————. "Sud'ba Sibiri." *Svobodnaia Sibir'* (Krasnoiarsk), 16 [3] November 1919.

————. *V bor'be za Rossiiu.* Harbin: Okno, 1920.

————. "Lik veka sego." *Okno,* no. 1 (November 1920): 25–29.

————. "Obmirshchenie." *Rossiia,* no. 9 (May–June 1923): 14–17.

————. "O nashei ideologii." *Al'manakh russkaia zhizn',* no. 4 (October 1923): 2–8.

————. "Sud'ba Evropy: Razmyshleniia k desiatiletiiu mirovoi voiny." *Rossiia,* no. 3 (1924): 121–32.

————. *Pod znakom revoliutsii.* Harbin: Russkaia mysl', 1925.

————. "Politicheskaia doktrina slavianofil'stva (Ideia samoderzhaviia v slavianofil'skoi postanovke)." *Vysshaia shkola v Kharbine: Izvestiia Iuridicheskogo fakul'teta,* no. 1 (1925): 47–74.

————. "Fevral'skaia revoliutsiia (K vos'miletnemu iubileiu)." *Vestnik Man'chzhurii,* 1925, no. 3–4:109–10.

————. "Dekabristy (Otryvki lektsii o dekabrizme iz kursa istorii russkoi politicheskoi mysli)." *Novosti zhizni,* 20 December 1925.

————. *Rossiia (u okna vagona).* Harbin: Tipografiia KVzhd, 1926.

————. "Rossiia (u okna vagona)." *Vestnik Man'chzhurii,* 1926, no. 1–2:82–97.

————. "U okna vagona (Moskva-Kharbin)." Parts 1, 2. *Novaia Rossiia,* 1926, no. 2:31–48, 3:25–38.

————. "O fundamente etiki (etiko-filosofskii etiud)." *Vysshaia shkola v Kharbine: Izvestiia Iuridicheskogo fakul'teta,* no. 3 (1926): 267–92.

————. *Pod znakom revoliutsii.* 2d enl. ed. Harbin: Politgraf, 1927.

————. "Etika Shopengauera." *Vysshaia shkola v Kharbine: Izvestiia Iuridicheskogo fakul'teta,* no. 4 (1927): 235–83.

————. "Ital'ianskii fashizm." *Vysshaia shkola v Kharbine: Izvestiia Iuridicheskogo fakul'teta,* no. 5 (1928): 29–200.

————. *Hic Rohdus [sic], hic salta!.* Harbin, 1929.

————. *Problema Pan-Evropy.* Harbin, 1929.

————. "Hic Rohdus [sic], hic salta!" Parts 1, 2. *Evraziia,* no. 25, (11 May 1929): 3–4, 26 (18 May 1929): 3–4.

————. "O politicheskom ideale Platona." *Vysshaia shkola v Kharbine: Izvestiia Iuridicheskogo fakul'teta,* no. 7 (1929): 145–90.

————. "Pravyi uklon." *Evraziia,* no. 29 (15 June 1929): 3–4.

————. *Na novom etape*. Shanghai: Tsenturion, 1930.

————. "O russkoi natsii." In *Sveslavenski zbornik spomenica o tisucugodnjici hrvatskogo kraljevstva*, 283–302. [Zagreb]: Zajednica slavenskih drutava u Zagrebu, 1930.

————. *Poniatie o gosudarstve*. Harbin: Vestnik kitaiskogo prava, 1931.

————. *Problema progressa*. Harbin: Khudozhestvennaia tipografiia, 1931.

————. *Elementy gosudarstva*. Harbin, 1932.

————. "Zarubezhnaia smena." *Utverzhdeniia*, no. 3 (October 1932): 107–18.

————. *Germanskii natsional-sotsializm*. Harbin: Chinarev, 1933.

————. *Nashe vremia*. Shanghai, 1934.

————. "Samopoznanie sotsializma." *Izvestiia*, 18 December 1936.

————. "Genii vekov." *Izvestiia*, 10 February 1937.

————. "Revoliutsioner-demokrat." *Izvestiia*, 6 April 1937.

Vainshtein, O. L. *Ocherki po istorii frantsuzskoi emigratsii v epokhu velikoi revoliutsii (1789–1796)*. Kharkov: Gosizdat Ukrainy, 1924.

Val'ter, Vl. "O starykh i novykh 'Vekhakh.' " *Spolokhi*, no. 2 (December 1921): 28–31.

Vania. "Smena vekh." *Krasnye ogni*, no. 5 (3 September 1922): 3–6.

Vardin, Il. "Smenovekhovskaia programma velikoderzhavnosti." *Pravda*, 8 July 1924.

Varshavskii, V. S. *Nezamechennoe pokolenie*. New York: Izd-vo imeni Chekhova, 1956.

Varvarin, D. "Smena 'Vekh.' " *Novyi put'*, 21 October 1921.

Vasilevskii, I. M. (Ne-Bukva). *Belye memuary*. Petrograd: 'Petrograd', 1923.

————. *General A. I. Denikin i ego memuary*. Berlin: Nakanune, 1924.

————. *Chto oni pishut? (Memuary byvshikh liudei)*. Leningrad: Krasnaia zvezda, 1925.

Vasilevskii, Vl. "Intelligentsiia i revoliutsiia (ezhenedel'nik 'Smena vekh')." *Petrogradskaia pravda*, 10 December 1921.

Vekhi: Sbornik statei o russkoi intelligentsii. Moscow: V. M. Sablin, 1909; Frankfurt am Main: Posev, 1967.

Vertinskii, A. "Chetvert' veka bez rodiny." In *V kraiakh chuzhikh: Literaturno-khudozhestvennyi sbornik*, 201–309. Berlin: Komitet za vozvrashchenie na rodinu i razvitie kul'turnykh sviazei s sootechestvennikami, 1962.

Ves' Leningrad na 1926 god: Adresnaia i spravochnaia kniga g. Leningrada. Leningrad: Organizatsionnyi otdel Leningradskogo gubispolkoma, 1926.

Ves' Peterburg na 1912 god: Adresnaia i spravochnaia kniga g. S.-Peterburga. Petersburg: A. S. Suvorin, 1912.

Vetlugin, A. *Avantiuristy grazhdanskoi voiny*. Paris: Sever, 1921.

————. *Tret'ia Rossiia*. Paris: Franko-Russkaia pechat', 1922.

Vishniak, M. "Na rodine." *Sovremennye zapiski*, no. 2 (1920): 268–97.

————. "N. Ustrialov, V bor'be za Rossiiu (Kritika i bibliografiia)." *Sovremennye zapiski*, no. 3 (1921): 271.

————. " 'Smena vekh' (Kritika i bibliografiia)." *Sovremennye zapiski*, no. 8 (1921): 380–85.

————. *Gody emigratsii 1919-1969: Parizh-N'iu-Iork (Vospominaniia)*. Stanford, Calif.: Hoover Institution Press, 1970.

"Vokrug 'Smeny vekh.' " *Petrogradskaia pravda*, 22 November 1921.

Volkov, A. "Polozhenie russkoi emigratsii (Beseda s V. N. L'vovym)." *Izvestiia*, 19 July 1922.

————. "Beseda s prof. Iu. V. Kliuchnikovym." *Izvestiia*, 17 August 1922.

Voronskii, A. "Vynuzhdennye priznaniia." *Pravda,* 6 April 1921.

———. "Starcheskoe slaboumie." *Pechat' i revoliutsiia,* 1921, no. 2:27–31.

———. "Na novom puti." *Pechat' i revoliutsiia,* 1921, no. 3:23–33.

Vsia Moskva na 1917 god: Adresno-spravochnaia kniga g. Moskvy. Moscow: A. S. Suvorin, 1917.

Vsia Moskva na 1923 god: Adresno-spravochnaia kniga g. Moskvy. Moscow: Moskovskii rabochii, 1923.

Vsia Moskva na 1926 god: Adresno-spravochnaia kniga g. Moskvy. Moscow: Moskovskii rabochii, 1926.

Vsia Moskva na 1929 god: Adresno-spravochnaia kniga g. Moskvy. Moscow: Moskovskii rabochii, 1929.

Vsia Moskva na 1936 god: Adresno-spravochnaia kniga g. Moskvy. Moscow: Moskovskii rabochii, 1936.

Wells, H. *Russia in the Shadows.* London: Hodder and Stoughton, 1920.

Zaitsev, A. *Ob Ustrialove, 'neo NEPe' i zhertvakh ustrialovshchiny.* Moscow: Gosizdat, 1928.

Zenzinov, V. M. *Gosudarstvennyi perevorot admirala Kolchaka v Omske, 18 noiabria 1918 goda: Sbornik dokumentov.* Paris: Rirakhovskii, 1919.

Zhakmon, P. *Pis'ma russkogo emigranta.* Warsaw: Slovo, 1921.

Zinov'ev, G. *Filosofiia epokhi.* Leningrad: Priboi, 1925.

———. *Leninizm.* 2d ed. Leningrad: Gosizdat, 1926.

———. "Manifest kulatskoi partii." *Bol'shevik,* no. 13 (1927): 33–47.

SECONDARY SOURCES

Acton, E. *Rethinking the Russian Revolution.* London: Edward Arnold, 1990.

Afanas'ev, A. *Polyn' v chuzhikh poliakh.* 2d rev. ed. Moscow: Molodaia gvardiia, 1987.

———. *Rossiiu nuzhno zasluzhit'.* Moscow: Sovremennik, 1990.

[Agurskii, M.] Agursky, M. "Dmitrievsky and the Origins of National Bolshevism." *Soviet Jewish Affairs* 7 (April 1977): 51–61.

[———] Agursky, M. "The Soviet Legitimacy Crisis and Its International Implications." In *The Many Faces of Communism,* edited by M. A. Kaplan, 146–93. New York: Free Press, 1978.

[———] Agurskij, M. "Lo sviluppo ideologico della nuova classe in URSS." In *I Nuovi Padroni: Atti del convegno internazionale di studi sui nuovi padroni,* 329–40. Milan: Edizioni Antistato, 1978.

———. *Ideologiia natsional-bol'shevizma.* Paris: YMCA-Press, 1980.

[———] Agurskij, M. "Existait-il une infiltration de droite dans le système politique soviétique?" *Cahiers du monde russe et soviétique* 21 (July–December 1980): 279–94.

[———] Agursky, M. "Defeat as Victory and the Living Death: The Case of Ustrialov." *History of European Ideas* 5 (1984): 165–80.

[———] Agursky, M. "The Prospects of National Bolshevism." In *The Last Empire: Nationality and the Soviet Future,* edited by R. Conquest, 87–108. Stanford, Calif.: Hoover Institution Press, 1986.

[———] Agursky, M. *The Third Rome: National Bolshevism in the USSR.* Boulder, Colo.: Westview Press, 1987.

————. "U istokov natsional-bol'shevizma." *Minuvshee: Istoricheskii al'manakh*, no. 4 (1987): 140–65.

Alekseev, P. V. *Revoliutsiia i nauchnaia intelligentsiia*. Moscow: Politizdat, 1987.

Alekseeva, G. D. *Oktiabr'skaia revoliutsiia i istoricheskaia nauka v Rossii (1917–1923 gg.)*. Moscow: Nauka, 1968.

Andreyev, C. *Vlasov and the Russian Liberation Movement: Soviet Reality and Emigré Theories*. Cambridge: Cambridge University Press, 1987.

Andreyev, N. "The Reality of National Bolshevism." *Soviet Jewish Affairs* 12 (February 1982): 76–80.

Arans, D. *How we Lost the Civil War: Bibliography of Russian Emigré Memoirs on the Russian Revolution, 1917–1921*. Newtonville, Mass.: Oriental Research Partners, 1988.

[Aucouturier] Okutiur'e, M. " 'Smena vekh' i russkaia literatura 20-kh godov." In *Odna ili dve russkikh literatury*, edited by Zh. Niva, 103–111. Lausanne: L'Age d'Homme, 1981.

Azrael, J. R. *Managerial Power and Soviet Politics*. Cambridge: Harvard University Press, 1966.

Bailes, K. E. *Technology and Society under Lenin and Stalin: Origins of the Soviet Technical Intelligentsia, 1917–1941*. Princeton: Princeton University Press, 1978.

Ball, A. M. *Russia's Last Capitalists: The Nepmen, 1921–1929*. Berkeley: University of California Press, 1990.

Barabokhin, D. A. "Bor'ba V. I. Lenina protiv burzhuaznoi ideologii v zhurnalistike v 1921–22 gg." *Vestnik LGU*, ser. 2, 1970, no. 8:100–110.

Baranov, V. *Revoliutsiia i sud'ba khudozhnika: A. Tol'stoi i ego put' k sotsialisticheskomu realizmu*. 2d rev. ed. Moscow: Sovetskii pisatel', 1983.

Barghoorn, F. C. *Soviet Russian Nationalism*. New York: Oxford University Press, 1956.

Barikhnovskii, G. F. *Ideino-politicheskii krakh beloemigratsii i razgrom vnutrennei kontr-revoliutsii (1921–1924)*. Leningrad: Izd-vo Leningradskogo universiteta, 1978.

Beilin, A. E. *Kadry spetsialistov SSSR, ikh formirovanie i rost*. Moscow: Soiuzorguchet, 1935.

Berdiaev, N. *Konstantin Leont'ev: Ocherk iz istorii russkoi religioznoi mysli*. Paris: YMCA-Press, 1926.

Beyer, T. R.; Kratz, G; and Werner, X. *Russische Autoren und Verlage in Berlin nach dem Ersten Weltkrieg*. Berlin: Arnold Spitz, 1987.

Beyssac, M. *La vie culturelle de l'émigration russe en France: Chronique (1920–1930)*. Paris: P.U.F., 1971.

Biehahn, W. "Marxismus und nationale Idee in Russland." *Osteuropa* 9 (1934): 461–76.

Birth, E. *Die Oktobristen (1905–1913), Zielvorstellungen und Struktur: Ein Beitrag zur russischen Parteiengeschichte*. Stuttgart: Ernst Klett, 1974.

Böss, O. *Die Lehre der Eurasier: Ein Beitrag zur russischen Ideeengeschichte des 20. Jahrhunderts*. Wiesbaden: Otto Harrasowitz, 1961.

Burbank, J. *Intelligentsia and Revolution: Russian Views of Bolshevism, 1917–1922*. New York: Oxford University Press, 1986.

Bychkov, L. "Iz istorii klassovoi bor'by v pervye gody NEPa." *Bor'ba klassov*, 1936, no. 10:82–91.

Carr, E. H. *The Bolshevik Revolution 1917–1923*. 3 vols. London: Macmillan, 1950–1953; Harmondsworth: Penguin Books, 1966.

————. *The Interregnum 1923–1924*. London: Macmillan, 1954.

————. *Socialism in One Country 1924–1926*. Vol. 1. London: Macmillan, 1958.

Carroll, E. M. *Soviet Communism and Western Opinion, 1919–1921*. Edited by F. B. M. Hollyday. Chapel Hill: University of North Carolina Press, 1965.

Chagin, B. A., and Klushin, V. I. *Bor'ba za istoricheskii materializm v SSSR v 20-e gody*. Leningrad: Nauka, 1975.

Chamberlin, W. H. *The Russian Revolution, 1917–1921*. 2 vols. New York: Macmillan, 1954; Princeton: Princeton University Press, 1987.

Champcommunal, J. *La condition des Russes à l'étranger et spécialement en France*. Paris: Recueil Sirey, 1925.

Charnyi, M. *Put' Alekseia Tolstogo: Ocherk tvorchestva*. 2d ed. Moscow: Khudozhestvennaia literatura, 1981.

Cherniak, E. I. "O smenovekhovstve v Sibiri." In *Materialy nauchnoi konferentsii, posviashchennoi 50-letiiu obrazovaniia SSSR*, 3:55–57. Tomsk: Izd-vo Tomskogo universiteta, 1972.

————. "K voprosu o vozniknovenii smenovekhovstva." *Iz istorii Sibiri*, no. 6 (1973): 55–64.

————. "Razgrom kontrrevoliutsii na vostoke strany i formirovanie osnovnykh elementov ideologii 'smenovekhovstva.' " In *Iz istorii interventsii i grazhdanskoi voiny v Sibiri i na Dal'nem Vostoke, 1917–1922 gg.*, edited by Iu. I. Korablev and V. I. Shishkin, 194–99. Novosibirk: Nauka, Sibirskoe otdelenie, 1985.

Cherniavskii, G. I., and Daskalov, D. "Sud'by russkoi beloemigratsii v Bolgarii." *Istoriia SSSR*, 1961, no. 1:109–17.

Chizhevskii, D. I. *Gegel' v Rossii*. Paris: Dom knigi i Sovremennye zapiski, 1939.

Chudakova, M., ed. "Neokonchennoe sochinenie Mikhaila Bulgakova." *Novyi mir*, 1987, no. 8:164–201.

Conquest, R., ed. *The Last Empire: Nationality and the Soviet Future*. Stanford, Calif.: Hoover Institution Press, 1986.

Daniels, R. V. *The Conscience of the Revolution: Communist Opposition in Soviet Russia*. Cambridge: Harvard University Press, 1960.

Delage, J. *La Russie en exil*. Paris: Delagrave, 1930.

Deutscher, I. *Stalin: A Political Biography*. London: Oxford University Press, 1949.

Diakin, V. S. *Russkaia burzhuaziia i tsarizm v gody mirovoi voiny (1914–1917)*. Leningrad: Nauka, Leningradskoe otdelenie, 1967.

Dumova, N. G. *Kadetskaia kontrrevoliutsiia i ee razgrom (oktiabr' 1917–1920 gg.)*. Moscow: Nauka, 1982.

Dumova, N., and Trukhanovskii, V. *Cherchill i Miliukov protiv Sovetskoi Rossii*. Moscow: Nauka, 1989.

Dunlop, J. B. *The Faces of Contemporary Russian Nationalism*. Princeton: Princeton University Press, 1983.

Dupeux, L. *'Nationalbolschewismus' in Deutschland, 1919–1933: Kommunistische Strategie und konservative Dynamik*. Munich: C. H. Beck, 1985.

Dvinov, B. L. *Politics of the Russian Emigration*. Santa Monica, Calif.: B. L. Dvinov, 1955.

Fediukin, S. A. "V. I. Lenin i problema privlecheniia burzhuaznykh spetsialistov k sotsialisticheskomu stroitel'stvu v pervye gody sovetskoi vlasti." *Istoriia SSSR*, 1950, no. 2:90–111.

————. *Sovetskaia vlast' i burzhuaznye spetsialisty.* Moscow: Mysl', 1965.

————. "Bor'ba za perevospitanie staroi tekhnicheskoi intelligentsii v vosstanovitel'nyi period." *Istoriia SSSR,* 1965, no. 4:106–20.

————. *Oktiabr'skaia revoliutsiia i intelligentsiia.* Moscow: Znanie, 1968.

————. *Velikii Oktiabr' i intelligentsiia: Iz istorii vovlecheniia staroi intelligentsii v stroitel'stvo sotsializma.* Moscow: Nauka, 1972.

————. "Iz istorii bor'by s burzhuaznoi ideologiei v pervye gody Nepa." *Voprosy istorii KPSS,* 1972, no. 1:80–88.

————. "Nep i intelligentsiia." In *Novaia ekonomicheskaia politika: Voprosy teorii i istorii,* edited by M. P. Kim, 220–38. Moscow: Nauka, 1974.

————. *Bor'ba kommunisticheskoi partii s burzhuaznoi ideologiei v pervye gody Nepa.* Moscow: Znanie, 1977.

————. *Bor'ba s burzhuaznoi ideologiei v usloviiakh perekhoda k Nepu.* Moscow: Nauka, 1977.

————. *Partiia i intelligentsiia.* Moscow: Izd-vo politicheskoi literatury, 1983.

————. *Deiatel'nost' KPSS po formirovaniiu sovetskoi intelligentsii.* Moscow: Znanie, 1984.

————. "Oktiabr' i intelligentsiia (nekotorye metodologicheskie aspekty problemy)." In *Intelligentsiia i revoliutsiia: XX vek,* edited by K. V. Gusev, 20–33. Moscow: Nauka, 1985.

Fedorova, O. P. "Zhurnal 'Novaia Rossiia' ('Rossiia') i otnoshenie burzhuaznoi intelligentsii k revoliutsionnoi deistvitel'nosti." *Problemy istorii SSSR,* 1973, no. 2:90–104.

————. *Zhurnal'naia publitsistika 20-kh godov kak istochnik po istorii sovetskoi intelligentsii.* Moscow: Izd-vo Moskovskogo universiteta, 1985.

Fel'shtinskii, Iu. *K istorii nashei zakrytosti: Zakonodatel'nye osnovy sovetskoi immigratsionnoi i emigratsionnoi politiki.* London: Overseas Publication Interchange, 1988.

Figurovskaia, N. K. "Smenovekhovstvo." In *Sovetskaia istoricheskaia entsiklopediia,* 13:73–75. Moscow: Sovetskaia entsiklopediia, 1973.

————. "Smena vek [*sic*], 'Changing Centuries Movement.' " In *Modern Encyclopaedia of Russian and Soviet History,* 36:19–21. Gulf Breeze, Fla.: Academic International Press, 1984.

Fischer, G., ed. *Russian Emigré Politics.* New York: Free Russia Fund, 1951.

Fischer, L. *The Soviets in World Affairs: A History of the Relations between the Soviet Union and the Rest of the World.* Princeton: Princeton University Press, 1951.

Fitzpatrick, S., ed. *Cultural Revolution in Russia, 1928–1931.* Bloomington: Indiana University Press, 1984.

Foster, L. *Bibliography of Russian Emigre Literature 1918–1968.* 2 vols. London: G. K. Hall, 1970.

Geller, M. " 'Pervoe predosterezhenie'—udar khlystom." *Vestnik R. Kh. D.,* no. 127 (1978): 187–232.

Geller, M., and Nekrich, A. *Utopiia u vlasti. Istoriia Sovetskogo Soiuza s 1917 goda do nashikh dnei.* Vol. 1. London: Overseas Publications Interchange, 1982.

Genkina, E. B. "Iz istorii bor'by bol'shevistskoi partii za ukreplenie ideologicheskogo fronta." *Voprosy istorii,* 1949, no. 1:16–38.

————. "Deiatel'nost' Gosplana v 1921-1925 gg. i bor'ba s burzhuaznoi ideologiei po voprosam planirovaniia." *Istoriia SSSR*, 1961, no. 6:38–59.

————. "O Leninskikh metodakh vovlecheniia intelligentsii v sotsialisticheskoe stroitel'stvo." *Voprosy istorii*, 1965, no. 4:21–42.

Gimpel'son, E. G. "Rabochii klass i privlechenie intelligentsii k upravleniiu Sovetskim gosudarstvom (noiabr' 1917–1920 gg.)." In *Intelligentsiia i revoliutsiia: XX vek*, edited by K. V. Gusev, 158–63. Moscow: Nauka, 1985.

Gladkova, T. L., and Ossorguine, T. A., comps. *L'Emigration russe, Revues et recueils, 1920–1980: Index général des articles*. Paris: Institut d'Etudes slaves, 1988.

Golinkov, D. L. *Krushenie antisovetskogo podpol'ia v SSSR*. 2d rev. ed. 2 vols. Moscow: Izd-vo politicheskoi literatury, 1978.

Gorlin, M. "Die philosophisch-politischen Strömungen in der russischen Emigration." *Osteuropa* 8 (1932): 279–94.

Gorodetskii, E. N. *V. I. Lenin—osnovopolozhnik sovetskoi istoricheskoi nauki: Istoriia sovetskogo obshchestva v trudakh V. I. Lenina*. Moscow: Nauka, 1970.

Gousseff, C., and Saddier, N. "L'émigration russe en France, 1920–1930." Mémoire de Maîtrise d'Histoire, Université de Paris I, 1983.

Grazhdanskaia voina i voennaia interventsiia v SSSR: Entsiklopediia. 2d rev. ed. Moscow: Sovetskaia entsiklopediia, 1987.

Grazhdanskaia voina v SSSR. 2 vols. Moscow: Voennoe izd-vo Ministerstva oborony SSSR, 1980–1986.

Grothusen, K.-D. *Die historische Rechtsschule Russlands: Ein Beitrag zur russischen Geistesgeschichte in der zweiten Hälfte des 19. Jahrhunderts*. Giessen: Schmitz, 1962.

Gurenkov, M. *Bez Rossii zhit' nel'zia: Put' A. Tolstogo k revoliutsii*. Leningrad: Lenizdat, 1983.

Gusev, K. V., ed. *Intelligentsiia i revoliutsiia: XX vek*. Moscow: Nauka, 1985.

Hagemeister, M. *Nikolaj Fedorov: Studien zu Leben, Werk und Wirkung*. Munich: Otto Sagner, 1989.

Halperin, C. "Russia and the Steppe: George Vernadsky and Eurasianism." *Forschungen zur osteuropäische Geschichte*, no. 36 (1985): 55–194.

Hammer, D. P. "N. V. Ustrialov and the Origins of National Bolshevism." Paper presented at the Third World Congress of Soviet and East European Studies, Washington D.C., 31 October–4 November 1985.

Hardeman, H. "De bundel en het tijdschrift 'Smena vech,' 1921–1922." Licentiaatsthesis, Katholieke Universiteit Leuven, 1985.

————. "The Journal 'Change of Landmarks' ('Smena vekh'), Paris 1921–1922: A Second Step Toward Reconcilitation with the Bolsheviks." *Slavica Gandensia*, no. 14 (1987): 49–67.

————. "A 'bourgeois' newspaper in the Russian revolution: 'Utro Rossii,' Moscow 1917–1918." *Rossiia/Russia*, no. 6 (1988): 61–80.

————. "Smenovekhovstvo." In *Modern Encyclopaedia of Russian and Soviet History*, 53:86–93. Gulf Breeze, Fla.: Academic International Press, 1990.

Hayes, N. "The Intelligentsia-in-Exile." Ph.D. diss., University of Chicago, 1976.

————. "Kazem-Bek and the Young Russians' Revolution." *Slavic Review* 39 (June 1980): 255–68.

Hogenhuis-Seliverstoff, A. *Les Relations franco-soviétiques 1917–1924*. Paris: Publications de la Sorbonne, 1981.

Huntington, W. C. *The Homesick Million: Russia-out-of-Russia.* Boston: Stratford, 1933.

Huskey, E. "The Russian Bar and the Consolidation of Soviet Power." *Russian Review* 43 (1984): 115–44.

Il'in, I. A. "Russkaia emigratsiia v tsyfrakh." *Russkii kolokol,* no. 2 (1927): 76–83.

Ilovaiskaia, I. "Tri goda spustia: Mikhail Geller otvechaet na voprosy glavnogo redaktora 'Russkoi mysli.' " *Russkaia mysl',* no. 3724 (13 May 1988): 4–5.

Ioffe, G. Z. *Kolchakovskaia avantiura i ee krakh.* Moscow: Mysl', 1983.

Jansen, M. *Een showproces onder Lenin: Het voorspel van de Grote Terreur.* Haarlem: De Haan, 1980.

Johnston, R. H. *New Mecca, New Babylon: Paris and the Russian Exiles, 1920–1945.* Kingston, Ont.: McGill-Queen's University Press, 1988.

Kaplan, M. A., ed. *The Many Faces of Communism.* New York: The Free Press, 1978.

Karlinsky, S., and Appel, A. Jr., eds. *The Bitter Air of Exile: Russian Writers in the West, 1922–1972.* Berkeley: University of California Press, 1977.

Kavtaradze, A. G. "Nekotorye itogi izucheniia problemy 'Oktiabr' i voennaia intelligentsiia.' " In *Intelligentsiia i revoliutsiia: XX vek,* edited by K. V. Gusev, 151–58. Moscow: Nauka, 1985.

Kenez, P. *Civil War in South Russia, 1918: The First Year of the Volunteer Army.* Berkeley: University of California Press, 1971.

———. *Civil War in South Russia, 1919–1920: The Defeat of the Whites.* Berkeley: University of California Press, 1977.

Khar'kovskii, A. "Chakhotinskaia odisseia." *Ogonek,* 1974, no. 8:6–7.

Khokhunova, O. I. "Partiinaia pechat' v bor'be s burzhuaznoi ideologiei smenovekhovstva v pervye gody novoi ekonomicheskoi politiki." In *Sbornik nauchnykh rabot kafedr marksizma-leninizma, politicheskoi ekonomii i ekonomiki i organizatsiia proizvodstva,* 1:71–93. Ivanovo: Ivanovskii energeticheskii institut imeni V. I. Lenina, 1958.

———. "Bor'ba Kommunisticheskoi partii protiv ideologii smenovekhovstva v gody vosstanovleniia narodnogo khoziaistva (1921–1925)." Kandidatskaia dissertatsiia, Moskovskii gosudarstvennyi universitet, 1967.

———. "Iz istorii bor'by kommunistischeskoi partii na ideologicheskom fronte (1921–1925 gg.)." In *Deiatel'nost' partiinykh organizatsii i sotsial'nyi progress,* 26–42. Ivanovo: Dom Politicheskogo prosveshcheniia Ivanovskogo Obkoma KPSS, 1968.

———. "Bor'ba Kommunisticheskoi partii s ideologiei kapitalisticheskoi restavratsii (1921–1923)." In *Deiatel'nost' partiinykh organizatsii i sotsial'nyi progress,* 149–65. Ivanovo: Dom Politicheskogo prosveshcheniia Ivanovskogo Obkoma KPSS, 1970.

———. "Iz istorii bor'by partii so smenovekhovstvom." *Vestnik MGU, Istoriia,* 1976, no. 4:3–21.

Khoruzhii, S. "Filosofskii parokhod. Kak eto bylo." Parts 1, 2. *Literaturnaia gazeta,* 9 May 1990, 6 June 1990.

Kim, M. P., ed. *Novaia ekonomicheskaia politika: Voprosy teorii i istorii.* Moscow: Nauka, 1974.

Kimerling, E. "Civil Rights and Social Policy in Soviet Russia, 1918–1936." *Russian Review* 44 (1982): 24–46.

Kliamkin, I. "Kakaia ulitsa vedet k khramu?" *Novyi mir,* 1987, no. 11:150–88.

Kolarz, W. *Stalin und das ewige Russland: Die Wurzeln des Sowjetpatriotismus.* London: Lincolns-Prager, 1942.

Komin, V. V. *Krakh rossiiskoi kontr-revoliutsii za rubezhom.* Kalinin: Kalininskii gosudarstvennyi universitet, 1977.

————. *Politicheskii i ideinyi krakh russkoi melkoburzhuaznoi kontr-revoliutsii za rubezhom.* Kalinin: Kalininskii gosudarstvennyi universitet, 1977.

Koons, T. B. "Histoire des doctrines politiques de l'émigration russe, 1919–1939." Thèse pour le Doctorat d'Université, Université de Paris, Faculté des Lettres, 1952.

Kopelev, L. *Derzhava i narod.* Ann Arbor, Mich.: Ardis, 1982.

Korablev, Iu. I., and Shishkin, V. I., eds. *Iz istorii interventsii i grazhdanskoi voiny v Sibiri i na Dal'nem Vostoke, 1917–1922 gg.* Novosibirsk: Nauka, Sibirskoe otdelenie, 1985.

Kostikov, V. *Ne budem proklinat' izgnanie . . . (Puti i sud'by russkoi emigratsii).* Moscow: Mezhdunarodnye otnosheniia, 1990.

Kovalevskii, P. E. *Zarubezhnaia Rossiia: Istoriia i kul'turno-prosvetitel'naia rabota russkogo zarubezh'ia za polveka 1920–1970.* 2 vols. Paris: Librairie des cinq continents, 1971–1973.

Kozlov, E. A. "Bor'ba kommunisticheskoi partii protiv velikoderzhavnogo shovinizma smenovekhovtsev v pervye gody Nepa." In *Bor'ba kommunisticheskoi partii Sovetskogo Soiuza protiv opportunizma i natsionalizma,* 124–32. Leningrad: Izd-vo Leningradskogo universiteta, 1978.

————. "Sovetskaia istoricheskaia literatura 50–70-kh gg. o politike Kommunisticheskoi partii v otnoshenii smenovekhovskogo techeniia burzhuaznoi intelligentsii." In *Rol' intelligentsii v postroenii i dal'neishem razvitii sotsialisticheskogo obshchestva v SSSR,* 2:23–29. Leningrad: Gosudarstvennyi pedagogicheskii institut, 1978.

Krasnikova, A. V. "Iz istorii razrabotki V. I. Leninym politiki privlecheniia burzhuaznoi intelligentsii na sluzhbu sovetskoi vlasti." *Vestnik LGU,* ser. 2, 1970, no. 8:32–43.

Kriukova, A. M., ed. *A. N. Tolstoi: Materialy i issledovaniia.* Moscow: Nauka, 1985.

Kulikowski, M. "A Neglected Source: The Bibliography of Russian Emigré Publications since 1917." *Solanus,* New Series, no. 3 (1989): 89–102.

Kupferman, F. *Au pays des Soviets: Le voyage français en Union soviétique 1917–1939.* Paris: Gallimard-Julliard, 1979.

Kustarev, A. Review of *The Third Rome: National Bolshevism in the USSR,* by Mikhail Agursky. *Russian Review* 47 (1989): 461–62.

Kvakin, A. V. "Mesto i rol' novovekhovstva v beloi emigratsii." Avtoreferat, Kalininskii gosudarstvennyi universitet, 1980.

————. "Osnovnye cherty novovekhovskoi ideologii." Avtoreferat, Kalininskii gosudarstvennyi universitet, 1980.

————. "Sovetskaia istoriografiia novovekhovstva." In *Istoriografiia i istochniki po istorii Oktiabr'skoi revoliutsii i sotsialisticheskogo stroitel'stva v SSSR,* 18–40. Kalinin: Kalininskii gosudarstvennyi universitet, 1980.

————. "Novovekhovstvo kak krizis beloi emigratsii." Kandidatskaia dissertatsiia, Kalininskii gosudarstvennyi universitet, 1981.

———. "Vliianie pobedy sovetskogo naroda nad belogvardeitsami i interventami na vozniknovenie 'smenovekhovstva.' " In *Iz istorii interventsii i grazhdanskoi voiny v Sibiri i na Dal'nem Vostoke, 1917–1922 gg.,* edited by Iu. I. Korablev and V. I. Shishkin, 199–203. Novosibirsk: Nauka, Sibirskoe otdelenie, 1985.

———. *Oktiabr'skaia Revoliutsiia i ideino-politicheskoe razmezhevanie rossiiskoi intelligentsii.* Saratov: Izd-vo Saratovskogo universiteta, 1989.

Lange, R. *La bianca Russia: Cenno di storia militare e politica del movimento russo antibolscevico dal 22 ottobre 1917 al 1935.* Florence: Bemporad, 1935.

Laverychev, V. Ia. "Vserossiiskii Soiuz Torgovli i Promyshlennosti." *Istoricheskie zapiski,* no. 70 (1961): 35–60.

———. *Po tu storonu barrikad: Iz istorii bor'by moskovskoi burzhuazii s revoliutsiei.* Moscow: Mysl', 1967.

Lavrov, V. V., comp. *Literatura russkogo zarubezh'ia: Antologiia.* Vol. 1. Moscow: Kniga, 1990.

Luks, L. "Die Ideologie der Eurasier im zeitgeschichtlichen Zusammenhang." *Jahrbücher für Geschichte Osteuropas* 34 (1986): 374–95.

Malevsky-Malevitch, S. "L'URSS et le mouvement eurasien." *La revue des deux mondes,* 1965, no. 14:208–17.

Mamai, N. *Kommunisticheskaia partiia v bor'be za ideino-politicheskoe vospitanie mass v pervye gody NEPa.* Moscow: Gospolitizdat, 1954.

Manuilov, V. "Dve paradigmy (Opyt sovremennogo prochteniia 'Smeny vekh')." *Polis,* 1991, no. 3:138–47.

Marrus, M. R. *The Unwanted: European Refugees in the Twentieth Century.* New York: Oxford University Press, 1985.

Masanov, I. F. *Slovar' psevdonimov russkikh pisatelei, uchenykh i obshchestvennykh deiatelei.* 4 vols. Moscow: Izd-vo Vsesoiuznoi knizhnoi palaty, 1956–1960.

Mawdsley, E. *The Russian Civil War.* Boston: Allen and Unwin, 1987.

Mel'gunov, S. P. *Tragediia admirala Kolchaka.* 3 vols. Belgrade: Russkaia tipografiia, 1930–1931.

Mierau, F., ed. *Russen in Berlin, 1918–1933: Eine kulturelle Begegnung.* Weinheim: Quadriga, 1988.

Miliukov, P. N. *Rossiia na perelome.* Vol. 1, *Proiskhozhdenie i ukreplenie bol'shevistskoi diktatury.* Paris: Imprimerie d'Art Voltaire, 1927.

———. *Rossiia na perelome.* Vol. 2, *Antibol'shevistskoe dvizhenie.* Paris: Imprimerie d'Art Voltaire, 1927.

Mukhachev, Iu. V. "K voprosu ob osobennostiakh klassovoi bor'by v SSSR v nachale NEPa: Proval 'novoi taktiki' rossiiskoi kontrrevoliutsii." In *Problemy sotsial'no-ekonomicheskoi i politicheskoi istorii SSSR,* 1:26–33. Moscow: Institut Istorii SSSR AN SSSR, 1975.

———. " 'Novaia taktika' rossiiskoi kontrrevoliutsii i ee proval, 1920–1922 gg." *Istoricheskie zapiski,* no. 99 (1977): 55–87.

———. *Ideino-politicheskoe bankrotstvo planov burzhuaznogo restavratorstva v SSSR.* Moscow: Mysl', 1982.

———. *Tri lika starogo mira: Ocherki po istorii beloi emigratsii.* Moscow: Nauka, 1990.

Mukhachev, Iu. V., and Shkarenkov, L. K. *Krakh 'Novoi taktiki' kontrrevoliutsii posle grazhdanskoi voiny.* Moscow: Znanie, 1980.

Nedoboeva, A. E. "Razoblachenie V. I. Leninym smenovekhovstva, men'shevizma i eserovshchiny v gody Nepa." In *Sbornik uchenykh trudov Sverdlovskogo iuridicheskogo instituta,* 11:78–91. Sverdlovsk: Sverdlovskii iuridicheskii institut, 1969.

Nielsen, J. P. *Miliukov i Stalin: O politicheskoi evoliutsii P. N. Miliukova v emigratsii (1918–1943).* Oslo: Universitetet i Oslo, 1983.

Nikitina, Z. A., and Tolstaia, L. I., comps. *Vospominaniia ob A. N. Tolstom.* Moscow: Sovetskii pisatel', 1973.

Nikolaev, S. *O pravovom polozhenii russkikh bezhentsev i o merakh k ego uluchsheniiu.* Prague: Ekonomicheskii kabinet professora S. N. Prokopovicha, 1928.

Nivat, G. "Du 'Panmongolisme' au 'mouvement eurasien': Histoire d'un thème littéraire." *Cahiers du monde russe et soviétique* 7 (July–September 1966): 460–78.

———. "La 'fenêtre sur l'Asie' ou les paradoxes de 'l'affirmation eurasienne.' " *Rossiia/Russia,* no. 6 (1988): 81–93.

[———] Niva, Zh. "Talisman emigranta: Chitaia knigu Marka Raeva 'Russkoe Zarubezh'e.' " *Literaturnaia gazeta,* 20 February 1991.

[———] Niva, Zh., ed. *Odna ili dve russkikh literatury?* Lausanne: L'Age d'Homme, 1981.

Oberländer, E. "Nationalbolschewistische Tendenzen in der russischen Intelligenz: Die 'Smena Vech'-Diskussion 1921–1922." *Jahrbücher für Geschichte Osteuropas* 16 (1968): 194–211.

Obichkina, L. G. "Iz istorii bor'by RKP(b) protiv antisovetskikh partii i techenii (1921–1923 gg.)." *Voprosy istorii KPSS,* 1969, no. 2:100–110.

Orekhova, L. G. "Klassovyi podkhod V.I. Lenina i sovetskikh istorikov k kritike filosofskikh i sotsiologicheskikh vzgliadov smenovekhovstva." In *Partiinost' istoriko-filosofskogo issledovaniia i kritika antikommunizma: Sbornik,* 145–61. Moscow: Izd-vo Moskovskogo universiteta, 1972.

Osipov, V. A. "Vozniknovenie smenovekhovstva i sozdanie gazety 'Nakanune.' " Avtoreferat, I.N.I.O.N., Moscow, 1989.

———. "Kto takoi F. Iks: Iz pisatel'skikh biografii." *Literaturnaia Rossiia,* 25 August 1989.

Ossorguine-Bakounine, T., comp. *L'émigration russe en Europe: Catalogue collectif des périodiques en lange russe, 1855–1940.* Paris: Institut d'Etudes slaves, 1976.

Petrovich, R. *Mladorossy: Materialy k istorii smenovekhovskogo dvizheniia.* London, Ontario: Zaria, 1973.

Pipes, R. *The Formation of the Soviet Union: Communism and Nationalism, 1917–1923.* 2d rev. ed. Cambridge: Harvard University Press, 1964.

———. *Struve: Liberal on the Right, 1905–1944.* Cambridge: Harvard University Press, 1980.

Poltoratskii, N. P. "Smena vekh (Change of Landmarks)." In *Handbook of Russian Literature,* edited by V. Terras, 427–28. New Haven: Yale University Press, 1985.

———. *Rossiia i revoliutsiia: Russkaia religiozno-filosofskaia i natsional'no-politicheskaia mysl' XX veka.* Tenafly, N.J.: Hermitage, 1988.

Pospelovskii, D. "Eshche raz o 'natsional-bol'shevizme': Tretii mezhdunarodnyi s"ezd slavistov—itogi odnoi diskussii." *Russkaia mysl',* no. 3599 (13 December 1985): 11.

Poznanski, R. *Intelligentsia et révolution: Blok, Gorki et Maïakovski face à 1917*. Paris: Anthropos, 1981.

Prianishnikov, B. *Nezrimaia pautina*. N.p.: B. Prianishnikov, 1979.

Proffer, E. *Bulgakov: Life and Work*. Ann Arbor, Mich.: Ardis, 1984.

Prokof'ev, V. S. "Bor'ba bol'shevistskoi partii s reaktsionnoi ideologiei smenovekhovstva." Kandidatskaia dissertatsiia, Leningradskii gosudarstvennyi universitet, 1951.

Raeff, M. "Institutions of a society in exile: Russia abroad, 1919-1939." *Rossiia/Russia*, no. 6 (1988): 95–117.

———. *Russia Abroad: A Cultural History of the Russian Emigration 1919-1939*. New York: Oxford University Press, 1990.

Read, C. *Religion, Revolution and the Russian Intelligentsia 1900-1912: The Vekhi Debate and its Intellectual Background*. London: Macmillan, 1979.

———. *Culture and Power in Revolutionary Russia: The Intelligentsia and the Transition from Tsarism to Communism*. London: Macmillan, 1990.

Reck, V. T. *Boris Pil'niak: A Soviet Writer in Conflict with the State*. Montreal: McGill-Queen's University Press, 1975.

Repiton, I. "L'Opinion française et les émigrés russes, 1920-1939, à travers la littérature de l'entre-deux-guerres." Mémoire de DEA, Institut d'études politiques, Paris, 1986.

Riasanovsky, N. V. "The Emergence of Eurasianism." *California Slavic Studies*, no. 4 (1967): 39–72.

Rimscha, H. von. *Der russische Bürgerkrieg und die russische Emigration 1917-1921*. Jena: Verlag der Frommannschen Buchhandlung, 1924.

———. *Russland jenseits der Grenzen 1921-1926: Ein Beitrag zur russischen Nachkriegsgeschichte*. Jena: Verlag der Frommannschen Buchhandlung, 1927.

———. "Probleme der russischen Emigration." *Wille und Weg* 4 (1 February 1929): 522–29.

Rogger, H. "Reflections on Russian Conservatism." *Jahrbücher für Geschichte Osteuropas* 14 (1966): 195–212.

———. "Nationalism and the State: a Russian Dilemma." *Comparative Studies in Society and History* 4 (April 1962): 253–64.

Rosenberg, W. G. *Liberals in the Russian Revolution: The Constitutional Democratic Party 1917-1923*. Princeton: Princeton University Press, 1974.

Rosenfeld, G. *Sowjetrussland und Deutschland, 1917-1922*. Cologne: Pahl-Rugenstein, 1984.

———. *Sowjetrussland und Deutschland, 1923-1939*. Cologne: Pahl-Rugenstein, 1984.

Sarkisyanz, E. *Russland und der Messianismus des Orients: Sendungsbewusstsein und politischer Chiliasmus des Ostens*. Tübingen: Mohr, 1955.

Savitskii, P. N. [S. Lubenskii, pseud.]. "Evraziiskaia bibliografiia 1921-1931: Putevoditel' po evraziiskoi literature." *Tridtsatye gody: Utverzhdenie evraziitsev*, no. 7 (1931): 285–317.

Scandura, C. "Das 'Russische Berlin' 1921-1924: Die Verlage." *Zeitschrift für Slawistik* 32 (1987): 754–62.

Schapiro, L. *The Origin of the Communist Autocracy: Political Opposition in the Soviet State, First Phase, 1917-1922*. Cambridge: Harvard University Press, 1955.

———. "The Vekhi Group and the Mystique of Revolution." *Slavonic and East European Review* 34 (1955): 56–76.

Schüddekopf, O.-E. *Nationalbolschewismus in Deutschland 1918-1933*. Frankfurt am Main: Ullstein, 1973.

Schulz, H. E.; Urban, P. K; and Lebed, A. I., eds. *Who was who in the USSR: A Biographic Directory*. Metuchen, N.J.: Scarecrow Press, 1972.

Senn, A. E. *Assassination in Switzerland: The Murder of Vatslav Vorovsky*. Madison: University of Wisconsin Press, 1981.

Sharoeva, G. G. "V. I. Lenin i bor'ba s burzhuaznoi ideologiei v zhurnalistike pervoi poloviny 20-kh godov." *Vestnik MGU, Zhurnalistika*, 1973, no. 2:15–22.

Shcherbina, V. *A. N. Tolstoi: Kritiko-biograficheskii ocherk*. Moscow: Khudozhestvennaia literatura, 1951.

Shkarenkov, L. K. "Dela i sud'by russkoi emigratsii." *Novyi mir*, 1967, no. 7: 255–58.

———. "Perekhod k Nepu i ego vliianie na proval antisovetskikh zamyslov beloi emigratsii." In *Novaia ekonomicheskaia politika: Voprosy teorii i istorii*, edited by M. P. Kim, 248–54. Moscow: Nauka, 1974.

———. "Belaia emigratsiia, agoniia kontrrevoliutsiia." *Voprosy istorii*, 1976, no. 5:98–120.

———. *Agoniia beloi emigratsii*. 2d rev. ed. Moscow: Mysl', 1986.

Shukman, H., ed. *The Blackwell Encyclopedia of the Russian Revolution*. Oxford: Blackwell, 1988.

Simpson, J. H. *Refugees: Preliminary Report of a Survey*. London: Royal Institute of International Affairs, 1938.

Somov, N. M. *Bibliografiia russkoi obshchestvennosti*. Part 1. Moscow: By N. M. Somov, 1927.

———. *Bibliografiia russkoi obshchestvennosti (K voprosu ob intelligentsii)*. Part 2. Moscow: Russkoe bibliograficheskoe obshchestvo pri 1-i MGU, 1931.

Soskin, V. L. *Ocherki istorii kul'tury Sibiri v gody revoliutsii i grazhdanskoi voiny (konets 1917–nachalo 1921 g.)*. Novosibirsk: Nauka, Sibirskoe otdelenie, 1965.

———. *Kul'turnaia zhizn' Sibiri v pervye gody novoi ekonomicheskoi politiki (1921–1923 gg.)*. Novosibirsk: Nauka, Sibirskoe otdelenie, 1971.

Spirin, L. M. *Klassy i partii v grazhdanskoi voine v Rossii*. Moscow: Mysl', 1968.

Struve, G. P. *Russkaia literatura v izgnanii*. 2d rev. ed. Paris: YMCA-Press, 1984.

Suvorov, L. N. "Bor'ba V. I. Lenina protiv restavratorskoi ideologii 'smenovekhovstva.' " *Vestnik MGU, Filosofiia*, 1960, no. 2:45–56.

———. *Bor'ba marksistko-leninskoi filosofii v SSSR protiv burzhuaznoi ideologii i revizionizma v perekhodnyi period ot kapitalizma k sotsializmu*. Moscow: Izd-vo Moskovskogo universiteta, 1961.

Szporluk, R. *Communism and Nationalism: Karl Marx versus Friedrich List*. New York: Oxford University Press, 1988.

Terras, V., ed. *Handbook of Russian Literature*. New Haven: Yale University Press, 1985.

Thaden, E. C. *Conservative Nationalism in Nineteenth-Century Russia*. Seattle: University of Washington Press, 1964.

Trifonov, I. Ia. "Smenovekhovstvo i bor'ba s nim." Kandidatskaia dissertatsiia, Leningradskii gosudarstvennyi universitet, 1948.

———. "Iz istorii bor'by kommunisticheskoi partii protiv smenovekhovstva." *Istoriia SSSR*, 1959, no. 3:64–82.

———. *Ocherki istorii klassovoi bor'by v SSSR v gody NEPa, 1921–1937*. Moscow: Gospolitizdat, 1960.

————. *Klassy i klassovaia borba v SSSR v nachale Nepa.* Leningrad: Izd-vo Leningrad-skogo universiteta, 1964.

————. *Lenin i bor'ba s burzhuaznoi ideologiei v nachale NEPa.* Moscow: Znanie, 1969.

Uchenova, V. V. *Partiino-sovetskaia pechat' vosstanovitel'nogo perioda (1921–25 gg.).* Moscow: Izd-vo Moskovskogo universiteta, 1964.

Uldricks, T. J. *Diplomacy and Ideology: the Origins of Soviet Foreign Relations 1917–1930.* London: Sage, 1979.

Ullman, R. *Anglo-Soviet Relations, 1917–1921.* Vol. 1, *Intervention and the War.* Princeton: Princeton University Press, 1961.

————. *Anglo-Soviet Relations, 1917–1921.* Vol. 2, *Britain and the Russian Civil War.* Princeton: Princeton University Press, 1968.

————. *Anglo-Soviet Relations, 1917–1921.* Vol. 3, *The Anglo-Soviet Accord.* Princeton: Princeton University Press, 1972.

Utechin, S. V. *Russian Political Thought: A Concise History.* London: J. M. Dent and Sons, 1964.

Volkmann, H. E. *Die russische Emigration in Deutschland, 1919–1929.* Würzburg: Holzner, 1966.

Wagemaakers, P. C. "N. V. Ustrjalov en het Russische Nationaal-Bolsjevisme." Doctoraalscriptie, Universiteit van Amsterdam, 1985.

Waignein, B. Het tijdschrift 'Novyj Grad' 1931–1939." Licentiaatsthesis, Katholieke Universiteit Leuven, 1988.

Walicki, A. *A History of Russian Thought: From the Enlightenment to Marxism.* Oxford: Oxford University Press, 1979.

White, S. *The Origins of Detente: The Genoa Conference and Soviet-Western Relations, 1921–1922.* Cambridge: Cambridge University Press, 1985.

Williams, R. C. " 'Changing Landmarks' in Russian Berlin, 1923–1924." *Slavic Review* 27 (December 1968): 581–93.

————. *Culture in Exile: Russian Emigrés in Germany 1881–1941.* Ithaca, N.Y.: Cornell University Press, 1972.

Zelikina, N. S. "Iz istorii bor'by sovetskoi publitsistike s burzhuazno-restavratorskimi ideiami smenovekhovstva." *Vestnik LGU*, ser. 2, 1983, no. 8:86–88.

Zimmerman, J. E. "The Political Views of the Vekhi Authors." *Canadian-American Slavic Studies* 10 (Fall 1976): 307–27.

————. "Russian Liberal Theory, 1900–1917." *Canadian-American Slavic Studies* 14 (Spring 1980): 1–20.

Znamenskii, O. *Intelligentsiia nakanune Velikogo Oktiabria, Fevral'–Oktiabr' 1917.* Moscow: Nauka, 1988.

Index

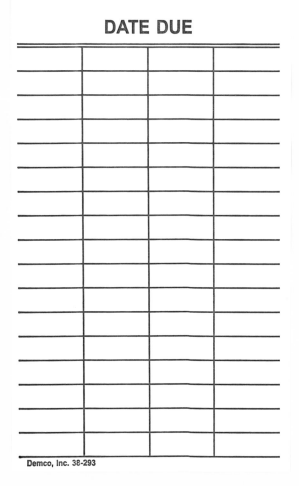

DATE DUE